MICHIGAN:

A History of the Wolverine State

Watercolors and Drawings
by Reynold Weidenaar

Michigan:

A History of the Wolverine State

by

Willis Frederick Dunbar

Professor of History
...higan University

WILLIAM B. EERDMANS PUBLISHING COMPANY
GRAND RAPIDS, MICHIGAN

977.4 D9llm5

C.2

JUN '70

First printing, March 1965
Second printing, July 1965
Third printing, August 1966
Fourth printing, May 1968

PHOTOLITHOPRINTED BY GRAND RAPIDS BOOK MANUFACTURERS, INC.
GRAND RAPIDS, MICHIGAN

WI FEB '76

*This book is dedicated to my
students in Michigan History*

PREFACE

Of all the states in the Union, Michigan is perhaps the least typical. It is unique geographically because it consists of two large peninsulas, because it lies in the midst of the upper Great Lakes, and because of the striking difference between the soils, climate, and vegetation in those parts of the state lying north of the 43rd parallel and in those lying south of this line. Its highly industrialized southeastern region is in sharp contrast to the sparsely settled Upper Peninsula and northern half of the Lower Peninsula. Michigan is heavily dependent on a single industry: automotive manufacturing. Portions of the state, however, rely on the tourist and vacation industry as the backbone of their economy. It is a state that has experienced boom periods in the fur trade, land speculation, mining, lumbering, and automobile manufacturing, each of which has been followed by severe depressions. Politically, it was for three-quarters of a century a stronghold of the Republican party, only to become, in more recent years, a state where party rivalry is intense and elections hotly contested.

Michigan is a state with a colorful past. The French voyageurs, missionaries, and empire builders were the first Europeans to come to this part of the country, at that time thinly populated by both Algonquin and Iroquois Indians. In due time the British replaced the French, and for a short time the Spanish flag flew over one

7

of the forts. The early American settlers included a preponderance of Yankees from western New York and New England. Their influence was felt in the names of cities and towns, and in the leadership Michigan gave in the field of public education. From Canada and Europe came foreign immigrants, such as the Finns, the Cornish, the Swedes, and the Italians, to work in the mines and lumber camps. Germans, Irish, and Dutch settled in the cities and the rich agricultural area of southern Michigan. The automobile industry attracted large numbers of immigrants from southern and eastern Europe during the first two decades of the 20th century. And the boom period from 1940 to 1955 brought a large influx of southern whites and Negroes. The intermingling of these many nationalities and racial stocks, their quest for greater economic opportunity, their exploitation of the state's natural resources, their constructive efforts to achieve social justice, their sacrifices to provide educational, religious, and cultural institutions, and their contributions to the nation and to the world constitute the warp and woof of Michigan history.

This book recounts the story of Michigan's past with the primary purpose of providing readers information and understanding that will help them contribute more effectively to the building of Michigan's future. History for history's sake is valuable only for the antiquarian or the hobbyist. For the great majority of people history is important because it is a guide to wise decision-making and planning for the years ahead. Not that history ever exactly repeats itself. What one receives from a study of history is a richer understanding of human beings in a social environment, and a better comprehension of how the present state of affairs actually came about. We can make sound decisions on where we are going and how we are to get there only if we know from whence we came and how we came.

In Michigan and elsewhere in the United States there has been a remarkable growth of interest in state and local history within the past two decades. It is not a little ironical that just at the time our nation has been more deeply involved than ever before in world affairs we should take such a keen interest not only in our national past but also in the history of our communities, neighborhoods, and states. Perhaps the American people, perplexed by the problems world leadership has thrust upon them, are instinctively falling back on their own origins to seek an understanding of their destiny. The new interest in state and local history reflects, too, a comprehension that here are the grass roots of our history as a nation. If one spent all his life in Washington, D.C., for example, he would gain a rather illusory picture of American life. The kind of people we are, our outlook on life, our ways of doing things, and our faults and foibles as well as our strengths can best be understood by carefully examining our cities, our rural areas, and our states.

This is why state and local history is important. This book is designed primarily for students of Michigan history and for adult readers. It seeks to interpret as well as to recount and describe the major events, movements, and personalities in Michigan's past. There are frequent references to books and articles for those who wish to explore more deeply in the field.

A few remarks as to how the book is organized may be helpful. For each of the four centuries within which Michigan's history falls there is a brief, preliminary summary of the chief developments. Each of these provides what might be called the "motif" for that century. The structure of the book up to the period of the American Civil War is loosely chronological. But for the last century the account is organized largely on a topical basis. It seems to the author that the history of the state during the last hundred years becomes more meaningful if subjects such as politics, the automobile industry, and the rise of cities are discussed as units.

The author wishes to express his thanks to many individuals who have been helpful in the preparation of this book. Reference librarians at the Michigan State Library, the Clarence M. Burton Historical Collections at the Detroit Public Library, the State Archives, the Michigan Historical Collections at the University of Michigan, the Western Michigan University Library, and the Kalamazoo Public Library have assisted in a variety of ways. I owe much to my colleagues in the history department at Western Michigan University, and in particular to Charles Starring, Alan Brown, and John Yzenbaard who read and provided helpful criticisms of the manuscript. My students in Michigan history at Western Michigan University, by asking searching questions, have stimulated new searches into the dark corners of Michigan history. My associates on the Michigan Historical Commission and my friends in the Historical Society of Michigan have contributed to my own growing enthusiasm for Michigan history. And the members of the historical profession who teach classes in Michigan history at other colleges and universities have encouraged the preparation of this book. To all these I am most grateful.

Willis F. Dunbar
Western Michigan University

TABLE OF CONTENTS

LIST OF MAPS

13

LIST OF FIGURES

THE SEVENTEENTH CENTURY

European adventurers reached Michigan at about the same time the Pilgrims landed at Plymouth. Waiting for them was a land largely covered with great forests of hard- and softwood trees, a land rich in mineral resources, some of it a land of great fertility. It was sparsely populated by native peoples living in a state of primitive culture. In due course these natives were compelled to yield this land to a race that exploited it far more than primitive peoples were able to do. But it was close to two hundred years before this finally came about.

The seventeenth century in Michigan history was first of all a century of discovery and exploration. It was the century of Marquette, Jolliet, and La Salle. By its close the white men knew the broad outlines of Michigan geography. They knew the lakes that surrounded Michigan, the shorelines, and the main rivers. They were less acquainted with the interior, though that, too, had been penetrated.

The seventeenth century was the French period of Michigan history. The first Europeans who came were Frenchmen, who brought with them the civilization and language of France. They laid claim to Michigan in the name of the king of France.

The seventeenth century witnessed the beginnings of the fur trade in Michigan, the launching of missionary activity among the Indians, and the persistent search for a waterway through the continent. Although there were, from time to time, threats to the French domination in Michigan, it was not until the next century that the British seriously challenged that domination.

The legend of the ghost ship *Griffin*

Dome-shaped dwellings of early Michigan Indians

I

MICHIGAN
WHEN THE WHITE MEN CAME

T he history of Michigan was conditioned by natural forces at work long before the seventeenth century. The iron, copper, salt, oil, and other mineral resources that have played so large a role in the development of Michigan were the results of geological forces operating during ages that are measured in millions of years. The shape of the land masses that constitute Michigan, the location of the lakes and streams, and the types of soil were determined during the glacial period that ended about ten thousand years ago. And there were human beings in Michigan long before the white men came. They, too, played a role in Michigan's history.

THE LAND AND WATERS

Time, as reckoned by the geologist, has little meaning to the ordinary person. He is unable to conceive a million years, to say nothing of a billion years, yet these are the time units that mark geological ages. In these dark recesses of time, when the earth was cooling, volcanic eruptions brought to the earth's surface deposits of copper that were mined by the white man and were used by the Indians before the white man came. During these ages, the deposits of iron, petroleum, and other mineral resources that have proved so useful to man were formed.

19

Relatively late in geological time, great icecaps covered the northern part of North America. Then, as the climate became warmer, these icecaps, or glaciers, retreated northward. The advance and recession of the glaciers occurred not once but four times. The underlying rock over which these great glaciers spread varied in character. A formation known as the Laurentian Shield embraced a large portion of the present province of Ontario and extended as far southward as Upper Michigan. It was the earliest land mass of North America. It was an area of crystalline rocks and granites, which do not erode easily. South of the Laurentian Shield the predominant rocks were sandstone, limestone, and shale, much softer, and hence more subject to erosion. The advancing glaciers swept the Laurentian Shield bare of its soils, depositing them helter-skelter over the area as far south as the Ohio River. Combined with these soils from the Laurentian Shield was that which was formed by the erosion of the limestone and shale. The net result was to create in southern Michigan, as well as in northern and central Iowa, Indiana, and Ohio, a belt of fertile land, diverse in character, but admirably adapted to agriculture, as well as to leave a region that embraces the northern portions of Wisconsin and all of Michigan with thin and sandy soils ill-suited to farming. Some of Michigan's most pressing economic problems in the 20th century arise from these consequences of glacial activity.

The configuration of the land of Michigan, the size and location of the lakes, islands, and peninsulas, resulted from varying degrees of resistance to erosion by different strata of rocks. Lake Huron, Lake Erie, and Lake Michigan owe their shape and position to the fact that they mark the location of easily eroded Silurian limestone, shale, and dolomite. The islands of the Great Lakes in most cases rest on outcroppings of harder rock. Until recently it was assumed that the Great Lakes were originally great ponds formed by the melting of the glaciers. A new theory, confirmed by holes drilled in the floor of Lake Superior in the summer of 1961 by a Michigan-Minnesota expedition, holds that the Great Lakes were originally carved by an ancient river system whose existence antedated the period of the glaciers. The Great Lakes region, according to this view, was drained by a mighty river that either emptied into the Hudson Bay or flowed down the St. Lawrence River Valley. The icesheets, or glaciers, are presumed to have plowed up the terrain and bulldozed dams and dikes of hills that obstructed this drainage and produced the Great Lakes in their present shape.[1]

[1] W. Sullivan, New York *Times,* July 19, 1961.

Whatever their origin may have been, the lakes that form the boundaries of Michigan today have had a powerful influence in determining its history. In every period of Michigan's development the existence of water on all sides but one has influenced the activities of its inhabitants. The Great Lakes have been invaluable as a means of transportation from the time when they bore the canoes of the Indians and French fur traders to the present day, when they carry the giant ore boats. They have been both an avenue of commerce and a barrier to commerce. They determined to a large extent the direction of the railroads and highways in the state. They have been an important source of food supply in the form of fish. They affect the climate and therefore agriculture. Prevailing westerly winds blowing across Lake Michigan make possible Michigan's fruit belt along the west coast of the Lower Peninsula. These winds, cool in the spring, prevent the premature development of the fruit buds and warmed by the Lake in the autumn, prolong the growing season. The opening of the St. Lawrence Seaway on April 25, 1959, made Michigan ports available to large ocean-going vessels because of their location on the Great Lakes and connecting waterways. And the almost limitless source of pure water they provide promises to play a vital role in the industrial development of Michigan in the future.

Glacial activity also scooped out the areas now covered by Michigan's 11,037 inland lakes. In early times there undoubtedly were more lakes, but their number has by this time been reduced by man-made drainage. The largest of these inland lakes is Houghton Lake, in Roscommon County, with an area of 30.8 square miles. Six others have areas of twenty or more square miles. There are so many lakes in Michigan that it has been difficult to find distinctive names for all of them. The state has 41 Long Lakes, 30 Little Lakes, 28 Big Lakes, 25 Round Lakes, 25 Bass Lakes, 18 Mud Lakes, 17 Crooked Lakes, and 15 Silver Lakes. These inland lakes, as well as the Great Lakes, constitute one of the foundations upon which Michigan's vacation and tourist industry is based, since they offer limitless opportunities for fishing, swimming, and boating.

As the glaciers retreated the present river system of Michigan came into being. Michigan rivers are unique in that they are extended rivers. The surfaces of the Great Lakes originally rested at a higher sea level than at present; when, after the glacial period, they receded to their present levels, the rivers were extended to flow to a lower lake outlet. The Huron River once flowed westward into other rivers that led to Lake Michigan; but when the lake levels receded, it made its exit by way of the Raisin River to Lake Erie, and finally through its own outlet. On the western side of the Lower Peninsula nearly all the rivers have outlets partially dammed by sand dunes, and hence the Kalamazoo, Black, Muskegon, and Manistee Rivers form lakes before flowing into Lake Michigan. These lakes were important during the period when Michigan's white pine was being harvested, as ideal locations for sawmills. Many Michigan rivers have rapids, and around these several early towns grew up, since they were places where canoes had to be portaged. There are 34 waterfalls in Michigan, mostly on the rivers of the Upper Peninsula, the falls of the Tahquamenon being the best known. The rivers were used extensively by the French fur traders and missionaries for transportation, and before the coming of the railroads they were invaluable to the American settlers for the same reason. They have also been important as sources of hydro-electric power; in 1934 forty Michigan rivers were producing electric power at 217 sites. The greater efficiency of "steam-generating" electric plants, using coal for fuel, and more recently the development of nuclear power plants make hydro-electric plants the size of those in Michigan less significant. Today, however, Michigan's river system is an asset second only to its lakes in the growth of the vacation and tourist industry.

Particularly important are the three rivers that connect the Great Lakes adjacent to Michigan. The St. Mary's River connects Lake Huron with Lake Superior. The latter lies twenty-two feet above the level of the lower lakes. To make it possible for ships to pass through this waterway, a canal with locks was built between 1853 and 1855. The St. Clair River, connecting Lake Huron with Lake St. Clair, and the Detroit River, connecting the latter with Lake Erie, are among the busiest waterways in the world. The Soo Canal on the St. Mary's River, which is ice-bound from December to April, carries more than twice the tonnage that passes through the Panama Canal. The importance of these narrow passageways was recognized by the early French explorers. The most important fortifications erected by the French, and the British who followed them, were built along these rivers and on the strategic Straits of Mackinac, connecting Lake Michigan and Lake Huron.

Other Michigan rivers deserve mention because of their historic associations. The St. Joseph, which rises in Hillsdale County and flows westward until it reaches St. Joseph County, and then makes a southerly bend into Indiana, only to return northward and find its outlet at St. Joseph, was one of the major routes of

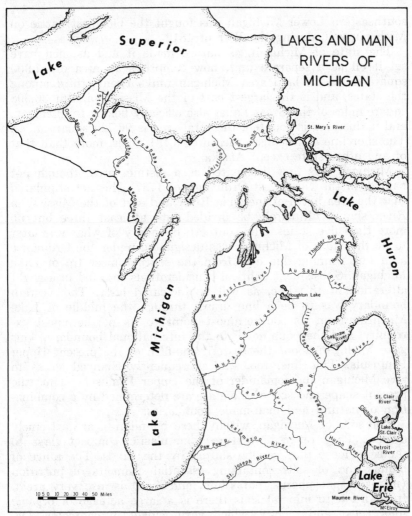

LAKES AND MAIN
RIVERS OF
MICHIGAN

travel for explorers, missionaries, and fur traders. Forts and a
mission were built along its banks. Only a short portage had to
be crossed to pass from the St. Joseph to the Kankakee River,
whose waters found their way into the Mississippi River. Fur
trading also was active on the Kalamazoo and the Grand Rivers,
the latter of which is Michigan's longest river (225 miles). The
Muskegon and the Manistee Rivers on the western side of the
Lower Peninsula, the Saginaw and its tributaries on the eastern
side, and the Menominee in the Upper Peninsula were the most
important rivers for the lumbermen. Near the Raisin River in

southeastern Lower Michigan was fought the bloodiest battle on Michigan soil, during the War of 1812.

The state of Michigan, as nature made it and as men have set it off as a separate unit, now comprises an area of 57,900 square miles. In land area Michigan ranks twenty-third among the states, and is the largest east of the Mississippi. But 36,698 square miles of the Great Lakes also officially belong to Michigan, and if this area is counted, the total area is 96,720 square miles. The shoreline of Michigan measures 3,121 miles, more than that of any other state except Alaska.

Michigan was first designated as a distinct area, though not named, in the Northwest Ordinance of 1787. This act stipulated that the area north of the Ohio River and east of the Mississippi River should ultimately be divided into at least three but no more than five states. The southern boundary of what was later to be the State of Michigan was designated under the Ordinance as a line running due east from the southernmost tip of Lake Michigan. Subsequent political considerations resulted in a slight alteration of this line, as will be indicated later. The western boundary was to be a line drawn through the middle of Lake Michigan from its southernmost point to its northernmost extremity, and then due north to the international boundary. This gave Michigan about the eastern one-fifth of the present Upper Peninsula. This line, too, was subsequently changed so as to give Michigan the remainder of the Upper Peninsula. Thus the present shape and size of the state are determined by a combination of natural and man-made boundaries.

The soils of Michigan, within these boundaries, are extremely diverse. They range in texture from plastic, compact clays to sands so loose they can be shifted by the winds. The range of humus and of soils containing essential elements of nutrition (nitrogen, phosphorus, potassium, and lime) is also very great. In addition to mineral soils there is a large acreage of organic soils (peat and muck), which vary widely in character. Deforestation, drainage, over-cropping, and other changes wrought by the white man have greatly altered the character of the land during the nearly three centuries that he has been in Michigan. The sand dunes along Lake Michigan and the many swamps in the interior gave the first Americans who came to see the area a low opinion of Michigan as a suitable place for agriculture. Later exploration revealed, however, many areas of rich and fertile land. But perhaps no state has such a wide diversity of soils as Michigan. For this reason, an unusually great variety of farm operations is characteristic of the state.

The land and waters of Michigan, as the first white men found them, must have been surpassingly beautiful. Yet there are few rapturous descriptions of the Michigan scene in the writings of the early explorers. They sometimes were wont to describe the wonders of this new country in exaggerated form, but most of them were too absorbed with the task at hand to rhapsodize on the beauties of nature. The early American pioneers, in the descriptions they wrote to friends and kinfolk in the east, tended to write about practical matters: the character of the soil, the question of whether or not the region was a healthful place to live, and the availability of rivers were their chief concerns. Of course we can never know whether the people who saw Michigan as it was before the white man began to change it felt more than they wrote.

Although the French demonstrated interest in the copper that the Indians dug out of Michigan's soil, no large-scale effort was made to exploit the vast mineral wealth beneath the soil until after the Americans took over. Explorations made by the first state geologist, Dr. Douglas Houghton, provided the first hint of the extent of these resources. The copper country, stretching through the Keweenaw Peninsula and southward, is located in what are now Keweenaw, Houghton, and Ontonagon Counties. Here the copper is found in its pure state, not as an amalgam with other metals. Mining operations, which began in 1842, yielded the largest single poundage during the year 1916, but since then the sizes of the yields have decreased. There are still great stores of copper ore in this area, but to obtain it deep shafts must be sunk, and the cost is so great that ore cannot be produced as cheaply as in the Rocky Mountain area. Iron ore mining, which began in 1844, still continues on a large scale. Michigan was the nation's largest producer of iron ore in the latter part of the nineteenth century, but was surpassed by Minnesota about 1900. Modern methods have enabled operators to utilize the low-grade ore, but in recent years many mines in the Upper Peninsula have been shut down because they could not be operated profitably. The three Michigan iron ranges, in the order of their development, are the Marquette, the Menominee, and the Gogebic. Michigan also has vast deposits of salt, and has been the nation's leading producer for many years. The brines pumped out of the earth are also the source of more than four hundred products made by the Dow Chemical Company of Midland. Michigan leads the nation in the production of gypsum, widely utilized in construction materials. The state also is a leading producer of limestone, an essential component in

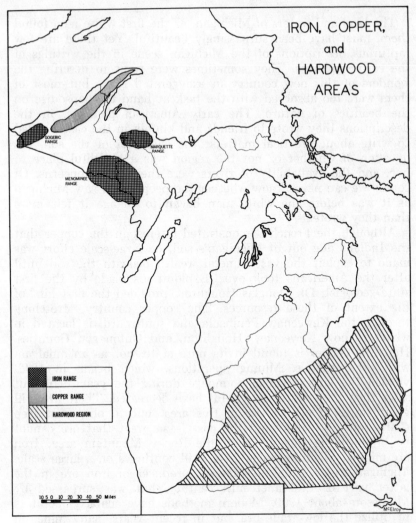

the manufacture of steel. Since 1928 Michigan has been a large producer of petroleum, some 239 oil fields having been discovered up to 1958. The state also has sizable deposits of low-grade coal, which has been mined in the past but cannot be mined profitably today. A small amount of silver and gold has been found in the Upper Peninsula. Sand and gravel constitute one of the most valuable nonmetallic mineral products of Michigan, due to their extensive use in highway construction. Michigan ranked second among the states in sand and gravel production in 1959. Cement is another mineral product important to the state. In fact, the value of cement produced in the state in 1959 outranked that of any other mineral product ($77,323,974 out of a total of $385,321,927). Reserves of mineral wool, talc, asbestos, and gem stones exist in the Upper Peninsula and on Isle Royale, but as yet there has been no production.

And finally, the climate of Michigan must be mentioned as a factor in the state's history. Michiganians,[2] unlike Floridans or Californians, do not boast of their climate. It is not a state for softies. The range of temperatures is extreme, the record high being 112 degrees (1936) and the record low 51 degrees below zero (1934). The sun shines only 30% of the time in the winter and 40% in the summer. The growing season varies from 180 days, in part of Berrien County, to 90 days, in a small portion of the Upper Peninsula. Rainfall varies from an annual average of 24 inches in Keweenaw County to 40 inches in the southern counties. The weather in Michigan is notoriously changeable. Though this may be unpleasant at times, one school of geographers holds that changeable weather conditions stimulate greater physical vigor and mental alertness.[3] Climatic conditions, combined with thin soils, militate against profitable agriculture in northern Michigan. On the other hand, as has been noted above, the westerly winds that moderate the climate on the western side of the Lower Peninsula are an asset. Michigan's climate may have something to do with the fact that the aviation industry has not developed in Michigan (except, of course, in wartime, when mass-production was essential), since weather conditions in the state are not conducive to plane-testing. The cool breezes of summer attract many vacationists to Michigan, and the heavy snowfall and cold weather in the North have made possible in recent years the development of skiing and winter resort operations. One must conclude, therefore, that the climate of Michigan is both a liability and an asset to the state and its people.

THE NATIVE PEOPLE

Before the white man came to Michigan the land was inhabited by a race of people known to us as Indians. We call them Indians because of a mistake made by the discoverer of the New World. Columbus firmly believed he had reached the

---

[2] I prefer the term "Michiganians" to "Michiganders," since the female counterpart of the latter might be presumed to be "Michigoose"!

[3] Ellsworth Huntington, *Mainsprings of Civilization*.

Indies, which was the name given to the dimly known Far East by the Europeans of that time. Hence he called the native peoples he found in this land Indians. Like so many misnomers, this one has persisted through the centuries.

The natives of Michigan sprang from ancestors who, many centuries before Columbus, had crossed the Bering Straits from Asia into North America and then had drifted southward to people the two continents of the New World. Many of their physical characteristics identify them with the Mongolian race: their bronze-colored skin, their straight, black hair, and their sparse beards. There is some reason to believe that Michigan was inhabited, at various times through the centuries, by groups of people whose culture differed from that of the Indians who lived here when the first Frenchmen arrived. For example, copper had been mined on Isle Royale by an earlier race,[4] but the Indians of Michigan at the time the French came were not doing so. A total of 1,068 Indian mounds have been identified by archaeologists in Michigan. Earlier writers presumed that these mounds were built by an earlier race of "mound builders," but it is now believed that they were the work of Indian peoples. They were utilized for burial purposes, in some instances, but they also appear to have been built for some other reason, perhaps as a speaking platform for Indian orators. The largest number of these mounds was found in the southern half of the Lower Peninsula. One of the largest was on the Rouge River. As described by Bela Hubbard, in his *Memorials of Half a Century*, it was forty feet high and several hundred feet long. A much smaller one, scarcely six feet high, was discovered by the pioneers of Kalamazoo and is still preserved in Bronson Park in that city. Far more remarkable than the mounds were southern and western Michigan's "garden beds," of which 31 have been identified. These most mysterious of all North American antiquities consisted of low ridges of soil about eighteen inches high, arranged in almost perfect geometric patterns (rectangular or circular), and covering as much as 120 acres. They were given their name because of their resemblance to a formal garden. Their function is a mystery. Were they simply artistic creations? Were they used for ceremonial purposes? Or were they used to kill buffalo, by driving the herds across the ridges, causing the beasts to stumble? No implements, pottery, arrowheads, or pipes have been found near these "garden beds." They had been abandoned long before the French came. Except for a few re-

---

[4] The many theories concerning the identity of these ancient miners range from Phoenicians to Indians and roving Norsemen.

ported in Indiana and Wisconsin, they have been found only in Michigan. All of them have been destroyed by farmers.

The Frenchmen who reached Upper Michigan somewhere between 1618 and 1622 found natives who spoke a language similar to that spoken by those along the Ottawa River far to the east, from whence they had come. The name of these Ottawa River tribes was "Algonkin" or "Algonquin." Hence the early French explorers applied the name Algonquin to all the Indians of the upper Great Lakes region who spoke a language like that spoken by the tribe of that name. The early French, by the way, seldom referred to the natives as "Indians," but called them *sauvages*. This word did not have quite the same connotation as our word "savages." It meant uncultivated or uncivilized, rather than bloodthirsty and cruel.

Later writers followed the lead of the early French explorers in calling Indians of Michigan whose language was similar to that of the Indians of the Ottawa River region Algonquins. By far the largest number of Michigan Indians belong in this linguistic grouping. The Algonquin area extended from the Atlantic coast to the foothills of the Rocky Mountains, and from Hudson Bay to the Ohio River. But within this area there were two other linguistic groups, each including a number of tribes, some of whose members at one time or another dwelt in what is now Michigan. On the west were the Sioux tribes, whose principal habitation was the region of the Upper Mississippi Valley. Ranging north and south of Lake Erie, and occasionally making forays into Michigan, were the powerful Iroquois peoples. Each of these linguistic groups, and each of the tribes within each group, had its own distinctive customs and characteristics. Hence one should not generalize too much about the Indians. Unfortunately, in our day the average person is apt to form a stereotype of Indian life and customs from western movies and television shows. Most of the Indians portrayed by these media are plains or mountain Indians, whose ways of life were in many respects quite unlike those of the Michigan Indians.

Few of the Michigan Indians lived in peaked tepees. Most of them built dome-shaped dwellings by pounding saplings into the ground, pulling them together at their tops, and covering them with skins, grass matting, boughs, and bark. A few built "long houses" as much as sixty feet long and twelve feet wide, sheltering several families, but usually the houses were only large enough for six or eight persons. Michigan Indians did not wear the elaborate feathered head-dress of the plains Indians. They did not fight on horseback, as the plains Indians did; in fact, they had few if any horses when the white man first came. Nor were they in a state of constant warfare against the whites; except for rare occasions the early settlers of Michigan were not attacked or harmed by the native peoples whose land they were appropriating for themselves. The Indians of Michigan were not the noble redmen of the romantic tradition, nor were they so treacherous, bloodthirsty, and bestial as they were regarded by the English and some early American pioneers. Essentially they were a primitive people living a semi-nomadic life, unable to read or write, superstitious, polytheistic, and the slaves of their customs and taboos.

An important fact about them that must be borne in mind constantly as we trace their relationships with the whites is that they had no conception of land ownership. To them the land and waters belonged to all alike. The fish, animals, berries, wild grains, and herbs that the waters and the land produced were for those who needed them. The Indians of Michigan practiced a crude sort of agriculture, growing corn, pumpkins, squash, peas, and beans. The land on which these crops grew *belonged* to no individual; it was simply utilized as long as needed to grow the crop. Hence, when the whites began to press the

Indians to sell them land, the natives did not understand what was meant. This accounts for many of the Indian troubles that arose. Even tribal ownership was vague, because the Indians moved about a great deal. A tribe generally regarded a rather vague, undefined area as its hunting grounds, but it had no conception of sovereignty over all the peoples within this area. Each tribe governed it own affairs. It claimed no right to rule other tribes.

Before the white man came each tribe was largely self-reliant. It provided all the essentials of life for its people. There was considerable commerce among the natives by swapping or barter, but the articles of this trade might be classified as "luxury goods": tobacco, sea shells, flint, copper, and feathers. A special tribe called the "Tobacco Indians," living in what is now the Province of Ontario north of Lake Erie, cultivated the tobacco plant and supplied the other tribes of the Great Lakes region. The Indian pipe, known as the calumet, was not generally smoked for pleasure, but rather was passed around following the conclusion of a parley to seal the bargain. (It is notable that tobacco is grown in large quantities in Ontario today, the very place where it was cultivated by the Indians.) Wampum also was used in connection with trade. But it was not money in our sense of the word. Wampum consisted of strings of shells and short sections of hollow bones of small birds and animals. It was a charm to protect the one who surrendered goods in an exchange from the evil influences that might be incident to the transfer. It was not "value received," but rather a sort of protective medicine.

Like other primitive peoples, the Indians had their medicine men, who were expected to know about the different kinds of spirits, especially how to eradicate the bad spirits that made people sick. Their stock in trade was a kind of mixture of religion and magic. They must have resisted, in subtle ways, the influence of the missionaries who came among the Indians with the object of converting them to the Christian religion, though there are not many references to this in the writings of the missionaries. Other habits and customs of the Indians made the work of the missionaries a difficult one. Because the natives were polytheistic they were inclined to think of the cross as just another kind of charm and found it difficult to grasp the meaning of monotheism. Since the Indians lived largely by the hunt, and since game was more plentiful in spring than in any other season, they were accustomed to gorge themselves on meat during the very time when Lent appeared on the Christian calendar. But perhaps the greatest difficulties encountered by the missionaries were the consequence of the intrusion of the white man into Indian culture. These will be dealt with subsequently in this narrative.

Emerson F. Greenman, one of the leading authorities on Michigan Indians, makes these general observations about the state of the culture of the Indians when the first white men arrived:

> The culture of both the Algonquin and Iroquois in the seventeenth century was static. About all they knew was what was handed down by one generation to another. The archaeological record going back two millenia suggests little technological change. The most important change, the loss of copper, was retrogressive. By 1600 the Indians of Michigan were no longer using copper. In the same period there were advanced cultures in Mexico where, although the Indians were still technically Neolithic, architecture in stone was developed, and the mixing of copper and tin to make bronze, a superior metal, was known though not widely used.
>
> The Indians of Michigan were far from the centers of the most highly developed New World cultures, and like all marginal peoples they were backward in some ways. They did not lack energy and intelligence. Their backwardness resulted from the conditions of their lives. They were dwellers in the forest in small social units far apart. Neither political nor religious authority was sufficiently centralized to require large buildings of stone, nor to organize the labor of their construction.[5]

The government of a tribe was entrusted to a chief and his council. There were no kings (hence no "Indian princesses") and no hereditary aristocracy. The chief was chosen on the basis of his ability as measured by tribal standards: his bravery and cunning in warfare, his eloquence as an orator, his skill in hunting, and his wisdom. Sometimes, but not always, the son of a great chief might succeed his father. The power of the chief depended on the amount of confidence the people of the tribe had in him. All matters of general welfare were discussed by the council. Often the deliberations were long and animated. A powerful orator was highly regarded, and because the language of the tribe grew out of a close contact with nature, Indian eloquence abounded in imagination, symbolism, and poetic speech. The loose government of the tribes, and the general lack of any inter-tribal organization (except among the Iroquois) made it difficult for the whites to reach agreements with the tribes. A tribe might not accept an agreement signed by its chief and, unless he was a man of powerful influence, he might not be able

[5] E. F. Greenman, "The Indians of Michigan," *Michigan History,* XLV (1961), 4.

to persuade or compel his people to abide by a treaty he had signed in their name.

War was a common occurrence in Indian life, but it was no more common than it had been in Europe for a thousand years before the discovery of the New World. Like the feudal lords, the native chiefs were ambitious for prestige, and one tribe often coveted the rich hunting grounds occupied by another, just as the feudal lords coveted the domains of others. Like feudal warfare, that of the Indians was desultory and more or less continuous. The Indians were more concerned with war as a means of demonstrating personal bravery than as a means of advancing the interests of the community, and that same observation might be made of feudal knights. Another similarity is that both feudal and Indian warriers adhered to strict codes of honor. The Indians were often cruel in inflicting torture upon their captives, but Indian cruelty cannot be compared to the excruciating tortures inflicted on the victims of the religious wars in Europe. Scalps were sometimes collected as trophies of war, but the practice of taking scalps was exploited and commercialized by the whites, who paid the Indians bounties for taking the scalps of their enemies. The Indians of Michigan were not normally cannibalistic. But a courageous fallen foe might have his heart cut out and devoured by his enemies because they thought this would impart some of his bravery to them. The Indians believed the vital force of one living thing could be imparted to another. Those who ate fish and waterfowl would become expert swimmers. To eat rabbit would make a man a good jumper; fox and weasel meat gave slyness to those who partook. Medicine men chose blood root to cure bleeding and Euphrasia, on account of its "eye spot," for sore eyes. Purely by accident some of these substances whose characteristic features were regarded as an indication of their medicinal value, have proved of actual therapeutic importance.

Each of the linguistic groups of Indians, such as the Algonquin, included inter-related sub-groups which are called "nations." Each nation was made up of several "tribes," each with its own chief. The Michigan Indians first encountered by the French were the Chippewa or Ojibway. Members of this nation inhabited the Upper Peninsula and sometimes visited the northern part of the Lower Peninsula. The French found them taking whitefish from the St. Mary's River.

The Potawatomi[6] are believed to have been located in eastern

[6] There are various spellings, Potawatomi, Pottawatomi, and Potawatomie being the commonest.

Wisconsin when the French first came, but they ultimately found their homes in southwestern Michigan, a region of small prairies and a kind of borderland between the forested area of the East and the great prairies further west.

The Miami also were found by the French in what is now Wisconsin, being called the Oumamik. In 1671 this nation, along with the Mascouten, dwelt around the headwaters of the Fox River in Wisconsin, but soon afterward moved to the valley of the Kalamazoo River and farther south.

A fourth Algonquin nation of importance in Michigan was the Ottawa. Members of this nation were first found by Champlain along the Ottawa River in Canada. After 1615, when Champlain found them, they began a westward trek, possibly due to the hostility of the Iroquois. The word "Ottawa" means "traders." The early French remarked on how the Ottawa traveled encumbered with goods and were not inclined to war. The goods included guns, powder, metal kettles, hatchets and knives, corn meal, sunflower oil, fur, tobacco, medicinal roots and herbs, and slaves obtained from the Illinois Indians. The Ottawa, by the end of the eighteenth century, lived mostly in the eastern, central, and northern parts of the Lower Peninsula.

Members of the fifth important Michigan Indian nation, unlike the others, were related to the Iroquois. They were the Huron or Wyandot. They were first found along the lower St. Lawrence River but by 1611 they were established in the Lake Simcoe area just south of Georgian Bay. At that time there were as many as 30,000 of them. But after the Jesuits had established missions among them, the other Iroquois made war against them and exterminated most of the tribe. A remnant moved westward, first to the area of the Mackinac Straits, then to Green Bay, Wisconsin, and finally to the far western side of the south shore of Lake Superior. Here this unfortunate people encountered the fierce Sioux, and was compelled to retreat eastward again. Some found refuge near the mission at St. Ignace in 1672. After the founding of Detroit the Huron, with the Ottawa, moved southward to take up their residence near the French fort and trading post there.

Indian nations other than the five principal ones mentioned above often are referred to in early accounts. For example, the Fox and Mascouten, whose hunting grounds were in Wisconsin, laid siege to Detroit in 1712 and the French and their Indian allies conducted a long, desultory war against them. Early records also include, in some cases, the names of tribes and of clans or bands within the tribes.

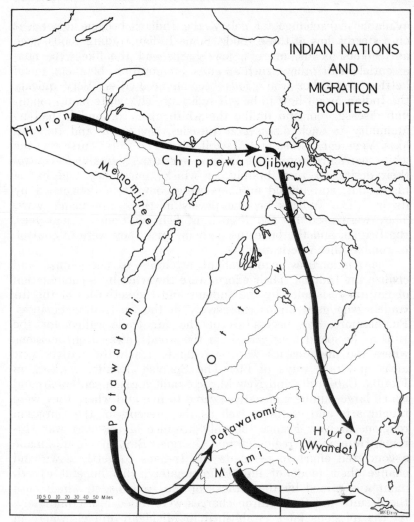

INDIAN NATIONS
AND
MIGRATION
ROUTES

Huron

Menominee

Chippewa (Ojibway)

Ottawa

Potawatomi

Potawatomi

Miami

Huron
(Wyandot)

10 5 0 10 20 30 40 50 Miles

McElroy

By any measurement Michigan was sparsely populated by the Indians at the time the first French explorers arrived. It has been estimated that the native population of Michigan at that time did not exceed 15,000. They made slight use of the resources of the area. Fish and wild game were killed for food, not for sport. Mineral resources were virtually untouched. Only a tiny amount of the land was cultivated in the growing of crops. To the European, Michigan was virtually unoccupied.

The coming of the white man quickly transformed the patterns of Indian life. As soon as the white man's goods became available in exchange for peltry, the Indians became dependent on a steady flow of these goods. Some Indian trading goods, such as trinkets, beads, mirrors, jews'-harps and the like were non-essentials. But others, such as guns, ammunition, blankets, metal kettles, and other iron goods became necessities. Very quickly the Indian forgot how to be self-sufficient. The white man brought him disease, too, and unlike the white man, the Indian had no immunity to such diseases as measles, small-pox, and tuberculosis. Venereal disease took its toll, also. The worst curse was the white-man's fire-water. The Indians were utterly unable to control their desire for rum, brandy, or whisky once they had had a taste of it, and untold numbers were completely debauched by its use. The Indians became pawns in the white man's wars. They were used by the French in fighting their ancient foes, the British, and the latter used them, once they were in control, to combat the Americans.

The missionaries made valiant attempts to christianize and civilize the Indians. Their efforts were thwarted by a combination of natural resistance by the Indians and the activities of the fur traders who used liquor extensively in the fur-trading business. Furthermore, the necessities of the fur trade called for the Indians to spend long periods in the woods, away from missions where the missionaries were striving to teach the natives new ideas and new ways of life. The Spanish Jesuits, working in Florida, California, and New Mexico, built mission centers around which large numbers of natives came to live and where they were taught arts and crafts as well as the precepts of the Christian religion. In New France the only instance of this sort was Huronia. Here, in the region around Georgian Bay, the Jesuits made a concerted effort to persuade the Indians to settle down and change their mode of life. Unfortunately, this hopeful experiment was ruined by the attacks of the Iroquois, in which both the Jesuits and their Huron charges were killed indiscriminately. At the missions later established in Michigan and elsewhere in the Great Lakes region the missionaries had to work under conditions that made their success impossible. The net result was to change very little either the nature or the mode of life of the Indian people.

The appearance, social customs, and habits of the Indians were studied and reported at length by the Jesuit missionaries who came to live among them. The reports of the Jesuits, transmitted to their superiors in France, are called the *Jesuit Relations*.[7] Many of the missionaries remarked upon the fact that the

[7] See R. G. Thwaites (ed.), *The Jesuit Relations and Allied Documents*.

Indians were handsome and well-proportioned, that their health and stamina were better than that of the Europeans, and that their senses were highly developed. The liberality and hospitality of the natives also received frequent comment. Parental love was carried so far that children were not disciplined, they reported. Among the characteristics of Indian life that shocked the Jesuits were sexual immorality, promiscuity, and lewdness. The Indian's lack of cleanliness, his gluttony, and his barbarity also were noted and condemned by the Jesuits. On the other hand, the stoicism of the natives and their capacity for suffering pain without wincing often excited the admiration of the missionaries. In his natural state the Indian seemed to be capable at once of high nobility and abysmal depravity.[8]

The contributions of the Indians to the white men who came into the land where they lived were of inestimable value. For one thing, Indians served as guides; without their knowledge of the lakes, rivers, and trails the progress of exploration would have been far slower. The Indians' birch-bark canoe enabled the French fur traders and missionaries to make long journeys with comparative ease. The trails over which the Indians led the white men were originally animal trails and unerringly followed the most practical routes. Later the pioneers built many of their highways and railroads along these Indian trails. For example, the Chicago Military Road, laid out in 1826, followed the route of the old Sauk trail, by which the members of the tribe of this name traveled to Detroit. Later the Michigan Southern Railroad was built along the same route, and today highway US 12 roughly parallels it. The Indians not only helped the whites travel around and through Michigan, but they also taught them how to subsist during their journeys. These Indians were skilled hunters, trappers, and fishermen. They taught the white man how to grow corn, or maize, a grain unknown to the old world. No single item of food was so important to the pioneer as corn. Pioneers encountered difficulty when they tried to raise wheat, rye, and barley on virgin soil, but corn was easy to grow and served a multitude of purposes.[9] The Indian taught the white man to know which of the wild berries and fruits were suitable for food, and which herbs were useful in treating diseases. The Europeans were also introduced to the pleasures of tobacco by the Indians. It is no accident that the figure of an Indian, carved out of wood, was long the sign of tobacco shops.[10]

[8] J. H. Kennedy, *Jesuit and Savage in New France*, p. 131.
[9] P. Weatherwax, *Indian Corn in Old America*.
[10] R. K. Heimann, *Tobacco and Americans*.

The Indians contributed many words to our language. Of Indian origin are such words as raccoon, opossum, moose, skunk, hickory, squash, caribou, pecan, paw-paw, persimmon, terrapin, catalpa, hominy, pone, toboggan, mackinaw, moccasin, sachem, powwow, maize, mugwump, and caucus.[11] In Michigan many rivers, lakes, counties, and cities bear Indian names: Huron, Michigan, Kalamazoo, Osceola, Chippewa, Saginaw, Muskegon, and Tecumseh are examples. It must be noted, however, that in most instances these names of Indian origin have undergone a considerable degree of modification. White men attempted to write down letters that would represent as closely as possible the sounds of Indian words. There followed many adaptations and alterations according to accident or convenience.[12]

The Indians were vital to the economy of New France, because that economy was based on the trade in furs, and the natives were skilled in trapping those animals that yielded the valuable pelts. Attracted by the trading goods the French had to offer him, and consumed by desire for the firewater they also provided, the Indian generally welcomed the first white men. No considerable number of Frenchmen came to Michigan to be farmers; hence the Indian had no fear of losing his hunting grounds to the French. Many of the French intermarried with the Indians. But the British, when they took over the management of the fur trade from the French, were less well received by the natives. The Britishers tended to be more aloof and to take a more condescending attitude toward the Indians. There was one serious revolt against British rule, but it ended in failure. In spite of their scorn for the natives, the British, like the French, recognized the importance of the Indian to their economy, and by the Proclamation of 1763 sought to keep farmers in the English colonies from moving across the Allegheny Mountains. In both the American Revolution and the War of 1812 the Indians of Michigan were generally on the side of the British because they had begun to fear that the coming of the American pioneer would mean the loss of their hunting grounds. The fear was well founded. By the use of force, by promising annual payments of goods, and by distributing intoxicating liquor freely, the Americans induced chiefs of the Indian tribes to sign a series of treaties by which they surrendered to the United States their claim to Michigan lands. The first treaty by which Indian lands

[11] H. L. Mencken, *The American Language*, pp. 104ff.
[12] See, for example, my book *Kalamazoo and How It Grew*, for the origin of the word "Kalamazoo."

in Michigan were ceded to the United States was signed at Greenville, Ohio, in 1795. The last major segment of Michigan land to be given up by the Indian tribes was ceded to the United States in 1842 by the Treaty of La Pointe.

To the American pioneer the Indian was of no importance to the economy. As the fur trade declined and agriculture took its place as the mainstay of Michigan economy, the Indian became a barrier to the exploitation of the area's land resources, and the consuming purpose of the pioneers was to get rid of him. Because there was no war with the Indians after the pioneers began coming to Michigan in large numbers, as there had been, for example, in Kentucky, there was no great antipathy among the settlers toward the Indians as individuals. Their thieving and drunkenness was often a nuisance, but no more. What the Michigan pioneer wanted was the Indian's land; what became of the Indian did not concern him.

The status of the Indian tribes under American law was that of nations within a nation. Each of the treaties with Indian tribes was subject to the approval of the United States Senate, just as were treaties signed with foreign countries. What is now the State of Michigan was included within the territories ceded to the United States by Great Britain in 1783. But the *land* of Michigan was the property of the Indian tribes, and was so recognized by law. It remained the property of those tribes until it was ceded to the United States by treaty. Furthermore, the United States government did not generally attempt to exercise sovereignty over the Indian tribes until much later. The people who belonged to these tribes were governed by their own customs and rules, not by the laws of the United States. A notable instance of this was the unsuccessful attempt to convict a chief of an Ottawa tribe of murder, after he had killed a tribesman in retribution for the death of another Indian whom the tribesman had killed. The court held that the chief had acted in accordance with Indian custom and that he could not be convicted under the white man's laws.

It is not correct to assume that the United States paid the Indians little or nothing for their land. Up to 1880 the total cost to the United States government of the public domain acquired from the Indians amounted to $275,000,000 and the surveys of the land had cost another $46,000,000. Total receipts from the sale of public lands up to that date were $120,000,000 less than the above expenditures.[13] The Indians received for their

---

[13] T. Donaldson, *The Public Domain: Its History*, p. 21.

lands cash, goods, and promises. Often the government agreed to pay annuities to a tribe over a period of years. In a treaty negotiated by Michigan Territorial Governor Lewis Cass and Solomon Sibley at Chicago in 1821, the government, in return for the cession of the southwest corner of Michigan, agreed to pay to the Ottawa Indians an annuity of $1,000 in cash and $1,500 annually in support of a blacksmith, a teacher, and an agricultural instructor, and for cattle and utensils; and to the Potawatomi a $5,000 annuity was paid for twenty years and $1,000 for fifteen years for a blacksmith and a teacher.[14] Treaties such as this were to lead to numerous suits against the government, brought by Indian tribesmen in later years, claiming damages on the ground that the government did not fulfill the obligations it assumed under the treaties, and in some cases that the Indian tribes had not been paid the fair value of their land at the time.

The earlier treaties by which the Indian tribes ceded lands in Michigan to the United States often provided for small tracts or reservations within the area granted on which the Indians might continue to live. For instance, in the Treaty of Chicago in 1821 mentioned above, by which the Indians ceded a huge amount of land in southwestern Michigan, five tracts were reserved, one of which included nine square miles. In 1827 the Indians agreed to exchange all the reservations they had secured in the Treaty of Chicago for a consolidated reservation called Nottawa-Sepee in Kalamazoo and St. Joseph counties. This also was surrendered in a treaty signed in 1833, also called the Treaty of Chicago. There were numerous instances of this same sort elsewhere in Michigan.

By 1833 the United States government had adopted a policy of eventually moving all the Indians of Michigan west of the Mississippi River. The policy was suggested by President Monroe early in 1825. He proposed that removal should be brought about only in such a way as to promote the interest and happiness of the tribes as well as the honor of the United States. Monroe advised that the government should seek to settle the Indians where they could be taught the arts of civilized society and to preserve peace and order among the tribes. Secretary of War John C. Calhoun, in a report that accompanied Monroe's proposals, suggested that the Indians of Michigan should not be removed west of the Mississippi, but rather that they be assigned land in the region west of Lake Michigan where the

[14] R. C. Buley, *The Old Northwest: Pioneer Period, 1815-1840*, I, 112-113.

climate and nature of the country were "more favorable to their habits." Calhoun probably thought that the region he had in mind, along with the vast area west of the Mississippi, then marked on maps as the "Great American Desert," would never attract white settlers. The "Permanent Indian Frontier" that was worked out in accordance with the suggestions of Monroe and Calhoun ran along the western boundaries of Louisiana, Arkansas, and Missouri, then swung eastward almost to the Mississippi. It then ran in a generally northerly direction to about the central part of the present state of Minnesota, after which it turned eastward again so as to include in the Indian country a large portion of the northern part of the present State of Wisconsin and a portion of what is now Michigan's Upper Peninsula.

The implementation of the new government policy began on August 29, 1825, when General William Clark and Michigan Territorial Governor Lewis Cass signed a treaty with the Sioux, Winnebago, and Chippewa Tribes at Prairie du Chien, in which these tribes agreed to accept definite boundaries and to recognize United States sovereignty. Other treaties followed, under which western tribes agreed to make way for eastern tribes and eastern tribes were induced to agree to move west. The treaties made with Michigan Indians after 1825 were all directed to this ultimate objective.

Of the principal Indian nations that were in Michigan when the French first came, the Miami moved outside the present boundaries of the state shortly after the beginning of the eighteenth century. By an act of Congress in 1809 the Wyandot, or Huron, were given possession of a tract of land in the southeastern part of Michigan, which they occupied for fifty years. Nine years later Governor Cass negotiated a treaty with them under which they agreed to give up this reservation and receive instead a tract of 4,996 acres along the Huron River in what is now Wayne County, to be held by them and their descendents as long as they should continue to occupy it. Sometime later the Wyandot left Michigan, however, and by a treaty signed in 1842 relinquished to the United States all their claims to land in Michigan.

The Potawatomi lived in the southwestern part of the Lower Peninsula when the United States began the process of securing the Indian lands. This nation ceded its last reservations in Michigan to the United States by the Treaty of Chicago in 1833, agreeing to move to the lands west of the Mississippi that had been assigned to it. The removal was delayed for several years, but between 1838 and 1840 government agents rounded up members of the tribe and started them on their long trek westward. At first located in Missouri opposite Fort Leavenworth, they were moved after two years to Iowa, near Council Bluffs. They stayed there for only a short time, after which they were again moved to Kansas. There they remained for about thirty years, after which they were transferred to Indian Territory.

A considerable number of Potawatomi remained in Michigan. Some eluded the government agents. Others escaped during the journey to the West and returned. In some of the treaties, grants of land were made to individual Indians, and although the recipients in many instances sold their holdings to white settlers, there probably was a considerable number who retained their land. In some cases the treaty grant withheld the power to sell for a time. Leopold Pokagon, a devout Roman Catholic, was able to get an exemption in the Treaty of 1833 that allowed him and his band to remain on the lands he had purchased in Silver Creek Township, Cass County. It is estimated that there were about 250 Potawatomi in this group. Pokagon later obtained lands in Van Buren County, around Hartford, where a group of Potawatomi made their homes. His son, Simon Pokagon, was born there in 1830. After the death of his father in 1841 Simon became leader of the Potawatomi band. In later life he was regarded as the best educated full-blooded Indian in America. He wrote several books, one of which, *Queen of the Woods*, contains much information on the Potawatomi language. The descendants of Pokagon's band still live in southwestern Michigan and northern Indiana and maintain a tribal organization.[15] Another group of Potawatomi, living near Athens in Calhoun County, refused to follow their fellow tribesmen west. In 1850 a committee of villagers in Athens managed to secure from the government the sum of $3,000 for these Potawatomi, and with the money purchased a small tract of land for them. Potawatomi still live on this tract in a settlement called "Indiantown."

The Ottawa, like the Potawatomi, resisted removal, and some of them, too, were able to escape the fate that befell many members of the tribe. A large number made their way to Canada, where they were welcomed by the Canadian government and provided with presents annually.[16] By the Treaty of Washington,

[15] A. B. Copley, "The Pottawattomies," *Mich. Pioneer and Historical Colls.*, XIV (1889), 256-268.

[16] R. F. Bauman, "Kansas, Canada, or Starvation," *Michigan History*, XXXVI (1932), 287-299.

in 1836, five tracts of land totalling 142,000 acres were reserved for the Ottawa and Chippewa tribes, and also several tracts north of the Straits of Mackinac for the Chippewa alone. Thus many of the members of these two nations were able to remain in Michigan. In 1854 and 1855 most of these reservations were given up, and by treaties made with the two nations the United States agreed to withhold from sale certain townships in which each head of family or single male over twenty-one years of age was to be entitled to an eighty-acre plot of land. More than a million dollars in money payments also were made under these treaties to the Indians.[17]

The number of Michigan Indians involved in the removal west of the Mississippi was probably considerably less than the number who remained in Michigan. Schoolcraft estimated that there were 7,737 Indians in Michigan in 1837 before many had been removed, although this figure probably is too low. The federal census of 1860 enumerated 6,172 Indians in Michigan. The state census of 1874 enumerated a total of 10,250 Indians, but the federal census six years later counted only 7,249. This indicates a considerable degree of variation, but leads one to conclude that the total number removed west could not have been very large. Disease took a heavy toll of Indian lives; as late as 1921 the Indian death rate was more than double the rate for the total population. By 1920 the total Indian population of Michigan was down to 5,614, although, of course, it is difficult to determine how many people of Indian ancestry had passed over into the white classification.[18]

Since 1920 the Indian population of Michigan has increased substantially. In 1940 it stood at 6,282; in 1950, 7,000; and in 1960, 9,701. The federal government policy of encouraging the break-up of tribes and the allotment of land to individuals was reversed in 1934 with the passage of the Indian Reorganization Act. An effort has been made under the provisions of this law to help the Indian regain sufficient land holdings for a self-sustaining economy and a self-satisfying social organization. Tribal reorganization has been encouraged. There are four reservations in Michigan today, consisting of a total of 22,721 acres of land.[19]

[17] A. Felch, "The Indians of Michigan and the Cession of Their Lands to the United States by Treaties," *Mich. Pioneer and Historical Colls.,* XVI (1894-95), 274-297.

[18] C. S. Larzalere, "The Red Man in Michigan," *Michigan History,* XVII (1933), 373.

[19] Although these tracts are called "reservations," the Indians are not required to live on them.

The largest of these is the Keweenaw Bay (L'Anse) Community, with 15,738 acres. The others are the Bay Mills Community in Chippewa County, Hannahville Community in Menominee County, and the Isabella Reservation in Isabella County. These lands are held in trust by the United States government for the benefit of the Indians. There is a tribal organization for each reservation, with a written constitution approved under the provisions of the Indian Reorganization Act. Some but not all of the members of the tribal organizations live on the reservations. In addition to these four reservations, a total of 4,349 acres of land are held by

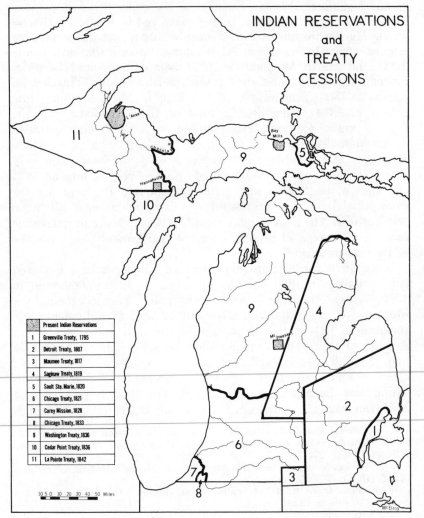

INDIAN RESERVATIONS
and
TREATY CESSIONS

	Present Indian Reservations
1	Greenville Treaty, 1795
2	Detroit Treaty, 1807
3	Maumee Treaty, 1817
4	Saginaw Treaty, 1819
5	Sault Ste. Marie, 1820
6	Chicago Treaty, 1821
7	Carey Mission, 1828
8	Chicago Treaty, 1833
9	Washington Treaty, 1836
10	Cedar Point Treaty, 1836
11	La Pointe Treaty, 1842

10 5 0 10 20 30 40 50 Miles

the Northern Michigan Ottawa Association, consisting of some 6,000 members living in widely scattered areas. In 1953 Congress adopted a policy of gradually terminating federal supervision over these tribal organizations.

In spite of the policy of the federal government after 1934 to encourage the Indians to retain tribal ties, Michigan Indians are being slowly assimilated into the population. On none of the reservations have the Indians been able or disposed to return to their ancient ways. Income from their lands is insufficient to sustain life. Many Indians have taken employment in non-agricultural lines. Wayne County has a sizable Indian population. But although the Michigan Indian is losing his identity as an Indian, the legends of his people and their words and names remain with us. Our roads follow their trails. They have transmitted to us some of their love of nature. Their ancient way of life has a great fascination for Michiganians of the space age, and particularly for children.

2

THE FRENCH EXPLORERS

Frenchmen were probably the first Europeans to see Michigan.[1] Samuel de Champlain, who founded Quebec in 1608, explored as far westward as Georgian Bay in 1615, but it is doubtful that he saw any of the land that is now part of the State of Michigan. One of his protégés, Etienne Brulé, went further and it is now regarded as probable that the latter reached the vicinity of Sault Ste. Marie in the winter of 1618-19. In 1621 or 1622 he and a companion named Grenoble paddled up the St. Mary's River into Lake Superior. On his way back to Quebec Brulé told the story of his journey to Gabriel Sagard, a lay brother of the Recollet missionaries who were working among the Huron Indians, and Sagard, in his *Histoire de Canada*, published in 1636, mentioned Brulé's discoveries. Two years before Sagard's book was published, Jean Nicolet, another of the young men who had been encouraged by Champlain to live among the Indians and learn their language and ways, had journeyed westward and had passed through the Straits of Mackinac.

[1] Occasionally it is claimed that Vikings and even Phoenicians reached Michigan much earlier. There certainly is no valid evidence in the case of the Phoenicians. The claim that the Vikings may have seen Michigan about the year 1362 is based on the so-called "Rune Stone" found near Kensington, Minnesota in 1898. An inscription on this stone was translated by a Norwegian-American scholar to relate that eight Goths and twenty-two Norwegians were in the vicinity in 1362. But the accuracy of the translation and the authenticity of the stone are rejected by most leading scholars. See E. Wahlgren, *The Kensington Stone, a Mystery Solved.*

47

The first Europeans reached Michigan about the same time the Pilgrims landed at Plymouth. But the French were slow to follow up their first discoveries. Not until 1660 did they have a fairly accurate knowledge of the size and shape of Lake Superior. By that time they had paddled their canoes along the southern shore of that lake, now a part of Michigan's Upper Peninsula, and they probably had penetrated somewhat into the interior. During the last forty years of the seventeenth century they explored the coastline of the Lower Peninsula of Michigan and gained some knowledge of the interior. Maps of the Great Lakes area drawn by the best European cartographers in 1704 located all the Great Lakes with some degree of accuracy, but the shape of the Lower Peninsula was grossly misrepresented, and indeed, maps drawn as late as the middle of the nineteenth century still did not show it accurately.[2] It is an odd fact that the most sparsely populated areas of Michigan today were the first to be found by the Europeans, while the more heavily populated southern portion of the Lower Peninsula was not explored until considerably later.

WHY THE FRENCH WERE THE FIRST EUROPEANS TO REACH MICHIGAN

The course of history has been influenced powerfully by geography. The Spaniards who colonized Mexico in the sixteenth century had explored far to the north of that country into what is now the United States, but they were unable to cope with the problems of the Great Plains and their settlements reached only as far northward as Texas and New Mexico. The English and the Dutch, who founded colonies along the Atlantic coast, were barred from the interior by formidable ranges of high mountains and by the strength of the Iroquois Indians who occupied the Mohawk Valley—the one major route by which easy access to the West was feasible. But the French, whose explorers discovered the St. Lawrence River, were lured into the interior through lakes and rivers whose waters eventually find their way to the Atlantic Ocean through the St. Lawrence. Because the French king gained title to the St. Lawrence River by reason of discovery, his subjects were the first Europeans to reach Michigan.

Jacques Cartier, a Breton pilot of the port of St. Malo, found the mouth of the St. Lawrence and ascended it above the present

[2] L. C. Karpinski, *Bibliography of the Printed Maps of Michigan, 1804-1880.*

site of the city of Quebec. His voyages for the king of France were made in 1534, 1535, and 1541-42. But nothing was done about these discoveries for many years. In the latter part of the 16th century France was engulfed in a long series of disastrous civil wars, involving religious and dynastic rivalries. Peace was restored in 1598, and a remarkably able monarch emerged from the terrible struggles in the person of Henry IV. He did much to encourage exploration and colonization in America. The first colonists were established in Acadia (later called Nova Scotia). Lacking funds to establish colonies himself, Henry IV granted a monopoly of the fur trade to a successful promoter, the Sieur de Monts, as a means of developing his American possessions. It was de Monts and his associates who brought the first settlers to Acadia. Among them was a French navigator, map maker, and friend of Henry IV—Samuel de Champlain. This was the man whose initiative was eventually to push French explorers far westward.

Champlain persuaded de Monts that a post up the St. Lawrence would be desirable for the fur trade, and on July 3, 1608, he founded Quebec. The death of Henry IV in 1610 resulted in the cancellation of de Mont's monopoly, but Champlain was retained by the new company formed by a group of French noblemen. His fascination with what lay beyond the horizon to the west was soon demonstrated.

The direction his explorations took and the route to the West the French were to follow for many years was determined the year after Quebec was founded. In order to cultivate the friendship of the Algonquin tribes and the Huron Indians who lived in the vicinity of Quebec, Champlain and a company of Frenchmen accompanied these Indians on a war party against their dreaded enemies, the Iroquois. They went up the Richelieu River to the lake that now bears Champlain's name, where they ran into a party of Iroquois. The firearms used by the French in the ensuing struggle threw the Iroquois into panic-stricken flight and incurred their lasting enmity. This powerful confederation occupied lands along the south shore of Lake Ontario and hence was in a position to block effectively the use of this waterway by the French. It is not certain that Champlain would have conducted his explorations of the West along the route of today's St. Lawrence seaway had it not been for the enmity of the Iroquois, but there can be no doubt that in the years that followed the French were prevented by the Iroquois time and time again from conducting explorations that might have taken them into southern Michigan, Ohio, and Indiana.

The mighty Ottawa River, which pours the waters accumulated along its 696 mile course into the St. Lawrence at Montreal, must have presented an inviting route to the West. Paddling against the current presented no great difficulty to the experienced canoemen who accompanied Champlain in 1613 on his first extended trip up the Ottawa River. Two years later Champlain and his party reached Georgian Bay by the Ottawa River route. They traveled up the Ottawa and into its tributary, the Mattawa, carrying their canoes and supplies through rapids, around waterfalls and over portages until they reached Lake Nippising, whence they followed the French River, which led them into Georgian Bay. At the head of the Bay, Champlain found Father Joseph Le Caron, a Recollet who had arrived there shortly before to start a mission among the Huron Indians. Joining an Algonquin war party, he traveled to the northern shore of Lake Ontario. The party then crossed the Lake into modern New York and fought a battle with the Iroquois in which Champlain was wounded. Returning to the Huron mission, he wintered there (1615-16). The Indians told him tales of a great lake forty days journey to the west. Though intrigued by this, Champlain returned to Quebec in the spring, thereafter leaving exploration to younger men. It was one of these, Etienne Brulé, who ventured much further westward in 1618, and reached the St. Mary's River.

WHAT THE FRENCH SOUGHT

Before describing the explorations by the French that revealed the shape and character of Michigan, it will be helpful to inquire what actuated these men. Curiosity about the unknown and the itch for adventure may be taken for granted as traits of the intrepid Frenchmen who braved the dangers and privations of the wilderness in order to discover what lay beyond the horizon. No doubt they thought there was always a chance that they would come to a land of immense riches, remembering the vast stores of gold and silver the Spaniards had discovered in Mexico and Peru. The Portuguese had found a source of great wealth in trade with the Far East, which Europeans of the time called "the Indies," and the French in their explorations westward persistently sought a water route that would lead them through the continent and provide a better way to the Indies. Francis I, when he commissioned Verrazano to sail under his flag, hoped that the expedition might reach "Cathay on the extreme coast of Asia." Champlain, when he heard of a people who dwelt beside the "Stinking Water" (which he thought meant salt water) and were called "People of the Sea," assumed that they were orientals or that they traded with residents of the Tartary visited by Marco Polo. So he equipped Jean Nicolet, before the latter left for an expedition westward, with a gorgeous robe of China damask "all strewn with flowers and birds of many colors" to put on when he arrived among them. When Nicolet, after passing through the Straits of Mackinac, reached Green Bay he thought he was on the verge of Cathay. We may imagine his disappointment when he found only the Indian villages.

But this was not the end of the quest; it was only the beginning. When the French heard of a great river further west, they jumped to the conclusion that this would lead them to the western sea. The prime objective of the famous expedition of Jolliet and Marquette in 1673 was to explore this river, the Mississippi. These explorers went far enough south to determine that it did not flow into the western sea, then returned. La Salle received permission from the king in 1677 to conduct explorations of the West by holding out the hope that he could find the route to Cathay and the East. It is amazing how long Europeans persisted in pursuing this will-o'-the-wisp. Long after they knew that rapids and falls blocked the passages inland, necessitating laborious portages, the search went on. An historical novel by Kenneth Roberts, *Northwest Passage*, revolves around the story of how Englishmen continued the quest. It is a bit difficult to see how such a waterway would have been of much use if it had been found. The dream must have been a sort of fixation, passed on from generation to generation long after it ceased to have any importance as a practical project.

Along with this purpose of finding a way through the continent and thus getting to the wealth of the East, was the desire to find a source of wealth in the new land itself. Already a thousand vessels were visiting the northern coasts of America each year and returning with valuable cargoes of fish. They also carried back furs, which they obtained in the trade with the natives. It was the fur trade that finally became the economic basis for New France. Possibilities of gain from this trade interested the king, numerous individuals and companies in France, and countless Frenchmen in the new world. Some of the chief explorers, Radisson and Groseilliers, for instance, were fur traders.

Other sources of profit were sought without success. Champlain, before he came to New France, had the unusual opportunity of going to Mexico, through the influence of an uncle in the service of the king of Spain. He became familiar while there with the vast harvest of silver and gold that had been reaped by the king of Spain in that country. He may have dreamed of similar mines in the interior of North America beyond the St. Lawrence. Of course they never were found. Father Claude Allouez did find specimens of pure copper along Keweenaw Bay, and Intendant Jean Talon sent Adrien Jolliet to find the mine where those specimens were produced. He found no such mine, and there are no records of any further effort by the French to exploit this rich resource of Michigan.

The vision of empire was another impelling force behind the French explorations. It was an unwritten law that unknown lands belonged to that monarch whose subjects found them first. The establishment of New France was actuated in part by the rivalry between France and Spain. Champlain must have hoped to build up a vast empire for his king comparable with that which he had seen belonging to the Spanish king. In the late seventeenth century, France became the leading power of Europe. The court of Louis XIV was the most brilliant of any in the world. In literature, art, and culture, as well as arms, France was pre-eminent. It was fitting that such a great monarch as Louis XIV should be able to boast of his far-flung possessions in America.

Another force that drove the French into the interior was the flaming zeal of the French missionaries to save the souls of the "savages." It is difficult for us to comprehend the attitude of these men. They regarded this life as a torture, and death as a great release. They not only endured hardship, they courted it. Even when living in France, or in Quebec, they permitted themselves no comforts. François de Laval, the great bishop of New France, who rivaled the governor in power, slept in a bed where he was tortured by fleas, kept meat until it was rotten, and shrunk from no humble or disgusting service. Such asceticism, such denial of the comforts and pleasures of the world, is not common in our time. It did not matter to the Jesuit how hopeless it might seem to convert the Indians to Christianity and to persuade them to accept civilized ways. His job was to carry out the will of God, to forego all bodily pleasures, and to labor unceasingly to convert the Indians, all as much for the sake of his own soul as for that of the Indian. When a man has not the slightest desire to live any longer than God ordains, he is not only unafraid to brave danger but he welcomes it. And thus we find men like Fathers Menard, Allouez, and Marquette blazing the trails that led into Michigan and the West. Of course there were among them rascals and men who were not above courting a little worldly fame for themselves, fellows like Father Hennepin who fabricated a wild tale of adventure and had historians duped by it for a long time. But for the most part the missionaries were intensely devoted to the single cause that dominated their lives.

OTHER CONDITIONING FORCES

The enmity of the Iroquois, which Champlain incurred early in his career in New France, forced the French, as has been noted, to use the "upper route" by way of the Ottawa River and Lake Nippising in their early explorations of the West. The Iroquois soon became allies of the Dutch, who settled in New York, and of the English when the latter took over the Dutch colony in 1664. Furnished by the Dutch with iron axes, awls, traps, and other implements, they quickly passed from the Stone Age to the Iron Age. The Dutch also provided them with guns and ammunition. Thus equipped, they crossed Lake Ontario in 1642 and set upon the missions established by the French among the Huron. Within a short time, they moved far enough northward to block the upper route to the West as well as the lower-lakes route. For almost two decades thereafter the French were able to make little progress in the further exploration of the West. Only the fearless *coureurs de bois*, or unlicensed fur traders, braved the dangers of the Iroquois fury. With the destruction of the Huron completed, the Iroquois turned against the Neutral, or Tobacco Indians of southern Ontario, burning their towns and slaughtering hundreds of the inhabitants. The effect of this was to drive the Indians of the Lower Peninsula of Michigan westward into Wisconsin to seek new homes. Lower Michigan was almost entirely depopulated. In 1653 a great Iroquois war party ventured west of Lake Michigan, but there it met disaster and almost complete destruction. A portion of that army was killed near Sault Ste. Marie; the name Iroquois Point still preserves the memory of that battle. Thereafter the Iroquois made a brief truce with the French and their Indian allies, allowing a great fleet of canoes from the West, richly laden with furs, to venture down the Ottawa River to Montreal.

But the truce did not last. Soon the Iroquois were on the war-path again, and in 1660 they moved to wipe out the French settlements along the St. Lawrence. A force of sixteen enlisted men and a few Huron and Algonquin under the leadership of a young nobleman named Dollard, who attempted to intercept them, was wiped out to a man, but so stubborn was their resistance that the Iroquois retired. Thoroughly alarmed now, the king sent a regiment of 1,200 soldiers to protect the colony. This force quickly reduced the Iroquois to submission and in 1667 a peace was signed that lasted almost two decades. It was in this interval between 1667 and 1688 that French exploration in the Great Lakes area was most active.

In addition to the enmity of the Iroquois, conditions in the homeland affected the exploration of the West. Champlain's work was made difficult by the misgovernment that followed the assassination of Henry IV in 1610. The great nobles who dominated the scene were interested only in personal profit and opposed expansion and settlement as injurious to the fur trade, which yielded them gains as high as forty percent. Cardinal Richelieu, who came to power in 1624, emphasized colonization and to some degree encouraged expansion. During his regime, however, England and France were at war, and the English sent an expedition that captured Quebec in 1629, holding it for three years. This episode quite necessarily called a halt to exploration for a time. Richelieu, in the closing years of his career, became deeply engulfed in European struggles for power and had less time to promote the interests of New France. Cardinal Mazarin, who was master of France during the years when young king Louis XIV was growing into manhood, also was engrossed in the struggle for power in Europe, as well as in civil conflict.

At Mazarin's death in 1661, Louis XIV assumed personal rule. He relied heavily, however, on the advice of his able finance minister, Jean-Baptiste Colbert. And Colbert was principally interested in the security of the French settlements along the St. Lawrence as a source of profit from the fur trade. He consistently opposed the establishment of posts in the interior on the ground that this would weaken the colonies along the St. Lawrence. This was definitely a handicap to western exploration. It explains why so much of that exploration was carried on by missionaries and by illicit fur traders rather than by official expeditions sent out by the governor of the colony. Some of the governors, notably Count Frontenac, undoubtedly profited personally from the fur trade in the interior and did all they could within the limits imposed by Colbert to promote it. Colbert was only willing to sanction exploration that was aimed at seeking the elusive waterway through the continent and at finding mineral wealth. Following his exploration of the Mississippi with Marquette, Louis Jolliet sought permission from the king to establish a settlement in the Illinois country but was refused. Repeatedly Frontenac was forbidden to issue permits to trade in the interior, although he disregarded the orders so far as he dared. Colbert wanted the Indians to bring their peltry to Montreal to trade there. But experience demonstrated that this was impractical, chiefly because the Iroquois and their English allies penetrated the West and threatened to get the fur trade away from the French. Had it not been for this threat to the backbone of New France's economy, the exploration of the West and the establishment of trading posts in the interior might have come about more slowly than it actually did.

UPPER MICHIGAN TAKES SHAPE, 1618-1668

Because of the route they followed to reach the West, the French became acquainted with Upper Michigan long before they were aware of the contours of Lower Michigan. The discoveries of Brulé and Nicolet gave them some knowledge of the St. Mary's River and the Straits of Mackinac. Brulé may have ventured some distance into the Lake Superior region, precisely how far we do not know. The next visitors to Michigan were two Jesuit priests, Fathers Isaac Jogues and Charles Raymbault. They traveled to the rapids of the St. Mary's River in 1641, where they found a great many Chippewa catching whitefish. They named the place Sault Sainte Marie. The word "sault" means rapids. Sainte Marie was the name of the chief mission in Huronia from which the two Jesuits had come. After a short time they returned to Huronia, intending to come back to the Sault and establish a mission there. But Huronia was attacked shortly afterward by the Iroquois, and the two priests were killed.

It will be recalled that Champlain had visited Father Le Caron, a Recollet priest who had started a mission among the Huron Indians at the head of Georgian Bay. He was one of three members of that Order who came to Quebec in 1615 at the invitation of Champlain. For several years Father Le Caron and two other Recollets studied the Huron language and baptized a few converts, but they found the undertaking too vast, and determined to invite the more powerful Jesuits to share it with them. The first Jesuits arrived in 1625. The English conquest of 1629 caused the withdrawal of all priests from New France and it was not until 1633 that Champlain returned with 200 colonists to restore the St. Lawrence settlements.

Included in Champlain's party were four Jesuits who were returning to the missionary work among the Huron that they had had to abandon four years before. They were joined by other priests and by lay brothers who undertook the systematic work of converting and civilizing the members of the Huron nation.

They brought blacksmiths, bakers, farmers, and other artisans, and built a fortified headquarters to serve as a safe retreat for the missionaries and their converts. Located near present-day Midland, Ontario, it was named Sainte Marie, in honor of the mother of Christ. A church and shrine are maintained there to-day, and are visited annually by thousands of devotees. From Ste. Marie the fathers went out to gradually expand their activities. Thus Fathers Jogues and Raymbault came to the place where the Chippewa were fishing in 1641, and the name they gave the spot was that of their principal mission in what was called "Huronia."

Although Huronia was a flourishing and successful enterprise, it was doomed to destruction. A feud had long existed between the Huron and the Five Nations of the Iroquois in present-day New York. Supplied by the Dutch with guns and gunpowder, as well as other implements of war, the Iroquois suddenly descended upon Huronia in 1642. They slaughtered the entire population of the first town they attacked. The attacks continued year after year, many of the Jesuits as well as their Indian charges falling victims to the bloodthirsty Iroquois warriors. Driven from Ste. Marie in 1648, the Jesuits built another fortified station, also called Ste. Marie on one of the Christian Islands in Georgian Bay. Thousands of Indians followed them, but there was no means of feeding so many. In despair the Jesuits abandoned the Huron mission in 1650. The Iroquois were now in a position to block the French from using the upper as well as the lower route to the West.

Not until the Iroquois were defeated by the Indians west of Lake Michigan in 1653 and forced to sign a truce was it possible for Frenchmen to venture westward from the St. Lawrence settlements. In 1654 a great fleet of Indian canoes laden with furs ventured down the Ottawa River to Montreal and was greeted with great rejoicing by the French. When the Indians returned to the western country "two young Frenchmen full of courage" went with them. It is generally assumed that these Frenchmen were Medart Chouart, Sieur de Groseilliers and his brother-in-law, Pierre Esprit, Sieur de Radisson. Groseilliers had spent several years in Huronia as an assistant to the Jesuits and Radisson, still a mere youth, had experienced some hazardous adventures among the Iroquois in New York. Some years later, Radisson wrote an account of his "third voyage" (the first two being those to the Iroquois), which probably refers to the one that began when he and his brother-in-law returned with the Indians who had brought the great flotilla of canoes to Montreal in 1654. The *Jesuit Relation* of 1656 mentions the return that year of two travelers who had spent two years in the interior of the country—referring, we may assume, to Radisson and Groseilliers. In 1659-1660 the two men journeyed to Lake Superior and far to the northwest. They returned with a large quantity of furs, but they were heavily fined by the governor of New France because they had undertaken the expedition without his permission. In disgust the two adventurers departed from New France and went to England, where Radisson wrote an account of his journeys and convinced the English that great wealth in the fur trade was to be gained in the country north and west of Lake Superior. As a consequence the English formed the Hudson's Bay Company, which has endured down to the present day and is the greatest fur company of all time.[3]

The extent of the discoveries of Radisson and Groseilliers is difficult to determine with any exactness. Radisson wrote his account in English, a language unfamiliar to him, and, furthermore, he wrote it some years after the journey took place. There would also appear to be a deliberate effort to make the narrative somewhat obscure and difficult to follow. It seems to be certain, however, that the two intrepid adventurers followed the southern shoreline of Lake Superior and ventured into the interior of what is now Michigan's Upper Peninsula in the course of a journey that took them also further to the west. Radisson describes Sault Ste. Marie, certainly identifies the Pictured Rocks (near present-day Munising) and a portage across the Keweenaw Peninsula, and indicates the presence of copper in the region.

Radisson brought word back to Montreal in 1660 that a remnant of the Huron who had escaped the fury of the Iroquois were living at the west end of Lake Superior. This report fired the zeal of 55-year-old Father René Menard, who had ministered to these people in the halcyon days of Huronia. He returned westward with the Indians, accompanied, it would appear, by a number of fur traders, determined to re-establish contact with the Huron and begin the work of restoring them to the Christian fold. Near the present site of L'Anse, Menard wintered with the Ottawa Indians with whom he had returned, although he was unceremoniously ejected from the hut of the tribal chief for rebuking the latter for his depravity. Menard survived and in the spring of 1661 found his way to Chequamegon Bay, at the head of which today stands the city of Ashland, Wisconsin. Here he found a large number of Indians who, it appears, were recep-

[3] L. P. Kellogg (ed.), *Early Narratives of the Northwest*, pp. 27-67.

tive to his religious teachings. But they were not his beloved Huron. These, he learned, were living some distance inland. With a single French companion he set out to find them. On the journey he became separated from the rest of the party and was never seen again.

Events were now transpiring in France and in the St. Lawrence settlements that speeded up the exploration of Michigan and the West. The aged Cardinal Mazarin died in 1661 and the ambitious young monarch, Louis XIV, became ruler of France in fact as well as name. That year, also, the French court read, in the *Jesuit Relation* written by Father Le Jeune, these words, addressed to the king: "When you consider, Sire, what the French name signifies, you will know that a great king who makes Europe tremble ought not to be held in contempt in America." Father Le Jeune in this way challenged the young monarch to take action to alleviate the desperate situation in New France. The Iroquois were on the warpath again and threatening the very bastions of French authority: Montreal and Quebec. Other warnings reached the king's ears, and in 1663 he inaugurated a revolutionary change. Up to this time New France had been hardly more than a preserve of the Company of New France, which was interested only in the profit it might gain from the fur trade. Now the king deprived the company of its rights and made New France a royal colony. Government was entrusted to a Sovereign Council, including the governor, bishop, and five others to be named by them. Two years later an official called an *intendant* was added. He ranked in importance with the governor and the bishop and had the duty of reporting to the king on the activities of the former. This remained the backbone of the government of New France during the remainder of its history. A new company was created to enjoy a monopoly of the fur trade. Assuming direct authority in France over the colony was Jean-Baptiste Colbert, as controller-general. In 1664 an adequate French force was dispatched to the St. Lawrence under the command of the Marquis de Tracy. Within three years, the Iroquois were humbled and defeated, and in 1667 they agreed to peace terms and gave hostages for their observance.

The stage was thus set for a much more vigorous and sustained French advance westward. After 1664, the Iroquois were forced to meet the threat and onslaughts of large French forces and no longer were in a position to block effectively the way west by the old route through Lake Nippising. The Jesuits were enabled to seek out the surviving Huron, and to undertake the task of spreading Christianity to the other tribes of the interior. Their wanderings revealed much of the nature of present-day Michigan. The French now were able, also, to seek out the elusive water route through the continent by which they hoped to reach the Indies and to search for mineral wealth in the western country. But so far as the fur traders were concerned, Colbert was determined that the Indians should bring their peltry to Montreal, and he opposed the establishment of colonies in the interior. As has been noted earlier, however, the fur traders were a lawless lot and seldom obeyed the rules laid down in distant France. Furthermore, officials of New France, as has been indicated above, frequently connived with them to permit fur trading in the West for a share of the rich profits. So the fur traders, along with the missionaries and those who searched for a waterway through the continent and for mineral wealth, brought back information about the configuration of the land and waters of Michigan, its resources, and its native peoples.

On the morning of August 8, 1665 the Indians who had come down the Ottawa to bring their furs to trade with the French started their return journey from Three Rivers, located on the St. Lawrence between Quebec and Montreal. They were followed by six Frenchmen manning a canoe in which sat a Jesuit priest, Father Claude Allouez. He had set out to retrace the route of Father Menard, to find the Huron, and to begin once more the work of spreading the Christian religion among the savages of the West. Allouez was, at the time, forty-three years of age. He had been a Jesuit since he was seventeen. His absolute devotion to the cause of Christ, his willingness and ability to suffer sustained privation and hardship, and his undaunted spirit made him an ideal missionary. Reaching the site of L'Anse, Allouez found two Indian women who remembered the instruction given them five years before by Menard. In the late autumn Allouez arrived at Chequamegon Bay and there established a mission at a place he called "La Pointe du Saint Esprit," or Holy Spirit Point. He erected a small bark chapel and adorned its sides with pictures of the infernal regions and of the judgment day. Large numbers of Ottawa as well as a few Huron listened to his teachings. He returned to Quebec in 1667, bringing word that help was needed to carry on his work, and incidentally telling the French authorities of copper deposits in the Lake Superior region.[4]

When Allouez returned to the West he brought with him another priest to work at La Pointe. These two were followed in the autumn of 1668 by Father Jacques Marquette and Brother

[4] G. Paré, *The Catholic Church in Detroit, 1701-1888*, pp. 33-37.

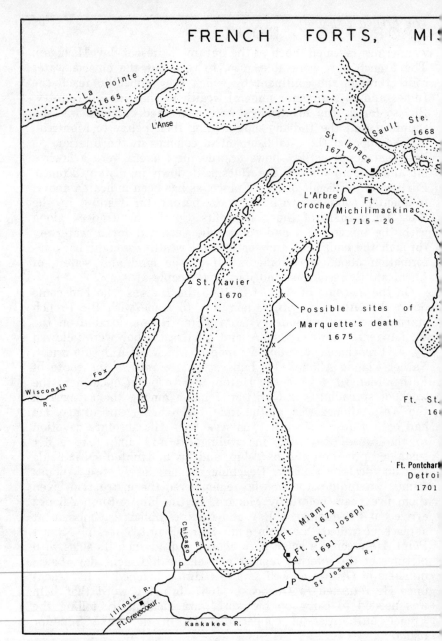

La Pointe
1665

L'Anse

Sault Ste.
1668

St. Ignace
1671

L'Arbre
Croche

Ft.
Michilimackinac
1715-20

△ St. Xavier
1670

x
Possible   sites   of
Marquette's death
1675

x

Fox

Wisconsin
R.

Ft. St.
16

Ft. Pontchart
Detroi
1701

Chicago R.

Ft. Miami
1679

Ft. St. Joseph
1691

St Joseph R.

P

P

Illinois R.
Ft. Crevecoeur.

Kankakee R.

Louis de Boêsme. With the restoration of peace with the Iroquois, Ottawa and Huron tribesmen began moving eastward to the hunting grounds they had deserted earlier to escape the Iroquois warriors. Father Marquette found many of the Ottawa and

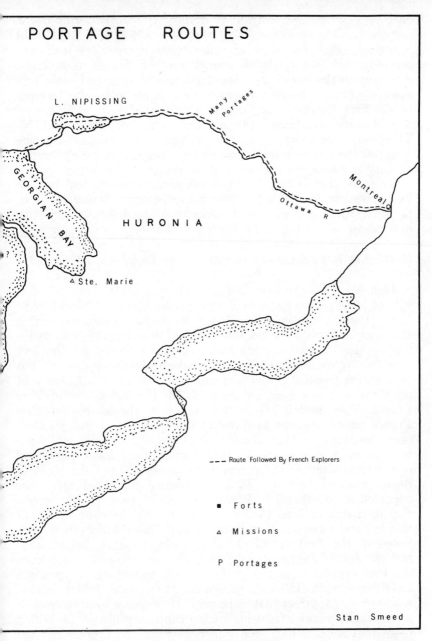

PORTAGE ROUTES

L. NIPISSING

Many Portages

GEORGIAN BAY

HURONIA

Ottawa R

Montreal

△ Ste. Marie

?

_ _ _ Route Followed By French Explorers

■ Forts

△ Missions

P Portages

Stan Smeed

Huron at the spot where Fathers Jogues and Raymbault had encountered large numbers of them twenty-seven years earlier, and hence he determined to establish a mission there. It was located on the American side of the St. Mary's River, below the rapids. A small enclosure of cedar posts twelve feet high was erected, and within it a chapel and a house were built. Adjacent to the enclosure, some land was cleared and grain was sown. Sault Ste. Marie, therefore, may claim to be the location of the first European settlement within what is now Michigan. The Jesuits maintained the mission until just prior to 1700. Then, for some years, there were no permanent settlers. But the spot was too strategic to be long abandoned, and in the eighteenth century it was again the scene of an established colony.

By 1668 what is now Michigan's Upper Peninsula had become well-known to the French. They had repeatedly traced its Lake Superior shoreline; they had penetrated the interior, and they had passed along the Lake Michigan shoreline to the south.

Early French explorers in the Lower Peninsula, 1669-1682

Jean Nicolet must have caught a glimpse of the Lower Peninsula of Michigan as he passed through the Straits of Mackinac in 1634. It was a hunting ground of many Indian tribes, but during the Iroquois wars it became almost deserted by its native peoples. In 1669 its eastern shoreline was followed for the first time, so far as we know, by a European. In the spring of that year an experienced trader and explorer, Adrien Jolliet, was sent on a mission westward by Jean Talon, the Intendant of New France. This official, one of the ablest in the history of New France, had ambitions to diversify the economy of the St. Lawrence settlements. He started shipbuilding, encouraged sheep raising, built a brewery to manufacture beer for export, and constructed a tannery. The reports of copper in the Lake Superior region brought back by Allouez intrigued him, and before he departed for a sojourn in France in 1668 he sent out an expedition in charge of Jean Péré to see what could be done to exploit this mineral resource. A supporting expedition under Jolliet followed in the next spring. It is doubtful whether Jolliet went further west than the Sault. He may have received word from the Péré expedition at this point that the mining of copper along Lake Superior would be impracticable. At any rate, Jolliet decided to return to Montreal that same year. He appears to have rescued an Iroquois prisoner from his Indian captors, probably by telling them that a peace had been signed between the French and the Iroquois. The Iroquois warrior, in gratitude, offered to guide Jolliet eastward by an easier route than that which had been followed by the French for many years. Accordingly, Jolliet and his Indian companion paddled southward along the Lake Huron shore of the Lower Peninsula, through the St. Clair River, Lake St. Clair, and the Detroit River to the northern shore of Lake Erie. Here they abandoned their canoe and proceeded overland across southern Ontario. Near the present city of Hamilton they encountered a party of French and Indians on their way west.

The principal members of this party were Father François Dollier de Casson, Father René Bréhant de Galinée, and Robert Cavelier de la Salle. La Salle, who later enters the stage of Michigan history, was on his way to search for a river to the south that might be the long-sought waterway to the Indies. The two priests were members of the Sulpician order, bound westward to start a mission among some band of Indians that had not yet heard the gospel. Jolliet told them of a large tribe called the Potawatomi living to the south of the Sault among whom no missionary had yet gone. Dollier and his companion at once determined to seek out this tribe and establish a mission among its members. La Salle, determined to press the search for the river of which he had heard, parted company with the priests and proceeded southward. Dollier and Galinée, together with about seven other men, continued along the shore of Lake Erie until winter caught up with them. They spent about five months near Port Dover in a snug retreat, which they built somewhat inland from the lake. Late in March they resumed their journey. But the journal of Galinée relates that a storm arose during the night, while the party was sleeping on shore, and swept away most of their packs, including those that contained the altar service. Without the sacraments the priests could not start their missionary work among the Potawatomi. Rather than return to Montreal for another service, they determined to proceed to Sault Ste. Marie and to come back with the Ottawa when the latter journeyed eastward with their furs. Had the Sulpicians carried out their objective of starting missions among the Potawatomi, southern Michigan, where these Indians lived, might have been explored earlier.

As the priests and their companions were paddling up the Detroit River, they beheld on shore a stone idol that the Indians worshipped in order to assure themselves a safe journey across Lake Erie. Since that Lake had been anything but kind to the Sulpicians, and because the idol was an object of heathen worship, Galinée demolished it with a consecrated axe, and the party carried the pieces of stone out into the middle of the river in their canoes to sink them. So far as is known, this was the occasion of the first visit of white men to the land of the Detroit area. The party then proceeded swiftly up the channel into Lake Huron

Fur trader's building on Mackinac Island

and from there to the Jesuit mission at Saulte Ste. Marie. Thus
in 1669 and 1670 the eastern shore of Michigan's Lower Peninsula
was traced by two different parties of French: that of Adrien
Jolliet, and that of Dollier and Galinée.[5]

The Lower Peninsula of Michigan continued for many years to
be a kind of no man's land between the fierce Iroquois warriors
of the East and the tribes that inhabited what is now Wisconsin
and Upper Michigan. This probably accounts for the fact that the
French did little for many years to explore this region. Both the
fur traders and the missionaries tended to concentrate where
the Indians were most numerous. During 1670 and 1671 there
was intense activity in the upper lakes area. Fur traders were
active at Sault Ste. Marie, the Jesuits established new missions,

---

[5] For many years historians assumed that the "Man Named Jolliet" in
Galinée's journal was the famous Louis Jolliet, leader of the Mississippi
expedition with Father Marquette in 1673. The fact that the Jolliet en-
countered by the Sulpicians in 1669 in Ontario was Louis' older brother
Adrien is convincingly demonstrated by T. Delanglez, *Life and Voyages of
Louis Jolliet, 1645-1700,* although several historians have disagreed with
Delanglez. See A. Godbout, "Louis Jolliet et son dernier historien," *Culture,*
XIV (1953), 223-246, and F. B. Steck, *Marquette Legends,* p. 255.

and a great ceremony designed to establish forever the French claim to the entire Great Lakes region was staged.

Early in 1670 Father Allouez journeyed to Green Bay, where he established the St. Francis Xavier mission. His place at the mission situated on Chequamegon Bay was taken by Father Marquette, while Marquette, in turn, was replaced by Father Claude Dablon at Sault Ste. Marie. The latter found that his charges were drifting to the straits area, and he followed them there, conducting a mission in the winter of 1670-71 at a site he called the "Ile de Michilimackinac." Presumably this meant Mackinac Island, but since the term "Michilimackinac" was commonly used by the French to describe the entire straits area, it is uncertain whether Dablon is referring to the island or the mainland.

The Indian population of the straits area was greatly increased in late 1670 and early 1671 as a result of an incident far to the west. In the summer of 1670 the Indians of Father Marquette's mission on Chequamegon Bay killed a Sioux chieftain and his four companions whom they were entertaining. Fearing retaliation by the Sioux, the Huron and Ottawa living around this mission fled eastward, the Ottawa taking refuge on Manitoulin Island, at the head of Lake Huron, and the Huron fleeing to the straits area, where many Ottawa later joined them. Father Marquette accompanied them and met Father Dablon at Sault Ste. Marie in the spring of 1671. Dablon instructed Father Marquette to establish a mission on the Upper Peninsula side of the Straits, which Marquette did in early 1671. It was called the mission of St. Ignace.[6] Father Dablon departed for Quebec shortly afterward to become Superior over all the Jesuit missions in New France.

The same year that saw the mission of St. Ignace established also witnessed the enactment of "the Pageant of the Sault," an impressive ceremony designed to establish French title to the interior of North America. This was a project of Jean Talon, intendant of New France, who recently had returned from a visit to the French court. It is possible that Talon had heard of the formation of the Hudson's Bay Company in England and chose this way of asserting France's title to an area whose vast fur resources the English might attempt to tap from Hudson's Bay. In the autumn of 1670 he sent out an expedition headed by a military officer named Simon François, Sieur de St. Lusson, to impress Indian tribesmen with the might and majesty of France. St. Lusson's expedition wintered on Manitoulin Island, and in the spring he sent out runners to summon the Indian tribes of the entire upper

---

[6]R. N. Hamilton, "Location of the mission of St. Ignace from 1670 to 1673", in *Michigan History*, XLII (1958), 260-266.

lake area to Sault Ste. Marie. Here, on June 14, 1671, surrounded by perhaps twenty of his fellow countrymen and a vast assemblage of Indians, he fulfilled his mission. First the *Te Deum* was chanted and a huge cross with the escutcheon of France above it was reared. Hymns and prayers for the king followed. St. Lusson then made a solemn declaration that all the lands "bounded on the one side by the Northern and Western Seas and on the other side by the South Sea including all its length and breadth"[7] belonged to the king of France, that all its people were the king's subjects, and that no other nation might intrude therein. Raising a piece of sod three times, he cried *"Vive le roi."* Father Allouez then addressed the Indians, relating the power and might of the French monarch. A great bonfire concluded the ceremony.

The year following the ceremony at the Sault, Intendant Talon determined to send out an expedition to discover the river west of the Great Lakes, referred to in the *Jesuit Relations* as the "Messipi," and to ascertain whether or not it would provide the long-sought water route to the western sea. As leader of the expedition, he selected a fur trader, skilled in navigation and map-making, Louis Jolliet, younger brother of Adrien Jolliet, whom he had sent west earlier to investigate the reports of a copper mine.[8] Before departing for the West, Louis Jolliet had a talk with Father Dablon, who suggested that Father Marquette be included on the exploring expedition. In May, 1673, Jolliet and Marquette, together with five other Frenchmen, departed from St. Ignace. They ascended the Fox River, portaged to the Wisconsin, and followed that stream to the Mississippi. They were borne southward by the Mississippi, continuing until they reached the mouth of the Arkansas River, at which point they concluded that the great river did not flow into the "western sea," but rather into the "southern sea." Having encountered Spanish-armed hostile Indians, they then retraced their course, paddling upstream. They proceeded as far north as the mouth of the Illinois River, and there they chose a different route for their return. By this time Father Marquette had become seriously ill and they probably

---

[7] P. Margry, *Découvertes et établissements des Français dans l'Amérique,* I, 96-99. For an English account, see *Wisconsin Historical Collections,* XI (1899), 26-28. There are three contemporary accounts of the pageant at the Sault. Besides the official state paper published by Margry (above), see the account of Nicolas Perrot in his *Memoir,* translated in full in E. H. Blair, *Indian Tribes of the Upper Mississippi and the Great Lakes Region,* pp. 77, and that given by the Jesuits in the *Jesuit Relations,* reprinted in L. P. Kellogg, *Early Narratives of the Northwest, 1634-1699,* pp. 211-221.

[8] Adrien Jolliet had never returned to Montreal. He was last seen when he and his companion left the Dollier-Galinée party in the fall of 1669.

hoped to find a shorter route homeward. By way of the Des Plaines and Chicago Rivers they at length reached Lake Michigan and paddled northwards along its western shore until they arrived at Green Bay. Here Marquette remained to recover his health, while Jolliet hurried back east to report his findings.

Father Marquette remained at Green Bay until the fall of 1674. He sought and received permission to return to the Illinois country in order to spread the gospel to the Indians whom he had found in that region. He remained there during the winter of 1674-75, but his illness recurred. Hoping to see his beloved mission at St. Ignace before death overtook him, he set out with two companions shortly after Easter. The party traveled along the western shore of the Lower Peninsula northward until it reached the mouth of a river flowing into Lake Michigan. There is some doubt whether this was the Pere Marquette, entering the lake at Ludington, or the Betsie, which flows into the lake at Frankfort. Marquette became so ill at this point that his companions put him ashore, where he died on May 18, 1675. He was only 38 years of age.[9]

Jolliet, on his way back to Quebec, had the misfortune of losing the journal he had kept and the maps he had drawn on the journey. Copies he had left at Sault Ste. Marie were destroyed in a fire. From memory he drew other maps of the country he had traversed. Father Marquette may also have drawn a map that, along with Jolliet's, ultimately reached France. At any rate, a map published in Paris in 1681 by Melckisidek Thevenot and believed to be based on the information of Jolliet and possibly also Marquette, shows the Mississippi River and the western shore of Lake Michigan. On earlier maps the latter had been called *Lac des Illinois;* this is the first map to call it *Lac de*

[9] Considerable controversy surrounds the Jolliet-Marquette expedition. One writer even casts doubt on whether Marquette ever went on the journey, suggesting that the story may have been a fabrication of Father Dablon (see F. B. Steck, *op. cit.*). A Michigan author has asserted that the description of the place where Marquette was put ashore and died and the changes that have occurred in the shoreline since that time indicate that the great missionary died, not near Ludington (where the river that bears his name, Pere Marquette, flows into Lake Michigan), but, rather, near Frankfort (see C. L. Stebbins, *Here I Shall Finish My Voyage*). Even the final resting place of Marquette's bones cannot be positively identified. Two years after his death, some Indians visited the spot where he was buried, disinterred his bones, and carried them to the St. Ignace mission where they were reinterred under the Mission House. Two centuries later the supposed site of the Mission House was located and some bits of bones taken from it that may have been those of Marquette. These are now preserved at Marquette University in Milwaukee. One author remarks that Allouez spent 22 years in the Western Country and is forgotten, while Marquette, far better known, spent only seven.

Michigami. The Jesuit map of 1672 shows only a small portion of
the eastern shore of *Lac des Illinois* along the northwest shore of
the Lower Peninsula. By 1688, however, maps drawn by French
and British cartographers begin to show the entire western shore
of the Lower Peninsula. These maps are based no doubt on information from the explorations of Robert Cavelier de la Salle.

La Salle was a protégé of Louis de Buade, Comte de Frontenac,
who served as governor of New France from 1672-1682 and from
1689-1698. Francis Parkman, the distinguished historian of New
France who produced his first works over a century ago, regarded
Frontenac as the greatest of French governors, and this opinion
has been accepted by many subsequent writers, although it has
been somewhat modified as the result of recent research.[10] Whatever the final verdict on Frontenac may be, there is no question
that he did much to encourage French exploration and French
fur trade in the West. He did so in the face of immense difficulties.
The French monarchy was spending large sums of money on wars
and subsidies to its allies. Little could be spared for America. For
this reason, expansion westward was discouraged and Frontenac
was repeatedly instructed to confine the fur trade to the St. Lawrence settlements. This he managed to evade. He was aware of
the encroachment of the Iroquois into the West, and that the Iroquois were being aided by the British. It was partly because Frontenac realized that unless the French were active in the West the
Ottawa and other tribes would not bring their peltry to Montreal,
but would sell it to the British, that he covertly encouraged fur
traders to venture into the Great Lakes region. But there is no
doubt that Frontenac also hoped to recoup his fortunes by sharing
in the profits of the *coureurs de bois.*

Although Louis Jolliet was refused permission by the king to
establish a fort in the Illinois region, La Salle was more fortunate
in his quest for the authority to explore, trade, and build forts.
La Salle had the backing of Frontenac when he went to France
in 1675 and sought permission to build a fort and establish a
settlement on Lake Ontario in return for a large grant of land
and the rank of an untitled noble. Returning to New France he
built the fort, naming it for his sponsor, Governor Frontenac. But
La Salle dreamed of greater things. In 1677 he once more crossed
the Atlantic to France where he received permission to establish
a colony in the Illinois country. It was to be accomplished at his
own expense and he was forbidden to trade in furs with the Ottawa or any of the other tribes that brought their furs to Montreal. He was to receive a grant of land and to have a monopoly on

[10] See, e.g., W. J. Eccles, *Frontenac, the Courtier Governor.*

the trade in buffalo hides. The bait La Salle used to obtain the grant was a promise to explore the lower Mississippi, to seek the waterway to the western sea, and to locate valuable minerals.

La Salle no sooner returned to New France than he openly violated his grant, probably with Frontenac's consent. He sent an advance party of fifteen men Henry de Tonty to trade with the Illinois Indians, so as to accumulate a cargo of furs. In early 1679 he built a shipyard above Niagara Falls and there workmen constructed the *Griffin*, the first sailing vessel to navigate the Great Lakes. When La Salle arrived at St. Ignace he discovered that his advance party had stopped there and that some had deserted. Two of the deserters were rounded up. A considerable quantity of furs was collected at an Indian village on Washington Island, near the outlet of Green Bay. The *Griffin* was loaded and on September 18, 1679, sailed out into Lake Michigan on her return voyage to Niagara. Her crew was instructed to return with all speed to a rendezvous at the mouth of the St. Joseph River on the eastern side of the lake. Exactly how La Salle knew of this river is uncertain.

With a party of fourteen men and four canoes, La Salle proceeded southward along the Wisconsin shore to the southern end of Lake Michigan, then followed the eastern shoreline of the lake until he reached the mouth of the St. Joseph on November 1, 1679. Here, on a bluff overlooking the lake in what is now the city of St. Joseph, La Salle had his men construct a stockaded fort. It was called Fort Miami, from the Indian tribes of that name, and the river also was called the Miami. It was the first French fort in the Lower Peninsula. On November 20 a party of twenty men arrived from St. Ignace. Its leader was Henry de Tonty, La Salle's lieutenant. Tonty, an Italian who had been taken in infancy to France, was known as "The Man with the Iron Hand." His right hand had been mangled in a naval engagement and he had cut the hand off himself, later replacing it with one made of iron. He had been introduced to La Salle when the latter was in France in 1678, and immediately enlisted in La Salle's service. He served his leader faithfully until the time La Salle was killed almost a decade later. Tonty brought word that the *Griffin* had not returned to St. Ignace, but it was late in the year and probably La Salle, though impatient, did not give up hope. Neither he nor anyone else was ever to see the *Griffin* again. It is presumed that the small vessel was lost in the storm-tossed lake on her return voyage.[11]

[11] Hardly a year goes by that some beachcomber does not turn up a bit of iron or some other object that is identified as a remnant of the *Griffin*.

La Salle now determined to proceed at once to carry out his design to build a fort in the Illinois country, as he had promised Louis XIV. Indians no doubt told him of the best way to reach his destination. On December 3 he left Fort Miami with thirty-two other men in eight canoes, paddling up the St. Joseph as far as present-day South Bend, where the canoes were carried for a distance of about five miles along a portage path long used by the Indians to the headwaters of the Kankakee River, whose waters eventually find their way to the Illinois River and by that river to the Mississippi. La Salle found an Indian village on the Illinois River, and here he had his men construct a fort, which he named "Crevecoeur" (meaning heart-break).[12] He also set them to work constructing a new ship, presumably to be used in descending the Mississippi. The *Griffin* was expected to bring back ironwork, sails, and rigging for the vessel, so, with only the lumber cut, La Salle determined to return to Fort Miami. When he arrived there, no sign of the *Griffin* was to be seen. Realizing that he must now return to the East for supplies, he sought the quickest way of making the journey. He determined that it would save time to cross the peninsula on foot.[13]

La Salle, with three or four men, set out from Fort Miami on March 22, 1680. So far as is known, they were the first white men to see any considerable part of the interior of the southern Lower Peninsula. La Salle's journal tells of crossing the prairies of southwestern Michigan, where the rank grass was set afire to hinder hostile Indians who were following the party. The present Kalamazoo, Calhoun, Jackson, and Washtenaw counties were crossed until the Huron River was reached at about where the village of Dexter now stands. Here a canoe was built, but when the border of the present Wayne County was reached, the river

A recent major find consisted of parts of a vessel that scientific tests show may well be three hundred years old. It was discovered near Tobermory in 1957 by Orrie Vail. Tobermory is located at the tip of the peninsula that separates Lake Huron from Georgian Bay (see *Telescope* [Detroit, Great Lakes Model Shipbuilders' Guilde], VI [December 1957]). Prior to this find it seemed most probable that the *Griffin* had been lost off the western tip of Manitoulin Island, not far north of Tobermory (see F. C. Bald, *Michigan in Four Centuries,* pp. 40-41). Countless stories and legends have been told to account for the *Griffin's* loss (see J. E. Johnston, "The Griffon, Ship of Tragedy," *Telescope,* VII [1958], 3-7). The spelling of the ship's name is variously given as *Griffin* and *Griffon*. The griffon, or griffin, is a legendary beast. The name was adopted by La Salle as a compliment to Frontenac, whose coat of arms bore two griffins.

[12] The name was that of a battle fought in Europe. See L. Kellogg, *French Regime in Wisconsin,* p. 289, note 4.

[13] F. Parkman, *La Salle and the Discovery of the Great West,* pp. 189-202.

was found blocked by fallen trees. The canoe was thereupon abandoned, and the party again proceeded on foot until it reached the Detroit River. By May 6 La Salle was back at Fort Frontenac.

One of the men who had accompanied La Salle as far as the Illinois country on his expedition was Father Louis Hennepin. From Illinois, La Salle sent Hennepin on a preliminary exploration of the Upper Mississippi. The priest went up that stream as far as the modern city of St. Paul, fell afoul of some hostile Indians, and was rescued by a French fur trader, Greysolon Duluth. Hennepin returned to France shortly afterward, where he published several accounts of his experiences. In one of them, he claimed he had reached the mouth of the Mississippi in 1680, but we know now that this, along with a great deal more that Hennepin wrote, was pure fabrication.

La Salle was confronted with many difficulties in carrying out his plans, of which the loss of the *Griffin* was only one. The next year, when he returned to Fort Crevecoeur where he had left Tonty in charge, he found it deserted and in ruins, victim of an Iroquois raid. After wintering at Fort Miami, he again returned east. The great explorer had many rivals who were jealous of the special privileges he had received from the king. But eventually, surmounting all obstacles, La Salle planted the royal arms of France at the mouth of the Mississippi on April 9, 1682. Returning up the river, he established a fort at the place called Starved Rock, later named Fort St. Louis. Confronted with a new governor at Quebec who was hostile to him, La Salle returned to France, where he was able to recruit an expedition to make a French settlement at the mouth of the Mississippi. Landing four hundred miles to the west of the great river's estuaries, La Salle was murdered by rebellious members of his crew before he was able to accomplish his purpose.

Maps published in Europe between 1683 and 1700 clearly reflect the knowledge of the lower lakes area and the Lower Peninsula of the present state of Michigan that La Salle had accumulated in his journeys through this area. By the time La Salle departed from Michigan for the last time, in 1683, the French were well-acquainted with the Lower Peninsula as well as the Upper Peninsula.[14] Having discovered and explored Michigan, the French were confronted with the problem of what to do with it. How they met this problem largely determined the history of Michigan for the next eight decades.

[14] L. Karpinski, *op. cit.,* pp. 99ff.

Wolverine

3

FRENCH EMPIRE BUILDERS, FUR TRADERS AND MISSIONARIES

Enormous profits were derived from the fur trade in the seventeenth century by the French. While the traders were reaping their great harvest of peltry, zealous missionaries labored with fanatical devotion to convert the natives to Christianity. Both fur traders and missionaries were associated with the quest for a waterway through the continent which fascinated the minds and enlisted the efforts of so many of the French explorers. And there had been the vision of empire, too, which had attracted Frenchmen to the West, illustrated by the Pageant of the Sault in 1671. In the years after 1682 imperial rivalry between France and England played a much greater role in determining French policy than it had earlier. The fur trade continued but was less profitable. The Jesuits maintained their efforts to spread Christianity among the Indians, though with not quite the same zeal that the earlier missionaries had demonstrated. The search for a waterway to the western sea was not wholly abandoned but it gradually faded into unreality. It is impossible to separate these three or four strands of French thought, planning, and activity with regard to Michigan. At many points they are interwoven. Not infrequently those primarily concerned with only one of these strands found themselves at odds with those principally attached to another. The history of Michigan from 1682 to 1750 can best be related by beginning with the vital role played by imperial rivalry between France and England. It is necessary to remind ourselves, in following this story, that no such entity as Michigan existed during this period, and that what is now Michigan was then part and parcel of the Great Lakes area that belonged to New France.

DISPERSION VERSUS CONCENTRATION, 1682-1696

The events that transpired in Michigan during the fourteen years after the departure of La Salle reflected a vacillating French policy with respect to the West. It hinged on whether to build forts and to encourage fur trading in the West or to concentrate as far as possible on the peltry trade in the St. Lawrence settlements and make these settlements stronger. This was not in reality a new issue. As we have noted, Colbert had consistently favored the concentration of French power along the St. Lawrence and had sent the governor repeated orders to do just this. Governor Frontenac managed to evade Colbert's directives by issuing special licenses to trade in the West and by supporting La Salle's schemes. On occasion the French court had departed from Colbert's policy, as it did when it authorized Jolliet's 1673 expedition and La Salle's enterprise. But the basic policy remained unchanged. In 1682 Frontenac was recalled to France and relieved of his duties as governor. Partly this was due to the courtier governor's quarrelsome and contentious nature, which got him into no end of trouble, but it was no doubt motivated in part also by the opposition of Colbert to Frontenac's persistence in dispersing the strength of New France.

Frontenac's successor as governor was Lefebvre de la Barre. Coming quickly under the influence of Frontenac's enemies, the new governor lost no time in adopting a new policy. He seized Fort Frontenac from La Salle's agents, and when the great explorer returned from his journey to the mouth of the Mississippi to obtain supplies for the fort he had built in Illinois, La Barre blocked his path, forcing La Salle to go to France itself for support. This La Salle did, and met with unexpected success. Colbert died in 1683 and his son, Seignelay, backed La Salle's plan to establish a colony at the mouth of the Mississippi. Hearing that Louis XIV was at the moment on the verge of war against Spain, La Salle told the king an army of many thousand Indians could be assembled at the mouth of the Mississippi for the conquest of Mexico and all its riches. That did it. La Salle had asked for two ships; he got four. Furthermore, Governor La Barre, who had seized Fort Frontenac and Fort St. Louis from La Salle's men, was ordered to restore them to La Salle. The policy of concentration, which appeared to have won out with Frontenac's recall, thus was modified within a year.

Still another modification of this policy in the same year is more closely related to Michigan history. Daniel Greysolon, Sieur de Duluth, who had traded for furs extensively in the region around Lake Superior and the Upper Mississippi Valley and who rescued Father Hennepin from hostile Indians—as related in the preceding chapter—went to France in 1683 and returned with a license that empowered him to trade with the Sioux. He came back to Lake Superior, building forts on the northwest shores of this lake and taking possession of the portage between the St. Croix and Brulé rivers across which the furs were carried on their long journey from the Northwest.[1]

But events were transpiring that were to force Duluth and other fur traders, as well as voyageurs and missionaries, to concentrate in the St. Lawrence settlements. The Iroquois were on the warpath again. As early as 1680 they had devastated Fort Crevecoeur, which La Salle had built in the Illinois country. In 1684, aided and supported by British fur traders and goaded into action by the aggressive governor of New York, Thomas Dongan, they boldly attacked the French. Striking far to the north and west against the Indians allied with the French, they forced Frenchmen in the West to flee for refuge. Concentration ceased to be a question of policy; it became a matter of necessity. The Iroquois carried the war to the very gates of Montreal.

Alarmed by these developments, the French court replaced La Barre as governor in 1686, sending out as his successor the Marquis de Denonville, a much abler and more energetic man. Denonville believed that the best defense is offense. He struck boldly into the Iroquois country, destroying a number of their villages. And he took steps to save the West from the domination of the Iroquois and their English allies. Word had reached Montreal that in 1685 English fur traders from Albany had reached the Straits of Mackinac with fifteen canoes laden with goods for trade with the natives. Denonville countered by making three moves. Nicholas Perrot, known as a skilled forest diplomat, was sent to build two forts on the Wisconsin River—along the route from Green Bay to the Mississippi—to impress the Indians of that area with French power and to hearten them to resist the Iroquois. Two Indian tribes, which had fled westward to escape the earlier onslaught of the Iroquois, had drifted back to northern Indiana and the St. Joseph River valley. To

[1] The modern city of Duluth, Minnesota, bears his name.

maintain their ties with the French, Denonville sought the aid of the Jesuits. On October 1, 1686 he granted to the Jesuit order an area of land a little less than a mile square along the St. Joseph River at any point they might select. It is probable that Father Claude Allouez was carrying on missionary work among the Indians on the St. Joseph River as early as 1683 and that Iroquois depredations had forced his withdrawal to St. Ignace.[2] Denonville apparently hoped by his grant to encourage the Jesuits to resume their missionary activity in this strategic area. The St. Joseph mission was established near the site of the present city of Niles. The exact date of its founding has been the subject of much speculation; it certainly existed as early as 1690.[3]

Denonville's third project also involved activity in what is now Michigan. Duluth, the experienced northwest fur trader, was commissioned to build a fort between Lakes Erie and Huron to block the passage of such English fur traders as had reached Michilimackinac the preceding year. Duluth chose the site of the modern city of Port Huron for the fort, which was constructed in 1686 and named Fort St. Joseph. The following year Denonville sent orders west to assemble a force of French and Indians at Fort St. Joseph to move from there to Lake Ontario and to join his expedition against the Iroquois. In obedience to his command some two hundred *coureurs de bois* and about five hundred Indians assembled at Fort St. Joseph in 1687. Henry de Tonty, La Salle's former lieutenant, brought in a party; Nicholas Perrot came from Wisconsin with another force. Olivier Morel de La Durantaye brought in from St. Ignace, not only a contingent of fighting men, but also an English trader and his party that had been captured. La Durantaye had been sent to St. Ignace in 1683 with thirty soldiers, who constituted the first French garrison at the great trading rendezvous and mission station. There were much rejoicing and wild demonstrations before Duluth and the other leaders could get the unruly force started for the meeting with Denonville's troops. On the way another English trading party was captured. Although Denonville's expedition did not bring the Iroquois to bay, it gave the French a psychological lift. Duluth returned to his fur trading in the Northwest, and Louis Armand de Lom d'Arce, Baron de Lahontan, was appointed as commandant at Fort St. Joseph.

The first French fort in the Lower Peninsula, Fort Miami at the mouth of the St. Joseph River, had been abandoned follow-

[2] G. Paré, *The Catholic Church in Detroit, 1701-1888,* p. 81.
[3] *Ibid.,* p. 85.

ing the departure of La Salle. Fort St. Joseph, at modern Port Huron, also had a short history. Lahontan, its commandant, was a young nobleman with considerable literary ability and a good sense of humor. He left a considerable body of writing descriptive of New France in his time. But he soon wearied of the lonely outpost, and decided late in the summer of 1688 it was not worth maintaining. He ordered it burned and made his way to St. Ignace.

The war with the Iroquois was by no means over. The St. Lawrence settlements were repeatedly raided, and on one of these forays the bloodthirsty Iroquois slaughtered two hundred people in the little village of La Chine. Then in 1689 the conflict was intensified as France and England began the first of a series of wars that was to last, off and on, for 126 years. When the Stuart king James II was deprived of the English throne by the Glorious Revolution of 1688, his place was taken by King William III, who, as stadholder of Holland, had been an implacable enemy of Louis XIV of France. War was inevitable. In Europe it was known as the War of the League of Augsburg, in America as King William's War.

In this emergency the French ruler recalled Frontenac from his retirement and sent the former governor back to resume his old post and to save New France. Frontenac had lost none of his quarrelsome propensities, but even his severest critics grant that he must be given credit for rescuing New France at this very perilous juncture. One writer describes his activities in these words:

> That grizzled old warrior threw himself into his task with an energy that belied his seventy years, perfecting defenses, whipping an army into shape, rebuilding decayed Indian alliances, and planning an invasion of the English colonies. Throughout Quebec hope displaced despair as the "Iron Governor" won over tribe after tribe in the Northwest; on one occasion Frontenac convinced a visiting party of chiefs to cast their lot with New France by interrupting a conference with a war whoop, seizing a tomahawk, and leading the excited natives in a war dance. Here were allies to carry the scalping knife against English settlements on the three fronts where the war was fought: the New York-New England borderland, the Great Lakes country, and about Hudson's Bay.[4]

In this narrative we are chiefly concerned with his strategy in the Great Lakes country.

[4] R. A. Billington, *Westward Expansion,* p. 110.

In his fight to save the West, Frontenac depended heavily on those Frenchmen already in the area and experienced in handling the delicate problems of Indian relations: Nicholas Perrot in the Wisconsin country; Henry de Tonty in Illinois; and Pierre le Sueur in the Lake Superior country. Perrot, who had been sent to establish French authority in Wisconsin by Denonville, had attained a position of great influence among the Indians. Tonty had remained in Illinois after La Salle's departure, where he contended against Iroquois war parties, traded in furs, and became a bulwark of strength in that region. Pierre le Sueur, another prominent fur trader, had built a fort at Chequamegon Bay, near the present Ashland, Wisconsin, and another on the Mississippi near the mouth of the St. Croix River. What chiefly concerned Frontenac was the strong possibility that the western tribes, lured by the prospect of cheap English goods and despairing that their French friends could protect them from the fierce Iroquois, would make peace with the latter. His strategy, therefore, was to demonstrate French strength, to promote the fur trade, and to cultivate all the ties of friendship that had existed through the years. This was no easy task, and it was complicated by the fact that French *coureurs de bois* carried on extensive trade further to the west with the Sioux, who also were the enemies of the Great Lakes Indians.

The center of French influence in the Great Lakes area was St. Ignace. The present city derives its name from the Jesuit mission established there in 1671. Around it the Huron and Ottawa had their villages. It became a center of activity in the fur trade, and the Jesuits often complained that the brandy the fur traders used in their barter debauched the Indians. Only the Jesuits referred to the place as "St. Ignace"; fur traders and official documents invariably call it "Michilimackinac." As early as 1683, as has been noted, a garrison of thirty soldiers had been sent there, under the command of La Durantaye. The commandant and his men left St. Ignace temporarily in 1686 to take part in the Denonville expedition described above. Following this, they returned. Durantaye was recalled, however, in 1690 by Frontenac, possibly because he was too friendly with the Jesuits to suit the governor. To replace him Frontenac sent out Louis de la Porte, Sieur de Louvigny, with 150 troops to impress the Indians at this all-important place. A fort was constructed and given Frontenac's family name, De Buade.[5] Fort De Buade was gar-

[5] The exact location of this fort is a subject of some controversy. It was long thought to have stood on the hill above the present Marquette Park, but some local historians believe it may have been situated on the waterfront, in the center of the present business district.

risoned for only six years, and the name seldom appears in French accounts. The place continued to be called "Michilimackinac."

Another strategic area in which Frontenac took measures to establish French authority was in southwestern Lower Michigan, among the Miami and Potawatomi Indians. It will be recalled that Denonville had encouraged the Jesuits to establish a mission among these peoples on the St. Joseph River. Frontenac now took steps to demonstrate French power in this region. Probably because of his experience among the Potawatomi in Wisconsin, Nicholas Perrot was sent by Frontenac to carry messages and presents to the Indian tribes in the St. Joseph valley in May, 1690. In October of that same year an English flotilla came up the St. Lawrence under the command of Sir William Phips, and Quebec was attacked. The French defenders, however, were able to beat off the attacking force, and the English flotilla retired. Frontenac lost no time in sending messages to the West telling how the English had been repulsed. In 1691 he sent Augustin le Gardeur, Sieur de Courtemanche, with a force to build a fort on the St. Joseph River. The site selected was near the mission, just south of the present city of Niles, and upstream some 25 miles from the mouth of the river, where La Salle, a dozen years earlier, had built Fort Miami. It was named Fort St. Joseph, but it is not to be confused with the temporary fort the French had built at the site of Port Huron in 1686 and that also was called Fort St. Joseph. The Fort St. Joseph erected by Courtemanche withstood attack by between three and four hundred Iroquois soon after it was established. In order to provide protection for the "Miami of the Maramek" (the Miami who lived in the Kalamazoo River Valley), Frontenac encouraged them to move to the St. Joseph Valley. While they were following the governor's instructions they were attacked by a body of Sioux warriors from the West. Southwestern Michigan assuredly was a dangerous place in which to live in those years.

In spite of continuing warfare with the Iroquois, the energetic measures taken by Frontenac to save the West for France began to bear fruit. In 1693 and again in 1695 huge flotillas of canoes heavily laden with furs arrived at Montreal. In 1694 Governor Frontenac sent one of his protégés, Antoine de la Mothe Cadillac, to take command of Fort De Buade. This young man, a native of Gascony, was destined to become the founder of Detroit. He was born of middle-class parents in 1658 and came to Acadia (now Nova Scotia) when he was twenty-five. For a time he was employed as a privateer. After a sojourn in France he returned to America in 1690. In Quebec he met Frontenac, who helped him to secure a lieutenancy in the colonial troops. He was later promoted to captain. At Fort De Buade he served as commandant for three years. Near the fort were sixty houses occupied by Frenchmen, the Huron and Ottawa villages, and the Jesuit mission. Father Nouvel, in charge of the mission, was the Jesuit Superior of all the western missions, while Cadillac had general supervision of the scattered forts in what is now Michigan, Illinois, and Wisconsin. During the trading season as many as five thousand Indians and hundreds of *coureurs de bois* made the vicinity of the fort and the mission their meeting place. During the short time he was at Fort De Buade, Cadillac made a small fortune from the fur trade.

Although the fur trade prospered, Cadillac soon became bitterly antagonistic toward the Jesuits, and they toward him. It arose in part because the effects of the brandy furnished by Cadillac to the Indians whom the Jesuits were trying to make into Christians. To celebrate an Ottawa and Potawatomi foray into the Saginaw region of the Lower Peninsula against Iroquois hunters, which netted thirty scalps and as many prisoners, Cadillac furnished the victorious Indians, on their return, with enough brandy so that two hundred of them staged an all-night orgy. Father Pinet, who denounced Cadillac as the cause of the disorders, was threatened by the commandant. Another Jesuit, Father Carheil, was described by Cadillac as the most violent and seditious person he had ever known. Frontenac staunchly backed Cadillac, but the story was different at the French court, where the Jesuit side of the case got a better hearing.

Meanwhile Frontenac, determined to bring the Iroquois to terms once and for all, led an army into their country. The chief village of the Onondaga, one of the Iroquois tribes, was destroyed, and a fort, together with several villages among the Oneida, another Iroquois tribe, were burned. Returning to Quebec on September 12, 1696, the seventy-six-year-old governor, weary from the exertions of the expedition but no doubt convinced that he had at last overcome the immense difficulties that had confronted him when he had arrived in Quebec six years before, found waiting for him a crushing decree from the French court, dated May 21, 1696. Settlers were no longer to go beyond the limits of the St. Lawrence settlements. Frontenac was to issue no more licenses to *coureurs de bois*. He was ordered to abandon and destroy the forts that had been built in the West, and to recall all the soldiers and settlers. He was also ordered to make peace with the Iroquois, even if it did not include the Ottawa and other western tribes whose allegiance Frontenac had fought so hard to retain.

The decree of 1696 constituted a return to the policy of concentration that Colbert had upheld for so long and that Frontenac never was willing to accept. Several reasons have been advanced for the court's decision. The Jesuits had great influence at court, which had been struck by a wave of austerity when the king married his mistress, Madame de Maintenon, who had many friends among the clergy. They pleaded for a chance to carry on their work among the Indians, unhindered by the demoralizing influence of the fur traders on the natives. Father Carheil provided a description of a western trading post, which he asserted had four features: cabarets where the Indians drank to excess; illicit carrying of brandy from post to post; scandalous vice with Indian women; and gambling so incessant it went on all night to the neglect of duty. There were other influences that probably induced the court to issue the decree of 1696. The intendant of New France, Champigny, with whom Frontenac was at odds, wrote to the court accusing the governor of wasting money and argued against maintaining posts in the West. The true policy, he urged, was to concentrate, not expand. Pontchartrain, the king's chief minister, asked why France should continue to take risks in America when, once victorious in Europe, she might do as she pleased in America. The decree also may have been motivated in part by a scheme to concentrate French forces at Quebec to constitute a land force that was to operate jointly with a naval force to capture Boston and New York. This ambitious project came to naught. Even before its failure was known the French agreed to the Treaty of Ryswick with the British, which restored the *status quo ante bellum* in America.

FRENCH REOCCUPATION OF THE WEST, 1696-1720

The decree of 1696 must have seemed to Frontenac a repudiation of everything he had fought for. But throughout his career he had never taken seriously the dictums from the French court with which he did not concur, and this decree was no exception. He made no peace with the Iroquois. He still gave licenses to *coureurs de bois* to trade in the West. And the *fleur de lis* still waved above the western forts. The crusty old governor even prepared two new military expeditions to be sent to the West. He was gratified when Cadillac arrived at Montreal accompanied by three hundred Ottawa, Huron, and Potawatomi warriors who, under the leadership of a Huron chief known as "The Rat" had defeated an Iroquois war party and were now prepared to lay before the governor their demands for arms and ammunition. Frontenac promised that such goods would soon be forthcoming. Whether he could have fulfilled his pledge cannot be known, for on November 28, 1698 the old governor died.

Although French troops were withdrawn from Forts De Buade and St. Joseph by Frontenac's successor, Chevalier de la Calliers, French fur traders continued to carry on their activities and the Jesuits to maintain their missions. The Iroquois tribes, alone in their war with the French after the Treaty of Ryswick, were at length ready to make peace. Since the western Indian tribes had to be included in the negotiations, messages were sent summoning them to Montreal. Between seven and eight hundred warriors, representing tribes from the West and Northwest, arrived on July 22, 1701 under the leadership of Courtemanche, who had been sent to collect them and bring them east. On the preceding day three hundred Iroquois delegates had arrived. The signing of the peace on August 4, 1701, was celebrated with a feast at which three roasted oxen were consumed and with the firing of cannon and fireworks. The French writer, La Potherie, was present at the great gathering and described the scene. A Huron chieftain, already stricken with a fatal disease, delivered a passionate, two-hour speech that so exhausted him that he died the same night. Other orators declared that they had now buried their instruments of war in a pit so deep that they should never be found, that the Iroquois were brothers of the other tribes, that the past should be forgotten. There was comic relief when one old chief, raising his hat in a ceremonial salute to the governor, lifted from his head an old French wig with tangled curls, which he had somehow acquired. The Iroquois solemnly agreed to remain neutral in any future war between the French and the British, and they kept their promise.

The Treaty of 1701 with the Iroquois ushered in a new era for the West. The menace of the Iroquois, that had so long been an obstacle to French activity in Michigan and the remainder of the West, was now at last removed. As the great ceremony at Montreal was in progress, an expedition already was enroute to the West to establish the French in a new area and to lay the foundations of the great Michigan city, Detroit. The leader of the expedition was Cadillac.

In 1699 Cadillac had gone to France with the purpose of convincing the court that the abandonment of the western country would be disastrous to New France. He attracted the attention of Count Pontchartrain, the king's chief minister, and convinced

him that a new start in the West was essential if that great
region were to be rescued from English domination. The attitude
of the court had undergone another change because of the likelihood of a new war with Britain. The king of Spain died in 1700
and Louis' grandson was one of the contenders for that throne.
Louis was determined that his grandson should become king of
Spain, but he realized that this would mean war with the other
European powers, including Britain, which would surely resist
seeing Bourbons on both the French and the Spanish thrones.
Cadillac's proposal was that a French colony be established
somewhere along *Le Detroit*, a name applied by the French for
many years to the waterway between Lakes Huron and Erie.
Around this colony the Indians were to be invited to come and
live, trading their furs and receiving instruction from the priests.
Through daily contact with the French, the natives would gradually adopt French customs and culture, Cadillac asserted. Cadillac received the rights of a landlord, and was authorized to make
grants of lands to French settlers, to charge them rentals for
these lands, and to collect certain dues characteristic of the
French feudal system. He also stood to profit by the fur trade.
He entered into a contract with the Company of the Colony of
Canada, the organization to which the king had given control of
the fur trade, to buy the furs traded at Detroit, and in 1705 he
bought out the rights of this company in the Detroit fur trade.
Cadillac had profited greatly from the trade in furs while he
served as commandant at Fort De Buade, and apparently expected to do likewise in the new colony.

Cadillac traveled to the site of his new colony by the old
Ottawa River route, since the peace treaty with the Iroquois was
not signed until after he had departed. With him were fifty
soldiers and fifty workmen, with provisions and tools. He chose
the present site of the city of Detroit for his colony for several
reasons. The river at this point is relatively narrow and unob-
structed by islands. The land a few rods west of what is now the
foot of Woodward Avenue rose some forty feet above the water.
To the rear a small river, the Savoyard, ran diagonally southwest. These conditions meant that this place would be easy to
fortify. The party landed on July 24, 1701, the date regarded as
marking the founding of Detroit.

Workmen immediately started felling trees for use in building
a palisade twelve feet high and two hundred feet square. It was
called Fort Pontchartrain, after the minister of Louis XIV who
had been influential in obtaining the grant for Cadillac. Inside
the palisade houses were built of logs set upright, in the manner

of the palisade itself. A church called St. Anne's was constructed. Two priests, a Jesuit and a Recollet, had accompanied Cadillac to Detroit. Madame Cadillac and Madame Tonty, the wife of Alphonse de Tonty who was second in command, reached Detroit that same fall. An impelling reason for bringing out the wives of the two leaders was to convince the Indians that Detroit was intended to be a permanent settlement.

A considerable number of farmers, called *habitants*, came to live around Detroit. Cadillac granted them frontage on the river and land extending for a considerable distance back into the interior. These were called "ribbon farms." The names of the owners of these farms, such as Beaubien, Dequindre, Aubin, and Chene are perpetuated in the names of Detroit streets today. Grants were made on both sides of the river. These *habitants* were a happy-go-lucky lot, often wandering out into the forest to trap the fur-bearing animals, fond of singing, dancing, and horse racing along the banks of the river in winter. Villages of Ottawa, Huron, Chippewa, and Miami grew up in the vicinity. Cadillac hit it off very well with the Indians, who called him "Our Father."

Cadillac remained in command at Detroit for nine years. In 1710 he was appointed governor of French Louisiana. He returned to France in 1717 and died there in 1730. During his stay at Detroit he made many enemies. He extracted the last penny possible from the *habitants*. The Company of the Colony of Canada hated him because he diverted so much of the fur trade to Detroit. And last but not least, he encountered the enmity of the Jesuits, who were opposed to the concentration of the Indians around Detroit, where they could be debauched by brandy and exploited by the fur traders.

The opinions of historians on Cadillac vary widely. One calls him an unworthy man, a shallow, crafty liar. Another refers to him as a "caustic-tongued Gascon." Even his patron in France, Count Pontchartrain, wrote him the year before his removal in these words:

> I note with much sorrow the little consideration which you have in your dealings with everybody, and all those who have dealings with you. I am surprised that, intelligent as you are, you do not foresee the consequences this will have for you, and that you should think that everybody should always be sacrificed to you . . . . Nobody can find any objection to the profits which you have made or will make at Detroit, as long as you are using

only just and legal means. I must say, however, that you show too much greed and that you should use more moderation. This will always make us fear to give you too much power.[6]

The Indians, disgusted by the high price and poor quality of French goods, traded more with the English. There was little drunkenness and debauchery at Detroit because Cadillac placed all the liquor in a central warehouse and charged a high price for it. There can be no denying that Cadillac had ability and that he got on well with the Indians. His letters are lucid and witty. And it must not be forgotten that his enemies consistently blackened his character, probably on many occasions quite unfairly.

Scarcely had Cadillac left Detroit than a crisis involving Indian relations arose. More than a thousand Fox Indians from Wisconsin arrived to accept an invitation Cadillac had extended some time before to come and live in the vicinity of Detroit. The other Indians were hostile toward them, and the new French commandant, Sieur Dubuisson, ordered them to leave. They refused to do so, and a fierce conflict between the Fox on the one side and the French and other Indians on the other broke out. Detroit was under siege for nineteen days. At length the Fox retreated, only to be overtaken by Huron, Ottawa, and Potawatomi warriors and almost completely annihilated. Enough escaped, however, to bring the story back to those Fox who had remained in Wisconsin. For many years, the Fox were able to prevent the French from passing through their Wisconsin territory to get from the Great Lakes to the Mississippi River. They defeated a number of expeditions sent out to chastise them, but in 1734 they finally were forced to flee across the Mississippi into Iowa. The Fox wars seriously sapped the strength of the French during this long and desultory conflict.

The exigencies of the war against the Fox may have been the motivating force for the re-establishment of a French fort at the Straits of Mackinac. Another explanation of the French decision to return to the "Upper Lakes" may be the fear of inroads by British fur traders operating out of Hudson's Bay. Part of the price Louis XIV had to pay to seat his grandson on the Spanish throne was to cede all French claims in the Hudson's Bay area to England. A fort at the Straits of Mackinac would more effectively check possible incursions from the North into the area which France regarded as its own. Missionaries had continued

[6] Quoted by S. C. Mitchell in "La Mothe Cadillac . . . a Stormy Figure of New France," *Bulletin of the Detroit Historical Society,* XI (July 1955), 9.

to work among the Indians at St. Ignace after the withdrawal of
the garrison from Fort De Buade, in accordance with the decree
of 1696. The place also continued to be a rendezvous for *coureurs
de bois*. Exactly when the French re-established a garrison at the
Straits is not certain. A veteran officer, De Lignery, was sent to
"Michilimackinac" in 1715 to enlist *coureurs de bois* to fight the
Fox. The following year the Sieur de Louvigny came out to the
Mackinac area with 225 soldiers, where he was joined by 200 fur
traders and a considerable number of Indians for a campaign
against the Fox, which was unsuccessful. De Louvigny may have
left some of the soldiers at the Straits when he returned to
Montreal. Father Pierre Charlevoix, who traveled throughout the
West in 1721, reported that the Fort and Mission House at that
time were occupied, but that the place was lightly held. He
apparently was referring to St. Ignace, although the habit of the
French in using "Michilimackinac" and "Mackinac" quite loosely
in referring to the whole straits area makes it uncertain. Sometime after 1715 Fort De Buade was abandoned and a new fort,
called Fort Michilimackinac, was constructed on the Lower Peninsula side of the Straits where Mackinaw City now stands. The
Jesuits apparently did not transfer their mission from St. Ignace
until 1741. There appears to be no good explanation for the
transfer of French power across the Straits.

The Jesuits continued their work at the St. Joseph mission,
near the present city of Niles, for some years following the withdrawal of the garrison. Although there appears to have been no
missionary there for a time, the mission was manned again by
1718, and in 1719 a garrison was sent to occupy the fort.

THE CALM BEFORE THE STORM: 1720-1744

France was at peace with Great Britain from 1713 to 1744.
Had it not been for the Fox wars, New France would have enjoyed
over three decades of peace. The Fox constituted a menace to
French communication, but the desultory conflict with them was
hardly more than a nuisance. In spite of this long period of peace,
New France grew very slowly in population. No considerable number of French came to live in the western country. Non-Catholics
were forbidden in New France, and, unlike the King of England,
the French monarch refused to encourage free enterprise in the
New World.

During the three decades following the siege of Detroit by the
Fox, life in that city was calm and uneventful. The fur trade was
practically the only business outside of retail merchandising. The

fertile soil yielded good crops without much labor and there were no markets for surplus products; hence the *habitants* took life easy. They raised large families, and their sons and daughters married at an early age. They were devoted to their church, but also were a merry lot, with their songs and dances and cart racing. There were occasional troubles with the Indians, but they did not take on a menacing aspect once the Fox had departed. A Jesuit missionary, Father La Richardie, ministered to the Huron Indians, transferring his mission to Bois Blanc Island in 1742. Schools were not regularly kept, and most of the *habitants* were illiterate. There were no democratic institutions, so politics were absent. And there were only occasional travelers to bring news of the outside world. All in all it was an isolated and, in a sense, idyllic life that Detroiters lived in this period.

Indian encampments, barracks, and traders' houses clustered around and within Fort Michilimackinac in these years. During the first few years after the establishment of the fort on the Lower Peninsula side of the Straits of Mackinac, the fur trade seems to have languished, because so many of the Indians had gone to live around Detroit. But in the 1730s and 1740s activity appears to have increased markedly. There also was a lively trade in furs at Fort St. Joseph, the center of the Potawatomi country. A French garrison was regularly maintained here, as well as a Jesuit mission. A glowing description of the St. Joseph Valley as it was in 1721 has been left to us by the French traveler Pierre-François-Xavier de Charlevoix, a Jesuit priest who was sent to New France by the King's Regent on the pretense of inspecting the missions, but actually to seek the elusive waterway to the western sea, which dreamers still assumed must exist. Charlevoix wrote:

> . . . we have a mission, and where there is a commandant with a small garrison. The commandant's house, which is but a sorry one, is called the fort, from its being surrounded with an in- different palisado [*sic*] . . . . We have here two villages of In- dians, one of the Miamis and the other of the Poutewatamies, both of them mostly Christian . . . . Several Indians of the two nations settled upon this river, are just arrived from the English colonies, whither they had been to sell their furs, and from whence they had brought back in return a great quantity of spirituous liquor . . . every night the fields echoed with the most hideous howlings. One would have thought a gang of devils had broken loose from hell, or that the two towns had been cutting one another's throats . . . .
>
> The River St. Joseph is so commodious for the commerce of all parts of Canada that it is no wonder it has always been

frequented by Indians. Besides, it waters an extremely fertile country, but this is not what these people esteem it for. It is even a great pity to give them good lands; which they either make no use of at all, or soon run out by sowing maize on them.[7]

Charlevoix reported that the fields around the fort were covered with sassafras to such an extent that the air was perfumed by the sweet-smelling shrubs. He was favorably impressed by the Indians, but witnessed their debauchery when intoxicating liquor was brought back by tribesmen who had returned from trading with the British.

Although some crops were grown by the *habitants* around Detroit and although there was a very limited amount of farming done around Forts Michilimackinac and St. Joseph, no appreciable number of Frenchmen came to live in Michigan during these years unless they were fur traders, missionaries, or soldiers. Indeed, the records show that supplies and provisions were transported westward to these posts from the St. Lawrence region. The western country was left to the Indians almost untouched.

THE FUR TRADE

The fur trade was the basis of the economy of New France and the great prize for which Britain and France contended in their long series of wars in America in the eighteenth century. The French king saw in the trade a source of revenues badly needed to forward his many ventures both in France itself and in making war against other nations. It was the practice to grant to individuals or groups of Frenchmen a monopoly in the fur trade of New France in return for a handsome flat payment. Cardinal Richelieu made such a grant in the name of Louis XIII to a company of one hundred associates. This grant stipulated that the associates should transport colonists to the new world and support each settler three years after his arrival. To what extent the grantees fulfilled these obligations is uncertain, but there is no doubt that they evaded their commitment as much as they could, being intent only on the profit to be earned. Another company secured a monopoly of the trade in 1664, only to be dissolved by the king ten years later. Although it appears that the king hoped to secure the revenues from the fur trade henceforth for himself, the temptation for immediate return was too great, and in 1675 he granted these revenues to another company for a flat payment of 350,000 *livres*. The policy of granting monopolistic rights in

[7] Quoted by Paré, *op. cit.*, p. 91.

the fur trade was continued in the eighteenth century, with such organizations as the Company of Canada (1701) and the Company of the West (1718) being formed to manage the trade.[8]

The regulation and control of the fur trade was never wholly successful. The exploration and occupation of Michigan would have proceeded much more slowly if the fur trading companies had been able to confine the trade to the St. Lawrence Valley. As has been indicated, Governor Frontenac granted special licenses to trade in the West. The lawless *coureurs de bois* paid little heed to any regulation, and even sold furs to British traders. And the king, from time to time, made special grants to individuals like La Salle and Cadillac that seemed to impinge upon the rights already granted to the monopoly. The settlers who were brought over to New France were not satisfied with being farmers. They habitually deserted their fields to engage in the fur trade on their own.

In seeking to understand the crucial importance of the fur trade in determining the destiny of the interior of North America, including Michigan, it is necessary to realize that the commerce of early modern times, unlike that of the twentieth-century industrial world, was largely in luxury commodities. The trade in foodstuffs, textiles, and other necessities was less important because such a predominant proportion of the population of Europe produced and processed the necessities of life for themselves and their families. The trade in peltry, while no small business even today, exerts no such powerful influence as it did in the seventeenth and eighteenth centuries. Furs at that time were worn by the French aristocrats and the members of the wealthy middle class, which aped the styles and manners of the lords and their ladies. Since France became the fashion center of Europe under Louis XIV, the wearing of furs spread to other European countries. Of special importance in creating a demand for furs was the vogue of the broad-brimmed beaver hat in the seventeenth century. A shift of style toward the close of the century created a crisis in the fur business. At the same time, an unusually large amount of peltry was being shipped to Europe by both French and English traders in America. This may have had something to do with the decision of the French king to withdraw traders from the western posts in 1696. During the eighteenth century there was a gradual stabilization of the market, partly due to restrictions placed on imports.

The pelts that were shipped to Europe included bear, elk, deer,

8 H. A. Innis, *The Fur Trade of Canada,* pp. 20-123.

martin, raccoon, mink, muskrat, opossum, lynx, wolf, and fox. Wolverine pelts were also shipped from Michigan trading posts, although it is not believed this ferocious animal ever had its habitat in Michigan.[9]

Far more important than any of these, or all of them together, was the beaver. It is estimated that there were about ten million beavers in America when the Europeans arrived. The number was rapidly depleted. The beaver's habits made it impossible for him to escape his enemies because he was not a migrant. He lived in lodges that could be attacked at any convenient time in all seasons. The beaver is not a very prolific creature; if left alone the beaver population increases only about twenty percent annually. As the beavers were exterminated in one region after another, the traders and trappers were forced to advance farther and farther inland to find them.[10] Even before the close of the seventeenth century Cadillac reported that beaver was very rare in the vicinity of Michilimackinac.[11]

The fur of the beaver consists of two parts: the guard hair, up to two inches in length, and the underhair or fur, at most an inch long. The pelts that commanded the highest prices were those that had been worn or slept in by the Indians and hence were known as *castor gras* or greasy beaver. The grease and sweat of the Indian's bodies and the smoke in their lodges made the pelts supple and loosened the long, coarse guard hairs, which were then easily removed, leaving the soft underfur for the finer quality of the pelt.[12] The beaver weighs from thirty to sixty pounds, and the pelt weighs from one and a half to two pounds. The flesh of the beaver was relished by the Indians for food. With the primitive weapons they possessed before the white man came, the natives could slaughter only a limited number of beaver; but with iron weapons and guns, and with the lure of the white man's goods, the Indian killed the little animals so rapidly that they soon disappeared.

The importance of Michigan in the fur trade during the latter

[9] See an interesting article on this subject by the famous University of Michigan football coach, F. H. Yost, in *Michigan History*, XXVII (1943), 581-589. Why the name of this beast, sometimes called the "glutton," was applied to Michigan is not positively known. It seems to have been employed as a term of derision by Ohioans in referring to Michiganians at the time of the Toledo War, 1836. See also *Michigan History*, XX (1936), 430-435.

[10] H. MacLennan, "By Canoe to Empire," *American Heritage*, XII (1961), 4ff.

[11] P. Margry, *Découvertes et établissements des Français dans l'Amérique*.

[12] W. J. Eccles, *Frontenac, the Courtier Governor*, p. 75.

part of the French regime was due chiefly to the fact that it contained three trading posts that were the focus and gathering place of traders venturing into or returning from the interior. The French establishments at the Straits of Mackinac (Fort De Buade in the seventeenth century and Fort Michilimackinac in the eighteenth— both referred to in the French records as "Michilimackinac") were the rendezvous for traders who had secured peltry from hundreds of miles to the north and northwest. Fort St. Joseph, near the present city of Niles, was the center of trade for the Illinois country and the region to the south. To Detroit traders and Indians from far to the west came with their peltry. There was a revival of the hunting and trapping of fur-bearing animals in Michigan in the early nineteenth century, but the emphasis by that time had shifted from beaver to muskrat and other types of wild animals.

Representatives of the monopolists at Three Rivers and Montreal during the French regime were forced to license traders to go into the West so as to combat competition from the English. The trade was by no means confined to those who obtained licenses, however, The famed *coureurs de bois* scorned all regulation and all restraint. They often lived among the Indians for years and took Indian wives. The free and adventurous life of the *coureurs de bois* had a fatal fascination for the youth of New France. It has been estimated that out of a population in New France of about ten thousand in 1680, over eight hundred young men had become engaged in the fur trade. The head of a trading post was called the *bourgeois*. Under him was a small army of traders sent out to secure the peltry. His duty was to secure food, traps, and blankets for them, supply them with articles such as brandy and firearms for use in the trade, see that the furs they brought in were properly cured and stored, and make arrangements for shipping the furs to the East. The *partisan* was the leader in charge of one of the parties sent out by the *bourgeois*. *Hivernans* (winterers) were men who spent the winter among the natives; they were the experienced and seasoned members of the trading fraternity. The recruits of the trade were dubbed *mangeurs de lard* (pork-eaters) because they could not subsist on the wild game of the forest but had to have food supplies from the post. At a large post there were clerks, boat builders, blacksmiths, and carpenters.

But the most colorful characters of the fur trade were the *voyageurs*, the hardy men who paddled hundreds of miles up swift streams and across lakes, carrying the canoes on their backs on portages from one stream or body of water to another. They were a gay lot despite their heavy labors, and loved to sing as they worked.[13] A hundred miles was a day's journey, but when competition was keen the paddles would dip on through the night. Sometimes out on the Great Lakes they did not put ashore for several days and nights, chewing pemmican (dried meat) for food and keeping themselves awake with singing. One of these *voyageurs* had this to say of his experiences,

> I have now been forty-two years in this country. For twenty-four I was a light canoeman. I required little sleep but sometimes got less than required. No portage was too long for me; all portages were alike. My end of the canoe never touched the ground till I saw the end of the portage. Fifty songs a day were nothing to me . . . . I saved the lives of ten *bourgeois* and was always a favorite because, when others stopped to carry at a bad step, and lost time, I pushed on—over rapids, over cascades, over chutes, all were the same to me. No water, no weather, ever stopped the paddle or the song. I had twelve wives in the country. . . . No *bourgeois* had better-dressed wives than I, no Indian chief better horses, no white man better harnessed or swifter dogs . . . . There is no life so happy as the *voyageur's* life; none so independent; no place where a man enjoys so much variety and freedom as in the Indian country. *Huzza! Huzza! pour le pays sauvage.* [14]

It was reckoned that one canoeload of Indian goods would buy four canoeloads of furs. Typical trading items were bright-colored beads, cloth, shawls, handkerchiefs, ribbons, sleigh bells, knives, jew's harps, shot, powder, tobacco, blankets, and brandy. There is no doubt that in many cases the Indians were unmercifully cheated by the traders, but it is possible that the extent of this has been exaggerated. Much of the trade was conducted on a credit basis. The trader usually went in debt for his supplies when he left for the woods. He paid a high price for the goods he bought from the Montreal merchants, partly due to the risk they took that he might not return. Food eaten by the fur traders consisted principally of corn and bear, pork, or other fat. The corn was boiled in strong lye, the hulls removed, and the kernels washed and dried. The ordinary allowance was a bushel of corn and two pounds of fat per man per month.

After the British took over New France the personnel of the fur trade continued to be largely French. And many French *voyageurs* and traders continued in the trade into the American pe-

[13] For some *voyageur* songs, see *Mich. Pioneer and Historical Colls.* I, 366-67.

[14] Quoted in C. L. Skinner, *Beaver, Kings, and Cabins,* p. 266.

riod. The descendants of these French fur traders may still be found in Michigan's Upper Peninsula. They were a colorful lot, immune to hardship, but given to song and storytelling when the occasion permitted. [15]

THE MISSIONARIES

As has been noted earlier, two Jesuits, Fathers Jogues and Raymbault, were the first French missionaries to reach Michigan. They were at the Sault in 1641, but the vicious attack of the Iroquois on Huronia prevented any immediate follow-up of their plan to establish a mission on the St. Mary's River. The first mission in Michigan was founded by Father Marquette at this location in 1668. Just how long the Jesuits continued their work among the Ottawa at the Sault is uncertain, but after 1671 their chief mission was at St. Ignace. Here they continued their work until 1705. Following the death of Father Marquette in 1675, Father Charles Albanel was sent to take charge of the mission among the Ottawa at St. Ignace. During this same time, Father Louis André worked among the Indians on Manitoulin Island, sometimes stewing the leather covers of his books to keep from starving, and when all was well playing his flute to teach hymn tunes to the Indians.[16] And there was Father Henri Nouvel, who ventured into the Lower Peninsula in 1675 upon the invitation of the Chippewa Indians. After the founding of Detroit in 1701, most of the Ottawa moved southward from the Straits of Mackinac, and in 1705 the Jesuit fathers set fire to the mission buildings at St. Ignace to prevent their profanation, and returned to Quebec. The Sault mission had been abandoned before 1700.

The name of Father Claude Allouez is closely associated with the beginnings of the Jesuit mission on the St. Joseph River near Niles. Here this great missionary is believed to have died in 1690. Sometimes called a second Francis Xavier, Allouez is reputed to have instructed more than one hundred thousand Indians and baptized more than ten thousand. In the year Allouez died Father Claude Aveneau was sent to work at the St. Joseph mission. He was followed by Father Jean-Baptiste Chardon. Because of the Fox wars the mission was abandoned for six years. Charles-Ange Collet, baptized at the St. Joseph mission in 1721, was the first native of Michigan to enter the priesthood. He had his preliminary schooling at Montreal, was ordained in 1747, and shortly thereafter took up his residence in France where he

[15] G. L. Nute, *The Voyageur.*
[16] Paré, *op. cit.,* p. 40.

remained until his death. The baptismal register of the St. Joseph
mission provides many sidelights on the events that took place
there. The priests ministered not only to the Indians but also
to the forty or fifty families that lived on or near the post. A
village of Potawatomi and one of Miami were located near
the mission, although the Miami moved into Ohio and northern
Indiana before the mission was abandoned. After the Jesuit
order was secularized by the French government, Father Pierre
Gibault was sent by Bishop Briand to the Illinois country. He
was at the St. Joseph mission intermittently between 1768
and 1773. He is often called the "Patriot Priest" because through
his influence the French population of Kaskaskia and Cahokia
supported George Rogers Clark during the American Revolution
when Clark took over the Illinois settlements from the British.
The last entry in the register of the St. Joseph mission is the one
made by Father Gibault in 1773.[17]

The mission at St. Ignace, abandoned in 1705, was rebuilt
the following year on specific orders from the king, Father Joseph Marest being sent to take charge of it. But it did not prosper.
It continued to exist more as a headquarters for traveling missionaries than for any good that could be accomplished in the vicinity.
The mission was moved to the vicinity of Fort Michilimackinac,
at the site of the present Mackinaw City, about 1741. About
this same time the Ottawa moved their village to the "land of
the crooked tree" (L'Arbre Croche), near the present Harbor
Springs, and the missionaries soon followed them. Father Pierre
Du Jaunay, last of the Jesuit missionaries among the Ottawa,
frequently traveled back and forth between L'Arbre Croche and
the St. Joseph mission.

A deep hostility had developed between the Jesuits and Cadillac during the latter's tenure as commandant at Fort De Buade.
This antagonism seriously affected the work of the Jesuits following the founding of Detroit in 1701. Cadillac was accompanied
to Detroit by a Jesuit as well as by a Recollet, but the Jesuit returned to Quebec before the end of the year. It was part of
Cadillac's plan to gather all of the Indians of the lake region to
live around Detroit and to do all their trading there. The Jesuits
were convinced that nothing was more certain to debauch the
natives, and refused to have anything to do with the project.
Cadillac tried in vain to induce Father Marest to move from St.
Ignace to Detroit. He accused the Jesuits of thwarting his plans by
urging the Indians not to come to Detroit. His removal from

17 *Ibid,* pp. 78-103.

Detroit in 1710 made it possible for the Jesuits to undertake missionary work among the Indians whose villages were located near Fort Pontchartrain. In 1727 Father Armand de La Richardie arrived at Detroit to start missionary work in the Huron village. He found that the Huron, while remembering some of the Christian practices they had learned from earlier missionaries, were quite indifferent to his efforts to persuade them to embrace the faith. Only after many months was he able to win a small band of converts. By 1735, however, there were six hundred fervent neophytes. Then the Huron had a quarrel with the Ottawa and abandoned their village at Detroit, moving to the vicinity of present-day Sandusky. Subsequently, the Huron were settled on Bois Blanc Island, and here Father La Richardie's mission was re-established. A large church, a priest's house, a forge, a house for the smith, another for the domestics, a refectory, barns, and a trading post were constructed. In 1749 the mission was transferred to Sandwich, on the Canadian side of the Detroit River. Meanwhile, a certain amount of missionary work was carried on by the Recollets who had charge of St. Anne's church, founded in Detroit in 1701. The first recorded baptism of an Indian child in St. Anne's occurred in 1706.

Missionary work was not entirely abandoned in Michigan after the dissolution of the Jesuit order. The coming of Father Gibault to the St. Joseph mission has been mentioned. Father Gabriel Richard, who came to Detroit in 1798, actively promoted education for the Indians. He was sent on a missionary tour to the northern lake region in 1799. In spite of the fact that they had no resident priest, the Indians of L'Arbre Croche had not abandoned the Christian faith, and efforts were made to provide them with a priest from time to time. Father Frederic Baraga started his missionary work at L'Arbre Croche in 1831. In 1832 he visited the Chippewa living on Beaver Island. Father Saenderl, a Redemptorist, took over the L'Arbre Croche mission in 1833, while Father Baraga established a new mission on the Grand River. In 1835 Father Baraga began his missionary work among the Chippewa of the Upper Peninsula. Thus the Catholic missionary labors, so nobly begun during the French period, were continued into the British and American periods.

THE EIGHTEENTH CENTURY

The eighteenth century on this continent was dominated by international wars for the possession of the interior of North America. What is now the state of Michigan was, in many ways, a focus of these conflicts. First there were the struggles between the French and the British, culminating in the Peace of Paris in 1763, which granted to Great Britain all the territory in North America east of the Mississippi River. A dozen years later the thirteen colonies began their war for independence, which we know as the American Revolution. France joined the United States in an alliance signed in 1778 against her old enemy, Britain. With the aid of France the patriots won independence, and Great Britain recognized the independence of the United States. What is now Michigan was part of the territory of the United States under the Treaty of 1783, which marked the close of the American Revolution. But Great Britain failed to evacuate Detroit and Fort Mackinac, and thus retained virtual possession of Michigan. She even administered the Detroit area as part of Canada. Eventually, however, John Jay persuaded the British in 1795 to agree to surrender the posts they had continued to hold within United States territory, and these posts were evacuated in 1796. Michigan thus came into the possession of the United States four years before the close of the eighteenth century. During the War of 1812 the British took both Detroit and Fort Mackinac, but Detroit was retaken by the Americans in 1813, and Fort Mackinac was returned to the United States by the terms of the Treaty of Ghent, which marked the end of the War of 1812.

The Indians were not passive in these wars waged by the white men. The Algonquin nations, which included most of the tribes in Michigan, fought alongside the French to the last. And in the very year that France ceded to Britain the territory that included Michigan, the Algonquin staged a formidable rebellion against the British troops who had taken over the forts and trading posts formerly controlled by France. Chief Pontiac, the leader of this uprising, was one of the ablest Indians ever to contest the white men who had intruded upon the Indian hunting grounds. But the Indian uprising was suppressed, and the Indians reconciled themselves to the new regime. The British won the Indians' support by endeavoring to prevent the intrusion of white settlers west of the Alleghenies and by imposing regulations upon the fur traders. When the American Revolution began the patriots sought to keep the Indians neutral, but with little success. The eventual transfer of Michigan to American control compelled the Indians to make another readjustment. During the War of 1812 they again fought on the British side. When the United States resumed possession of Michigan after that war, the Indian threat subsided.

Reconstruction of Fort Michilimackinac, currently a tourist attraction

Voyageurs

4

THE DUEL FOR EMPIRE

Between 1689 and 1815 there were eight wars between France and Great Britain; the two nations were at war for almost sixty out of the one hundred twenty-six years between these two dates. As has been noted earlier, the outbreak of the first of these conflicts was occasioned by the Glorious Revolution in England, which brought about the downfall of the Stuart kings and made bitter enemies of King Louis XIV of France, and William of Orange, and his wife Mary, the rulers of England. The second war, called the War of the Spanish Succession in Europe and Queen Anne's War in America, was the result of the ambition of Louis XIV to place his grandson on the Spanish throne. It was concluded by the Treaty of Utrecht, signed in 1713, in which the British gained possession of Hudson's Bay. This had a repercussion in Michigan, for the decision of the French to re-establish a fort at the Straits of Mackinac was probably made in part to meet the competition of British fur traders operating out of Hudson's Bay. A long interval of peace followed the Peace of Utrecht; indeed, it was not until thirty-one years later that the two nations were once more involved in conflict. This third war was called King George's War in America and the War of the Austrian Succession in Europe. In this war Britain and France were drawn into conflict as a result of a war between Prussia and

101

Austria, France being an ally of Prussia and Britain being allied with Austria. There was fighting in America during this war, but its result was indecisive. The fourth war, unlike the others, had its origin in America. This struggle, called the French and Indian War in America and the Seven Years' War in Europe, was truly a world war, for there were battles in America, in Europe, and in India. Its outcome determined the fate of North America and India. On both sides of the globe the British won overwhelming victories and laid the foundations of the mighty British empire. New France disappeared from the map of North America. The territory claimed by France west of the Mississippi river was ceded to Spain and all the region east of the Mississippi to Britain. France retained only two islands in the Caribbean and two tiny islands for her fishermen at the mouth of the St. Lawrence. Although the French people in the St. Lawrence settlements and in the West no longer were subjects of the French king, they remained in America and constituted an influence with which the British had to reckon once they began the process of ruling the vast region they had acquired.

PRELUDE

During the long period of peace preceding King George's War (1744-1748) the French occupied nine major posts in the Great Lakes region. In what is now Michigan, there were Fort Detroit, Fort Michilimackinac, and Fort St. Joseph. In what is today Wisconsin, were Fort La Baye at the site of Green Bay and Fort La Pointe, far to the north on Chequamegon Bay. Fort Chartres on the Mississippi River in Illinois was perhaps the finest fort in the West. In what we call Indiana were Fort Ouiatenon on the Wabash River, Fort Vincennes, further south on the Wabash, and Fort Miamis on the Maumee. Of these forts, Michilimackinac and Detroit were by far the most important. From these two points the influence of France radiated, the fur traders carried on their business, and the missionaries went out to convert the "savages." Near these two fortified places many Indians had their villages. A census taken in 1736 revealed that around Detroit some 200 Ottawa, 200 Huron and 100 Potawatomi braves lived with their families. At Michilimackinac were 180 Ottawa, who moved a few miles south with their families to L'Arbre Croche (Cross Village) about 1742. There were 100 Potawatomi braves who resided near Fort St. Joseph and thirty Chippewa at St. Mary's Falls (the Soo), where the French were to establish a settlement again in 1750. The Miami had mostly moved out of

Michigan, some 200 Miami braves residing near Fort Miamis. Apparently the largest number of Chippewa lived in villages close to La Pointe, in what is now northern Wisconsin.[1]

All these Indians were nominally attached to the French. But some of them had learned that they could make a better bargain for their peltry with the British than with the French. The Miami had been trading secretly with the British for years. In 1738 a band of Huron, fearful of the enmity of the Ottawa and Chippewa toward them and not satisfied with the way the French at Detroit treated them, moved their village down to Sandusky Bay in northern Ohio, where British traders operating out of Albany had little difficulty reaching them. Unlike the French traders, the British were not hampered by monopolies and by having to pay license fees. This was the situation when King George's War broke out in 1744. The following year Chief Nicolas of the Huron band living on Sandusky Bay allowed the British to build a "strong-house" near his village, and the Iroquois, at the instigation of the British, urged the Huron warriors to attack Detroit. Five French traders returning to Detroit were captured and killed in June, 1747. This incident and a timely warning received by the French commandant at Detroit from a squaw alerted him to the danger. He called the nearby French *habitants* into the fort for protection, but the Indians living near Detroit promptly disavowed any connection with the plot. Even though the proposed foray against Detroit was thus foiled, several more French traders were killed or plundered during the summer of 1747. There was trouble at Fort Michilimackinac, too, but when reinforcements arrived the rumblings among the Indians died away. Deserted by his fellow Indians, Chief Nicolas moved his village southward and the British had to abandon their trading place on Sandusky Bay.[2]

The peace that came in 1748 was hardly more than a truce. The fourth and decisive war between France and Great Britain for the possession of North America did not break out along the border between New France and New England, nor on the borderland between the Carolinas and Georgia on the one side and Spanish Florida on the other, where most of the fighting had taken place in the earlier wars. Instead, it was in the valley of the Ohio River that the rivalry between the two powers brought about the clash that started the French and Indian War.

Conflicting claims for the Ohio Valley were not of recent origin when the French and Indian War broke out. As early as 1671

[1] H. Peckham, *Pontiac and the Indian Uprising*, p. 30.
[2] *Ibid.*, pp. 30-33.

at the famous "Pageant of the Sault," St. Lusson had laid claim
for the King of France to all the lands drained by the lakes and
rivers of the interior. British claims went back even further.
In 1609 King James of England had granted to the London Company a charter for Virginia, which included a vast interior tract.
The boundary along the seacoast was to include a two-hundred-
mile stretch north of Point Comfort and a two-hundred-mile
stretch south of that point. And the grant included "all that Space
and Circuit of Land, lying from the Sea Coast of the Precinct
aforesaid, up into the Land, throughout from Sea to Sea, West
and Northwest." The description, though vague, was later to be
interpreted as giving Virginia title to Kentucky and the territory
north of the Ohio River. When King James dissolved the London
Company in 1624, the crown assumed this claim. Subsequent
charters, granted to Massachusetts and Connecticut, also ran from
sea to sea and partially overlapped the Virginia claim. These,
however, were considerably north of the Ohio Valley.

Although both Britain and France had laid claim to the Ohio
Valley in the seventeenth century, it was not until after King
George's War that much attention was given to the fact that
these claims were in conflict. Few British colonists had ventured
west of the Allegheny Mountains up to that time. But in 1747
a group of Virginians formed an association to promote settlement
in the Ohio Valley. And at about the same time Pennsylvania
fur traders were boldly venturing westward into the Ohio Valley
and were challenging the French control over the fur trade with
the Indians of that region. These two developments aroused the
French to action.

The association of Virginians, called the Ohio Company, obtained in 1748 a grant of 200,000 acres of land along the Ohio
River, with the provision that 300,000 acres more would be
granted if one hundred families were settled on the land within
seven years. An agent of the Company, Christopher Gist, established a storehouse and laid out a trail to the region of the grant.
Although the effort to secure settlers failed, the French were
alarmed at the prospective intrusion into a region they considered
to be outside the limits of the English colonies. Several other
land companies were formed in Virginia and Pennsylvania during
this same period, with the purpose of seeking land grants for
speculative purposes.

The Pennsylvania fur traders found a golden opportunity to
benefit when, during King George's War, the British navy disrupted French trade to the extent that Montreal merchants were
unable to obtain adequate supplies of trading goods required

to secure peltry from the Indians. A tough Irish trader from Pennsylvania, George Croghan, was operating trading centers on the Upper Ohio by the close of 1744. From these bases trading expeditions were traveling as far west as the Illinois country. Other traders ventured up the rivers flowing into the Ohio. And in 1748 Croghan had a palisaded fort constructed at the Miami Indian village of Pickawillany, the site of the present Piqua, Ohio. With the help of Conrad Weiser and with the approval of the Pennsylvania Assembly, Croghan lured chieftains of several Indian tribes of the Ohio Valley to Logstown, Pennsylvania, where they signed a treaty pledging their allegiance to Great Britain rather than France.

In 1749 the French reacted to these challenges to their claims on the Ohio Valley by sending Celeron de Blainville with two hundred soldiers into the region. He did not have a sufficient force to attack Pickawillany and, instead, planted at the mouths of several of the rivers flowing into the Ohio lead plates proclaiming that the land belonged to the King of France.

Another move made by the French to check British inroads had a more direct connection with Michigan. This involved the building of a fort and the establishment of a settlement on the St. Mary's river. Site of the earliest mission in Michigan, the Soo had been a natural stopping place for fur traders during and after the time when the Jesuits maintained a mission there and, as has been indicated, a small number of Chippewa lived there. The passage through the St. Mary's River afforded a means whereby Indians from the far North could avoid Fort Michilimackinac and carry their peltry to British traders. To forestall this the governor of New France, La Jonquière, in 1750 granted a seignory eighteen miles square bordering on the St. Mary's River to a man who had proved his prowess by conducting a successful raid into New York, Louis le Gardeur de Repentigny. The grant was to be shared by Captain Louis de Bonne, a nephew of the governor, but the latter never visited the property, so far as is known. Repentigny erected three buildings enclosed in a stockade, and established Jean-Baptiste Cadotte and his Indian wife as tenants. He had horses and cattle brought from Fort Michilimackinac for their use. Repentigny gave the Chippewa a belt of wampum and persuaded them to deliver to him a belt that had been sent them by the British.[3]

Although Repentigny's fort and the symbol of French authority that it provided probably served to maintain the allegiance of the Chippewa to the French cause, it had little significance in the im-

[3] F. C. Bald, *Michigan in Four Centuries*, pp. 58-59.

pending struggle. Much more important was that the long line of incompetent governors of New France was broken in 1752 when the Marquis Duquesne assumed that position. He was a naval officer of ability, imposed firm discipline, and took decisive action to strengthen New France. Lacking sufficient French personnel, he undertook to enlist France's remaining Indian allies to meet the British threat. Under his orders a half-breed trader named Charles Langlade organized at Detroit a band of Ottawa braves to attack Pickawillany. The fort was utterly destroyed and the local chieftain, who was among those who had gone over to the British, was killed, boiled, and eaten by the Ottawa. Here was more than a gentle hint to the British to keep out of the French preserves. The Indians, too, were impressed, and the Miami, Huron, and most of the Shawnee returned to French allegiance.

Duquesne quickly followed up this advantage. In 1753 he ordered a string of forts erected south of Lake Erie on French Creek and the Allegheny River to protect the portage by which the French could take a shortcut to the Mississippi Valley. The forts were named Presqu'Isle, Le Boeuf, and Venango. They were on Pennsylvania soil, but the Quakers who dominated the Pennsylvania Assembly would not take any step that might lead to war. Governor Robert Dinwiddie of Virginia had no such qualms. Clearly the French were seeking to assert their title to the Ohio Valley, which Virginia claimed under its charter. Dinwiddie sent a promising young Virginia surveyor named George Washington to warn the French to get out. Washington visited Forts Venango and Le Boeuf, and was received with the greatest of politeness and hospitality by the French commandant, but was told in no uncertain terms that the French did not propose to leave. When Dinwiddie received this news he decided that Virginia would try her hand at fort building. Washington was given a company of Virginia militia and sent back to build a fort at the strategic point where the Allegheny and Monongahela Rivers flow together to form the Ohio. Washington's guide was Christopher Gist, who had been the advance agent of the Ohio Company. A small contingent of Washington's party was sent ahead and was beginning work on the proposed fort when a great fleet of canoes appeared carrying five hundred Frenchmen. The party of about forty men was allowed to depart and the French then proceeded to construct a strong fort, naming it Fort Duquesne in honor of the governor.

Meanwhile Washington was advancing with his mainforce of about 150 militiamen. When the French commandant at Fort Duquesne, the Sieur de Contrecoeur, was advised by Indian allies of the approach of Washington's force, he decided to send forward a party of forty men to warn Washington that he was intruding on French territory and that he should return forthwith to Virginia. Washington also learned through an Indian runner that the French had driven off his advance party and were sending forward an armed force to meet him. After marching all night Washington and his men came upon the French party, and without any parleys firing began. Each side claimed the other fired first. The officer in charge of the French party, Jumonville, and nine others were killed. The remainder were taken prisoner. Thus the French and Indian War began. The British historian Horace Walpole wrote of this skirmish, "A volley fired by a young Virginian in the backwoods of America set the world on fire."

The French commander who was killed in this engagement spent his boyhood in Michigan. Jumonville was the surname of Joseph de Villiers. He and his brother Louis were sons of the Sieur de Villiers, who was the commandant of Fort St. Joseph from 1724 to 1730. Louis and Joseph had played on the banks of the St. Joseph River as boys. Louis was at Fort Duquesne when he heard of the death of his brother, and he straightway organized a party to take revenge for what the French regarded as a massacre. Washington, anticipating an attack from the larger French force, had thrown up an entrenchment, which he called Fort Necessity. After fighting fiercely an all-day battle against overwhelming odds, Washington signed a capitulation under which his men were allowed to march out of the fort with the honors of war, but were to abandon the Ohio Valley. The articles of capitulation recited that Washington had wrongly invaded the realm of France and had killed Jumonville in violation of the recognized laws of war. Washington claimed afterward he was not correctly informed by the interpreter of the meaning of the statements he had signed. His horses had been stolen so his men were compelled to return home carrying their sick and wounded on their backs and harassed by Indians who had happily returned to their allegiance to the French.

The die was now cast. The war that was to decide the fate of a continent had begun in the backwoods of Pennsylvania with the killing of a former resident of Michigan by a Virginia military company commanded by the man who was destined to become the first president of the United States.

DECISION

Surprisingly enough, France and Britain remained officially at peace until 1756. The reason was that the two countries were in the process of reshaping their alliances. Great Britain, which had made common cause with Austria in the previous war, signed an alliance with Frederick the Great of Prussia, the archenemy of Empress Maria Theresa of Austria. And France, which had supported the Prussian cause previously, now entered into an alliance with Austria. When this "diplomatic revolution" was complete, war was declared.

But the conflict in America did not wait upon the completion of the diplomatic revolution in Europe. Britain sent General Edward Braddock to take command of two regiments of regulars and whatever colonial forces he could muster. Unfortunately for the British cause, Braddock divided his forces into four parts, one of which he himself led in an attempt to capture Fort Duquesne. It was an ill-starred venture. The story of Braddock's defeat and death in western Pennsylvania is one of the famous episodes of the French and Indian War. When he set out, Braddock had a force of 1,400 regulars, 450 Virginia militiamen under Washington, and fifty Indian scouts. A French force of only about 250, with 600 Indians, was sent out from Fort Duquesne with the design of delaying rather than defeating the oncoming Britishers. Only seven miles from Fort Duquesne the two forces clashed head-on. The French were able to occupy a hill and a ravine on either side of the British from which they could pour a murderous fire into the confused redcoats and militiamen. The retreat Braddock ordered, after he had been mortally wounded, turned into a rout. The stunning defeat of Braddock has sometimes been attributed to the unfamiliarity of the British regulars with wilderness fighting. But modern military historians who have studied the engagement have concluded that Braddock's army was woefully mismanaged. One of them has written of the cause of the defeat thus:

> It was incompetent leadership, judged not by modern standards, but by contemporary. There was far too little space between the various parts of the army; the flanking parties and the guides were inadequate to give timely warning of an enemy's approach; a strategic point along the line of march was left unoccupied; the main body, divided by the column of wagons, had its mobility seriously decreased; and the main body was either ordered or permitted to advance, contrary to European rules, before its officers knew what lay ahead. For all these reasons, and not because of the strangeness of the woods or of Indian methods of fighting, the troops became panic-stricken.[4]

[4] S. Pargellis, "Braddock's Defeat," *American Historical Review,* XLI (Jan. 1936), 269.

A native of Michigan played perhaps a decisive role in bringing about Braddock's defeat. He was the half-breed trader, Charles Langlade, who two years before had commanded the force that successfully assaulted and destroyed Pickawillany. Langlade was born about 1732. His father was a Frenchman, said to have been descended from an aristocratic family, who had come to Fort Michilimackinac to recoup the family fortune in the fur trade. His mother was a young Ottawa Indian woman, the sister of a chief. There is a story that when Langlade was a boy of five his mother's brother had a dream in which the Great Spirit directed him to take a little boy with him on a war party, and promised victory if he did so. The chief did as he was told in the dream; the victory that was won was attributed to the presence of the little boy, Charles Langlade. For whatever cause, Langlade had a powerful influence over the Indian tribesmen who were allied with the French. He led a force of Ottawa and Chippewa from northern Michigan, and possibly some Ottawa of Detroit as well, to defend Fort Duquesne against the British. His braves were included in the force sent out to meet Braddock. And according to one account it was his repeated urging that finally persuaded the French commander of the force, Captain Daniel de Beaujeu, to attack the superior British army at the place where the latter was at a great disadvantage. Two British officers later testified that the defeat of Braddock could be attributed to Langlade.[5]

Following the defeat of Braddock, Langlade and his warriors returned to Michigan. Possibly as a reward for his services, Langlade received from the commandant at Fort Michilimackinac, Captain Lewis Herbin, an authorization to trade for furs in the Grand River Valley, and to make his headquarters there at a place called "Gabagonache." He and his descendants were to carry on the fur trade in the Grand Valley until 1821. This remarkable man continued to support the French cause against the British, and later aided the British in the American Revolution. He had an uncanny way of turning up at crucial moments in both conflicts.

The two years following the defeat of Braddock were dismal ones for the British cause. The Indians, having returned to their allegiance to the French, harried the back country of the thirteen colonies relentlessly, forcing the colonies to construct forts all along the Allegheny frontier. The Earl of Loudon, characterized by one writer as a "pompous windbag," succeeded Braddock in command of the British forces, and accomplished almost nothing.[6]

[5] C. T. Hamilton, "Western Michigan History," *Michigan History*, XIII (1929), 211-218; *Wisconsin Historical Collections*, III, 213.
[6] R. Billington, *Westward Expansion*, p. 108.

Fort Pontchartrain, first settlement, Detroit

Meanwhile the French were led by a brilliant new commander, the Marquis de Montcalm, to a series of victories that opened the Mohawk Valley in New York to frequent Indian raids from Canada.[7] Detroit played a major role in the French military campaigns. Food supplies from Detroit and from the Illinois country sustained Fort Duquesne. Detroit was the gathering place, not only for supplies but for Indian and French fighting men.

Late in 1757 the tide began to turn. In the fall of that year a new British ministry headed by William Pitt injected fresh vigor into the British cause. Subsidies were sent to Frederick the Great to help him keep French armies tied down in Europe. British naval power, destined to be a deciding factor in the British victory, was strengthened by the addition of more ships. Most important, Pitt was able to rid the British army and navy of many incompetent officers, who had been raised to power through the purchase of commissions, seniority, or social rank, and to put in their places brilliant young commanders. Military leaders of the stamp of Colonel Jeffrey Amherst, General James Wolfe, and General John Forbes won North America for Britain. In July,

[7] W. Edmonds, in his historical novel *Drums Along the Mohawk,* gives a vivid description of this phase of the war.

1758 the French stronghold of Louisburg on Cape Breton Isle was captured. About the same time, another British force swept up the St. Lawrence and captured Fort Frontenac, cutting the communication and transportation route between Detroit and the St. Lawrence settlements. And later the same year General Forbes led an expedition across Pennsylvania, captured Fort Duquesne, and rechristened it Fort Pitt.

News of General Forbes' advance against Fort Duquesne was brought to Detroit and a fighting force of Ottawa, Potawatomi, and Chippewa was assembled to go to the defense of the fort. The Michigan warriors arrived while Forbes was proceeding slowly westward. He purposely moved slowly because he knew that the longer he delayed, the more impatient the Indian allies of the French would become to return to their homes. But an advance British force under Major James Grant virtually invited attack. On September 14 it was surprised and driven back, with losses of 270 killed, 42 wounded, and 100 taken prisoner. While the French commandant waited impatiently for Forbes to come up with the main body of his force and launch the attack, his Indian allies began to melt away. At length, so many had gone that he despaired of holding out against a British attack. On November 24 he blew up the fort and burned it, retiring up the Allegheny River to Fort Venango.

The evaporation of the Indian force that led to the abandonment of Fort Duquesne may have been influenced by a cunning deal made with the Indians. At Albany in 1754 the Iroquois confederacy had ceded the lands occupied by the Delaware west of the Susquehanna River to the British. Now to pacify these Indians a treaty was signed at Easton, Pennsylvania in which a promise was made to the Delaware and the other Indians that all the lands west of the mountains would be respected as Indian property. This concession on the part of the British may have helped persuade the Indians to leave Fort Duquesne in its hour of need. On November 25, 1758 the British flag was raised at the site, which henceforth was to be known as Fort Pitt.[8]

In 1759 the British moved in for the kill. Amherst captured Forts Crown Point, Ticonderoga, and Niagara. And on September 17 the principal city of New France, the supposedly impregnable Quebec, fell to British arms after the most celebrated battle of the war, fought on the Plains of Abraham in front of the city. Wolfe, the British leader, and Montcalm, the French commandant, both lost their lives in the engagement. Among the defenders of Quebec

[8] R. C. Downes, *Council Fires on the Upper Ohio*, p. 89.

were Charles Langlade and some 400 Indian warriors led by him. Langlade already had been of inestimable aid to the French. He had temporarily abandoned his fur trading in Michigan, and in 1757 he had won a battle from Major Robert Rogers and his famous rangers on Lake Champlain. Langlade and his Indian followers helped Montcalm capture Fort William Henry on Lake George in New York. He had now become a lieutenant in the French army. At one stage in the siege of Quebec Wolfe landed 3,000 of his men in an exposed position, separate from the rest of his army. Langlade quickly saw that this was a golden opportunity to inflict a stinging defeat on the British expedition and he sent an appeal to the commander to come to his support. It went unheeded, and although Langlade's Indians attacked anyway and inflicted considerable loss on the British force, the chance for a knockout blow was lost. Later Wolfe moved his forces above Quebec, then crossed the river and scaled the cliffs in front of the city by using a narrow unguarded pathway. The battle that followed resulted in a British victory and Quebec was surrendered.[9]

Earlier the same year, when the British were attacking Fort Niagara, Indians from Detroit and the Illinois country came to the relief of the fort. This time, however, it was the French and Indian forces that were ambushed by the British. After sustaining heavy losses the Detroit Indians fled across Lake Erie back to their villages. With the tide of the war turning, the Indians now began to waver in their support of the French. A delegation of Huron, Ottawa, and Chippewa went to Fort Pitt and smoked the pipe of peace with George Croghan, representing the British. Even so, the majority of the tribesmen co-operated with the French commandant at Detroit, who, after the fall of Fort Niagara and Quebec, prepared for a last ditch stand against what he thought might be a British foray against Detroit. Although he had only 45 regulars and 655 militiamen under his command, they were joined by 150 Frenchmen who came from the Illinois country with a supply of provisions. Some 600 *habitants* of the region also were potential defenders, and he could count on 550 Indian warriors living in nearby villages. Prominent among these braves was the Ottawa chieftain Pontiac, who was destined to become the central figure in the most formidable Indian uprising the British ever faced in America.[10]

The French cause was not without hope in the spring of 1760

[9] M. M. Quaife, "The Romance of the Mackinac Country," *Michigan History*, XIII (1929), 392.

[10] H. Peckham, *op. cit.*, p. 55.

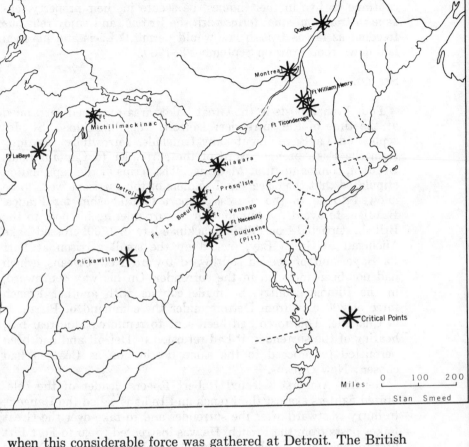

FRENCH AND INDIAN WAR

Quebec

Montreal

Ft William Henry

Ft Ticonderoga

Ft Michilimackinac

Ft LaBaye

Niagara

Detroit

Ft Presq'Isle

Ft La Boeuf

Venango

Ft Necessity

Duquesne (Pitt)

Pickawillany

Critical Points

Miles 0 100 200

Stan Smeed

when this considerable force was gathered at Detroit. The British in Quebec faced near-starvation before the ice went out of the St. Lawrence, enabling a British supply fleet to rescue them. At the very time the British fleet arrived, Quebec was under attack by the Chevalier de Lévis, Montcalm's successor as commander of the French forces, and a stinging defeat had been inflicted upon the British at the battle of Sainte-Foy. But the coming of the British fleet with men and supplies completely reversed the situation. Lévis retreated to Montreal where three British armies converged early in September. It was the Marquis de Vaudreuil, last governor of New France, who decided to surrender. Most of the Indian allies of the French already had melted away and

even some of the regulars had deserted. All the French possessions
in North America except New Orleans were surrendered. Amherst,
the British commander, promised that the French people might
continue to live in their homes, be secure in their property, engage in trade on equal terms with the British, and enjoy religious
freedom as far as British law would permit.[11] Lévis and his men
laid down their arms on September 8, 1760.

SEQUEL

Four French posts in the Great Lakes area remained garrisoned
at the time of the surrender: Detroit, Michilimackinac, St. Joseph, and La Baye. Lieutenant Langlade, sorrowfully returning
from the East, brought word of the surrender to Captain Louis
Beaujeu, commandant at Mackinac. The terms of the capitulation
stipulated that the officers and soldiers of the garrisons were to be
allowed to go to the nearest seaport to take ship for France.
Beaujeu, to avoid the humiliation of surrendering his post to the
British, departed from Michilimackinac late in 1760, crossed Lake
Michigan to Green Bay, picked up the small garrison at Fort
La Baye, and proceeded southward toward New Orleans, which
had not been included in the surrender. On his way southward,
in the Illinois country, he made contact with another French
force of 200 men from Detroit under the command of Pierre de
la Chapelle. This force had been sent to reinforce Montreal but,
hearing of the surrender, it had returned to Detroit and had been
permitted to proceed to the same destination as Beaujeu had
chosen: New Orleans.[12]

General Amherst selected Robert Rogers, leader of the celebrated fighters against the French and Indians called the Rangers,
to hurry westward after the surrender and to take over the Great
Lakes posts from the French. He was instructed to go to Fort Pitt
first to pick up a company of British regulars to garrison Detroit.
General Robert Monckton at Fort Pitt assigned the duty to a
company of the 60th Regiment of Royal Americans, under Captain
Donald Campbell. Rogers' responsibility was chiefly that of dealing with the Indians and winning them over to the British side.
Along the shores of Lake Erie, the expedition made contact with
the pro-English band of Ottawa that already had smoked the
pipe of peace with George Croghan. Rogers wrote an account in

[11] G. M. Wrong, *The Rise and Fall of New France,* II, 872.
[12] L. P. Kellogg, *The British Regime in Wisconsin and the Old Northwest,* pp. 4-6.

later years that told of meeting Chief Pontiac at this point. He gave a careful description of Pontiac and the ceremony, which was accepted as authentic by Parkman and later writers, but which now appears to have been a mere figment of Rogers' imagination.[13] Probably, however, Pontiac was among the chiefs who welcomed the British force when it reached the mouth of the Detroit River. The formal surrender took place on November 29, 1760, when the French commandant, Captain François de Bellestre, gave up his arms and his men. The *fleur-de-lis* of France came down and the British colors were raised.

Captain Campbell and George Croghan, who accompanied the expedition, thought Fort Pontchartrain was the finest they had ever seen. Pickets were twelve to fifteen feet in height, and the area they enclosed was very large. Inside the stockade were houses and shops, Ste. Anne's church, and a barracks. The commandant's house stood on a stone foundation measuring 43 by 32 feet and all the rooms were plastered. The other houses had sharply sloping roofs, dormer windows, and board siding over hewn logs. The *habitants* witnessed the ceremony of surrender with seeming indifference. The Indians, in contrast, appeared to be happy with the change, probably anticipating cheaper goods and better trading conditions. However, they reminded the British that "this country was given by God to the Indians" and expressed the hope that "you would preserve it for our joint use."[14] Rogers secured the release of a total of 57 English prisoners held by the natives. Having thus secured Detroit, Rogers ordered a small party of Rangers to proceed southward to take possession of Forts Miamis and Ouiatenon. He led another party northward to take over Fort Michilimackinac. He was turned back by ice, however, and returned to Detroit, then marched overland to Fort Pitt, which he reached on January 23, 1761.[15]

Captain Campbell and his men spent a pleasant winter in Detroit. The *habitants* willingly furnished them with foodstuffs, and accounts indicate that there was a good deal of dancing, card playing, and conviviality at the commandant's house. Apparently the British were infected with the robust, vivacious spirit of the French *habitants*. But Captain Campbell had his worries. The Indians were demanding more and more; there even were hints of a plan to attack the fort, which was now called Fort Detroit

---

[13] H. Peckham, *op. cit.*, pp. 59-63.
[14] Croghan's journal in *Massachusetts Historical Collections,* fourth series, IX, 375, quoted in Peckham, *op. cit.*, p. 66.
[15] Peckham, *op. cit.*, pp. 63-67.

by the British. Campbell did not feel that he could weaken his garrison by sending an expedition to take over the forts in the North. English traders, arriving in the spring, did not bring the goods the Indians wanted, and their prices were high. Furthermore, Campbell forbade the sale of rum to the natives. Finally, Campbell learned that the Seneca, one of the Iroquois tribes, had hatched a conspiracy to unite all the western Indians in an attack on the British posts at Detroit, Pittsburgh, Presqu'Isle, and Niagara. Although they were becoming unhappy with the British, the western tribes were not yet ready to revolt. The Seneca plot thus failed. Campbell sent word of the situation to General Amherst. It was decided that a large reinforcement of British regulars would be sent to strengthen Detroit and to take over the other French posts, and that Sir William Johnson and Croghan would accompany the troops and hold a grand council in Detroit to pacify the Indians.

Sir William Johnson was a man of immense influence among the Indians. A native of Ireland, he had come to America in 1737 to manage a tract of land in the Mohawk Valley of New York that had been acquired by his uncle. He later added a tract of his own, traded with the Indians, erected a store and a mill as well as a beautiful Georgian mansion. The fort and the house still stand. He was adopted by the Mohawk and learned their language. It was his influence that held the Iroquois allegiance to the British during the French and Indian War. For his victory over the French in the Battle of Lake George he received the thanks of parliament and was created a baronet. In 1756 he was appointed as Indian agent for all the tribes living north of the Carolinas and the Ohio River.[16] The expedition to Detroit was under the command of a thirty-two-year-old man who had won his laurels in the war just ended: Henry Gladwin. The arrival of Johnson, Croghan, Gladwin, and his men at Detroit early in September was the occasion of much festivity. Johnson related that there were frequent balls, where dancing continued on one occasion until five in the morning, and on another until seven. Johnson was especially attracted to a handsome young woman named Angelique Cuillerier dit Beaubien, daughter of a prosperous French trader. She was the belle of Detroit. The grand council with the Indians opened September 9. There was a great deal of speechmaking on both sides. Johnson did not dare mention an alarming communication he had received from General Amherst en route, instructing him that henceforth there would be no

[16] J. T. Flexner, *Mohawk Baronet: Sir William Johnson of New York.*

more presents for the Indians. Spokesmen for the Indians proclaimed their loyalty to the British, reminded the British of the services to their cause rendered by the Indians in the late war, and confessed to some shortcomings. One chief admitted some horse stealing, but said it had been done "by some of our idle young men, who you know are very difficult to restrain."[17] All in all, the conference appeared successful, though Johnson must have had misgivings for the future in view of the new policy of Amherst on presents, to which the Indians had become accustomed during the war. And he may have been concerned that Chief Pontiac of the Ottawa took no part in the council; at least there is no record indicating that Pontiac spoke. The council was topped off by an exchange of wampum belts and a huge feast, at which the *pièce de résistance* was an immense roasted ox provided by Johnson.[18]

Gladwin sent Captain Henry Balfour to take possession of the northern posts on September 9. Arriving at Fort Michilimackinac on September 28, he found the garrison had fled, as indicated above. Lieutenant Charles Langlade had been left in command, and he officially handed the fort over to Balfour. At the post were a number of French half-breed traders and a few hardy English traders who had arrived in advance of the soldiers. Balfour left Lieutenant William Leslye and 28 men to garrison the fort. The fort at the time was described as being roughly square, containing five long barracks for soldiers and traders, a few houses and storerooms, a church, a priest's house, a powder magazine, a guard house, and a few other buildings.

Balfour then crossed to Green Bay, where he left a small garrison to occupy Fort La Baye. From there he proceeded southward to the mouth of the St. Joseph River, on the eastern shore of Lake Michigan, and up that stream to Fort St. Joseph. Here he left fifteen men under the command of youthful Ensign Francis Schlosser to hold the fort, and returned overland to Detroit with the remainder of his small force. The following year, Lieutenant John Jamet, with a small contingent, was sent to occupy Repentigny's fort at the Sault, which had been abandoned by the French.

This completed the British occupation of the French posts throughout the West, except for the Illinois country. Forts Vincennes and Chartres were included within the jurisdiction of New Orleans and were considered part of French Louisiana. They were not included within the surrender by Lévis in 1760. Hence the British made no attempt to occupy them until after the conclusion

[17] Peckham, *op. cit.*, p. 82.
[18] *Ibid.*, p. 84.

of peace in 1763. The strong fortification called Fort Chartres was under the command of Pierre Joseph Neyon de Villiers. It was not taken over by the British until 1765.

The victory of Britain over France in the duel for empire in America may be attributed to several factors. British sea power played a major role. The sparse population of New France and the fact that it was scattered over such a huge area was important. So was the success of Frederick the Great in Europe, which had the effect of limiting the number of men and the resources France could spare for the war in America. The genius of William Pitt and the ability of the commanders he selected turned the tide in 1758 and paved the way for victory in 1760.

Although the fighting in America ended with the surrender of Lévis in 1760, the war in Europe continued until 1763. This meant that the situation in America remained uncertain for three years. France had surrendered her empire along the St. Lawrence and around the Great Lakes in America, but there was always the possibility that it might be restored if victory could be won in Europe. This, however, was not to be the case. Frederick the Great and his Prussian army held their own against an alliance consisting of most of the other European powers, and when the Peace of Paris was signed in 1763 the loss of the French empire in America was confirmed. Great Britain received all the former French possessions east of the Mississippi, while Spain was given New Orleans and all the lands claimed by France west of the Mississippi.

The victory won by Britain in the French and Indian War was to prove a decisive one. But that war did not end the duel for empire. In 1778 France saw an opportunity to revenge her defeat by joining with the thirteen colonies in their revolt against the mother country. Although Britain was forced to recognize the independence of the United States in the Treaty of 1783, France did not win back her empire. Following the excesses of the French Revolution, France and Britain again went to war in 1793. This conflict continued, with one brief interruption, until 1814. Napoleon Bonaparte, the military genius of France, was able to defeat all the great powers of Europe but he could not rival British sea power. During the conflict between Napoleon and Great Britain the United States became involved in a second war against the mother country. Peace came in 1814. The following year Napoleon escaped from captivity and again briefly challenged Britain and her continental allies. But he was defeated and exiled. This brought to a close the series of wars between France and Britain which had begun 126 years before. Never since have these two great nations engaged in war against each other.

The British, having won a great new empire in America, were confronted with the problem of how to rule it. As already indicated, grave problems related to Indian affairs arose even before the occupation of the French posts in the Great Lakes region was completed. The next chapter in the history of Michigan covers the thirty-six-year period during which the British ruled the Great Lakes area.

Fort Mackinac

5

UNDER THE BRITISH FLAG

The British flag flew over Michigan for thirty-six years, from 1760 to 1796. During the last thirteen years of this period the British continued to occupy Detroit and Fort Mackinac even though they had ceded the region to the United States. Doubtful of the ability of the thirteen states to form a union strong enough to hold and control the western regions, and desirous of continuing to enjoy the profits derived from the fur trade, the British delayed their evacuation of posts that they agreed, in the Treaty of 1783, to hand over to the United States.

During the first three years after the British flag was raised in Detroit it remained uncertain whether Britain would retain control of what her armed forces had won from the French. But, as already indicated, the Treaty of Paris in 1763 gave the British a clear title to the area. The whole region of the Great Lakes remained under military control until 1774, when parliament passed the Quebec Act, which provided for civil government. The coming of the American Revolution, however, meant that a large measure of military rule would be continued. In 1791 another act of parliament made Michigan a part of Upper Canada, and for the five remaining years of British control civil government was provided under the terms of this act.

Throughout the British period, the Indian tribes continued to roam the forests of Michigan and to trade the pelts of the fur-bearing animals that they killed for British goods. Few Britishers came to live in Michigan; indeed, the British Proclamation of 1763 prohibited settlers from entering the territory west of the Alleghenies. The French people who lived in Michigan when the British took control continued their carefree ways, and provided manpower required in the fur trade, now managed by English and Scottish merchants. When the British finally handed over Michigan to the United States in 1796 there were remarkably few differences in the way of life of the Indians and whites who lived here from what it had been when the French relinquished control three dozen years earlier. But there were many stirring events, exciting episodes, and colorful personalities that make the story of the period worth telling.

THE INDIANS STRIKE BACK

In 1763 the British garrisons occupying the forts they had taken over from the French in the West were compelled to meet the most formidable Indian uprising in American history. The uprising is generally known as "Pontiac's conspiracy," from Francis Parkman's classic *History of the Conspiracy of Pontiac*, published originally at Boston in 1851. Parkman makes Chief Pontiac of the Ottawa the instigator and strategist of the entire uprising, but this interpretation has been disproved by Howard Peckham, whose *Pontiac and the Indian Uprising* was published originally in 1947. Peckham holds that Pontiac's role was that of uniting the Indian nations living around Detroit in a determined effort to capture that post.

For almost a century the British had been endeavoring to gain the favor of the western tribes. They had sold the Indians liquor when the French refused to do so, had given them presents, and had paid them higher prices for their peltry than had the French. The natives expected this to continue. But, as has been noted in the preceding chapter, Sir Jeffrey Amherst, commander of the British forces in America, was opposed to any coddling of the Indians. He decreed that the giving of presents to them must stop. They were to get goods only for what their peltry brought them. They must be punished for misbehavior. The sale of liquor was to be rigidly restricted. Amherst lacked any real comprehension of the problems involved in dealing with these proud native peoples.

The abolition of the French fur trading monopoly gave independent traders free rein and opened the way for an orgy of cheating, fraud, and dishonest dealing that quickly infuriated

the Indians. The traders dispensed shoddy goods at high prices
and taunted the natives for their gullibility. In spite of restrictions, whisky or rum were offered as an inducement, but even
this was diluted with water, tobacco being added to give it the
desired "kick." The new rules compelled the Indians to come
to the forts to sell their furs. The soldiers and British traders
were haughty and scornful, treating the Indians in such a manner as to wound their pride. Another development that alarmed
the Indians was the entrance into Kentucky, western Pennsylvania, and Tennessee of settlers from the East. If this kept up
how long would it be before they would be crowded out of their
hunting grounds? And finally, the French *habitants* and fur-
trading personnel in the West were sympathetic with the dis-
gruntled natives. The latter were assured that the king of France
was asleep and that he would presently awake and scatter these
usurpers. That the resumption of French control still was a
possibility was substantiated by the fact that at the time the
Indian uprising was in the making, no treaty of peace had yet
been signed by Britain and France.

It appears quite likely that both the French in the Illinois
country and those living along the St. Lawrence were involved
in encouraging the Indians to strike back against the British.
In the fall of 1762 George Croghan in Pittsburgh learned from
a Detroit Indian that during the preceding summer there had
been a secret war council at the Ottawa village along the Detroit
River, attended by chiefs of the Ottawa, Huron, and Potawatomi
as well as the Chippewa from the Lake Superior region. The
latter had brought with them two Frenchmen in Indian dress.
The council plotted to attack the British, the informer related,
and had sent deputies to the tribes on the Wabash and along the
Ohio River to the south. Croghan later received another report
that the Shawnee in the Ohio Valley had received a war belt
from Detroit and that the tribes in that region were being stirred
emotionally by a "prophet" among the Delaware nation, a psy-
chotic who claimed to have had visions in which a spirit told him
that the Indians, by purifying themselves and returning to their
ancient ways, would be able to drive the white men out of their
country.[1] Meanwhile in the East the Seneca, who had tried to
make trouble for the British two years before, were hatching a
definite conspiracy. There is reason to believe that the Seneca
were inspired and encouraged by the French along the St. Law-

---

[1] Although the Indian leaders that are best-known are those that led
revolts against the whites, it is noteworthy that almost every formidable
native revolt was inspired by a "prophet" with spirit visions.

rence. The Seneca passed a war belt on to the Delaware, who conveyed it to the Shawnee and the Miami. The Seneca sent another war belt to Detroit. Thus the Detroit Indians were prompted from both west and east to attack the British.

There can be no question that Chief Pontiac was the moving spirit in the plot devised to capture Fort Detroit. Probably in his forties in 1763, he was distinguished for his intellect, his shrewdness, and his oratorical prowess. His plan called for gaining entrance into the fort on the pretext of desiring a parley, and, at a given signal, to have the Indians who accompanied him and those waiting outside fall on their enemies. Unfortunately for the Indians the commandant of the fort had been forewarned. There are many stories about how Major Henry Gladwin, who had succeeded Campbell in command, learned of Pontiac's scheme. Gladwin never revealed who had warned him. The most persistent legend is that it was a squaw, sometimes called young and beautiful, sometimes old and homely, and that her name was Catherine. A famous painting by J. M. Stanley, an artist who came to Detroit in 1834, depicts a handsome Catherine delivering the warning to Major Gladwin. But recent historians generally accept the theory that Gladwin learned of the plot through Angelique Cuillerier, the same girl who had caught Sir William Johnson's eye at the balls held in Detroit during his visit there in 1761. Angelique was now being courted by James Sterling, a local merchant. Her father, Antoine, was a friend of Pontiac and it is known that Pontiac held at least one council in the Cuillerier home. The presumption is that Angelique overheard the revelation of the plot by Pontiac, that she warned her lover for fear he might fall victim to the Indian fury, and that Sterling in turn relayed the news to Gladwin.[2]

Pontiac's plan called for about sixty of his best warriors to accompany him, carrying tomahawks, knives, and sawed-off muskets under their blankets. The rest of the Ottawa would be spread around, also carrying concealed weapons. Pontiac would speak to Gladwin and hold up a belt of green and white wampum. When he turned it over it would be a signal for the Ottawa to fall upon the British soldiers and traders. On Saturday morning,

[2] H. Peckham, *Pontiac and the Indian Uprising,* pp. 122-25; see also the "Haldimand Papers," *Mich. Pioneer and Historical Colls.,* XIX (1891), 310. These papers, located in the Dominion Archives at Ottawa, Canada, have been printed in Volumes IX and X of the *Mich. Pioneer and Historical Colls.* Haldimand succeeded Sir Guy Carleton as governor general of Canada in 1778 and served until 1785. His papers are an important source of information for Michigan history before and immediately after the American Revolution.

May 7, 1763 some 300 braves and squaws, almost all of them wearing blankets, crossed the river to the fort. They were admitted through the gate, and then small groups began to move through the town. They found merchants had closed and locked their shops. And on the parade ground, they saw soldiers drawn up with muskets ready. Major Gladwin and Captain Campbell stood waiting, wearing pistols and sabers. Pontiac soon gathered that Gladwin had found out about the plot and was ready. When the crucial moment came, Pontiac failed to give the signal to attack, and the Indians left the fort. Two days later he tried again, but this time the braves were not even admitted to the stockade. Meanwhile, Gladwin hastened to move into the fort all the food supplies the French farmers would sell.

After a week in which the Indians killed or captured some thirty Englishmen outside the fort, Pontiac asked for a day's truce. Captain Campbell and Lieutenant George McDougall went out to meet him, hoping to restore peace, but Pontiac broke the truce and kept them prisoner. Later when one of the officers, during a sortie from the fort, killed a son of Chief Mackinac and then proceeded to scalp the young man and to wave the bloody trophy insolently at the Indians, the old Chief was so enraged that he rushed to the lodge where Campbell was held prisoner, tore off his scalp, cut out his heart, and ate it.

The siege of the fort was now on in earnest. Gladwin had only 123 soldiers, about twenty English traders and a few Frenchmen who would aid him to defend the fort. The besieging force probably numbered more than 500. Gladwin did not fear a direct assault on the stockade so much as he did fire from burning arrows. Every precaution was taken to make ready water supplies to extinguish fires. Two ships with small cannon, the sloop *Michigan* and the schooner *Huron*, could help defend the fort from the river side, although it became necessary to use these vessels to bring in supplies and reinforcements. In response to a plea sent to Niagara for help, about a hundred men with barrels of meat and flour were sent in ten small boats. Discovering these moving along the north shore of Lake Erie, Indians made ready and attacked the men when they had landed for a night's sleep. Only forty of the men escaped, but some provisions were brought in. By using larger vessels Gladwin could depend on securing troops and provisions from the East, and this was what enabled him to hold out. Detroit could be held against an attack only if the lakes could be controlled. This was to be demonstrated again during the War of 1812.

Having failed in his attempt to surprise Detroit, Pontiac sent runners to urge Indians to attack other British forts in the West. So successful were these efforts that of all the British posts only Forts Pitt, Niagara, and Detroit were able to hold out. The capture of Fort Michilimackinac was effected by a clever stratagem, engineered by Minavavana, chieftain of the Chippewa. This crafty leader first saw to it that all his followers not wholeheartedly against the British were sent away. He then cultivated the friendship of the post commandant, now Captain George Etherington. Langlade warned Etherington that a plot was afoot to capture the fort, and Alexander Henry, a young English trader, also warned the commandant, but the latter was not convinced there was any danger, being completely duped by the wily Minavavana. The chief proposed that a celebration be held on King George's birthday, June 2, which was to occur two days later. The Indians would show their loyalty by staging a ball game for the amusement and enjoyment of the garrison to observe the occasion. Captain Etherington thought this was a fine idea. The spot chosen was just outside the gates of the fort, along the shores of Lake Michigan. Near the gates squaws squatted or stood, wrapped in their blankets. Underneath these blankets they had concealed tomahawks, knives, clubs, and sawed-off guns. The ball game got under way. It was all very amusing. The soldiers and even the commandant watched the game idly without even taking the precaution to arm themselves. The game played was similar to lacrosse. A wooden ball was used and this was clouted by any member of the team in the general direction of a goal post by means of a four foot bat terminating at one end into a circular curve, netted with leather strings. After the game had gone on for some time, the ball was gradually worked towards the gates and finally was hit over into the fort. The players dashed after it, but as they got to the gates the squaws passed them the weapons that had been concealed and the massacre began. The French traders went to their houses and were not harmed. Twenty British soldiers and one trader were killed. The goods of the other traders were plundered. The remainder of the garrison, including Captain Etherington together with the other traders, were made prisoner. One who escaped was Alexander Henry, who concealed himself in the attic of Langlade's house. He survived to leave to posterity a vivid eyewitness account of the frightful massacre:

> Through an aperture which afforded me a view of the area of the fort, I beheld, in shapes the foulest and most horrible, the ferocious triumphs of barbarian conquerors. The dead were scalped and mangled; the dying were writhing and shrieking under the

unsatiated knife and tomahawk; and from the bodies of some, ripped open, their butchers were drinking the blood, scooped up in the hollow of joined hands and quaffed amid shouts of rage and victory.[3]

With Captain Etherington at Fort Michilimackinac were Lieutenant William Leslye, whom he had succeeded in command, and Lieutenant John Jemay. The fort at the Sault, built originally by Repentigny, had burned the preceding December, and Jemay and his little force had sought refuge at Fort Michilimackinac. Jemay was killed while defending himself with his sword during the massacre. Both Leslye and Etherington were made prisoner. Fifteen soldiers, in addition to the officers and three traders, were held as prisoners by the victorious Chippewa. Just why they were spared is not known. One source claims that Langlade interceded in their behalf.[4] It is probable, however, that they would have suffered the same fate as the others had it not been for the intercession of the Ottawa of L'Arbre Croche. These Indians had been sent a war belt by Pontiac but had not made up their minds to join in the war against the British. They had not been notified either by Chief Minavavana, who planned the attack, or by Chief Matchekewis, who carried it out, that the Chippewa were going to try to capture the garrison. Furious because they had not shared the plunder, the L'Arbre Croche Ottawa set out for Michilimackinac, which they reached on June 4, only two days after the massacre. They immediately seized all the British prisoners, but after a conference they let the Chippewa keep five, while they retained custody of the other fifteen, including Etherington and Leslye. A Chippewa chief who arrived too late for the foray killed four of the five prisoners held by his nation. One body was cut up and boiled for feasting.

The Ottawa carried their prisoners back to L'Arbre Croche with them. There they were joined by the garrison of Fort Edward Augustus in Wisconsin.[5] The Sauk, Fox, Menominee, and Winnebago Indians of Wisconsin had long been at odds with the French and accordingly had made no trouble for Lieutenant James Gorrell and his garrison at Fort Edward Augustus. Gorrell, however, had been sent word by Etherington, who now considered himself and his men safe among the L'Arbre Croche Ottawa, to join him.

[3] J. Bain (ed.), *Travels and Adventures of Alexander Henry*, p. 72. See also R. McCoy, *The Massacre of Old Fort Mackinac*.

[4] C. T. Hamilton, "Western Michigan History," *Michigan History*, XIII (1929), 218.

[5] The British had given this name to the French Fort La Baye at Green Bay, after they occupied it.

Gorrell and his men were accompanied on the journey across Lake Michigan to L'Arbre Croche by several friendly Indians from Wisconsin who came to urge the Ottawa to take their prisoners to Montreal, and who suggested that the Ottawa might receive a large reward for so doing. In spite of the opposition of the Chippewa, the Indians started for Montreal with their prisoners on July 18, and in less than a month they reached their destination by the old Ottawa River route. Among the prisoners they delivered was Ezekiel Solomon, the first Jewish trader in Michigan. He had been among the traders who had arrived at Fort Michilimackinac ahead of the British garrison; after the suppression of the Indian uprising he returned to Michilimackinac and remained there for many years.[6]

About a week before the Chippewa treacherously obtained possession of Fort Michilimackinac, Potawatomi warriors had overwhelmed the small garrison at Fort St. Joseph. Here Ensign Francis Schlosser was in command. He was so addicted to the bottle that frequent complaints reached his superiors. He apparently paid no heed to the warning of Louis Chevalier, a French resident of the St. Joseph Valley for more than thirty years, that the Indians intended to attack the fort. On May 25 a group of about a hundred Potawatomi from Detroit appeared, saying they had come to visit relatives. They notified Schlosser they wished to bid him good morning. A Frenchman warned the commandant that the Indians had come with "ill designs," and Schlosser hastened to put his men under arms. But it was too late. The garrison already was swarming with Indians. Schlosser was seized and the Indians began butchering the soldiers. Ten were quickly killed; only three were spared. They, along with Schlosser, were taken to Detroit, where they were handed over to Gladwin.[7]

Even though the Indians were successful in capturing every British post west of Niagara except Detroit, Pontiac's inability to take this crucial fort spelled the doom of the great Indian uprising. Captain James Dalyell reached the besieged fort at the end of July with 250 redcoats to assist in its defense. Dalyell, contemptuous of the Indians, at once urged upon Gladwin that a surprise attack be made on Pontiac's camp in the night. Gladwin demurred but at length gave his consent. The emergence of the British force was quickly reported by Indian spies and about

---

[6] I. I. Katz, "Ezekiel Solomon: The First Jew in Michigan," *Michigan History*, XXXII (1948), 247-256.

[7] A rich storehouse of information on the Indian uprising is contained in "The Gladwin Manuscripts," *Mich. Pioneer and Historical Colls.* XXVII (1896), and "The Haldimand Papers," *ibid.*, XIX (1891).

two miles from the fort Dalyell and his men fell into an ambush. The fighting took place along Parent's Creek, thereafter called Bloody Run. Before the Britishers could get back to the fort, twenty of their number, including Captain Dalyell, lay dead, and forty-two others were wounded. In spite of this success Pontiac was in trouble. Detroit continued to receive supplies by ship and there seemed to be no prospect that the siege could be successful. Delegations of Indians from beyond Detroit began to come seeking peace with Gladwin. On September 9 seventy Potawatomi from the St. Joseph region arrived and asked for peace. Pontiac's force began to melt away. News came from the east that Colonel Henry Bouquet had inflicted a defeat on the Indians at the Battle of Bushy Creek. In desperation the Ottawa chieftain sent a messenger to the French commandant at Fort Chartres, Major de Villiers, to seek help. The reply from de Villiers advised Pontiac to stop the fighting and to smoke the pipe of peace. De Villiers had learned that the Treaty of Peace had been signed and that France had ceded all her lands east of the Mississippi to Great Britain, and he was only anxious for the British to take over the fort so he could return to France. During October one after another of the Indian chiefs smoked the pipe of peace with Gladwin. On October 31 Pontiac sent his capitulation, then journeyed sadly to the Illinois country, hoping to continue the fight there. The lack of ammunition was perhaps the only consideration that deterred him from resuming the war against the British in 1764. Had he done so it would have been a futile gesture. Colonel John Bradstreet was sent by General Thomas Gage, who had succeeded Amherst as commander-in-chief of the British forces in America, on an expedition that marched across northern Ohio and reached Detroit, where representatives of the western tribes were assembled. They acknowledged the sovereignty of King George, agreed to surrender all their captives, and promised to make war on any tribe that turned against the British. Another expedition from Fort Pitt, led by Colonel Bouquet, was necessary to finally pacify the natives and convince them that further resistance was futile. At Oswego, New York, Sir William Johnson presided over a great peace council in July, 1766, which confirmed the agreements the Indians had made with Bradstreet in Detroit. Pontiac himself was present at this council. In 1769 Pontiac was assassinated by a member of the Peoria tribe in Illinois.

Following Colonel John Bradstreet's arrival at Detroit in August, 1764, Gladwin returned to England, where he lived the life of an English country gentleman until his death in 1791. Brad-

street sent Captain William Howard to reoccupy Fort Michilimackinac. Charles Langlade, who had done what he could to
save the British garrison, now carried out a plan he had made
before the uprising to move his headquarters to Green Bay,
where he had numerous relatives. Here he spent the remainder
of his life, although during the American Revolution he fought to
uphold the British cause against the thirteen colonies as vigorously as he had earlier aided the French cause. However, he
became reconciled to American control and lived until early in
the nineteenth century, continuing his fur-trade business along
the Grand River in Michigan. He became known as the "father of
Wisconsin," and a county in that state is named for him.[8]

The British did not re-establish permanent garrisons after the
Indian uprising either at Sault Ste. Marie or at Fort St. Joseph.
Around the latter place the Potawatomi villages continued to be
occupied and it continued to be a rendezvous for fur traders.
Louis Chevalier, who had warned Ensign Schlosser of the Indian
plot against the fort during the Indian uprising, was entrusted
with the responsibility of guarding British interests in the St.
Joseph Valley following the suppression of the Indian outbreak.
He was under the supervision of the commandant at Fort Michilimackinac.

BRITISH MILITARY RULE

Having acquired a vast new territory from the French under
the peace treaty signed at London on February 20, 1763, the
British were confronted with the problem of how to govern it.[9]
The responsibility for formulating a policy was entrusted to the
Earl of Shelburne, a young Irishman destined to be a key factor
in the determination of British policy at three critical times
during the British regime in the Old Northwest. In 1763 he was
president of the Board of Trade. He had been a friend and disciple
of General James Wolfe, who had perished in the attack on
Quebec in 1759. Unlike many of his contemporaries who spent

[8] L. P. Kellogg, *The British Regime in Wisconsin and the Old Northwest*, pp. 3, 4, 13, 35, 226, 253, 329.
[9] There had been a lively debate in Britain during the peace negotiations
whether to demand that the French cede to Britain their territory east of
the Mississippi or the West Indies Islands of Guadeloupe and Martinique,
which were heavy producers of sugar. Although Britain finally decided
against demanding the islands, it is indicative of the small value the
British then placed upon a region that later proved to be so fabulously
rich in agricultural and mineral resources, that they should have equated
it with two small islands in the West Indies.

their time at drinking and gambling, Shelburne was industrious and well-read. On June 8, 1763 he proposed the policy that was adopted by the British government and announced in October, 1763. It is known as the Proclamation of 1763.

Shelburne drew up his plan before news of the Indian uprising led by Pontiac had reached England. Nevertheless, its provisions were based primarily on considerations related to the Indian problem. It will be recalled that during the French and Indian War the British, in order to secure Indian support, had signed the Treaty of Easton with several chiefs, pledging that the region west of the Alleghenies would be reserved for the natives. A warning of the determination of the Indians to keep possession of their hunting grounds was given by means of an uprising of the Cherokee nation in the South between 1759 and 1761. The British had pacified the Cherokee by making a pledge similar to the one they had made to the northern tribes at Easton. Hence the British government, if it were to keep its pledges to the Indians, had to reserve the trans-Allegheny region for them. The need to take steps to counter the menace of Indian revolt was underscored when news reached England of Pontiac's attack on Detroit and the Indian assaults on other British-held posts. This news hastened the issuance of the Proclamation by the British authorities.[10]

The Proclamation reserved all the lands west of the Alleghenies for the use of the Indians, and no purchases of Indian lands were to be made except through imperial agents. Traders were required to take out licenses from the governor or commander-in-chief of the colony where they resided. The Proclamation provided for civil government in the Province of Quebec, but that province was to include only the French settlements along the St. Lawrence. This left the entire Great Lakes area under military rule.

Several of the thirteen colonies had claims under their charters on the region west of the Alleghenies, as has been noted earlier. The Proclamation nullified these claims, and this nullification became one of the basic causes for the animosity against the mother country that led to the American Revolution. The Proclamation was not intended to be permanent, but rather was designed as a temporary expedient to quiet hostile Indians. The British appear to have contemplated a gradual and orderly acquisition of Indian lands through purchase by imperial agents, which lands would

[10] The fullest account of how the British met their responsibilities is found in C. V. Alvord, *The Mississippi Valley in British Politics.*
A more recent treatment is found in L. H. Gipson, *The Triumphant Empire.*

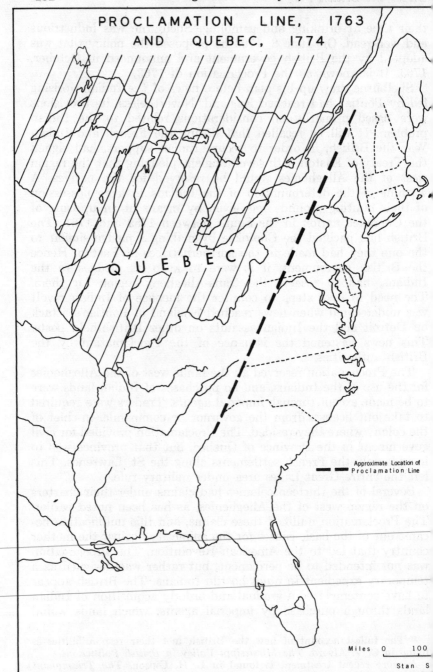

PROCLAMATION   LINE,   1763
AND   QUEBEC,   1774

Q U E B E C

Approximate Location of
Proclamation Line

Miles   0   100

Stan S

then be opened to settlement. By failing to provide civil government for Detroit, Michilimackinac, and other western posts, the Proclamation left the French people who resided at these places, as well as the Britishers who came to them, under military rule until the passage of the Quebec Act in 1774.

The method of regulating the fur trade was a major problem facing the British after the defeat of Pontiac. As early as 1756 the British government had appointed two imperial agents, one in the North and the other in the South, to regulate the fur trade. The appointee in the North was Sir William Johnson, whose prestige and influence among the Indians has been commented on previously. Johnson proposed in November, 1763 a comprehensive plan for the management and regulation of the fur trade. His plan was to put the fur trade and Indian affairs entirely in the hands of the two imperial agents, himself in the North and Captain John Stuart in the South, to be administered by their agents, who were called commissaries. These commissaries were to control prices, keep the traders from cheating the natives, and see that the rules of the trade were enforced. They were to act in cooperation with the military commandants at the various posts, who were subject to the orders of the commander-in-chief of the British forces in America. Johnson advised that all trade be confined to the posts and that each trader be licensed. This plan was received with favor by the Board of Trade in London, but unfortunately it never received full approval. In January, 1765 General James Murray issued a proclamation declaring hostilities with the natives at an end and opening the fur trade at designated posts, including Detroit and Michilimackinac, to licensed traders. In spite of the fact that no authorization had been received from London, Johnson's plan was partially put into effect. It evoked a storm of protest from Montreal merchants, particularly that part of it that prohibited trade outside the posts. Spanish and French traders operating out of New Orleans and St. Louis would capture a large part of the peltry trade, it was feared, if the British traders were confined to the posts. At Fort Michilimackinac Captain Howard issued permits to a few individuals to conduct trade outside the post, an action for which he was harshly criticized by those who were denied the coveted permits.

One of the factors that created delay and uncertainty in America was the frequent changes in ministries at the British capital. Shelburne, who had been responsible for the Proclamation of 1763, was replaced by Lord Hillsborough even before the Proclamation was issued. But in 1767 Shelburne was back in office. He did not share Johnson's view that the West should be kept per-

manently as a reserve for Indians and fur traders. He had never
intended that the Proclamation should be more than a temporary
policy. He saw in the West a great area for future settlement and
colonization, whereas Johnson thought of it only in terms of
peltry and Indian relations. Shelburne suggested the formation
of three new colonies: one around Detroit, another in the Illinois
country, and a third on the Ohio River. He proposed to let the
thirteen colonies control the fur trade, to withdraw the troops
gradually, and to open the area for settlement in orderly fashion.
Before the talented Shelburne could press the plan upon the king
there was another political overturn and Hillsborough once more
replaced him. Hillsborough's plan was neither to follow a determined policy of imperial control nor to put the responsibility
squarely on the colonies. The Indian agents were retained, but
with reduced authority. The colonies were to pay the salaries of
the lesser officials at the posts and were to supply presents for the
Indians, a wholly impractical idea. No new colonies were to be
authorized. The plan utterly failed to give the colonies any stake
in the West, yet, for reasons of economy, it made imperial control
ineffective.

The Proclamation of 1763 had virtually invalidated the claims
and dashed the hopes of the land speculation companies that had
been formed just prior to the French and Indian War in Virginia
and Pennsylvania. But there was a rash of new schemes in the
years following 1763, based on the expectation that the terms of
the Proclamation would be modified or reversed. A pamphlet that
appeared in Edinburgh in 1763 suggested the formation of a new
colony in the West in which discharged soldiers and sailors, craftsmen, poor farmers, and prisoners taken from the jails might be
settled. A Virginia group, allying itself with the Mississippi Company and including on its roster of members the Washingtons and
the Lees, and a Pennsylvania company that included Benjamin
Franklin among its members, sought to induce the British government to grant large tracts of land for purposes of settlement.
Several other such companies were formed in America. Captain
Robert Rogers, commandant at Fort Michilimackinac during part
of the period, and Jonathan Carver, one of his subordinates, each
made a proposal for a new western colony. Mention already has
been made of Shelburne's plan to establish three new colonies.
Largely through pressure from land speculators and the companies
they formed, the Imperial agents negotiated with the Indians for
an extension westward of the Proclamation line. Although the
larger schemes of the land speculators seemed at times close to
realization, they failed to materialize prior to the outbreak of the

Revolution. It is interesting to speculate whether men like Washington and Franklin would have been more reluctant than they were to back the stroke for independence in 1776 if the British government had taken a more favorable attitude toward the land companies with which they were associated. The opposition of the great fur merchants in London, and the probability that any large scale colonization would have sparked a new Indian revolt probably were the principal factors in bringing about the failure of the land speculators.

Thus Michigan and the entire Great Lakes area remained Indian country, with the British asserting their authority only at a few isolated posts. In the interests of economy garrisons were maintained after 1771 only at Detroit and Michilimackinac. Trade revived at Detroit, where Indians from the entire lower lakes region brought their annual catches to exchange for clothing, guns, ammunition, trinkets, and—whenever possible—intoxicating liquor. The French *habitants*, scattered along both banks of the Detroit River, appeared quite indifferent to the change in masters, so long as they could enjoy their little farms and orchards, have a hand in the fur trade, sing their songs, and worship in their beloved church. A number of the French held Indian slaves. Although Detroit remained under military rule, a magistrate was appointed and petty disputes were settled by suits at law.

The most colorful figure appearing at Michilimackinac during the British regime was Captain Robert Rogers. After he had successfully carried out his assignment to accept the surrender of Detroit to the British in 1760, he was sent to the Carolinas to help put down the revolt of the Cherokee. While there he met Governor Arthur Dobbs, the aging governor of North Carolina, who long had been fascinated by the lure of the imaginary Northwest Passage. He appears to have found an ardent disciple in Rogers, who accepted his belief that there was a waterway between Hudson's Bay and the Pacific Ocean. In 1765 Rogers went to London in quest of authority and financial backing to make a search for this passage. He had resigned his military commission, having gotten into the ill graces of both General Gage and Sir William Johnson. But he made quite a hit in England, got some influential backers, and won an appointment as commandant at Michilimackinac. When he left England he was confident that his extravagant requests for financial backing, together with permission to undertake the search for a northwest passage, would be forthcoming, although he had no positive assurance of either. He assumed command at Michilimackinac in 1766. In the fall of that year he sent out an expedition under Captain Jonathan Carver, from whose pen we have vivid descriptions of the West of that day,[11] to look for the passage. Carver got only as far as the Grand Portage, north of Lake Superior, when lack of supplies forced him to return.

Soon after the return of Carver, Rogers fell upon evil days. Gage and Johnson, both distrustful of Rogers, sent a commissary to watch over his activities. The man chosen was Lieutenant Benjamin Roberts, with whom Rogers already had quarreled. Roberts found that the traders were very favorable to Rogers, for the latter knew the Indian thoroughly and understood every aspect of the fur trade. Disregarding the injunction to confine the trade to an area near the fort, Rogers granted permission to the traders to venture in all directions. In 1767 thirty-two outgoing canoes carrying traders' goods left Michilimackinac for Lake Superior sixty canoes for Green Bay, and twenty-nine for Lakes Huron and Michigan. Being heavily in debt Rogers traded on his own account, though this was forbidden. He allowed liquor to be used in trading, another violation of his orders. Needless to say, he was soon involved in a bitter quarrel with Roberts. The two managed to compose their differences when a new element entered the picture. Rogers was accused of conspiring to join hands with the French traders operating out of St. Louis. For this he was arrested and brought to Montreal for trial, although he was acquitted of the charge of treason. He went to England once more was again lionized for a time, then ceased to be the "fashion" and sank into obscurity.

The British also made an effort during this period to exploit the mineral wealth of the Lake Superior region. Much earlier the French had realized that the shores of the great northern lake abounded in copper, and had sought without much success to discover and open mines. Apparently through his acquaintance with Rogers, Charles Townsend, a British official and author of the famous Townsend Acts, became interested in the possibility of exploiting the mineral wealth of this region. Townsend commissioned Rogers to investigate the possibilities, and Roger

[11] *Travels Through the Interior Parts of North America in the Year 1766, 1767, and 1768.* The original edition of this work appeared in London in 1778. Its popularity was so great that it went through many editions in England. An American edition appeared in 1784. French and Dutch translations were made. Europeans gained their ideas of Indians largely from Carver's book. Yet in 1904 an American historian proved that large portions of it were plagiarized, and that possibly it was not written by Carver at all, but rather by another from Carver's notes. See *American Historical Review,* XI (1906), 287-302, for a paper by E. G. Bourne on this subject.

responded to the commission by engaging Henry Bostwick, a British trader, and Jean Baptiste Cadotte, who was acquainted with the Indian legends and the stories of the French attempts at mining, to make an exploratory trip. Alexander Baxter, Jr., son of the Russian consul at London, also appeared at Michilimackinac, probably because of his interest in the project. Baxter was a mining expert and upon examining the data and specimens collected by Bostwick and Cadotte became convinced there were great riches to be gained by exploiting the area. A company was formed for the purpose by a group of English noblemen and funds were subscribed. A shipyard was set up near Sault Ste. Marie, a fort was constructed, an assaying furnace was begun, and men were sent out to collect ores. It was confidently expected that gold and silver, as well as copper, would be found.

The fur traders disliked all this hubbub and looked askance at the establishment of a fort near the Sault. Meanwhile Lieutenant John Nordberg, another Russian mining expert, found a stone that assayed in London 75% silver. The promoters were elated and redoubled their efforts. Workmen were first taken to the mouth of the Ontonagon River, but prospecting was shifted in 1772 to the northeast shore, where a shaft thirty feet deep was sunk. But the vein did not prove profitable, and the next year the project was suspended. Thus ended the British effort to exploit a source of wealth that one day was to prove far richer than the commerce in peltry.

CIVIL GOVERNMENT COMES TO MICHIGAN

Persistent reports of disorder and even disloyalty in the West reached the British commander, General Gage, but nothing was done to meet repeated demands from Detroit, and even from the Illinois country, for civil government. An alternative, seriously considered and favored by General Gage, was to deport the French residents of Illinois, and perhaps others in the West, in the manner in which the British earlier had uprooted the Acadians from Nova Scotia and sent them to Louisiana. There were grave doubts about the loyalty of the French in Illinois to the British sovereign, and persistent reports that they were in league with the Spanish and French in New Orleans. Gage actually issued an order in July, 1772 for the people of Vincennes to move at once, probably as a first step to the removal of other French residents in the West. "Let the savages enjoy their Deserts in quiet," advised Gage. But when the Earl of Hillsborough, who favored Gage's plan, was succeeded as president of the Board of Trade by the Earl of Dartmouth, whose ideas were quite different, the policy of deportation was abandoned.

In 1774 Parliament passed the Quebec Act, which extended the boundaries of the Province of Quebec west to the Mississippi River and south as far as the Ohio River. French civil law was to be applied, but in criminal cases British law would prevail. Complete toleration was to be enjoyed by Roman Catholics, whereas only limited toleration was the rule in England at the time. Four lieutenant governors were to be appointed, one each for Detroit, Michilimackinac, the Illinois settlements, and Vincennes. The governor of Quebec was to have an appointed legislative council, but there was no elected assembly provided for, since the French people were ignorant of representative government. The act was of great importance when the Revolution broke out in retaining the allegiance of the French people of Quebec to Great Britain, and in causing them to turn a cold shoulder to proposals of the continental congress that they join in the revolt against the mother country. Their priests felt that the full freedom of worship accorded Roman Catholics in the Quebec Act might be more than they could expect were the Puritan New Englanders to have a voice in their affairs. But so far as the thirteen colonies were concerned, the Quebec Act was associated with the other "coercive laws" passed in 1774 to discipline the colonies. In fact it is the only British act specifically referred to in the Declaration of Independence. The omission of any provision for an elected assembly in the Quebec Act was cited in the Declaration as evidence of the intent of the king' government to impose tyranny on America. The Quebec Act also, by extending the boundaries of the Province of Quebec, further invalidated the claims of Virginia, Massachusetts, and Connecticut, under their charters, to western lands.

Sir Guy Carleton, who became governor of Quebec, appointed Henry Hamilton as lieutenant governor at Detroit the year following the passage of the Quebec Act. Inferior courts of jurisdiction were to be established both at Detroit and at Michilimackinac, with appeals possible to the superior courts at Quebec and Montreal. This was the extent of civil government in Michigan. The revolt of the thirteen colonies, which started in 1775 made it impractical to fully carry out the plans for civil government. Hamilton became the commander of the British forces around Detroit as well as the chief resident civil official, and so there was little real modification of military rule, except that marriages could now be legally registered, petty disputes could be resolved by civil process, and matters such as the inheritance of property could be handled in a legal manner.

How the tea was brewed

For a long time American history was written chiefly by New Englanders. To them the events in and around Boston that led to the American Revolution were of paramount importance. This emphasis still persists in many histories of the United States. It is clear that the Revolution was directly precipitated by disputes over taxes and the right to tax. But why were these taxes levied? What occasioned the bitter disputes over the power to tax? The Boston Tea Party and other protests on the part of the Americans were not the real causes of the Revolution. Before you can have a tea party you have to brew the tea.

It had cost the British taxpayer a pretty penny to pay for the French war. Even before the peace treaty ending that war had been signed large additional expenditures were required to take steps to suppress the Indian uprisings. The national debt of Britain more than doubled. The cost of maintaining garrisons and officials at places like Detroit and Michilimackinac meant a further drain on the British treasury. It was about time, the British government concluded, that the colonies paid part of the bill. This explains why the British sought greater tax returns from America after 1763. The Americans protested partly because of their natural aversion to any taxes, especially new ones. But they contended that they received no benefits from the maintenance of British garrisons in the West, which the taxes were designed to pay for; rather, that the profits from the fur trade, which these garrisons protected, went into the pockets of London merchants. The colonists were denied the legal right to settle on the western lands by the prohibitions in the Proclamation of 1763, although these were not fully observed. Virginians especially were piqued by this aspect of British policy since their mode of agriculture wore out the land rapidly. Furthermore, many of them had ambitions to speculate in lands of the Ohio Valley, which the British regulations thwarted. The resentment of the Virginians against the closing of the West to settlement persuaded them to join forces with the New Englanders, who were aroused against the new taxes. This combination of New England and Virginia made possible the American Revolution and the patriot victory.

Thus the disputes between the thirteen colonies and the mother country stemmed mainly from the problems of the West. The

stamp tax and the other taxes that aroused determined resistance on the part of the patriots were laid to obtain revenue
to defend and administer the western country from which the
patriots felt they derived no benefit. It turned out that the advocates of Guadeloupe and Martinique as opposed to Canada
were right when they prophesied trouble if the French were
removed from North America and the colonials no longer needed
British arms for their defense.

MICHIGAN DURING THE WAR FOR INDEPENDENCE

During the French and Indian War, Detroit and Michilimackinac
had been the major centers of French power in the West; during
the American Revolution they played a comparable role in British
hands. The British did not take the two great Michigan forts by
force of arms during the French and Indian War, but occupied
them after the French surrendered in 1760. Likewise, in the
American Revolution the patriots never were able to oust the
British from these forts during the war, but received title to them
in the treaty of peace.

The Indians played a key role during the Revolution, just as
they had during the French and Indian War, but once more they
found themselves on the losing side. Since British policy after
1763 had been designed to keep the Indians contented and to
prevent encroachment on their lands by colonial settlers, it was
inevitable that the natives should side with the British in their
conflict with the thirteen colonies. The continental congress never
entertained any hope that they could persuade the natives to
support the patriot cause, but rather bent its efforts to keeping
as many Indian nations neutral as was possible. Even with this
limited objective, only the Shawnee and the Delaware could be
persuaded to promise to remain neutral.

In violation of the Proclamation of 1763 settlers had filtered
into Kentucky, then recognized as part of Virginia, in the years
prior to the American Revolution. Their settlements were clustered
around rude fortifications at Boonesborough, Harrodsburg, and St.
Asaph's. The Indians, of course, resented this invasion of their
hunting grounds, and the Revolution afforded them an open invitation to attack these settlements. Indians around Detroit
demanded that Governor Hamilton furnish them with arms, ammunition, and supplies preparatory to forays against the Kentuckians, and to reward them for success by paying them a
bounty for such scalps as they might bring back. Although reluctant to let loose the barbarism of Indian war, Hamilton really

had no alternative if he were to retain the adherence of the Indians to the British cause.[12] This was no excuse in the eyes of the Kentuckians, who called Hamilton "the hair-buyer."

Tiring of the constant raids, George Rogers Clark, a young Kentuckian, determined that the best defense was offense. Accordingly, he journeyed to the Virginia capital in the winter of 1777-1778, where he obtained approval and some assistance from Governor Patrick Henry to attack the British-held posts in the Illinois country and ultimately to capture Detroit. By this time an alliance with France had become a certainty and Clark hoped to use this as a lever to secure the backing of the French inhabitants of these settlements. His little army reached Kaskaskia on July 4, 1778, approaching the place so stealthily that its defenders had little chance to resist. Nearby Cahokia was occupied by Clark's force without any resistance. The local priest, Father Pierre Gibault, was among those whom Clark won over to the American cause, after the latter assured him that the Americans would not interfere in any way with the Catholic worship. Gibault not only helped convert the local French inhabitants to the patriot cause, but also journeyed overland to Vincennes, where his persuasion was important in securing the support of the local French inhabitants for Clark. Ever after Father Gibault was known as the "patriot priest." He had come to the Illinois country in 1768, stopping at Michilimackinac and at Fort St. Joseph to hear confessions, to baptize, and to perform marriage ceremonies. Although Kaskaskia became his residence, he made at least two more missionary trips to Michigan. He was at Fort St. Joseph in 1773 and at Michilimackinac in 1775, returning from the latter by way of Detroit.[13]

By August, 1778 Clark was in control of the Illinois country. He won over the Indians of the region through his confident manner, his blustering speeches, and his distribution of presents. The Indians had come to respect the fighting qualities of the "Big Knives," as they called Clark's men. When word reached Detroit of Clark's victories, Governor Hamilton hastened to summon the Indians, gather supplies, and enlist the militia for a retaliatory blow. He left Detroit on October 7 with 243 men. The route taken was down the Detroit River to Lake Erie, up Lake Erie to the Maumee River, up that stream to its source, over a short portage to the Wabash, and down that river to Vincennes.

---

[12] J. D. Barnhart, *Henry Hamilton and George Rogers Clark in the American Revolution, with the Unpublished Journal of Henry Hamilton,* pp. 93-101.

[13] G. Paré, *The Catholic Church in Detroit, 1701-1888,* pp. 99, 229-231.

Hamilton arrived at Vincennes before Fort Sackville after a journey of 71 days. Since Captain Leonard Helm, whom Clark had sent to take possession of Fort Sackville, had but one man to help him, the former had no recourse but to surrender. The 621 inhabitants were summoned by Hamilton and renewed their oath of allegiance to Britain.[14]

The capture of Vincennes by Governor Henry Hamilton was the prelude to one of the most heroic exploits in American history. When Clark received the news that Vincennes had fallen to Hamilton, he decided that, since his own small force was no match for Hamilton's, the only hope was a surprise attack. He reasoned that Hamilton would not think the Americans could move on Vincennes in mid-winter, but that is exactly what Clark did. With 172 men he struck out overland on February 6, sending supplies by the water route down the Mississippi to the Ohio, up the Ohio to the mouth of the Wabash, then up that river to Vincennes. Clark's men, half-starved, waded through deep mud in driving, cold rains, often fording streams where they had to break the ice with their shoulders as they waded across. Hamilton was ignorant of Clark's approach until the latter opened fire on the fort. The townspeople were easily won over, and furnished the Americans with supplies of ammunition and food which they had hidden away. The Kentucky riflemen, with deadly accuracy, picked off the British defenders, and on February 25, 1779 Hamilton surrendered the fort and its 79 defenders to Clark.[15]

Clark's amazing victory created a new situation in the Old Northwest. Indian allies of the British began to waver in their allegiance. Colonel Arent De Peyster, in command at Fort Michilimackinac, had called Charles Langlade from Green Bay and Charles Gautier, another trader, to get an Indian force together to co-operate with Hamilton in a concerted attack on Kaskaskia and Cahokia. Proceeding as far as the present city of Milwaukee, Wisconsin, the expedition got word of Hamilton's surrender. At once the Indians turned insolent and refused to go further. Already they had been somewhat affected by agents sent among

---

[14] N. V. Russell, *The British Regime in Michigan and the Old Northwest, 1760-1796*, pp. 195-198.

[15] There are several good biographies of Clark: Temple Bodley, *George Rogers Clark*; J. A. James, *The Life of George Rogers Clark*; W. Havighurst, *George Rogers Clark, Soldier of the West*; J. Bakeless, *Background to Glory*. See also M. M. Quaife, *The Capture of Old Vincennes*; J. A. James (ed.), *George Rogers Clark Papers*; and D. Van Every, *A Company of Heroes, The American Frontier, 1775-1783*. A magnificent monument has been erected by the federal government on the site of Fort Sackville at Vincennes.

them by Clark. De Peyster received reports that the Ottawa and Chippewa had promised agents of the Americans that they would remain neutral in the event of an attack on Fort Michilimackinac. At Detroit the military commander, Captain Richard Lernoult, was told by the Wyandot that they intended to make peace with the Virginians. At a council held in June, 1779 Ottawa, Chippewa and Potawatomi chieftains made similar declarations. Lernoult hastened to strengthen the defenses of Detroit by building a new fort in back of the town. The stockade was extended back to the forward extremities of Fort Lernoult, which had high earthen ramparts.

Colonel De Peyster was transferred from Fort Michilimackinac to take command at Detroit, with Major Patrick Sinclair replacing him at Michilimackinac. Sinclair believed he would be in a better position for defense against the attack by Clark's forces, which he feared was coming, if he transferred his troops to Mackinac Island. Between 1779 and 1781 a new fort, called Fort Mackinac, was built on Mackinac Island, and old Fort Michilimackinac at present-day Mackinaw City, originally built by the French sometime after 1715, was destroyed.

In 1780, however, the British took the offensive. Clark failed to secure the reinforcements he needed for a proposed attack on Detroit. The British worked out a plan for an attack on the Illinois settlements, to be launched from Michilimackinac. A large Indian force was raised through the efforts of Langlade and other traders, with supplies being provided from Michilimackinac. The force, which included Sioux warriors, assembled at Prairie du Chien, where the Wisconsin River joins the Mississippi. The foray was directed against Spanish St. Louis as well as Kaskaskia and Cahokia, since Spain had joined in the war against Great Britain in 1779. The British-led force assaulted both Cahokia and St. Louis on May 26, 1780, but both places were successfully defended.[16]

Early in 1781 an emissary from the French government, Colonel Mottin de la Balme, arrived in the Illinois settlement to rally the French people in the war against Britain. As a result of his efforts an expedition was organized that captured the British post on the Maumee River near the present Fort Wayne, Indiana, and carried off the traders goods found there. But Miami Indians under Chief Little Turtle pursued La Balme and killed almost all the invaders, including La Balme himself. Of more interest to students of Michigan history is a side expedition consisting of 16 men that marched against Fort St. Joseph at present-day Niles.

[16] L. P. Kellogg, *op. cit.,* pp. 162-169.

There had been no garrison there since the 1763 uprising, and the Indians who lived nearby were away on their winter hunt. Some fifty bales of goods were seized and several traders were made prisoner. But as the raiders were retreating down the shore of Lake Michigan they were overtaken near the present site of Michigan City, Indiana, by a pursuing band of British militiamen and traders. Four were killed, two were wounded, seven surrendered, and three escaped in the woods. The goods and captives they had carried off were retaken.[17]

Fort St. Joseph, though not garrisoned, was a place of some importance to the British during the Revolution. In 1779 De Peyster had sent his second-in-command at Michilimackinac, Lieutenant Thomas Bennett, with a force of twenty soldiers and sixty traders and Indians to Fort St. Joseph to intercept an American detachment that, he had been informed, was coming up the Wabash to occupy the place. The rumor did not prove to be based on fact. Bennett arrived at Fort St. Joseph, which apparently was in ruins, and is believed to have thrown up a fortification on the western side of the river. His attempt to obtain pledges of support for the British cause from the neighboring Potawatomi ended in failure. Even the arrival of Langlade with a reinforcement of 60 Chippewa did not change the insolent attitude of the natives, and Bennett returned to Michilimackinac. The following year Sinclair, who had succeeded De Peyster in command at Michilimackinac, decided it would be best for the British cause if the inhabitants at the site of Fort St. Joseph were removed. Louis Chevalier, the trader on whom the British had relied, was now suspected of secretly favoring the American cause. He and his wife were brought to Michilimackinac along with the others. Subsequently he was taken to Montreal, where he was tried and acquitted.

Apparently some traders were left at Fort St. Joseph, and they were the ones who were captured by the French raiding party from Cahokia, and later were released by the force which overtook and broke up the raiding party. The British force was under the command of Lieutenant Dagneau de Quindre who had been sent from Michilimackinac by Sinclair to safeguard the place. He and his men appear to have been encamped some distance from the old fort when the raiding party arrived. As soon as the news of the disaster which had befallen the raiding party reached Cahokia and Spanish St. Louis, across the Mississippi River, a

[17] "The Haldimand Papers," *Mich. Pioneer and Historical Colls.,* X, 450-51.

retaliatory force was recruited. Don Euginio Pourée, a militia captain at St. Louis, was given command by the Spanish commandant at St. Louis, Don Francesco Cruzat, who organized the party. It included 65 militiamen, both Spanish from St. Louis and French from Cahokia, and at least 60 Indians. Setting out in the dead of winter, the party arrived at Fort St. Joseph after following the portage from the Kankakee to the St. Joseph River. One of the members of the party was Louison Chevalier, son of the trader now under suspicion by the British. The fort was taken and the Spanish flag was run up, giving Niles the distinction of being the only place in Michigan which has been under four flags. After gathering all the loot it could carry away, the party made its way back to Cahokia and St. Louis.

The object of this 1781 raid on Fort St. Joseph has been the subject of many historical researches and investigations, and to this day it is not entirely clear. Older historians inclined to the view that it was designed to give Spain a claim on the lands east of the Mississippi. Some of the more recent investigators, who have had access to the Spanish archives, reject this theory, having found no evidence that the raid was officially inspired or ordered by the Madrid government. Another suggestion is that it was planned to forestall another possible attack on Cahokia and St. Louis from Michilimackinac, by destroying supplies that were presumed to have been deposited at Fort St. Joseph for such an expedition. Most writers, however, now view the raid as inspired by the hope for loot and a wish to revenge the defeat suffered by the raiding party of the preceding year.[18]

The British in Detroit continued to plan expeditions against both Clark in the Illinois country and against Fort Pitt, while there were plans both by Clark and by the commander at Fort Pitt to capture Detroit. None of these plans succeeded, although there was a great deal of fighting in the Old Northwest even after the Battle of Yorktown in the fall of 1781, which virtually ended hostilities in the East. Not until De Peyster received word in April, 1783 that a treaty of peace had been signed did hostilities come to an end in the western country.

[18] See L. Kinnaird, "The Spanish Expedition Against Fort St. Joseph in 1781: A New Interpretation," *Mississippi Valley Historical Review,* XIX (1932) 173-192; F. Taggart, "The Capture of St. Joseph, Michigan (*sic*) by the Spaniards in 1781," *Missouri Historical Review,* V (1911); and C. M. Alvord, "The Conquest of St. Joseph," *Missouri Historical Review,* II (1908), 195ff. In support of the older theory that the Spanish sought to establish a claim on the Old Northwest by the raid, see Van Every, *op. cit.,* p. 272.

During the war there was an episode in Michigan history that demonstrated the plight of those who chose not to fight on either side. A religious group called Moravians, who came originally from Germany to settle at Bethlehem, Pennsylvania, had established some missions among the Indians near the present town of Tuscarawas, on the Muskinghum River in southern Ohio. The missionaries had taught the Indians arts and crafts, as well as their religion, which, like that of the Quakers, was opposed to war. When the Revolution broke out the Moravians and their Delaware charges attempted to stay neutral. This was difficult because the patriots regarded all the western Indians as openly or secretly disposed toward the British. In order to escape the tide of conflict the settlement was moved northward to the neighborhood of Sandusky on Lake Erie. Late in 1781 some of the Delaware, called "Christian Indians," returned to their town in southern Ohio, Gnadenhutten, to harvest the grain they had planted. While there a party of Virginians and others deceived them into surrender by telling them they would be taken east for protection. Then the Americans murdered ninety of them in cold blood. David Zeisburger, leader of the mission, had conferred with Major De Peyster at Detroit regarding the removal of his community to Michigan. Hearing the news of the frightful massacre at Gnadenhutten, Zeisburger and his followers started for Detroit, carrying all their possessions with them.

For a time the Moravians and their Delaware charges lived in or near Detroit. Zeisburger leaves us this description of the town in April, 1782:

> It is something wonderful here, and pleasant if anyone is found who shows a desire for God's word, for the place here is like Sodom, where all the sins are committed. The French have, indeed, a Church here and a Priest, who, however, is quite old, and never preaches, but merely reads mass. The English and Protestants have neither church nor preacher, and wish for neither, although they could have them if they would.[19]

Somewhat later the Moravians and their Delaware converts were allowed to build a community on the Clinton River near present-day Mount Clemens. It consisted of 27 log cabins and a meeting house. Land was cleared, crops were raised, and a road was built—the first inland road in Michigan—between the settlement and a

[19] Quoted by J. E. Day, "The Moravians in Michigan," *Mich. Pioneer and Historical Colls.,* XXX (1906), 55.

mill situated within the present city of Detroit. The community prospered between 1782 and 1786. But when it became clear that Michigan would ultimately be taken over by the United States, most of the group removed to Canada, where they built a new town called New Gnadenhutten on the Thames River. Here again a successful and thriving community was built, only to be destroyed once more as a result of war when the armies of General William Henry Harrison swept through the area during the War of 1812.

MICHIGAN HANGS IN THE BALANCE

The end of the Revolutionary War found the Americans in control of Kentucky and the Illinois country and the British still in firm possession of the Great Lakes region, including Michigan. Therefore, had each side kept the territory it controlled at the close of the war, Michigan would have remained in British hands. That this did not happen was due largely to certain aspects of European politics at the time.

Several generations of historians held that the conquests of George Rogers Clark saved Michigan and the Northwest for the United States. But a careful study of the peace negotiations has led the foremost authority on the subject and many other writers in recent years to deny that such was the case. They have concluded that Clark's hold on the Illinois country at the time the peace was negotiated was very weak; there even is some doubt about whether the negotiators were fully acquainted with Clark's earlier victories. And it now seems clear that, in any event, the principal reason the United States was able to obtain title to the area between the Alleghenies and the Mississippi was that Great Britain preferred to see the United States get all this region rather than allowing Spain to obtain a portion of it.[20]

The disaster the British suffered at Yorktown and a change in the ministry combined to make the British government ready to negotiate for peace. A peace commission was appointed and proceeded to Paris, where it met the American negotiators, including Benjamin Franklin, John Adams, John Jay, and Henry Laurens. The American commission had been instructed by congress to negotiate jointly with the French. But when Jay learned that

[20] S. F. Bemis, *The Diplomacy of the American Revolution*, pp. 172-228. For the older view see R. G. Thwaites, *How George Rogers Clark Won the Northwest*; J. A. James, "To What Extent Was George Rogers Clark in Military Control of the Old Northwest at the Close of the Revolution?" *Annual Report* of The American Historical Association for 1917.

the French foreign minister, Count Vergennes, had sent an aide to London to confer with British officials, he suspected that the French were dealing separately with Britain, and persuaded his fellow commissioners that this justified them in also proceeding with separate negotiations. Franklin proposed to the British commission that it would be desirable for Britain to cede all of Canada and Nova Scotia to the United States. But news that the Franco-Spanish assault on the British-held Rock of Gibraltar had failed served to stiffen the British attitude, and it became evident that it was out of the question for the United States to secure Canada. The question then was how much territory south of Canada the United States would be able to get, and where the boundary lines would be drawn.

The Count of Aranda, Spanish minister at the French court, now attempted to persuade Vergennes to back a plan that would not only return Florida to Spain (it had been lost to Britain in 1763), but also would give Spain a large area east of the Mississippi, extending from the Ohio River to the Gulf of Mexico. Under Aranda's plan the United States would have retained parts of what are now the states of Kentucky, Tennessee, and Ohio. The remainder of the region north of the Ohio would have been allowed to remain in British hands while Spain would have received the area south of Tennessee. The British rejected this proposal, and instead agreed to cede all the region between Canada and Florida, east of the Mississippi to the United States. One writer explains this choice by Britain as follows:

> In the first place, Prime Minister Shelburne had long been kindly disposed towards the colonials. He was eager to close the bloody chasm and avert future friction, particularly over the inevitable westward expansion of the American republic. He likewise desired to establish profitable commercial relationships, to wean the United States away from French post-war influence, and perhaps to lure the Americans into a loose tie with the British Empire . . . . Finally, the attractive British terms must be considered in the light of the European conflagration. At the time when Jay opened separate negotiations, Britain was in desperate straits. Here was a golden opportunity to improve her position by seducing America from the ranks of the enemy.[21]

Thus Michigan, which hung in the balance in the peace negotiations, was to become part of the new United States of America.

But the question remained as to exactly where the boundary between Canada and the United States would be located. The

[21] T. A. Bailey, *A Diplomatic History of the American People*, p. 51.

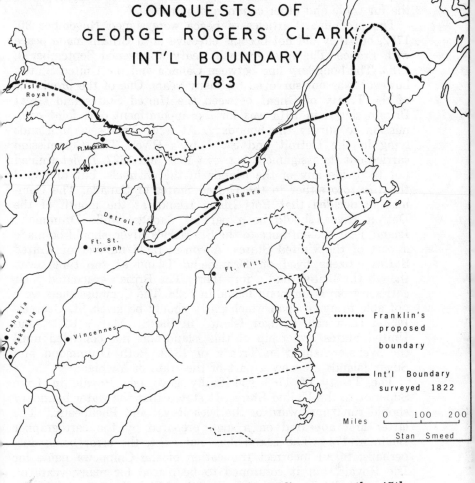

CONQUESTS OF
GEORGE ROGERS CLARK
INT'L BOUNDARY
1783

Isle
Royale

Ft. Mackinac

Niagara

Detroit

Ft. St.
Joseph

Ft. Pitt

Cahokia
Kaskaskia

Vincennes

•••••••• Franklin's
proposed
boundary

———— Int'l Boundary
surveyed 1822

Miles   0   100   200

Stan Smeed

Americans gave the British a choice of two lines: one, the 45th parallel from the St. Lawrence River to the Mississippi, the other, through the middle of Lakes Ontario, Erie, Huron, and Superior, and the rivers connecting these lakes. Had the British accepted the first option, the United States would have secured what is now southern Ontario, but the northern tip of Lower Michigan, all of Upper Michigan, northern Wisconsin, and northern Minnesota would have remained British. Great Britain would have had title to all the rich iron and copper deposits of the Lake Superior region. The British selected the boundary through the middle of the Great Lakes and their connecting waterways probably because this left them free to use these lakes and waterways for the fur trade and other commercial purposes.[22]

The preliminary articles of peace were signed November 30, 1782, but they did not become effective until Britain made peace with France. The Anglo-French treaty was signed September 3, 1783. The boundary line between Canada and the United States, however, was not surveyed for many years. One of the provisions of the Treaty of Ghent between the United States and Great Britain signed in 1814 was for the appointment of a joint commission to survey the boundary. At issue were several islands lying in the Detroit and St. Mary's River. The Commission carried out its assignment between 1822 and 1827. It determined not to divide any of the islands in the channels, but to award them *in toto* either to the United States or Canada. The Commission decided that Bois Blanc Island, at the mouth of the Detroit River, should be a part of Canada, while Drummond Island, near the entrance to the St. Mary's River, should be made a part of the United States. A considerable number of United States citizens lived on Drummond Island at the time, even though the British had a fort there. The British evacuated their garrison from Drummond Island in 1828. The Commissioners were not able to agree upon which party should be given St. George's Island (now called Sugar Island) in the St. Mary's River, and United States ownership of this island was not conceded until the Webster-Ashburton Treaty of 1842. Both Drummond and Sugar Islands are now a part of the state of Michigan.[23]

The Treaty of 1783 specifically gave Isle Royale in Lake Superior to the United States. It stated that the water boundary should run "northward of the isles Royal and Phelipeaux." The latter first appeared on a map prepared by the cartographer Bellin in 1744. The island does not exist, the error being due, perhaps, to an incorrect translation of the Chippewa name for Isle Royale, but it continued to be placed for many years on maps of Lake Superior, including the Mitchell map used in the Paris peace negotiations of 1783.[24] Many writers have perpetuated the tradition that Franklin, knowing of the existence of rich copper deposits on Isle Royale, managed to include the island

[22] S. F. Bemis, *op. cit.*, p. 233.

[23] A. M. Soule, "The International Boundary Line of Michigan," *Mich. Pioneer and Historical Colls.*, XXVI (1896), 597-632; J. and E. Bayliss, *River of Destiny*, pp. 1-144.

[24] L. C. Karpinski, "Early Michigan Maps: Three Outstanding Peculiarities," *Michigan History*, XXIX (1945), 506-507. Karpinski errs in stating that the Treaty of 1783 gave the mythical Phelipeaux Island to Great Britain.

within the United States for that reason. This notion has now been pretty well disproved. Mitchell's map shows both Isle Royale and the mythical Phelipeaux Island considerably to the south of where Isle Royale is actually located. The natural water dividing line, according to this map, would run north of Isle Royale, and this was no doubt the reason why the Treaty specified that the boundary should run to the north of that island, and hence include the island within the United States.[25] After Michigan became a state Isle Royale was attached to Ontonagon County, later was transferred to Houghton County in 1845, and to Keweenaw County in 1861 In 1875 it was made a separate county, but since 1891 it again has been a part of Keweenaw County. It was made a national park by an act of Congress in 1931.[26]

CANADIAN MICHIGAN

Although Great Britain had agreed in the Treaty of 1783 to withdraw all its garrisons from the territory ceded to the United States, this promise was not carried out. British soldiers continued to occupy Detroit, Fort Mackinac, and the other "northwest posts," including Niagara, Oswego, and several other forts extending as far east as Lake Champlain. The retention of these posts continued until 1796.

Even before the treaty had been ratified, influential fur merchants in London urged the British government to retain the posts for two or three years in order to give them time to readjust their trade and their trade routes. An order went out to America to retain possession of the posts the day before George III proclaimed the Treaty. But instead of keeping the posts for two or three years, the British clung to them for thirteen years, offering as justification the claim that the United States had violated certain terms of the Treaty. It had been agreed that the United States should "earnestly recommend" to the states the restoration of the confiscated properties of the loyalists who had fled from the colonies during the Revolution. Congress made the recommendation but the states paid it no heed. The Treaty also specified that there was to be no impediment placed in the way of the collection of debts owed by Americans to Britishers prior to the Revolution. This provision of the Treaty was unquestion-

[25] Soule, *op. cit.*, pp. 612-617; J. C. Starbuck, "Ben Franklin and Isle Royale," *Michigan History*, XLVI (1962), 157-166.
[26] H. E. Fredeen, "The Story of Isle Royale," *Michigan History*, XXV (1941), 331-353.

ably violated by the states. But the United States could also point out that the British had not kept their promises either. They had agreed not to carry away any slaves when their armies left the United States, but in spite of this pledge some 3,000 slaves were taken along by the departing Britishers. At any rate, the facts demonstrate that the British had determined to retain the northwest posts before they knew whether or not the Americans were going to observe the treaty. The weakness of the United States under the Articles of Confederation made many Europeans doubt that a republic could be held together with such loose ties. And finally there was the question of whether the United States could cope successfully with the Indians. As will be discussed in the next chapter, the new republic at first suffered a number of serious setbacks in its efforts to control the Indians within its borders.[27]

The British not only kept their troops in Detroit and Fort Mackinac, they also took measures to establish institutions of civil government in what is now Michigan. During the Revolution thousands of loyalists had settled in "Upper Canada," the region we call today southern Ontario. Almost at once they began to demand the traditional British rights, such as *habeas corpus*, trial by jury, British commercial law, and an elective assembly. To meet some of these demands Governor Sir Guy Carleton established four administrative districts in the region inhabited by the loyalists in Upper Canada. Detroit, whose civilian population was still predominantly French, was included within the District of Hesse. A court of common pleas, sheriff, and justices of the peace were provided for each district. Judge William D. Powell presided over the court of common pleas, which held its sessions at Sandwich on the Canadian side of the Detroit River.[28]

A more comprehensive plan for the government of Canada was enacted by the British parliament and became effective in 1791. It established two provinces: Lower Canada (so-called because it was on the lower reaches of the St. Lawrence River), with a predominantly French population, and Upper Canada, whose people were mainly English. The relatively small number of French people in Michigan were far outnumbered by some 20,000 Britishers in the region of Kingston and Niagara. Each province was to have an elected assembly. John Graves Simcoe, who had fought for the British cause in the Revolution and was an ardent imperialist, was appointed as chief executive of Upper

[27] T. Bailey, *op. cit.*, pp. 56-58.
[28] W. R. Riddell, *William Dummer Powell and Michigan Under British Rule: Law and the Law Courts, 1760-1796.*

MICHIGAN DURING
THE AMERICAN
REVOLUTION

Fort
Michilimackinac   Fort Mackinac

Moravian Settlement

Detroit

Fort
St. Joseph

10 5 0 10 20 30 40 50 Miles

McElroy

Canada with the title of lieutenant governor. Soon after his arrival at Kingston, then capital of the province, counties were set
up from which representatives were to be chosen to the assembly.
Simcoe bestowed good English names upon the counties as well
as the towns. The Detroit area was divided between counties of
Kent and Essex. In 1792 the first election in Michigan history
took place. From the Detroit area William Macomb, François
Baby, and David W. Smith were elected to the assembly, which
met at Niagara. Alexander Grant was appointed to the lieutenant
governor's council. Laws were passed for the introduction of

English civil law, trial by jury, and a system of courts. Another law legalized all marriages irregularly contracted because of the absence of clergy in the remote settlements.[29]

After the Revolution, life went on much as it had before the war in Detroit. The Indians continued to bring their peltry from great distances, to exchange for the usual trade goods and for firewater when they could get it. The value of the fur trade for 1785 was estimated by one British official at £180,000, of which well over half came from territories belonging to the United States. After 1785, however, the fur trade at Detroit declined. Indians of the Old Northwest were on the warpath, resisting the tide of settlers which had begun to flow over the mountains into the West. At Mackinac the volume of the trade continued high. The trade in the north was largely in the hands of the Northwest Company, formed in 1783. Headquarters were on Mackinac Island, adjacent to the fort, which had been moved to the island from the Lower Peninsula side of the straits during the Revolution.[30] By 1793 the French Revolution was having an injurious effect upon the fur trade. The French aristocrats, who always had been heavy buyers of furs, were fleeing the country or falling victim to the guillotine. Keeping the forts in repair and providing for their garrisons entailed a heavy expense for the British government. The decline of the fur trade as well as mounting costs were factors in the decision of the British to evacuate their posts within the United States. However, the involvement of Great Britain in a new war with France in 1793 and a brilliant victory by an American general, Anthony Wayne, over the Indians were the decisive factors. During the summer and fall of 1796 Detroit and Fort Mackinac finally were handed over to the Americans, and the stars and stripes at last flew over Michigan.

---

[29] C. Wittke, *A History of Canada,* pp. 65-77.
[30] However, the British continued to call the fort as well as the island "Michilimackinac."

Beaver

6

MICHIGAN
AND THE OLD NORTHWEST, 1783-1805

W hile Michigan was still being governed as part of Canada, decisions that were to play a major role in its future were being reached by the United States. The states that had claims to western lands surrendered those claims to the United States. A plan for the survey and sale of the land was adopted. A revolutionary political policy was evolved, making it possible for segments of the American West, after passing through certain stages of development, to become states with all the rights and powers of the original thirteen. The region lying between the Pennsylvania boundary to the east, the Ohio River to the south, the Mississippi River to the west, and the Canadian boundary to the north was formed into the Northwest Territory.[1] Then at Philadelphia in the summer of 1787 the plan for a federal union was devised, giving the new nation greater strength. After several false starts the Indians of the Northwest Territory were defeated by an American army under General Anthony Wayne, and the process of purchasing the land from the Indians was begun. For four years following the evacuation of Detroit and Mackinac by the British in 1796 Michigan was administered as a part of the Northwest Territory. From 1800 to 1803 it was divided between

---

[1] The region is often referred to nowadays as "the Old Northwest" to distinguish it from the northwest part of the present United States.

157

the Northwest Territory and the newly created Indiana Territory. From 1803 to 1805 all of Michigan was included within the Territory of Indiana. Finally in 1805 the Territory of Michigan was established by an act of Congress.

THE STATES GIVE UP THEIR CLAIMS TO MICHIGAN

Five of the original thirteen states had claims on all or part of the Old Northwest. The claims of New York and Pennsylvania were based on treaties they had signed with the Indians granting them certain lands in the West. Those of Virginia, Massachusetts, and Connecticut arose from provisions in colonial charters. Virginia claimed all of the Old Northwest as well as Kentucky; the two New England states claimed strips of land extending from east to west. Massachusetts laid claim to the western part of New York as well as the strip extending further west. The Carolinas and Georgia had claims to lands in the West to the south of Kentucky.

The impetus for the surrender of these western claims originated with Maryland. That state, along with six others, had no western land claims. When the Articles of Confederation were proposed in 1778, Maryland announced it would not ratify even this loose bond of union until the landed states gave up their claims to the central government. It was argued that the West was being fought for by all the states, and that all should share it. Several circumstances gave support to the Maryland case. The fortunes of war were at a low ebb, and it was apparent that the new states must form a firm union if they were to make good on their stroke for independence. It was recognized that the Indian problem in the West was too big for any one state to handle. Then in 1780 the continental congress made one of the most important policy decisions in American history as a means of persuading the states to cede their claims. A promise was made that the land in the West, if ceded, would be "formed into separate republican states, which shall become members of the federal union, and have the same rights and sovereignty, freedom, and independence as the other states." This was an ingenious and unique plan. Perhaps the method by which Greek city-states established colonies that became independent is the closest analogy, but in the case of the Greeks there was no federal union to bind the new states to the old. The British Commonwealth of Nations, which evolved later, also bears some resemblance to the American system of establishing new states, but it lacks the cohesion of the United States.

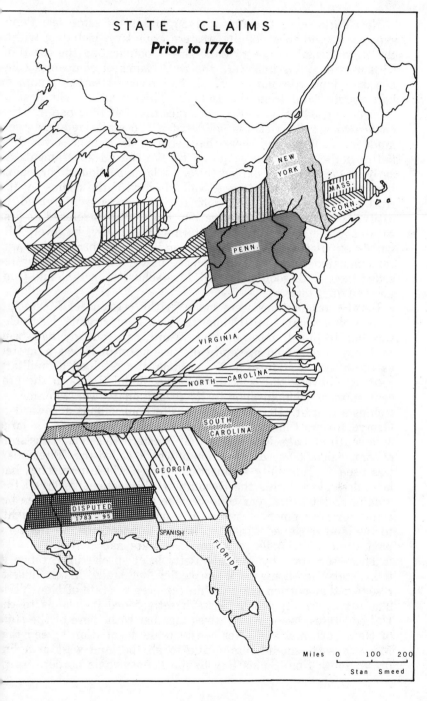

STATE CLAIMS
Prior to 1776

NEW YORK

MASS.

CONN.

PENN.

VIRGINIA

NORTH CAROLINA

SOUTH CAROLINA

GEORGIA

DISPUTED
1783 - 95

SPANISH

FLORIDA

Miles 0 100 200

Stan Smeed

New York ceded its claims in 1780, and in the same year Pennsylvania agreed to a definite western boundary, including within the state a small outlet to Lake Erie. Complicating the situation with regard to Virginia were the rival claims of companies composed of land speculators, which had received earlier grants or had bought land from the Indians. There was a great deal of intrigue carried on by those companies that felt they had a better chance to get their claims validated if the states retained their lands in the West, and those that believed their chances would be better if the lands were acquired by the central government. As early as 1781 Virginia agreed to cede a large portion of her claims if congress would agree not to validate any of the claims by the rival companies. This was sufficient to persuade Maryland to ratify the Articles of Confederation, but Congress refused at first to accept the cession on those terms. Eventually, however, Virginia's stipulation was agreed to, and in 1784 her cession was consummated. This was the decisive move, and the other states ceded their lands soon afterward, Massachusetts in 1785 and Connecticut in 1786.

Certain reservations were made in the cessions of Massachusetts, Connecticut, and Virginia. In the case of Virginia, Kentucky was not included; most of that future state already had been sold and it remained a county of Virginia until it was admitted as the fifteenth state in 1792. Virginia also retained a "military reserve" between the Scioto and Little Miami Rivers in the present state of Ohio to allot to its revolutionary war veterans, as well as a plot of 150,000 acres opposite Louisville as an award to George Rogers Clark and his men. Connecticut reserved a large area south of Lake Erie called the "Western Reserve," consisting of some 4,000,000 acres, a portion of which, called the "Firelands," was used to indemnify Connecticut people whose properties had been destroyed during the Revolution. Connecticut governed this area until 1803, the year Ohio became a state. The area then became, for governmental purposes, a part of Ohio, but the rights to the land remained with the state of Connecticut and the companies and individuals to whom that state had sold it.

The reservation by Massachusetts is of special importance in the history of Michigan. When ceding her lands, Massachusetts reserved that portion lying within the present state of New York. The same year in which Massachusetts ceded its claims to the United States, its representatives together with those of the state of New York met and after considerable negotiation agreed that Massachusetts should retain title to all the land west of a line drawn south from Sodus Bay to the Pennsylvania border, except for a mile-wide strip along the Niagara River. Massachusetts also was awarded a tract of 230,400 acres east of the Sodus Bay-Pennsylvania line (called the "pre-emption line"), along the upper reaches of the Susquehanna River. The state of New York, however, retained *sovereignty* over the entire area within her present boundaries; Massachusetts merely retained *title to the land*. Massachusetts disposed of its lands to speculators, who, in turn, sold them to individual settlers. Most of the people who bought these lands were from Massachusetts, Connecticut, and Rhode Island. Due to the poor soil and growing population of New England a mass exodus took place in the years after 1786 to western New York, which became a little New England. The sons and grandsons of these pioneers and their wives and children were destined to be the ones who, half a century afterward, were to constitute the largest segment of the great influx to Michigan. Michigan, in its early and formative years, was to be peopled more than any other state in the Old Northwest by New England yankees who came not only from New England itself, but also from western New York. It was relatively easy to reach Michigan from western New York by canal boat and lake vessels. This predominant New England element in Michigan's population is one of the most important and significant aspects of the state's history.

A PUBLIC LAND POLICY ADOPTED

The Congress under the Articles of Confederation, now that the states had ceded the largest part of their lands to the United States, faced the necessity of deciding what would be done with these lands. Its decision was embodied in the Ordinance of 1785, one of the most important policy measures in American history.

From the beginning there were several points of view on what policy was best. One faction favored the "southern system," by which the purchaser would obtain a warrant, select the tract he wanted, and then have it surveyed. The "New England system," in contrast, called for a survey of the land in advance of sale. As early as 1781 a pamphlet written by Pelatiah Webster advocated this policy, and the Ordinance of 1785 adopted it. Another and more basic difference of opinion related to whether the land should be sold in large tracts to wealthy individuals and companies, who in turn would sell it to individual settlers, or whether it should be sold directly by the government to the settler. Related to this issue was the question of whether the land should be made available rapidly and on easy terms to promote settlement, or be regarded as a great national resource to be husbanded primarily for the income it would bring to the treasury. The Ordinance of 1785 represented a compromise on all these questions.

The Ordinance provided that the land belonging to the United States should be surveyed, in advance of sale, into townships six miles square, each containing 36 "sections" one mile square. A uniform system of numbering the sections was adopted. The townships were to be surveyed from an east-west line called a "base line," and a north-south line called a "prime meridian." The land was to be sold at auction, with a minimum price of $1.00 per acre. The least amount a buyer could purchase was 640 acres. Alternate townships were to be sold intact, while the others were to be sold by sections. Section sixteen in each township was to be reserved from sale for the benefit of schools. Although certain modifications were later made, the Ordinance of 1785 established the policy followed by the United States government for the disposal of all its lands in the West, including Michigan.

The subsequent changes in the policy pertained mainly to the minimum amount that could be purchased, the minimum price, and the convenience of the purchaser. A land law passed in 1800 established the minimum price at $2.00 an acre, but made it possible to buy the land on the installment plan, with a down payment of one-quarter the purchase price, and with one-quarter due and payable at the end of one, two, and three years. Because this plan led many buyers to purchase more land than they could pay for, another change in 1820 provided for a cash price of $1.25 an acre. This is the price for which most of the United States government land in Michigan was purchased. In 1862 the Homestead law was enacted, which made it possible for a person to receive 160 acres of government land upon payment of a small fee, by residing on the land for five years. A considerable amount of land in northern Michigan was taken up under the Homestead law. The minimum amount of land that could be purchased from the government was lowered to 320 acres in 1800, to 160 acres in 1804, and to 80 acres in 1820. The Harrison land law, passed in 1800, provided for land offices in the West; until that time government land could be purchased only in the eastern states. Quite often settlers would build a cabin and start clearing land before it was surveyed, hoping to be able to purchase it when it was placed on the market. These people were called "squatters." In 1841 a "preemption law" gave a person who had settled on land, erected a dwelling, and made certain improvements, the right to purchase 160 acres at the minimum price when the land went on the market.

The reservation of four sections of land for future disposal, as provided in the Ordinance of 1785, was subsequently abandoned. But the reservation of section sixteen in each township for schools became a settled policy. It became the practice of Congress to hand over title to the states, at the time they were admitted into the Union, to the sixteenth section in each township for the support of schools. These sections were then sold, the proceeds of the sale going, in some states, to the townships in which they were situated. Michigan was the first state to use these proceeds to build up a *state* fund, the income from which was designed as a permanent endowment for schools. The reservation of section sixteen for schools, as provided in the Ordinance of 1785, initiated "federal aid to education." As will be indicated subsequently, the federal government later granted the states additional public lands for education and other purposes.

The base line for the Michigan public land surveys was established east and west along the northern boundaries of the second tier of counties in the Lower Peninsula (Van Buren, Kalamazoo, Calhoun, Jackson, Washtenaw, and Wayne). The prime meridian for Michigan was established south from Sault Ste. Marie on longitude 84 degrees, 22 minutes, and 24 seconds west. All land surveys in Michigan numbered townships east or west and north or south of these lines. Thus "T2N, R3W" means the second township north of the base line and the third west of the prime meridian. The sections within each township are numbered from one to 36, beginning with number 1 in the northeast corner, continuing westward to number 6 in the northwest corner. Directly south of section 6 is section 7. The numbering continues back and forth to section 36 in the southeast corner.[2]

A GOVERNMENT POLICY FOR THE OLD NORTHWEST.

Better known than the Land Ordinance of 1785 and equally important was the Ordinance of 1787, which established policies with respect to government. Because the Ordinance of 1787 applied only to the Old Northwest, it is known as the Northwest Ordinance. In 1784 Congress adopted an ordinance based on recommendations by Thomas Jefferson that divided the Old Northwest into ten future states. Jefferson proposed for them such names as Pelisipia, Polypotamia, and Illinoia. One was to be called Michigania, but it was located in part of what is now Wisconsin. The area within the present state of Michigan was divided among the states of Metropotamia, Cherronesus, and

[2] R. M. Robbins, *Our Landed Heritage*; B. H. Hibbard, *A History of Public Land Policies.*

Sylvania in Jefferson's plan. The Ordinance of 1784, however, never went into effect, being superseded by the Ordinance of 1787.[3]

The impetus for the passage of the Ordinance of 1787 came from a group of Massachusetts veterans of the Revolution who had formed an organization called the Ohio Company at a meeting held in the Bunch of Grapes tavern in Boston on March 1, 1786. The plan for this company originated with Brigadier General Rufus Putnam. It was based upon the idea of using depreciated paper money, with which the veterans had been paid off, to buy a tract of land in the West. The job of negotiating with Congress for the purchase was entrusted to the Reverend Manasseh Cutler. Cutler's success was achieved through a shady deal he made with Colonel William Duer, an official of congress who handled all land sales. The scheme was to combine the request of the Ohio Company with a petition for an option to purchase an enormous tract of land by the Scioto Company, the latter consisting of Duer and certain key congressmen. This arrangement was consummated, although the Scioto Company never was able to make the payments to take up its option. The Ohio Company, however, went forward and some of its members established in 1788 the first American settlement in the Old Northwest on the tract that had been purchased, founding the city of Marietta (named for Queen Marie Antoinette of France) on the Muskingum River in the southern portion of what is now the state of Ohio.

While negotiating for the land purchase of the Ohio Company Cutler insisted that Congress take action to provide for the government of the region in which the tract was located. The Ordinance of 1787 was the outgrowth of this demand. One of the most significant documents in American history, it appears to have been drafted and passed principally to facilitate the deal made by Cutler and Duer. A committee was formed on July 9, 1787, which reported its recommendations two days later. On July 13 Congress passed the Ordinance. That policy decisions of such magnitude and of such importance to the future development of the United States were made so hastily is one of the most amazing facts in American history. Congress, as has been noted, already had committed itself to the formation of new states in the West. The Ordinance of 1784, based on Jefferson's recommendations, was available as a starting point, although Jefferson himself was now in France to take over the duty of representing the United States from the aging Benja

[3] For a map setting forth Jefferson's plan and a further description of it see F. L. Paxton, *History of the American Frontier, 1763-1893*, pp. 61-63.

min Franklin. The greatest defect of Jefferson's plan was its failure to provide any orderly procedure for the evolution of western states. Congress had debated this matter for years, many members distrusting the capacity of frontiersmen for self-government. The time had come for decision, and Cutler's proposal provided the stimulus for making a decision.

There is a serious question whether the Ordinance of 1787 was ever legally adopted. In the congress under the Articles of Confederation votes were taken by states, each state having one vote regardless of how many delegates it had in congress. The Articles of Confederation required the assent of nine states on all important matters. Although the vote by states on the Ordinance of 1787 was unanimous, only eight states were represented when the vote was taken. A number of modifications were made as the principles of the Ordinance were applied in subsequent years by the congress under the Constitution. But in the main the outlines of the Ordinance of 1787 were followed in providing for government, not only in the Old Northwest, but also in the vast area west of the Mississippi that the United States acquired later. So the question of its legality becomes only a matter of academic interest.

Disregarding some of the portions of the Ordinance of 1787 that were not of lasting importance, its poorly organized provisions may be grouped under three headings: first, it provided for the division of the Old Northwest into not less than three nor more than five states and set forth the boundaries of these future states; second, it stipulated three stages of development through which these divisions would pass as they progressed toward statehood; and third, it contained a statement of rights guaranteed to the people who settled in the region. A brief survey of these three groupings will indicate their significance in Michigan history.

With regard to the future states, the Ordinance provided that the minimum number (3) should be formed by drawing two north-south lines, one northward from Vincennes on the Wabash River and the other northward from the mouth of the Miami River, both lines continuing to the international boundary. One state would thus consist of the region west of the line northward from Vincennes, another would include the region east of the line northward from the mouth of the Miami, and the third would take in the area between the two lines. The Ordinance provided that Congress might create one or two additional states from the area lying north of a line drawn due east and west through the southernmost tip of Lake Michigan, which would then become the northern boundary of the first three states.

The Ordinance set up the entire region of the Old Northwest as the Northwest Territory. It was to be governed by a governor, secretary, and three judges, all appointed by Congress.[4] The five territorial officials were empowered to adopt such laws of the original states as were best suited to the territory. Thus at first the people of the territory would not enjoy self-government. However, the Ordinance went on to provide that when the territory had a population of 5,000 free, adult males, partial self-government would be inaugurated. This became known as the second stage of territorial development. At this stage the voters of the territory (males who owned at least 50 acres of land) were to have the right to elect a house of representatives. In addition, there was to be a legislative council which was to consist of five men selected by Congress from a list of ten nominated by the territorial house of representatives. The laws of the territory were henceforth to be made by the house of representatives, the legislative council, and the governor, the consent of all three being required. The house of representatives and the legislative council were to have the right to choose by joint ballot a delegate to the Congress of the United States, which delegate was to have the right to participate in debates, but not the right to vote.

The right to eventual statehood was guaranteed. The Ordinance stated that "whenever any of the said states shall have sixty thousand free inhabitants therein, such state shall be admitted by its delegates into the Congress of the United States, on an equal footing with the original states in all respects whatsoever; and shall be at liberty to form a permanent constitution and state government: provided the constitution or government so to be formed, shall be republican and in conformity to the principles contained in these articles. . . ." This right to statehood applied to each of the states into which Congress might eventually determine to divide the Northwest Territory. It was not clear from the Ordinance whether each of the future states should pass through the three stages leading to statehood, but this became the accepted policy.

The rights guaranteed to the people who might settle in the Old Northwest conformed to those that had been regarded as the traditional rights of Englishmen, their origins reaching back to the Magna Carta. These included the benefit of the writ of *habeas corpus* to safeguard against arbitrary arrest, the right to trial by

---

[4] After the Constitution of the United States went into operation these appointments were made by the President with the advice and consent of the Senate.

jury, security of property, and religious freedom. Slavery was prohibited. However, this latter provision was not rigidly enforced. Considerable numbers of slaves were owned and kept in the southern parts of the Old Northwest, and even in Michigan slavery was not unknown. And it must be remembered that when a state was admitted into the Union it had all the rights of the original states, which included the right to legalize slavery. In fact there was a close contest in both Indiana and Illinois between anti-slavery and pro-slavery forces, although neither state actually legalized the slave system.

One of the most famous phrases in the Northwest Ordinance pertains to education: "Religion, morality, and knowledge being necessary to good government and the happiness of mankind, schools and the means of education shall forever be encouraged." This much-quoted phrase was adopted as the first section of the article on education in the constitution framed by the 1961-62 Constitutional Convention in Michigan.[5] Far more important for the future of education than this purely *verbal* support in the Northwest Ordinance was the reservation of section sixteen in each township for the financial support of schools, contained in the Ordinance of 1785.

MEETING THE INDIAN PROBLEM

Congress under the Articles of Confederation had achieved success in dealing with two important problems, land disposal and government, in the territory between the Alleghenies and the Mississippi that had been ceded to the United States by Great Britain in 1783. But it was not able to contend successfully with two other problems that were even more pressing at that time: how to deal with the Indians and how to meet the challenge presented by the continued occupation of the northwest posts by the British, as well as Spanish intrigue aimed at detaching the West from the new nation. The lack of a strong executive, the difficulties encountered by a weak central government in dealing with foreign nations, and particularly the totally inadequate powers to lay taxes for providing revenue to maintain an army account in large part for the failure of the Congress under the Articles of Confederation to deal effectively with these problems. The framing of the Constitution of the United States, its ratification, and the inauguration of the national government under its provisions

[5] Oddly enough, there were strong objections to this article on the ground that it might be interpreted as being in conflict with the separation of church and state.

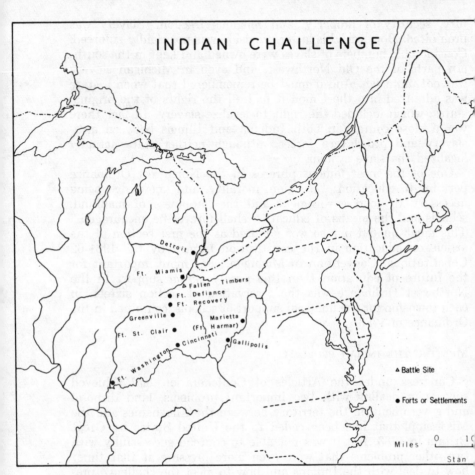

INDIAN CHALLENGE

Detroit
Ft. Miamis
△ Fallen Timbers
● Ft. Defiance
● Ft. Recovery
Greenville ●
Marietta
(Ft. Harmar)
Ft. St. Clair ●
● Cincinnati
Ft. Washington ●
● Gallipolis

△ Battle Site

● Forts or Settlements

Miles 0 10

Stan

in 1789 were, therefore, of major importance in meeting the unsolved problems of the West.

An effort was made to cope with the Indian problem prior to
1789. Commissioners appointed by Congress persuaded the Iroquois in 1784 at Fort Stanwix to cede all their claims to the Old
Northwest to the United States in return for a few presents. Early
the following year several Algonquin tribes, including the Chippewa and Ottawa of Michigan and the Wyandot or Huron, signed
a treaty at Fort McIntosh agreeing to give up all their lands in
the present state of Ohio except for a reservation. But Ohio tribesmen resented the treaty their chiefs had signed, and the important Shawnee refused to agree to it at all. On threat of war the

Shawnee did consent to the terms of the agreement in the Treaty of Fort Finney, at the mouth of the Miami River, early in 1786, but as soon as they returned to their villages they repudiated it. Meanwhile, settlers were pouring across the Ohio River and settling on lands that had not been surveyed, even on the lands not yet ceded by the Indians. The attitude of the Indians now became extremely threatening. Since Congress was unable to supply troops to keep the rebellious natives in order, militiamen were assembled, one detachment under George Rogers Clark and another led by Benjamin Logan. Clark's force mutinied before a single Indian was sighted; Logan's men destroyed some Indian villages and 15,000 bushels of corn belonging to the Indians, but did not engage the natives in any battles. Both the Iroquois and Algonquin nations now openly repudiated the treaties they had signed and declared that they would concede nothing to the whites west of Pennsylvania and north of the Ohio River.

At this stage the Indian problem merged with that of the continued occupation of the Northwest posts by the British. General Haldimand, the British governor-general of Canada, with an eye to assuring Britain possession of these posts, sought to encourage the Indians to form a strong federation to unitedly refuse any cession of land in the West to the United States. The Indians, true to their strong tribal loyalties, refused to adhere to any such federation; they were so divided, in fact, that Arthur St. Clair, first governor of the Northwest Territory, was able to persuade them to sign a treaty at Fort Harmar, situated at the mouth of the Muskingum River, confirming the treaties of Fort McIntosh and Fort Finney. While the governor was talking peace, however, frontiersmen were sending raiding parties against the Indians. Naturally, the latter struck back. By the fall of 1789 a new Indian war had broken out.

The new government under the constitution entrusted the task of disciplining the Indians to General Josiah Harmar. Starting out from Fort Washington (Cincinnati) in October, 1790, Harmar moved so slowly that the Indians easily eluded him. Then, late in October, a detachment was ambushed and lost 183 men. The following year a force of about 3,000 men under the command of Governor St. Clair set out in the late summer from Fort Washington. When his tired army finally reached the Maumee River and pitched their tents for the night without posting adequate guards, the camp was quietly surrounded, then furiously attacked. St. Clair and a part of his army slipped through the Indian cordon, but left 630 dead and 283 wounded behind. The retreating force reached a small fort that had been built on the way north—Fort

Jefferson—in twenty-four hours, whereas it had taken them ten days to cover the same ground on the northward march.

The Indians now fell mercilessly on the Ohio settlers. Marietta and Cincinnati were the only places where safety was assured. They readily agreed to a new British proposal that they concede nothing north of the Ohio to the Americans. President George Washington, who throughout his life had been deeply interested in the development of the West, now called upon "Mad Anthony" Wayne, a man who had made a brilliant name for himself during the Revolution by his reckless courage and daring exploits. There is little doubt that Washington was convinced that the desperate situation in the West called for the same bold and dashing action he himself had used in crossing the Delaware and surprising the British on Christmas night, 1776. Wayne accepted the command, and an army was collected for him at Pittsburgh. It was the same sort of army that Harmar and St. Clair had had and numbered about 2,500. Wayne realized that any sort of effective action was impossible without thorough organization and strict discipline. While the nation waited impatiently, Wayne calmly drilled his men for over a year. He enforced strict obedience to orders and even trained his men to yell like the Indians.

Wayne's advance from Fort Washington began in October, 1793. Halting at Fort Greenville, the site of the present Greenville, Ohio, he sent out spies and did some more drilling. This time supposedly friendly Indians, who had been permitted into the camps of Harmar and St. Clair, were excluded. The soldiers were not allowed to take their women friends along as they had on the St. Clair expedition. There followed an advance to the site of St. Clair's defeat where Fort Recovery was built. Meanwhile an Indian force had been gathered by the intrepid warrior Little Turtle. This numbered perhaps 2,000 braves. Desirous of repeating their previous success at this place, the Indians attacked in a determined fashion. They suffered severe casualties, were unable to carry out their objective, and had to retreat.

In his report on this engagement, Wayne wrote that he had virtual proof that there were a considerable number of Britishers and Detroit militiamen mixed with the savages in the attack on Fort Recovery. There is unmistakable evidence that the British supplied the natives with provisions and ammunition. The old French fort on the Maumee, near the present Perrysburg, Ohio, was occupied by a British force and named Fort Miamis. This was such an open violation of the peace that it was made the subject of a strong protest, communicated through John Jay, who at that time was in England attempting to negotiate a treaty between Great Britain and the United States.

After receiving reinforcements Wayne moved forward on July 28, 1794. At the confluence of the Auglaize and Maumee Rivers, Fort Defiance was built. Little Turtle, now thoroughly alarmed, urged Blue Jacket and other chiefs to make peace, but they would not listen to him. Tecumseh, a young Shawnee warrior of whom much will be heard later, was a member of the Indian force. On August 20, 1794 a pitched battle between Wayne's army and the Indians took place some dozen miles south of the present Toledo, Ohio, on the Maumee. It was a place where trees had been uprooted by a violent tornado, giving the engagement the name "Battle of Fallen Timbers." Wayne was completely victorious. Only 33 of his men were killed and about a hundred wounded. After burning some native villages he marched into what is now Indiana and built a fort named in his honor at the site of the present Fort Wayne. Then he retired to Greenville.

The victory at Fallen Timbers broke the back of the Indian resistance. What discouraged the Indians most was that the battle had been fought within two or three miles of Fort Miamis, and the British had made no move to come to their aid. Wayne now called for a conclave with all the Indian leaders at Greenville. Runners were sent to remote points to summon the chiefs. Some of these messengers came to Michigan. There is an account telling of the meeting of one of Wayne's envoys with a Britisher sent out from Detroit to sound out Indian sentiment at the trading post near the present city of Kalamazoo. In the summer of 1795 the chiefs together with a thousand or more braves assembled at Greenville. Chief spokesman for the Indians of Michigan was the Chippewa chieftain variously called Matchekewis, Mash-ipi-nash-i-wish, or Bad Bird. He had led the attack on Michilimackinac during the Indian uprising of 1763, had fought for the British cause during the Revolution, and was dignified with the title of general prefixed to his Indian name. At Greenville Matchekewis spoke for the Ottawa, Chippewa, and Potawatomi of Michigan and pledged that they would make war no more on the Americans. After a considerable amount of oratory and palaver the Indians signed the Treaty of Greenville on August 3, 1795, in which they ceded to the United States all of Ohio except a strip along Lake Erie. They also ceded a triangle of land in Indiana and sixteen small areas for trading posts on strategic waterways. These latter included the first land in Michigan ceded to the United States by the Indians: a strip six miles wide along the Detroit River between the Raisin River and Lake St. Clair, all

of Mackinac Island, that part of the mainland along the Straits
of Mackinac to which Indians had given the French or English
title, and a six mile strip on the mainland north of the island
extending three miles inland.[6]

It is noteworthy that the cessions made by the Indians at
Greenville were not simply the spoils of war. They received payment in goods to the value of $20,000 and a promise that they
would receive goods in the amount of $9,500 every year forever
from the United States. It is a common misconception that the
Americans simply confiscated the Indian lands and gave nothing
in return. Actually, in the Treaty of Greenville and in the many
treaties by which later purchases were made, very considerable
amounts were paid for the lands that the Indians regarded as
their own but of which they cultivated only a tiny amount.[7]

The transfer of Michigan to the United States.

Had the British garrison in Fort Miamis come to the aid of the
Indians at the Battle of Fallen Timbers, it probably would have
meant war between the United States and Great Britain. The
British might have been willing to risk war a few years before,
but by 1794 the situation in Europe had so changed as to cause
the British government to avoid any chance of a conflict in America. The French Revolution, which had begun in 1789, entered its
radical phase in 1792, and early the next year the frenzied revo-
lutionaries executed their king, Louis XVI. European monarchs
saw in the French excesses a menace to their security. A wave
of anti-French sentiment swept England. Sensing this hostility and
confident of its ability to contend with the armies of its enemies,
the French Republic declared war on Great Britain and Holland.
The other European powers soon were involved, but against the
combined armies of their enemies the French began to win start-
ling victories by the end of 1793.

In 1794, as French successes continued, the United States sent
John Jay as its special envoy to London in an attempt to persuade
the British to end discrimination against American commerce and
to evacuate the Northwest posts. He was cordially received and

[6] The text of the treaty may be found in *Mich. Pioneer and Historical
Colls.*, XX (1892), 410-419.

[7] Biographies of Wayne provide a fuller account of his campaign, the
Battle of Fallen Timbers, and the Treaty of Greenville: T. A. Boyd, *Mad
Anthony Wayne;* H. E. Wildes, *Anthony Wayne, Trouble-shooter of the
American Revolution;* R. C. Knopf, *Anthony Wayne, a Name in Arms.*
Important source materials may be found in *Mich. Pioneer and Historical
Colls.*, XXXIV (1904), 341-741.

prospects seemed good for a favorable outcome. The British were disposed to make concessions to the Americans in order to prevent them from joining the league of "Armed Neutrals" that was forming to resist Britain's usual depredations against neutral commerce in wartime. But the ground was cut from under Jay by Alexander Hamilton, pro-British Secretary of the Treasury in Washington's cabinet. Hamilton told the British minister in Philadelphia that the United States would under no circumstances join the Armed Neutrals. When this was reported to London the British attitude immediately stiffened. Jay was unable to get a treaty that would open British ports to American commerce on fair and equal terms. The British even balked at agreeing to evacuate the Northwest posts until news arrived of Wayne's successes. The treaty Jay eventually signed included an agreement that these posts would be turned over to the United States no later than June 1, 1796, but the United States had to allow Canadian traders to continue to operate south of the border, agree not to tax the furs they carried back to Montreal, and promise not to levy any higher tax on the trading goods of the Canadians than on those of United States nationals.

The commercial provisions of Jay's Treaty were so unsatisfactory that there was a danger it might not be ratified by the United States Senate. But the treaty, which had been signed on November 14, 1794, was approved by a narrow margin, with the exception of the article relating to trade with the British West Indies, on June 22, 1795. The British were ready to surrender Detroit and Fort Mackinac on June 1, 1796, as they had agreed to do in the Jay Treaty, but the American forces did not arrive to take them over until later. Wayne sent one regiment of his army under Lieutenant Colonel John Francis Hamtramck to occupy Detroit. An advance detachment of sixty-five men under Captain Moses Porter was the first to arrive. On July 11, 1796 the Union Jack that had flown over Fort Lernoult was lowered and the United States flag was raised in its place. Colonel Hamtramck and the remainder of the American occupational force arrived a couple of days later. After a visit to his home in Pennsylvania, Wayne came to Detroit on August 13. He remained there until November, then started out again for home. On his way he was suddenly taken ill and died at Erie, Pennsylvania. At the time of his death he was 51 years of age. It is appropriate that Michigan's most populous county and one of its universities should bear the name of Anthony Wayne. Largely through his efforts the United States had won possession of the Old Northwest.

The remaining British garrison in Michigan was withdrawn

when Major Henry Burbeck with 110 men occupied Fort Mackinac on Mackinac Island September 1, 1796. But events were to prove that the United States was not yet free from foreign intrigue. From Fort Mackinac the British garrison was removed to St. Joseph Island at the mouth of the St. Mary's River, where ground had been cleared and preparations made to build a new British post. Across the Detroit River the British built Fort Malden. British and Canadian fur traders continued to roam through American territory, and Indians living within the United States took large quantities of fur to sell at Fort Malden. Not only the British but also the Spanish still harbored the hope that they could eventually get possession of western lands belonging to the United States. Although the Spanish signed a treaty with the United States in 1795 giving the United States the right to export the products of the West through the port of New Orleans, which they held, Spanish intrigue that was aimed at separating the West from the United States and attaching it to Spanish Louisiana continued for many years. It is noteworthy that General James Wilkinson, who served as commander of the western armies after Wayne's death, was long an agent of the Spanish government, receiving secretly large amounts for his services. It was not until after the Louisiana Purchase in 1803 that the schemes connected with separating the West from the United States finally ended in failure.

MICHIGAN AND THE OLD NORTHWEST IN 1796

By 1796 a sizable group of settlements had sprung up in the Old Northwest. The founding of Marietta by members of the Ohio Company in 1788 already has been noted. Here the whole process of settlement was supervised by the Ohio Company, which had purchased the land. Each settler received a town lot, an eight-acre field near the town, and a 116-acre pasture along the river. Waterpower sites were offered to gristmill and sawmill operators. Lands were donated to "warlike Christian men" who would settle at dangerous spots in the interior. The company planted shade trees along the streets and even donated half a pint of whisky to each settler as an aid to the celebration of the first fourth of July in their new homes. Not relying on nearby Fort Harmar for protection from the Indians, a large fortification called Campus Martius was constructed. It included lodgings for many of the settlers and the home of their leader, Rufus Putnam, which is still preserved in the Campus Martius Museum at Marietta. Prehistoric Indian earthworks, which were found on the townsite, were carefully preserved and still may be seen.

Downstream from Marietta was the town of Gallipolis, settled by Frenchmen who had purchased lands from an agent of the Scioto Company, and who had found when they arrived that they did not even have title to the lands they thought they had purchased. Congress took pity on them and in 1795 granted them a 24,000 acre tract called the "French grant." Still further down-river was a settlement first called Losantville and later Cincinnati, established on land purchased by John Cleves Symmes of New Jersey. Inland the Virginia Military Reserve had been settled by a considerable number of Virginia veterans. The settlers were not aristocrats, but came largely from the more democratic western part of the state. Manchester was founded in 1791, but Chillicothe, established after Wayne's victory, soon became the chief center. Though from Virginia, the people in the Military Reserve were not strongly in favor of slavery. Shortly after Wayne's victory settlers from Connecticut began pouring into the Western Reserve along Lake Erie. Some 500,000 acres of this tract were reserved for Connecticut veterans. The surname of Moses Cleaveland, one of the leaders, was given to the principal town (though the spelling was changed). In the extreme eastern part of present-day Ohio a considerable number of settlers had drifted across the Pennsylvania line and had come up from Virginia. Fort Steuben (now Steubenville) was the center of this settlement.

In addition to these new American settlements the Northwest Territory contained forts and trading posts around which the population consisted largely of French-speaking people. In the Illinois country there were Kaskaskia, Cahokia, and Vincennes. In Wisconsin there was a settlement at Green Bay. In Michigan Detroit and Mackinac Island were the chief centers of population. A few whites were scattered among remote trading posts on the St. Joseph, Kalamazoo, and Grand Rivers. South of Detroit a number of French farmers made their homes along the Raisin River.

At Detroit in 1796 there were about 500 inhabitants. Most of them were of French ancestry, spoke the French language, and observed the rites of the Roman Catholic Church. The merchants and Indian traders were mainly English and Scotch. There were a few Americans already in the town while it was in British hands. Both Indian and Negro slaves are noted in the records, and there were some free Negroes. The Indians who were slaves had been taken captive in inter-tribal wars and sold to the whites. Those who held slaves when the Americans took over were allowed to retain them.

Among the principal merchants and traders in Detroit in 1796 were John Askin, William Macomb, James May, James Abbott, and Joseph Campau. The latter was a Frenchman. These men provided the Indians with arms, blankets, and other supplies in the fall, and were paid with furs, which the Indians brought in the following spring. These merchants did business with dealers in Montreal, who forwarded the furs to London and advanced to the traders in Detroit the goods required for the Indian trade. Ste. Anne's Church, where most of the people worshipped, was a community center. Some leading residents had libraries of considerable size. There was no newspaper, but John McCall operated a printing press as early as 1796. There also was a Masonic lodge, called Zion Lodge Number 10, which was formed during the British period. The French lived in a world of their own. Their customs had changed very little during the imperial struggles. There was much dancing to the tune of the fiddle, and a kind of Mardi Gras was held each year just before the beginning of lent. Christmas was not observed, but New Year's day was a joyous holiday.

The fort, called Fort Lernoult by the British and re-named Fort Detroit by the Americans, was the center of the town. Within it were wooden barracks for the garrison and shops for the carpenter, baker, and armorer. The town lay below the fort and consisted of about a hundred houses. Looking out from the fort, one could see the French farms on the opposite shores of the river and many kinds of craft, ranging from sloops and schooners to canoes, plying the river. Most of the houses were built of logs, although there were some frame dwellings. There were shops and taverns in the town and several stores.[8]

Far to the north of Detroit was Mackinac Island. It is described as it was in 1796 by a contemporary, Major Caleb Swan:

> On the south side of this Island, there is a small bason [*sic*], of a segment of a circle, serving as an excellent harbour for vessels of any burden, and for canoes. Around this bason the village is built, having two streets of nearly a quarter of a mile in length, a Roman chapel, and containing eighty-nine houses and stores; some of them spacious and handsome, with white lime plastering in front, which shews to great advantage from the sea. At one end, in the rear of the town, is an elegant government house, of immense size, and finished with great taste. It is one story high, the rooms fifteen feet and a half in the clear. It has a spacious garden in front, laid out with taste; and extending from the

[8] F. C. Bald, *Detroit's First American Decade, 1796 to 1805.*

house, on a gentle declivity, to the water's edge. There are two natural limpid springs in the rear of the house, and a very lovely grove of sugartrees, called the park. Suitable out-houses, stables, and offices are added; and it is enriched on three sides with beautiful distant prospects. Twenty rods from the rear, there is a sudden and almost perpendicular ascent of about a hundred feet of rock, upon the top of which stands the fort, built of stone and lime, with towers, bastions, etc., occupied by our troops and commanded by Major Burbeck.[9]

One of the houses that stood on the island in 1796 was acquired later by Edward Biddle, a leading trader of the area. Parts of it may have been built as early as 1780. Constructed in the typical Quebec rural style, this old house was restored in 1959 by the Michigan Society of Architects and is listed in the *Historic American Buildings Survey*. The "Biddle House" is probably the oldest surviving house in Michigan, if not in the entire Old Northwest.

Among the white inhabitants of Michigan outside Detroit and Mackinac in 1796 mention must be made of William Burnett. Precisely where he came from is not clear, nor is the date of his arrival in the St. Joseph Valley precisely established. Apparently he was trading there during the American Revolution, for in 1782 he was married to the daughter of a Potawatomi chief. He continued his business through all the vicissitudes of strife between the United States and Britain until his death in 1814. He was strongly pro-American, a fact that created for him no end of difficulties with the British who dominated Mackinac Island where he sold his furs, until 1796. His house and trading post were situated on the west bank of the St. Joseph River, about one and a half miles upstream from its mouth.[10] Upriver, beyond old Fort St. Joseph at Niles, another trader, John Kinzie, had his headquarters. He removed to Chicago in 1804 and became known as "the father of Chicago." His post was taken over by Joseph Bertrand, whose name has been given to a Berrien County town near the site of his old trading post. On the Kalamazoo River a trader named Pepan had his headquarters near the modern city of Kalamazoo. On the Grand River near the present site of Ada Joseph La Framboise and his bride, an Ottawa Indian maiden, established a trading post in 1796.[11]

[9] Quoted by E. O. Wood, *Historic Mackinac*, I, 280.
[10] W. M. Cunningham, *Land of Four Flags*, pp. 89-100.
[11] V. L. Moore, "A Pocahontas of Michigan," *Michigan History*, XV (1931), 71-79.

Biddle House, Mackinac Island

AND FINALLY, MICHIGAN

All of present-day Michigan, after the departure of the British officials in 1796, was officially under the control of Governor Arthur St. Clair and the other officials of the Northwest Territory until 1800. Under an act that became effective July 4, 1800 the Territory of Indiana was created, consisting of that portion of the Northwest Territory west of a line drawn from the mouth of the Kentucky River to Fort Recovery, then due north to the Canadian border. This divided Michigan between the Indiana Territory and the Northwest Territory, although the Detroit area, which included most of the population, remained within the Northwest Territory. Then in 1803 Ohio became the first state to be carved out of the Old Northwest, and all of Michigan as well as the remainder of the Old Northwest became part of the Indiana Territory. Finally, on January 11, 1805 Congress passed an act creating the Territory of Michigan, and on June 30, 1805 that act became effective. Michigan's career as a separate political entity began on that day.

Governor St. Clair was a man of considerable ability, a Federalist in politics and quite undemocratic in his views. When news arrived at Cincinnati, the territorial capital, that the British were about to evacuate the northwest posts, St. Clair was outside the territory. Hence it fell to the lot of Winthrop Sargent, the territorial secretary, to accompany Wayne's army to Detroit and to install civil government. Upon his arrival he proceeded to officially establish the County of Wayne, and included within its boundaries practically all of the present state of Michigan, as well as portions of northern Ohio and Indiana, and those parts of Illinois and Wisconsin bordering on Lake Michigan. In casting about for local officials, Sargent found that the French were inclined to be more loyal to the United States than the people of British ancestry. The trouble was that few of the French could read or write. He compromised by appointing some of each. Seven justices of the peace were designated. Sitting together, they were to constitute a "Court of General Quarter Sessions." A "Court of Common Pleas" was also set up. George McDougall was appointed as sheriff. Peter Audrain, the only American civilian and one· of the few residents who had a knowledge of both French and English, was appointed to four offices. Sargent found that land titles were in a state of terrible confusion. Even what records there were had been carried off by the British, and Sargent had to send word requesting the officials of Upper Canada to return them.

Having done what he could at Detroit, Sargent sailed to Mackinac Island, arriving there after a voyage of more than a month. So illiterate and uneducated were the inhabitants that Sargent could find only two "proper persons" outside the military garrison to appoint as justices of the peace. The commandant was also made a justice of the peace to serve the needs of the many fur traders who periodically visited the post. After trying in vain to settle the troublesome problem of land titles, Sargent returned to Cincinnati by way of Detroit.

The laws to be enforced by the justices at Detroit and Mackinac were those enacted by the governor, secretary, and three judges at Cincinnati. These defined crimes and punishments, commanded the strict observance of Sunday as a day of rest, prohibited swearing and drunkenness, and regulated marriages. Murder and treason were the only capital crimes; flogging, fines, and standing in the stocks were prescribed as punishments for lesser infractions. A court house and a jail were to be provided by each county, with separate compartments for debtors and for women prisoners. Fees charged by probate judges and justices of the peace were regulated. It was stipulated that a minister or judge who performed a marriage ceremony was entitled to a fee of $1.10. Another law followed New England precedent by providing for the organization of townships within the counties. Wayne County officials in December, 1796 divided the county into four townships: St. Clair,

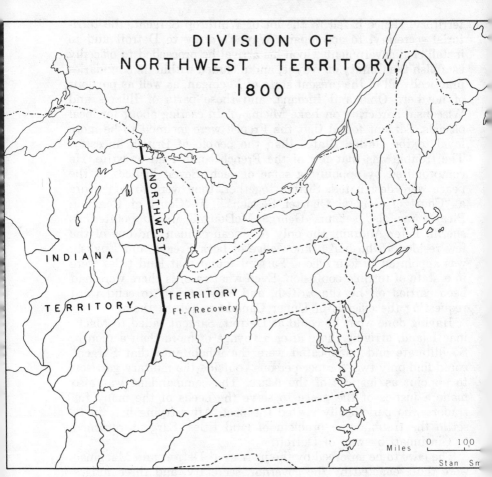

DIVISION OF
NORTHWEST TERRITORY,
1800

NORTHWEST

INDIANA

TERRITORY

TERRITORY
Ft. (Recovery)

Miles   0   100

Stan Sm

to the east, Hamtramck on the north, and Detroit and Sargent to the south. Constables, overseers of the poor, and highway inspectors were appointed for each township.[12]

Settlers pouring into the Ohio Valley, the area around Steubenville, and the Western Reserve swelled the population of the Northwest Territory by 1798 to well over 5,000 free adult males, the number required under the Ordinance of 1787 for the second stage of territorial development. Accordingly, Governor St. Clair ordered elections held for a house of representatives. At Detroit

[12] A careful distinction must be made between a "survey township," as provided under the Ordinance of 1785, which was always 6 miles square, and a "government township," which might be of any size.

this first American election was held in John Dodemead's tavern. It extended over three days: December 17, 18, and 19, 1798. Since each voter announced the candidate of his choice, it was known throughout the three days of balloting how each stood. James May, a former British subject, who was supported by the British residents, and Solomon Sibley, who was favored by the Americans and many of the French, were the two rival candidates. According to May, the defeated candidate, Sibley won because he passed out liquor to the voters and had soldiers armed with clubs who threatened to beat anyone who cast his vote for May. Early in January Sibley set out on horseback for Cincinnati to take his seat in the legislative body. Then word arrived in Detroit that the census returns entitled Wayne County to two additional representatives. At an election held on January 14 and 15, 1799 James May ran again and once more was defeated. The successful candidates were Jacob Visger and François Joncaire de Chabert. Neither the December nor the January election centered around partisan lines, since the new political party that was forming around Thomas Jefferson in opposition to the Federalists was still unorganized in Detroit.

Division of the Northwest Territory was now being debated. Governor St. Clair at first opposed this move, but when he recognized it was inevitable, proposed a division that would have placed the Western Reserve and Marietta, both solidly Federalist, into a single territory, and would have divided the remainder of the Old Northwest into two separate territories so as to delay statehood in the area that favored the Jeffersonian Democrats and to speed up statehood in an area that might be expected to vote Federalist. But Congress rejected St. Clair's proposal, and in 1800 decreed that the Northwest Territory should be divided by a line that closely approximated the present Ohio-Indiana line extended north to the Canadian border. This brought a large proportion of the settled areas within the eastern portion, with the result that Federalist strength in Marietta and the Western Reserve was offset by the Democratic preferences of Cincinnati, the Virginia Military Reserve, and other settlements where the New England element was less strong.

This first division of the Old Northwest was promoted in Congress by William Henry Harrison. Harrison had been chosen by the general assembly of the Northwest Territory as delegate to Congress in 1798. Though he had no vote, Harrison not only was influential in getting the territory decided in a manner favorable to the Democrats, but also succeeded in obtaining a revision of the land laws that made it possible to purchase government

land on the installment plan and provided for the opening of
land offices in the West. When the law dividing the territory was
passed Harrison was appointed governor of the new Territory of
Indiana, with its capital at Vincennes. St. Clair remained as governor of the Northwest Territory, the capital of which was moved
to Chillicothe so as to be closer to the center of population.

An important event in Michigan history occurred on January
18, 1802, when a bill for the incorporation of Detroit as a town
was approved by the general assembly of the Northwest Territory.
It provided for a five-member Board of Trustees, other town
officers, and annual meetings of the voters. The trustees were
authorized to take whatever action they deemed necessary for
the health and welfare of the inhabitants. Their first act was to
adopt a code of fire regulations consisting of seventeen articles
that were almost identical with a voluntary agreement adopted
four years earlier by 73 householders. Regular chimney-sweeping
and the provision of barrels, buckets, and ladders were required
of all those who owned buildings. All citizens were required to
turn out to fight fire. Between 1802 and 1805 the trustees levied
fines on several citizens having defective chimneys or otherwise
failing to observe the fire regulations. In spite of all these precautions the town was destined to be destroyed by fire in 1805.
The second ordinance passed by the trustees regulated trade in
the town. There was no holding with the economic doctrine of
laissez-faire, for several of the regulations were quite exacting.
Bakers, for instance, were required to sell a three-pound loaf of
bread for six pence, New York currency, and to stamp their
initials on each loaf. The town government was conducted on lines
of strict economy. During the fiscal year 1803-1804 the income
of the town government, derived chiefly from fines, amounted to
$137.25. After paying fees to officers and $15.00 to repair the fire
engine the town ended the year with a neat balance of $35.36!

Agitation for statehood now became lively in the eastern part
of the divided territory. St. Clair opposed it with vehemence and
finally became so obnoxious that he was removed from office. On
April 30, 1802 Congress passed an act enabling the people of
Ohio to write a constitution and form a state government. The
act for the first time definitely committed the federal government
to create more than three states out of the Old Northwest, for it
set the northern boundary of Ohio at a line drawn due east from
the southernmost extremity of Lake Michigan, as the Northwest
Ordinance had provided in case Congress decided to create more
than three states. Politics played a part in this decision. It was
believed in Washington that Detroit would vote Federalist. By

excluding it from the new state the Jeffersonian Democrats would have a better chance to carry Ohio. The western boundary of Ohio was also in accord with the Northwest Ordinance: a line drawn due north from the mouth of the Miami River. All the Old Northwest that remained when the state of Ohio was removed was made part of the Territory of Indiana. This, of course, included Michigan. The change was anything but popular in Detroit. The people had not been consulted about it. Vincennes was further away than Chillicothe. Because Indiana was still a territory of the first grade it had no elected legislature. The dissatisfaction led to the circulation of a petition asking that Wayne County be set up as a separate territory. Over 300 signatures were obtained.

Governor Harrison visited Detroit in company with one of the territorial judges in May, 1804. Little is known about his visit, but it is now definitely established that he came.[13] His appearance did nothing to halt the movement for a separate territory. Congress was at first unresponsive but, following receipt of a petition from the "Democratic-Republicans of Michigan," a more favorable attitude was taken. This petition declared it was the "unanimous opinion" of the people that "good order and prosperity" depended on the grant of a separate territorial government. The petitioners argued that the proximity of the British in Canada, the general lack of "patriotic attachment" to the United States, and the lack of a safe route of communication between Detroit and Vincennes all supported the plea. Congress passed an act approved by President Jefferson on January 11, 1805 setting off the Territory of Michigan, and taking effect June 30, 1805.

This act committed Congress to carve 5 states out of the Old Northwest. The western boundary of the new Territory of Michigan was established at a line drawn northward from the southern extremity of Lake Michigan through the lake to its northernmost point, from there due north to the international boundary. This line put the eastern tip of the present Upper Peninsula within Michigan. The southern boundary was to be that specified in the Northwest Ordinance: a line drawn due east through the southernmost extremity of Lake Michigan. The government of the Territory of Michigan was to be that set forth in the Northwest Ordinance for a Territory of the first grade.

MICHIGAN'S FIRST AMERICAN DECADE

No great changes had taken place since the British flag was hauled down in 1796. Few people had come to live in Michigan.

[13] F. C. Bald, *op. cit.*, p. 211.

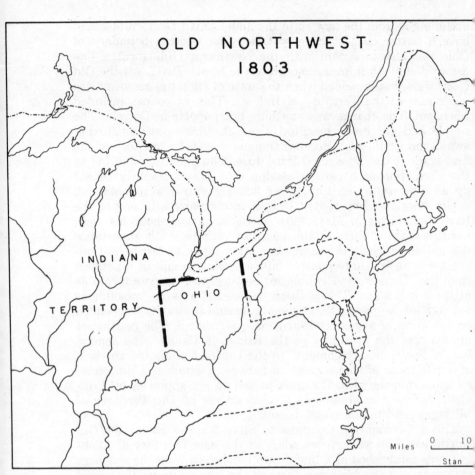

The region was remote from the Ohio River, which was the route of travel utilized by most settlers coming into the West. For New Englanders lands were available in western New York and in the Western Reserve in Ohio, much less remote than Michigan. Furthermore, the Indian title to lands in Michigan had been extinguished only in the areas around Detroit and Mackinac Island, and no government surveys had yet taken place. Hence little land was available for settlers.

The fur trade continued to remain, for the most part, in British hands. Fort Malden, on the Canadian side of the Detroit River, rapidly replaced Detroit as the nucleus of trade in the lower lakes region. Some Britishers in Detroit moved to the other side of the River. The fort continued to dominate the town. Colonel John Francis Hamtramck served as commandant until he was ordered by Secretary of War Henry Dearborn to establish a fort at the mouth of the Chicago River. The fort was duly built and named after Dearborn. Shortly afterward Hamtramck died suddenly, and his passing was deeply mourned in Detroit. A Michigan city today bears his name.

In June, 1798 Father Gabriel Richard, a Sulpician priest, arrived at Detroit to assist the resident pastor of Ste. Anne's Church, Father Levadoux. Driven from France by the excesses of the French Revolution, Richard was destined to become one of the most important forces for cultural and educational advancement in the early history of Michigan. The first Protestant missionary, the Reverend David Bacon, reached Detroit in 1800. Detroit had five doctors of medicine by 1805. There were a number of private schools, but no public schools. Although postal service had been extended to the town the mails were slow. Considering the distance from the East and the difficulties of transportation it is surprising to find that the people of Detroit were able to obtain almost every sort of merchandise that one could find in Boston or New York. A tannery provided leather for shoes, harness, and other goods, but most manufactured goods had to be imported. Coffee, tea, almonds, figs, and candy were among the many articles that could be bought.[14]

The fur trade continued to be the dominating motif of life on Mackinac Island. Although some Americans took part in the trade its management was almost wholly in the hands of Britishers. The fort, with its small garrison flying the American flag, was the only symbol of United States sovereignty over the region. There was a church, but no resident priest. Father Gabriel Richard paid a visit to Mackinac Island in 1799, and in his report to his superior lamented the fact that liquor was so prevalent and so generally used in trading with the Indians. Many Indians, he wrote, were drunk in the streets. He found a profound indifference to religion; former converts had even forgotten the sign of the cross. About a thousand traders come to the Island in the summer time, he reported. Richard also visited the Ottawa at L'Arbre Croche, finding about 1,300 living there. Only one out of this whole number had been baptized. The Catholic priest visited St. Joseph's Island, to which the British garrison had retired from Mackinac, and Sault Ste. Marie, at which place he found a number of Frenchmen living with Indian wives.[15]

---

[14] Bald, *op. cit.*
[15] G. Paré, *The Catholic Church in Detroit, 1701-1888,* pp. 283-85.

In spite of the fact that the conditions of life had not greatly changed during Michigan's first American decade, the groundwork had been laid for the development that was to come in later years. Between 1783 and 1805 the claims of the several states to lands in the Old Northwest had been ceded to the United States, and provisions had been made for the distribution of land and for government. The Indians had been pacified and the British had evacuated the Northwest posts. American authority had been established at Detroit and Mackinac. And Michigan, after being a part of the Northwest Territory, divided between that Territory and Indiana Territory, and then a part of Indiana Territory, had at last become a separate political unit as the Territory of Michigan. But before any great influx of settlers would occur, Michigan was to pass through another troubled period, during which the British flag once more flew over Detroit and Mackinac for a brief time.

THE NINETEENTH CENTURY

Michigan in 1796, when the United States took possession of it, was much the same as it had been a century and three-quarters earlier, when the first Europeans arrived. The face of the land had not been materially altered except in the immediate vicinity of a few forts and trading posts. The same native peoples inhabited the forests and traversed the lakes and rivers. Their economy had been affected by the white man's trade in peltry, and they had become dependent on the white man's goods. Otherwise the pattern of their lives was much the same as when the French first came.

During the next century, however, profound changes occurred. Large tracts of land were cleared and placed under cultivation. Forests were cut down and the wood was sawed into lumber. Mines were opened and exploited. These changes were wrought by a great surge of immigrants who came to make Michigan their home. The newcomers displaced a large portion of the Indian population. They laid out highways, constructed railroads, and built cities. They founded schools, colleges, churches, and other cultural institutions. Whereas the Indians had used Michigan's natural resources sparingly, the white men dug and slashed and burned with tragic wastefulness.

At the dawn of the nineteenth century Michigan had been under the American flag for only four years. It was part of the Northwest Territory of the United States, but in 1805 it was designated as a separate territory by Congress. After passing through the stages of development provided under the Northwest Ordinance it was admitted as a state into the federal union in 1837.

During this century Michigan men fought in four major wars, not to mention countless forays against the Indians. There were times of boom and times of depression. But through it all there was dynamic growth by every measure. The American pioneer who came to Michigan possessed boundless energy, ingenuity, and ambition. He was a rank individualist, yet he had the will and capacity to cooperate voluntarily with others to accomplish purposes beyond the strength of one individual. He had religious faith, but he was no mystic; his religion seemed to stimulate his determination to get ahead. He had boundless faith in the future: his own, his children's, his state's, and his country's. His hand, his mind, and his spirit transformed Michigan into a prosperous and confident American commonwealth.

MacArthur Lock at Sault Ste. Marie, Michigan

Detroit Harbor

7

MICHIGAN'S
FIRST TROUBLED DECADE, 1805-1815

Even before Michigan's first territorial officials arrived at Detroit, that town had burned to the ground. This disaster inaugurated a troubled decade for the new Territory. The governor, secretary, and judges appointed to govern Michigan quarreled among themselves and proved to be singularly inept. Relations with the Indians steadily deteriorated. Few people came to live in Michigan. Then in 1812 the United States declared war on Great Britain. Within a few weeks both Detroit and Mackinac Island had fallen to the British. Detroit was regained in 1813 by the Americans, but the British still occupied Mackinac Island at the close of the conflict. Again, however, the United States took advantage of conditions in Europe to sign a favorable peace treaty, and under the provisions of that treaty, Mackinac Island and the rest of Michigan once more was in American hands. After Detroit was recaptured in 1813 a new governor was appointed. This man, Lewis Cass, held that position for eighteen years and did much to promote Michigan.

THE MICHIGAN FUR TRADE

The fur trade, so important in the early periods of Michigan history, played a major role in the events leading up to the War of 1812. As has been noted in the preceding chapter, the trade in peltry remained largely in British hands even after the British withdrew their troops from Detroit and Mackinac in 1796. Both the United States government and American merchants made a determined effort, however, to break that hold. In 1795 Congress enacted legislation which during the next years inaugurated the government Indian "factory" system. Under this plan stores operated by agents of the United States government were to be opened at important trading centers in the West, where goods were to be sold at cost to the Indians in exchange for their furs. The purpose was to promote better relations with the Indians and to combat the British fur traders. Private trading was still permitted, but it was expected to slowly decline. A government "factory" was opened at Detroit in 1802 and placed in charge of Robert Munro, but it was abolished in 1805. A similar establishment was opened on Mackinac Island in 1808, and operated until the Island was captured by the British in 1812. It was not reestablished after the war, and in 1822 the entire system was abandoned.

Several reasons account for the failure of this system. Private traders roaming the woods could reach the Indians before the latter could get their furs to a government factory. Furthermore, the private traders sold rum to the Indians, while this was prohibited in the government factories. American-made goods, which were sold at the government factories, were higher in price and inferior in quality to the British goods. After the war the bitter opposition of private trading interests was primarily responsible for the decline and finally the abandonment of the system.[1]

The principal threat to British control of the fur trade was John Jacob Astor's American Fur Company, chartered by the state of New York in 1808. Prior to 1806 a company owned by British and Scottish merchants operating out of Montreal and called the North West Company, dominated the fur trade at Mackinac. In that year, however, a new company was formed named the Michilimackinac Company (or the Mackinac Company, as it was usually called). The organizers included several of the owners of the North West Company, and they proceeded at once to divide up the trade between the two companies. Practically all of Michigan fell within the area assigned to the Mackinac Company. When Astor, an immigrant from Germany who had engaged in the fur trade in New York, formed his American Fur Company and started trading at Mackinac, there was bitter rivalry with

[1] O. B. Peake, *A History of the United States Indian Factory System, 1795-1822.* Also on the fur trade, see I. A. Johnson, *The Michigan Fur Trade*; W. E. Stevens, "The Michigan Fur Trade," *Michigan History,* XXIX (1945), 489-505; M. M. Quaife (ed.), *The John Askin Papers.*

the British firm. However, in 1811 Astor made an arrangement with the North West and Mackinac companies under which the former was to confine its trade to Canada, and the latter was to conduct its trade on a joint account with Astor's American Fur Company. Mackinac Island was the headquarters of the joint operation. Thus by the time of the War of 1812 the great fur trading companies had made peace with each other.

For many years, however, the Americans had been irked by the prevalence of British traders on American soil. They traded not only at Mackinac, but also at several places in what is now Wisconsin, including Green Bay and Prairie du Chien. Zebulon Pike, who led an American expedition to explore the headwaters of the Mississippi River in 1805, found British traders everywhere in the northern woods who were not even aware they were on American soil. The Americans were convinced that the British were arming the Indians and constantly urging them to resist the settlement of the West. This was an important factor in building up the resentment that led to the declaration of war in 1812.

Astor was able to keep his property on Mackinac Island during the period of British occupation from 1812-1815, but his business there came practically to a standstill. The peace treaty signed in 1814 restored Mackinac Island to the United States. Then in 1816 Congress passed an act confining the fur trade within the United States to American citizens. This made it possible for Astor in the following year to buy out the properties of his Montreal rivals within the United States. Henceforth for seventeen years the American Fur Company enjoyed a near-monopoly on the Michigan fur trade.

FIASCO AT DETROIT

Michigan's first territorial governor was William Hull of Massachusetts. He was a graduate of Yale, a lawyer, and a veteran officer of the Revolution. Fifty-two years of age at the time of his appointment by President Thomas Jefferson, he was a Jeffersonian Democrat from the land of Federalism. He was a man of considerable ability, but was handicapped by a total lack of acquaintance with the life and problems of the frontier. Jefferson appointed as secretary of the territory Stanley Griswold, a former Connecticut minister who had been unpopular with his parishioners because of his fondness for Jefferson's ideas, which were commonly considered atheistic in New England. He proved himself in Michigan to be a contentious and opinionated man. The

most prominent of the three judges appointed to office in Michigan Territory was Augustus Elias Brevoort Woodward. Born in
New York, he had attended Columbia College but had not graduated. He had moved to Virginia when he was 21 years of age,
locating in Rockbridge County, where he "read for the law" and
began practice in 1799. He met Thomas Jefferson in Virginia, and
a close friendship grew up between the two men. Both were deeply
read in the classics and both were disciples of the 18th century
Enlightenment. They shared a fondness for devising elaborate
and often highly complicated plans for the betterment of mankind, although Jefferson was far more practical than his younger
friend. Broad generalizations based on rational theories, scientific
investigations, and systems for the classification of knowledge
were interests common to both men. Woodward moved to Washington when his idol became president in 1801, and there he
mingled with the best society. He was an intimate of the President during these years and it was natural that Jefferson should
offer him an opportunity for public service in the new Territory of
Michigan. Like Hull, young Woodward was profoundly ignorant
of conditions in a frontier area like Michigan. He was extremely
aggressive, very sensitive, and quite domineering in his attitudes.
A bachelor with slovenly personal habits, Woodward was endowed
with a fine mind. His grandiose projects appeared utterly impractical, but in his expansive visions of the future greatness of
the West, Woodward was in accord with frontier psychology.[2]

The other judges first appointed were Frederick Bates and
Samuel Huntington. Bates was the only one of the territorial
officials who had lived in Michigan prior to 1805. He had settled at
Detroit in 1797, had established a prosperous business, and had
been appointed as first postmaster of his adopted city in 1803.
He had read law and was an altogether admirable choice. The
other judge, Huntington, was chief justice of the Ohio supreme
court, and declined the appointment. So at first there were only
four territorial officials. John Griffin, a native of Virginia and one
of the judges of Indiana Territory, was appointed to be the third
judge in Michigan Territory in 1806. But he no sooner took
office than Bates resigned to accept appointment as secretary of
Louisiana Territory. So Michigan was left once more with only
four territorial officials. The two New Englanders—Hull and Griswold—were usually at odds with the two Virginians—Woodward
and Griffin. In 1808 James Witherell of Vermont was appointed

[2] F. B. Woodford, *Mr. Jefferson's Disciple: a Life of Justice Woodward*;
W. L. Jenks, "Augustus Elias Brevoort Woodward," *Michigan History*,
IX (1925), 515-546.

to take the place of Bates, giving the New Englanders a 3 to 2 advantage on the governing board.

Just before the arrival of the new territorial officials a fire that practically levelled the town of Detroit took place. On June 11, 1805 John Harvey, the town's baker, had—so the story goes—harnessed his pony to go to the mill for flour. A gale of wind, which was roaring up the river, caught sparks from his pipe and the still burning tobacco was blown into a pile of hay. In a moment the hay and the barn in which it was stored were ablaze. The pony with the cart attached, dashed from the barn while Harvey spread the alarm of fire. Soon men with buckets, poles, and other crude fire-fighting equipment were at hand, but despite all they could do the blaze spread from building to building, and soon the town was a mass of smoldering ruins. Only the fort and a few large buildings along the river belonging to the navy were left. Food was scarce and the country was scoured to supply the sufferers. Shelter was found in the fort, the naval buildings, and improvised tents and shacks. A supply of lumber was obtained from the region of present-day Port Huron, sawed by hand, and floated down the river to rebuild the town.[3]

Arriving shortly after the disaster, Hull and Woodward saw it would be wise to rebuild Detroit on a new plan, since the old town had been too compact and the streets too narrow, the broadest being no more than 20 feet wide. Before permitting the erection of permanent structures the two officials went to Washington, where they secured from the federal government a grant of 10,000 acres of land for the new town. The grant provided that each citizen over the age of seventeen was to receive a city lot of not less than 5,000 square feet, with the remainder of the land to be sold and the proceeds used to build a court house and a jail.

While in Washington Woodward secured the plan for the national capital that had been made by Pierre L'Enfant. Using this plan as a guide, Woodward laid out on paper his scheme for the new Detroit. A number of circular parks ("circuses") were to form the centers of municipal districts or wards. Radiating from these, as spokes from the hub of a wheel, were to be wide and spacious avenues and streets. The grand avenues were to be 200 feet wide, and at their intersections were to be located the grand circuses, 1,000 feet in diameter. Other main streets were to be 120 feet in width. An open "campus" (like the present Campus Martius in Detroit) would be laid out wherever the 120 foot streets intersected the grand avenues. Had Woodward's plan been

[3] G. Catlin, *The Story of Detroit,* ch. 23.

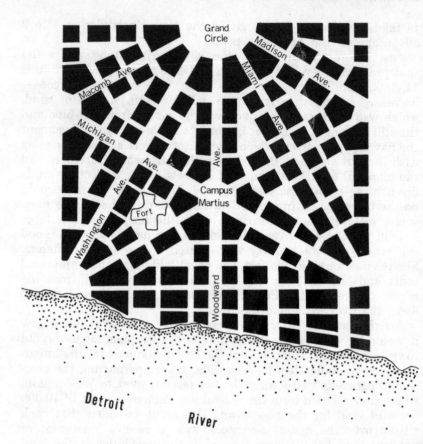

Judge Woodward's Map of Detroit

carried out it would have done much to solve the modern city's traffic problem. But Woodward was far ahead of his time. Only about 900 people lived in Detroit at this time and it seemed to them fantastic to have streets 120 or 200 feet wide. Possibly to get Hull's support the judge had the governor's brother Abijah draft the plan. It was adopted by the governing board in Detroit and forwarded to Washington for approval.

In spite of local opposition the reconstruction of Detroit was carried out in accordance with Woodward's plan. But several years later, while Woodward was in Washington on a visit in 1817, Judge Witherell joined with Lewis Cass, who had become territorial governor, to wreck Woodward's plan for what is now downtown Detroit. Some streets were narrowed to 66 feet and others were made to veer or were cut off in such a way as to avoid penetrating certain farms, among them that belonging to Cass. One of the streets was named "Witherell Avenue." In a letter of protest Woodward wrote "You have well named that main avenue as Witherell, for you have withered my beautiful plan of Detroit and have spoiled the beauty and symmetry of the city of Detroit for all time."[4] In later years the abandonment of Woodward's plan was to cost Detroit millions of dollars spent in widening streets.

In his administration of territorial affairs Hull seems to have disregarded the fact that a majority of the inhabitants were of French extraction and understood neither the customs nor the language of the Americans. The governor established American local government institutions and appointed justices of the peace and militia officers in the four districts into which Wayne County was then divided: Erie, Detroit, Huron, and Michilimackinac. The code of laws adopted by the governing board was largely the work of Judge Woodward and was called the Woodward Code. It consisted of 31 laws. The Ordinance of 1787 had specified that the laws enacted by the governor, secretary, and judges of a territory must be adapted from those of the original states, but much of Woodward's code was original. The laws were altogether too complicated and elaborate for a pioneer community. A detailed treatment of judicial procedures might have been a blank page so far as the French were concerned, and most of them could not read anyway. The code provided for taxes to be levied on each wheel of a pleasure vehicle, sleds, dogs, horses, and mules. License fees were required of innkeepers, ferry operators, retail merchants, and auctioneers.

The problem of land titles was a particularly troublesome one. Few French *habitants* had written deeds to their lands in the neighborhood of Detroit, and the fire of 1805 complicated and delayed the settlement of property rights inside the town. There was friction between the American newcomers and the French. The Americans complained of certain habits of the French, such as dumping dead animals in the river and racing live ones pell-mell down the streets of the town. A grand jury in 1806 complained of gambling, of "disorder and scandal" on Sunday, and of insults from the British across the river. The territorial officials responded by passing 26 more laws. One of these appropriated $20,000 for a new court house and jail, an amount regarded as

---

[4] For the complete text of Woodward's protest, see *Mich. Pioneer and Historical Colls.*, XII (1887), 473-483.

grossly extravagant by the people of Detroit, and another made the already elaborate judicial system still more complicated.

Included in the new laws was one that incorporated the Bank of Detroit. Hull had become interested in the plan of a group of Boston speculators to establish a fur-trading company and bank in the West. Woodward was enthused when he heard of it, too. He conjectured that somehow such an institution might lure the fur trade away from Fort Malden and back to Detroit. On September 15, 1806 the governing board of the territory granted a charter to the Bank of Detroit, and forwarded it to Washington for approval. Without waiting for congressional action the bank opened for business. Woodward was elected president. Capital stock was set by the charter at $100,000, with $19,000 paid in. Woodward bought one share, on which he made a down payment of $2.00. The charter had a life of 30 years, but this was not to Woodward's liking. He persuaded the governing board to extend the charter to 100 years and to increase the capitalization to $1,000,000. A structure commensurate with the ambitious plan for the bank was erected at a cost of $8,000 and equipped with impressive iron doors. But it turned out that the real purpose of the eastern manipulators was not to promote the fur trade in Michigan Territory. They quickly ran off $165,000 in notes on the Bank of Detroit, which the charter stipulated it might circulate as legal tender, and sold these notes in the East at discounts varying from 10% to 25%. After these were taken up $1,500,000 more in notes was printed. When these notes found their way back to Detroit and were presented for payment in gold or silver, it turned out that the bank had no means of making such payments. Congress, horrified by this skulduggery, vetoed the act of incorporation and the bank quickly passed out of existence. After careful investigation it was proved that neither Woodward nor Hull had any substantial financial interest in the Bank and that they had not profitted from its operation. But the episode gave Michigan a bad reputation in the East, and those who had invested their cash in the worthless scrip were not ready again for a long time to touch any investment related to Michigan.

Nothing illustrates Hull's poor judgment better than his provisions for a territorial militia. After making himself a major general of the militia he issued an order prescribing uniforms to be worn by the officers: dark blue coats, "long and faced with red, with a red cape, white buttons and lining, white under cloathes, and silver epaulettes." Their adornment was to be set off with cocked hats topped with black plumes, red tipped; red sashes, swords, pistols, and bearskin holsters. The riflemen were

required to wear "short green coats, turned up with buff, buff
capes, round hats, black cockades and green feathers; in the warm
season white vest and pantaloons with black gaiters; in the cold
season green pantaloons edged with buff."[5] There being no cloth
in Michigan to make such uniforms, Hull had quantities shipped
from the East for sale to the militiamen. It was rumored Hull
made a profit on the transactions. Most Detroiters could not
afford such outfits; some who wouldn't or couldn't buy them were
arrested and publicly flogged.

Woodward and Hull could never get along with each other.
As early as 1806 the former wrote a lengthy letter to the government in Washington condemning the acts of the territorial government. He tried to persuade officials not to reappoint Hull,
whose term was to expire in 1808. When criticism of the bank
scandal swirled up around him, Woodward left Detroit and retired to a farm on the River Raisin, which he named Monticello
in honor of his friend Jefferson. Here he sulked for more than a
year. While he was away the governing board, now controlled by
the New England faction, repealed the Woodward Code and
adopted 46 acts named the Witherell Code, drafted by Judge
Witherell. One of these acts authorized a road to be laid out
southward from Detroit to the foot of Maumee Rapids (where
Toledo stands today), a much needed improvement. The sum of
$6,000 to finance the work was to be raised by holding a lottery.
Some other laws in the Witherell Code were more in accord with
the needs of Michigan than the Woodward Code had been. The
familiar crimes of horse-stealing as well as forgery and counter-
feiting were made punishable by severe penalties.

In spite of complaints made against him, Hull was reappointed
in 1808, and Woodward, swallowing his chagrin, returned to Detroit. Hull also secured the dismissal of Griswold as secretary;
Griswold had been a critic of both Hull and Woodward. His successor as secretary was Reuben Atwater, a Vermonter and hence
a welcome ally for Hull. Nevertheless in 1810, while Witherell
was absent from the territory, Woodward persuaded the governing board to repeal the Witherell Code, and to re-enact the
Woodward Code.[6] This must have created even more confusion.
It is little wonder that one writer has called the regime of the

---

[5] B. Bond, *The Civilization of The Old Northwest*, pp. 234-35.

[6] Source material dealing with the early territorial period may be found
in C. Moore (ed.), "The Beginnings of Territorial Government in Michigan; Manuscripts in the Department of State, Washington, D. C.," *Mich.
Pioneer and Historical Colls.*, XXXI (1901), 510-612; VIII (1885), 548-
601; C. E. Carter (ed.), *Territorial Papers of the United States*, X.

governor and judges in Michigan Territory between 1805 and 1812 a "fiasco."[7]

While there is much to criticize in the government of Michigan from 1805 to 1812, it must be borne in mind that those in authority worked under extreme difficulties. Michigan was overrun with British traders who were openly hostile to the United States, and even many citizens of Detroit were only lukewarm in their loyalty. With only a tiny area cleared of Indian title, and with no government surveys there was no chance of the kind of vigorous growth that was being enjoyed at the time by Ohio and Indiana. Michigan was isolated from the rest of the country. Furthermore, Congress made no real effort to understand Michigan's problems and gave little aid. In spite of these difficulties the period was not barren of constructive accomplishments. Father Richard was proving to be an extremely useful citizen. He devised a plan for the education of Indian children, providing training in crafts as well as common-school education at a school he established at Springwells, below Detroit, in 1808. Richard succeeded in persuading the government in Washington to provide a modest subsidy for the school. He also brought a printing press to Michigan, the first product of which was a child's spelling book. And on August 31, 1809 there issued from Father Richard's press the first Michigan newspaper, *The Michigan Essay* or *Impartial Observer*. It is doubtful, however, that much interest was shown in the venture, because, so far as is known, only one issue was published. Several books came from the press.

Woodward, though impatient and often impractical, was an able judge. One case that he tried involved slavery. Most well-to-do Detroiters owned one or more Indian or Negro slaves; William Macomb at one time was the owner of 26 slaves. The case that came before Woodward, however, involved slaves that had been brought into Michigan from Canada; their owners, seeking to recover them, brought suit. Woodward denied their petition, averring that the Ordinance of 1787 had prohibited slavery, and that slaves could be held in Michigan only if they had been owned before the end of the British regime in 1796, or were fugitives from another American state. His decision was widely acclaimed throughout the northern states and was popular in Detroit, where antislavery sentiment partially involved the common man's jealousy of wealthy people who owned them.[8]

Governor Hull's outstanding achievement while governor of Michigan was a treaty he negotiated with the Ottawa, Chippewa,

[7] Bond, *op. cit.,* p. 207.
[8] F. Woodford, *op. cit.,* pp. 84-91.

Wyandot, and Potawatomi Indians. In 1806 and 1807 rumors of an Indian uprising reached Hull, and he called out the militia to strengthen the fort and to repel a possible attack. Instructions were sent to Hull from Washington to negotiate a treaty with the Indians as commissioner for the United States. A council of chiefs was called to meet at Brownstown, on the river below Detroit, and on November 7, 1807 a treaty was signed by Hull and the chieftains of the four Indian nations.[9] In return for a payment of $10,000 in goods and money and an annual payment of $2,400, the Indians ceded to the United States an area that included roughly the southeastern one-quarter of the Lower Peninsula. The Indians retained the right to hunt and fish on the lands. This was the first major cession of Indian lands in Michigan. Although there is no indication that there was any unusual difficulty in persuading the natives to make this cession, resentment against the United States government was building up, and was to constitute a major factor in bringing about war between the United States and Britain.

TECUMSEH, TIPPECANOE, AND THE WAR HAWKS

The Indians found an able leader in the person of Tecumseh, a chief of the Shawnee. His name meant "shooting star," and was bestowed upon him because a meteor streaked across the sky the night of his birth. He had a handsome face, a noble bearing, and a high degree of intelligence. Born in Ohio, he fell in love, it was told, with the daughter of James Galloway, a scholarly Pennsylvanian who lived in Chillicothe. She is said to have promised to marry him if the would desert his Indian life and adopt the white man's ways. After due consideration he refused to do so, for he had developed a bitter hatred toward the Americans. His oratory made him the idol of his people. He had a brother, a one-eyed mystic who became known as The Prophet, and who proclaimed with great fervor that if the Indians would revert to their primitive way of life and cease their dependence on the white man they could drive the latter from their hunting grounds. His influence was enormously enhanced by the performance of a miracle. Sometime earlier he had learned from a British trader that a total eclipse of the sun would take place on June 6, 1806. On that day he appeared wearing a dark robe, a crest of raven's wings in his hair, and a black scarf over his sightless eye. Pointing his finger at the sun, he ordered it to disappear, which

[9] The treaty is sometimes called the Treaty of Brownstown, sometimes the Treaty of Detroit.

Tecumseh

the sun obediently did. Later he called out to the Master of Life to lift the shadow from the face of the sun, and soon the sun shone again. The combination of a skilled warrior who was highly respected and intelligent with a brother who was regarded as a miracle worker had the effect of rallying not only the Shawnee but many other Indian nations to resist the United States.[10]

The Americans in the West were convinced that the rumblings among the Indians were the consequence of British intrigue. The extent to which this was true is difficult to estimate, but regardless of this factor there was substantial basis for Indian alarm and resistance. Year by year, through bribes, threats, doubletalk, and the covert use of liquor, the United States had gained title to more and more of the Indian lands. The most aggressive and effective United States agent in negotiating the treaties in which the natives gave up their lands was William Henry Harrison, governor of Indiana Teritory. Showing little sympathy or humaneness toward the Indians, Harrison would deal with whatever chiefs he could persuade to sign a treaty. Sometimes a parley would be called at the insistence of the Indians to protest against a cession made without the approval of all the Indians con-

[10] G. Tucker, *Tecumseh*, pp. 35-92.

cerned; on other occasions Harrison would take the initiative to assemble the chiefs to right an alleged wrong. The result never varied: more lands were surrendered. Governor Hull was simply following the pattern set by Harrison when he secured a vast tract of land in Michigan from the Indians in 1807. The squeeze on the Indian's hunting grounds was intensified by the movement of the Sioux into Wisconsin in search of peltry, forming a barrier to the expansion of the woodlands Indians in that direction.[11]

Beginning in 1806 Tecumseh bent all his effort to organize a confederation of Indian nations to resist the Americans. Although his attempt to enlist the Iroquois in his cause failed, he succeeded in uniting the northern Algonquin peoples. While he was in the South trying to persuade the natives of that region to rally to his cause, Harrison assembled a force and moved against the Indian settlement that was the center of the resistance movement: Prophetstown, at the confluence of the Tippecanoe and Wabash rivers, near the present Lafayette, Indiana. The Prophet, who was in command, had been instructed by his brother not to begin hostilities under any circumstances, but he unwisely disregarded this advice. Early on the morning of November 7 the Indians attacked. Harrison's men, whom the Prophet had proclaimed would be rendered helpless by his magic, successfully repelled the onslaught, losing 38 dead and 150 wounded. The Indian losses were about the same. Prophetstown was evacuated by the Indians and later burned by Harrison's men. Harrison's force outnumbered the Indians by almost three hundred. It was not a decisive victory by any means, but Harrison wrote the Secretary of War that the Indians had sustained the most severe defeat in the history of their relations with the whites, and this notion became enshrined in myth and legend. Twenty-nine years later Harrison was to win a campaign for the presidency of the United States as the hero of Tippecanoe.

Even though the idea that Harrison had won a great victory became generally accepted, it was clear that he had not solved the Indian problem. Depredations against American settlers increased rather than diminished. After Tippecanoe the belief became general in the West that the only way to eradicate the Indian menace was to drive the British out of Canada. Harrison reported that each of the Indians at Tippecanoe had received a gun, a scalping knife, a war club, and a tomahawk from the

[11] F. Cleaves, *Old Tippecanoe: William Henry Harrison and His Times*; D. B. Goebel, *William Henry Harrison*; J. A. Green, *William Henry Harrison: His Life and Times*.

British; that some of the guns were so new that the wrappings had not been removed. On the frontier the feeling was universal that British incitement was at the base of the Indian troubles. About a month after the battle of Tippecanoe a group of young men from the West and South who zealously advocated this view took their seats in Congress. Known as the War Hawks, they included Henry Clay of Kentucky, Felix Grundy of Tennessee, and John C. Calhoun of South Carolina. They were full of confidence that the United States could defeat the British; Clay declared that the Kentucky militia alone could win Canada. Their efforts won success when, on June 18, 1812, Congress declared war. The war resolution passed in the House of Representatives by a vote of 79 to 49, in the senate by 19 to 13. Congressmen from New England, New York, and New Jersey voted against war; the heavy vote in favor of war by western and southern congressmen was decisive.

For many years there had been a diplomatic conflict between Great Britain and the United States over the rights of neutrals on the high seas in time of war. The British had been engaged since 1793 in a war against France, except for one brief period of truce. Although the United States had disputes with France as well as with Britain over American rights to trade with belligerents, the controversy was more heated with Britain because of the greater sea power of the British. The War of 1812, which climaxed this hostility, was called the fight for a free sea by several generations of American historians.[12] There is some indication, in recent scholarly writings, of a return to the view that the war was caused basically by the dispute over neutral rights.[13] Beginning in 1911, however, historians began to stress the role of the south and the west in precipating the conflict. They pointed out that the very section of the country whose congressmen voted against war had the largest stake in shipping and maritime commerce. They cited the irrefutable evidence that in the decisive vote in congress, it was western and southern congressmen who led the forces favoring war.[14]

There is no doubt that resentment against the British, based on the conviction that they were principally responsible for

[12] R. D. Paine, *The Fight for a Free Sea*; H. Adams, *History of the United States During the Administrations of Jefferson and Madison*, vol. IX.

[13] R. Horsman, *The Causes of the War of 1812*; B. Perkins, *Prologue to War. England and the United States, 1805-1812*.

[14] J. Pratt, *The Expansionists of 1812*; W. H. Goodman, "The Causes of the War of 1812: A Synthesis of Changing Interpretations," *Mississippi Valley Historical Review*, XXVIII (1941).

Indian troubles, was a major cause of the western desire for war. But there were other components. Several writers assert that "land hunger," manifested in greed for Canadian lands, pushed the westerners to cry for war. They point out that the pioneers considered the ample prairie lands of the West unfit for settlement because they lacked timber and rivers with adequate supplies of water for running mills, and because they were remote from centers of communication.[15] Such writers neglect to recognize the enormous amounts of wooded lands still unsettled in Michigan and Wisconsin. They assert that the desire of southerners for Florida lands, which it was hoped might be secured through war, reinforced the western desire for Canadian lands. Whatever impact this feeling may have had, it was inseparable from the belief that the Spanish in Florida as well as the British in Canada must be eliminated in order to control the Indians. Another element may have been the economic distress that prevailed in the West for several years prior to 1812. Westerners were disposed to blame the British blockade and British interference with American shipping for the low prices they received for their grain.[16]

Ironically enough, the British government had decided prior to the date Congress declared war to remove the regulations it had imposed on neutral shipping, but this news had not yet reached Washington. Never did a nation enter a war with such supreme confidence in ultimate victory or such lack of organized military strength to win such a victory as did the United States in 1812. Actually the only hope for the American cause lay in the deep involvement of Britain in the long conflict with France and Napoleon Bonaparte. It appears to have caused no misgivings among Americans that in warring against Britain they were fighting on the side of aggression as personified by Bonaparte. In part this was because Bonaparte professed to champion liberty, equality, and fraternity—watchwords of the French Revolution, and principles consonant with those of the American Revolution.

1812: YEAR OF DISASTER

The year 1812 was a convulsive one both in the United States and abroad. While Napoleon was leading his troops on a fateful invasion of Russia, the United States and Great Britain again found themselves in the throes of a major war. For Michigan,

[15] L. M. Hacker, "Western Land Hunger and the War of 1812," *Mississippi Valley Historical Review*, X (1924).
[16] R. A. Billington, *Westward Expansion*, pp. 268-269.

however, that year is chiefly remembered for the loss to the British of its two major centers, Detroit and Mackinac Island.

Governor Hull, alarmed by the hostility of the Indians and the defenseless position of Detroit, had traveled to Washington in quest of assistance in October, 1811. He pleaded with the authorities to make some provision for the safety of Detroit. He warned them that Detroit could not be held by the Americans in a war if the British were in control of Lake Erie. At the nation's capital, however, all thoughts centered on the defense of the Altantic seabord and on various wild schemes for conquering Canada. In spite of his misgivings, Hull accepted appointment as commander of operations in the West, with the rank of brigadier general.

Three regiments of militia, commanded by Duncan MacArthur, James Findlay, and Lewis Cass were raised in Ohio. These troops, together with a regiment of regulars—a total force of some 1,200 —moved northward toward Detroit in the early summer of 1812. On June 26 Hull received a dispatch from the Secretary of War, William Eustis, dated June 18, but it failed to inform the commander that war had been declared that day. On June 30 after a hard march the army reached the mouth of the Maumee, still without word of the declaration of war. To ease the remainder of the journey Hull secured a small schooner on which baggage, camp supplies, entrenching tools, and hospital stores were placed. Contrary to Hull's orders there also was placed aboard the vessel a chest containing his military papers, muster rolls, and official correspondence. When this ship appeared under the guns of Fort Malden the British, aware that war had been declared, forced it to surrender, thus securing invaluable information on the size and strength of Hull's army. Hull had advised the ship's captain to pass Bois Blanc Island on the American side. But since the captain did not know war had been declared and hence felt no apprehension, he chose the less difficult channel on the Canadian side.

Not until July 2 did Hull learn that the fateful decision for war had been made. He received this information before his troops had reached Frenchtown (the site of the present city of Monroe), in a letter dated June 18, the same date as that which he had received six days earlier. Hull arrived at Detroit on July 5, where he found that Acting Governor Atwater had collected a small militia force, which, together with the 94 regulars stationed at Detroit, brought Hull's total force to about 1,800. On July 12, Hull invaded Canada. The troops crossed the river just below the foot of Belle Isle and landed without opposition. Hull issued a confident proclamation to the Canadian people, announcing that he had come to free them from British tyranny and that volunteers would be accepted. A few deserters from the British army and some civilians cast their lot with the American cause, but the proclamation had little effect on most Canadians. Hull treated the civilians in such a manner as to win their favor, doing the best he could to prevent looting by his troops. In his diary, John Askin, a British subject, praised Hull for protecting his property. Askin had four sons in the British service, but his wife and three sons were in Detroit, while a son-in-law was a member of the Michigan militia. Askin's divided family was typical of many in Canada at the time.

It was Hull's intention to attack Fort Malden, which at that time was not strongly held. Its defenders have been estimated at between 80 and 270 regulars, 300 to 600 militiamen, and perhaps as many Indians. Hull may have overestimated the strength of the fort. However, the British had three warships based at Amherstberg that could have raked a besieging force with their cannon. At a council of war Hull and his chief officers decided to delay the attack until gun carriages for the artillery could be brought across the river. In spite of Hull's efforts to hasten this operation, it was August 7 before the gun carriages were ready. Nine days before this Hull had received a message that had had the effect of raising grave doubt that he could carry out his objective or even hold Detroit. It told that Mackinac Island had fallen to the British and that a horde of Indians and Britishers would likely move southward to attack Detroit.[17]

The capture of Fort Mackinac less than a month after the declaration of war was largely due to the initiative and ability of Captain Charles Roberts, who was in command of the British forces on St. Joseph's Island, the British stronghold built after the surrender of Mackinac Island to the Americans in 1796. Roberts also had forces that had been raised by Robert Dickson and John Askin, Jr. in Wisconsin, in anticipation of a war. Curiously enough, the prompt notification Roberts received that a state of war existed was brought to him by an agent of John Jacob Astor, who sought to safeguard trade goods he had in storage on St. Joseph's Island before word reached the remote point through official channels. The messenger he selected, however, turned out to be a loyal British subject who promptly relayed the news to Captain Roberts. The latter at once began preparations to attack Fort Mackinac. He commandeered a schooner

[17] A. R. Gilpin, *The War of 1812 in the Old Northwest;* F. C. Hamil, *Michigan in the War of 1812.* For source materials see *Mich. Pioneer and Historical Colls.,* XV (1890), 1-210, and XL (1929), 242-740.

belonging to a British fur-trading company, helped himself to guns and supplies belonging to Astor's company, organized *voyageurs* to the number of about 150, and enlisted the help of John Johnston of the Soo and other traders. Roberts had less than fifty regulars, but his force was swelled by over three hundred Indians, impatient to attack Mackinac. Lieutenant Porter Hanks, the American commander at Fort Mackinac, had a force of 57 men. The war department in Washington was as dilatory in notifying him that war had been declared as it was in the case of Hull. Whereas Roberts had learned unofficially on July 1 and officially on July 8 of the state of war, Hanks had no word of it until he was called upon by the British to surrender.

For several days, however, Hanks had sensed a growing sullenness among the Indians who had come to Mackinac Island to trade. Suspecting something was afoot, he sent a resident of the Island who was also a militiaman—Michael Dousman—to St. Joseph's Island to investigate what was happening. Dousman, being a civilian, would arouse no suspicion, he thought. On his way, on the night of July 16-17, Dousman ran into the entire force Roberts had gathered, on its way to attack Fort Mackinac. He was taken prisoner, but was released when he promised that he would return to Mackinac Island and, without revealing the invasion force to Hanks, would warn the civilian inhabitants to seek safety in an abandoned distillery on the west side of the Island where they might escape the wrath of the war-drunk Indians. Roberts' force landed at 3 A.M. in a cove on the northwest shore of the Island, since then called British Landing. Roberts had brought with him two six-pound artillery pieces, and the strong *voyageurs* managed to drag one of these to the high ground that rises well over a hundred feet immediately back of the fort. Thirty years before, a British officer, sent to inspect the fort, which had just been constructed, pointed out that it would be at the mercy of artillery from this high ground. Hanks had made no attempt to safeguard the hill that rose in the rear of the fort, perhaps because he had so few men, or because he doubted that artillery could be landed from the north side of the Island on account of the shallow waters. The fort, constructed of eight-foot-thick stone walls on a high cliff, appears formidable from the harbor even today, and no doubt it gave the Indians of 1812 an impression of great strength. Actually, it was vulnerable not only because of the high ground to its rear, but because it had no well, leaving its defenders dependent for a water supply on sources outside the fort.

When Hanks learned of the strength of the attacking force,

and saw that the fort could be raked with artillery fire from above, he knew there was no chance for a successful defense. He also was warned that once an attack was launched the blood-thirsty Indians could not be restrained from murdering prisoners and civilians alike. Hence he decided to surrender without firing a shot. His force was allowed to march out of the fort with the honors of war, and was sent to Detroit under parole.[18]

While Fort Mackinac was being handed over to the British without resistance, General Hull was readying his attack on Fort Malden. Two expeditions sent into the interior had returned with arms, provisions, and supplies. On the day the British force set out for Mackinac Island (July 16) word came to Hull that a British force had crossed to the north side of the Canard River, about six miles above Fort Malden. Hull sent Lewis Cass with 300 men to investigate the rumor, but with orders not to attack. Cass disregarded these orders and drove the enemy from a bridge over the Canard. He was disgusted when Hull ordered him to withdraw because his force would be exposed to fire from a large British warship anchored in the Detroit River off the mouth of the Canard. Two British pickets were taken prisoner, both were wounded, and one died soon after. This was the first battle cas-ualty of the campaign and possibly of the war.

On July 28, after hearing of the fall of Fort Mackinac, Hull sent word to Captain Nathan Heald, in command at Fort Dear-born, located where the city of Chicago now stands, ordering him to withdraw to Fort Wayne in Indiana. Heald began the evacu-ation on the morning of August 15. A small group of friendly Miami Indians escorted the 54 regulars, 12 militiamen, 9 women, and 18 children as they set out on their journey. Heald had been warned by one of the fur traders, John Kinzie, not to leave the fort, but he disregarded the warning. After the party had pro-ceeded about a mile, it was attacked by a band of some 600 Pot-awatomi. The Miami quickly fled and over half the whites were killed before the rest surrendered. Two women and twelve children were tomahawked. Captain Heald and his wife survived, and were taken to Fort Mackinac as prisoners. Another survivor, James Van Horne, wrote an account of the massacre, which was published in 1817.[19]

About a week after the news of the fall of Fort Mackinac was brought to General Hull, he suffered an ominous setback. He had been requested to send a force to the Raisin River for the purpose of escorting 70 packhorses laden with flour, 300 cattle,

[18] E. O. Wood, *Historical Mackinac*, I, 284ff.; G. S. May, *War 1812*.
[19] W. M. Cunningham, *Land of Four Flags*, pp. 83-89.

and reinforcements of militiamen to Detroit. Captain Henry Brush, in command of this supply train, when he learned that his way was blocked by Tecumseh's Indians, sent to Hull for help. The latter picked Major Thomas Van Horne to lead 200 men by a back trail from the mouth of the Ecorse River through the site of present-day Ypsilanti to rescue Brush and his men and to bring the much-needed provisions to Detroit. The roundabout route was chosen so as to avoid Tecumseh's Indian force, reported to be at Brownstown. Leaving on the afternoon of August 4, Van Horne camped for the night at Ecorse, but the next morning failed

MICHIGAN DURING THE WAR OF 1812

to find the back trail. He proceeded instead along the river trail. Although two of his force were ambushed and killed by the Indians, Van Horne started to cross Brownstown Creek without sending scouts ahead. A sudden burst of gunfire came from the brush, and the militiamen fled in terror back to the Ecorse. Eighteen of Van Horne's force were killed and twelve were wounded. And the Indians captured Hull's dispatches to Washington telling that his position was precarious. These were taken promptly to the British at Fort Malden. The defeat of Van Horne took place just beyond the Indian village of Monguagon, now the city of Trenton.

After learning of Van Horne's defeat, Hull held a council of war, and it was decided to attack Fort Malden at once. A few hours later Hull learned that the British General Isaac Brock was on his way from Niagara with heavy reinforcements. This apparently caused him to abandon the plan to attack. On August 8 the main body of troops was moved back across the river to Detroit, leaving only a small garrison in a temporary fortification at Sandwich. The colonels of the Ohio militia again protested, but to no avail. Hull, then moved promptly to bring the convoy from the River Raisin to Detroit. He sent Lieutenant Colonel James Miller with 280 regulars and more than 300 militiamen down the road to Frenchtown. A British and Indian force was encountered at Monguagon, and after a lively fight the opposing force fled. Miller lost 20 killed and 60 wounded. He sent word to Hull asking for rations and boats to evacuate the wounded. Although these were sent, Miller made no move to advance to the Raisin, and on August 12 Hull ordered him to return to Detroit. Late on August 13 Hull sent out a picked force of 400 men under MacArthur and Cass in a final, desperate effort to join forces with Brush. Shortly afterward General Brock arrived at Fort Malden with heavy reinforcements. Preparing to take the offensive, Brock superseded Colonel Henry Procter in command.

Brock's arrival with additional manpower was made possible by the inactivity of General Henry Dearborn, in command on the Niagara frontier. Dearborn disregarded an order from the Secretary of War to make a diversion at Niagara and Kingston to keep the British forces tied down there. Instead on August 8 he entered into an armistice agreement with the British general in which Hull was not included. Brock was thus able to go to Fort Malden with reinforcements. He was a man of commanding presence, with a long and brilliant military record. He made a very favorable impression on Tecumseh and the other Indian chiefs.

On August 15 he called upon Hull to surrender, warning the American commander of the danger of an Indian massacre if there was resistance. At first, Hull refused, whereupon the town and the fort were bombarded by shore batteries and the guns of two ships. The Americans suffered several casualties. Lieutenant Porter Hanks, who had surrendered Fort Mackinac, was killed, as was Dr. James Reynolds. Dr. Hosea Blood was seriously wounded. The American batteries returned the fire, and the artillery duel lasted until ten in the evening. The next day British regulars joined the Indians who already had landed on the American side to assault Detroit. At this juncture Hull determined to surrender. In the absence of Cass and MacArthur he had only a few more than a thousand men to defend the fort. The threat of an Indian massacre of the civilian population was an important determinant in Hull's decision to give up Detroit, as it had been in that of Hanks to surrender Fort Mackinac.

Brush had been ordered to move his supply train on the inland trail to Godfroy's trading post (Ypsilanti), where it was to be met by MacArthur and Cass. Brush, however, refused to take the chance of running into an Indian ambush, and remained at Frenchtown. Failing to find Brush at the appointed place, the two Ohio militia colonels led their force back toward Detroit and camped for the night only three miles from the town. They made no move to go to Hull's assistance, as the British bombardment continued. This may have been due to the fact that both were involved in a plot to displace Hull, or to the fear that if they returned they would be surrendered. It is a moot point whether Hull's decision would have been different had they brought their men back to the fort. The terms of surrender included both the men under Cass and MacArthur and the detachment under Brush. The latter, however, refused to permit the British to seize his men and supplies, withdrawing southward. Cass and MacArthur brought in their men, but bitterly condemned Hull for the surrender. Militiamen were paroled and sent home, promising not to serve again in the war unless exchanged. Hull and the regulars were sent to Montreal as prisoners of war. Leaving Procter in command at Detroit, Brock returned to Niagara in time to take command of the British forces when the Americans attacked Queenstown Heights on October 13. Unfortunately for the British, this brilliant officer was killed during that attack.

Hull was paroled in the fall of 1812, and at once demanded a military inquiry into his conduct. A court martial opened in Albany, New York on January 3, 1814. Hull was accused of cowardice, neglect of duty, conduct unbecoming an officer, and treason. He was acquitted on the treason count, but convicted on the remaining charges and sentenced to be shot. The sentence was commuted, however, by President Madison in consideration of Hull's services during the Revolution. He retired to his home in Newton, Massachusetts, where he lived for the rest of his life. Shortly before his death in 1825, Lafayette, while on a visit to America, called on Hull and offered his condolences on the treatment his old comrade in arms had received.

That Hull was indecisive and that he was unsure of himself in a time of crisis cannot be denied. But from the distance of a century and a half, the decisions of the court martial and the sentence imposed upon him appear utterly unjustified. General Dearborn, whose failure to exert pressure on the British at Niagara had enabled Brock to reinforce Fort Malden and to take command there, was chairman of the courtmartial that tried Hull. Hull's own papers had been destroyed, and he was denied access to government records in his defense. Witnesses against him, which included Cass, MacArthur, Miller, and some of his other subordinate officers, were allowed to testify in each other's presence, an unusual procedure. The conduct of the trial leaves little doubt that the war department was bent on making Hull the scapegoat to bear the blame for its own failures and shortcomings as well as that of other commanders.[20]

For the American cause, the year 1812 closed ingloriously. Not only had the British captured Mackinac and Detroit, but they had also repulsed two attempts to invade Canada from Niagara and Lake Champlain. In Europe, as the year closed, Napoleon was in retreat from Russia, his campaign an ignominious failure, and his once great army half starved and half frozen. England, Napoleon's most dogged enemy, prepared to move in for the kill. For Britishers the war in American was strictly a sideshow, but it appeared at the close of 1812 that victory was assured. Fortunately for the Americans, most of Britain's might was to be concentrated during the next year on the defeat of Napoleon rather than on achieving victory over its former colonies in the new world.

1813: THE TIDE TURNS

William Henry Harrison was appointed Hull's successor in command of the American army in the Northwest, and he immedi-

[20] J. G. Van Deusen, "The Detroit Campaign of Gen. William Hull," *Michigan History,* XII (1928), 568-584; "Court Martial of Gen. William Hull," *ibid.,* 668-684.

ately began raising troops in Ohio to retake Detroit. In January, 1813 an advance detachment of Kentucky militiamen under General James Winchester had advanced as far as the rapids of the Maumee, a short distance from the present Toledo, Ohio. On January 17 Winchester sent Colonel William Lewis with almost seven hundred men over the ice of frozen Lake Erie to Frenchtown (Monroe), from whose inhabitants he had received an urgent appeal for protection against the threat to their lives and property by the Indians. Lewis found a force of British militia and Indians in the settlement and succeeded in driving them out and forcing them to retire to Fort Malden some 20 miles away. He then sent to Winchester for reinforcements. The latter arrived on January 20 with 300 more men, and made himself comfortable before the hearth of Colonel François Navarre, the principle citizen of the place. His men who encamped in an open field, were surprised early on the morning of January 22 by an attack of Britishers and Indians. Rushing to the battlefield, Winchester tried in vain to rally the panicky soldiers, only to be captured himself. However, the Kentuckians in the town fired with such deadly accuracy that the enemy retired. Colonel Procter then took a leaf out of Brock's book and warned Winchester that unless he surrendered his force in the town the Indians could not be restrained from murdering the prisoners that had been captured. On Procter's promise that his men would be safeguarded by the British from the Indian fury, Winchester agreed to surrender. The British commander then retired to Fort Malden with his troops and with the prisoners who could walk, fearing that he might be attacked by Harrison. The wounded who were left behind were put under the care of two army surgeons. Early the next morning some 200 Indians, crazed with liquor, roared into the town, murdered and scalped the prisoners, and set fire to the houses in which they were lodged.

This frightful affair aroused bitter hatred against Procter for what was considered purposeful neglect. Throughout the West the battlecry became "Remember the River Raisin." Even in Detroit Procter was so maligned and criticized that he declared martial law and arrested several prominent citizens, including Father Gabriel Richard. Judge Augustus B. Woodward, who had remained in the town after the British took possession, labored manfully to protect the lives and properties of American citizens from British reprisals and Indian fury. The battle of the River Raisin was the bloodiest battle ever fought on Michigan soil. Only about sixty survivors of the force of around a thousand men found their way back to the Maumee. The battle and its terrible aftermath marks the high point of British success in the Old Northwest.

The defeat and capture of Winchester threw Harrison on the defensive. A few miles above the present city of Toledo on the Maumee, Harrison built a fort named in honor of Governor Return J. Meigs of Ohio, where artillery, ammunition, food supplies and clothing for his army were collected. Flushed with his victory on the River Raisin, Procter led a force of about 2,500, over half of it consisting of Indians, in an assault on Fort Meigs on April 23, 1813. The attack was successfully withstood. After a siege that lasted until May 9, Procter retired to Detroit, disappointed that he had not won another easy victory. In July a second attempt to capture Fort Meigs also ended in failure. A clever ruse designed to draw the Americans out of the fort was tried by Tecumseh. He dressed some of his warriors as frontiersmen moving in to reinforce the fort and staged a sham battle between them and the Indians. A rainstorm, however, forced the Indian leader to halt the "battle" and the ruse failed. To salvage some prestige after his failure to take Fort Meigs, Procter attempted to capture a stockaded post near Lower Sandusky called Fort Stephenson. The American commander there was Major George Croghan, a 21-year-old Kentuckian. His garrison was small and his artillery was limited to a single six-pound cannon. Nevertheless he rejected a demand to surrender. In reply to a warning by the British that the Indians could not be restrained from slaughtering the entire garrison in the inevitable fall of the fort, Croghan replied, "When the fort shall be taken, there will be none to massacre. It will not be given up while a man is able to resist."[21] Harrison, who had his army in camp nearby, refused to come to Croghan's aid, believing Procter had an army larger than his own. But the heroic Kentuckian held out against the assaulting force. He lost only one man killed and seven wounded, while the attacking force lost fifty men and two officers.[22] Croghan was the hero of the hour, and Harrison joined in singing his praises.

Officials in Washington had become convinced after the fall of Detroit that Hull had been right when he had pressed for the construction of a fleet on Lake Erie, and that Detroit never could be held unless the United States dominated the water routes by which that place, as well as Fort Malden, were supplied. The construction of vessels had been started at Presque Isle, the present site of Erie, Pennsylvania, but it made little progress until the arrival of Lieutenant Oliver Hazard Perry in March, 1813.

[21] A. R. Gilpin, *The War of 1812 in the Old Northwest,* pp. 206-7.
[22] J. A. Caruso, *The Great Lakes Frontier,* pp. 282-284.

Using planks sawed from trees felled in neighboring forests, Perry soon had two brigs and three schooners completed. American successes on the Niagara frontier enabled Perry to get five other vessels to join his force. Armament had to be transported overland from Pittsburgh and Philadelphia. Still short of manpower, Perry's next problem was to get the two brigs he had built across a sandbar and out to sea. A British fleet under the command of Commodore Robert H. Barclay hovered offshore, ready to pounce on Perry once the opportunity presented itself. But on July 31 Barclay was compelled to sail back to Amherstberg to replenish his supplies, and Perry had his chance. Guns were removed from the two ships to lighten them. Then a flat-bottomed scow was run alongside one of the ships on each side, filled with water, and sunk. Strong timbers were laid across the scows and thrust through open gunports. The water was then pumped out of the scows, which rose under the timbers and lifted the ship out of the water so it could be floated across the sand-bar. The operation was repeated for the other brig, and the cannon were quickly remounted. Perry then put to sea and took his small fleet to Sandusky Bay.

Conferences with General Harrison followed. Harrison now had 7,000 men and was ready for an assault against the British in Detroit as soon as the British fleet could be defeated. Lieutenant Jesse D. Elliott arrived with 102 officers and men to help man the ships, and Harrison detailed about a hundred Kentucky riflemen, who had probably never seen a ship before, to serve in place of those on Perry's sick-list. But Commodore Barclay hesitated to leave the protection of the guns of Fort Malden until construction had been completed on a large new British naval vessel, the *Detroit*. It is probable that the need for food supplies at Malden, which could not be obtained so long as Perry remained vigilant, prompted Barclay to sail for Long Point, chief deposit base for supplies on the Detroit River. Perry saw his opportunity and at once took his fleet out into the lake to challenge Barclay. Perry had nine ships to Barclay's six, and had more guns. But the British outclassed the Americans in long-range guns. For this reason Perry instructed the officers in command of his ships to close in as rapidly as possible. He showed the men who were to fight the battle a blue flag, bearing in white letters the words "Don't give up the ship," the dying words of Captain James Lawrence, who had commanded the *Chesapeake*, an American naval vessel that had participated in a battle off Boston harbor earlier the same year. At 11:45 a.m. Perry hoisted his flag to the top of his flagship, the *Lawrence*, and the battle was on.

Well before Perry could reach the British with his guns they had started pounding his flagship with their long-range cannon. The *Lawrence* continued to approach Barclay's flagship, the *Detroit*, until the vessels were blasting at each other almost side by side. The *Detroit* was joined in the attack on the *Lawrence* by two smaller British vessels as well as by the *Queen Charlotte*, second largest of the British ships. Lieutenant Elliott, in command of the *Niagara*, Perry's second brig, instead of closing with the *Queen Charlotte* as he had been instructed by Perry to do, stood off and fired only his two long-range guns. The British ships attacking the *Lawrence* suffered severe damage. The *Queen Charlotte* lost both her commander and her second-in-command. Captain Barclay aboard the *Detroit* was severely wounded and his second-in-command was killed. The *Lawrence* was in even worse shape. Her rigging was shot to pieces, and by 2:30 p.m. every one of her guns had been knocked out of action. Of her 103-man crew, 83 had been killed or wounded. Perry, still unscathed, now made a daring decision. Hauling down his flag, he embarked in a rowboat and was transported through a hail of gunfire to the *Niagara*. Taking command of this vessel, he sent Elliott to bring the smaller American ships into action, then brought the *Niagara* into the thick of the battle. This vessel, so far virtually untouched, turned the tide. Although the *Lawrence* had struck her colors she had done such damage to the British ships that the *Niagara* and the smaller American vessels quickly finished them off. On orders from Barclay the entire British fleet surrendered. The British lost 41 killed and 94 wounded in the engagement; the American loss was 27 killed and 96 wounded. Perry then penned his famous message to Harrison: "We have met the enemy and they are ours, two ships, two brigs, one schooner and one sloop."[23]

The victory won by Perry opened the road to the capture of Detroit. Harrison transferred his main force to the Canadian side. Procter evacuated Fort Malden on September 24. Two days later the British forces were pulled out of Detroit after burning the public buildings. Procter retreated eastward toward the Thames River, hotly pursued by Harrison, whose progress was facilitated by an early frost that hardened the ground. Tecumseh, having lost faith in Procter, tried to halt Harrison's advance, but his Indian warriors were brushed aside. Forced to give battle, Procter chose a position on the north side of the Thames River. An impetuous charge by the Kentucky mounted regiment was completely successful. Procter fled eastward with a small number of mounted

[23] C. J. Dutton, *Oliver Hazard Perry.*

men, while his British army facing Harrison surrendered. Th
Indians under Tecumseh put up a harder fight, but when thei
great leader was killed the natives fled into a swamp, pursued b
Kentuckians seeking vengeance for the massacre of the Rive
Raisin. Procter, like Hull, was court-martialed. He was foun
guilty on several counts of poor leadership, was publicly repr:
manded, and suspended from rank and pay for six months.

Meanwhile Perry had arrived at Detroit on September 29 an
found it had been evacuated by the British. The same day Ger
eral Duncan Mac Arthur, in command of 700 men, occupied th
town. He declared an end to British martial law, and again place
Detroit under American civil government. Colonel Richard M
Johnson, commanding the mounted Kentuckians who were t
lead the charge that won the Battle of the Thames on Octobe
4, also arrived in Detroit on September 29. Johnson's mounte
regiment was part of a force of 3,500 Kentuckians that had bee
raised by the governor of that state, Isaac Shelby, and marche
to northern Ohio. The fort at Detroit, which had been called Fo:
Lernoult and later Fort Detroit by the British, was now rename
Fort Shelby in honor of the Kentucky governor.

Harrison, lacking the supplies and equipment for continuin
his invasion of Canada, led his forces back to Detroit, and th
Kentucky militiamen returned to their homes. Harrison an
Perry were now national heroes; bonfires and "illuminations
lighted many a western town in their honor; Congress vote
Harrison the thanks of his countrymen and a gold medal. Bu
it had been Perry's great victory that had opened the way fc
the defeat of the British at the Battle of the Thames and th
American reoccupation of Detroit. On October 19 Perry an
Harrison left for the Niagara frontier, leaving Colonel Lewis Ca:
in command at Detroit. Ten days later, President James Madiso
appointed Cass governor of Michigan territory, a position tha
he was to retain for 18 years.[24]

The recapture of Detroit by the Americans and the contr
of Lake Erie that they now enjoyed posed a serious problem fc
the British at Fort Mackinac. Captain Richard Bullock, who ha
succeeded the aging and ailing Roberts as commandant, had onl
a small force at his disposal. And a horde of western Indians wh
came to Mackinac in the summer of 1813 had exhausted his scar

[24] Harrison continued to be a public figure and was elected President
the United States in 1840; Perry died of yellow fever on the island
Trinidad only six years after he had won his famous victory. A beautif
monument to honor Perry and his men was erected in 1913 through sta
and federal appropriations at Put-in-Bay on the centennial of the battl

store of provisions. In mid-October a vessel belonging to the North West Company arrived, after barely escaping capture by the Americans in the St. Clair River. Harrison had planned to send an expedition north to take Fort Marckinac in the fall of 1813, but it was so late in the season before the expedition was ready that plans to send it were postponed. The British garrison at Fort Mackinac was in desperate straits that winter for food, in spite of the provisions that were bought from Islanders.

Thus ended the year 1813. The tide had turned in the West in favor of the American cause. But in the East, in spite of some successes, the picture was far less bright. Two days before the close of the year the British captured Fort Niagara. And in Europe the defeat of Napoleon seemed assured. When that was accomplished the British could be expected to make the American war something more than a side issue.

1814: Peace without victory

The United States had some dark days in 1814. The national capital was sacked and burned by the British. The eastern seacoast was terrorized by the British navy. New England, opposed to the war from the start, threatened to disrupt the Union. And in the West an American attempt to retake Fort Mackinac ended in failure while the British solidified their control of Wisconsin and the entire region north of Detroit.

British strategists recognized the vital importance of Fort Mackinac, and early in 1814 took decisive steps designed to hold onto it. They dispatched large quantities of flour, biscuits, pork, salt, rum, and armaments to Nottawasaga Bay in Georgian Bay, since American control of Lake Erie prevented them from sending supplies by the usual route. A regiment of 100 men under Lieutenant Colonel Robert McDouall, a Scotsman who was a veteran of eighteen years in the British army, was sent to the embarkation point. The reinforcements and supplies reached Mackinac Island in May, and McDouall superseded Bullock in command. The latter had already taken measures to strengthen Fort Mackinac, and during the winter and spring had also constructed a fort on the high ground in back to prevent the Americans from using the same tactics Captain Roberts had employed in 1812 to capture Fort Mackinac. The British position thus was much stronger by the summer of 1813 than it had been the preceding fall.

In June news reached McDouall that the Americans had captured Prairie du Chien, situated where the Wisconsin River joins the Mississippi. This was in the heart of an area long dominated by British traders. The attack had come from Missouri militiamen, under the command of Brigadier General William Clark, who had moved up the Mississippi from St. Louis some six hundred miles to occupy Prairie du Chien as a means of forestalling a possible attack on Illinois and Missouri from that direction. McDouall, when he heard what had happened, quickly organized a force of 75 whites and 136 Indians at Mackinac Island, placed them under the command of Major William McKay, and sent them to retake Prairie du Chien. The force was almost doubled by acquisitions at Green Bay and at other points along the old Fox-Wisconsin portage route, which it followed. Clark had foolishly assumed that sixty men could defend the fort, but after holding out three days they were compelled to surrender to the overwhelming strength of the attackers. McKay considered continuing southward to attack Illinois and Missouri, but the desertion of many of his Indian allies caused him to abandon the idea.[25]

News of the victory at Prairie du Chien reached Mackinac in July about the same time as the report that an American expedition was approaching. It had left Detroit on July 3. The naval commander was Captain Arthur Sinclair, and in his fleet were the *Lawrence*, the *Niagara*, and other smaller ships that had participated in the Battle of Lake Erie the preceding year. Also included among his ships was the *Caledonia*, a vessel used by Captain Roberts to transport his men and guns from St. Joseph's Island in 1812. The ship had been captured by the Americans late in 1812 and thus had the unique distinction of participating in both the British and America expeditions against Fort Mackinac. The troops aboard the vessels were under the command of Colonel George Croghan, the hero of Fort Stephenson, with Major Andrew Hunter Holmes as second-in-command. The operation was bungled and mismanaged from the beginning. Sinclair and Croghan had orders to destroy on their way north the British installations supposedly built at Matchadash Bay to supply Fort Mackinac, but after the ships arrived in Lake Huron it turned out that no one knew how to get there! Instead of moving against Mackinac Island the ships entered the St. Mary's River. The fort on St. Joseph's Island that the British had abandoned was burned. A party under Holmes then proceeded to the Soo, where it seized a ship belonging to the North West Company and goods that were the property of the trader John Johnston.

When the expedition finally got around to its major objective, that of taking Fort Mackinac, there seems to have been no thought given as to how to go about it, and this in spite of the

[25] J. W. Pratt, "Fur Trade Strategy and the American Left Flank in the War of 1812," *American Historical Review,* XL (1935), 246-274.

fact that former residents of the Island and soldiers who had served at the fort were aboard. A party sent to reconnoiter from Round Island was chased off by Indians from Mackinac. The next day it was found that the guns on the *Lawrence* and the *Niagara* could not be elevated sufficiently to hit the fort, high up on a cliff. After several days of hesitation, prolonged by bad weather, a landing was made about where the British had gone ashore in 1812. But this was no surprise. Every move of the Americans was watched. When the troops started to advance inland the Indians were lying in ambush. Major Holmes was killed in the fighting that ensued, and the Americans were forced to retreat and take to their ships.

The Americans had learned that the British were supplying Mackinac from Nottawasaga Bay, and on their way back to Detroit with the main fleet, Sinclair and Croghan attempted to destroy 'this base. Sailing up the Nottawasaga River for two miles, they destroyed a blockhouse and captured a schooner laden with supplies destined for Fort Mackinac. Two of the smaller vessels were left in the vicinity of Mackinac Island to keep the supply lines cut until winter set in. These were discovered by the British, and in a daring move, they managed to surprise and board each of the ships and capture them.

The capture of the *Scorpion* and the *Tigress* on September 3 and 5, 1814 brought to an end the fighting in the Great Lakes area. It was a crowning indignity to the American cause, and left the entire north part of the Great Lakes area under British domination. With Fort Mackinac and Prairie du Chien in their hands the Britishers were in complete control north of Detroit. It was an American victory won on Lake Champlain just a week after the capture of the *Tigress* that salvaged the American cause. Commodore Thomas Macdonough defeated a British fleet that was guarding and supplying a British invasion expedition, and thus brought about the failure of this ambitious British project. It was the turning point in the war, for when news of this victory reached Europe Great Britain recognized it could demand no spoils of war without making a further all-out effort. The Duke of Wellington, victor over Napoleon, turned down an offer to take command in Canada. Heavily in debt and tired of war, the British agreed to make peace on the basis of *status quo ante bellum*. Thus Mackinac Island, Prairie du Chien, and all the northern Great Lakes area was restored to the United States. The brilliant victory of Andrew Jackson in the Battle of New Orleans came after the peace had been signed. The Treaty of Ghent was

signed on Christmas Eve, 1814, while Jackson's victory was won
on January 8, 1815.

Once more Europe's distresses had spelled American successes.
Michigan territory was restored to the United State, not through
military victory but through shrewd negotiation and war weariness
in Britain. Mackinac Island was turned over to American forces
on July 18, 1815 and the British garrison withdrew to Drummond
Island. The exact location of the international boundary as defined
in the Treaty of 1783 had not been determined at that time, and
the British assumed that Drummond Island lay within their
territory. As has been noted earlier, the international boundary
commission determined later that Drummond Island should go to
the United States. The British occupied the Island from 1815 to
1828, and constructed a fort called Fort Collier. This was abandoned when the British withdrew, though traces of it may still
be seen on the Island.[26] On Mackinac Island the fort that the
British had constructed on the high ground back of Fort Mackinac and had christened Fort George was now renamed Fort
Holmes, in honor of the brave officer who had been killed in
the futile American assault of 1814. Lieutenant Colonel McDouall,
the commandant at Mackinac, wrote: "Our negotiators have been
egregiously duped, as usual; they have shown themselves profoundly ignorant of the concerns of this part of the Empire. I
am penetrated with grief at the restoration of this fine Island—
a Fortress built by nature for herself."[27]

A PEACE THAT PROVED LASTING

The United States did not achieve its objective of securing
British guarantees of the freedom of the seas in the War of 1812.
The Treaty of Ghent made no mention of this, and it was to remain a subject of contention during the years that followed. On
many occasions after 1815 the United States and Great Britain
were involved in disputes that seemed likely to result in war, but
in every case conflict was avoided and a peaceful method of settling these disputes was found. Today the longest unguarded international boundary in the world is that which separates Canada
and the United States. The first step toward bringing this about
was an executive agreement reached in 1817 between Britain
and the Monroe administration, called the Rush-Bagot Agreement.
It provided that neither country would maintain armed vessels

[26] See Chapter V.
[27] McDouall to Lieut. Bulger, *Wisconsin Historical Colls.,* XII, 143.

on the Great Lakes, except small craft for the regulation of commerce. This pact was not always observed to the letter in the years that followed, and land fortifications along the border were not only maintained but increased in the period immediately afterward. But it was the first step toward disarmament along the international boundary Along the 5,425-mile boundary line between Canadian and United States territory today there are more than eight thousand markers and monuments of various sorts, but not a single manned fortification. The last small garrison at Fort Mackinac was removed in 1894.

Charcoal kiln

8

EXIT THE FUR TRADER:
ENTER THE FARMER

For about fifteen years after the War of 1812 the fur trade enjoyed a brief period of boom in Michigan. It was dominated during this period by John Jacob Astor and his American Fur Company. After 1830 it declined rapidly, as trappers and traders transferred their activities further west. About the same time that the fur trade went into a decline, agricultural pioneers began to come into Michigan in large numbers. Between 1815 and 1830 much was accomplished under the leadership of Governor Lewis Cass to prepare the way for these pioneers. More lands were secured from the Indians. Government surveys were carried on that made the land available for sale. In New York, the Erie Canal was opened, facilitating access to Michigan. Many factors played a part in determining those parts of Michigan that were first settled: the quality of the soil, transportation facilities, the kind of timber on the land, and the distance from the place of entry, to mention a few. These first Michigan pioneers were largely of New England stock, and this fact had much to do with shaping the future development of the state and its institutions.

THE FUR TRADE BOOMS, THEN DWINDLES

For fully two centuries after Jean Nicolet first set foot on Michigan soil, men were attracted to this *peninsulam amoenam* by the lure of profit to be gained from the fur trade.[1] First the French, then the British, and finally the Americans came to engage in this business. The Treaty of Ghent radically altered the situation with respect to the fur trade, even though there were no territorial changes under its provisions, for there was no renewal in it of the right granted British citizens in the Jay Treaty to trade in United States territory. And in 1816 Congress passed an act confining the fur trade in American territory to United States citizens.

The period from 1800 to 1840 has been described as the "golden age" of the Michigan fur trade One author describes these four decades of Michigan history in these words:

> It was a period of systematic, wholesale exploitation of the furred creatures of her forests by factory, fur-trading company, and independent traders, without thought of reservation or preservation; a period when the dollar took the place of the beaver pelt, salaries the place of the credit system and the Yankee the place of the Briton; a period when her splendid forests and Indian hunting grounds were transformed into pastures and farms, her trading rendezvous became the sites of villages and thriving cities; when the trapper and hunter and savage gave way to the man with the axe, the hoe, the lumberman, the merchant, and the farmer.[2]

During this period the trade rose to its greatest heights, and then very rapidly declined, so that by 1840 it was no longer a major industry and employed relatively few men. The lumber industry, as we shall see, followed a similar pattern later.

As was related in the preceding chapter, John Jacob Astor had entered into an agreement with the Canadian fur-trading companies in 1811 to share the trade within the United States. During the war, Astor, as an American citizen, was of course under a severe handicap, for Mackinac was in British hands from 1812 until 1815. Promptly upon the cessation of hostilities he resumed his fur-trading activities at Mackinac. An act passed by Congress on April 29, 1816 forbade the granting of licenses to trade with the Indians or even to serve as clerks or boatmen to any but citizens of the United States, unless by express direction of the President of the United States. This placed Astor in a position

---

[1] The motto on the state seal of Michigan is *"Si quaeris peninsulam amoenam circumspice"* (If you seek a beautiful peninsula, look around you). It may be added that this motto is valid whether you happen to be in the Upper Peninsula or the Lower.

[2] I. A. Johnson, *The Michigan Fur Trade*, p. 102.

to squeeze his Canadian associates out of the American trade, which he promptly proceeded to do. Early in 1817 he purchased for an unrevealed amount the goods, buildings, and business of the South West Company, which was the name of the organization that he had formed jointly with the Canadians.

Astor then set about eliminating all his competitors. Through political influence at Washington he was able to persuade Congress in 1822 to abolish the government "factories" or trading houses. Thomas Hart Benton, a newly elected senator from Missouri, was retained as an attorney by the American Fur Company; it was he who led the fight against the government trading houses. While eliminating competition from this source, Astor also was ruthlessly destroying the independent traders. Through the intervention of Michigan Governor Lewis Cass, he secured exemptions from the prohibitions against the use of foreigners in the fur trade for the many traders, clerks, and boatmen in his employ who were Canadians, while making it extremely difficult for his competitors to obtain such exemptions. It was Astor's practice to select his best traders, send them to locations where they competed with independent traders, and authorize them to sell trade goods to the Indians at extremely low prices. By such means most of the independents were squeezed out of business and forced to become vassals of the American Fur Company. Where the independents combined into strong rival companies, Astor, instead of fighting them, would buy them out. Although some of the traders who worked for Astor traded at the risk of the American Fur Company, it was Astor's aim to put them all on a share-trading basis, which allowed them to share in any profit earned in their transactions, but also required them to share any loss. Trade goods were supplied by the Company at the highest market price, while the furs were bought from the traders at rates that allowed for possible declining values.[3]

In Washington Astor wielded enormous political influence. Not only was he able to secure the passage of legislation that would benefit his company, but he also had so much influence and power that he could have the laws administered in such a manner that they would serve his ends. If the laws got in his way he seemed to be able to evade or violate them with impunity. Lewis Cass, as governor of Michigan territory during the heyday of the American Fur Company, time and time again acted in such a manner as to serve Astor's interests. After the passage

[3] K. W. Porter, *John Jacob Astor, Businessman,* II, 686-852; J. V. Terrell, *urs by Astor,* pp. 243-389.

by Congress of the law of 1816 prohibiting foreigners from engaging in the fur trade but giving the President the power to grant exemptions, President Madison delegated this authority to Cass, as governor of Michigan territory and to the Indian agents of the United States at Mackinac, Green Bay, and Chicago. Cass, in a letter to the Indian agent at Mackinac, instructed him in veiled language to provide Astor's agent there with all the licenses he asked for, while granting only a small number to other traders. Perhaps Cass should not be blamed too much for this favoritism, since the War Department had instructed him to afford Astor's agents "every facility in your power consistent with the laws and regulations."[4] But this was only one of many ways in which Cass served Astor's interests. The unusual favors granted to Astor's company by Cass as governor of Michigan territory and later as secretary of war led many traders to assume that the American Fur Company was actually a quasi-official institution.

It has been claimed that Cass received a bribe of $35,000 to allow Astor's agents special privileges.[5] This claim is based on two newspaper accounts describing items in the account books of the American Fur Company, one published in 1892 by the New York *Press,* the other in 1909 by the New York *Times.* Both tell that an entry in these account books stated that Cass took about $35,000 of Astor's money from Montreal to a place in Michigan—one says Mackinac, the other Detroit. But a careful scrutiny of these account books about 1930 by Kenneth W. Porter, an able scholar, revealed no such entry, although in one account book Porter found a page had been torn out following the entry of May 12, 1817. The New York *Times* account gave May 13, 1817 as the date of the entry in question. Although it must be admitted that these circumstances are mysterious, if not suspicious, the fact remains there is no solid evidence that Cass took a bribe from Astor. Even the newspaper accounts, if taken at face value, do not prove Cass accepted a bribe, but only that he took the money from Montreal to Michigan for Astor. To assume that Cass accepted a bribe from Astor is not consonant with the character of this great statesman, although one must acknowledge that ethical standards in such matters were different in the early nineteenth century from what they are today. Senator Benton's reputation did not suffer because he accepted attorney's fees from Astor while serving Astor's interests in Congress, nor was Daniel Webster condemned for having accepted retainers

[4] Porter, *op. cit.,* II, 702.
[5] G. Myers, *History of the Great American Fortunes,* I, 130; A. D. H Smith, *John Jacob Astor,* pp. 201, 213.

from the Bank of the United States while fighting that institution's battles in Congress.[6]

Astor's principal agents at Mackinac during the height of the fur trade were Robert Stuart and Ramsay Crooks, both Scotsmen. Each received an annual salary of around $2,500, but they profited in other ways from the enterprise. At the lowest level of the economic scale were the boatmen, who were paid about $83.00 per year, out of which they had to buy their clothes and supply their personal wants, including tobacco. Astor squeezed the traders so hard that few of them made any money, and many incurred losses. One writer states: "That the business continued at all was apparently due to sheer inertia and the unfitness of the traders for any other form of occupation."[7] Although the enormous Astor fortune was derived largely from his investments in real estate, it is estimated that he cleared from the fur trade during the seventeen years he was head of the American Fur Company between one and two million dollars.[8]

The use of intoxicating liquor in the fur trade was the greatest evil connected with it, as far as the Indians were concerned. Having no conception of moderation, the Indians were debauched and degraded by the traders' fire-water. As early as 1802 Congress passed an act designed to prevent the use of liquor in the fur trade. A regulation imposed by the President in 1817, another congressional act in 1822, and still another in 1832 failed to eradicate this curse. In one way or another the various regulations were evaded or violated. In 1832 liquor in the amount of 8,776 gallons was delivered to Mackinac. The following year, in spite of a new and stringent law passed by Congress, 5,573 gallons were imported. There is evidence that Astor actually would have preferred to bar liquor from the trade. He was convinced the Indians would be more productive trappers were they denied strong drink. But he was forced to meet the competition of independent traders who, driven to desperation by the policies of his company, used liquor to attract the Indians to their trading posts. Astor also claimed he was compelled to use liquor in trading to meet the competition of the Hudson's Bay Company.

Although Astor maintained a trading post at Detroit, Mackinac

[6] A most thorough discussion of the claim that Cass took such a bribe is found in Porter, *op. cit.,* II, 723-725.

[7] R. G. Thwaites, "The Fur Trade in Wisconsin, 1812-1825," *Wisconsin Historical Colls.,* XX (1911), 66-79.

[8] This included both the "northern division" and the "western division" with headquarters at St. Louis, which was established in 1822. Porter, *op. cit.,* II, 823.

Island was the principal center of the Michigan fur trade in this era. In the fall traders set out in all directions, their boats filled with goods for trade with the Indians, such as blankets, beads, hats, traps, spears, hooks, and firearms. Most traders had several assistants, often including one or more Indians. Each was assigned to a trading post where he would remain for the winter, exchanging his goods for the peltry brought in by the Indians. In the spring the furs were put aboard craft called "Montreal barges," capable of carrying about eight tons in smooth water. They were propelled by oars or sails and when they reached the Great Lakes they clung to the shore. There were high jinks aplenty on Mackinac Island when these traders arrived one by one, received their remuneration, and sought release from the loneliness of a long winter in the woods. Dances and banquets were given, the merrymaking invariably continuing until daybreak. The man or group being honored would return the courtesy the following night. As many as 3,000 Indians sometimes camped along the beach, their wigwams often two or three rows deep. Woodsmen, clerks, voyageurs, and adventurers from many European countries met and mingled here. Their lives were rough and adventurous, punctuated by drunkenness, brawling, and not infrequent murders.

The American Fur Company had a barter room in which most of the buying and collecting was done.

> In these quarters the peltries were examined and paid for, after considerable haggling over price and quality with each individual seller. After the skins had been thoroughly dried, they were beaten, to expel dust and vermin, and then sorted, counted, and repacked in the warehouse for shipment. A hundred skilled men were employed during July and August to grade the pelts according to size, fineness of fur, and shades of color.[9]

At the height of its success the American Fur Company employed between two and three thousand boatmen and trappers and more than four hundred clerks on the Island. Four large white-frame buildings, situated on Market Street, were utilized by the company. Two of these survive, one has been restored, and the fourth has been torn down. Oldest of the four was the warehouse built in 1810 with hand-hewn beams. This building is now used as a community hall. The Agency House, built in 1817, was the home of Robert Stuart and Ramsay Crooks, the principal company agents, and lodged many clerks and traders as well at the height of the season. It is now a museum. The third building was called the

[9] *Michigan, a Guide to the Wolverine State*, p. 619.

Clerk's Quarters and was used to house clerks and warehousemen in the summer months. These three structures were linked together and made into a hotel in 1871. It operated as the John Jacob Astor House until 1929. In 1941 the unit was separated and restored to single buildings, as they originally had been. The Clerk's Quarters fell into decay and the structure was removed about 1960. A post office built in the same style as the other structures now stands on the site.

The fourth of the Astor buildings on Market Street, somewhat separated from the others, was the retail store After the decline of the fur trade it was completely altered, but in 1954 it was rebuilt in its original style. Along the same street is the old court house, built in 1839 and now used as a city hall, and the Biddle House, oldest house on the island and perhaps in the Old Northwest, now restored with the original structure still, in part, retained. All these buildings help make Market Street one of America's most historic thoroughfares. And the exclusion of automotive vehicles from the Island helps to create the illusion, as one walks or rides in horse-drawn carriage along the street, that he is making an excursion into the past.

Some of the traders at Mackinac had remarkable careers. One such was Gordon Saltonstall Hubbard, a Vermonter who was employed as a clerk on Mackinac Island in 1818. He was only sixteen years old at the time. He conducted a trading post on the Kalamazoo River and later was assigned to a post on the site of the present city of Chicago. After leaving the employ of Astor in 1827 he became a meat packer and merchant. At one time he was a member of the Illinois legislature. Before his death in 1886 he was interested in plans for a huge hotel on Mackinac Island, which later materialized as the Grand Hotel.[10] Rix Robinson, who conducted the fur trade for Astor's company on the Kalamazoo and Grand Rivers for many years, was well-educated and had partially completed his preparation for a legal career. His departure for the West is attributed by his biographers to "personal reasons." He came to Detroit and later to Mackinac as a sutler in the army. Here he met John Jacob Astor who, much impressed by the young man, employed him as a trader. He was first assigned to the Illinois country. Later he conducted the fur trade for Astor on the Kalamazoo River, then transferred to the Grand, where his trading

---

[10] Hubbard to H. G. Wells in a letter written in 1875, quoted by S. W. Durant, *History of Kalamazoo County,* pp. 82-83. Hubbard's *Autobiography,* dictated toward the close of his life, contains an excellent description of the fur trade. It was published in 1888 and has been reprinted in the Lakeside Classics series.

post was situated near the present township of Ada. He continued to make his home there for the rest of a long and useful life. He married an Indian woman to whom he was deeply devoted. He read widely, was active in political affairs as state senator for four terms and as a member of the Constitutional Convention of 1850, and came to be one of the most prominent and highly respected citizens of the state.[11]

Among the independent traders was Louis Campau, a native of Detroit, one of a large family of French-Canadians engaged in the fur trade. He was employed soon after the close of the War of 1812 by Detroit merchants to trade with the Indians in the Saginaw valley and was described as an intelligent, shrewd, farsighted operator. He helped negotiate the Treaty of Saginaw by which further lands were obtained from the Indians, befriended the first white settlers, and in 1822 plotted the "Town of Sagina." In 1826 he shifted his trading operations to the present site of Grand Rapids and is regarded as the first settler of that city. A square in the present city is named in his honor. In 1831 he purchased from the land office at White Pigeon a 72-acre tract that now lies in the heart of Grand Rapids.

John Jacob Astor sold his American Fur Company in 1834, possibly because of advancing age and ill health. The "northern division" was acquired by Ramsay Crooks, who continued fur trading on Mackinac Island for some years under the same company name. But in 1834 the fur business was definitely shifting westward, with St. Louis rather than Mackinac becoming the major center of the trade. The substitution of silk for beaver skins in the manufacture of high hats was decreasing the demand for furs at about the same time. The trapping of fur-bearing animals continued, however, on a somewhat smaller scale down to the present.

In dollar value the income from the sale of pelts in Michigan in the early 1960s was about twice the amount paid at Mackinac by the American Fur Company during its busiest year. The total value of the "ranch mink" pelts (pelts from mink raised in captivity) sold in Michigan in 1960 was $5,595,000. It is estimated that Astor bought $3,000,000 worth of pelts at Mackinac in 1822 —one of his best years. In addition to the income derived from the sale of ranch mink, Michiganians are paid a considerable sum each year for the pelts of wild animals. Licensed trappers in the 1961-62 trapping season realized $566,402 from the sale of pelts, according to the Department of Conservation. These included 309,000 muskrat, 13,600 mink, 11,500 raccoon, 3,700 opossum, 100

[11] G. H. White, "Sketch of the Life of Hon. Rix Robinson," *Mich. Pioneer and Historical Colls.*, XI (1888), 186-200.

badger, 2,560 skunk, 3,400 weasel, 923 otter, and 16,471 beaver. In addition to this, a total of $238,500 was realized from bounties paid for the pelts of predatory animals (34,255 red fox, 753 bobcats, and 3,638 coyotes), making a grand total for a single year of $6,399,902.

Around the same time that Mackinac Island was becoming a mecca for fur traders a Presbyterian mission was founded on the Island and a school was opened to train Indian youths to be teachers and interpreters in the mission work in the country's interior. This school, which was founded in 1823, was supported by missionary societies in the East, and was superintended by the Reverend William Ferry.[12] In 1825 a structure was raised known as the "Mission House," for use by the school and as a boarding house. This house later became a hotel. A second church, built in the New England style, was constructed in 1830 and still stands today as one of the oldest church structures in the Middle West. The Catholic parish, Ste. Anne's, dates back to 1695, when it was founded on the Lower Peninsula side of the Straits. An old log church was moved to the island in 1780; the present frame church, surmounted by a tower and spire, was built in 1874.

Mackinac Island became known very early for its healthful climate. By 1838 it was well-established as a summer resort, with visitors being turned away for lack of accommodations. Several hotels and boarding houses were erected within the next few decades. That part of the Island not privately owned became a national park in 1875. The Grand Hotel, with its extensive front porch—longest in the world—was opened to the public in 1887. Francis Stockbridge of Kalamazoo, a prominent lumberman and United States senator, was the leading figure in its construction, which was financed by railroad and steamship companies. The Grand became one of the nation's most fashionable summer hotels, with noted national and world figures as frequent guests. When the garrison at the fort was removed the national government transferred the fort and the Island (except for the privately owned property) to the state of Michigan. The legislature placed it under the supervision of the Mackinac Island State Park Commission.

During the time when the Island was the great mecca for fur traders an incident occurred that was to lead to one of the most famous and unusual research studies in medical history. On the morning of June 6, 1822 a young voyageur named Alexis St. Martin was accidentally shot while in the Astor retail store. The young

---

[12] While the Ferrys were on the Island a son was born to them, Thomas W. Ferry, later destined to be a United States Senator and a prominent citizen of Grand Haven.

man received the entire shotgun charge in his chest and upper abdomen at point-blank range. Dr. William Beaumont, the fort surgeon, was summoned, and arrived twenty minutes later. Beaumont, a native of Connecticut, had studied medicine in the manner then customary: by associating himself with a practicing physician. He was 36 years of age in 1822, and had been surgeon at the fort for two years. When he first saw St. Martin he described the patient's condition as "an appalling and hopeless case." Membrane and muscle the size of a man's hand had been blown off, the diaphragm and left lobe of the lung had been lacerated, and the stomach had been perforated. Beaumont thought the young man could not live 36 hours. In this he was wrong. With constant care and attention by Beaumont, St. Martin miraculously withstood the shock, and after fighting a violent fever for ten days he began to improve. By the fourth week his appetite became good and healing was well under way. Instead of falling back into the abdomen to its natural position, the protruded portion of the stomach adhered to the chest wall. By that means the orifice in the wounded stomach remained in contact with the external wound. By April, 1823 St. Martin was well enough to walk about and do light work. But he was not in a condition to support himself and he became a pauper. Local authorities proposed to escape the burden of supporting him by sending him in an open boat to Montreal. Beaumont, aware this would mean death for the young man, took St. Martin into his own family, which he had to support on his meager salary of $40 a month. It was not until 1825 that the idea crystallized in his mind that he had a unique opportunity to observe the processes of digestion. For, strange as it seems, the way the wound had healed permitted free access to the interior of the stomach without impairing its functions.

Thus began a series of experiments and observations which were to extend over a period of years. St. Martin became known as "the man with a window in his stomach." He was fed different types of foods by the doctor, who then observed exactly how digestion took place. The first report on his observations was published in 1826 in a magazine called the *Medical Recorder*. In 1833 Beaumont's *Experiments and Observations on the Gastric Juice and the Physiology of Digestion* was published as a 280-page book. This work is one of the classics of medical research, and with the passage of time it has assumed progressively greater importance. To honor Beaumont the Michigan Medical Society in 1954 restored the Astor retail store where St. Martin was wounded, and made it a depository for artifacts related to Beaumont's discoveries. Actually, St. Martin was moved from the store as soon as it was possible and taken to the fort hospital.

Beaumont was transferred from Mackinac Island in 1825, but managed to take St. Martin along so the experiments could be continued. At his own expense Dr. Beaumont maintained St. Martin until 1834. The latter on several occasions unceremoniously departed for Canada, where he had found a wife, and Beaumont had to foot the bill for his return. Dr. Beaumont petitioned Congress for a grant of $1,323.75 to compensate him for the time he had spent and the expense he had incurred in treating St. Martin, since he had made the experiments "for the benefit of the public and the advancement of science," but Congress turned him down. He resigned as army surgeon in 1839 and became a medical practitioner in St. Louis, Missouri. He was the recipient of many testimonials and honors for his work prior to his death in 1853. The man whose life he had saved survived him for 27 years. St. Martin died in 1880 and was buried in Quebec. He sired a huge family of children; the count recorded by historians varies from seventeen to twenty.[13]

OBSTACLES TO SETTLEMENT ARE REMOVED

It was not possible to obtain title to Michigan lands except those in the vicinity of the two principal settlements (Detroit and Mackinac) until 1818, when a government land office was opened in Detroit. There were "squatters," of course: pioneers who helped themselves to the land with the expectation of securing ownership when it was placed on the market. Often these squatters would band together to prevent others from obtaining lands that they had cleared and on which they had built homes when the land office made them available for purchase. Any prospective buyer who might try to bid higher than the minimum price was discouraged from doing so by the possibility that he might receive a coat of tar and feathers and a free ride on a rail. Pioneers agitated repeatedly for "pre-emption" rights, that is, the right for a settler to buy the land on which he had settled at the minimum price when it was offered for sale by the government. Congress occasionally passed special acts of this character, but it was not until 1841 that a general pre-emption law was enacted. At best the pioneer took a risk when he invested his time and labor on the improvement of land that was not his property.

[13] H. B. Selleck, *Beaumont and the "Mackinac Island Miracle,"* C. B. Burr (ed. and comp.), *Medical History of Michigan, I,* 165-180. Dr. Beaumont's famous book was reproduced in facsimile in 1941 and recently has been made available in a paperback edition.

The first step toward settlement was to persuade the Indian nations to relinquish their claims. As has been indicated in Chapter I, the United States recognized that the Indians owned the land. Treaties were negotiated with the several Indian nations under which, in return for goods and money, they would transfer ownership of tracts of land within specified boundaries to the United States. The first Michigan lands had been obtained from the Indians by the Treaty of Greenville (1795), and a much larger tract had been secured by the Treaty of Detroit (1807). The next cession was a small area along the Ohio border just to the west of the portion of land described in the Cession of 1807. This was obtained in 1817. Two years later by the Treaty of Saginaw another immense tract lying to the north and west of that which had been obtained in 1807 was ceded. Thereafter, through a series of treaties the Indian title was gradually relinquished. By the time Michigan was admitted to the Union in 1837 only the western part of the Upper Peninsula and a few tracts called "reservations" had not been obtained, and the United States had adopted the policy of moving the tribesmen to lands west of the Mississippi. The final major cession was made by the Treaty of La Pointe in 1842.

The story of the Treaty of Saginaw may perhaps be taken as typical of the manner in which these Indian land cessions were secured. The incentive for the treaty came from individuals who had visited the Saginaw Valley, believed the area had a great future, and hence were ambitious to secure lands for settlement or speculation. They made their desires known in Washington and the government responded by instructing Governor Cass to act as a United States Commissioner, directing that he negotiate with the Indians for the Saginaw Valley tract, and providing him with $10,000 to defray the costs. Pursuant to these instructions Cass sent word for the Ottawa and Chippewa to meet with him near the junction of the rivers flowing into the Saginaw. The date set was in the full of the moon in September, a time when the Indians had gathered their harvests but before they had set out on winter hunting. Two ships were loaded in Detroit with provisions and liquor for distribution at the proper time, and a company of soldiers was put aboard to protect the negotiators. Louis Campau was instructed to build a council house; this consisted of a roof of boughs supported by trees, the sides and ends left open, and in the middle a long platform with rustic benches for Cass and the other officials. Cass arrived on September 10 with a staff of assistants and interpreters. Preliminaries lasted for about two weeks, during which time Indians whose numbers were estimated between 1,500 and 4,000 assembled. Cass led things off with a lengthy speech, with necessary pauses for translation by interpreters. In his remarks he made known the extent of the lands that he desired to purchase. Indian orators replied at length, and meanwhile the Indians pondered the question of whether they would cede their lands.

The tract Cass proposed to buy from the Indians consisted of some six million acres. The Indians would receive a lump sum of $3,000 in cash, and an annual payment of $1,000 plus "whatever additional sum the Government of the United States might think they ought to receive, in such manner as would be most useful to them." This flexible provision was rather unusual, and apparently was inserted by Cass. He justified it in a letter to Secretary of War John C. Calhoun as a measure of justice to the Indians, intimating that he was uncertain just how much should be paid for the lands.[14] The government also agreed to furnish the Indians with the services of a blacksmith, and to supply them with farming implements, as well as teachers to instruct them in agriculture. Calhoun had suggested to Cass that he endeavor to persuade the Indians to migrate further west, but the governor quickly perceived that they were in no mood to entertain such as a proposal, so he dropped it. Reservations for the various bands were provided in the treaty, so the Indians could still live in the area. Cass sensed that even with these inducements the natives were not disposed to agree to the treaty. It was discovered by his assistants that a trapper named Jacob Smith, who had lived among the Indians for many years and had won their friendship and trust, was using his influence against the proposed treaty. They suspected that he might have his price, and this proved to be the case. Eleven sections of land (640 acres each) were set aside for Smith and his friends, after which the chiefs appeared much more favorable.

On the table of the council room the $3,000 in silver coin was stacked. Louis Campau, however, claimed that the Indians owed him $1,500 of the money for goods advanced and proposed to take half the silver to fulfill that debt. This was vastly disappointing to Smith and two other traders who were present with goods to sell the Indians when the latter were paid. They urged the chiefs to take all the money, without deducting what they owed Campau, and the chiefs so demanded. Campau was furious, attacked one of the other traders, and the two had to be pulled apart. The treaty was then signed. To celebrate the occasion, Cass authorized five barrels of whiskey to be opened and the contents distributed among the natives with dippers. Campau now had his

[14] F. B. Woodford, *Lewis Cass, the Last Jeffersonian*, p. 125.

revenge. He opened ten barrels of his own whisky and began passing it out. The Indians became roaring drunk, of course, and their violence alarmed Cass. "Louis! Louis!" he cried, "Stop the liquor." Campau replied "General, you commenced it; you let Smith plunder me and rob me." But after another plea Campau restrained the Indians and got them back to their wigwams, saying, "I lost my money; I lost my fight; I lost my liquor; but I got good satisfaction."[15]

As the Indians lost more and more of their lands through treaties, there was bound to be a certain amount of resentment. To safeguard the frontier against possible Indian troubles and to protect the settlers as they came in, the United States built and garrisoned several additional forts in the Old Northwest after 1815. Fort Gratiot, named for its first commandant, Captain Charles Gratiot, was built at the site of Port Huron in 1816. Fort Saginaw was established in 1822 at the site of the present city of Saginaw, and in the same year Fort Brady (named for its first commandant, Captain Hugh Brady) was constructed at Sault Ste. Marie. Fort Dearborn at Chicago and Fort Howard at Green Bay, Wisconsin, along with Fort Shelby at Detroit and Fort Mackinac helped to overawe the Michigan Indians. As has been noted in Chapter I, there was little trouble with the Indians when settlers began coming to Michigan after 1815. The one remaining conflict with the natives in the Old Northwest, the Black Hawk War of 1832, hardly deserves to be called a war at all, for it consisted in the pursuit, defeat, and virtual annihilation of about five hundred Sauk and Fox warriors and as many of their women and children by a force of regulars and militia on the banks of the Mississippi in what is now Wisconsin, but what was then part of Michigan territory. Nevertheless, it created great alarm on the frontier for a short time.

With the Indian title virtually extinguished and the frontier protected from any Indian uprising, the next step toward settlement was the survey of the lands. None of the government lands in Michigan acquired by Hull in 1807 were surveyed until after the War of 1812. The government surveyors began their work in 1815. Their first task was to establish accurately the location of the base line and the prime meridian. The surveys then began where the two lines intersected. By 1825 most of the southern third of the Lower Peninsula had been surveyed. This was the area first settled, and surveys north proceeded slowly from 1825

[15] E. S. Williams, "The Treaty of Saginaw in the Year 1819," *Mich. Pioneer and Historical Colls.*, VII (1886), 262-270; see 140-144.

to 1835 as the government concentrated on road building. Between 1835 and 1840 the survey of the Lower Peninsula was virtually completed and a start was made on the eastern side of the Upper Peninsula. In 1851 the surveys of the entire state were completed, except for some necessary resurveys of some of the inland lakes, rivers, and islands. The surveys were conducted by individuals under contract with the Surveyor General of the United States. The land was marked off into one-mile-square sections and into townships six miles square, in accordance with the provisions in the Ordinance of 1785. A hardwood stake was driven into the ground at each section corner, with about a foot length of the stake being left above ground. Nearby trees were deeply notched and marked to identify the location of these stakes. Individuals examining lands with the thought of purchasing them could thus locate sections indicated on the maps provided in the land offices.

The task of the surveyor was to run a line exactly straight in a given direction and to measure that line in units of one mile. He required two chainmen to measure the line and an axeman to clear the line of brush and to mark corners. The surveyor worked with a compass set on a tripod. William A. Burt, one of the government surveyors in Michigan, invented the solar compass in 1835, although it did not come into general use until after 1840. Burt also is credited with the discovery of iron in Michigan's Upper Peninsula, his attention having been attracted by the strange behavior of the magnetic needle on his compass.[16] Surveyors were required to mark all trees along the line and to carefully record the crossing of streams, ravines, and hills, the character of the soil, timber, and minerals, and a description of each township that they surveyed. The surveyor was paid by the mile of line surveyed, the rate varying from $2 to $6.50 at various periods. Working eight months a year, living in the open, and providing his own food, a surveyor might earn as much as $3,000 out of which his assistants had to be paid.[17]

The survey of the public land had progressed sufficiently by 1818 so that a government land office was opened in Detroit. The most desirable sites were sold first at auction. The minimum price, payable in four annual installments, was $2.00 an acre at first, but Congress reduced it in 1820 to $1.25 per acre payable in

[16] A. S. Brown, "William Austin Burt: Michigan's Master Surveyor," *Papers of the Michigan Academy of Science, Arts, and Letters,* XLVII (1961), 263-275.
[17] K. Jamison, "The Survey of the Public Lands in Michigan," *Michigan History,* XLII (1958), 197-214.

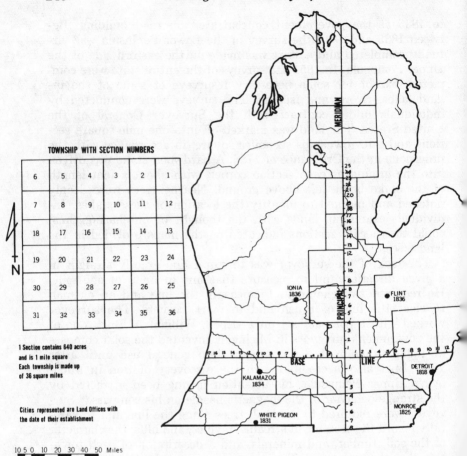

TOWNSHIP WITH SECTION NUMBERS

6	5	4	3	2	1
7	8	9	10	11	12
18	17	16	15	14	13
19	20	21	22	23	24
30	29	28	27	26	25
31	32	33	34	35	36

1 Section contains 640 acres
and is 1 mile square
Each township is made up
of 36 square miles

Cities represented are Land Offices with
the date of their establishment

10 5 0 10 20 30 40 50 Miles

EARLY LAND OFFICES AND SURVEY
INFORMATION

cash. At the same time the minimum amount of land that could be bought was reduced from 160 to 80 acres. Thus for $100. a settler could buy an 80-acre farm. Another land office was opened at Monroe, in 1825, and a third at White Pigeon in 1831. The latter, however, was moved to Kalamazoo in 1834. Two additional offices were opened in 1836, one at Ionia and the other at Flint. Each land office was assigned a given segment of public lands.

At the land offices the prospective buyer could obtain maps showing the sections available, with the letter "S" marked on those sections or parts of sections that had been sold. It also was possible to obtain the surveyor's notes so as to get a general idea of the quality of the land. Almost invariably the buyer or someone representing him would proceed on foot or on horseback to look over the lands available, using maps and a compass to guide him. He then returned to the land office, and "entered" the lands he wished to buy. He paid for them in silver, gold, bank notes, or drafts and was given a receipt. A record of the sale was then sent to Washington and after some delay (often a year or more) he would receive a "patent," signed by the President of the United States giving him title to the land he had purchased. When a given area was first put on the market the law required that bids be taken. On rare occasions speculators attempted to bid up the price of desirable plots, but they incurred the wrath of settlers if they did so, and few of them made the venture. During the 25 years the land office in Kalamazoo was open the average price received by the government was $1.28 per acre—just three cents above the minimum.[18]

Even though Michigan lands had been cleared of Indian title, surveyed, and made available for purchase at the government land office by 1818, the amount sold at first was small. It was necessary to clear other obstacles before the great land boom in Michigan could begin. There had been adverse reports concerning the quality of Michigan and there were doubts concerning health conditions. In 1814, for example—General Duncan MacArthur, who was stationed at Detroit, wrote William Woodbridge, who was considering whether to accept an appointment as secretary of the territory, "I have no hesitation to say that it would be to the advantage of Government to remove every inhabitant of the Territory, pay for the improvements, and reduce them to ashes, leaving nothing but the Garrison posts. From my observation, the Territory appears to be not worth defending, and merely a den for Indians and traitors. The banks of the Detroit River are handsome, but nine-tenths of the land in the Territory is unfit for cultivation."[19] Another disparaging report on Michigan came from Edward Tiffin, Surveyor General of the United States. Congress had enacted a law which provided that 2,000,000 acres of land were to be awarded to veterans of the War of 1812, and Tiffin sent surveyors north from Defiance, Ohio into

[18] Kalamazoo *Gazette,* June 16, 1929. For a first-hand account of the process by which an investor selected and purchased lands in Michigan in 1836, see J. M. Gordon, "Michigan Journal, 1836," *Michigan History,* XLIII (1959), 10-42, 129-149, 257-293, and 433-478.

[19] Quoted by F. C. Bald, *Michigan in Four Centuries,* p. 144.

the southeastern part of the Territory of Michigan in 1815 to see whether the land was suitable. Their report to Tiffin was unfavorable, and the latter, in turn, reported that Michigan apparently consisted of swamps, lakes, and poor, sandy soil not worth the cost of surveying. He declared that in his opinion not more than one acre in a hundred, or perhaps a thousand, would admit of cultivation. Congress, as a result, designated land in Illinois and Missouri for the veterans.

As the surveys continued it was discovered that Tiffin was wrong. Just how much damage Tiffin's report did to the reputation of Michigan is a moot point. Most historians have assumed that it was influential in slowing settlement. But it is possible that the influence of Tiffin's report has been exaggerated. In a paper read before the Historical Society of Michigan in 1961 Professor Madison Kuhn, on the basis of extensive research, expressed the opinion that Tiffin's report was not widely publicized or widely read, and that other much more favorable reports were more generally circulated. The Detroit *Gazette*, a newspaper that began publication on July 25, 1817, carried many favorable articles concerning the character of Michigan, rebutting derogatory opinions concerning it. These articles were widely copied in eastern newspapers. Three visitors to Detroit in 1818, one an authority on agriculture, gave glowing accounts of Michigan lands in books and articles printed in the East.[20] Geography books of the time generally lauded the potential of Michigan for agriculture.

However the prospective pioneer may have appraised these conflicting accounts of the quality of Michigan lands, he probably was discouraged about migrating to Michigan by rumors that the climate of the Detroit area was unhealthy. Hundreds of soldiers had died of disease at Detroit during the fall and winter of 1813. The most common ailment was malaria, which the people of the time attributed to the prevalence of swamps and bogs in Michigan. In 1823 "intermittent fever" and typhoid fever took such a toll among the garrison at Fort Saginaw that the post had to be abandoned.[21] In the East the warning about unhealthful conditions in Michigan was put into rhyme:

> Don't go to Michigan, that land of ills;
> The word means ague, fever, and chills[22]

Governor Cass helped undo the bad publicity Michigan had received by several means. He appraised its natural resources and

[20] F. R. Dain, *Every House a Frontier*, pp. 73-75.
[21] B. F. Emery, "Fort Saginaw," *Michigan History*, XXX (1946), 476-503.
[22] R. C. Buley, *The Old Northwest*, I, 242.

Early settlers' house

its attractiveness for settlers, and sized up the mood of the Indians by seeking and obtaining permission from Secretary of War Calhoun in 1820 to conduct an exploring expedition. Illinois had become a state in 1818, and Congress then added to Michigan Territory all the rest of the Old Northwest, including what is now Wisconsin and part of Minnesota. Hence Cass' itinerary took him beyond the present boundaries of Michigan. His party consisted of 42 men, including 10 soldiers and an officer, 2 interpreters, 9 Indians, 12 voyageurs, a physician, a geographer and 2 assistants, a geologist, a reporter, and a private secretary. Captain David B. Douglass was the geographer and Henry R. Schoolcraft was the geologist. The party left Detroit in three large canoes on May 25, 1820. Proceeding northward after a brief stop at Mackinac Island, where 23 more soldiers were added to the party, Cass reached Sault Ste. Marie. Here he discovered a large band of Chippewa Indians, with their chiefs in a hostile mood. Still under British influence, now exerted from Drummond Island, the Indians' principal chief appeared wearing the red coat of a British officer, denounced the Americans, and kicked aside the presents Cass had brought. A little later a British flag was raised over the Indian camp. This was more than Cass could take. He walked into the camp, accompanied only by an interpreter, pulled down the British flag, and told the chief that no foreign flag could be flown over American territory. John Johnston, Indian agent at the Soo, was away at the time, but his wife, the daughter of a chief, intervened to warn the Indian leaders that if they harmed Cass' party it would mean a war of extermination against them. Apparently her words were effective, for the chiefs met Cass, recognized American sovereignty, and acknowledged the American right to a tract along the St. Mary's River that had been ceded by the Indians at the Treaty of Greenville. The experience led to the establishment of Fort Brady there two years later.

Skirting the southern shore of Lake Superior, the party gazed on the famed Pictured Rocks near present-day Munising and reached the Ontonagon River. Schoolcraft ascended the Ontonagon to see the copper boulder that had been reported by earlier travelers. Cass then proceeded westward by streams and portages to the Mississippi River, which he ascended, seeking its source. He was unable to find the source, however, and turned downstream again as the summer waned.[23] The party returned east by way of the familiar Wisconsin-Fox portage route.

Sending a contingent to follow the coast of Green Bay and the northern shore of Lake Michigan, Cass proceeded with the rest of the party by canoe down the Lake to Fort Dearborn. Schoolcraft and Douglass continued along the eastern shore of Lake Michigan and returned to Detroit by way of Lake Huron, while Cass and the others traveled on horseback across Lower Michigan from Fort Dearborn to Detroit by way of the Old Sauk Trail (now U.S. 12). The report of the expedition, which was published soon after the parties returned, helped give Michigan a better reputation. Making light of the hardships and dangers involved, Cass stressed that the Indians were peaceful and the land promising. Schoolcraft reported numerous traces of iron and copper in northern Michigan. An important by-product of the expedition was the interest Schoolcraft developed in the Indians. Through Cass' influence he was appointed as Indian agent at the Soo in 1822. The next year he married Jane Johnston, daughter of John Johnston and his Indian wife. For many years thereafter he studied every aspect of Indian life and became recognized as the greatest authority of his day on the American Indian. His work *Algic Re-*

[23] The true source of the Mississippi, Lake Itasca, was discovered by an expedition led by a member of Cass's 1820 party, Henry R. Schoolcraft, in 1832. See P. P. Mason (ed.), *Schoolcraft's Expedition to Lake Itasca.*

searches, published in 1839, contained the material used by Longfellow in writing his famous poem *Hiawatha*.[24]

One of the factors that was most important in delaying any large-scale movement into Michigan was the difficulty involved in reaching the territory. In the years immediately following the War of 1812 transportation to Michigan by water was "dangerous, unreliable, and fraught with discomfort."[25] Navigation on Lake Erie was regarded as more dangerous than on the Atlantic. Accommodations for passengers were very poor. To reach the Detroit area from the south by land it was necessary to cross the Black Swamp. During the war a military road was laid out through it, but by 1815 this had all but disappeared. In rainy periods the swamp was virtually impassable. The horrors of the Black Swamp were widely publicized. While there was still plenty of land to be had in Ohio, Indiana, and Illinois, there was little incentive for the pioneer to take the trouble to come to Michigan.

Although the first steamboat in America dates back to 1809, it was not until 1818 that steam navigation on the Great Lakes began. In that year a steamship of 330 tons burden, rigged with sails to supplement steam power, was launched at Black Rock (Buffalo) and was named the *Walk-in-the-Water*. The appearance of this ship did a great deal to improve transportation between Detroit and Buffalo. Cabin passage cost $18.00, steerage fare was $7.00. The vessel was wrecked in 1821, but her engine was salvaged and placed in a new ship, the *Superior*. Until 1825 there was only a single steamship between Detroit and Buffalo. Two additional ones were launched in that year, and soon afterward there were more. There was a marked increase in the number of sailing vessels in the 1820s, too. The safety of navigation on Lake Erie, furthermore, had been promoted by federal appropriations for lighthouses and harbor improvement.

The completion in 1825 of the Erie Canal, connecting Lake Erie with the Hudson River, was an event of major importance in Michigan history because it greatly facilitated the transportation of passengers and freight between the eastern seaboard and Michigan ports. The canal, built at a cost of $7,000,000 by the state of New York, was such a success financially that within three years toll charges had paid the cost of construction plus interest charges. For the first time New England families, anxious to leave rocky and

[24] Schoolcraft's most extensive work was his *Historical and Statistical Information Respecting the History, Condition and Prospects of the Indian Tribes of the United States.*

[25] F. Dain, *op. cit.*, p. 9.

infertile fields for richer lands in the West, had a practicable route for reaching the "promised land." To the sons and grandsons of an earlier generation of New Englanders who had settled in western New York after the American Revolution, the Erie Canal beckoned westward from a land that already was becoming too crowded to suit them. And the waterway provided not only an easier way to move to Michigan, but it also made available for the first time an inexpensive method of moving Michigan products to markets in the East.

Important as it was, the Erie Canal did not cause the great migration to Michigan; it only facilitated that movement. This is shown clearly by the fact that sales of public land at the Detroit land office reached a high point in 1825, the year the Erie Canal was completed, and thereafter declined. Whereas 92,232 acres had been sold in 1825, only 70,441 acres were disposed of in 1830.[26] Sales at the Monroe land office also declined in these years.[27] There can be little doubt that this decline was due to rising prices in the East, a depression in 1828-1829, and the "tight money" policy of the United States Bank, which made it difficult for prospective settlers to obtain the cash to buy land, to finance the journey westward, and to obtain the capital needed for successful pioneering.[28] It was not until the improvement of economic conditions in the East and the availability of easier credit that the pioneers in large numbers could take advantage of the Erie Canal to move to Michigan.

For the improvement of land transportation within the Territory Michigan relied heavily on the federal government. In 1816 troops of the Detroit garrison began building a road to the rapids of the Maumee River, near the present city of Toledo, Ohio. By 1819 it was "cut through" and bridges over runs and marshes had been built, but the road was poorly located and almost impassable for wagons. Congress made an appropriation of $20,000 for the construction of a new road from Detroit to the Maumee Rapids and it was completed after a supplementary appropriation of $12,000 by Congress in 1827. A road across the Black Swamp from the settled part of Ohio to the Maumee Rapids was completed the same year through a grant of land to Ohio for financing its construction. Thus by 1827 land transportation to Detroit from the south had been greatly improved.

[26] G. N. Fuller, *Economic and Social Beginnings of Michigan,* p. 67.
[27] *American State Papers,* Finance, V, 529, 642.
[28] A. M. Schlesinger, Jr., *The Age of Jackson,* pp. 32-33.

Roads from Detroit into the interior were required, however, before any large-scale settlement was possible. In addition to the road southward, two roads from Detroit to the north and three to the west were projected during the Territorial period. The Territorial legislature in 1816 launched a project to build a road northward from Detroit, but the road was inadequate and by 1822 had only reached as far as Pontiac. A post-road from Pontiac through Flint to Saginaw was laid out in 1823, and an appropriation was made by Congress in 1829 to construct it. Intervening swamps made progress difficult, and by 1835 it had been extended only about five miles beyond Flint. This is now the route of US10. Another congressional appropriation in 1829 provided funds to begin work on a military road between Detroit and Fort Gratiot (Port Huron). Although it was quite inadequate it was of some use to settlers.

The first road westward also was a military road, designed to connect Detroit with Fort Dearborn (Chicago). An act of Congress, passed in 1825 at the behest of Father Gabriel Richard (then Michigan's delegate in Congress), provided for the laying out of such a road. Funds were provided in 1827 to extend the road to the Indiana line. It followed the path of the Old Sauk Trail and is the approximate route of the present highway US12. It ran westward from Detroit to Ypsilanti, then veered to the south, and continued westward through the southernmost tier of Michigan counties. The eastern portions of this road were in use in the later 1820s, and by 1835 two stagecoaches a week were operated between Detroit and Fort Dearborn. This highway, known as the "Chicago Military Road," became "practically an extension of the Erie Canal and . . . a great axis of settlement in southern Michigan."[29] In 1829 the Territorial council provided for another road westward into the interior, branching off the Chicago Military Road at Ypsilanti and running through the second tier of counties to its terminus at St. Joseph, approximately the present route of highway I-94. It was laid out in 1830, and by 1834 a stage line, running over it from Detroit to St. Joseph and connecting there with steamers for Chicago, enabled the traveler to complete the entire journey in five days. Although heavily traveled, it was not kept in as good condition as the parallel route to the south. The third of the roads westward was known as the Grand River Road. It branched off the Saginaw Road at Pontiac, but it was hardly better than a trail until the end of the Territorial period. Some

[29] G. N. Fuller, *op. cit.*, p. 76.

federal aid apparently was secured for work on this road. Surveyed to Grand Rapids in 1832, it had been completed only as far as Howell by the time Michigan was admitted into the Union as a state. It followed in general the route of the present highway I-96.

These roads were a far cry from the modern highway. In fact it can hardly be said that they were "built" at all, as we think of highway building today. Surveyors selected the route, often following Indian trails, axemen cut away the brush and felled trees along the path low enough so wagons could pass over the stumps, and workmen constructed crude bridges over streams which could not easily be forded. Logs were laid crosswise of the road across bogs and swamps to prevent wagons and animals from miring. This was known as a "corduroy road." Other than this, little was done to provide a surface for the roads. They were notoriously bad. The noted British author Harriet Martineau, who made a journey over them when she visited the "Wild West" in 1836, wrote of the experience: "Juggernaut's car would have been 'broke to bits' on such a road . . . . such hopping and jumping; such slipping and sliding; such looks of despair from the middle of a pond; such shifting of logs, and carrying of planks, and handing along the fallen trunks of trees."[30] One story that went the rounds was that a person found a beaver hat on the Detroit-Pontiac road, and when, at the risk of his life, he waded out to it, he found a man under it and yelled for help. But the man under the hat protested: "Just leave me alone, stranger, I have a good horse under me, and have just found bottom."[31] Settlers along the roads took a proprietary interest in the mudholes, and the right to pull wagons out of one of them for a price was recognized as belonging to the man who lived nearest to it. It was said that these mudholes were fostered carefully in dry weather; one tavern-keeper found a buyer for his property partly, it was said, because he had nearby an especially profitable mudhole.[32] Since the roads were laid out to follow the routes having the fewest obstacles, they seldom were straight. A description of the Chicago Military Road states that it "stretches itself by devious and irregular windings east and west like a huge serpent lazily pursuing its onward course utterly unconcerned as to its destination."[33]

[30] *Society in American,* I, 318, 322, 325, 326, quoted in *ibid.,* p. 77.
[31] *Mich. Pioneer and Historical Colls.,* VI (1884), 16.
[32] R. C. Buley, *op. cit.,* II, 461.
[33] *Mich. Pioneer and Historical Colls.,* I (1876), 231, quoted by C. E. Pray, "An Historic Michigan Road," *Michigan History,* XI (1926), 338.

Bad as they were, these roads were of the utmost importance in the early settlement of Michigan. A major role in their construction was played by the soldiers stationed in the garrisons.[34] Along the routes followed by the major roads, trails branched off, which served to guide the traveler to a destination beyond the main roads. Along the chief roads taverns were built and towns sprang up.

With the relinquishment of Indian claims to the land, the rapid progress of the surveys, the opening of land offices, and the improvement of transportation facilities, Michigan became attractive to settlers.

Ho for Michigania!

From 1830 to 1837 Michigan was the most popular destination for westward moving pioneers. An "Emigrant's Song" expresses the spirit of the time:

> Come all you Yankee farmers who'd like to change your lot,
> Who've spunk enough to travel beyond your native spot,
> And leave the village where pa and ma do stay,
> Come, follow me and settle in Michi-gan-i-a.
>
> What country ever growed up so great in little time,
> Just popping from the nursery right into-like its prime?
> When Uncle Sam did wean her, 'twas but the other day,
> And now she's quite a lady, this Michi-gan-i-a.
>
> Then come, ye Yankee farmers, who've mettle hearts like me,
> And elbow grease in plenty to bow the forest tree.
> Come take a quarter section, and I'll be bound to say,
> This country takes the rag off, this Michi-gan-i-a.

There were many more verses, contrasting the rich soil of various parts of Michigan with the rocky and worn-out lands of New England.[35] The census figures indicate the size of the influx of the early 1830s. The federal census of 1820 enumerated only 8,765 persons in Michigan Territory. The number had grown to 31,640 by 1830. This included the persons residing in the region west of

[34] The many ways in which military personnel of these garrisons served the early settlers are described in F. P. Prucha's *Broadax and Bayonet: The Role of the Army in the Development of the Northwest, 1815-1860.*

[35] For the complete song, see S. W. Durant, *History of Kalamazoo County,* pp. 106-61. It is included among Michigan folk songs recorded by Duane Starcher (Western Michigan University Aural Press, 1964).

Lake Michigan now embraced within Wisconsin and part of Minnesota. In the next four years the population almost tripled. A total of 87,278 were counted in a Territorial census taken that year, of which 85,856 lived in the Lower Peninsula. Three years later another Territorial census showed that there were 174,543 within Michigan. Although the influx slowed down after 1837, Michigan had the largest percentage increase between 1830 and 1840 of any state or territory, as indicated by the census of 1840, which listed 212,267 persons living in Michigan.

The majority of the newcomers came by way of the Great Lakes, making the journey from Buffalo to Michigan by steamship or sailing vessel. Detroit was the major point of entry. There the pioneer secured a wagon, if he had not brought one along, and necessary supplies for the subsistence of his family until the land he proposed to clear and cultivate started producing. Some settlers landed at Monroe and smaller ports, and sizable numbers came northward overland from Ohio and Indiana into the southern counties of Michigan. Some used the "Michigan Road," which was built by the federal government between Madison, Ohio and the foot of Lake Michigan.

Usually a man who proposed to settle in Michigan would come west alone to look over the land, decide where he wanted to settle, and purchase the tract if it had been put on the market. Then he returned east, packed up his family and his possessions, and brought them to the new home. These men were keen judges of the quality of the land. They did not like stony soil, for obvious reasons. Good drainage was important, and the settler preferred to avoid swampy, marshy land in part because it was regarded as "unhealthy." Land was called "heavy" if its clay content was high, or "light" if it was sandy. To some extent the pioneer was attracted to the kind of land he was accustomed to cultivate. To a considerable degree the soil was judged by the kind of trees that grew on it. The best soils were supposed to lie under a covering of black walnut, whitewood, ash, and sugar maple.[36] Burr oaks denoted good land, too, but land on which pine grew was generally sandy and infertile. Although the pioneers avoided for many years the vast prairies of Indiana and Illinois, they were quickly attracted to the small prairies of Calhoun, Cass, and Kalamazoo counties in southern Michigan because timber and water were available nearby. There was the advantage of not having to clear the land of trees on these prairies, though it

[36] J. H. Lanman, *History of Michigan,* p. 322.

was very difficult to break up the soil, the task often requiring several yoke of oxen. Grass on these prairies grew waist-high, and naturally the root growth was heavy and went deep. But the soil, once made cultivable, was fabulously rich.[37] The settlers were also attracted to "oak openings." Here the oak trees grew so tall and shaded the ground so completely that little or no brush or other vegetation grew underneath. It was possible to drive an ox team through oak openings for miles along an unblazed trail.[38]

A number of factors besides the quality of the soil entered into the pioneer's decision where to settle. Proximity to the main roads and the larger rivers was an advantage because it facilitated the bringing in of supplies and the marketing of products. Particular care was used to seek a location that was regarded as healthful. An abundant water supply was essential. And, finally, locations were naturally preferred as close as possible to the point of entry—in most cases, Detroit.

The spread of settlement in Michigan may be judged by the establishment of counties. When a considerable number of settlers had bought land in a given area, the Territorial legislature generally provided them with a county government. Often the legislature would "establish" a county, specifying its boundaries and giving it a name, and then temporarily attach it to another county for governmental purposes. When the population had reached the point where the lawmakers decided to separate government for a county was justified, they passed an act providing for the "organization" of the county, which meant the election of county officials and the institution of a separate county government. In 1837, at the time Michigan was admitted into the Union as a state, there were 38 counties that had been established. Of these, 23 had been organized and 5 others were organized before the end of the year. The total of 28 organized counties at the close of the year 1837 included all those in the four southernmost tiers with the exception of Barry. North of these Saginaw, Mackinac, and Chippewa counties had been organized, but the latter two embraced huge areas that were later divided. It is obvious from the progress of county organization that sizable settlements had been established in the first four

[37] A. F. Butler, "Rediscovering Michigan's prairies," *Michigan History,* XXI (1947), 267-286; XXXII (1948), 15-36; XXXIV (1949), 117-130, 0-231.

[38] James Fenimore Cooper's novel *The Oak-Openings* (1848) has a Michin setting.

tiers of counties, but that the population north of these, except in the Saginaw country, was small.[39]

The largest number of inhabitants of Michigan in 1837 lived in Wayne County (23,400, or over 13%). However, the City of Detroit accounted for about 10,000 of these; the rural parts of Wayne County were less thickly settled than those of neighboring counties. Second in size was Washtenaw County, lying directly west of Wayne, with a population of 21,817. Here the soil was excellent and the Territorial Road and the Huron River made access easy. The earliest towns were Ann Arbor, Ypsilanti, Saline, Dexter, and Manchester. Close behind Washtenaw was Oakland County, lying north and somewhat west of Wayne, having a population of 20,176. The county received its name from the large number of oak-openings that attracted settlers. The soil was very desirable, too. The towns were small, Pontiac and Rochester being the chief ones. Fourth in size was Lenawee County with 14,540 inhabitants. Tecumseh, Adrian, and Clinton were the principal centers. Adrian and Tecumseh first grew up as lumbering towns.

The area covered by Monroe, Wayne, Macomb, and St. Clair counties along the shores of Lakes Erie and St. Clair and the Detroit and St. Clair Rivers was not as attractive to early settlers as the three inland counties among the four just mentioned. The soil in the shore counties varied widely; some of it was stiff clay and some was sandy. It was heavily timbered. The founders of the town of Monroe, named for the fifth president of the U. S., who visited it in 1817, predicted a great future for it, anticipating that it would become the great metropolis of the West. Its location was favorable and its prospects were considered at the time to be better than those of Chicago. Mt. Clemens was the chief town in Macomb County, while in St. Clair County Port Huron, Marine City, Algonac, and St. Clair were founded at an early date.

Even though the Chicago Military Road had been opened before the Territorial Road, the counties that were laid out along the latter, except for Van Buren, contained a larger population in 1837 than those in the south. Washtenaw, as has been noted, was second only to Wayne. The importance of the relative distance of a county from Detroit is shown by the fact that

[39] For the dates and circumstances of the establishment of Michigan's counties, see W. L. Jenks, "History and Meaning of the County Names of Michigan," *Mich. Pioneer and Historical Colls.*, XXXVIII (1912), 439-477. For dates of county organization and the census of 1837 by townships and counties, see G. N. Fuller, *op. cit.*, pp. 531-539.

each county in the second tier had a larger population than its neighbor immediately to the west. West of Washtenaw, Jackson was the largest, its chief town being called at first "Jackson-burg." Calhoun and Kalamazoo counties, to the west of Jackson, were attractive to settlers because of the abundance of small, fertile prairies. The early towns in these counties included Marshall, Battle Creek, and Kalamazoo (at first named Bronson). In the southernmost tier of counties many settlers entered over-land from the south; hence distance from Detroit was less important in their peopling. Hillsdale and Branch counties, lying west of Lenawee, were hilly and heavily wooded, factors that tended to retard their growth. Jonesville, an important point on the Chicago Road, was the most important town in Hillsdale County, while Coldwater was the chief center in Branch. St. Joseph County was the most populous county in the first tier west of Lenawee, with White Pigeon, Mottville, Constantine, Centreville, and Three Rivers being its principal towns. The St. Joseph River, which wound its way through this county, was of vital importance as a means of carrying products to market and bringing supplies and merchandise back into the interior. St. Joseph County, as well as Cass County to the west, had several small prairies that, as has been indicated, were highly prized by the settlers. Edwardsburg and Cassopolis were Cass County's chief towns. In Berrien County the soil along Lake Michigan was sandy and its potential for fruit-growing was not recognized until a little later. St. Joseph was an important town chiefly because of its port. Further south along Lake Michigan the name of the town of New Buffalo is indicative of the soaring ambitions of its founders. Niles and Bertrand were the chief inland towns.

To the north of Berrien County along Lake Michigan lay Van Buren, Allegan, and Ottawa counties. They were remote and their lands were less fertile, particularly near Lake Michigan where the sand drifted in for some distance. All three of these counties were thinly settled in 1837.

The counties in the third tier west of Oakland all had small populations. Although they contained fertile lands, they were distant from the main routes of travel and lacked ready access to rivers for transportation. Livingston was the most thickly settled, with Howell and Brighton being its chief towns. Ingham, Eaton, and Barry had only a few hundred inhabitants each. The fourth tier of counties was more sparsely settled, but towns of some size had grown up at Grand Rapids, Ionia, and Grand Haven. Lapeer and Shiawassee counties on the eastern side of the fourth tier were in the Saginaw Valley and constituted a unit, along with Saginaw County to the north, distinct from Clinton, Ionia, and Kent to the west. These latter counties were settled in part by pioneers coming over the crude Grand River Trail, but mainly by those moving northward from the Territorial Road.

The Saginaw River Valley contained lands that were densely forested, with occasional oak-openings. The soil was considered somewhat inferior by the early settlers. Lumbering subsequently became a major industry in this region, but the earliest settlers regarded the giant pines as a nuisance rather than a resource. Fur traders in the area in some cases frowned on settlers and because of the many marshes the Saginaw country was regarded as unhealthful. Its chief advantage lay in its easy access by water.[40]

THE MICHIGAN PIONEER

What sort of people were these early Michigan settlers? In many respects they shared the characteristics of the American frontiersman wherever he was found. They were eager to better their lot in life and sought more abundant opportunity for themselves and their children. James Truslow Adams has called this quest the Great American Dream. Such men and women were courageous and venturesome. Those who were well-to-do and comfortable in the East were less likely to become pioneers in the raw western country. But it is not true that the westward-moving pioneers were the scum of the eastern states. Many men, no matter how poor their condition, preferred to accept things as they were, lacking the energy and ambition to better their lot. Such persons did not go west. The men who left the eastern communities for the hardships of frontier life were those with abundant vitality, the will to get ahead in life, and enough resources to obtain the essential supplies for the journey. They were neither the very rich nor the very poor. They were usually young and were looking ahead to the future, not so much living in the present as in their dreams of what the years ahead might bring. Generally they were married, for women had a vital role in the success of the venture.

They abounded in self-confidence and in many cases were rugged individualists. Individualism frequently went to the point of eccentricity. But it was blended with neighborliness, hospital-

[40] J. T. Blois's *Gazeteer of the State of Michigan* is a valuable source of information on early settlements.

ity, and a large measure of tolerance. The pioneer had to be versatile enough to subsist with little dependence on the outside world. Mainly, these people were farmers in the East. The older notion that the West furnished a "safety valve" for underpaid workers in the East has been exploded.[41] A factory worker did not possess, as a rule, the financial means to move west; furthermore, he lacked the skills and experience demanded of the farmer.

The pioneers were democratic, although they did not necessarily believe that all men were created equal. The hardships of frontier life emphasized the weakness of the weak and the strength of the strong. These pioneers did believe passionately in equal opportunity and they were scornful of certain marks of distinction in the East such as superior cultural and social attainments.

In all these traits the Michigan pioneers resembled their counterparts elsewhere in the American West. But in some respects they were distinctive. First and foremost was the fact that they were predominantly New Englanders or sprang from New England stock. The largest numbers came from western New York, but as has been explained earlier, these people were largely the descendants of Yankees who had settled in this region after the American Revolution. Nowhere in the West did Yankee stock predominate to the degree that it did in Michigan. The influence of this dominant New England element on the history of Michigan has been profound. That Michigan was in the forefront of the anti-slavery crusade and other reforms of the 1840s and 1850s was due in large measure to this fact. It also accounts in part for the extraordinary strength of the Republican Party in Michigan from 1854 to 1932. Michigan's leadership in public education is directly attributable to the Puritan zeal for schools, which was part of the New England heritage. The names of towns like Vermontville, Bangor, and Hartford, the strength of the Congregational Church in Michigan, and the leadership of New Englanders in the early legislatures, schools, and churches attest to the influence of the New England element.

A sizable segment of Michigan's 1837 population came from the neighboring states of Ohio and Indiana. These people settled mainly in the Detroit area and in St. Joseph, Cass, and Berrien counties. Many of them had been born in Virginia and North Carolina. In and around Detroit and Monroe the French Canadian influence was still observable in 1837; French was still spoken by many persons. Here and there throughout the territory were

[41] F. A. Shannon, "A Post-mortem on the Labor-safety-valve Theory," *Agricultural History*, XIX (Jan. 1943), 31-37.

colonies of settlers representing distinctive nationality or religious groups. Generally such settlers clustered together in a neighborhood and a number of them came into Michigan together as a community. For instance, there were numerous German colonies in Shiawassee and Washtenaw counties, a "Pennsylvania Dutch" colony in Cass County, Irish settlements, and colonies of Quakers. The proportion of foreign-born, however, appears to have been slight. The number coming from below the Mason-Dixon Line also was small. The pioneers were predominantly Protestant in religion, the main exceptions being the Irish and some of the Germans.

PIONEER LIFE IN MICHIGAN

The first concern of the settler after he arrived with his family on the land he had selected was to find shelter. Sometimes a neighbor would take in the family until it could secure its own quarters; otherwise, the pioneer would build a temporary shelter by using two trees to support a cross timber, and sloping down from this to a large log, poles made of saplings to form a crude roof. This was an "open faced camp." But soon he was likely to build a log house. For this job he required help; "house raisings" were among the many tasks that were performed by voluntary cooperation on the frontier. Ash, beech, maple, or poplar logs of nearly uniform size were cut and dragged to the cabin site. Prior to the day of the raising the pioneer might prepare timbers for window and door frames, roof poles, and chimney slats. Ofttimes the earth served as a floor for the log cabin, but the more energetic settlers prepared "puncheon floors" by splitting and hewing logs. When the neighbors arrived, the best axeman in the crowd fitted the notches at the corners, as the logs were skidded up with forks and hand spikes. Openings for doors and windows and the fireplace were sawed or chopped out after the logs were in place. The longitudinal roof poles were pegged on, and the job of preparing the "shakes" for the roof (clapboards split from oak or ash three or four feet long) was left to the settler. The energies and spirits of the workmen were stimulated by liberal draughts of whisky, while the women prepared a bountiful repast to satisfy mighty appetites.

The next progression from the primitive log cabin was the hewn log cabin, with the hewn logs replacing the rounded, bark covered timbers. In Michigan, sawmills appeared relatively early in many communities, so that the log cabin stage was brief and frame houses soon predominated.[42]

Some settlers arrived with only the bare essentials: their clothing, a small amount of flour and salt, an axe, rifle, iron pot, a few tools, some seeds, and bed clothing.[43] Many families arrived better-equipped, however. Frequently a choice piece of furniture, a flute, a fiddle, a few dishes, or some other prized possession was brought from the East. Beds were built by driving crotched posts in the ground or holes in the floor and running rails to the cabin walls, with a deer hide to support a grass tick. Three-legged stools, benches, sturdy chairs, and wooden pegs to be inserted into the walls to hang things on, were home-made. Dishes were fashioned from wood. Gourds of many sizes and shapes were highly prized by the pioneer, who always planted a liberal supply. They could be used as bowls, dippers, wash pans and even as rattles for the baby.

Food for the pioneer family was often a problem, for stores were generally far distant, and money scarce to buy supplies if they chanced to be nearby. Heavy reliance was placed on wild game, fish, honey, maple syrup, and wild fruits. Pioneer accounts tell of fabulous numbers of fish that could be secured from lakes and streams with a seine. Hunting in the woods for deer, bear, and smaller game—at first a necessity—provided a welcome release from the humdrum of hard work on the pioneer farm, so that many of the pioneers continued to hunt long after they were able to provide for their tables otherwise. Some of the pioneers became so enamored of hunting that they followed it as a business and gave up farming. They were called "professional hunters." The honey of the wild bee was especially prized by the settlers.[44] If possible, the settler brought along a cow to supply milk, butter, and cheese for the family. A few chickens to provide eggs and geese to provide feathers were also frequently included in the original inventory. Hogs, which could survive on acorns, were regarded as almost a necessity. They were butchered in the

[42] The restored pioneer village at New Salem, Illinois provides a good idea of earlier log cabins. There are a number of restored log cabins in Michigan, too. See W. Nowlin, "The Bark-covered House, or Pioneer Life in Michigan," *Mich. Pioneer and Historical Colls.,* IV (1881), 480-541. This was reprinted as *Back in the Woods Again* in 1937 and subsequently under its original title in a paperback by the Dearborn Historical Society. Other material on pioneer life in Michigan may be found in the *Mich. Pioneer and Historical Colls.,* XIV (1890), 431-483; XXII (1903), 236-246; XXXI (1902), 178-227; XXIX (1900), 609-624.

[43] R. C. Buley, *op. cit.,* I, 138-240.

[44] The central character of Cooper's novel *The Oak-Openings* is a bee-hunter.

fall, provided fresh meat during the winter, and salt pork could be packed in barrels for use the next summer. Corn was almost always the first grain grown. "Hog and hominy" became the standard pioneer diet.

Clearing the land of trees was the most arduous task that confronted the settler. First the brush was cleared away and the large trees were "girdled" by stripping the bark from around the trunk, causing the tree to die. Later the dead trees would be felled in windrows and burned. The colossal waste of such a process appalls those of us who live in the twentieth century, but the supply of timber in these early days seemed inexhaustible. The pioneer's faithful axe was his most useful tool. The crosscut saw was unknown to early Michigan pioneers. With his axe the settler felled the trees, chopped firewood, and split rails to build fences. Fences around cultivated fields were a necessity to keep out roving livestock, both wild and domesticated. During the growing season, women and children were required to keep constant watch to guard against squirrels, birds, raccoon, bear, deer, and other marauders from ruining the growing grain.

There were a few necessities that had to be obtained from the world beyond the pioneer homestead. One of these was salt. Most of this vital commodity came from salt springs, or salines, where a hundred gallons of water had to be boiled down to produce a bushel of salt. Much of the salt used by Michigan pioneers, however, was imported from New York. Prices frequently were high.

Wheat did not grow well in the virgin soil of cleared forest lands, but the small prairies of southern Michigan proved to be ideally adapted to this grain. Unlike the corn harvest, which could be carried on in a leisurely manner, wheat had to be cut and threshed within a rather short period. The wheat was cut with a "cradle"; this consisted of a scythe with a sort of basket attached. Two men, one cradling and the other binding the bundles, could harvest about two acres a day. Cyrus Hall McCormick invented a reaper in 1831, but it was not perfected and produced in quantity until after 1850. Obed Hussey of Ohio invented a reaper about the same time as McCormick, and a long war over patent rights began. In Kalamazoo County, Michigan, John Hascall and Hiram Moore developed a combine, an immense contraption for the operation of which 12 to 20 horses were required. Developed in 1836, this machine was demonstrated on Climax Prairie. It cut and threshed the grain in a single operation. But it was far too large, unwieldy, and expensive to be of practical use.[45]

Clothing brought from the East was not well-suited to the rigors of pioneer life. The pioneer quickly learned that deerskin was a valuable material in his environment. Moccasins of tanned buckskin, breeches and skirts made of dressed skin worked soft and thin by hand and sewed with sinews, and coonskin caps provided a dress that could withstand the wear and tear of briars and brush, repel cold winds, and ward off snake bite. Flax seed was sown in the spring, and the plants produced fibers that, with an immense amount of labor and skill, could be used to make women's clothes. Wool obtained from sheep raised on the farm provided another fiber. The spinning wheel and the hand loom kept everyone in the family busy throughout the long winters. Other tasks included candle-making, the manufacture of soft soap with wood ashes and lye, and tapping maple trees and boiling down the sap to make maple syrup.

Of primary importance to the pioneer was the construction of mills for the grinding of grain. These usually appeared within a few years after the first settlements, but often it was a long journey to mill and back. Another trade that was important to the early settlers was that of the blacksmith. His forge was a center of social as well as industrial activity. He produced nails, chains, bullet molds, yoke rings, axles, traps, hoes, augers, bells, shears, locks, adzes, plowshares, and metal parts for just about anything. The tanning of hides was a difficult process requiring much skill, and the pioneer welcomed the establishment of a tannery to take over this job for him.

The pioneer is often thought of as a strong, healthy specimen, but accounts of pioneer life in Michigan give the impression that there was a great deal of sickness. What the settlers called fever and ague was so prevalent that it was rather unusual to escape it. "He ain't sick, he's just got the ager" was a common remark. This ailment was actually malaria and was spread by the mosquitoes that bred in the marshes and swamps that were so prevalent before the land was drained. Quinine, commonly used today in the treatment of this disease, was then known as "Peruvian bark." It was expensive and many doctors refused to prescribe it. Most victims just endured the ailment, which was debilitating but seldom fatal. The victim first yawned and stretched a great deal, felt tired, and then began to have fierce chills. After an hour or so of this a raging fever would come with racking headache and back pains. Then after copious sweating

[45] W. F. Dunbar, *Kalamazoo and How It Grew,* pp. 71-72.

the sufferer would feel as well as ever. These attacks usually occurred at a certain time each day, or on alternate days, or even every third day. Work schedules were arranged to accommodate a person's "shakes."

> And on every day there, as sure as day would break,
> Their neighbor "Ager" came that way, inviting them to shake.[46]

Late summer usually was the most sickly time for the pioneers. Various types of "billious fevers," typhoid epidemics, "milk sick," and digestive upsets were common, caused in the main, no doubt, by lack of refrigeration, unpasteurized milk, and contaminated water. Epidemics of erysipelas (called St. Anthony's Fire) occurred in Michigan in early times. Contagious diseases such as scarlet fever, diphtheria, measles, mumps, and smallpox took a heavy toll. Infant mortality was high. Pneumonia, or "lung fever," was most prevalent in winter. Rheumatism was common, and probably was caused in part by exposure in all kinds of weather, the practice of drying wet clothing on the body, and decaying, unrepaired teeth. Worst of all was the frightful epidemic of Asiatic cholera that struck Detroit in 1832 and again in 1834. Most of the deaths from this terrible visitation, however, were in the towns and not among the pioneer farmers. While illnesses of various kinds were rampant in pioneer times, it is a strange fact that there are several instances of persons suffering from a disease that threatened to be fatal who came to Michigan and recovered their health. One such was Charles T. Harvey, builder of the Soo Canal.

The pioneers treated many ailments with roots and herbs. The lore that contained prescriptions of these remedies was brought from the East or learned from the Indians. Hideous concoctions of foul materials were resorted to; the worse the illness the more repulsive the remedy.

> For fevers, they recommended sweating and snake root with a purge of white walnut bark peeled upward, sassafras, dogwood, willow, or a glass of pearl ash and water. The breaking out in eruptive fevers, such as measles, was hastened by the use of sheep-dung tea, popularly known as "nanny tea." For pleurisy, if no bleeder was at hand, catnip or penny-royal, or butterfly

[46] A. D. P. VanBuren, "The Fever and Ague—'Michigan Rash'—Mosquitoes—the Old Pioneers' Foes," *Mich. Pioneer and Historical Colls.*, V (1882), 300.

tea, applications of boiled hot nettles, or brimstone, sulphur, and eggs . . . .[47]

There were a considerable number of doctors in pioneer Michigan, but often a long journey was necessary to summon a physician, and when he came his remedies might be no better than those devised by the pioneer and his wife. Copious bleedings and the use of calomel were favorite procedures of these early doctors, and the effect was frequently little more than to sap the strength of the patient. The doctor could be of use in setting bones and, of course, the psychological effect of having the advice of a doctor was helpful. Few of the doctors had studied at a medical school; most of them had learned the secrets of their profession through an apprenticeship with an established doctor. The physicians of this early period in some cases did not devote their full time to the practice of medicine. Some operated farms or engaged in business. The first postmaster of Kalamazoo was a doctor. As early as 1819 the governor and judges had passed a law authorizing the formation of county medical societies to pass on the qualifications of persons aspiring to practice medicine. But little was accomplished; few doctors apparently bothered to secure a license to practice and quackery abounded. There were several different "schools" of medicine, one of which was called the "botanical." The first medical journal and perhaps the first magazine produced in Michigan was the *Vegetable Herald,* published in Kalamazoo and devoted to the advocacy of "botanical medicine."[48] In spite of his shortcomings the pioneer country doctor had a more intimate relationship with his people than the lawyer or the minister. "Though frequently short of learning, intolerant of rivals and given to petty quarrels, he was abundantly possessed of those qualities which made his humanity triumph over both nature and human selfishness, and himself usually a figure feared, loved, and venerated."[49]

When sickness and death afflicted the family there were always neighbors ready to lend a helping hand. On happier occasions when there were social gatherings such as a barn- or house-raising, husking bee, or "town meeting," strenuous sports were the order of the day. Running and jumping contests, wrestling,

---

[47] R. C. Buley, "Pioneer Health and Medical Practices in the Old Northwest Prior to 1840," *Mississippi Valley Historical Review,* XX (1934); see also M. E. Pickard and R. C. Buley, *The Midwest Pioneer: His Ills, Cures, and Doctors* and C. B. Burr, *Medical History of Michigan,* I, 682ff.

[48] W. J. Bonk, "The *Botanic Luminary,* a Michigan Incunabulum," *Mich. Alumnus Quarterly Review,* LXVII (1961); see also F. Anderson, *Doctors Under Three Flags,* and Pickard and Buley, *op. cit.*

[49] R. C. Buley, *The Old Northwest,* I, 271.

tug-of-war, and pitching quoits were popular. Horse racing appeared early, and betting on the nags was a common accompaniment. After a husking bee the floor was cleared for a "barn dance," unless the neighborhood was dominated by ultra-religious folk who considered it wicked. In almost every neighborhood there were fiddlers who knew not a note of music, but could rip off such a tune as "Money Musk," "Zip Coon," or "The Devil's Dream" with great gusto. For those who frowned on dancing there were always the popular marching and singing games. Social occasions, of course, found young people engaged in the age-old quest for a mate. Although the girls frequently sang a little ditty that announced,

> I am too young, I am not fit,
> I cannot leave my mamma yit,

they often said "yes" at the age of fourteen or fifteen if the right young man popped the question. Weddings were big events on the frontier, occasions for visiting, feasting, drinking, and making merry. Following the ceremony the young couple was serenaded with all sorts of noisemaking paraphernalia a night or two after the wedding. This was called a "shiver-ee."[50] The settlers were fond of spelling schools, Fourth-of-July celebrations, camp meetings, and singing schools.[51]

Sexual irregularity was harshly condemned in pioneer days. There were taboos on sex applied to conversation: male animals were euphemistically named in the presence of women, but it was respectable enough to talk about mares, sows, ewes, and cows. Pregnancy was not mentionable in mixed company. Any departure from the moral code met stern rebuke and social isolation by one's neighbors. Nevertheless, individuality to the point of eccentricity in speech, manner, and dress was tolerated and even admired. Whisky was in universal use, being obtainable at general stores at 15 to 20 cents a gallon. But in the 1830s the temperance movement was gaining momentum, and many families frowned on spirituous liquors, advocating instead the use of beer, cider, and wine.

Pioneer life in Michigan was fraught with danger. If one escaped the prevalent types of sickness, he might die of rattlesnake bite

[50] *Ibid.*, 332-333.
[51] E. Gardner and G. J. Chickering (comps.), *Ballads and Songs of Southern Michigan.* See also C. M. Kirkland, *A New Home or Life in the Clearings.* Originally published in 1839, this description of pioneer life in Michigan by a cultivated eastern woman is one of the finest descriptions of the new settlements when Michigan was young.

or as the result of being struck by a falling tree. The pioneer had little time or disposition to admire the wild beauty of the primeval forest or the prairies covered with wildflowers in springtime. The life of the pioneer, though hard, had its rewards, and the chief one was the feeling that he was getting ahead in the world, that he could look forward to better days for himself and his family as his land came into production. The settler also was exhilarated by the feeling that he was part of a growing community, that he was sharing in the creation of a new society.

THE URBAN FRONTIER

Most of the writings on pioneer life deal with the experiences of pioneer farmers in rural neighborhoods. Less has been written about the beginnings and growth of towns, and the common problems they had to solve. No account of pioneer Michigan, however, would be complete without some reference to life in the new towns.

Detroit was not exactly a new town when the rush of settlers to Michigan began. In fact it was a century and a quarter old. But even so, it was hardly more than a frontier outpost until the population of Michigan began to grow at a rapid pace in the late 'twenties and early 'thirties. In 1816 it had only 850 people, and a dozen years later the number had increased only to 1,517. But by 1834 the city could boast of 4,968 inhabitants, and by 1840 it had grown to 9,192. The people were principally engaged in wholesale and retail trade; there was very little manufacturing except for local use. The city's port had become a busy place by 1836; ninety steamboats and an even larger number of sailing vessels used its facilities; an estimated 200,000 people entered and left the town that year. Hotels and boarding houses sprang up for their accommodation, while stores did a lively business in supplying settlers venturing westward. The Bank of Michigan was established in 1817, and by 1837 the city had a second bank. The most important center of activity was the government land office, where thousands of settlers and speculators came to examine records and to purchase a tract either for a homestead or with the purpose of reselling at a profit.

The city's growth created problems with which other urban communities had to wrestle as they developed. One of these was fire protection. Laws were passed after the fire of 1805, requiring each property owner to make certain preparations for the fighting of fire, but they were not well observed. Before the end of the territorial period three active voluntary fire companies had been formed. There was a great deal of rivalry among them to see which could reach a fire first and not infrequently they obstructed each other. The members wore red flannel shirts and blue pants tucked inside high boots, and girded their waists with ornamental belts. The city government provided them with fire engines, hoses, and other equipment, and grateful citizens whose property was saved from destruction by their efforts often provided them with a feast in return. A reward of $5 was voted by the common council in 1836 to the first person who gave the alarm of a fire. To sound an alarm the bell in the steeple of the Presbyterian Church at the northeast corner of Woodward and Larned Streets was rung by pulling a rope that dangled down into the open porch under the spire.

Water to quench the flames was pumped from the river or nearby cisterns. For domestic use, water was obtained from the river or from open wells, which were often a hazard when left without protection. As early as 1823 Peter Berthelet was authorized to build a wharf from the shore out to deep water and to install a pump to supply water that would be "free from contamination" by the debris commonly dumped into the river. Two years later Bethuel Farrand was given the right to install water mains. These were made from bored-out tamarack logs, mortised together and connected to an elevated tank at the wharf. A reservoir was erected at the corner of Jefferson Avenue and Randolph Streets to provide pressure, and the citizen obtained water from "penstocks" attached to the mains by withdrawing a wooden plug and allowing the water to pour into a bucket. Before the end of the territorial period other reservoirs were erected and service pipes were run into a number of homes.

In a growing urban community, especially in one so close to the frontier, there was certain to be a sizable number of miscreants. A public whipping post was erected near the intersection of Jefferson and Woodward Avenues where evildoers were flogged. Several public executions took place in Detroit during the territorial period, mostly of Indians. On September 24, 1830 one Stephen G. Simmons was publicly hanged for killing his wife while drunk. A grandstand was erected in front of the gallows for the accommodation of a huge throng of spectators who came from miles around to witness the event. There was some revulsion of feeling as a result of an eloquent confession of his faults by the victim and his rendition of a hymn just before he was executed. One result was the abolition of the public whipping post. A jail for the confinement of persons who had been arrested had been built before the War of 1812, a new one was constructed in 1819, and a larger one in 1830. No professional police force was maintained until later; however there was a voluntary night watch.[52]

Detroit had been incorporated as a town by the legislature of the Northwest Territory in 1802, and its government had been entrusted to a board of trustees. In 1805, however, this board was abolished and the new governor, secretary, and judges of Michigan Territory took control of the government of the town. Following the War of 1812 the governing board of the Territory adopted an act on October 24, 1815 incorporating Detroit as a city, with an elected board of trustees. In 1824 the governing body came to be known as the common council. The city government provided a public market and a weighmaster to see that people got honest weight. Some of the streets were paved with cobblestones. One of the persistent problems with which the city fathers had to deal was the roaming of livestock through the streets; under an act of 1817 hogs were allowed to run at large so long as rings were kept in their snouts to prevent them from rooting up lawns and gardens. The days of big government were still a long way off, however, for the total city tax collections in 1817 amounted to only $1,787.37. The growing city acquired several churches, schools, and newspapers, as will be detailed in the next chapter.

There were many exciting events in Detroit during territorial times. President James Monroe visited the city in 1817, and the event was a gala occasion. The arrival of the first steamboat, the *Walk-in-the-Water*, the following year was greeted by a large crowd. The building of a territorial capital building at the head of Griswold Street began in 1823, but the structure was not completed until 1828. Fort Shelby was abandoned by the army garrison in 1825, and the towering embankments that had dominated the town for many years were removed.

The year 1832 brought Detroit both excitement and tragedy. The excitement was induced by the so-called Black Hawk War, which actually was not a war at all. The threat to the settlers of Michigan was greatly exaggerated, and there were wild stories that Black Hawk and his warriors might ravage western Michigan in a desperate attempt to reach Fort Malden. A call for 300 volunteers from Michigan was sent out and in Detroit two amateur military groups responded—the Detroit City Guards and the Light Dragoons. On May 24 they started westward across the territory, but the infantry was recalled when it got no further than Saline. The dragoons went on to Chicago. Black Hawk was easily crushed. A disgraceful episode occurred when 150 of the

[52] G. B. Catlin, *The Story of Detroit*, pp. 261-263; 289-294.

Indians laid down their arms, approached a steamboat flying flags of truce, and the captain of the ship opened fire on them with a battery of guns. The fighting took place in what is now part of Wisconsin, but it was at that time attached to Michigan Territory. Black Hawk surrendered on August 2; he and nine other chiefs were kept as hostages to guarantee the good behavior of the Indians. Taken east, they were held prisoners in Fortress Monroe, then taken on a tour of the larger cities of the country to demonstrate to them the futility of any further resistance. Black Hawk met and conferred with President Andrew Jackson; returning west in 1833, he visited Detroit on July 4. The curious townspeople saw a man who was striking in appearance, eloquent in speech, and noble in bearing.

Just one year before, on July 4, 1832, the steamer *Henry Clay* had arrived at Detroit with several companies of soldiers under the command of General Winfield Scott, en route to meet the threat of Black Hawk's warriors. Several cases of Asiatic cholera had broken out, and when the ship stopped at Detroit, the extremely contagious disease was spread to the townspeople. It had appeared in Russia in 1831, had spread to western Europe, and was brought to America by a passenger on an emigrant ship. It soon made its appearance in cities on the eastern seaboard, where many deaths were reported. At Detroit there were 58 cases, and 28 deaths took place within two weeks. The upper story of the territorial capitol was utilized as a hospital for the victims, and the townspeople were in a state of panic.[53] Outstate towns set up guards to prevent travelers from Detroit from using the public roads. A stage coach with passengers, attempting to elude the road block east of Ypsilanti was fired upon and one of the horses was killed. In spite of all these precautions the disease spread beyond Detroit; eleven died at Marshall. The disease took its victims quickly; persons in excellent health were suddenly stricken with a feeling of uneasiness, shortly were consumed with burning fever and a craving for cold drinks, after which came vomiting, intestinal spasms, general debility and death. The cause of the disease was a comma-shaped germ discovered by Dr. Robert Koch of Germany in 1883. It grows entirely within the stomach and intestinal tract. The high rate of fatalities was due to the tremendous loss of body fluids and minerals; the blood stream literally dries up. The disease runs its course in three to five days. The modern treatment is to support the patient over this period by intravenously injecting fluids and minerals into the

[53] C. M. Burton, "Detroit in the Year 1832," *Mich. Pioneer and Historical Colls.*, XXVIII (1898), 163-171.

blood stream, and applying medications to keep him comfortable. But the treatment of the disease by the physicians of 1832 was to use counter-irritants and astringents, which only made the patient worse.[54] Among those who died at Detroit in 1832 was Father Gabriel Richard; he did not succumb to cholera but to exhaustion caused by wearing himself out nursing and comforting the sick. A second epidemic of cholera broke out in Detroit in 1834; it was of relatively short duration but more deaths occurred than in 1832. Seven percent of the city's population died in August. Many widows and orphans were left without means of support, and were sent to a poorhouse that had been opened the preceding year, largely through the efforts of the Reverend Father Martin Kundig.[55]

Much of the business done in Detroit came as a result of the flow of immigrants through the city. The demand for ships for the transportation of passengers and freight to Michigan from the East greatly stimulated the shipbuilding industry. A small steamship was built at Detroit in 1827, and in 1833 the steamer *Michigan*, pronounced the largest and finest on the lakes, was built at the foot of Wayne Street. Her construction was financed by Oliver Newberry, who owned the largest warehouse on the lakes; Newberry was a pioneer in lake transportation and a prominent and successful Detroit businessman for many years. He was a bachelor, let his hair grow long, always had his tall hat stuffed with business papers of all sorts, and was regarded as a shrewd operator. The arrival of settlers, speculators, businessmen and others created a demand for lodging and meals. A total of nine hotels were meeting this need by 1835. Several physicians, headed by Dr. Douglas Houghton, practiced in the city. More than a dozen lawyers handled the many legal problems connected with the sale and exchange of property as well as other civil cases and criminal cases. The town was not without its amenities. Major David C. McKinstry operated a theater, a modest museum, and a summer "pleasure garden" where ice cream and other refreshments were served and where there was a small zoo.[56]

No other town in Michigan approached Detroit in size or importance. In fact, it was the only incorporated city in Michigan when the state was admitted to the Union in 1837. Fifteen vil-

[54] J. S. Chambers, *The Conquest of Cholera, America's Greatest Scourge.*
[55] C. E. Rosenberg, *The Cholera Years;* A. Praus (ed.), *The Cholera in Kalamazoo.*
[56] For sidelights on the Detroit of the 1820s and 1830s see *Mich. Pioneer and Historical Colls.,* IV (1881), 89-99; 459-479.

lages had been incorporated by 1837, however: Monroe (1827),
Ypsilanti (1832), Ann Arbor (1833), Niles, Adrian, Pontiac, St.
Joseph, Tecumseh, Centreville, Constantine, White Pigeon, New
Buffalo, Marshall, Mount Clemens, and Coldwater. The state
census taken in 1837 lists the population of the townships in the
various counties, but not the towns proper. Estimating the size
of the towns from the number of inhabitants of the townships in
which they were located, we may conclude that the ten largest
towns in Michigan in 1837, in decreasing order of their size, were
Detroit, Ann Arbor, Monroe, Tecumseh, Ypsilanti, Adrian, Marshall, Pontiac, Grand Rapids, and Niles.

The location of towns was due to a variety of factors. Many
grew up along the Chicago Military Road (Ypsilanti, Coldwater,
Jonesville, White Pigeon) and the Territorial Road (Jackson-
burg, Marshall, Battle Creek, Kalamazoo). A town sometimes
developed around a tavern on one of these highways (Clinton) or
where a stream could be most easily forded (Kalamazoo). Marshall
was located at the head of navigation on the Kalamazoo River.
Towns often grew up around early forts (Saginaw, Niles) or
trading posts (Ypsilanti). Some towns were the result of the
work of promoters who hoped to profit from the sale of town
lots (Ann Arbor, New Buffalo, Albion). A town was apt to grow
up at a promising mill site (Galesburg), or at a favorable point
on an important river. Constantine was situated on the St. Joseph
River and became an important shipping point for grain; Grand
Rapids, as its name indicates, grew up at a point on the Grand
where rapids made it necessary to interrupt travel. The growth
of some towns was promoted by the location of a land office
(Monroe, White Pigeon, Kalamazoo, Ionia, Flint).

By the close of the territorial period, as has been indicated, a
few of the growing towns had been incorporated as villages and
hence had local governing bodies to meet the needs of citizens
for regulations to control the running at large of livestock, to
provide for the fighting of fires, and to maintain law and order.
In the unincorporated towns local government was in charge of
township officials. Most of the towns had one or more churches,
a school, several general stores, a sawmill, and a gristmill. Streets
were deep in mud during the spring season and dusty in summer-
time. As will be noted in the next chapter, several of the towns
had newspapers. Lawyers and doctors maintained offices, often
serving the people of an extensive area. In some towns promoters
set aside squares for public parks, and since the people who
built the towns were largely Yankees, they tended to use the
New England village as a model.

The names of the towns were selected from many different sources. Indian names were common (Kalamazoo, Pontiac, Tecumseh, Saginaw). Some took their names from geographical features (Grand Rapids, Saline, Coldwater). The names of the founders were often utilized: Kalamazoo was first called Bronson, from the name of Titus Bronson, its founder; the present Bronson was named for Jobez Bronson; Dexter took its name from Samuel Dexter. New England names were popular (Quincy, Vermontville, Lawrence), and the New York influence was reflected in the names of such towns as Utica, Rochester, and New Buffalo. Other names had more esoteric origins. The name of Ypsilanti, suggested by Judge Woodward, was that of two brothers who were heroes of the Greek war of independence; Niles was named for the publisher of a popular eastern newspaper; and Ann Arbor derived its name from the wives of the two founders, both of whom were named Ann. Adrian, Constantine, and Homer derived their names from classical antiquity. Monroe and Jackson were named for United States presidents, and Marshall for a chief justice.

These towns growing up in the interior of Michigan were of great importance to the early settler. The story of their development is quite as significant as that of the pioneer farmers. In 1837 the majority of Michiganians lived on farms, but within a century the city dwellers outnumbered those dwelling on farmsteads.

Walker Inn

9

POLITICAL DEVELOPMENT
AND CULTURAL BEGINNINGS

Life in Michigan during the two decades following the War of 1812 was intensely dynamic. Nothing was fixed or static. The boundaries of the Territory of Michigan were changed repeatedly. Territorial government underwent change when Congress acknowledged the right of the people to elect a delegate to Congress and a territorial legislature. The area open to settlement was enlarged as new purchases were made from the Indians. A system of education was provided and schools were opened. Churches appeared, representing different denominations and several formed territory-wide denominational organizations. Newspapers were founded. Various kinds of associations were formed. The population, which grew slowly in the 1820s, increased during the first half of the 1830s to the number that entitled Michigan to statehood.

The eyes of men and women were on the future, not the past or even the present. Everyone expected to work hard; it is remarkable that, in spite of this, these pioneers found time to devote to many activities not essential to survival in a new environment. There was a profound confidence in the competence of the individual to carve out of the wilderness a home for himself and his family that would be, after the passage of years, better than the one he had left. Not only was there unbounded confidence in the individual, but also in the capacity of free men

271

to make decisions and act collectively in a democratic way so as to produce a government and a society superior to any designed and controlled by kings and aristocrats. To this end farmers and urban pioneers organized and sustained educational, religious, social, and cultural institutions that were to have a lasting impact on the history of Michigan.

TERRITORIAL BOUNDARIES

As noted above, the extent of the Territory of Michigan did not remain the same during this period. When first organized in 1805, Michigan Territory included the eastern tip of the present Upper Peninsula. The western boundary, as specified by Congress when Michigan Territory was created, was a line drawn through the middle of Lake Michigan from its southerly bend to "its northern extremity, and thence due north to the northern boundary of the United States." Thirteen years later when Congress admitted Illinois into the Union as a state it attached to Michigan Territory all the region north of Illinois and east of the Mississippi, subject to the future disposition of Congress. In 1834 the western boundary of Michigan was extended west of the Mississippi as far as the Missouri River. This vast expansion placed all of what is now the State of Iowa under the jurisdiction of Michigan. Two years later in 1836, however, Wisconsin Territory was set off and organized to include all this western country. What was to become the Upper Peninsula of Michigan was not included. Wisconsin's northern boundary was left so indefinite that its precise location remained a matter of dispute down into the twentieth century. It is difficult to say exactly what Michigan included after Wisconsin was set off. The act organizing the Wisconsin Territory clearly carried the intent to give it an outlet on Lake Superior. The following year Michigan was admitted to the Union with its present boundaries, including the entire Upper Peninsula.

The southern as well as the western boundaries of Michigan also underwent modification. The Northwest Ordinance had specified a line drawn due east and west through the southernmost tip of Lake Michigan. The framers of the Ohio constitution, fearing that such a line, as yet unsurveyed, might leave the mouth of the Maumee River outside Ohio's boundaries, inserted a proviso that if, when the boundary was surveyed, this proved to be the case, then the northern boundary of Ohio, with the assent of Congress, should be along a line drawn from the southern end of Lake Michigan to the northernmost cape of Maumee Bay. Congress admitted Ohio into the Union under this constitution and then two years later, in 1805, created Michigan Territory with its southern boundary that which was set forth in the Northwest Ordinance, and without any proviso for changing the line in accordance with the Ohio constitution. Surveys of the Ordinance line were eventually made, and it was discovered that it would place the mouth of the Maumee River in Michigan. As Michigan approached statehood this problem created the contest with Ohio that will be described in the next chapter.

In 1816, when Indiana was ready for admission to the Union, its citizens asked Congress to move the northern boundary of the new state ten miles north, so that Indiana would have as its northern boundary a line running parallel with the original line—due east and west—but ten miles north of that original line. Congress

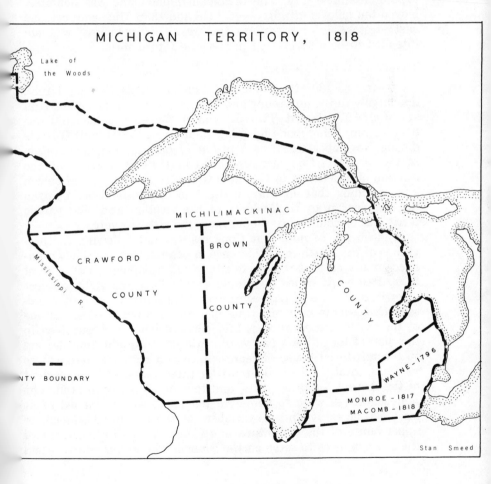

MICHIGAN TERRITORY, 1818

Lake of
the Woods

MICHILIMACKINAC

CRAWFORD
COUNTY

BROWN
COUNTY

COUNTY

MISSISSIPPI R.

WAYNE - 1796

MONROE - 1817
MACOMB - 1818

COUNTY BOUNDARY

Stan Smeed

admitted Indiana with that provision, and hence Michigan lost the region between the original line and the new one. This gave Indiana, instead of Michigan, the present Michigan City, Gary, and Indiana Harbor along the lake. Illinoians were even more ambitious when, two years later, they prepared for admission of Illinois as a state into the Union. They requested and received permission to move the original line *sixty* miles to the north. This area includes the present city of Chicago, and a considerable area to the north.

To summarize, then, during the territorial period there was uncertainty about the permanent Michigan-Ohio boundary, with Ohio claiming a line not due east and west, but on a "bias," projected from the southern tip of Lake Michigan to the northernmost cape of Maumee Bay. The Michigan-Indiana line was definitely moved ten miles north. Between 1818 and 1836 Michigan included vast stretches of territory to the west that obviously was not intended to be a permanent part of the future state.

TERRITORIAL GOVERNMENT

As early as 1809 there was agitation for an elective legislature, due largely to the quarreling and bickering between Governor Hull and Judge Woodward. Two years after the war the demand was heard again, being made by "Cincinnatus" in the Detroit *Gazette* during November, 1817, as a means of encouraging immigration to the territory. Congress responded in 1819 by authorizing the election of a delegate to Congress from the Territory of Michigan and providing that all white males who had resided in Michigan for one year prior to the date of the election and who paid a territorial or county tax should have the right to vote.

It is worthy of note that Congress was not following the provisions of the Northwest Ordinance in passing this act. The Ordinance stipulated that when a territory had a population of at least 5,000 free adult males its people should have the right to elect a territorial house of representatives. The right to vote for representatives was to be confined to men who had been citizens of one of the states, owned at least fifty acres of land, and had lived in the district for at least two years. In order to qualify for election to the territorial house of representatives a man was required to be a citizen of the United States for three years, to be a resident of the district for three years, and to own 200 acres of land. The representatives were to nominate ten men, each possessed of at least 500 acres of land, as members of the territorial council, or upper house of the legislature, and Congress was to select five of the ten nominees to serve on the council. The representatives and the council sitting together were then authorized to elect by joint ballot a delegate to Congress who was to have the right to participate in debates but not to vote. Michigan did not have 5,000 free adult males in 1817 (its total population in 1820 was only 8,765), nor did Congress authorize the election of a territorial house of representatives and a territorial council in 1817. Rather, it provided that a delegate to Congress might be elected, and required of all voters residence in the territory for one year and the payment of some kind of tax.

Congress was discouraged from going the full distance in giving Michigan the powers of a territory of the second grade, first because the territory did not as yet have 5,000 free adult males, and second, because a vote taken the preceding year at the behest of Governor Cass, who believed wholeheartedly in democratic processes, had shown a majority of the voters in the territory to be unfavorable to a change from the existing system. Most of the inhabitants of Michigan were still of French origin; they were satisfied with Cass' administration and were uninterested in elections and "democratic processes." The action taken by Congress was, therefore, in the nature of a compromise: Michigan would have a non-voting delegate in the Congress of the United States, but its laws would continue to be made and administered by the governor and judges.

In 1823, however, Congress definitely raised Michigan to a territory of the second grade when it authorized the voters to nominate eighteen persons for a territorial council, from which number the President of the United States, with the advice and consent of the senate, was to select nine to serve on the council. The lawmaking power in the territory was then to be transferred from the governor and judges to the territorial council. The governor was still to enjoy the power of veto and Congress might disapprove any act passed by the council. It is notable that Congress made no provision in this law for the election of a territorial house of representatives or "general assembly," as provided in the Northwest Ordinance. The act did contain, however, a provision that the territorial council might at any time submit to the people of the territory the question of whether a "general assembly" should be chosen in accordance with the provisions of the Northwest Ordinance. This provision is evidence that Congress still regarded itself as bound by the provisions of that Ordinance, at least in a general way. Four years later in 1827 Congress passed another act, this one increasing the size of the territorial council from nine to thirteen members and making it wholly elective by the people of the territory.

As a result of these acts Michigan had a non-voting delegate to Congress in Washington after 1819, and Michigan's laws were made after 1823 by a Territorial Council, consisting of nine men until 1827, when the number was increased to thirteen. No action was taken during the territorial period, however, to provide a general assembly or house of representatives for Michigan, as stipulated in the Northwest Ordinance. Hence Michigan had a unicameral, or one-house, legislature until it became a state.

The settlers who trickled into Michigan in the fifteen years after the War of 1812, and who then came in a torrent during the early 1830s, had none of the apathy toward democratic institutions that was characteristic of the French who constituted the large part of the population prior to their coming. These newcomers demanded not only a voice in the government of the territory, but also clamored for local self-government. They were fully supported by Governor Cass. The rapid development of county organization from 1815 to 1837 has already been noted. An act of Congress passed in 1825 provided that the qualified voters in each county should choose all the county officials except the judges. The governor and council also were permitted to divide the counties into townships. In the townships the town meeting, in which all adult males had the right to take part, became the governing body. The inauguration of township government in Michigan followed the pattern sent in Ohio and Indiana. No townships were formed in the early years in southern Illinois, but they developed in the northern part of the state. The township was modeled after the New England "town," which is not really a town in the sense the word is used in the Middle West, but an area that may or may not include some sort of a municipality. New York also had "towns" but in the Old Northwest the term "township" supplanted "town" as the connotation for a local governmental unit. The township unit of local government exists in less than half the states (22 out of 50 in 1962). Outside of New England, where it originated, the system has been adopted by New York, Pennsylvania, New Jersey, eleven north-central states, and to a limited extent by South Carolina and Washington.

TERRITORIAL POLITICS AND POLITICIANS

Political rivalry in territorial Michigan was of the knock-down-and-drag-out variety. A fierce spirit of liberty and individualism is evident in the political contests of the day. Newspapers were rabidly partisan, asking of and giving to the other side no quarter. The pioneers were intensely interested in politics. Religion and political partisanship provided emotional outlets that were important as a release from toil and loneliness.

Michigan was represented in Congress by some very able men during the territorial period. The first delegate chosen was William Woodbridge, a native of Connecticut who had come to Michigan as Indian agent of the United States, and was serving as secretary of the territory at the time of his election. He took his seat in Congress on December 10, 1819 and served for one year. He then resumed his position as territorial secretary, later was appointed to one of the judgeships, and after statehood was achieved was elected governor (1839) and then United States senator. Solomon Sibley, a lawyer, native of Massachusetts, and long-time Michigan resident, was chosen to replace Woodbridge when the latter resigned as a result of a clamor against him for retaining his position as territorial secretary while serving in Congress. Sibley also served later as a territorial judge. There were six candidates for the office of delegate to Congress in 1823. The leading ones were Colonel John Biddle, clerk of the Detroit land office and brother of Nicholas Biddle (head of the Bank of the United States); Father Gabriel Richard, the pastor of Ste. Anne's church who had been born in France; and Austin Wing, sheriff of Monroe County and native of Massachusetts. Richard had the solid support of the French element and was declared the winner in the election. An attempt was made by an agent of Biddle to contest his election on the ground that he was not a citizen, but a congressional committee decided in favor of Richard. He thus became the only Roman Catholic priest ever to serve as a member of the Congress of the United States.

Richard was at first quite a curiosity in the national capital: his French accent and his personal appearance attracted considerable attention. He wore knee breeches, silk stockings, a long black coat very short in the waist and voluminous in the collar, and a huge skirt extending almost to his ankles. He is said to have been a good listener and to have been addicted to snuff. Both President Monroe and Secretary of War Calhoun were fascinated by the stories he told of the Indians. When he came back to Detroit after Congress adjourned in the spring of 1824, he was put in jail. Somewhat earlier in the pulpit of Ste. Anne's he had condemned as an adulterer and excommunicated a man named Labadie, who had divorced one wife and married another. Labadie brought suit for damages against Richard, and in 1821 the court awarded the former a judgment of $1,116. Richard refused to pay the amount, because to have done so would have acknowledged, as he saw it, the power of civil authorities over purely ecclesiastical concerns.

Hence he was jailed. After spending about three weeks behind bars he was released when some of his friends gave bond to insure his remaining in Wayne County. He was informed, however, by Henry Clay, Speaker of the House, that he could claim immunity from arrest as a member of Congress, so he was allowed to return to Washington in the late fall. The judgment remained to plague him for the rest of his life. Richard spoke in Congress only on rare occasions but he did a great deal of lobbying for measures beneficial to Michigan, sought to get more lands put on the market, and was active in promoting the measure by which Congress authorized the construction of the Chicago Military Road.[1]

Richard ran for re-election in 1825, and he was once more opposed by Biddle and Wing. The votes were so evenly divided that the outcome was long in doubt. There were claims and counterclaims of rascality, coercion, and fraud. The board of canvassers, in its report, gave the election to Wing. The latter was given 728 votes to 724 for Richard and 689 for Biddle. A congressional committee reopened the investigation and after lengthy consideration decided Wing had 725 legal votes, Richard 722, and Biddle 714. The same contestants had it out again in 1827, 1829, and 1831. Wing retained his seat until 1831 when Biddle was the winner. Lucius Lyon was elected in 1833. He declared his residence to be Bronson (later named Kalamazoo), but his activities as a surveyor and land speculator kept him on the move a great deal. He was the first delegate to come from the western part of the territory. After statehood was attained, he was chosen as one of Michigan's first two United States senators.[2] The last territorial delegate elected was George W. Jones, who came from that part of Michigan Territory which is now the State of Wisconsin.

The contests for the election of members of the Territorial Council appear to have been somewhat less exciting than those for delegate to Congress. There were six elections between 1823 and 1833. Members were chosen to serve two-year terms and the Council met annually.[3] Among those who served on the Territorial Council were the scientist and Indian authority Henry R. Schoolcraft; noted surveyor William A. Burt; Major Abraham Edwards, a physician, who was president of the first four Councils, who won his military rank during the War of 1812 and later served

---

[1] F. B. Woodford and A. Hyma, *Gabriel Richard, Frontier Ambassador*, pp. 101-141.

[2] See the letters of Lucius Lyon in *Mich. Pioneer and Historical Colls.* XXVII (1896), 412-604.

[3] The laws passed by the Council are included in *Laws of the Territory of Michigan*, published in 4 vols., 1871-1884.

as register of the land office at White Pigeon and Kalamazoo; Calvin Britain, a prominent figure in the early history of Berrien County; and John McDonnell of Detroit, president of the last two councils.[4]

The people of the Territory had no voice in the selection of the governor, secretary, and judges. These were chosen by the President of the United States. Augustus B. Woodward, the most prominent of the territorial judges, served from 1805 to 1824. President Monroe refused to reappoint him in 1824 because of charges of intemperance that had been brought; but upon receiving a letter from Governor Cass stating that he had never known Woodward to be intoxicated, the president appointed the latter as one of the judges in the Territory of Florida. He died there in 1827. His grave is unmarked. Judge James Witherell, Woodward's archfoe, outlasted the latter, serving from 1806 to 1828. Later appointees to the court included William Woodbridge and Solomon Sibley, each of whom had been delegate to Congress for a single term. Woodbridge was secretary of the Territory from 1818 to 1830. He was succeeded by John T. Mason of Virginia, who resigned the following year to go abroad. His successor, appointed by President Andrew Jackson, was his son, then only 19 years of age, Stevens Thomson Mason. Whenever the governor was out of the territory, as happened quite frequently, the secretary became the acting governor. Upon the resignation and departure of Governor Cass young Mason became acting governor of the territory, and he served in this capacity later on several occasions. He was destined to become the first governor of the State of Michigan and to hold that position for two terms.

Governor Cass resigned in 1831 to accept appointment as secretary of war in President Jackson's cabinet. His career as governor of Michigan Territory had been eminently successful. Later he was to be elected twice as United States senator from Michigan, to contend unsuccessfully for the presidency of the United States in 1848, and to serve as secretary of state in President Buchanan's cabinet. President Jackson appointed George B. Porter to be Cass's successor as governor of Michigan Territory. Porter reached Detroit on September 17, 1831, taking over the reins of government from Acting Governor Stevens T. Mason. He was absent frequently from the territory during the next three years, during which interims Mason again assumed the duties of governor. In 1834 he fell victim to the cholera. Stevens once more became acting governor on July 6 of that year. Since Michigan was

---

[4] For a list of members of the six Councils, see *Michigan Manual* (1963-54), pp. 92-94.

moving rapidly toward statehood, President Jackson did not at
once appoint a successor to Porter. But in 1835, as a result of the
squabbles connected with Michigan's battle for statehood, the
President made an attempt to oust Mason from office. He appointed Judge Charles Shaler as secretary and acting governor on
August 29, but Shaler had the good sense to decline. On September 15, Jackson appointed John S. Horner to the same position. By
the time Horner arrived in Detroit a state constitution had been
framed, and a conflict with Ohio over the southern boundary was
in progress. Horner was snubbed socially and officially. At a public meeting a resolution inviting him to "return to the land of his
nativity" was endorsed, and on November 2 and 3 the new state
government was inaugurated. The following May Horner was
appointed secretary of the newly formed Wisconsin Territory and
left Detroit.[5]

EDUCATIONAL BEGINNINGS

Michigan long has been recognized as a leader in the field of
public education. The groundwork for this position of leadership
was laid during territorial times.

Schools had been maintained during the British regime for
children of the troops garrisoned in the fort and others. From 1790
private schools were conducted by itinerant ministers and school-
masters. The Reverend David Bacon, a New England Protestant
missionary, opened a school at Detroit in 1801, but it was short-
lived, partly because of the prevalent prejudice at that time
against Yankees. Other private schools were conducted in 1806
by John Guff, in 1810 by Daniel Curtis, in 1812 by "Mr. Payne,"
and in 1813 by "Mr. Rowe" There was little continuity in these
efforts, each schoolmaster accommodating all who paid the fee he
asked, regardless of age. Father Gabriel Richard was deeply concerned about education and fostered several schools in and around
Detroit. His school at Spring Hill was primarily for the vocational
training of Indian children. As early as 1806 he petitioned the
governor and judges for a parcel of land on which to build a
"college." Judge Woodward and Governor Hull both expressed interest in providing schools, and on February 26, 1809 the governor

[5] W. Jenney, "Governors of Michigan Territory," *Mich. Pioneer and
Historical Colls.,* III (1881), 119-120. On Cass, see A. C. McLaughlin,
Lewis Cass, and F. B. Woodford, *Lewis Cass, the Last Jeffersonian.* B
Hubbard, *Memorials of a Half Century,* is a valuable source for this period
For official records of the territorial period, see *Mich. Pioneer and Hist
Colls.,* XXXVI (1908), 100-620 and XXXVII (1909-10), 17-507, and C. E
Carter (ed.), *Territorial Papers of the United States,* X, XI, and XIII.

and judges passed an act authorizing the overseers of the poor to establish school districts, to act as trustees of the same, and to lay an annual tax of two to four dollars per school child. But it does not appear that any schools were established under this law.

The first serious effort to promote public education in Michigan came on August 26, 1817, when the governor and judges established "a Catholepistemiad or University of Michigania." This act was the brain child of Judge Woodward and, as might be expected, was grandiose in conception as well as name. It was not a university in the usual sense of that term, but rather a complete system of education for the territory, under centralized control. Control was vested in thirteen "didactors," each representing a field of knowledge that was given an outlandish name invented by Woodward and based on Latin or Greek derivatives. The year before, Woodward had published a book entitled *A System of Universal Science*, in which he had organized all human knowledge into thirteen divisions. The "didactors," also called "professors," were to be appointed by the governor and were empowered to establish "colleges, academies, schools, libraries, museums, atheneums, botanical gardens, laboratories, and other useful literary and scientific institutions throughout the territory." They were authorized to employ as many "instructors and instructorixes" as was necessary to staff these institutions. Modest fees for instruction were stipulated, but those unable to pay them were to be educated at public expense. The principle of tax support was established, and lotteries were authorized to provide funds.

The Catholepistemiad was greeted by hoots of derision at the time and frequently has been the butt of ridicule since. Governor Cass couldn't even pronounce its name, referring to it as the "Cathole-what's its name."[6] But the fact remains that the plan set forth a number of principles that later became basic in the Michigan system of education: (1) public education extending from the lowest grade through the college and university level; (2) tax support; (3) non-sectarian control; (4) low tuition in public institutions. The system, however, contemplated one principle that has proved impractical: centralized control.[7] Although the authorship of the act must be credited to Judge Woodward,

[6] Even today those who attempt to pronounce it vary in their renditions; Cath-ol-a-pist-eem'-ead seems to have the most favor.

[7] E. B. Isbell, "The Catholepistemiad of Michigania," *Mich. Alumnus Quarterly Review*, XLIII [1937], 590-602; W. F. Dunbar, "Centralized State Control of Education," *loc. cit.*, XLVI (1940), 256-266; W. B. Shaw (ed.), *The University of Michigan, an Encyclopedic Survey*, Part I, pp. 3-39.

historians have pointed out that both Father Richard and Governor Cass were equally desirous of taking steps to promote education.

All the "didactorships" or "professorships" were conferred by Governor Cass on two men. The Reverend John Monteith, a graduate of Princeton and pastor of the Detroit Protestant church, was assigned seven didactorships and the presidency, while six didactorships and the vice-presidency went to Father Gabriel Richard. About a month after the passage of the law a treaty was made with the Indians (Treaty of Fort Meigs), one of the series of treaties by which the natives surrendered their lands in Michigan; in this treaty they deeded six sections of their lands in equal shares to Ste. Anne's Church and the "college at Detroit." As yet there was no "college at Detroit" but Monteith and Richard, acting as didactors of the Catholepistemiad, moved to remedy this deficiency by decreeing that "there be established in the City of Detroit, a College, to be denominated the First College of Michigania."[8] The college did not materialize, but a primary school and academy were established in 1817 at the behest of the two didactors, and these schools operated more or less continuously until about 1827. Monteith and Richard also took steps to establish schools at Monroe and on Mackinac Island, but the inhabitants of these places seem to have shown little interest in the proposal.

The governor and judges amended the act of 1817 by passing another act in 1821. The strange verbiage of the Catholepistemiad was abandoned, but the feature of the original act that placed the responsibility for schools in the hands of a central body rather than in local communities was retained. Within a few years this plan proved impractical, partly, at least, because the central body lacked the funds to make any program of education effective.

In 1827 the Territorial Council, which had succeeded the governor and judges as the lawmaking body, abandoned the centralized policy by enacting a measure to enable townships to maintain schools. Townships containing at least fifty families were to employ a schoolmaster of good morals to teach the children to read and write, instruct them in the English and French languages, and teach arithmetic, orthography, and good behavior. Schools were to operate at least six months a year, taxes might be levied for their support, and the poor were to be instructed without cost. In townships having at least two hundred families, a "grammar school" was to be maintained and a master employed who could teach Latin. A board of not more than five commissioners was to have charge of schools in each township. The law contained an odd pro-

[8] University of Michigan, *Records of the University, 1817-1837*, pp. 31f.

vision that townships not complying with the requirements might be fined, but that any township might be exempt from these requirements if two-thirds of its electors so voted! Except for this "escape clause" the law closely resembled the famous Massachusetts Law of 1647. Obviously it was a compromise between those who wished to require townships to establish schools and those who preferred to make it optional. But it was a definite departure from the laws of 1817 and 1821 in that it placed the responsibility for starting and maintaining schools squarely on local communities rather than on a central body.

Two years later in 1829 another law passed by the Territorial Council provided for the laying off of school districts within a township. Five school inspectors were to be elected whose duty would be to examine teachers and to grant certificates to those whose good moral character and preparation indicated they were fit to teach. This act provided that the costs of maintaining schools were to be borne by those whose children were taught, but poor children were to be taught at the expense of the district. There were no schools in Michigan in which all children were taught at public expense until 1842, and then only in Detroit. Parents of school children paid what were called "rate bills," based on the number of children they had in school and the number of days that each attended. The schoolmaster was lodged and fed by the parents in turn.

The laws of 1827 and 1829, as well as another passed in 1833, were not rigidly enforced, and most of the actual teaching during the territorial period was done in private schools opened for various lengths of time and then abandoned. Most of these were elementary schools. Above this level there were numerous "academies" that gave advanced instruction, mainly in Greek, Latin, and mathematics. The Territorial Council passed laws authorizing groups of citizens to form corporations for the purpose of founding and operating academies. Thirteen such acts were passed prior to the admission of Michigan into the Union. One of these corporations is still in existence. The Michigan and Huron Institute, which received a charter in 1833 and opened its doors in 1836, later became Kalamazoo College. It was founded by Baptists. Spring Arbor Seminary, incorporated in 1835 under a charter granted to a group of Methodists, was the forerunner of Albion College. The other eleven academies were community projects, most of which were later absorbed into the public school system.[9]

[9] L. Salmon, *Education in Michigan During the Territorial Period*; Sister Mary Rosalita, *Education in Detroit prior to 1850*; W. F. Dunbar, *Higher Education, the Michigan Record*.

In the pioneer schools the subjects usually taught were reading, spelling, writing, and arithmetic, with some small amount of attention to grammar and geography. Writing was done with pens made of quills. One of the requirements of a schoolmaster was the ability to make these quill pens; more important was his capacity for keeping order and maintaining strict discipline. The birch rod was an indispensable part of his equipment, and no pupil who strayed from the straight and narrow path of good conduct could long escape its sting. The democracy of frontier life was not reflected in the school room, for there the master was an autocrat of autocrats. In the summer term, when boys old and strong enough to work on the farm were busy in the fields, women teachers might be employed; but during the winter term, when these boys attended, men were usually employed as teachers. Only women with strength and courage could manage a school in those times.[10]

The pioneer schoolhouse was apt to be located at an intersection of roads or on the brow of a hill. It was made of logs, sometimes roughly hewn, and was generally about 18 feet wide and 24 feet long. The openings between the logs were chinked with pieces of wood, stones, or any convenient material, and plastered with mortar made from the earth nearby. The door was made of rough boards, hung on wooden hinges, and fastened with a wooden latch. Windows were made by cutting out spaces and fastening oiled paper over the opening, thereby admitting some light and keeping out some cold. An ample fireplace provided heat, in its immediate vicinity at least. Slabs mounted on legs were used for seats, and desks were constructed by placing boards upon pins driven into the walls of the building. The teacher's agreement usually stipulated that he would teach the school for a specified number of weeks, from six to eight hours a day, six days a week, for which parents agreed to pay him a stipulated sum for each pupil sent.[11]

Although such schools were crude and the teachers, in many instances, inadequately prepared to teach, it is remarkable that the pioneers devoted as much time and money for schools as they did when one recalls that sheer survival was often a problem. The New England element, which formed such a large proportion of the settlers who came in during the early 1830s, was especially devoted

[10] Several vivid accounts of pioneer schools have been written by A. D. P. VanBuren and published in *Mich. Pioneer and Historical Colls.*: "The Log-Schoolhouse Era," XIV (1892), 326ff.; "The Old Academy and Seminary, the Classic Schools of our Pioneer Days," XVIII (1896), 397ff.; and "A Quarter-Century of Teaching," X (1888), 24-29.

[11] *Forty-fourth annual report of the Supt. of Public Instruction.*

to education. It was the Yankee habit to equate learning with godliness, and ignorance with deviltry.

THE EARLY CHURCHES

As long as the French element formed the dominant part of the population, the Roman Catholic Church continued to be the most important religious organization in Michigan Territory. The work of the Jesuits and other early missionaries has been described at some length in an earlier chapter. There is a tradition that Cadillac's party, after landing at Detroit on July 24, 1701, began the construction of a chapel, which was completed two days later on July 26, the feast of Ste. Anne and dedicated in her honor, but George Paré, the foremost historial of the Catholic Church in Detroit, doubts that the tradition is accurate. The two priests who accompanied Cadillac did not remain long, but one of them seems to have returned in 1702, and the history of Ste. Anne's parish may be regarded as beginning in that year. The earliest baptismal records were lost, and the first entry in those that still exist is dated 1703. This register, continuous since 1704, is the oldest continuous Catholic register in this country with the single exception of that of St. Augustine, Florida. The present Ste. Anne's Church is the seventh edifice bearing that name. In 1708 a Potawatomi chief granted land for a "house of prayer" near Monroe, and two years later Father Frechette of Detroit organized a parish there. The church edifice was built about two and a half miles west of Monroe and was called St. Anthony's. Some years later the center of the parish was moved to Monroe and a new church, called Ste. Mary's, was erected. The third Catholic parish in Michigan was St. Peter's at Mount Clemens, dating from 1799 when a log chapel was built near the mouth of the Clinton River.[12]

The history of the Roman Catholic Church in Michigan during the first third of the 19th century, centers around the figure of Father Gabriel Richard. Though he is remembered for his work in education, his printing press, and his career in Congress, his passion was the Church. His residence was Detroit but his charge included not only all of Michigan but also what is now Wisconsin. Ste. Anne's Church, destroyed in the fire of 1805, was not rebuilt until 1818, services in the interim being held in farm houses and rented buildings. In 1822 Father Richard reported that his parish included 926 families, averaging six to a family, mostly French-Canadians. There were about 150 Irish Catholic families, widely scattered, and there were six Catholic churches in the territory.

[12] G. Paré, *The Catholic Church in Detroit, 1701-1888,* pp. 141-278.

Old Mission Lighthouse, built in 1870

Four years later Richard reported 7,000 Catholics and nine churches. In 1831 Irish Catholics around Ann Arbor worshipped in the first English-speaking Catholic church in the territory. Many of the Germans who started arriving about 1830 were Catholic. In that year Assumption, the first German Catholic parish, was formed. By the end of the territorial period Detroit had a second Catholic parish, largely for Irish Catholics and called Holy Trinity.

One of the tragedies of Father Richard's life was that, in spite of his manifold services and the growth of Catholicism in Michigan, he never was consecrated as a bishop. After the American flag was raised over Detroit, Michigan was attached to the diocese of Baltimore. Then in 1808 it became part of the diocese of Bardstown, Kentucky, and in 1821 it was made a part of the diocese of Cincinnati. As early as 1827 the erection of a Michigan diocese was considered. Perhaps Father Richard's involvements in a number of controversial matters, such as the Labadie case, caused the hierarchy to hesitate to make him a bishop. Within a year after his death, the diocese of Michigan and the Northwest was erected, the first bishop being Frederick Rese, a native of Hannover, Germany.

The first Protestants in Michigan were probably members of the British garrison that occupied Detroit in 1760, but no Anglican church was founded until much later. The next Protestants were the Moravians, who lived briefly in Michigan during the Revolution at Mount Clemens. Their little meeting house on the Clinton River was the first Protestant church, though it was only a temporary place of worship. The Reverend David Bacon made his way to Michigan as an agent of the Congregational churches of Connecticut as early as 1800, conducted religious services in Detroit, but found that all but a few of the people were firmly attached to the Catholic faith, so he shortly returned to the East.[13] Three years later the first Methodist preacher, Nathan Bangs, visited Michigan. He had been appointed to the Circuit of Upper Canada including Detroit by the New York Conference of the Methodist Episcopal Church. In Michigan, as elsewhere on the frontier, the Methodist circuit-rider was one of the most useful and tireless figures in the new country. Tramping or riding miles through the wilderness, he brought to lonely cabins not only spiritual consolation but also news of the outside world, books, and guidance in manners and morals. He held religious meetings wherever the opportunity presented itself, performed marriage ceremonies, buried the dead, and baptized the young.

The first Methodist society in Michigan was formed in 1810 by Methodists living on the River Rouge. Until 1818 services were held in homes, but in that year a hewn-log chapel was constructed on a site covered in later years by the vast Ford Motor Company plant. Except for the Moravian chapel on the Clinton River, which was built and used for a short time during the American Revolution, this chapel was the first Protestant house of worship in Michigan. The great influx of settlers in the 1830s brought many Methodists to Michigan, and Methodist churches had sprung up by 1837 in Ypsilanti, Adrian, Port Huron, Niles, Jackson, Coldwater, Kalamazoo, Flint, Ann Arbor, Marshall, and Detroit. Almost 5,000 members were reported by 1835 and the next year the Methodist Conference of Michigan was established.[14]

The arrival of the Rev. John Monteith in 1816 was an important event in the history of Protestantism in Michigan. A graduate of Princeton, Monteith was sent into the West by a home missionary organization that represented the joint efforts of the Presbyterians and Congregationalists. Since 1801 these two denominations had been under a "Plan of Union" in their work on the frontier. The plan envisioned that Presbyterians and Congregationalists in pioneer communities would establish a single church and that the membership would decide whether to adopt the Presbyterian or the Congregational mode of worship and organization. A public meeting of Protestants was held soon after Monteith came to Detroit, and he was engaged to remain one year, the sum of $800

[13] S. Farmer, *History of Detroit and Michigan,* p. 715.
[14] E. H. Pilcher, *History of Protestantism in Michigan,* pp. 16, 56, 88, 109, 115, 129, 175-178.

being subscribed to supplement the amount he received from missionary sources in the East. At the close of the first year the First Protestant Society of Detroit was organized. It consisted of Congregationalists, Presbyterians, Methodists, and Episcopalians, as well as people of no particular denomination. Monteith remained as pastor, and a church edifice, started in 1818 and dedicated in 1820, was erected at a cost of $7,000. Monteith and Father Richard were warm personal friends, both interested in education, active in the establishment of the Catholepistemiad, and appointed as president and vice-president respectively of that institution.

Methodists in Detroit became sufficiently numerous in 1821 to form their own society and build their own church. The Episcopalians organized separately in 1824 and also built a church, which was finished in 1828. The First Protestant Society was reorganized as the First Presbyterian Church in 1825. Monteith was instrumental in organizing a Presbyterian church at Monroe in 1820, and other churches of this denomination were founded at Pontiac in 1824, Farmington in 1825, and Ann Arbor in 1826. These churches formed the Detroit Presbytery, which was organized in 1827. The Presbyterian Church grew rapidly in the early 1830s, and by 1834 the St. Joseph and Monroe Presbyteries had been formed. These and the Detroit Presbytery constituted the Presbyterian Synod of Michigan, organized in 1834.

The Congregational Church regards the Rev. Isaac Ruggles, who came from Connecticut and established himself near Pontiac, as the pioneer Congregationalist in Michigan. Next to "Father Ruggles," the Rev. John D. Pierce of Marshall was perhaps the first Congregational minister in Michigan. There were eight churches in Michigan formed under the Plan of Union prior to 1835 that adopted the Congregational polity and never relinquished it. The path of co-operation between the Congregationalists and the Presbyterians was not a smooth one, and in 1837 a split occurred in the latter denomination over whether the Plan of Union should be continued. Most Michigan Presbyterians adhered to the "New School," which favored the Plan of Union, and this helped to maintain the co-operative program. As a result there was either a Presbyterian or a Congregational church in most pioneer Michigan towns, but seldom both. Fewer churches chose the Congregational affiliation than the Presbyterian, and it was not until 1842 that the Congregationalists formed a state association.

The first Baptist church in Michigan was organized by a group of New York immigrants who settled near Pontiac in 1819. The pastor of the church was paid $100 a year, one-third in cash and the remainder in produce. The Rev. Elon Galusha was probably the first Baptist minister in Michigan; he came as a missionary to the new church at Pontiac. By 1826 there were three other Baptist churches: Stony Creek (Oakland County). Troy, and Farmington. A Baptist church was founded in Detroit in 1827, and Ypsilanti and Ann Arbor Baptists organized churches the following year. In 1836 the Michigan Baptist Convention was formed by 55 delegates from 27 churches in Michigan. Close relations were maintained with the New York Baptist Convention. The Baptist Church was especially strong in western New York, and since so many Michigan pioneers came from that area, this denomination enjoyed a rapid growth.[15]

Of major importance in promoting the growth of Protestant churches in Michigan was the home-missionary movement. New England leaders for some years opposed the expansion of the nation westward, but when they realized that the westward movement was irresistible they determined to do what they could to civilize and christianize the new states by encouraging the founding of churches and schools. To this end they organized home-missionary societies in several of the New England states. This led to the formation of the American Home Missionary Society in 1826 as a co-operative venture of the Congregational, Presbyterian, and Reformed Churches. In 1832 the American Baptist Home Missionary Society was organized. The Methodists had no comparable society, but they were very effective along the same lines through the work of the circuit riders.[16] Among the leading home missionaries who came to Michigan were the Rev. John D. Pierce, who became the first state superintendent of public instruction, and Thomas W. Merrill, a Baptist, who was instrumental in founding the institution that became Kalamazoo College. There can be no doubt that churches were established in pioneer Michigan communities earlier than would otherwise have been possible as a result of the work of the home missionaries, who received their meager stipends in whole or in part from eastern missionary agencies.[17] The reports to the American Home Missionary Society contained in letters written by the scores of home missionaries who came to Michigan provide an intimate glimpse of pioneer times, although they no doubt overstressed the prevalence of drunkenness,

[15] M. E. D. Trowbridge, *History of the Baptists in Michigan*; C. Hayne, *Baptist Trail-makers in Michigan.*
[16] R. C. Crawford, "Reminiscences of Pioneer Ministers in Michigan," *Mich. Pioneer and Historical Colls.*, XVII (1890), 226-238.
[17] C. B. Goodykonntz, *Home Missions on the American Frontier.*

gambling, swearing, sabbath-breaking and other sins as a means of encouraging continued support from the East.[18]

The home missionaries, unlike the earlier Catholic missionaries, did not work among the Indians. However, several Protestants established Indian missions in the 1820s and 1830s. Notable among these were Isaac McCoy, who conducted the Carey Mission at Niles, and Leonard Slater, whose Indian mission on the Grand River was later moved to a location near Hastings. Both these men were Baptists. The Methodist Church had missionaries working among the Indians of the Upper Peninsula. The Presbyterian mission on Mackinac Island has been mentioned earlier.

The Episcopal Church was represented in Michigan by a sizable membership during the territorial period. St. Paul's Church in Detroit, formed in 1824, was the first Episcopal church in Michigan. The first pastor received $150 from his parishioners and $150 from the church mission board as his annual salary. Services were first held in the Council House, but a new church edifice was dedicated in 1828. Other Episcopal churches were established at Ann Arbor (1827), Troy (1829), Ypsilanti, Tecumseh, and Monroe (all 1831). The edifice built by the members of St. Peter's Church at Tecumseh and dedicated in 1833 was a fine example of church architecture. It was demolished in 1963 to make way for a new structure. In 1832 the Episcopal Diocese of Michigan was set up, although it had no bishop until 1836.[19]

Thus by the end of the territorial period the Roman Catholic Church and four Protestant denominations—the Methodist, Baptist, Presbyterian, and Episcopal—had set up ecclesiastical bodies embracing all of Michigan. A number of other denominations were represented. The Congregationalists have already been mentioned. German settlers around Ann Arbor formed a Lutheran church in that town in 1833, and by 1850 there were twelve Lutheran houses of worship in Michigan. A number of "Friends" (Quakers) settled near Adrian, and there the first "monthly meeting" of Quakers in Michigan was held in 1831. Shortly thereafter, "preparative meetings" of Quakers were held at Farmington (Oakland County), and Palmyra (Lenawee County). The Quakers were strongly opposed to slavery and the first antislavery society in Michigan was organized by the Quakeress Margaret Chandler in 1837. One of the most noted leaders of this faith was Laura Smith Haviland, affectionately known as "Aunt Laura," who was an ardent worker in

---

[18] Many of these letters are reproduced in M. Cole, *Voices from the Wilderness.*

[19] C. C. Trowbridge, "History of the Episcopal Church in Michigan," *Mich. Pioneer and Historical Colls.,* III (1881), 213-221.

the Underground Railroad, a name given to the clandestine smuggling of slaves from the South to Canada. The Universalist Church was represented in Michigan during territorial times by a society organized at Ann Arbor in 1828 and by 1850 seven Universalist churches were open in the state.

The religious life of early Detroit found expression not only in the formation of church bodies and the building of churches, but also in inter-church efforts of several kinds. A Bible Society was formed in 1816 and was supported by such notables as Governor Lewis Cass. A religious society for seamen was started in 1830, and a tract society was formed the following year. Detroit also had a German Evangelical church, organized in 1833. Thirteen ex-slaves voluntarily withdrew from the First Baptist Church to organize the Second Baptist Church in 1836.

A smaller percentage of the population belonged to churches than is true today, but there were stricter rules for members. It was not uncommon for a member to be excommunicated for not living up to the code of conduct demanded by church rules and practice. Although there were many pioneers who were unchurched, partly from preference and partly from the lack of any accessible church, there was a universal acceptance of the church as a cornerstone of society.

The early newspapers

The first newspaper in Michigan came from Father Richard's press in 1809, but it is doubtful whether more than one issue was published. Beginning with the establishment of the Detroit *Gazette*, the first issue of which appeared on July 25, 1817, newspaper publishing in Michigan has been continuous. It was established by John P. Sheldon and Ebenezer Reed. Although it was an English-language newspaper, most of the important articles were also printed in French on the last page. The paper measured 16½ x 9½ inches, and each page was made up of 4 columns. The subscription price was $4.00 per year to city subscribers and $3.50 by mail. It was issued weekly. The primitive character of the paper is implied by this description in Farmer's *History of Detroit and Michigan*:

> Occasionally the type-cases were overtaxed, and the number for October 18, 1822, gives the names of signers to a call for a public meeting in so many kinds and sizes of type that one might imagine that the compositor had just returned from a wake.[20]

[20] I, 671.

That the editorial policy was quite different from modern standards is shown by a statement in the issue of September 11, 1818. After warning the people against a person who had defrauded him, the editor made this announcement:

> Citizens who have been wronged by scoundrels have only to send a notice of their wrongs and the name of the scoundrel to this office in order to put the public on guard. Such notices will be published gratis.

Editor Sheldon published in 1829 an editorial bitterly assailing the territorial supreme court, by which he was convicted of contempt and fined $100. Upon his refusal to pay the amount he was put in jail. Townspeople were aroused by this and held a public meeting resulting in 800 people adopting a resolution upholding the editor. He continued to write for the paper while in jail, and a public banquet was given for him in the jail. He was at length released when citizens insisted on paying his fine, promptly taken to a hotel and given a gala luncheon.[21]

The Detroit *Gazette* printed its last issue in 1830. Other Detroit papers that came and went during the territorial period were *Michigan Herald* (1825-1829), the *Gazette Française* (1825), the Detroit *Telegraph* (1829), the Detroit *Courier* (1830), the *Herald of Literature and Science* (1831), the Detroit *Journal* (1835), and the *Michigan State Register* (1836-37). Two newspapers were being published at the end of the territorial period: the Detroit *Daily Advertiser*, which was founded in 1829 under a different name and became a daily in 1836, and the *Democratic Free Press and Michigan Intelligencer*, founded in 1831. The latter became a daily in 1835, and thus became Michigan's first daily newspaper. It is the lineal ancestor of the present Detroit *Free Press*, Michigan's only morning newspaper (1962). The first editor of the paper was John P. Sheldon, who had been editor of the *Gazette*. He had gone to Pontiac in 1830, where he started publication of the *Oakland Chronicle*. He returned to Detroit the following year to launch his new venture. The *Free Press* thus has the further distinction of being the oldest existing newspaper in the state. It also had the first power press used in the West. The *Free Press* was for many years a staunchly Democratic newspaper, while the *Advertiser* took the Whig, and later the Republican side.

Detroit was the only town in Michigan with daily newspapers. Several weeklies had been started outside Detroit, however, b

21 G. Catlin, *op. cit.,* pp. 286-287.

the close of the territorial period. The first of these was the Monroe *Sentinel,* which started publication in 1825. Second was the *Western Emigrant,* published at Ann Arbor beginning in 1829. The *Oakland Chronicle* of Pontiac, which was launched in 1830 and moved to Detroit the next year to become the *Free Press,* was the third newspaper outside Detroit. In November, 1833 the *Michigan Statesman and St. Joseph Chronicle* was established at White Pigeon by Henry Gilbert. It was the fourth outstate newspaper to be published. Gilbert was attracted to White Pigeon, it may be assumed, by the printing business that the local government land office would provide. When the land office was moved to Kalamazoo in 1835 the printer went along and started publication of the *Michigan Statesman* in Kalamazoo. He changed its name to the Kalamazoo *Gazette* in 1837, and this newspaper is still being published. Since there is no newspaper in existence today that can trace its beginning back to the Monroe *Sentinel* and the *Western Emigrant,* and since the *Oakland Chronicle* was moved to Detroit, the Kalamazoo *Gazette* has the distinction of being the oldest existing newspaper in Michigan outside Detroit.

Monroe had a second newspaper in 1834, the Monroe *Advocate,* and the present Monroe *Evening News* is the descendant of that paper. Ann Arbor also had a second newspaper, the *State Journal,* which started publication in 1835. St. Clair, Niles, and Adrian had their first newspapers in 1835; Tecumseh, Constantine, Marshall, and Saginaw in 1836; Jackson, Mount Clemens, and Grand Rapids in 1837.

St. Clair had a second newspaper by the end of 1837, and before the close of the 1830s, rival newspapers had also been established in Kalamazoo, Jackson, Marshall, Mount Clemens, and Pontiac. In the latter town the short-lived *Oakland Chronicle* was followed by the Pontiac *Courier* (1836) and the Pontiac *Jacksonian* (1838). The intense partisanship of the late 1830s, with friends and foes of President Jackson and his successor in office, Martin Van Buren, contending against each other, encouraged partisan journalism. Many newspapers were started purely as partisan organs, and some were published only for a few months during a campaign.[22]

Newspaper publishing in Michigan began in earnest at a time when American journalism was at a low ebb. One authority on

[22] D. McMurtie, *Early Printing in Michigan;* W. Stocking, "Prominent Newspaper Men in Michigan," *Mich. Pioneer and Historical Colls.,* XXXIX (1929), 153-168; T. S. Applegate, "A History of the Press in Michigan," *Mich. Pioneer and Historical Colls.,* VI (1883), 62-98.

the subject writes: "Indeed the whole period of 1801-1833 was in many respects disgraceful—a kind of 'Dark Ages' in American journalism. Few papers were ably edited; they reflected the crassness of the American society of the times. Scurrility, assaults, corruption, blatancy were commonplace."[23] Hezekiah Niles, one of the most reliable observers of the time, wrote: "The press is now so conditioned in the United States, that nearly every publisher is compelled to take a side in personal electioneering."[24] In many cases newspapers depended for their support mainly on subsidies from political parties.

In spite of their shortcomings these early newspapers kept the people of Michigan in touch with the outside world. In addition to biting editorials and usually some bad fiction and worse poetry, they brought news from Europe (usually two or three months old) and information on happenings in the East. The advertisements advised readers on merchandise available in the stores. The papers contained some territorial news, but relatively little on local events. The reader was expected to know as well as the editor what had gone on in the community where the newspaper was published. This lack of a record of local happenings, though understandable, often is vexatious to the researcher who expects or hopes to find in old newspaper files full accounts of an important event of territorial times.

CULTURAL INTERESTS

The cultural life of Detroit in territorial days found expression in a variety of interests and activities. The citizens of the town formed a library society in 1817, and in 1831 the Detroit Athenaeum was established to maintain a club reading room. Governor Cass and John Biddle were chosen president and vice-president respectively. The Detroit Young Men's Society was formed in 1833 to "devise means for greater intellectual improvement"; meetings were held each Friday evening during the winter, at which time debates were conducted and "elocutionary exercises" were presented. A library was also maintained. Incorporated in 1836, the Society continued to exist for almost half a century. A lyceum was organized in 1818 under the leadership of Judge Woodward and Secretary Woodbridge. As usual with anything in which Woodward had a hand, this club was too grandiose in design for practical purposes. Dr. Douglas Houghton announced a series of 26 lectures on chemistry in 1830; admission was $2.00

[23] F. L. Mott, *American Journalism*, p. 169.
[24] Quoted in *ibid.*, p. 168.

for the series, or $4.00 for a family of three. A local newspaper offered a prize of $25 to the apprentice who submitted in writing the best summary of the series. The Historical Society of Michigan was incorporated in 1828, with Lewis Cass as president. At the meetings of the Society, Cass, Henry R. Schoolcraft, and others lectured. However, the Society soon passed out of existence, to be revived in 1874 as the Michigan Pioneer Society. Later the name was changed to Michigan Pioneer and Historical Society; the original name, Historical Society of Michigan, was adopted in 1949.

There was scant time for the cultivation of the arts in pioneer Michigan, but interest in music, the visual arts, and the theater were not lacking. Music was an adjunct to the worship of God at Ste. Anne's Church in Detroit, and there is evidence that the church had a chorister as early as 1755. To celebrate the end of the siege of Detroit during the Pontiac uprising of 1763 an "instrumental concert" was given. Shortly after 1800 a small pipe organ was installed in the church; the instrument so amazed and fascinated the Indians that they stole the pipes![25] The organ must have been repaired, or else Father Richard obtained a new one. In 1832 the organ that had been used by Ste. Anne's was given to Trinity Church. St. Paul's Episcopal Church acquired a new organ in 1831, on which a "concert" was performed by "Mr. Newell" on September 30 of that year.

There was at least one harpsichord in Detroit prior to the nineteenth century. The first piano arrived in 1803. It was an instrument that had been played by Mrs. Solomon Sibley prior to her marriage while attending a school in Pennsylvania. It was transported on horseback to Marietta, Ohio; just how it was carried from Marietta to Detroit the records do not tell. Another piano was brought to Ann Arbor from Detroit by ox team in 1827. The teamster was somewhat fearful of the contents of the box in which it was packed because "it thundered so." This was the first piano taken west of Detroit. It had only five octaves and was manufactured in New York. The Indians were also greatly attracted to this instrument, so the story goes, and the chief is said to have offered half a dozen ponies for the instrument and the young lady who played it.[26]

Singing was popular among the pioneers. Many of them sang at their work. Some were noted for their good voices or their extensive repertoire of songs, and these were called upon to perform at social gatherings. Mothers sang to put their children to sleep,

[25] S. Farmer, *op. cit.,* I, 354.
[26] *Michigan History,* XXIV (1940), 290.

songs they had heard their mothers sing. Mostly the words and tunes were just remembered. There were books containing the words of songs, but since only a very few people could read music the names of the tunes but not the notes were included. Singing schools were popular with the young people and were not frowned upon by the pious, as were dancing and some other kinds of amusement. More often than not the songs and ballads were sung unaccompanied; occasionally the performer would provide his own accompaniment with the dulcimer or guitar. The singer and the audience were more enraptured by the story told by a ballad than by the tune. In these stories the tragic element predominated, although happier themes were not entirely lacking. Some told of disasters and tragedies, others dealt with unrequited love. A number were in a humorous vein, and some of the love ballads had a happy ending.

The history of the theater in Michigan begins with the amateur theatricals performed by the soldiers in the Detroit garrison. Life in the western military posts was dull and monotonous for the lively young men who manned them, and to while away the hours they rehearsed and presented plays, taking both male and female roles and using improvised scenery. The plays were designed mainly for the amusement of the participants, their families, and friends. The officers of the Detroit garrison formed an amateur troupe in 1798, and produced such favorites as *The Rivals* and *The Mock Duke*. These plays continued to be presented for many years. Traveling players may have visited Detroit as early as 1810. In 1816 a theater was fitted up on the second floor of a large brick warehouse at the foot of Wayne Street. There were several other buildings used for theatricals during the next two decades, indicating that there must have been quite a lively interest in dramatics. A company of players arrived from Buffalo in 1827, was granted a license to perform, and apparently presented an entire season of plays. In 1833 another company came for the summer season, and the next year two more arrived.[27] The *Free Press* in 1837 told of a rapid succession of "sterling comedy, showy melodrama, gorgeous spectacle, broad farce, and delightful vaudeville and drama."[28]

Without any pretense of artistic expression, the pioneers, in many of the tools and utensils they made by hand, demonstrated sound ideas of design. Simple but beautiful geometric and representational designs are found in the carved and turned wood fashioned by early craftsmen. Simple furniture made by pioneers

[27] R. C. Buley, *op. cit.*, II, 574.
[28] August 9, 1837.

in many instances reflects skill of workmanship and an eye for beauty. In the homes and public buildings they constructed, after sawmills made lumber available, the pioneer carpenters produced structures of lasting beauty, aesthetically far superior to the ornate monstrosities that were built later in the nineteenth century by a wealthier and more sophisticated generation. The style of pioneer houses, after the log-cabin stage was passed, was determined to a large degree by the New England and New York origins of most of the Michigan settlers. New England colonial architecture was widely copied. The houses were rectangular in plan and placed parallel with the street; they usually had a low gabled roof, molded cornice, small-paned sash, and doors framed with slender pilasters. The Snow house in Paw Paw, the Medor Tromble house in Bay City, and the Agent's house on Mackinac Island are surviving examples of the use of the New England colonial style by Michigan builders.[29] The style was also copied in some of the early churches.

Before the end of the territorial period the Greek Revival style had been introduced into Michigan and it continued to be popular throughout the 1830s and 1840s. A number of examples of it may still be seen in the surviving homes constructed during that period. The central portion of these houses was built on the order of a Greek temple, but they vary greatly in form and composition. Builders apparently used standard designs, in the absence of architects, then added their own ideas. Heavy cornices and columns, generally of wood, were distinctive features of the Greek Revival houses. The southeastern part of Michigan, which was most thickly settled in this period, is particularly rich in examples of this type of house, though many are found in towns as far west as Kalamazoo. More have survived in rural areas and small towns than in the cities, for with urban growth old houses are often sacrificed in the name of progress. At Cambridge Junction along US 12 stands the Walker Tavern, erected by Ezra Blood in 1832. It is basically a New York farmhouse, but the narrow veranda around two sides, with heavy, square columns supporting the roof, is a crude but typically Greek Revival characteristic. The Elijah Anderson house and the Yawger house in Tecumseh, built in the 1830s, the Charles M. Croswell house in Adrian, and the Wilson-Wahr house in Ann Arbor are excellent examples of various aspects of the Greek Revival style.[30] Perhaps the finest Greek Revival house in Michigan

[29] E. Lorch, "The Development of Architecture," *Michigan, a Guide to the Wolverine State*, p. 164.
[30] H. Taylor, "Michigan's Pioneer Architecture," *Michigan History*, XXXVII (1953), 19-26.

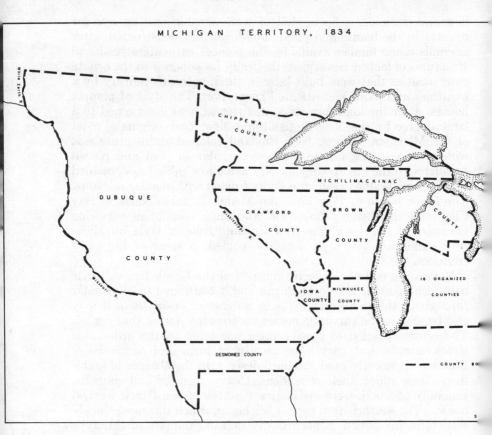

MICHIGAN TERRITORY, 1834

CHIPPEWA COUNTY

DUBUQUE COUNTY

MICHILIMACKINAC

CRAWFORD COUNTY

BROWN COUNTY

COUNTY

IOWA COUNTY

MILWAUKEE COUNTY

16 ORGANIZED COUNTIES

DESMOINES COUNTY

COUNTY BO—

was built near Dexter by Samuel Dexter; this house has been pictured and described in many architectural journals.

The first professional artist in Michigan was probably James O. Lewis, who arrived at Detroit in 1824. A steel engraver and painter, he employed both these media in his portraits of Father Gabriel Richard and Governor Lewis Cass. He was one of the artists who submitted designs for the seal of the City of Detroit, and the first seal of the State of Michigan (1835) is ascribed to him. He went with the Cass expedition in 1820 and made many drawings of Indian chiefs. His work went to the Smithsonian Institution in Washington, but the drawings were destroyed by fire in 1865. Two portfolios of lithographs of his Indian subjects were sold by subscription, and copies of these have been preserved.

Shortly after Lewis came to Detroit he was followed by another painter, Gildersleeve Hurd. Hurd came to visit his brother, who had married a daughter of Judge James Witherell. His portraits of the judge and members of the Witherell family have survived and show considerable skill. He opened a decorator's studio in Detroit and specialized in decorating the plastered walls of houses with paneled landscapes, surrounded by ornamentation.

Several itinerant artists turned up in Detroit in the 1830s. One was J. M. Stanley, who came to Detroit after being employed at Buffalo painting medallions and landscapes on farm wagons. He produced many landscapes which were purchased by Detroiters to hang in their homes, and, like Lewis, he painted many Indian chiefs. His "Indian Telegraph" is in the permanent collection of the Detroit Institute of Arts. T.H.O.P. Burnham, nicknamed "Alphabet Burnham" for obvious reasons, is best known for his "State election scene" of 1837. It depicts Campus Martius in Detroit on election day, and includes portraits of Governor Mason and other notables. Critics have compared this painting to the work of Hogarth and feel that it reveals an artist of keen perception and artistic understanding. Alvah Bradish, a portrait painter who arrived in 1837, set up a studio and for more than fifty years produced portraits of famous Detroiters. His style was that of the English portraiture of the eighteenth century. Several other artists came to Detroit prior to 1837. The popularity of portraits before the advent of photography created a lively demand for artists. It was not confined to the great or the near-great either. Itinerant "limners" roamed Michigan, equipped with an assortment of canvases, complete except for the face. The person desiring to have his portrait done would select a background, body, and dress, after which the artist would quickly finish the work for a small fee, sometimes accepting board and lodging in lieu of money.[31]

Although Detroit had a greater variety of cultural activities and civic associations than was found elsewhere, the new outstate towns manifested an early interest in such fields. Bible societies, temperance societies, and antislavery societies were established in many places. Lyceums had been organized in several towns outside Detroit by 1837.

[31] C. H. Burroughs, "Painting and Sculpture in Michigan," *Michigan History,* XX (1936), 395-411; XXI (1937), 39-55 and 141-158.

Governor Stevens T. Mason

IO

A STORMY ENTRANCE
INTO THE UNION

W hen Michigan celebrated the centennial of its admission into
the Union as a state, the observance had to be extended over a
three-year period. Although a state government was formed and
put into operation in 1835, it was not until 1837 that President
Andrew Jackson signed a bill passed by Congress making the
State of Michigan a member of the federal union. The delay was
occasioned by a border dispute between Michigan and Ohio, which
erupted into what has been called the "Toledo War." Armed men
were mobilized on both sides of the border, but fortunately this
was one war in which no one was killed. In the end Ohio received
the area involved in the controversy while Michigan received in
return the extensive tract of land that now forms the greater part
of the Upper Peninsula.

STATEHOOD WITHOUT AUTHORIZATION

As Michigan's population grew by leaps and bounds in the early
'thirties it was natural that the possibility of statehood should be
broached. A vote on the expediency of forming a state government
was taken in 1832. It carried, but only by a small margin. Nevertheless the territorial council formally requested Congress in 1833
to pass an enabling act for Michigan. The usual procedure had
been, when a territory was ready for statehood, for Congress to

301

pass such an "enabling act" authorizing the election of a constitutional convention. After a constitution had been written it was then submitted to Congress, and the state was admitted under that constitution. The reason for this procedure lay in the fact that the United States constitution guarantees to each state a "republican" form of government, and thus Congress, before admitting the state, had to be assured it would have such a government. However, Tennessee, which was admitted to the Union in 1796, had framed a constitution without any enabling act and had demanded statehood as a right that Congress could not deny. A governor, congressman, and two senators were elected. The congressman and senator proceeded to Philadelphia, then the seat of the federal government, and demanded to be seated. There was considerable debate over the propriety of this procedure, and political interests were involved. The Federalists opposed the admission of Tennessee because they were certain the state would favor the Jeffersonian anti-federalist party. However, they were outvoted and Tennessee was granted statehood.

Although Tennessee was not part of the Northwest Territory, its claim to statehood rested upon a census that showed it had more than 60,000 people, the number set forth in the Northwest Ordinance as a prerequisite for statehood. The Northwest Ordinance stated, ". . . whenever any of the said states shall have sixty thousand free inhabitants therein, such state shall be admitted by its delegates into the Congress of the United States, on an equal footing with the original states in all respects whatsoever; and shall be at liberty to form a permanent constitution and state government." Whether this provision in an ordinance enacted for the "government of the territory of the United States, northwest of the River Ohio" applied also to Tennessee was debatable, but there could be no question of its applicability in the case of Michigan. However, the Constitution of the United States provides that "New States may be admitted by the Congress into this Union . . . ;" which would appear to give Congress the power to exercise discretion in the matter of admitting a state. As has already been indicated, there always was some question of the validity of the Northwest Ordinance, and there can be no doubt that Congress departed in several respects from its provisions. Michigan's contention was, however, that the Northwest Ordinance represented a compact that gave the people who settled in the Old Northwest rights that could not be violated even by Congress. The Ordinance itself stated that "the following articles shall be considered as articles of compact between the original states and the people and states in the said territory, and for ever unalterable, unless by common consent . . . ," and one of the articles that followed guaranteed statehood when "any of the said states shall have sixty thousand free inhabitants therein."

The federal census of 1830 had enumerated 31,639 persons in the Territory of Michigan, but so great was the influx after 1830 that there could be little question that there were at least 60,000 by 1833. Michigan was fortunate to have as its delegate in Congress at the time an unusually capable man in the person of Lucius Lyon. He had a wide circle of friends and he ably supported the petition of the Territorial Council that an enabling act be passed. The House committee on territories reported that it was "inexpedient" to grant the petition at the time, but a bill was introduced in the senate to authorize the people of Michigan to form a state government. This bill was debated between May 9 and 12, 1834, then laid on the table by a vote of 20 to 19. Lyon could accomplish little in the face of hard political facts.

The difficulty centered around a boundary dispute between Michigan and Ohio that had lain dormant for many years but now, for a variety of reasons, had become heated. Politicians are notoriously reluctant to deal with a hot issue such as this was unless compelled to do so. In many respects, as will be indicated below, Michigan had a strong case, but on the other hand, Ohio had more voters than did Michigan; from the political standpoint, if one side or the other was to be offended it should not be Ohio. The result was that Congress did nothing about statehood for Michigan.

Back in the territory the cholera epidemic took Governor George Porter as one of its victims, and this once more made young Stevens T. Mason acting governor. He promptly called the Territorial Council into special session and sent the members a message in which he called attention to the inaction of Congress and proposed a course of action designed to attain statehood for Michigan. He asked the Council to authorize a census to ascertain the size of the population of Michigan, which, he wrote, "is beyond doubt, over sixty thousand," and then to proceed to call a convention to institute a state government, to elect a representative and two senators, and to send them to Washington to *demand* admission into the Union.[1] The Council readily assented to Mason's proposal. A census was ordered and the returns indicated there were 85,856 persons in the Lower Peninsula, with another 6,817 in the vast area north and west of Lake Michigan that was then part of the Territory of Michigan. Early in 1835, the Council reconvened and on January 26 ordered an election

[1] *Messages of the Governors of Michigan,* I, 121-124.

to be held on April 4 of delegates to a constitutional convention, who were to assemble at Detroit on May 11. The convention consisted of 91 delegates: 17 from Wayne County, 15 from Washtenaw, 14 from Oakland, 9 each from Monroe and Lenawee, and the remainder from the other counties of the territory.

The convention completed its work in 45 days. It drafted a constitution that was brief, simple, and suited to the temper of the time, and submitted the document to a vote of the people. A schedule was drawn up that called for the voters to pass judgment on the proposed constitution on October 5, 1835. On the assumption that the verdict would be favorable, it was provided that an election should be held on the following day—October 6—at which a governor, lieutenant governor, state representatives, state senators, and a representative to Congress would be chosen. And finally, the legislature so elected was called to assemble on November 1. This timetable gave the people of Michigan a little over three months to consider the proposed constitution, after which time the process of choosing officials and inaugurating a new state government was to be compressed into a period of less than one month. The reason for this haste no doubt was that the border controversy with Ohio was reaching a climax, and as a consequence neither the delegates nor the people were in a mood to delay asserting the right of Michigan to statehood.

The political parties during the summer nominated their candidates for state office. The Democrats chose Stevens T. Mason as their candidate for governor, while the Whigs named John Biddle, former territorial delegate to Congress.[2] Then on September 10 Mason received a letter from Washington signed by Secretary of State John Forsyth apprising him of his dismissal as secretary (and therefore as acting governor) of Michigan Territory for failing to preserve the "spirit of moderation and forbearance" that President Jackson deemed "necessary for the preservation of the public peace." The President was alluding to Mason's leadership of armed resistance against Ohio's attempts to take over jurisdiction of the disputed strip by Michigan militiamen. Mason, who at the time was watching a dress parade of his troops, at once called for attention, and announced he was no longer their leader. On September 19 John S. Horner arrived at Detroit to assume Mason's position as secretary and acting governor of the territory.

Although Mason himself made no move to resist the President's decision, the people made life miserable for Horner. They re-

[2] The Whigs held no formal convention, but Biddle was their leading candidate.

garded him as a puppet of Washington politicians who had rejected their appeal for statehood. Horner himself was immensely fat, wore a sour expression, and had a raspy voice—characteristics that only intensified the contempt in which he was held by Michiganians. Even worse, he released from jail those Ohioans who had been apprehended trespassing on what Michigan regarded as its territory, giving rise to the suspicion that he was in league with Governor Lucas of Ohio. These suspicions were well-founded, for Horner kept Lucas informed on developments in Michigan, broadly hinting that affairs would be managed in such a way as to redound to the benefit of Ohio. He could find no one to carry out his orders. His appearance was greeted with boos and clods of dirt, and he was dubbed "Little Jack Horner." Finally he left Detroit in disgust and went to Ypsilanti, where the people, hearing he had freed the Ohioans, gathered beneath his window and woke him up with a barrage of stones and blobs of horse dung. Terrified, he returned to Detroit, where he was simply ignored.[3]

On the appointed day in October the voters approved the proposed state constitution by an overwhelming majority: 6,752 in favor and 1,374 against. And the following day they elected Mason as governor and Edward Mundy of Ann Arbor as lieutenant governor. Both were Democrats. Mason received 7,508 votes, while his leading Whig opponent, John Biddle, was given only 814. The newly elected legislature convened on November 1. In his inaugural Governor Mason vigorously upheld Michigan's right to form a state government. But he recommended that the legislature pass few laws, and pointed out that the new constitution provided that territorial laws not in conflict with it should remain in effect until they expired or were altered and that all territorial officials except for governor and lieutenant governor should remain in office "until the legislature, giving due time for the legislation of Congress on the subject of our admission into the union, may deem it expedient to organize a State judiciary, and to authorize the election or appointment of other officers, under the constitution." The lawmakers heeded the advice of the governor, confining itself to the passage of only seven laws, mostly dealing with fiscal matters, and the election of Lucius Lyon and John Norvell as United States senators. Mason made only one appointment, that of Kintzing Prichette as secretary of state. It is apparent that there was some reluctance to proceed in the absence of approval by Congress and in the face of a denial

[3] K. Sagendorph, *Stevens Thomson Mason, Misunderstood Patriot*, pp. 207-211.

by President Jackson that the people of Michigan possessed the right to set up a government that would supersede the territorial government.

The legislature met only one day, then adjourned to February 1, 1836. Meanwhile it was hoped that Congress would take action to admit Michigan into the Union. The hope proved vain, because it was mid-June before any definite action was taken. When the legislature reassembled on February 1 there were many who had grave doubts on the advisability of completing the organization of the state government. An act calling on the territorial auditor general and treasurer to hand over the books, papers, and funds in their custody to state officials was passed by the legislature and approved by the governor on February 19; but Levi Cook, treasurer of the territory who was appointed to the corresponding position in the state government, not only declined the appointment but refused to deliver the books, papers, and funds of the territory to the state. The three territorial supreme court judges were renominated by President Jackson and confirmed by the Senate late in February. The territorial courts continued to function through June. But the legislature, in spite of considerable opposition, took action in February and March to establish a state judiciary, headed by a state supreme court. It also enacted other laws that provided for a complete organization of the state government, the methods of selection, duties, and salaries of state officers, and the dates on which persons still holding office under the territorial government would be removed. Opposition to the organization of a state government without prior approval by Congress continued, however. Curiously enough, the Whigs led the opposition, while the Democrats favored going ahead in defiance of the party's leader: President Jackson.[4]

The tension was somewhat relieved by the departure of John S. Horner, who had continued to stay on in Detroit in spite of the fact that no attention was paid to him. On April 20, 1836 an act passed by Congress establishing a territorial government in Wisconsin became law. Horner was appointed as its secretary and he left Detroit soon afterward for his new post. Meanwhile Congress was wrestling with the knotty problem of the Michigan-Ohio boundary and Michigan's application for statehood. The debate and its outcome can be better understood by reviewing the struggle that took place in 1835 over the boundary between Michigan and Ohio.

[4] C. F. Norton, "Michigan Statehood, 1835, 1836, or 1837?" *Michigan History*, XXXVI (1952), 321-350.

THE MAUMEE MELEE

The clash between Ohioans and Michiganians that took place in 1835 has been called the Toledo War. Since the city of Toledo was not chartered until 1837 and since the fracas was not actually a war, "Toledo War" is a misnomer. The crucial issue, so far as Ohio was concerned, was whether the mouth of the Maumee River (then called the Miami of the Lake) should be in Ohio or Michigan. Numerous projects for the building of canals were being advanced, and the outlet of one entire system of such canals would be the Maumee River. Hence, the unpleasantness of 1835 might more aptly be called the Maumee melee.

The origin of the dispute between Michigan and Ohio dates back to the Ohio constitutional convention of 1802. There is a story to the effect that a hunter who happened to be present asserted that the southern end of Lake Michigan was actually further south than was indicated on the maps of the time.[5] To be certain that the mouth of the Maumee River would be included within Ohio, a proviso was inserted in that part of the Ohio constitution dealing with boundaries. It stated

> that if the southerly bend or extreme of Lake Michigan should extend so far south that a line drawn due east from it should not intersect Lake Erie, or if it should intersect said Lake Erie east of the mouth of the Miami River of the Lakes [i.e., the Maumee] then and in that case, with the assent of the Congress of the United States, the northern boundary of this state shall be established by and extend to a line running from the southerly extreme of Lake Michigan to the most northerly extreme of the Miami [Maumee] Bay.

Congress admitted Ohio to the Union in 1803 under this constitution but with no specific assent to the change in boundary stipulated in the proviso just quoted. As soon as the Ohio congressmen were seated they began to work to obtain the assent of Congress to the boundary proviso, but to no avail. The case of Michigan rested strongly upon this failure by Congress to accept specifically the altered boundary proviso in the Ohio constitution.[6] In 1805, when the Territory of Michigan was established,

[5] Several of the maps of that time, all showing the southern tip of Lake Michigan further north than it actually is, may be found in L. C. Karpinski, *Bibliography of the Printed Maps of Michigan, 1804-1880*, pp. 186ff. The story of the hunter is told in C. S. Larzelere, "The Boundaries of Michigan," *Mich. Pioneer and Historical Colls.*, XXX (1906), 13.

[6] A. M. Soule, "The Southern and Western Boundaries of Michigan," *Mich. Pioneer and Historical Colls.*, XXVII (1897), 849.

Congress provided that its southern boundary should be that set forth in the Northwest Ordinance, completely disregarding the proviso in the Ohio constitution.

Ohioans in Congress continued to agitate for acceptance of the altered northern boundary of their state, but despite their efforts, Congress in 1812 passed a resolution providing for the survey of the line as established in the Ordinance of 1787: a line drawn due east from the southerly extreme of Lake Michigan. The War of 1812 intervened, at this point, and the survey of the line was put off until 1817. By that time the Surveyor General of the United States was a former Ohio governor, Edward Tiffin. He employed a surveyor named William Harris to survey the boundary, but instructed him to run 'it in accordance with the provision in the Ohio constitution! Governor Cass of Michigan Territory promptly lodged a spirited protest to President Monroe, and as a result a new survey was made in 1818, this one by John A. Fulton, in accordance with the Ordinance provisions. This survey line intersected Lake Erie east of the mouth of the Maumee, leaving the river's outlet in Michigan. The area between the two lines, commonly called the "Toledo strip," was about eight miles wide on the east, five miles wide on the west, and contained 468 square miles.

Oddly enough, the dispute quieted down after 1818. The Ohio legislature declared the Harris line was the official boundary, but jurisdiction in the disputed area was quietly assumed by Michigan. The Territorial Council in 1825 organized the Township of Port Lawrence in the very heart of the area without causing any Ohio protest. County courts were held in the strip, and residents voted in Michigan elections. A land company bought a tract that included the mouth of the Maumee and laid out two towns: Port Lawrence in 1817 and Vistula in 1832. They were united under the name of Toledo in 1833, but the place was not incorporated as a city until after the boundary question was settled. During this "quiet period," Governor Cass had attempted to negotiate a compromise with Ohio, permitting that state to retain the mouth of the Maumee and compensating Michigan by conceding additional territory to the west, but the effort came to naught.

The dispute was resumed in earnest on December 11, 1833, when Lucius Lyon, Michigan's delegate to Congress, presented the first formal petition for the admission of Michigan as a state. Then someone discovered certain technical shortcomings in the Fulton survey, and a new one was ordered. This time the line was run by Captain Andrew Talcott, whose chief assistant in the project was a young lieutenant named Robert E. Lee, later to gain fame as commander of the Confederate armies in the Civil War. The Talcott line, when run, coincided with the Fulton line.[7] Meanwhile in Washington, the senate, after a lengthy debate, passed a bill upholding Ohio and accepting the Harris line as the official boundary. In the House of Representatives, however, the bill encountered stiff opposition and was referred to a committee, where it still reposed when Congress adjourned. Shortly afterward Governor Porter died and Acting Governor Mason at once took steps, as has been related, to have a census taken as a first step toward statehood.

In the next session of Congress, beginning in December, 1834, Ohio's senators revived the boundary bill, and this time added a section confirming the northern boundaries of Indiana and Illinois. It will be recalled that in 1816, when Indiana had achieved statehood, Congress had moved Indiana's northern boundary ten miles north of the Northwest Ordinance line, and that two years later, when Illinois was admitted, the northern boundary of that state had been moved sixty miles north of the Ordinance line. There was no necessity to reaffirm these boundaries, but the Ohioans, by including such a provision in the bill to establish Ohio's northern boundary at the Harris line, sought support from their neighbors to the west. The inclusion constituted an inference that if Michigan were to make the Ordinance line stick in its dispute with Ohio, then the Indiana and Illinois lines might be of questionable legality. The senate again passed the bill establishing the Harris line, with the additional provision confirming the northern boundaries of Indiana and Illinois, but once more the House of Representatives failed to uphold the Senate action.

While Congress was grappling with the dispute, the Michigan Territorial Council, in a conciliatory gesture, passed an act on December 26, 1834 for the appointment of three commissioners to negotiate with Ohio a settlement of the boundary dispute. Governor Robert Lucas of Ohio promptly rejected any such negotiation, ordered permanent markers to be placed along the Harris line, and proceeded to organize the area into a new Ohio county, bearing his own name. The Michigan Territorial Council countered with a resolution imposing a fine of $1,000 or five years' imprisonment on anyone except Michigan or federal officers who should accept office or exercise official functions in the disputed strip. Undaunted, Lucas appointed a sheriff and judges to hold court in his newly created county, whereupon Governor Mason mobilized

[7] W. Millis, "When Michigan was Born," *Michigan History,* XVIII (1934), 208-224.

the territorial militia, called for volunteers, and placed himself at the head of these forces.

The danger of an armed clash between Ohioans and Michigan-ians now became a matter of concern to President Jackson. He sought the opinion of his attorney general, who upheld Michigan's claim. This was no comfort to Old Hickory, who had his eye fixed on the next election and worried no end about all those votes his party would lose in Ohio, Indiana, and Illinois if he came out in support of Michigan. Not knowing what else to do, Jackson ap-pointed two commissioners to go west and try to settle the con-

MICHIGAN BOUNDARIES AND THE
TOLEDO STRIP QUESTION

troversy. They went first to Detroit and saw Mason, who said he w ˙ˀ refrain from using force as long as Lucas stayed out of the ɑᵤˏ ₑd strip. When they transmitted this proposal to Lucas, the latter quite naturally rejected it. Then they went back to Mason and told him Jackson would remove him from office if he started arresting Ohioans who tried to exercise authority in the disputed strip. Mason wouldn't back down: he told the commissioners, in effect, that it would be usurpation and tyranny to remove him for enforcing the law!

Mason was not bluffing. At the head of his militia, he proceeded to the Toledo strip and arrested any Ohio officials he found who refused to leave by a specified time. He also arrested nine surveyors who were re-marking the Harris line for Ohio. The rest of the surveying party was permitted to escape, the retreat of its members being speeded by the firing of a gun high over their heads. When they got safely back within Ohio, they told a tale of a hairbreadth escape from bloodthirsty Michiganians that aroused great indignation.

The story of the Michigan-Ohio fracas during the next few weeks is full of comic-opera incidents that no doubt were regarded seriously at the time but, at a distance of more than a century, appear uproariously funny. For example, when the Ohio legislature voted $300,000 to defend the Toledo strip, the Michigan Territorial Council voted $315,000. An Ohio flag, torn down by irate Michiganians, was referred to by a Michigan newspaper as "the disgraceful badge of treason," and was burned "with suitable demonstrations of contempt." There is a report that Ohio produced its own Barbara Fritchie, who unfurled the dishonored flag or one like it.[8] Then there is the story of the judges appointed by Governor Lucas who were sent to hold court in the disputed strip as a means of establishing Ohio's claim to jurisdiction. In spite of the fact that the judges were accompanied by a small armed guard, they were half scared out of their wits by fear of the Michigan militiamen. In the dead of night they crept into a schoolhouse, blacked out the windows, lit a tallow dip, went through the motions of holding court, and hastily repaired to a nearby tavern to refresh their spirits. As they were about to have a second round, a local wag dashed in and shouted that a company of Michigan militiamen was about to arrest them. They dropped their glasses, dashed to their horses and made off at top speed. After they had gone a short distance the clerk of the court discovered his tall stovepipe hat was missing. In it he had stowed the official records

[8] C. Wittke, "The Ohio-Michigan Boundary Dispute Re-examined," *Ohio Archaeological and Historical Society Quarterly*, XLV (1936), 299-319.

of the court session. Nerving themselves to a possible clash with the Michiganians, the party retraced its route, and the lost hat was discovered under a tree, where it had been knocked off by an overhanging branch during the hasty retreat. So great was the joy in recovering the hat and its contents, that two salutes were fired to celebrate the victory. The spot was close enough to the border so that escape would be possible if the volleys were heard by the enemy.

It is surprising that no one was killed in the clashes between the two sides. Miraculously there were no casualties, with the single exception of a Michigan sheriff who was stabbed with a jackknife in a tavern scuffle by an Ohioan by the name of Two Stickney. He was the son of B. F. Stickney, an ardent Buckeye who fancied himself a military genius. His two sons were named, respectively, One and Two. In spite of the fact that no one was killed, the rumors that circulated through Ohio depicted Michiganians as bloodthirsty villains of the deepest dye. One explanation for the origin of the name "Wolverines" for Michiganians is that it was invented by the Ohioans during the Maumee melee as a suitable nickname, since the wolverine is a particularly vicious and ornery animal.

The danger of an armed conflict evaporated in September, 1835, when Mason received word of his removal by President Jackson. Bowing to the president's authority, Mason took leave of the Michigan militia, and General Joseph W. Brown, its commander, immediately disbanded the troops. This left the decision squarely up to Congress.

STATEHOOD WITH AN "IF"

Although Stevens T. Mason may appear, in retrospect, to have taken some rash and precipitate actions during the crisis just described, he made the most sensible and rational proposal for settling the matter that was put forward during the entire controversy. He proposed that the dispute be referred to the United States Supreme Court for a decision. Unfortunately, at that time the power of the Supreme Court to settle boundary disputes between the states had not been clearly established. However, in 1838—the year after Michigan was admitted to the Union, the Supreme Court itself held that it did have jurisdiction in a boundary dispute between Rhode Island and Massachusetts. Had the Michigan-Ohio dispute been referred to the Supreme Court, as Mason suggested, it is likely that the justices would have accepted jurisdiction and would have settled the dispute. Probably the

reason Mason's proposal went unheeded was that a presidential-
election year was in the offing. President Jackson, who was completing his second term, was grooming Martin Van Buren as his
successor. He had little taste for a situation in which his party
might suffer the loss of support in three western states because of
Michigan's stubbornness. Hence he exercised his powerful influence
to persuade Congress somehow to settle the question in such a
manner that Ohio, Indiana, and Illinois would be happy.

The battle began early in the session that opened in December,
1835. Lucius Lyon and John Norvell, who had been chosen as
Michigan's first two United States senators, and Isaac E. Crary,
who had been elected as representative, were on hand to take their
seats, but after considerable debate they were allowed to be seated
only as "spectators" and were thus compelled to listen to Ohio's
congressmen set forth that state's claims in the ensuing debates
without any chance to reply. In the Senate the bill to admit Michigan was referred to a committee of which Senator Thomas E.
Benton of Missouri, a staunch backer of Jackson, was chairman.
It was from this committee that there emerged, in due course, a
compromise that called for the acceptance of the Harris line to
satisfy Ohio, but gave to Michigan a large area in what is now the
Upper Peninsula. This compromise may have been suggested by
the feeling in some quarters that the fifth state to be carved out
of the Old Northwest would be too large. Acceptance of the compromise was foreshadowed in April, 1836, when the Territory of
Wisconsin was established by law with its northern boundaries
fixed along the lines of the Menominee and Montreal Rivers. But
the debate on the admission of Michigan to the Union dragged
on, with southern senators resorting to delaying tactics designed
to postpone the admission of Michigan until Arkansas also was
ready for admission. It had been the practice for some years to
admit a free state and a slave state at the same time so as to
preserve the balance in the Senate. During the debates an amendment to the bill was inserted requiring the assent to the compromise of delegates elected by the people of Michigan before the
state could be admitted. The great debate in the Senate came to
a close on April 2, 1836, when the compromise bill as amended was
passed.

The battle now shifted to the House of Representatives. The
result was a foregone conclusion, but the vote was delayed by a
three-hour speech upholding Michigan's contention by a former
president of the United States, now a Massachusetts representative,
John Quincy Adams. Said Adams: "Never in the course of my life
have I known a controversy of which all the right was so clear on

one side and all the power so overwhelmingly on the other." The bill carried 143 to 50 and was signed by President Jackson on June 15. It meant Michigan would be admitted into the Union *if* its people would accept the boundary compromise.

THE FINAL HURDLE

While Congress was debating the question of how Michigan might be admitted to the Union, the state government installed in November, 1835 was at least partially in operation. The state legislature met at Detroit on July 11, 1836, and two weeks later passed an act calling for the election of delegates to a convention that was to meet at Ann Arbor on September 26 for the purpose of deciding whether Michigan would consent to the compromise Congress had voted.

Sentiment against the proposed compromise was almost universal at first. A resolution adopted in March had dismissed the area that was to be Michigan's consolation prize as a "sterile region on the shores of Lake Superior, destined by soil and climate to remain forever a wilderness." And the editor of the Detroit *Free Press* wrote that it was "a region of perpetual snows—the *Ultima Thule* of our national domain in the north." Senator Lyon said the region could furnish the people of Michigan with Indians for all time and now and then with a little bear meat for a delicacy, but he was nonetheless one of the few who thought Michigan might eventually find it got the better of the bargain.[9] There was resentment of the fact that Arkansas had been granted statehood unconditionally the same day Michigan had been offered admission only on conditions most people regarded as politically motivated and disadvantageous to Michigan.

If Michigan did not want the huge area in the northland that Congress offered, it is no less true that the few people in that area did not want to be a part of Michigan. Congress had received a number of petitions from persons in this region asking that the area south of Lake Superior be organized as the Territory of Huron. As was noted earlier, Michigan Territory originally included Sault Ste. Marie and a small portion of the eastern Upper Peninsula. Thus the statement, often made, that Michigan received the Upper Peninsula in return for surrendering the Toledo strip is not correct. It was approximately the western three-quarters of the present Upper Peninsula that was involved in the compromise. Even people in the eastern section, already part of Michigan, expressed a preference to become a part of the proposed

[9] R. C. Buley, *The Old Northwest,* II, 201, note 151.

Huron Territory, pointing out that Sault Ste. Marie was cut off from Detroit for six months each year and that the region was treated by Michigan as a remote and neglected colony. Congress, however, paid no attention to these proposals. Politics was more important!

The members of the convention who were to consider the proposed compromise, elected September 12, assembled at Ann Arbor two weeks later. The 49 delegates, representing 27 counties, required four days to reach their decision, which was to reject the compromise. Those opposing the compromise had a majority of seven, but even the minority favored acceptance only on the ground that once Michigan were a state it would be in a position to carry the boundary issue to the Supreme Court.

Hardly had the convention adjourned than sober second thoughts began to be expressed. What was to be gained by rejecting the deal Congress had approved? It was obvious that Ohio, now in complete control of the Toledo strip, could not be evicted by Michigan. Lucrative federal appointments might be available to Michigan Democratic leaders, following the victory of the Democratic party and the election of Van Buren to the Presidency. If Michigan were a state it would receive 5% of the enormous proceeds from the sales of public lands in Michigan. And if the state were admitted to the Union by January 1, 1837, it would stand to share in the distribution of the surplus from the United States treasury, which Congress had voted. It was estimated that Michigan's share would amount to about $400,000. Governor Mason refused to call another convention but said the people "in their original capacity" had the right to reverse the decision of the convention of assent "if found prejudicial to their interests." On October 29, 1836 Wayne County Democrats held a meeting and resolved in favor of a second "convention of assent." Washtenaw Democrats followed suit, and as a result a "Committee of the People" was formed, which called for delegates to meet at Ann Arbor December 14. These delegates were chosen quite irregularly, and the Whigs refused to participate on the ground that the whole proceeding was illegal, which it probably was. Eighteen counties were represented, and the delegates took just two days to draw up and pass a resolution accepting the compromise proposal of Congress. All but 10 of the 72 delegates who attended signed the resolution. The meeting was dubbed by its opponents as the "Frost-bitten Convention."

When the resolution of assent reached President Jackson, he promptly sent it to Congress with a message stating that Michigan had "complied with the regulations of the conditional act of admission." A bill to admit Michigan into the Union was duly presented. There was a debate of several days duration in the Senate over the propriety of the frost-bitten convention, but the bill was finally passed 23 to 10. The debate in the house was a brief one. On January 26, 1837 President Jackson signed the bill that made Michigan the twenty-sixth state in the federal union. Lucius Lyon and John Norvell were at once seated as members of the United States Senate and Isaac E. Crary was recognized as a member of the House of Representatives. At long last statehood had been achieved.

MICHIGAN'S FIRST STATE CONSTITUTION

Michigan's first state constitution came out of a convention of 91 delegates who deliberated at Detroit from May 11 to June 24, 1835. In its call for the convention the Territorial Council had stipulated that every free white male resident of the territory over the age of twenty-one should be entitled to vote in selecting the delegates. Most of those chosen were men of small or moderate means. Almost exactly one-half (45) were farmers. The next largest group (20) included merchants, mill operators and lumbermen. Surprisingly, there were only ten lawyers among the delegates. Included also were three physicians, two surveyors, an editor, an architect, a school teacher, and eight persons whose occupations are unknown. A majority were Democrats, but there were a few Whigs. Few of the delegates had any parliamentary experience and it is surprising that they were able to draw up and approve a constitution within a period of six weeks. After considerable floundering, a committee of 19 was selected to prepare a first draft. A subcommittee consisting of five of the 19 produced a draft in only four days and this was submitted to the convention. Several standing committees were then chosen to study carefully the various sections of the draft. When these committees gave their reports the delegates debated some controversial issues, but there was remarkably little dissension. The articles dealing with the right to vote, the bill of rights, amendments, and education aroused the greatest amount of debate.

The first article, consisting of 21 sections, was actually a bill of rights, although it was not labeled as such. The provisions were copied largely from the Connecticut bill of rights and the first ten amendments to the United States Constitution. Freedom of worship, trial by jury, the writ of *habeas corpus*, compensation for property seized for public use, freedom of speech, freedom of assembly, and the subordination of the military to the civil power were guaranteed to the people and placed beyond the reach of state government to destroy. The necessity for a bill of rights in a state constitution rests upon the fact that most of the guarantees contained in the first ten amendments to the United States Constitution protect the citizen from the violation of basic rights by the Congress of the United States, not the states.

There was little new in the form of government provided. The constitutions of the older states were freely used as models. The unicameral Territorial Council was to be replaced by a bicameral state legislature, in accordance with the universal custom of other states. The legislature was to consist of a house of representatives numbering not less than 48 nor more than 100 and a senate having one-third as many members as the house. Members of the house of representatives were to be elected annually, but senators were to hold office for two years. The positions of governor and lieutenant governor were also made elective for two-year terms, and the election of these officials, as well as of senators, was to take place in the odd-numbered years. Except for the representatives, senators, governor, and lieutenant governor, all other state offices were to be filled through appointment, usually by the governor with the consent of the senate or the legislature required. Even the judiciary was to be manned by judges appointed by the governor. It was to consist of a supreme court, probate courts, justices of the peace, and such other courts as the legislature might ordain. An ultra-democratic feature was the power granted to the legislature to remove judges by a two-thirds vote.

The hottest debates in the convention centered around the question of who should have the right to vote. There were some delegates who wished to restrict the franchise to property holders, but in the end they were defeated. Every white male over the age of 21 who resided in Michigan at the time the constitution was ratified was qualified to vote. A six-months' residence was required of those who came later. Even aliens were permitted to vote under the 1835 constitution.

Of all the articles in the Michigan constitution, the one on education was probably the most enlightened and farsighted. It stipulated that the legislature should encourage "the promotion of intellectual, scientific, and agricultural improvement." It provided for the appointment of a state superintendent of public instruction. Michigan's was the first state constitution to contain such a provision. Some states had established by law a similar office, but in such cases it was always possible for the legislature to abolish the position. By giving constitutional status to the office of superintendent of public instruction, the constitution-makers of 1835 placed it beyond the power of the legislature to destroy. The article on education also contained safeguards against diverting to other uses the income from the land grants by the federal government to the state for education. In several other states proceeds from the school lands had been dissipated and not used for their intended purpose. Another unique provision of this article placed the proceeds from the sale of section 16 in each township, which had been reserved from sale for school purposes, into a perpetual primary school fund, the interest on the fund to be divided annually among school districts conducting a school for at least three months a year. In some other states each township had received the proceeds from the sale of its 16th section. Since the value of section 16 in different townships varied widely, this gave some townships a sizable amount and others virtually nothing. Michigan, by placing the proceeds from all the sections into a state fund and distributing the interest on the fund according to the number of pupils in each school, took the first step toward equalization of educational opportunity.

Among the other provisions of the Michigan Constitution of 1835 was one that authorized the state government to engage in works of "internal improvement," that is, the building of roads, canals, and railroads. Acts of incorporation were to require a two-thirds vote of the legislature. Lotteries were prohibited, and there were a few other specific provisions. One limited the compensation of legislators to $3.00 a day. This was continued in later constitutions and was not abolished until 1948.

The Constitution of 1835 has been lauded by political scientists, and it has been claimed by some that it was the best constitution Michigan has ever had. Among the provisions most often praised is the popular election of only the legislators, governor, and lieutenant governor, with other state offices filled by appointment. Advocates of the short ballot regard this as far better than choosing so many state officials by election that the voter can scarcely be expected to know the qualifications of all the candidates. The election of the governor, lieutenant governor, and senators in the odd-numbered years has been praised because it scheduled the chief state election at a time when the attention and interest of the voters are not diverted by national election contests and issues. As has already been observed, the article on education has been regarded as wise and forward-looking. The brevity and simplicity of Michigan's first state constitution has been especially acclaimed by political scientists. It placed few restrictions upon the legislature or the governor and left much to the discretion of these elected officials. Later constitutions were to be far more specific, thus destroying to a great degree that freedom of choice and action possible under the first constitution. As the years passed citizens found more and more policies that they wished to place beyond the power of the legislature to change; therefore they added appropriate provisions to the constitution as amendments. Many critics believe there are too many such restrictions. The new state constitution, drafted in 1961-62 dropped some of these, but retained many others and inserted some new ones. Whatever may be the conclusion as to the wisdom of such clauses in the state's present constitution, there can be no doubt that the constitution-makers of 1835 were wise to reduce them to a bare minimum and to leave many matters to the wisdom and the judgment of future legislatures and governors.

Clinton Canal passing over the Clinton River

II

A CYCLE OF
BOOM, BUST, AND RECOVERY

Speculative booms followed by economic depressions or "panics" have occurred throughout American history. The business cycle operates in other countries, too, but nowhere else have people been so reckless when gambling on the future and nowhere else have the "busts" been so precipitous. The presence of large, unsettled areas within or adjacent to the nation had the effect of stimulating great hopes for future development. And the frontier seemed to nourish the habit of intemperance in all things. The pioneers performed gargantuan labors and when the opportunity came they drank, danced, and gambled to excess. When they "got religion" at camp meetings they carried that to extremes also. So far as the future of the western country was concerned, the sky was the limit. Easterners caught the same spirit, and speculators who had no thought of settling in the West themselves invested their money recklessly in all sorts of ventures, on the confident expectation that big profits could be made.

In the early 1830s Michigan enjoyed such a boom. Prospective settlers and eastern speculators bought public lands, as they came on the market, then resold them at a price considerably above the $1.25-an-acre they usually cost. It was not uncommon for a purchaser to double his money within a few weeks. And the person to whom he sold might do likewise. The individual fortunate enough to have acquired land at a site deemed promising for a town could make a fabulous profit by selling it to one of the many individuals and companies engaged in town development. The new state legislature, infected by the universal confidence in the future, launched an ambitious program of railroad and canal building at state expense.

The year Michigan was admitted into the Union there was a financial crash in the East called the "Panic of 1837." Although land sales slowed down, there was little loss of confidence in Michigan, and there was even a brief period of recovery the next year. In 1839, however, came a much more serious collapse. Land values tumbled, the prices of commodities went down, money became very scarce, and the influx of immigrants was radically reduced. Progress in the building of the state-financed railroads and canals ground to a halt. Ultimately the canals were abandoned and the railroads that had been built were sold to private investors. Distress continued into the 1840s and recovery was slow. It was not until the middle of the decade of the 'forties that business began to recover and hope take the place of despair.

A BOOM IN THE MAKING

The rush of settlers into Michigan and the rapid growth of population have been described in the last chapter. Some of the causes of Michigan's rapid growth in the early 'thirties have been noted. It was a period of prosperity in the East, enabling many families to acquire the funds needed to make the move to the West and yielding to factory owners and merchants handsome profits for investment. Low tariffs and reciprocal trade treaties helped cause imports and exports to double between 1830 and 1836. Factory owners made unprecedented profits by employing women and children to work long hours at low wages. The cost of living increased 70% in three years, but wages failed to keep pace. These conditions gave rise to the spread of trade unionism between 1834 and 1837. Relatively few factory workers moved west, but many farm families that might have moved to the cities were repelled by the declining status of the factory worker and chose to become pioneers.

One of the major factors in the Michigan land boom in the early 'thirties was easy credit. Until 1833 the Bank of the United States had dominated the banks of the nation; conservatively managed by Nicholas Biddle, its president, its notes circulated as money and drove from circulation the notes of shaky state banks. But in 1832 President Jackson launched his "war on the Bank," vetoing an act passed by Congress to renew the charter of the Bank, which was due to expire in 1836. Jackson's triumphant re-election in

1832 indicated that he had popular support. Prospective settlers and speculators who found it hard to borrow money clamored for easier credit, and they were confident that if the Bank of the United States, dominated by the rich and well-born of the East, could be destroyed, money would become more abundant and would be easier to borrow. In this they were right. The amount of paper money per capita circulating in 1830 was only $6.69; by 1835 it had risen to $9.86, and two years later it went up to $13.87.

Jackson halted the deposit of government funds in the Bank of the United States even before its charter expired, and directed that the monies be deposited in selected state banks, which his enemies promptly called "pet banks." This had the effect of encouraging the establishment of state banks. Between 1829 and 1837 their number increased from 329 to 788, their note circulation rose from $48,000,000 to $149,000,000, and their loans went up from $137,000,000 to $525,000,000.[1] The result was inflationary. Prices rose, debtors paid off their loans with cheap money and borrowed more for speculative purposes. Government income from the sale of public lands and other sources increased to the point where in 1835 the entire national debt was paid off. Congress then passed an act decreeing that the surplus in the treasury should be distributed among the states.

President Jackson viewed the flood of paper money with considerable apprehension. At his suggestion Congress passed a series of acts between 1834 and 1836 to increase the supply of gold coins in circulation and to ban notes of small denomination. The states, however, refused to co-operate in curbing inflation. Banks sprang up with little capital or specie (gold or silver coin) but ready and eager to make loans in the form of notes bearing the promise of the bank to pay the bearer in specie. These notes could be used at government land offices to pay for land purchases. With prospects bright for reselling land bought at $1.25-an-acre for several times that amount within a matter of months or even weeks, the temptation to borrow to the hilt was irresistible.

MICHIGAN'S WILDCAT BANKS

Many bona fide settlers as well as speculators obtained funds for the purchase of land in the East before coming to Michigan. In the territory itself the oldest financial institution was the Bank of Michigan, which had operated successfully since 1817. By 1834

---

[1] H. J. Carman and H. C. Syrett, *A History of the American People*, , 384.

there was another bank in Detroit and one at Monroe. In that year the Bank of Michigan established a branch in Kalamazoo (then called Bronson) to which the government land office in White Pigeon was moved. Under the constitution and laws of the new state a special act of the legislature was required to charter any corporation. In addition to the Bank of Michigan, whose charter had been granted by the Governor and Judges, the Territorial Council had incorporated nine banks and the state legislature in 1836 chartered nine more. Of this total of 19 banking corporations, at least one apparently did not establish a bank and one other was located in the Green Bay country, which was set off as the Territory of Wisconsin in 1836. Of the remaining 17 banks, two were established by railroad companies through amendments to their charters. Three banks had also been permitted to establish branches.[2]

This would appear to have been sufficient banks to have met the needs. But there was a demand for still more banks and easier credit. As a consequence of Jackson's bitter condemnation of the Bank of the United States it had become the fashion to regard banks as being monopolies of the monied interests and to view with suspicion the charters granted by state legislatures. It was widely believed that such charters granted special privilege to the few. These factors combined to produce Michigan's General Banking law of 1837. Enacted by the legislature and approved by Governor Mason on March 15, 1837, it empowered any twelve landowners to form a banking association by applying to a county treasurer and clerk. Capital stock to the amount of not less than $50,000 was to be subscribed and 30% was required to be paid in specie before the bank could start operating. These provisions and a "safety fund" system, modeled after that which New York had adopted the previous year, appeared to provide sufficient security for the soundness of the banks to be established under the new law. The General Banking law of Michigan was the first of its kind in the nation.

Under the provisions of this law 49 banks were organized and 40 of these are believed to have started operation. It would have been quite impossible for such a large number of banks to have been established if the law concerning paid-in capital stock had been strictly enforced. But all sorts of dodges as well as wholesale fraud were resorted to by the organizers of these banks in order to evade the law. Specie was sent ahead from one bank to another in advance of the bank inspectors. Instead of actually paying in the

² A. Felch, "Early Banks and Banking in Michigan," *Mich. Pionee. and Historical Colls.*, II (1880), 111-114.

specie, the organizers got by with "specie certificates," certifying that the specie had been received to be held on deposit. Sometimes specie was borrowed for the occasion, then immediately returned to its owner. These were Michigan's "wildcat banks," about which fabulous stories have been told.[3] In spite of their lack of hard cash, they issued handsome bank notes that pledged the bank to pay to the bearer on demand so many dollars in hard money. And they issued them in enormous quantities.

A contemporary reported that the notes of the different banks organized under the General Banking law were called "wild cat," "tom cat," "red dog," and other names according to the fancied solvency of the different institutions.[4] Seven of these banks were established in Washtenaw County, which had at the time a population of about 20,000. Many of them were located in towns like Singapore (Allegan County), Goodrich (Genesee County), and Auburn (Oakland County), which do not exist today. The story was told that a stranger lost his way in the woods of Shiawassee County, and toward nightfall was following what he thought was a trail through the woods when suddenly he came to a clearing that contained a large frame structure across the front of which was a conspicuous sign proclaiming it was the Bank of Shiawassee. For a brief time the demand for borrowed money was so great that almost none of the notes were presented for redemption in specie. One Detroiter made his way to one of these obscure banks planning to exchange notes for specie. The president of the institution received him with cordiality, wined him and dined him, and told him he couldn't redeem the notes just then, but was expecting a shipment of gold and silver coin within a few days.

UNREAL ESTATE

With credit so easily obtainable speculation ran riot. In 1836 every ship arriving at Detroit was packed with immigrants and speculators, with 500 to 700 often arriving on a single vessel. Land offices at Detroit and Kalamazoo were swamped with business. Long lines formed before their doors, and purchasers sometimes paid fancy prices for a place further up in the line. In Kalamazoo a sea of tents and makeshift shacks sheltered the men who sought to buy land. Dozens of associations were formed to purchase land for speculation. Many such associations would purchase land at the mouth of a river or at some other likely spot for a town, en-

[3] H. M. Utley, "The Wildcat Banking System in Michigan," *Mich. Pioneer and Historical Colls.*, V (1884), 209-222.
[4] *Mich. Pioneer and Historical Colls.*, I (1877), 190.

gage a draftsman to draw up a town plan, divide the tract into town lots, and proceed to sell them at a fancy price. Often the purchaser was shown drawings that depicted homes, stores, churches, schools, and factories already built, and lots were no doubt purchased by many who labored under the impression that the town actually existed. In some cases speculators gambled on a vast expansion of a town that really did exist. St. Joseph, for instance, had an almost unbelievable speculative boom. Lots there sold at from $1,800 to $5,000 each, whereas they could be had at Chicago for $100. A plat of the town, according to a local historian, showed streets extending for miles into what was then a wilderness. The Paw Paw River, for more than thirty miles above its mouth at St. Joseph, was to be lined with mills and factories. A great university was planned—on paper.[5] The speculative fever probably got to the point where, as in most speculative manias, sober people realized that the whole thing was bound to blow up sooner or later, but in the meantime they could see no reason they should not take advantage of the opportunity to buy one week and sell the next at a big profit.

A visitor to one of the paper cities describes it in these words:

> The annals of this place constitute one of those chapters of romance of which the records of 1835 and 1836 are so replete. Before the rage of real estate speculation was at its height and all through the wild fever we had known of "White Rock City." Maps executed in the highest style of the typographer's art, displayed in hotel barrooms and other places, where congregate the thousand seekers after fortune that courted the happy possessor of valuable lots and water privileges—had announced its unrivalled situation and advantages. They depicted the magnificent harbor at the mouth of the large stream into which steamboats were entering. Saw mills were converting the forests into houses; around the public square clustered a court house, churches, and other public buildings, not omitting the inevitable bank; and the air of prosperity which pervaded the place was evident at a glance. Auctioneers had sounded its praises and struck off its lots at fabulous prices to anxious buyers. None of the rising cities for which Michigan had become famous had so wide a celebrity and distributed stock so freely.
>
> And now we were to see with our own eyes this western marvel. A large white boulder in the lake marked the entrance, and gave name to this modern Karnac.
>
> We found the entering river: it hardly admitted our canoe. Harbor there was none. Churches, houses, mills, people were all

[5] S. B. Reber, *History of St. Joseph,* p. 17.

a myth. A thick wilderness covered the whole site. Even those
marks of advancing civilization, the surveyor's marks, were
wanting.[6]

It must not be assumed that everyone who bought land in
Michigan in the early 'thirties was duped by promoters. Thousands
were bona fide settlers, buying land on which to settle and to make
homes. And there were many who regarded the purchase of public
lands in Michigan as an investment rather than as a speculation.
Such investors carefully examined the land before they bought
it and expected to hold it for a period of years. This is illustrated
by the journal of John M. Gordon, a rising young Baltimore lawyer and banker, who came out to Michigan in 1836 to buy land.
He brought with him not only funds of his own but amounts entrusted to him by friends and associates. Besides providing a vivid
picture of Michigan in 1836, this journal shows how carefully a
prudent eastern investor sized up and evaluated lands before buying them. Making his way on horseback over crude trails, and
guided by a map that he obtained at the Kalamazoo land office,
showing unsold lands, Gordon made meticulous notes on the quality of the soil, the types of trees, and many other factors that
entered into the value of any given tract of land.[7] Only then did
he decide which tracts to buy.

AND "INTERNAL IMPROVEMENTS"

Michigan's boom times in the early 1830s came in a period when
the whole nation was buzzing with excitement over new methods
of transportation. Hundreds of projects for the construction of
canals and railroads were afoot. Eastern states vied with each
other to establish links with the West by canals, railroads, or a
combination of both. And within the western states themselves
there was hardly a town or city whose citizens did not hatch
schemes involving railroads or canals. Dozens of corporations
were formed to advance such plans, but the western states, like
those in the East, were not willing to entrust the responsibility
to private enterprise alone. One shortcoming was that projects
financed by private capital were helter-skelter and offered little
prospect of providing an integrated transportation system. Even
more important was the fact that capital which could be raised
by private companies was hardly adequate to finance the hoped-for

[6] B. Hubbard, "A Michigan Geological Expedition in 1837," *Mich.
Pioneer and Historical Colls.,* III (1881), 200.
[7] J. M. Gordon, "Michigan Journal, 1836," *Michigan History,* XLIII
(1959), 10-42, 129-149, 257-293, 433-478.

improvements. Hence in both East and West states undertook to construct and operate railroads and canals.

It was the state of New York that set the pattern. Largely through the efforts of Governor DeWitt Clinton, that state had built the Erie Canal, a 363-mile stretch connecting the Hudson River at Albany with Lake Erie at Buffalo. This waterway, which was 40 feet wide at the top, 28 feet wide at the bottom, and four feet deep, cost the state about $8,000,000. Tolls collected during the first few years of operation more than paid for the cost of construction. Its success led to the building of many branches. The importance of the Erie Canal in facilitating the settlement of Michigan has already been noted. More than any other factor, perhaps, it was responsible for making New York City the leading metropolis of the nation. Western grain, lumber, and other prodducts now found an outlet in the East as well as at New Orleans. The cost of shipments from Buffalo to New York was reduced from $100 to $8 a ton.

Only two years after the opening of the Erie Canal the Baltimore and Ohio Railroad Company was incorporated. The idea for the railroad originated in the mines and quarries of England, where cars were let down an inclined plane by gravity and pulled back up by horses. Soon the idea of using steam to propel wheeled vehicles gave rise to experiments on both sides of the Atlantic. The Baltimore and Ohio Railroad was Baltimore's answer to the Erie Canal. That city hoped, like New York, to promote its growth by means of better transportation facilities to the West. There were many skeptics whose minds were conditioned to water transportation, and so Baltimore people, not content with their railroad venture, saw in 1828 the first shovelful of dirt thrown by President John Quincy Adams to launch construction of the Chesapeake and Ohio Canal, designed to connect Baltimore with the West by water as well as rail. Pennsylvania, not to be outdone by New York and Maryland, spent $10,000,000 between 1826 and 1834 to construct a combined canal-and-railway system to connect Philadelphia with Pittsburgh. Canal boats were hauled over the Alleghanies on a 33½-mile portage railway.

The simultaneous development of canals and railroads gave rise to the term "internal improvements" to embrace both of these new methods of transportation. Canals, having been started first and having proved their worth by the success of the Erie, were initially favored. A canal stockholder had dire predictions about the railroad:

> He saw what would be the effect of it; that it would set the whole world a-gadding. Twenty miles an hour, sir—why you will not be

able to keep an apprentice boy at his work! Every Saturday evening he must have a trip to Ohio to spend a Sunday with his sweetheart. Grave plodding citizens will be flying about like comets. All local attachments will be at an end. It will encourage flightiness of intellect. Veracious people will turn into the most immeasurable liars. All conceptions will be exaggerated by the magnificent notions of distance. Only a hundred miles off—tut, nonsense, I'll step across, madam, and bring your fan! . . . . Upon the whole, sir, it is a pestilential, topsy-turvy, harumscarum whirligig. Give me the old, solemn, straight forward, regular Dutch Canal—three miles an hour for expresses, and two rod jog-trot journeys—with a yoke of oxen for heavy loads! I go for beasts of burden; it is more formative and scriptural, and suits a moral and religious people better—none of your hop skip and jump whimsies for me.[8]

In the Old Northwest the major canal projects were designed to connect the Great Lakes with the Ohio and Mississippi Rivers. The Ohio legislature adopted a canal act in February, 1825, and the first spade of dirt was turned the following July 4. Because of local jealousies the legislators were not able to confine their plans to a single canal. Instead, provision was made for three canals connecting rivers flowing into the Ohio with those flowing into Lake Erie. By 1850 canals and rivers connected Cincinnati, Portsmouth, and Marietta on the Ohio with Toledo and Cleveland on Lake Erie. Having plunged heavily into canal construction at an early date, Ohio was content to leave railroad construction to private companies.

Indiana leaders were intrigued by the idea of building a canal to connect the Wabash River, which reached the Ohio River at Evansville, with the Maumee River, flowing into Lake Erie at Toledo. It may have been the fact that this involved both Ohio and Indiana that led to efforts to obtain federal aid. In 1827 Congress voted to donate to the State of Indiana a strip of land consisting of alternate sections five miles on each side of the proposed canal. The portion of the grant lying in Ohio was transferred to that state. The project was completed in 1845.

A canal to connect the Great Lakes and the Mississippi River by way of the Illinois River had been suggested by the French explorer, Louis Jolliet. It was inevitable that such a canal should be proposed as a practical project during the 1820s when canal building was at the height of popularity. In 1827 Congress gave Illinois a grant similar to that made to Indiana to facilitate the

[8] *Western Sun and General Advertiser,* July 24, 1830, quoted in R. C. Buley, *The Old Northwest,* I, 515.

building of this canal. Political and sectional bickering, however, delayed for a considerable period the start of construction.

The prospect of federal aid for internal improvements was shattered in 1830 when President Jackson vetoed a bill to provide federal funds to build a road between Lexington, Kentucky, and Maysville in the same state. In his veto message Jackson indicated his opposition to lavish expenditures for internal improvements and recommended instead that the national debt be paid. Although there were grumblings of dissent, the veto was upheld. Henceforth federal appropriations for internal improvements were few and far between. Partly as a result of this the national debt was paid, a surplus was accumulated in the treasury, and Jackson approved a bill passed by Congress in 1836 to distribute the surplus among the states in quarterly payments starting January 1, 1837.[9] In anticipation of these funds many states adopted extravagant plans for the building of canals and railroads. Even before the distribution of the surplus was assured, the Indiana legislature in February, 1836 adopted a system of internal improvements estimated to cost $13,000,000—one-sixth of the wealth of that state. The following year the Illinois legislature enacted a similar law providing for an extensive railroad and canal system. Other states also plunged headlong into internal-improvements projects. Only seven states failed to contract debts for roads, canals, and railroads. State debts that had amounted to only $12,790,728 in 1820 rose to $170,000,000 in 1837, a prodigious sum for the time.

Michigan inevitably was caught up in the mania for internal improvements. During the 1820s attention was focused on the building of roads radiating out of Detroit into the interior, and work on these roads continued into the 1830s. Improvement of the Chicago Military Road in 1832, completion of the Territorial Road so that stage coaches could operate over it between St. Joseph and Detroit by 1834, and construction of the Grand River Road were matters of more immediate interest to the pioneers than plans for future canals and railroads. Nevertheless, enterprising business men were manifesting an active interest in railroad development. Up to 1837 the territorial and state legislatures granted charters to no less than 20 railroad corporations, with an aggregate capital of $10,000,000.[10] The first of these incorporated

[9] A provision in the bill approved January 26, 1837 permitted Michigan to receive the first quarterly payment of the distribution in spite of the fact that its status as of January 1 was still that of a territory.

[10] L. A. Chase, "Michigan's Share in the Establishment of Improved Transportation Between the East and the West," *Mich. Pioneer and Historical Colls.*, XXXVIII (1912), 596.

First U. S. railway locomotive

the Pontiac and Detroit Railway Company; this was the first railroad charter granted in the Old Northwest. The charter was approved on July 31, 1830.[11] This railroad, like the Ohio and Steubenville chartered by Ohio later the same year, never advanced beyond the charter stage. It was reincorporated as the Detroit and Pontiac Railroad in 1834, but it was not until 1838 that it began to run trains between Detroit and Birmingham. The cars were pulled by horses at first, but a locomotive was brought to Detroit in 1839 and went into operation on the line August 16.[12] The second railroad company to be chartered in Michigan was the Detroit and St. Joseph, which was incorporated under an act approved in 1832. That the legislators were thinking about the possibility of a state-owned railroad system as early as that date is indicated by a provision in the charter of this company that gave Michigan the right to purchase the railroad at cost plus 14% interest. Although this company was not operating any trains by the time Michigan was admitted into the Union, it had secured a right of way, had graded several miles beyond Detroit, had purchased a locomotive, a passenger car, wheels and iron for six freight cars, and had bought spikes and rails for 30 miles of track.

[11] G. N. Fuller, *Economic and Social Beginnings of Michigan,* p. 79; *Laws of the Territory of Michigan,* III, 844.
[12] G. Catlin, *The Story of Detroit,* p. 365.

The most noted and successful of Michigan's pioneer railroads, however, was the Erie and Kalamazoo, which was incorporated April 22, 1833. This project was initiated by pioneers of Adrian. The 33 miles between Adrian and Toledo (then called Port Lawrence) was traversed by a trail cut through forests and swamps that during the wet seasons was so deep in mud and water that it was impassable even with oxen. If some better way to transport goods and passengers over this route could be found, Adrian and Lenawee County would clearly enjoy great advantages. But the promoters, emulating those in other states who were planning internal improvements, did not limit their vistas to the local scene. They envisioned a railroad that would connect Lake Erie at Port Lawrence with the waters of the Kalamazoo River at Marshall, below which that stream was believed to be navigable to Lake Michigan. The total distance was about 180 miles. The nominal capitalization of the company was set at $1,000,000. About $100,000 of this was actually paid in, principally by six Adrian and Port Lawrence subscribers. Construction was started at Port Lawrence, and was completed to Adrian in the fall of 1836. Rails were made of white oak, and on top of them were nailed iron "strap rails" about five-eighths of an inch thick and 2 ½ inches wide. Unfortunately, these iron strap rails often came loose while a train was passing over them, and sometimes plowed up through the floor of the cars, endangering the passengers, who called them "snake heads." On the morning of November 2, 1836 the first car to run on this railroad departed from Port Lawrence, to the boom of cannon, arriving safely at Adrian several hours later. Horses pulled the car and were driven tandem, with relays every four miles. It was the first railroad to operate west of Schenectady, New York.[13] The first passenger coach on the Erie and Kalamazoo was called a "pleasure car," a top-heavy affair with ornamental openings that made it look like a traveling chapel. Later, passenger cars were provided with benches along the sides, and the entrance door on one side. Double-decker coaches also were used, the upper deck being furnished somewhat more lavishly than the lower deck and reserved for ladies. In 1837 the Erie and Kalamazoo received at Toledo a locomotive manufactured by the Baldwin Works in Philadelphia. This was the first locomotive to operate on a railroad west of the Alleghenies. Although the Erie and Kalamazoo never was completed to Marshall, it did build two branch lines. Some years later it was leased to the Michigan Southern Railroad, but the Erie and Kalamazoo continued to exist, its directors receiving annually a rental of $30,000 to be distributed among the stock-holders.

Of the twenty railroad companies chartered prior to 1837, the Erie and Kalamazoo was the only one in actual operation by that date. With the prospect in view of sharing in the distribution of the federal surplus there were demands that the state government take action to speed up internal improvements. Much was made of the fact that settlers along the line of the Erie and Kalamazoo could buy eastern commodities, such as salt imported from New York, at greatly reduced prices, and also that they could sell their products more readily. The clamor for state action was irresistible. The spirit of the time is illustrated by the report of the internal improvements committee of the House of Representatives, made on January 24, 1837:

> The progress of centuries in other lands is here realized in as many years . . . . Internal improvements is the great lever which is opening the sealed-up fountains of national wealth and civilization. The question for Michigan to decide is whether she will by her own enterprise sieze [*sic*] the present opportunities to avail herself of these vast viaducts of wealth and prosperity, and lead them laden within her own borders, or whether her timidity or apathy will allow them to pass her by to swell the power and abundance of her wiser neighbors.
>
> The more the subject is investigated, the wider extends the field and the more worthy it appears of attention . . . . A few leading routes in successful operation will excite the enterprise of every section of the country, while it will create and allure capital for the more rapid fulfillment of every design.

On the basis of what were purported to be prudent estimates, it was asserted that an internal-improvements system would pay for itself and yield a net profit of $3,000,000 to the state in twenty years.

Governor Stevens T. Mason recommended that the state become a subscriber in the stock of private companies organized to build railroads and canals, borrowing money for the purpose. The legislature, however, preferred to proceed by state action alone. On March 20, 1837 the internal improvements bill became law. It authorized surveys to be made of three railroads across the Lower Peninsula. The southern railroad was to extend from Monroe across the southernmost tier of counties to New Buffalo on Lake Michigan. The central railroad was to connect Detroit and St. Joseph by a line through the second tier of counties, and the rights and properties of the Detroit and St. Joseph Railroad Company, which had been chartered to build a line

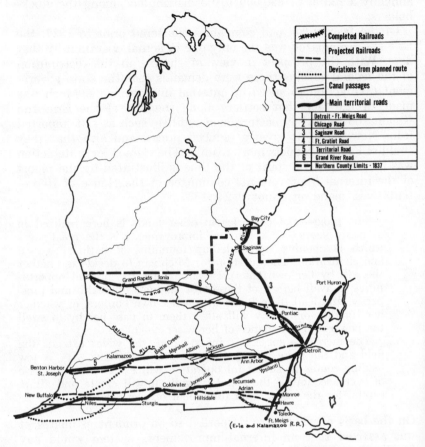

INTERNAL IMPROVEMENTS ABOUT 1837

between these two points, were to be acquired by purchase. A
third railroad was to be laid out from the town of St. Clair (then
called "Palmer") on the St. Clair River to the navigable waters
of the Grand River (Grand Rapids) or to the mouth of that
river. Two canals also were to be surveyed, one connecting the
Clinton and Kalamazoo rivers, the other joining the waters of
the Saginaw and Grand. The Havre Branch Railroad was to be
acquired. This was a line, still in the planning stage, that was
designed to connect the terminus of the southern railroad at
Monroe with the new town of Havre, which had been founded

seven miles north of Toledo within Michigan, and which had ambitions to become the rival of the city Michigan had lost to Ohio. In a separate act, a survey of a canal route around the falls of the St. Mary's River at Sault Ste. Marie was also authorized. A board of internal improvements consisting of seven members was established to manage these enterprises. And on March 21 a bill to authorize the governor to negotiate a loan of $5,000,000, secured by the faith and credit of the state at the best terms possible, became law. It would have been more prudent for the legislature to have adopted a program calling for the building of a single railroad and a single canal across the state, but to have done so would have incurred opposition from those communities not fortunate enough to be located on the selected route. The political appeal of the act was that it had something for just about every settled part of the new state.

Ironically enough, this ambitious program was adopted on the very eve of the Panic of 1837. By the time Governor Mason could reach New York to begin negotiations for the loan that he had been authorized to make, the great boom had collapsed and moneylenders had suddenly become extremely cautious.

THE BIG BUST

Looking back on a boom period, it is difficult to understand why the people of the time could have ignored clear indications that they were riding for a fall. The speculation in Michigan land values in the early 1830s, for example, was clearly fantastic. The enormous note issues of the banks were obviously out of proportion to their resources. And the internal improvements programs adopted by the states were far beyond their ability to finance. The nation was importing, largely from Great Britain, much more than it was exporting, piling up a steadily mounting debt to British merchants and manufacturers. The South was overplanting cotton. Inevitably there would be a day of reckoning.

In July, 1836 President Jackson issued his "Specie Circular," which stated that henceforth only gold and silver would be accepted in payment for public land, except for bona fide settlers, who, until December 15, were to be allowed to pay for no more than 320 acres in bank notes. This indicated the lack of faith by the government in the soundness of the paper money that had been issued in such vast amounts. It did not stop private speculation, however, and did not immediately check the buying of land. About the same time, British exporters began to refuse to extend new credits to American buyers and to demand payment of overdue debts. This resulted in a drain of specie from

American banks. Then on January 1, 1837, when the distribution of the government surplus began, banks were called upon to pay over to the states specie that the federal government had deposited with them. The second quarterly payment exhausted their resources, and in May, 1837, banks throughout the nation suspended specie payments. This meant that no longer could a bank note be presented for payment at full value in gold and silver. Very quickly these notes—the paper money of the time—depreciated in value, and within a short time many of them became virtually worthless.

By the middle of 1837 thousands of people in the eastern part of the nation were unemployed. Hundreds of firms went bankrupt and business was almost at a standstill. In the West, however, there was less distress and a considerable measure of confidence in the future remained. The Kalamazoo land office, which had sold 1,634,511 acres in 1836, found purchasers for only 313,885 acres in 1837, but even this was three times the amount sold in 1834 and about one-third the total sales in the entire Territory of Michigan up to 1832. Governor Mason encountered difficulties in floating the $5,000,000 loan, but he at length succeeded, and surveys went forward rapidly on the various internal improvements projects. The nation's new president, Martin Van Buren, summoned Congress into special session and proposed measures designed to strengthen the financial structure. Movement of settlers into Michigan slowed down but by no means halted. The population, which stood at 174,543 in 1837, had increased to 212,267 by 1840, a gain for the three-year period of almost as many people as constituted the entire population in 1830. It was not until 1839 that the full impact of the hard times reached Michigan. A train of circumstances then set in that sharply reduced prices on all commodities and plunged the nation into a new economic crisis. This time the West suffered more severely than the East.

DISILLUSIONMENT

Following the passage of the Internal Improvements Act, surveyors and engineers set out from Detroit with instruments and equipment to blaze the way for the railroads and canals that were expected to transform the wilderness into prosperous farms and bring magical rewards to the towns along their routes. It proved easier to locate the route for the northern railroad than for the others, because there were not so many towns contending that the railroad should be laid out to accommodate them.

The line was surveyed to Grand Haven, a distance of 201 miles, and the cost of construction was estimated to be $1,409,015.75. The southern route was found to be 183 miles long, and the cost of building this railroad was estimated at $1,496,376.39. The cost of the central railroad was set at about $1,700,000 and the distance was 153 miles. These surveys, as well as those to be followed by the canals, were completed by January 1, 1838. The board for internal improvements by that date had bought the property of the Detroit and St. Joseph Railroad Company, had let contracts for the beginning of construction on all three of the projected state railroads, and had spent at least $415,000.

The preliminary work done by the Detroit and St. Joseph Railroad Company made it feasible to start construction on the central line first. Before the end of 1837 the railroad was in operation as far west as Dearborn, and on February 3, 1838 there was a memorable celebration when the first train made the run from Detroit to Ypsilanti. The locomotive hauled several flat cars, all loaded with passengers, and two passenger coaches having the appearance of Concord coaches with doors on each side. One of these, named the "Governor Mason," had been built in Detroit. Aboard the train were the governor, Senator Cass, and many other dignitaries. A light snow had fallen that morning, and as the throng at Ypsilanti watched the train approach they witnessed two men, one sitting on each side of a crossbar in front of the engine equipped with a broom with which he brushed the snow off the track. The visitors were welcomed by a brass band, and were invited to a barbecue, at which an ox was roasted over a huge log fire. After partaking of the feast and much speechmaking the Detroiters got aboard for the return trip to Detroit. But at Dearborn the engine refused to start, and the engineer—driven to a frenzy by a storm of sarcasm, declared himself to be "clean beat." Horses were obtained to pull the engine on a siding, then were hitched to the principal car and hauled it back to Detroit.[14] The locomotive eventually was repaired, and regular operation between Detroit and Ypsilanti was provided. The fare was $1.50. Trains departed from the depot, then located at the southwest corner of Michigan Avenue and Griswold Street, at 6 A.M. and 1 P.M.

Another celebration took place at Mount Clemens the following May when ground was broken for the Clinton and Kalamazoo Canal. Visitors flocked into the town for the affair, which included

[14] T. E. Potter, "A Boy's Story of Pioneer Life in Michigan," *Mich. Pioneer and Historical Colls.,* XXXV (1907), 394-95; G. Catlin, *op. cit.,* pp. 370-71.

a 13-gun salute, band music, a parade, appropriate oratory, and finally the turning of the first spade of earth by Governor Mason.[15]

Considerable progress was made during the year 1838 on the entire internal-improvements program. In his report to the legislature in January, 1839 the governor maintained an optimistic note. The central railroad was completed to Ann Arbor and under contract for construction as far west as Jackson; the southern railroad was ready for the laying of iron on the first 30-mile stretch from Monroe to Adrian; the two Lower Peninsula canals and the northern railroad were reported to be in "active progress," while the contract had been let for the canal at Sault Ste. Marie.[16]

Beginning in 1839 the various construction projects, begun so hopefully, began to bog down. The principal difficulty was lack of money to pay for the improvements. At Sault Ste. Marie, however, the contractor encountered difficulty when the commandant at Fort Brady halted the digging because it interfered with a millrace of a sawmill used by the post. Although the state and the War Department agreed in August on the route of the proposed canal, the contractor refused to resume work. It is believed that he feared the state would not be able to pay him for the work, and possibly that the sum for which he had agreed to build the canal would be insufficient to pay the cost, and hence that he intentionally caused the interference of the commandant by digging where the millrace would be endangered. At any rate, work was suspended, not to be resumed until 1853, when a federal grant made possible the Soo Canal.

Financial problems, which slowed down the other internal improvements, arose from difficulties surrounding the $5,000,000 loan and the deepening financial crisis in the nation. By the time Governor Mason could reach New York in the spring of 1837, following the authorization of the $5,000,000 loan by the legislature, financial stringency already was being felt, and he encountered difficulty in selling the bonds that were to be issued to secure the loan. It was not until June 1, 1838 that he finally made an agreement with the Morris Canal and Banking Company, then regarded as a sound institution, whereby it undertook to sell the bonds. Meanwhile, the legislature had passed an act authorizing an interest rate of 6%, instead of 5½% as originally provided, but stipulating that the bonds must be sold at par.

---

[15] J. N. Ingersoll, "The Clinton and Kalamazoo Canal Celebration," *Mich. Pioneer and Historical Colls.*, V (1882), 469-471.

[16] O. C. Comstock, "Internal Improvements," in *Mich. Pioneer and Historical Colls.*, I (1875), 46.

In order to induce the Morris Canal and Banking Company to sell the bonds, Mason agreed that it should receive a commission of 2½%, thus in effect reducing the proceeds from the bonds to a figure below par. For this action he was later criticized, but at the time he felt it was necessary in order to obtain the much-needed funds to advance the internal improvements program. Bonds in the amount of $1,300,000 were deposited with the Company, but Mason did not receive the equivalent amount in cash. Payments were to be made to the state by the Company as the bonds were sold. Mason carried back to Detroit notes of the bank to the amount of $110,397, locked in a small trunk. After he returned to Detroit it was discovered that $4,630 in these notes had disappeared from the trunk. Subsequently a package containing all but $50 of this amount was received at the office of the Company in New York, and Mason made good from his own pocket the remaining $50. The mystery of the disappearance was never solved.

When Mason returned to Detroit in the summer of 1838 he was confident that he had negotiated a fair arrangement for the sale of the bonds and that income from them would be forthcoming at regular intervals. In November, 1838 the Company proposed to Mason that it would buy one-fourth of the bonds itself and that the remainder would be bought by the former Bank of the United States, now chartered as a Pennsylvania bank. Payments of $250,000 each quarter were promised until the bonds were paid for. Mason thereupon delivered the balance of the bonds to the Company, certifying the indebtedness of Michigan of $3,700,000, or a total (including the first delivery of bonds) of $5,000,000. When the legislature met in the spring of 1839 it was informed of this arrangement and raised no objection to the delivery of all the bonds in advance of payment. The payments were made as agreed during 1839 but a dispute arose over whether the state should pay interest on the total amount of the bonds or only on that portion for which it had received payment.[17]

This was the situation in the fall of 1839 when the state election was held. By this time Van Buren's panacea for the depression—the independent treasury bill—had been buried in an avalanche of party wrangling between Whigs and Democrats. Michigan's "wildcat banks" had folded, and the paper notes they had issued, which were held by thousands of Michigan citizens, had become worthless. Little public land was being sold and im-

[17] W. L. Jenks, "Michigan's Five-Million-Dollar Loan," *Michigan History,* XV (1931), 575-634.

migration into the state had sharply declined. Prices for farm products had dropped disastrously. A wave of sickness, most of it malaria (or "fever and ague," as the pioneers called it), swept the new state and added further misery.[18]

As is usual in such circumstances, the party in power was blamed for the woes of the people. Mason, once a popular figure, was bitterly maligned. The reaction politically was strongly in the direction of conservatism. Mason himself declined to run for re-election, and his party turned to Elon Farnsworth, an able but conservative Detroit lawyer, as its candidate for governor. The Whigs nominated William Woodbridge and campaigned for him on a platform of "retrenchment and reform." On election day Woodbridge received 18,195 votes while his opponent was given 17,037.[19] The Whigs also elected a majority in both houses of the legislature.

Early in 1840 the legislature met and promptly passed an act forbidding the commissioners of internal improvement from entering into any further construction contracts. The deadline for paying 1839 taxes was extended, some offices were abolished, and the salaries of some officials were reduced. But such measures were insufficient to solve the state's problems. On April 1, 1840 the Morris Canal and Banking Company defaulted on its payments to the state, and in the following year the former Bank of the United States, which had purchased three-quarters of the Michigan bonds, went into bankruptcy. There ensued a series of negotiations and dealings extending over a long period of years that were so complicated as to defy description. When Michigan demanded the return of the bonds for which it had received no payment it was found that the two companies had deposited them with bankers in England as security for loans of their own. They were, of course, an obligation of the State of Michigan, but the state never received any proceeds from them. In 1842 the legislature declared that the state would contest the payment of interest and principal on those bonds for which it had received no compensation. In the end, however, the bonds for which the state had not received payment were redeemed at around one-third their face value, while interest and principal on the others were paid in full. It is possible that the state might have been able to recover a larger portion of the amount due from the bonds had it not been for the intense party rivalry of the 1840s. The five-million-dollar loan became the focus of bitter disputes be-

[18] B. Hubbard, *Memorials of Half a Century*, p. 103.
[19] F. B. Streeter, *Political Parties in Michigan, 1837-1860*, p. 21.

tween Whigs and Democrats, and between those who favored full payment and those who were willing to settle for "partial repudiation."

Michigan was by no means the only state that was unable or unwilling to pay the debts so recklessly incurred in the 1830s. Mississippi, Louisiana, Maryland, Pennsylvania, and Indiana as well as Michigan repudiated their debts in whole or in part. One result was to seriously injure the credit standing of American states in Europe, where many of these obligations were held.

The internal-improvements program would have been halted for lack of funds in 1841 had it not been for a grant of 500,000 acres of public land to the state by the federal government in that year. Contractors and workers were frequently paid in "land scrip" rather than money. Only a small portion of the Saginaw-Grand Canal had been dug when that project was abandoned. A 12-mile stretch of the projected Clinton-Kalamazoo Canal was completed between Mount Clemens and Rochester, and canal boats were operated for a few years from Mount Clemens to Utica. But it never got any further. Some right of way was obtained and a considerable amount of grading was done on a part of the proposed northern railroad before it, too, was abandoned. The reduced resources of the state were then concentrated on the southern and central railroads.

The scandals and partisan bickering over the $5,000,000 loan, hard times, and slow progress on construction had by this time created a revulsion against the entire internal-improvements program. In 1843 the legislature decided to extend the southern railroad no further than Hillsdale, which it had by that time reached, and to build the central railroad no further than Kalamazoo. Work was continued on the latter project by the state until 1846, when the first train reached Kalamazoo. Agitation for the sale of the two railroads had been growing for some time. In 1846 it was estimated that the state had spent almost four and a half millions in cash and had granted 305,000 acres of the 500,000 acres of public lands donated by the federal government to pay for the internal-improvements program. Proceeds from the operation of the southern and central lines were being used for the repair and rehabilitation of the parts of the railroads that had been poorly constructed. It was estimated that the interest charges alone would require a one percent tax on property. For these reasons it was agreed to sell the lines. The southern railroad was sold to a private company for $500,000, while the sale of the longer central line brought $2,000,000. Thus ended the state's experiment in railroad and canal building and operation. To prevent any subsequent projects of this kind the framers of the Constitution of 1850 wrote into that document a clause that forbade the state government from engaging in any program of internal improvement.

Disillusionment of the people with banks was as profound as that with state railroads and canals. By the end of 1839 only three of the older banks having special charters (one of which had a branch) and four of the "general-law" banks were still in operation. In 1838 the legislature suspended for one year the general banking law under which the "wildcats" had been organized, and the following year decreed that no more banks could be formed under its provisions. A case brought before the state supreme court in 1844 resulted in a decision that the general banking law had never been constitutional! The legislature in April, 1839 established a State Bank of Michigan with nine branches, modeled after the State Bank of Indiana, but before the end of the year it too was winding up its affairs. By 1845 only three banks remained in the entire state. There had developed a deep antipathy toward banks and bankers among the people, an attitude that continued to the time of the Civil War. During the 1840s practically the only money in circulation consisted of coinage of the United States mint: gold coins with a limited number of silver dollars and smaller coins.

The Whigs, who came into power in the state in 1839, quickly demonstrated that they had no cure for Michigan's ills. But Michigan voters, along with those of the rest of the nation, reacted against the administration of President Van Buren, Jackson's Democratic successor, in the hotly contested presidential election of 1840. Van Buren, as candidate for re-election, was opposed by the Whig candidate, William Henry Harrison. A native of Indiana, still famed for the glorious victory he was reputed to have won at Tippecanoe in 1811, and credited for having saved Michigan from the British in 1813, Harrison proved to be a strong candidate. While his supporters chanted that "Van, Van, is a used-up man," the Democrats sought to cast derision on Harrison by claiming that he had retired after the Battle of the Thames to his cabin on the Ohio, where he had drunk hard cider and nailed coonskins upon the logs of his cabin. Harrison men promptly adopted these symbols for their candidate to prove that he was one of the common people. On election day in Michigan Harrison received 22,933 votes to 21,096 for Van Buren. Michigan's electoral votes combined with those of other states put Harrison in the White House, where the old frontiersman lasted only a month before office-seekers drove him to his grave.

Even before Harrison was inaugurated Michigan's Whig legislature elected Governor Woodbridge as United States Senator in place of Democrat John Norvell, whose term was expiring. It did not leave a good taste in the mouths of voters when Woodbridge deserted his position as governor in such hard times to go to Washington. When Woodbridge resigned as governor to accept his new position, Lieutenant Governor James W. Gordon, a native of Connecticut who had settled in Marshall in 1835, became acting governor. In the meantime the Democrats succeeded in healing the schism within their party and united upon the nomination of John S. Barry for governor in 1841. Barry, a native of New Hampshire, had become a prosperous merchant in Constantine, a town located on the St. Joseph River in St. Joseph County. He had a reputation for scrupulous honesty and stood for conservative principles. He was elected by a plurality of over 5,000 votes. Disillusioned with the Democrats, the voters had turned to the Whigs. Now, disillusioned with the Whigs, they turned back to the Democrats. For the next dozen years the Democratic candidate for governor won every election. Barry himself served three terms, the only 19th-century governor to do so. He stood for rigid economy in state government. It was even told that he had the grass on the capital yard cut and sold, turning the proceeds into the hard-pressed state treasury.

By the middle 1840s confidence began to return. There was no repetition of the wild speculation of the early 1830s, but Michigan citizens began to take a somewhat more optimistic outlook on their future. A few men in Saginaw were proving that Michigan pine had an eastern market. A copper rush to the Upper Peninsula and the discovery of iron in another part of this area that Michigan people had scorned when they had been compelled to accept it in lieu of the Toledo strip, helped to give the state the "lift" it needed to emerge from the doldrums of the late 'thirties and the early 'forties.

DEMOCRACY AND THE "PATRIOT" CAUSE

President Andrew Jackson was the symbol of democracy to frontier Americans of the 1830s. His election was made possible by the adoption of universal manhood suffrage by most of the states. His war against corporations and banks was popular in the West. The United States was a young nation, and its people believed that American democracy was better than any other form of government. Americans cheered the new Latin American Republics, and in 1830 they applauded as Greeks and Poles struck for freedom and independence. The Texas revolt from Mexico, which, after the setback of the Alamo, brought the Lone Star Republic into being, was viewed as another victory for free men from tyranny.[20] Antislavery forces, however, opposed granting the petition of the Texans for annexation to the United States because of their distaste for the prospect of another slave state, and President Jackson held up his approval for fear it would hurt the chances of his favorite, Martin Van Buren, in the election of 1836.

It was in this atmosphere that the Canadian Rebellion of 1837 took place. In Lower Canada the predominant French population sought independence from British rule, while in Upper Canada the people who were descended from the Loyalists that had fled from the thirteen colonies during the American Revolution sought relief from the domination of a small clique of governing officials called the "Family Compact." The British government put down the rebellion in Lower Canada rather promptly, but the trouble in Upper Canada was prolonged by persistent attempts made from across the border to aid the "patriots." William Lyon Mackenzie, a Toronto editor and leader of the Upper Canada rebels, fled to Buffalo when the attempt of the rebels to capture Toronto failed in December, 1837. Here he was given a noisy welcome, and received offers of both money and manpower to harass the Canadian authorities. Guerilla bands, consisting of both refugee Canadians and Americans, conducted frequent raids into Canada. And this, of course, was something about which the federal government could not avoid being concerned, since it was a violation of British territory by American citizens and Canadians operating from the American side.

Shortly after the rebellion broke out, Governor Mason was instructed by the State Department to arrest anyone engaged in hostile acts against the British government. Mason obediently issued a proclamation reminding Michiganians of their duty under international law, even though he was personally favorable to the rebel cause. The people of Michigan, and especially the Irish immigrants, sympathized with the patriots. In spite of the governor's warnings, a mass meeting was held in Detroit on New Year's day, 1838, and funds were collected to aid the patriots. A few days later 450 stands of arms were stolen from the Detroit jail, where they had been placed for safekeeping.

[20] One Kalamazoo County township formed in the 'thirties was named "Alamo," another, "Texas."

Volunteers then seized the schooner *Ann* and sailed down the Detroit River for Gibralter, opposite the Canadian shore. General Hugh Brady, United States army commander for the Great Lakes area, had his headquarters at Detroit, but he had no troops. Therefore he called upon Governor Mason for militiamen to pursue the *Ann* and capture the men who had taken her. Mason obeyed, but the militiamen had to be marched to the United States arsenal at Dearborn for arms before they could start for Gibralter. By the time they secured the arms and arrived at Gibralter the raiders already had left for Canada. The force of 132 men had crossed the river, where Canadian defenders had shot down the mainsail of the *Ann*, permitting the ship to drift aground, where the entire rebel force was captured.

Before the end of January three companies of United States regulars arrived at Detroit, but they did not prevent another band of patriots from crossing the river on the ice on February 24 to Fighting Island, which belonged to Canada. General Brady, when he learned of the foray, led his troops down the river to a point opposite the island with orders to arrest any armed men attempting to reach the island or to return to United States territory from it. The British attacked the invaders the next day and drove them back across the river, killing 15 and wounding 40. Angered at this rebuff, patriot sympathizers vented their spleen by collecting all the books in the city written by a noted British author, Captain Frederick Marryat, who was then visiting in Detroit, and making a bonfire out of them in front of his hotel.

The most serious violation of Canadian soil by Detroit raiders took place in December, 1838. A band of about 135 men seized a steamer, the *Champlain*, crossed to the Canadian side, marched on Windsor, and about two o'clock in the morning set fire to the military barracks, guardhouse, and the steamer *Thames*, which was moored at the dock. Several soldiers sleeping in the barracks were burned to death; others were shot as they escaped the burning building. When news of the marauding expedition reached Sandwich a strong Canadian militia force stationed there moved against the invaders. The raiders broke and fled; 21 were killed in the attack and the four taken prisoner were lined up and shot in reprisal against the alleged atrocities of the invaders. Detroiters watched this "Battle of Windsor" from across the river. The execution of the four prisoners perpetuated bad feeling for many years. In 1841 the United States government built Fort Wayne on the Detroit River to guard the border. It was completed in 1851. But it never fired a hostile shot. Civil War volunteers were quartered within its walls, and the fort served as a

troop-training center. The historic portion of the fort was transferred to the city of Detroit in 1949 for use as a museum.[21]

Efforts to aid the Canadian rebels in 1837 and 1838 were not
confined to Detroit. Everywhere along the border secret organizations known as "Hunters' Lodges" sprang into being to aid the
patriot cause. An attempt was made to seize arms, ammunition,
and artillery at Fort Gratiot in Port Huron, but the plot was
foiled.[22] Not until the signing of the Webster-Asburton Treaty
between the United States and Great Britain in 1842 did the
border disorders cease. During the border raids Great Britain
violated its pledge in the Rush-Bagot Agreement of 1817 not to
maintain armed vessels on the Great Lakes except for a limited
number of small ships to enforce customs laws. And the United
States launched an iron warship, the *Michigan*, at Erie, Pennsylvania, in 1844. Fortunately, however, these violations proved to
be temporary and unimportant. The spirit of the Rush-Bagot
Agreement was maintained and later led to the abandonment
of land fortifications as well as armed ships.

EPILOGUE

Michigan's "Boy Governor," Stevens T. Mason, moved to New
York City after the completion of his second term in 1839. He
had married a New York girl, and went there to take up the
practice of law. His life was tragically short. On January 4, 1843
Mason died before reaching his 31st birthday. Bitter partisanship
had resulted in many aspersions against him in the years that
followed his retirement from office. But Michiganians could not
forget this handsome young man, his winning manner, the brave
and confident leadership he had provided during the exciting days
of the big boom, the "Toledo War," and the struggle for statehood. There can be little doubt that his youth and lack of experience led him to make errors of judgment, but in most respects
he had epitomized the strengths and weaknesses of the Michigan
of his time. On June 4, 1905 his remains were brought from
New York to Detroit and interred on the site of the old state
capitol with appropriate ceremony. A bronze statue was erected
in his honor. With the modernization of downtown Detroit in
the 1950s it became necessary to move his remains once more.
There was considerable agitation at the time for their removal
to Lansing, but Detroiters staunchly opposed this. They had

[21] Catlin, *op. cit.*, pp. 338-342.
[22] G. C. Bates, "Reminiscences of the Brady Guards," *Mich. Pioneer
and Historical Colls.*, XIII (1888), 530-546.

come to regard Mason as one of their own. One of the office buildings at Lansing bears his name, as do one of Michigan's counties and one of the state's cities today.

The depression that began in the East in 1837 and spread to Michigan in 1838 and 1839 had many effects upon the state's growth. Movement into Michigan was reduced, and when the westward movement again swelled to large numbers in the later 1840s, major segments of the newcomers bypassed Michigan and went to Wisconsin, Iowa, and Minnesota. The less fertile soils of northern Michigan could not compete for settlers with the richer soils to be found further west. The experiences of the years following 1837, as has been indicated, created a fixed prejudice among Michiganians against state-owned railroads and canals. It also created a prejudice against banks that could not be eradicated for many years. But in the long view, the hard times were no more than an interlude in the growth of Michigan from a wilderness to a great industrial and agricultural state.

Abandoned mine shaft

12

OUT OF THE WILDERNESS, 1835-1860

During the quarter-century that elapsed between the time
Michigan assumed statehood and the beginning of the American
Civil War a large portion of the southern half of the Lower Peninsula was cleared of forests and placed under cultivation, while in
the North the exploitation of timber and mineral resources began.
The building of railroads, the invention of the electric telegraph,
and the extension of postal service established closer connections
between the new state and the eastern seaboard. Recovery from
the economic collapse that took place in the late 1830s was slow,
but by the mid-'forties immigration into Michigan was on the up-
grade and a large measure of confidence had been regained.
Population almost doubled in both the 1840s and 1850s. The
state's capital was permanently located at Lansing. A new state
constitution was written and adopted. Whigs and Democrats contended for political honors until 1854, when antislavery elements
in both parties combined to form the Republican party, and henceforth the partisan battles were between Democrats and Republicans.

Along with other Americans the people of Michigan had boundless faith in the future of the nation and its mission in the
world. They believed in "Manifest Destiny," although some were
inclined to be suspicious that some of the projects for expansion
to the South were plots for the extension of the area of slave-

holding. The evils of slavery were much discussed and condemned. To show their distaste for slavery Michiganians joined in spiriting escaped slaves to freedom via the Underground Railroad, and their legislature passed "personal liberty laws" to withhold the co-operation of state and local officials in the capture of escaped bondsmen. The cause of temperance and the women's-rights movement attracted almost as much attention as the antislavery crusade. In these years, too, Michigan became a leader in public education.

By 1860 southern Michigan was emerging from the wilderness, although unbroken forests covered most of the northland. Some Michiganians, smitten by the restless spirit of the pioneer, moved further west to the rich prairie lands of Iowa and Kansas, and a large number took part in the gold rush to California. But the places of those who left were filled by a steady stream of newcomers from the East and from foreign lands.

MORE PEOPLE

The population of Michigan, which stood at just under 175,000 in 1837, grew to 212,267 in 1840, to 397,654 in 1850, and to 749,113 in 1860. This represents a substantial growth. But whereas Michigan had had the largest percentage increase in population of any state or territory in the decade of the 'thirties, it slipped to fourth in the 'forties and to ninth in the 'fifties. The older states of Illinois and Missouri had far larger numerical increases in population in both decades than did Michigan. So did Wisconsin, Michigan's western neighbor.

After settlement had reached northward in the state to approximately the Muskegon-Bay City line, heavy growth of pine was encountered under which the soils were generally sandy. Frosts came earlier in the autumn and later in the spring. The rich prairie soils of Illinois and the warmer climate of Missouri were preferred by many settlers. Another factor that probably retarded the movement into Michigan was the relative slowness of railroad construction. Railroads were becoming the principal means by which products could be moved to market. Bounded on two sides by the Great Lakes and on another by unbroken forests, southern Michigan presented serious obstacles to the railroad builders. A successful railroad should connect major cities and run through a settled area. East-west railroads were blocked in Lower Michigan by the Great Lakes, and building north-south railroads into the unsettled northland was impractical. Although the export of lumber from Michigan had begun by the time of the Civil War, it was not until after 1860 that the great days of lumbering in the state's northland began.

Some indication of the origins of the people who came to Michigan during this quarter century may be found in the reports of the United States Census of 1860. The census reveals that more than one-third of the residents of the state on the eve of the Civil War had been born in Michigan. Of those born elsewhere, by far the largest number claimed New York as their native state. More than one-quarter of the people in Michigan in 1860 were born in the State of New York. Somewhat less than 5% were natives of Ohio, which ranked third as the state of origin. Pennsylvania was fourth with about half as many as Ohio. Then followed three New England states—Vermont, Massachusetts, and Connecticut, with considerably smaller numbers. The dominance of New Yorkers in the population of Michigan is especially notable. And it must be remembered that most of these were second- or third-generation New Englanders, since western New York, from which so many came, had been settled so largely by people moving west from New England.

A little less than 20% of the people of Michigan in 1860 were born outside the United States. Of these the largest segment consisted of people born in the British Isles: 30,049 in Ireland, 25,743 in England, and 5,705 in Scotland. Those born in one of the several separate states into which Germany was then divided constituted the second largest group: 38,787. There were almost as many who were born in Canada: 36,482. Another significant foreign element was the Dutch, who numbered 6,335, and who settled mostly in western Michigan.

Smaller numbers of Michiganians in 1860 claimed other foreign countries as the land of their birth. The state contained a sizable number of Belgians, French, Norwegians, Swedes, and Swiss. There were even four from the "Sandwich Isles"! The census takers enumerated a total of 6,172 Indians in Michigan in 1860, indicating that a large number had escaped the government agents who had been detailed to move them beyond the Mississippi River in 1840. Counties having the largest Indian population were Emmet, Isabella, Leelanau, Mackinac, and Oceana. The Negro population of Michigan in 1860 numbered 6,799. Of these the largest number (1,673) lived in Wayne County, while Cass County contained the second largest number (1,368).

The lure of fertile land, available at a relatively low price, was undoubtedly what attracted most of the people who came to Michigan in these years. There were also businessmen who saw in the new state opportunity for profitable investments in mercantile establishments, lumbering, mining, and manufacturing. And there were professional men—lawyers, doctors, teachers and others —who sought a more promising field for their endeavors. There were railroad builders, miners, lumbermen, and fishermen who came. And many were simply unskilled laborers who hoped to earn a stake to buy a farm, start a business, or in some other way improve their lot in life.

Yankees, forsaking the rocky lands of New England, and New Yorkers—descendants of earlier westward-moving Yankees—finding it more and more difficult to acquire good land, moved to Michigan in such numbers as to constitute the dominant element in the population of almost every county in the new state. Practically all of them used the Erie Canal and the sailing vessels or steamers of the Great Lakes to reach Detroit, from where they moved into the interior of the state either by railroad or by horse or ox team. The route of foreign immigrants into Michigan was essentially the same. Many German settlers moving into Wisconsin also landed at Detroit, traveled to Grand Haven by the Detroit and Milwaukee Railroad, and across Lake Michigan by ship. Ohioans and Pennsylvanians, as well as immigrants from the southern states, came overland from Ohio or Indiana into southern Michigan.

The influence of the predominant New England-New York element in the population of Michigan is evident in many ways. Some of these have already been indicated.[1] Such leaders in the early development of Michigan as Lewis Cass, the Reverend John D. Pierce, General Isaac E. Crary, Lucius Lyon, and Elon Farnsworth were natives of New England. All but two of the governors of Michigan between 1835 and 1860 were born in New York or one of the New England states. The New York township, varying somewhat from its New England progenitor, was transplanted to Michigan, and here the New England town meeting was combined with the New York idea of a county board.[2] The judicial system of Michigan was copied almost entirely from that of New England and New York, and the early supreme-court justices were from this region.[3] The New England influence is clearly evident in Michigan's leadership in education and in the strong antislavery sentiment demonstrated in the state. New York and New England names such as Rochester, Utica, Albion, Bangor, Hartford, and

[1] See Chapter VIII.

[2] L. K. Mathews, *Expansion of New England*, p. 236.

[3] W. V. Smith, "The Puritan Blood of Michigan," *Mich. Pioneer and Historical Colls.*, XXXVIII (1912), 355-361.

many others were adopted for Michigan towns. One writer characterizes the New Englanders and New Yorkers in Michigan's early population as "homeseekers, a thrifty, enterprising, plucky people, with high ideals of religion, morality and education" who "brought with them the New England home, the church and the school to transplant their superior culture in the wilderness of Michigan," adding that "in spite of their venturesome spirits, they retained their hardheaded individualism, preserving that essential incentive to progress and prosperity, which would, in time, produce a better standard of living."[4]

Of the immigrants who came to Michigan from other countries, the English and Scots were quickly and easily assimilated due to the absence of a language barrier and the similarity of British and American institutions. The Irish, however, tended to retain their identity longer. Most of them were Roman Catholics, whereas a large preponderance of the other immigrants were Protestants. The Irish brogue and the utter poverty that most of them endured also tended to set them apart. Thousands had escaped to America to avoid starvation at the time of the terrible potato famine of the 1840s. The Irish tended to settle in the cities, where the men became common laborers while the women were engaged as household servants. The labor force for the building of Michigan railroads in this period was made up largely of Irish immigrants. Because they were poor and obscure, seldom attaining positions of eminence, little has been written about the Irish immigrants into Michigan. They were anti-English in sentiment and many of them were involved in the clandestine organizations formed along the border to aid the rebels in Canada during the Patriot's War of 1837 and afterward.

The large migration from Canada into the United States during the period from 1835 to 1860 was due in part to unfavorable economic conditions in Canada. The failure of the rebellion of 1837 undoubtedly stimulated the exodus from Canada of many who had become disgusted with the ruling class. But more than anything else it was because Canada's Middle West is a cold, infertile, and uninviting country, sparsely settled even to this day, that so many Canadians seeking better lands migrated to Michigan during this period. The adoption of free trade by Great Britain between 1846 and 1849 was a serious blow to Canada, and caused a severe economic depression, which encouraged emigration. A considerable degree of prosperity returned after a

[4] J. H. Stevens, "The Influence of New England in Michigan," *Michigan History*, XIX (1935), 351-352. See also S. H. Holbrook, *The Yankee Exodus, An Account of Migration from New England*, pp. 77-96.

trade reciprocity treaty with the United States was signed in 1854.[5]

German immigrants, who came to Michigan in such large numbers during this period, were welcomed because of their sturdy, industrious habits as well as the cultural contributions they made to the state. Among the German states most heavily represented in Michigan in 1860 were Prussia, Württemberg, Bavaria, Baden, and Hesse. There was a sizable number of Germans in Washtenaw County by 1837. One of their number, the Reverend Frederick Schmid, who had arrived in 1833 as a Lutheran missionary, was instrumental in settling a colony of 15 Germans from Bavaria in Saginaw County, where they established the town of Frankenmuth. Another German colony in 1847 established the settlement of Frankentrost.[6] The following year still another colony of Germans, this one from Hannover, arrived in the Saginaw Valley. Other German immigrants found homes in Clinton County. In sharp contrast to these were the German intellectuals and professional classes who fled from Germany when the revolutionary movements of 1848 collapsed. A great many of these people settled in the cities. Representative of them was Dr. Herman Kiefer, a physician who became a prominent civic leader in Detroit.[7]

Wherever they settled the Germans brought their love of music, organizing bands, orchestras, and singing societies. At Detroit their devotion to choral music led them to form the Harmonie Society in 1849. Four years later they formed a society for physical development and political discussion, and another to produce German plays. A German language newspaper, the *Allegemeine Zeitung*, was published in Detroit as early as 1844. The large influx of well-educated Germans to Detroit caused several other German language newspapers to be published in the 1850s. Some of these Germans also were active in the publication of English language papers.

Though Michigan received a large number of German immigrants during the 1840s and 1850s, an even larger number migrated to Wisconsin. It is altogether likely that if northern Michigan had offered better farm lands, most of these settlers would not have gone further west. German immigrants were eagerly sought by Michigan as well as other western states. Land obtained through federal grants for education and internal improvements could be sold to swell the revenues of a state, and

[5] C. Wittke, *History of Canada*, pp. 134-149.

[6] The names Frankenmuth and Frankentrost suggested that the original settlers were from Franconia, a district of Bavaria.

[7] J. A. Russell, *The Germanic Influence in the Making of Michigan.*

most states needed such revenues badly. Heavily burdened with debt incurred during the 1830s, and with citizens averse to paying high taxes, the states found in land sales a welcome source of revenue as well as an added base for taxes in the future. In many instances, the federal land grants were disposed of at a low price to attract settlers, thus dissipating funds intended for education. In this respect, Michigan was less shortsighted than most of its sister states, due perhaps to the greater regard for education among its heavily New York-New England population. But even so, in the early 1840s especially, school and university lands were sold cheaply to attract settlers to Michigan. In 1845 an act of the legislature empowered Governor Barry to employ an agent to reside in New York for the purpose of encouraging immigration to Michigan. The agent appointed to this position, John Almy of Grand Rapids, published a six-page pamphlet extolling the attractions of the state. In 1848 Governor Epaphroditus Ransom strongly recommended action to encourage immigration to Michigan. Ransom appointed Edward H. Thompson of Flint to represent the state in New York City, where most of the emigrants from Europe arrived, and the latter published a 47-page pamphlet in both English and German entitled *The Emmigrant's Guide to Michigan*. Similar efforts to attract immigrants, especially Germans, continued to the Civil War and were resumed thereafter.[8]

The Michigan legislature demonstrated its interest in the first German colonies in the Saginaw country by appropriating 8,000 acres of land granted to the state by the federal government for internal improvements to construct roads to their settlements. Another 2,000 acres were set aside, the proceeds to be used to build a road to the German settlements in Clinton County. Other grants were made for the aid of the Dutch settlers who settled at Holland. To build a wharf or pier at the mouth of the Black River for their use, the proceeds from 4,000 acres were appropriated, and funds derived from the sale of 3,000 acres more were set aside to build roads to Holland from Allegan, Grandville, and Grand Haven.

The first Dutch settlers comprised a colony whose leader was the Reverend Albertus Van Raalte. One reason for the migration of this first group and several subsequent ones was religious. Their members objected to conforming to the state church of the Netherlands, the National Reformed Church. These seceders had been compelled to surrender their churches and to worship in

[8] W. L. Jenks, "Michigan Immigration," *Michigan History,* XXVIII (1944), 69-100.

barns and stables. But the economic reason for the Dutch emigration was probably more compelling than this religious factor. During 1845 the potato rot hit the Netherlands and destroyed so much of the crop upon which the poor chiefly relied for food that many faced starvation. The country was crowded and the more ambitious sought greater opportunity for themselves and their children than their small homeland afforded. The importance of the economic motive for emigration may be judged by noting that of those who came to America in 1847 nearly twice as many were members of the state church as were members of the seceding group.[9]

The leader and pastor of the first colony of Dutch settlers in Michigan, Albertus Van Raalte, was a man small in stature, possessed of an indomitable will, unflinching courage, considerable executive ability, and implicit trust in God. His group of 53 members arrived at New York November 17, 1846, after a month and a half on the stormy Atlantic. Van Raalte originally intended to settle in Wisconsin, where several Dutch families had arrived in 1845 and 1846. After arriving at Detroit the men of the party found work while Van Raalte continued westward to look over the land. After considering the possibility of selecting lands in Iowa, Missouri, and Wisconsin, Van Raalte finally decided upon a location at the mouth of the Black River in Michigan, where the town of Holland was founded. The colony consisted of the members of Van Raalte's congregation, and it was governed to a large extent by the congregation's governing body, the Classis.[10]

Unaccustomed to the use of the axe, the most important tool used by pioneers in clearing the forest, the members of the colony endured great hardships the first year. They were quickly followed by other Dutch settlers, who migrated in some instances as congregations, in others as families or individuals. Zeeland was founded in 1848 by a congregation from the Dutch province of that name led by the Reverend C. VanderMeulen. Scores of these Zeelanders received financial aid from Jannes Van de Luijster. The first Dutch settlers of Kalamazoo came in 1850 under the leadership of Paulus den Bleyker. Shortly after the arrival of the party, cholera broke out among its members and spread among the townspeople of Kalamazoo. The Dutch newcomers were isolated in a pest house on the edge of the town, where several

---

[9] A. Mulder, *Americans from Holland*, p. 118.
[10] *Classis Holland Minutes, 1848-1858.*

of their number died before the disease subsided.[11] Other Dutch immigrants found homes in Grand Rapids, Muskegon, and Allegan, while some formed their own communities.[12]

The Dutch were a sturdy, hard-working lot, zealously devoted to their churches, and inclined towards theological disputation. A split in the Reformed Church in America, to which most of the Dutch immigrants belonged, took place before the Civil War and resulted in the formation of the Christian Reformed Church. The Reformed Church and the Christian Reformed Church remain today the principal denominations that consist largely of people of Dutch origin, though there have been other smaller offshoots. The faith in education among these Dutch pioneers was strong. By 1851 they had established the school in Holland that ultimately developed into Hope College. Many of the Dutch leaders were opposed to assimilation, and preferred that the Dutch settlers retain their identity and traditions. In Kalamazoo the Dutch farmers were the ones who first developed bleached celery and made that city famous for this herb. Politically, the Dutch tended toward conservatism as did the New Englanders, although both were radical in their opposition to slavery.

In the mines that were opened in the Upper Peninsula during this period, a large portion if not a preponderance of the workers were foreign born. It was possible for immigrants from Europe to reach the Upper Peninsula by an all-water route, using the Great Lakes waterway. Cornishmen were the most important of these workers.

> From the beginning, the Cornishman established himself as the backbone of the underground force and the supervisor of both underground and surface developments. His educational background was not likely to be as good as that of the early German, but he had mined copper, and experience was what counted. As early as 1844, 20 Cornish miners were working for the Lake Superior Copper Company, and in 1849 most of the miners at the Cliff were Cornishmen. But the real stream began in the fifties after the California gold boom set off an exodus of mining men from England.[13]

[11] A. Praus (ed.), *The Cholera in Kalamazoo.*

[12] M. L. D'Ooge, "The Dutch Pioneers of Michigan," *Mich. Pioneer and Historical Colls.,* XXXVIII (1912), 204-212. See also a series of articles on the Dutch pioneers in *Michigan History,* XXXI (1947), 353-416; H. S. Lucas, *Netherlanders in America: Dutch Immigration to the United States and Canada, 1789-1950*; A. J. Pieters, *A Dutch Settlement in Michigan*; and A. Hyma, *Albertus Van Raalte and His Dutch Settlements in the United States.*

[13] W. B. Gates, Jr., *Michigan Copper and Boston Dollars,* p. 95.

Other foreign stocks represented in sizable numbers in the copper mines were Irish and German. In Houghton County five persons out of seven were of foreign birth in 1850 and two out of three in 1860.[14] Cornishmen also came to work in the iron mines. Antagonism between the Cornishmen, or "Cousin Jacks," and the Irish in the mining towns became traditional.[15] An important element in the iron mining industry were the French Canadians, especially in the preparation of charcoal for smelting.[16]

According to the census of 1860, Wayne County contained 75,547 inhabitants, or approximately 10% of the total population of the state.[17] Only four other counties contained as many as 30,000. Three of these— Oakland, Washtenaw, and Lenawee —were clustered in the southeastern part of the state. The other one, Kent, contained the growing city of Grand Rapids. By 1854 lumber-sawing had become an important industry, and on the eve of the Civil War Grand Rapids was a boom town.

Except for Kent County, the population was heavily concentrated in the two southernmost tiers. Of the counties in this group, only Van Buren had fewer than 20,000 people. In the third tier only Oakland and Macomb had that many inhabitants, Barry being the most sparsely settled. In the fourth tier Kent County was the largest, followed in order by St. Clair and Genesee, both of which had over 20,000. Saginaw was the largest county north of the four southern tiers with 12,557. In the Upper Peninsula the largest concentration of population was in Houghton County, heart of the copper country, with 8,893 inhabitants. Total population of the Upper Peninsula in 1860 had grown to more than 20,000.

NEW SOURCES OF WEALTH

Between 1835 and 1860 the exploitation of Michigan's timber and mineral resources got under way, though lumber, copper, and iron production was to rise far higher in the years after the Civil War. Even by 1860, however, the products of the state's mines and forests were making a major contribution to its economy. Sawmills sprang up early in the history of every Michigan

[14] *Ibid.*, p. 96.

[15] L. A. Chase, "Michigan's Upper Peninsula," *Michigan History,* XX (1936), 327.

[16] P. White, "The Iron Region of Lake Superior," *Mich. Pioneer and Historical Colls.,* VIII (1885), 152.

[17] The 1960 population of Wayne County, 2,435,235, was almost one-third of the total population of Michigan.

community to provide sawed lumber for the building of houses, barns, stores, and shops. These mills were a profitable investment and provided jobs for many workers. By 1854 a total of 889 sawmills employing 4,579 persons were in operation in Michigan. But the lumber industry as usually conceived may be said to have begun when sawed lumber was produced beyond the quantity required to meet local demand, with the excess shipped elsewhere. The first region in which large scale lumber production took place was the Saginaw Valley. In this valley and in the valleys of the tributaries of the Saginaw—the Cass, the Shiawassee, and the Tittabawassee—were thousands of acres of white pine forests. Because of its beauty, and because it was a soft wood, easy to work, white pine was the most highly prized of all lumber. For many years lumbermen confined their cutting to the areas in proximity to rivers, down which the logs could be floated to the sawmills. The Saginaw country was threaded by rivers suitable to the needs of the lumbermen. And at the mouth of the Saginaw River access was easy to distant markets by use of Great Lakes shipping.

Harvey Williams is said to have set up the first steam sawmill in the Saginaw Valley in 1834, the engine being one salvaged from the *Walk-in-the-Water*, the first steamboat on the Great Lakes. Not for more than 10 years, however, was any appreciable amount of lumber sent from this region to outside markets. It was in 1847 that a shipment of Saginaw pine reached Albany, New York, by way of the Great Lakes and the Erie Canal, and attracted favorable notice from lumber dealers who pronounced it the equal of pine from the Maine woods, long regarded as the best obtainable. From this time forward the export of pine lumber from the Saginaw Valley grew rapidly. There were 29 mills in this valley by 1854, with a capacity of 100,000,000 board feet per year; by 1860 the number of mills had increased to 72. Detroit, Cleveland, Toledo, and Buffalo provided ready markets for lumber. By 1860 a wholesale migration of lumbermen from Maine to the Saginaw Valley was taking place. Loggers, sawyers, teamsters, rivermen, and capitalists came, bringing with them their tools and techniques. A future governor of Michigan, Henry H. Crapo, was among those who came from the East and invested their capital and labor in the lumber business. Within a decade from the time of his arrival he had amassed a fortune and had been elected governor of the state.[18]

[18] M. D. Lewis, *Lumberman from Flint, the Michigan Career of Henry H. Crapo, 1855-1869.*

Commercial lumbering was also well under way on the western side of the Lower Peninsula by 1860. Huge quantities of logs were being floated down the Grand River to sawmills in Grand Rapids, the lumber from these mills being shipped on river boats to the mouth of the Grand until the railroad arrived in 1858. Muskegon was producing the largest amount of lumber of any point on the west coast, its mills, the first of which had been started in 1838, turning out 75,000,000 board feet in 1860, as compared with 131,000,000 board feet turned out by the Saginaw Valley mills.[19] Sawmills had also been established by 1860 at the mouths of the Pere Marquette, the Manistee, and the Boardman rivers. In the Upper Peninsula lumber was being sawed by mills at Escanaba and Menominee by 1860. Large amounts of hardwood were also being cut in the Upper Peninsula to feed the charcoal kilns that were erected by the iron smelters.

Copper mining had become an important segment of the Michigan economy by the time of the Civil War. As has been recounted earlier, the French and the British knew of the existence of copper in the Lake Superior region and had made unsuccessful attempts to develop the mining of the red metal on a profitable scale. Henry R. Schoolcraft, who had accompanied the Cass expedition in 1820, mentioned in his account (written in 1821), the copper deposits of the area. He told of seeing the boulder of pure copper imbedded in rock on the Ontonagon River, which had been discovered in 1771 by Alexander Henry, the trader who luckily escaped being slaughtered by the Indians when they attacked Fort Michilimackinac in 1763. Schoolcraft visited the area again in 1831 and 1832. With him on these visits was a young Detroit physician and scientist, Dr. Douglas Houghton. Houghton hacked off a piece of the Ontonagon boulder as a souvenir. He also found traces of copper in the rocks of the Keweenaw Peninsula. In 1837 Houghton was appointed as Michigan's first state geologist. His report to the legislature in 1841 indicated there were extensive copper deposits along the Lake Superior shore, and although Houghton warned that quick riches were not to be had, news of his findings resulted in a copper rush to the Keweenaw Peninsula.[20] Houghton's life was snuffed out when a boat in which he was a passenger capsized on Lake Superior off Eagle River on October 14, 1845. He was only 36

[19] F. C. Bald, *Michigan in Four Centuries*, pp. 228-229.
[20] E. K. Rintala, *Douglass Houghton, Michigan's Pioneer Geologist*.

years of age at the time of his death. His name is borne by a city, a county, and the state's largest inland lake.

Attention was attracted to the copper country, too, by the determined efforts of Julius Eldred, a Detroit businessman, to transport the Ontonagon boulder from the Upper Peninsula and to display it as a natural wonder. He made his first trip to the site of the boulder in the summer of 1841. At that time, the whole western part of the Upper Peninsula was still Indian land, but in 1842 the United States government acquired title to it by the Treaty of La Pointe. Because the boulder lay on Indian land when he found it, Eldred paid a local chieftain $150 for it. He returned the next summer to secure the 6,000 pound combination of copper and rock but was unable to move it with the apparatus at hand. The following year he was back again, with a small railroad car and tracks, only to find that another claimant to the boulder had taken possession. After paying the latter $1,365 Eldred succeeded in moving the boulder by loading it on his flat car with a block and tackle, pushing the car ahead a short distance, then taking up the track behind it and laying a stretch in front. In this way the expensive prize was transported to Lake Superior, where it was put aboard a ship and taken to Detroit. But Eldred's troubles were not over. The boulder was seized by the United States government, taken to Washington, and displayed in the Smithsonian Institute. Eldred, however, did receive compensation. The boulder was later removed to the Natural History Building of the National Museum in Washington where it is still on exhibit. The publicity that was given the Ontonagon boulder served, along with Houghton's report, to focus attention on the Michigan copper country.[21]

The great copper rush began in 1843 and reached its height in 1846—three years before the gold rush to California. A few prospectors arrived at Copper Harbor in the summer of 1843, and workers from the Wisconsin lead mines began digging for copper in the vicinity of the Ontonagon River the same year. The following spring the influx began in earnest. Every ship brought parties of men from the East, certain that they would return home with vast wealth. These copper hunters had little equipment: usually it consisted of a small tent, two blankets per man, a camp kettle, frying pan, tin plates and cups. Actually there was very little real mining during the first two years. Equipped with a pick and some gunpowder, hundreds of men tramped through the forests,

[21] F. C. Bald, *op. cit.,* pp. 232-234.

fighting off hordes of gnats and mosquitoes, picking up copper lying on the surface or easily blown free from overcropping rocks. Mostly they were searching out the most promising lands for purposes of speculation. In these mining camps of the copper rush many of the same conditions existed that were later to be found in the gold mining camps of California.[22] Although American history books relate the story of the gold rush to California in detail, they seldom mention the great Michigan copper rush. Yet the Michigan copper rush came first, and the value of the copper taken from the Lake Superior mines over the years probably was greater and contributed more to the growth of the nation than all the gold mined in California.

After Indian rights in the land had been acquired by the Treaty of La Pointe, the question arose as to how rights to mine copper could be secured. It was decided to grant leases under provisions of an act passed by Congress in 1807 for the purpose of permitting lead mining. The War Department was in charge of granting the leases, and in the summer of 1843 an agent was stationed at Copper Harbor to issue permits to prospectors. Nearly a hundred such permits had been granted by the end of 1843. At first it was possible to obtain a permit to explore nine square miles, but the area was reduced to one square mile in 1845. After a location had been made, the holder could apply for a lease, accompanied by surety bonds in the amount of $20,000. The lessee was allowed a year for exploration and three years to mine, with the privilege of two renewals of three years each. He was required to pay the government a royalty of six percent of the value of the minerals taken during the first three-year period and ten percent thereafter. In 1846, however, it was found that the issuance of these permits had been illegal, and thenceforward the lands could be acquired only by purchase. An act passed by Congress in 1847 provided for the designation of mineral lands in the Lake Superior region and stipulated that they should be sold for not less than $5.00 an acre. The price was reduced, however, in 1850 to $1.25 an acre—the same minimum price as that charged for agricultural lands.[23] The rights of those to whom permits had been granted were safeguarded. Altogether about a thousand such permits had been issued.

[22] A. Murdoch, *Boom Copper: The Story of the First U. S. Mining Boom*; R. J. Hybels, "Lake Superior Copper Fever, 1841-47," *Michigan History*, XXXIV (1950), 97-120; 224-245; 309-327.

[23] L. A. Chase, "Early Days of Michigan Mining: Pioneering Land Sales and Surveys," *Michigan History*, XXIX (1945), 166-179.

Prior to the sale of lands for copper mining, it was necessary that they be surveyed. Douglas Houghton conceived the idea of conducting the usual topographical surveys with a geological survey, and in 1844 he contracted with the United States government to take charge of these surveys. At the time of Houghton's untimely death the following year, a good start had been made, and the running of section lines and the identification of mineral resources were continued according to his plans.

It soon became apparent that the individual miner, working with hand tools, could accomplish little. Accordingly, copper companies were formed early, some actually to conduct mining operations, and others only to sell stock to speculators. Two companies were organized in 1844, mainly by Boston capitalists. One of these went bankrupt five years later. The other one, the Pittsburgh and Boston, also nearly expired before it hit "pay dirt." Some of its workmen opened a mine near Eagle River that was given the name Cliff Mine. From it masses of pure copper and many nuggets of silver were taken. This was the richest mine discovered before 1860. Before it was discontinued in 1870, it had paid the stockholders of the company a total of more than $2,500,000, a profit of some 2,000% on their original investment. Many other companies, however, were less fortunate, and failures were common.

Three major copper-producing areas had been located by 1860, all of them in the western part of the Upper Peninsula. Near the end of the Keweenaw Peninsula were the mines that centered around Copper Harbor, Eagle River, and Eagle Harbor. Considerably to the southwest were the workings in the region of the Ontonagon River. The third and richest area to be developed was around Portage Lake in the middle of the Keweenaw Peninsula.

Mining in the Ontonagon area had begun in 1843, almost at the same time as in the Copper Harbor region. In the Minesota Mine, opened in this area in 1847, there was found the largest single mass of native copper ever discovered.[24] The National Mine in the same area was paying good dividends by the time of the Civil War. The Cliff and the Minesota contained the richest mass copper deposits ever discovered. A copper mass is a solid piece of native or pure copper weighing 100 pounds or more, surrounded by a rock matrix. These mass copper deposits, which were regarded at first as the only lodes worth mining, were actually geological freaks. Much more important in the long run were the deposits of finely disseminated metal in amygdaloid and conglomerate rock. An

[24] The spelling "Minesota" is reputed to have come from a clerical error made in a charter application.

amygdaloid rock is one that often contains pure copper in the amygdaloids, or almond-shaped cavities. Conglomerate is a rock formation held together with pure copper metal.

Another mine that was to become world-famous was the Quincy, opened in 1848. It was situated on Portage Lake in the middle of the Keweenaw peninsula. Christopher C. Douglas, a cousin of Douglas Houghton, and his brother-in-law, Ransom Sheldon, were the men who are credited with opening the Quincy Mine. Although its production at first was discouraging, it was beginning to be profitable by 1860, and was destined in future years to earn the nickname "Old Reliable" for its large and sustained production. The rich Pewabic mine was opened in the same vicinity in 1856. It was in this mine that the great amygdaloid vein was found, and this type of formation was the foundation for the amazing production record of the Quincy as well. Also in production by the time of the Civil War was the Franklin mine in the Portage Lake area. And finally, there was the Calumet and Hecla Mine, opened in 1859, but not put into production until 1866. It became the most famous copper mine in the world.[25]

The companies that were formed to exploit the discoveries that had been made not only supplied the necessary capital but also provided trained personnel. Dr. Charles T. Jackson was one such man, though his enthusiastic reports to the first company formed, Lake Superior Copper Company, proved unfounded; it operated at a loss until 1849 when it became bankrupt. Men with practical experience in the lead mines of Wisconsin and Illinois, James K. Paul, Nicholas Miniclier, and others, came to the Ontonagon region and were the key figures, along with a prospector, William W. Spaulding, in developing the copper resources there. Paul purchased the land on which Ontonagon was located and platted the town. The name was an adaptation of a Chippewa word. Ransom Sheldon, a key figure in the development of the Quincy Mine, opened a store on the south side of Portage Lake in 1852, and around this the town of Houghton grew up. On the opposite side, Christopher C. Douglas built a store in 1858 and the following year platted the town of Hancock, named for John Hancock, signer of the Declaration of Independence. Capital provided by eastern capitalists proved indispensable in sinking shafts and making the mines pay. Up to 1860 over $900,000 had been invested in the Quincy Mine, and although it was beginning to be productive, op-

[25] D. S. Coon, "The Quincy Mine," *Michigan History,* XXIV (1940), 91-104; W. H. Pyne, "Quincy Mine: the Old Reliable," *Michigan History,* XLI (1957), 219-244; A. S. Wax, "The Calumet and Hecla Copper Mine," *Michigan History,* XVI (1932), 5-41.

erations were still in the red. But in the years ahead the investors got back their money many times over. The name of the Quincy Mine, taken from that of a town in Massachusetts, symbolizes the importance of eastern capital in mining Michigan copper. By 1860 no less than 33 companies were engaged in mining in the Michigan copper country. They had invested over four million dollars and were employing 3,681 workers.

The federal government played an important role in laying the foundations for copper production in Michigan. It purchased the land from the Indians under treaties signed in 1842 and 1854, had it surveyed, and sold it at a low price to those who wished to engage in mining. Fearing that the Indians of the area might be resentful of the intrusion of the prospectors and miners, the War Department built Fort Wilkins at the tip of the Keweenaw Peninsula between Lake Superior and an inland body of water, Lake Fanny Hooe. The first stockade was built in 1844. The Indians proved friendly, however, and far less dangerous than the boisterous prospectors and miners. The troops were pulled out in 1846 at the time of the Mexican War. The fort was unoccupied thereafter, except for a brief period between 1867 and 1870. In recent years the site of the old fort has been acquired by the Michigan Conservation Department, and the stockade and barracks have been restored. The buildings house an interesting museum, made possible through the unflagging efforts of Mrs. Carroll Paul of Marquette.

A third new source of wealth to Michigan, developed during the quarter-century between statehood and the Civil War, was iron ore. Although the existence of copper in the Lake Superior region had been known for centuries, and although Houghton's 1841 report had suggested that there was iron ore in the region, it was not until 1844 that the existence of the latter was confirmed. The discovery was made by a government land surveyor, William A. Burt. Burt was associated with Douglas Houghton in the combined linear and geological survey for which a contract had been signed with the government June 25, 1844. Burt formed a survey party, which started its work in August, one of his assistants being Jacob Houghton, a brother of Douglas. On September 19 Burt was puzzled by the peculiar movements of the needle of his magnetic compass. In seeking the reason for this, numerous outcroppings of iron were discovered south of Teal Lake near the site of the present city of Negaunee. Though Burt is remembered by Michiganians chiefly because of this discovery, he took far more pride in his invention of a solar compass, which enabled the surveyors to run the section lines accurately in a region where iron ore deposits were numerous.[26]

The year after Burt and his party discovered iron ore near Teal Lake, Philo M. Everett of Jackson found his way to the same spot. It is quite probable that he did not know of the finding by Burt. He had been infected by the copper fever and, through the intervention of United States Senator John Norvell, had secured a permit to lease a square mile of land in northern Michigan just before the granting of such permits was discontinued. Setting out for the Upper Peninsula, he met a French Canadian who had been a clerk in the fur trade and was thoroughly acquainted with the Lake Superior region. It is just possible that this man, Louis Nolan, had heard something about Burt's discovery, although the news had not yet been made public. At any rate, Nolan told him that there was a mountain of ore near Teal Lake, and when Everett showed him some copper ore, Nolan shook his head and indicated it was not that kind of ore. Everett engaged Nolan to accompany him. The party was guided to the location of the iron ore by a Chippewa chieftain named Marji-Gesick, who also may have gained his information from one of Burt's party. After entering the location in the office of the United States mineral agent at Copper Harbor, Everett returned to Jackson with samples of his ore, the fine quality of which was soon confirmed. The officers of the company Everett formed, the Jackson Mining Company, gave Marji-Gesick a small share in the company for his services in guiding Everett to the location. After the death of the chieftain, his daughter, Charlotte, found a paper certifying the gift, and its validity was confirmed in a famous trial before the Michigan supreme court. The Jackson Mining Company took its name not from the city from which its founders came but from that of a Boston geologist, Professor Charles T. Jackson, whose geological reports were the indirect source of Everett's original interest in the Upper Peninsula and its mineral resources.[27] The original iron was dis-

---

[26] A. S. Brown, "William Austin Burt: Michigan's Master Surveyor," *Papers* of the Michigan Academy of Science, Arts, and Letters, XLVII (1962), 263-275; H. E. Burt, "William Austin Burt, Inventor," *Michigan History*, VI (1922), 175-193; W. A. Burt, "Autobiography," *Mich. Pioneer and Historical Colls.*, XXVIII (1898), 646-647; G. H. Cannon, "The Life and Times of William A. Burt," *Mich. Pioneer and Historical Colls.*, V (1882), 115-123.

[27] P. M. Everett, "Recollections of the Early Explorations and Discovery of Iron Ore on Lake Superior," *Mich. Pioneer and Historical Colls.*, XI (1888), 161-174. In the above account Everett does not acknowledge his debt to Marji-Gesick. See H. Hatcher, *A Century of Iron and Men*, and R. D. Williams, *The Honorable Peter White*, p. 17.

covered clinging to the roots of a fallen tree. The stump of this tree, a drawing of which forms part of the seal of the City of Negaunee, was preserved until 1900 as an historical relic. A monument of native stone now marks the spot where the old stump was located.[28]

The Jackson Mining Company, which had been formed as a copper-mining business before Everett made his original trip to the Upper Peninsula, at once took steps to produce iron instead. The company sent an expedition to Teal Lake in 1846, and it brought back enough of the ore to test. It was made into a bar of fine iron at a forge located at Hodunk, north of Coldwater—the first iron ever to be made from Lake Superior ore. Steps were taken at once to get together materials needed for a forge, and in 1847 the forge was transported to the site of the company's operation near Negaunee. The first iron was made from this forge in February, 1848. Fuel for the forge was charcoal, made in kilns from hardwood. Because of the extreme difficulty of transportation, especially before the construction of the Soo Canal, the early iron companies set up forges to smelt the iron before it was shipped to market.

A second association, the Marquette Iron Company, began mining ore in 1849 at the site of the present city of Ishpeming. This company also built a forge. It was situated on the shore of Lake Superior in Marquette. Here three officials of the firm—Robert Graveraet, Dr. Edward Clark, and Amos R. Harlow—set up the forge, built some cabins, and thus started the settlement that grew to be the city of Marquette. A young man named Peter White, then only nineteen years of age, was one of the party. In due time he became a leading citizen of the Upper Peninsula. Like so many other young men of his time, he had been caught up in the enthusiasm of the copper boom. The officials of the Marquette Iron Company ran into him at Mackinac Island on their way north and hired him to accompany them. He was later put in charge of the company store. In 1853 he opened a bank in Marquette, and three years later he was elected to the state legislature.[29]

The Cleveland Iron Company, later to take the name of Cleveland-Cliffs, was formed in 1847, its leading organizers being a young lawyer, Samuel L. Mather, and a physician, Dr. Morgan L. Hewitt. Like the other two companies, the Cleveland Iron Com-

[28] R. A. Brotherton, "The Discovery of Iron Ore: Negaunee Centennial, 1844-1944," *Michigan History*, XXVIII (1944), 198-213.

[29] R. D. Williams, *op. cit.*; P. White, "The Iron Region of Lake Superior," *Mich. Pioneer and Historical Colls.*, VIII (1885), 145-161.

pany built a forge and produced "bloom iron." But it was the common experience of all that this was an unprofitable business, and they turned to shipping the raw ore, to be smelted in the large blast furnaces in the lower-lakes region. A blast furnace—first in the Upper Peninsula—was built at Negaunee in 1858 by the Pioneer Iron Company. Later other blast furnaces were constructed —25 in all—in various parts of the Upper Peninsula. Some of these operated for many years. But the leading producers by 1860 were shipping the ore elsewhere to be smelted. The Cleveland Iron Company was able to establish in court its prior occupancy of the same outcropping at Ishpeming as that claimed by the Marquette Iron Company, and in 1853 the latter was taken over by the Cleveland firm.[30]

The distance between Negaunee and Marquette is only about a dozen miles and Ishpeming is about three miles further. Yet this short gap between the mines and the Lake Superior port where the ore could be shipped proved to be a difficult obstacle. The road went through a dense forest and across a high range of hills. At first ore was transported only during the winter months when sleighs could be used. A railroad was projected as early as 1851, but six years were required to complete it. In the meantime a plank road was built, over which wagons piled high with ore could be hauled.

At Marquette there were more problems. Shallow water near the shore made it necessary to transfer mining equipment and supplies from ships to barges, or else to float them ashore. The problem of loading iron ore onto ships lying offshore can readily be imagined. A dock built out into the lake in the early 1850s was shattered by the winds and waves of the lake. The first modern dock was built by the Cleveland Iron Company in 1859. Resting on piles driven to solid rock, it extended 400 feet. Railroad tracks were laid on a trestle constructed on the dock, and railroad cars could then discharge their cargoes of iron ore into chutes leading to pockets from which the ships could be loaded. The completion of the Soo Locks in 1855 removed another bottleneck in the transportation of iron ore to market. Thenceforward ore carriers could proceed directly from Marquette to lower lake ports.

Until 1870 the mining of iron was a relatively simple process. After the trees, sod, and soil were scraped away, the ore could be broken off by use of the pick, hand drill, and sledge hammer. Black powder was used to break up the ore-bearing rock. It was not until the 1870s that shafts were sunk for underground mining. Thus, once the transportation problem was solved, it was relatively

[30] W. Havighurst, *Vein of Iron: The Pickands-Mather Story.*

PRESENT
AND
ORIGINAL
COUNTY NAMES

easy to increase production by leaps and bounds. Shipment of iron ore from the Upper Peninsula jumped from 1,449 tons in 1855 to 114,401 tons in 1860. Marquette County had a population of 2,821 in 1860. Marquette, Negaunee, and Ishpeming had been founded as towns. Marquette, founded July 13, 1849, was originally called Worcester, but the name was later changed to honor the great Jesuit missionary. The mines worked before the Civil War were all located in what is called the Marquette Range. Michigan's two other iron ranges—the Menominee and the Gogebic—were not developed until later.

THE SOO CANAL

The glaciers in prehistoric times determined the shape and size of the Great Lakes. They left Lake Superior at a level some 22 feet above Lakes Michigan and Huron. Connecting Lake Superior with the lower lakes is the St. Mary's River, through which the waters rush over rapids to the lower level. Indians, skilled in the management of canoes, were able to guide their frail craft through these rapids, but they formed a barrier to the passage of larger craft. As early as 1797 the Northwest Company had built a lock to lift small vessels from the lower lakes to the level of Lake Superior and to lower downbound vessels, but the size of the canal limited its use to the canoes and boats used by the fur traders. When copper and iron were discovered in the Upper Peninsula, a tramway was built around the rapids to transport ore. Lack of materials and skilled labor made shipbuilding above the rapids a difficult task. During the winter of 1839-40 the schooner *Algonquin* was moved around the rapids on greased rollers. In 1845 and 1846 two steam-powered vessels, the *Independence* and the *Julia Palmer*, were transferred to Lake Superior by the same laborious process. As copper and iron production increased, the movement of ore around the rapids and the transfer of supplies and equipment bound for Lake Superior called for the employment of many men. But it was cumbersome and expensive at best. Quite clearly, a canal was what was needed.

As already has been related, the construction of such a canal was one of the projects undertaken in the state internal-improvements program, but the contractor refused to start work when he became convinced the canal could not be built for the amount he had agreed to build it for and when he became skeptical, too, about the ability of the state to raise the money to pay him. He found a ready excuse for discontinuing the undertaking when he ran into difficulty with the commandant at Fort Brady concerning the location of the canal. Shortly thereafter Michigan senator John Norvell, in December, 1839, introduced a bill into Congress for a donation of public lands for the purpose of constructing the canal. The Michigan legislature in 1840 officially requested such a grant of land. It required twelve long years of struggle to get such a bill enacted by both houses of Congress. The great Senator Henry Clay derisively commented that the canal would be "a work quite beyond the remotest settlement of the United States if not in the moon." Three times a bill passed the Senate only to meet defeat in the House of Representatives. The opening of copper and iron mines in the Upper Peninsula was a factor in the eventual suc-

First Soo lock

cess of the effort. A bill was passed by both houses and approved by President Millard Fillmore on August 26, 1852.

Under the provisions of this act, a right of way through the United States military reservation was granted for the canal, which was to be at least 100 feet wide and 12 feet deep, with locks at least 250 feet long and 60 feet wide. Public lands in the amount of 750,000 acres were granted to the state of Michigan to build the waterway, but the proceeds were to be forfeited unless the construction of the canal was started within three years and completed within ten years.

At the time the bill was passed a young man named Charles T. Harvey was at Sault Ste. Marie seeking to regain his health after an attack of typhoid fever. He had visited the iron and copper mines of northern Michigan and realized how vital a canal was. Harvey was employed by the Fairbanks Scale Company. In the belief that the canal would be of great public benefit and at the same time might prove to be a profitable venture for its builders, he wrote to officials of his company suggesting that they undertake the project. Without waiting for their response, Harvey obtained the services of an engineer to make a preliminary survey, then went to Detroit where he sought the help of James F. Joy, a lawyer for the Michigan Central Railroad who was well-acquainted with the members of the legislature. A bill was drawn up and passed in February, 1853. It specified a canal with locks 350 feet long and 70 feet wide. The governor was authorized to appoint five commissioners and an engineer to prepare plans and superintend the construction of the canal. And it offered to grant the 750,000 acres of land that had been donated for the purpose by the federal government to a company that would build the canal within two years.

The Fairbanks brothers, who had invested in Upper Peninsula mines, were for this reason interested in Harvey's proposal that they form a company to seek the contract. A corporation was formed under the name of the St. Mary's Falls Ship Canal Company. Among its subscribers were such prominent eastern capitalists as Erastus Corning and August Belmont. The investors' trust in Harvey was indicated by their appointment of him as their agent at the Soo to take charge of construction. An agreement between the company and the State of Michigan was signed on April 5, 1853. Harvey immediately went to Detroit where he bought tools, supplies, and horses and engaged workmen. Then he took ship for the Soo, where he rented the Indian Agency building (which is still standing) for his residence and headquarters, contracted for the construction of shanties to lodge the workers and a mess hall to feed them. He also had a hospital built and engaged the services of a physician. Early in June, almost two months to the day from the time the contract was signed, the first excavation was made.

Formidable obstacles had to be overcome. Workers for the Chippewa Portage Company, which transported goods around the rapids, were opposed to a canal because it would cost them their jobs. Harvey pacified them by giving them work on the canal at good wages. During the long winters, of course, no progress could be made. In 1854 an epidemic of cholera hit the Soo and felled many of the workers. A constant stream of new laborers had to be brought in from the East. Enormous supplies of blasting powder—a total of 3,157 kegs—were required. And just when the work was nearing completion it was found that the rise and fall of Lake Superior would require the canal to be dug a foot deeper—through solid rock. The heavy expenditures and the difficulties encountered caused some of the investors in the St. Mary's Falls Ship Canal Company to become skeptical of the project. Although he had been the General Agent of the Chippewa Portage Company, John T. Whiting undertook a midwinter trip to the East to reassure the company members and succeeded in persuading them to continue the work. On May 31, 1855—less than two years from the time the work was started—the locks and canal were turned over to the superintendent appointed by the state. The first ship to pass through the locks, the steamer *Illinois*, was lifted to the level of

Lake Superior on June 18, 1855. Later the same day or early the next the steamer *Baltimore* made passage through the locks and the canal downward toward Lake Huron.[31]

The total cost of construction was just under one million dollars —about double the amount estimated when the project was undertaken. The company, however, realized a large return from its investment. Empowered to select from the unsold public lands the 750,000 acres to which it was entitled, the company obtained title to some of the best mineral and timber lands in northern Michigan. Charles T. Harvey chose 140,000 acres for the company in the Upper Peninsula. One of the sections he selected was the site of the fabulously rich Calumet and Hecla mine, although the company sold the quarter-section on which the mine was situated for only about $60,000.

For 26 years the locks were operated by the state of Michigan. A toll of four cents per registered ton was charged until 1877, when the rate was reduced to three cents. United States government ships and ships carrying troops or government supplies were exempt. The year after the locks were opened, Congress appropriated $100,000 for deepening the St. Mary's River. President Pierce vetoed the bill, but it was passed over his veto. The use of the locks increased steadily from the time they were opened. The tonnage of ore passing through the channel increased from 1,449 in 1855 to 114,401 in 1860. Upbound freight in the year 1857 included foodstuffs, dry goods, powder, coal, railroad iron, tools, building materials, livestock, and 6,650 passengers.[32] In 1881 the operation of the locks was taken over by the United States government and passage was made toll free. A new lock, the Weitzel Lock, was opened that same year. The Poe Lock, opened in 1896, replaced the original "State Lock." Also in 1896 a lock was opened on the Canadian side of the St. Mary's River. The Davis Lock was put into operation in 1914 and the Sabin Lock in 1919. Finally during World War II the MacArthur Lock was built to replace the Weitzel Lock.

[31] C. Moore (ed.), *The Saint Mary's Falls Canal . . . Semicentennial,* pp. 91-129; F. C. Bald, *The Sault Canal Through 100 Years;* C. F. Norton, "Early Movement for the St. Mary's Falls Ship Canal," *Michigan History,* XXXIX (1955), 257-312. Some writers assert that Harvey claimed too much credit for building the canal, that actually the construction was completed largely through the efforts of John W. Brooks. See article by E. H. Rankin, in *Inland Seas,* XIX (Winter, 1963), p. 311.

[32] E. Calkins, "Report of St. Mary's Falls Ship Canal, 1857," *Michigan History,* XXXIX (1955), 71-79.

ECONOMIC PATTERNS

Although the export of lumber and the mining of copper and iron gave Michigan three new sources of wealth in the quarter-century after statehood was achieved, agriculture remained the backbone of the state's economy. Large numbers of men found employment and sources for the profitable investment of capital in lumbering and mining, but far more people invested in land and earned a living by cultivating the soil. By 1850 Michigan was producing over 5,500,000 bushels of corn and a little less than 5,000,000 bushels of wheat—more than twice the production of ten years before. Nearly 3,000,000 bushels of oats were grown in 1850, over 2,000,000 pounds of wool, 2,000,000 bushels of potatoes, 8,000,000 pounds of butter and cheese, and 2,500,000 pounds of maple sugar. Rye, barley, buckwheat, tobacco, and hops were grown in smaller quantities. The somewhat primitive state of farming in 1850 is indicated by the fact that almost as many oxen (55,350) as horses (58,506) were in use on the farms of the state.

Statistics of production do not tell the whole story of agriculture. Farming in the 1840s and 1850s was a way of life. To a far greater extent than was true a century later the farm family was self-sustaining. Most of the food and fiber needed for the family unit was produced and processed. The farm family was dependent for little on the outside world. Shoes and hats or caps were often secured from the general store, and also cloth for the ladies' best dresses. Salt, coffee, tea, and sugar, harnesses for the teams, tools and wagons were also usually purchased at the nearest trading center. Perhaps a few books and other nonessentials might be bought by the families that were better off. In the southern counties the first stage of frontier life had passed. Pioneers were moving from log houses into frame houses, the lumber being supplied by a nearby sawmill. There was still plenty of wild game in the woods and fish in the streams and lakes to supplement the family diet. On the whole, the farm family was largely independent of the ups and downs of the economic cycle, although when prices for farm products fell, less profit was made. But no one needed to go cold or hungry or unhoused. Poverty existed, but it was usually due to physical or mental defects, misfortune, illness, or just plain laziness.

There were ready markets for the farm products of Michigan. Some of them were shipped to the growing urban centers of the Middle West like Chicago, Milwaukee, or Detroit. Some found their way to eastern cities. With the repeal of the English corn laws, American agricultural products were being shipped abroad in ever-increasing amounts. The vast wheatfields of the prairie states had not yet been put under the plow, and Michigan for many years was a major producer of the nation's wheat.

All but fourteen counties in Michigan reported lumber-sawing as the chief industry outside agriculture in 1860. Even in Wayne County the sawing of lumber was second in size and importance only to the manufacture of machinery. In the northern counties almost the entire male population was engaged in various phases of the lumber business, although the total so employed was far smaller than that in the southern agricultural counties.

Another industry that was promoting the growth of northern Michigan by 1860 was fishing. In Mackinac County alone in 1860 there were 32 fishing companies employing 130 people. In Mason, Manitou, Leelanau, Huron, Grand Traverse, Delta, Chippewa, Berrien, Bay, Alpena, and Alcona Counties fishing appears in the census report of 1860 as the most important industry outside agriculture and lumbering, and in some of them it outstripped these occupations in the number of persons employed as well as in the value of the product. In the entire state 186 fishing companies are listed, employing 929 men and 63 women. Fishing was already a source of profit on Lake Superior by 1833. Commercial fishing began on Lake Huron in 1835. Even earlier, fish were taken from the St. Clair and Detroit Rivers for sale in Detroit. In the early period whitefish, lake trout, and perch constituted most of the catch. Total production of fish in 1859 was estimated at 18,000,000 pounds with a value of $650,000. The American Fur Company in the waning years of the fur industry engaged in commercial fishing operations. Seines were used at first, but gill nets were introduced as early as 1835. In the days before refrigeration the fish had to be cleaned, and then packed in salt in barrels for shipment. By being salted and packed in barrels, the fish could be preserved for a long period of time.[33]

There was considerable manufacturing in Michigan by 1860. Apart from lumber the principal products were boots and shoes, flour, cooperage, staves, hoops (for barrels), shingles, sashes, doors, furniture, saddlery and harnesses, wagons and carts, agricultural implements, clothing, and metalware.

The advance of civilization by 1860 is shown by the number of persons enumerated in the census of 1860 engaged in what might

[33] J. Van Oosten, "Michigan's Commercial Fisheries of the Great Lakes," *Michigan History,* XXII (1938), 107-143.

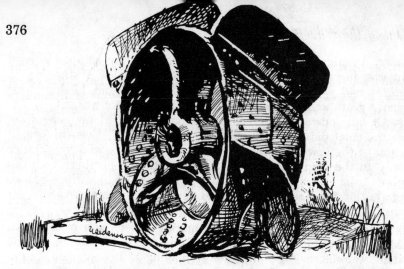

Propeller from the Independence, *an early Great Lakes steamship*

be called luxury occupations. There were 23 actors, 23 ice dealers, 178 music teachers, seven florists, and 617 gardeners and nurserymen. But there were only five paper hangers and seven undertakers in the entire state of Michigan in 1860. The census lists, however, no less than 14,193 persons as "servants." Among the professional classes there were 4,222 teachers, 1,266 physicians, 6 oculists, 791 lawyers, and 855 civil and mechanical engineers. The number of printers was surprisingly large (496). Blacksmiths, carpenters, masons, and brewers are reported in considerable numbers. And the state had 198 professional hunters.

TRANSPORTATION SPELLS PROGRESS

The improvement of transportation was one key to the progress of Michigan in the quarter-century preceding the Civil War. It is difficult for one living in an age that has such rapid and diverse methods of transportation to understand what it meant in these earlier times to be isolated from the outside world, and what a boon it was when transportation became available. The principal cities of the state grew up along the lakes where there were good ports, at important points along navigable rivers, and along the line of the chief roads and railroads. By means of improved transportation the movement of both goods and people was facilitated, and Michigan emerged from the wilderness into closer relations with the outside world.

In discussing improved transportation, the logical place to start is the Great Lakes. It was by canoes paddled along the shores of the Great Lakes that the explorers, followed by the fur traders and the missionaries, came to Michigan. The sailing vessel and the steam-ship made it possible to move persons and products in large numbers to Michigan, and from Michigan to the East. The Erie Canal continued to constitute the principal link between the Great Lakes and the eastern seaboard throughout this period, although rail connections were imminent by 1860. The amount of traffic carried by the railroads was small in comparison to that carried on the Great Lakes in the ante-bellum period. In 1850 a total of 2,341 vessels with a tonnage of 671,545 and crews numbering 31,784 entered the port of Detroit. Ten years later the number of ships had increased to 3,351, and the tonnage to 731,419. By 1860 Great Lakes vessels had crossed the ocean with cargoes for the European market. This was made possible by the Welland Canal, constructed between 1829 and 1833 to allow ships to bypass the Niagara Falls. Throughout the period both sailing vessels and steamships were used. The Detroit and Cleveland Navigation Company, organized in 1850, had docks in various ports of the Great Lakes, and there were many other companies. As will be noted later, the railroads had their own fleets of passenger and freight vessels to connect with their rail-heads. The importance of the Soo Canal to Great Lakes shipping and to the development of the Upper Peninsula of Michigan has already been noted. At ports all along the coast of the Lower Peninsula ships picked up the products of Michigan farms and delivered goods from the East, as well as carrying passengers.[34]

The quarter-century prior to the Civil War was the heyday of river transportation in Michigan. River boats carried passengers, but their chief usefulness was in transporting grain, salted meats, dairy and other products of the farm to the lake ports, from whence they could be picked up by Great Lakes vessels. On the return trips the river boats brought back to the inland towns groceries, hardware, and general merchandise. The rivers of the Saginaw country were used extensively for transportation because of bad roads. Midland, on the Tittabawassee, grew up at the head of navigation.[35] As early as 1837 a cargo of flour was shipped by boat from Owosso to Saginaw. Boatbuilding became a sizable industry in the latter city. On the western side of the state the St. Joseph, Paw Paw, Kalamazoo, and Grand Rivers were all used for transportation. David Walbridge started a line of flat-

[34] G. A. Culbertson, *Freshwater*; J. H. Beers, *History of the Great Lakes*; W. Havighurst, *The Long Ships Passing*.

[35] The head of navigation of a river was located at the first falls above the river's mouth.

boats from Kalamazoo to the mouth of the Kalamazoo River in 1841 and thereby made it possible for the farmers of the area to get a much higher return for their grain. Grain was also shipped from the village of Paw Paw down the river of that same name to its mouth at St. Joseph. Steamers carrying passengers shuttled between Grand Rapids and Grand Haven on the Grand River.

On the St. Joseph River traffic was heavy for many years. Building boats for use on the river was a lively industry in St. Joseph even before Michigan became a state. Two firms began operations in 1832. Schooners were also built at Berrien Springs and Niles for use on the Great Lakes and floated down the river. The first steamboat built for use on the St. Joseph was the *Newburyport*, built in 1832. Unfortunately, it proved to be too large for river use, and in 1833 the *Matilda Barney* was built and put into use. Within a short time several steamboats were plying up and down the river as far as Elkhart. At one time fifty keelboats were reported operating on the St. Joseph. These boats were poled upstream and floated down with the current. A captain and from eight to sixteen men constituted the crew. The operation of a keelboat has been described thus:

> The crew was divided, even numbers to a side and again divided so that half were at the bow and half at the middle of the boat. When the captain gave the word, the bow men placed their poles in the water to the river bed and pushed with all their might as they slowly walked the boat ahead. When the bow men reached the middle the stern men took up the push while the bow men raced back to the bow. The captain stood at the steering oar and repeated over and over again his commands, "Ahead, behind, ahead, behind, ahead, behind." Old residents who lived near the river tell of hearing these monotonous commands every day and often far into the night . . . . Occasionally a complacent steamer captain gave the keel boat a tow and the tired crew a rest.[36]

Canoes, flat-bottomed rowboats and flat-bottomed scows called "arks" were other types of boats in use on the St. Joseph.

The men who operated these river boats were a rough-and-ready lot, heavy drinkers and great fighters. Some of these river men became almost legendary characters. Typical was "Stormy" Davis, six feet tall, strong as an ox, and forever singing. He sang so loudly that "farmers were alarmed, setting hens left their nests, and cattle hoisted tails and fled for life." Later "Stormy" got religion and took up preaching. He always preached barefoot

[36] J. B. Reber, *History of St. Joseph,* p. 65.

in the pulpit. Needless to say, his sermons were "sin-searing, hell-blasting, heart-stirring."[37]

The extent of the traffic on the St. Joseph River may be gained by the record of shipments from the port of St. Joseph during the year 1843, most of which consisted of products that had come down the river to St. Joseph from as far upstream as Constantine: 79,915 barrels of flour (129,33 barrels in 1844), 88,539 bushels of wheat (263,116 bushels in 1844), 99 barrels of cranberries, 3,100 cords of wood, 1,150 casks of wine and whisky (2,721 in 1844), and 1,130 kegs of lard. At this time St. Joseph outstripped Chicago as a shipping point for grain and flour, and in Michigan was exceeded only by Detroit.[38]

Although river traffic was heavy, little was done to connect rivers by canals after the breakdown of the state internal-improvements program. Projects for the building of canals that would connect rivers on the eastern side of the Lower Peninsula with those on the western side persisted for many years but failed to materialize. The great canal craze rapidly disappeared in the 1840s as railroads became more and more popular. The Illinois Canal, connecting the Great Lakes with the Mississippi, was completed in 1848, but it carried relatively little Michigan produce to market. The building of the Soo Canal in 1853-1855 marked virtually the end of the canal era in the Middle West.

In railroad building during the two decades from 1840 to 1860 Michigan lagged far behind its neighboring states. In the decade from 1850 to 1860 2,325 miles of railroad were built in Ohio, 1897 miles in Indiana, 2,757 miles in Illinois, 902 miles in Wisconsin, 817 miles in Missouri, 679 miles in Iowa, and only 475 miles in Michigan. The total railroad mileage in Michigan in 1860 was 799.3. The reasons for this slowness to build railroads in Michigan are rather obvious: the Great Lakes to the east and west blocked the building of through lines, while the sparseness of population in the North made it unprofitable to build railroads from south to north.

The principal Michigan railroad lines in 1860 followed the routes set forth in the internal-improvements program of 1837, with some important variations. In addition there were three shorter lines connecting cities and towns on the southern and central railroads, another short line connecting Flint and Saginaw, and two short lines in the Upper Peninsula built by mining companies.

The central railroad was sold by the state in 1846 for $2,000,000

[37] *Ibid.*, p. 67.
[38] *Ibid.*, p. 69.

after it had been extended as far west from Detroit as Kalamazoo, a distance of 143 miles. Henceforth it was known as the Michigan Central Railroad. The purchase of the line by private investors was the work of a young man of 26, a native of Massachusetts: John W. Brooks. Failing to obtain the capital he sought in Boston, he turned to New York bankers who held some of the Michigan $5,000,000 bond issue. By facilitating the purchase of the railroad they hoped to provide Michigan with funds to pay off at least some of the bonds. After receiving favorable reactions from the New York bankers, Brooks returned to Detroit where he sought the aid of another native of New England, James F. Joy, a lawyer. The two men bargained with the legislators and finally reached an agreement. The purchase was consummated under an agreement that required the new owners to replace the wooden strap-rails with 60-pound iron T rails and to extend the tracks from Kalamazoo to Lake Michigan within three years. It is noteworthy that the agreement did not stipulate St. Joseph as the western terminus, which was the original state plan. Brooks was given six months to raise the necessary capital. He now returned to Boston, where he received a more friendly hearing because of the promise of New York capital. His biggest catch was John Murray Forbes, a friend of Ralph Waldo Emerson and a prominent and respected New England businessman. Other Bostonians who invested in the Michigan Central were John E. Thayer, Thomas H. Perkins, Josiah Quincy, and Erastus Corning. The largest part of the capital was subscribed in Boston, Forbes was elected president, and for many years the company's chief office was in Boston.[39]

Earnings of the railroad for the first year under private ownership were $200,000, while expenses totaled only about half that amount. In 1848 receipts were almost double those of the preceding year, with about 60% of the revenue derived from freight. A total of 80,000 passengers were carried in 1848. The profitable operation of the line encouraged the investors to extend the tracks rapidly and to make the improvements specified in the charter, which included a relocation of the tracks entering Detroit and the erection of a new depot there. In extending the line west from Kalamazoo the company veered the route to the south from that marked out by the state, aiming at New Buffalo rather than St. Joseph as its objective. The tracks reached Niles in 1848 and New Buffalo on April 23, 1849. From New Buffalo the company operated a line of steamers to Chicago, so that

[39] A. F. Harlow, *The Road of the Century,* pp. 218-220.

passengers could travel from Detroit to Chicago in between 33 and 36 hours. A traveler over the railroad in 1851 wrote that trains maintained a uniform speed of 18 miles an hour, and were punctual and safe. He described the railroad's route through primeval forests, occasional cleared fields, and "neat and thriving villages half smothered in luxuriant foliage." Wild turkeys, quail, wild pigeons and other game could be seen from the car windows. Freight cars were 15 feet long, had no brakes, and freight trains had no conductors. Fuel for the locomotives was wood, piled along the right of way by farmers for sale to the railroad. Locomotives were identified by such names as Ranger, Rover, White Cloud, Trade Wind, Foxhound, Corsair, and Arab rather than by number.[40]

The coming of the railroad was generally hailed with enthusiasm by the people of the towns and villages along its route. But shortly after the Michigan Central passed into private ownership, a strong tide of opposition manifested itself in what has been called "The Great Railroad Conspiracy." The trouble arose because the trains killed livestock that strayed onto the tracks. When the old strap rails were replaced by iron T rails, the trains could run faster and the carnage of livestock increased. At first the Michigan Central paid the farmer the full value of his livestock killed by the trains, as the state had done, but in 1849 the management announced that henceforth only one-half the value would be paid. A storm of protest arose. East of Jackson, around Grass Lake, lawlessness broke out. Woodpiles were burned, freight cars were derailed, heavy obstructions were placed on the tracks, and engineers and firemen were targets of guns in the hands of enraged farmers. In the autumn of 1850 the interference became so serious that detectives were hired by the railroad to discover the ringleaders and bring them to justice. The lawless acts reached a climax when, on the night of November 18, 1850, the freight house of the railroad in Detroit was burned. The following April, through revelations by the detectives, two ringleaders and 36 others were arrested at Michigan Centre, near Jackson. A trial lasting until September followed these arrests. It was a remarkable trial, with the best legal talent available engaged by the opposing sides. For the defense no less a personage than Senator William H. Seward of New York was retained. Two of the chief defendants died before the trial was over. Twelve were convicted and sentenced to prison terms. This stopped the

[40] *Ibid.,* pp. 220-223; A. S. Hill, "The Romance of a Railway," *Michigan History,* XXIII (1939), 53-76.

violence along the line, but for many years there was great bitterness against the railroad.[41]

The officers of the Michigan Central were much more concerned in the early 'fifties with the problems of eastern connections and the difficulties of extending their line into Chicago than in their troubles with Michigan farmers. As soon as Lake Erie froze over so ships could not shuttle between Detroit and Buffalo, freight traffic dropped off sharply. The Michigan Central's owners were eager to see the Great Western Railway completed across Canada to Windsor. Their corporate charter, however, prevented the company from investing in a foreign corporation. To get the railroad built, John W. Brooks, aided by a number of prominent Detroiters, succeeded in persuading New York capitalists to buy stock in the Great Western, and it was completed to Windsor in 1854. The following year the great suspension bridge over the Niagara River was completed, and railroad cars could be run from Albany to Windsor. Passengers and freight were ferried across the Detroit River to the Michigan Central line. It was not until 1867, however, that the first ferry carried railroad cars across the river, and not until 1910 that the tunnel under the river was completed.

To reach Chicago proved an expensive feat for the Michigan Central. It had to contend with the rivalry of the Michigan Southern for a route around the end of Lake Michigan and into Chicago, and also with a host of petty, self-seeking politicians in both Indiana and Illinois. Entrance to Chicago was finally attained by buying the charter of a nonexistent, Indiana-chartered railroad for $500,000 and reaching an agreement with the Illinois Central for joint use of tracks into the city. It was on May 20, 1852 that the first Michigan Central train chugged into a temporary depot in Chicago. The Southern had run its first trains into the future metropolis of the West three months before. The effect on Chicago of the coming of these two railroads from the East was to greatly increase both property values and population. By 1855 the completed 269-mile Michigan Central line was doing a $2,500,000 business. The Michigan Central became widely known for its profitable and efficient operation. By the latter 'fifties it was running some of the fastest trains in America. In 1855 it began stringing telegraph lines to be used in the operation of its trains, far in advance of the railroads in the East.

[41] C. Hirschfield, *The Great Railroad Conspiracy,* and an article by the same author with the same title in *Michigan History,* XXXVI (1952), 97-219.

The state's southern railroad, which had reached as far west as Hillsdale, was sold for $500,000 in 1846. A Detroit attorney, Elisha Litchfield, was the chief organizer of the Michigan Southern Railroad Company, which negotiated the purchase. The company was required by its charter to extend the line to Coldwater along the route mapped out by the state, but west of Coldwater it might veer from that route provided it did not build into Indiana before reaching the St. Joseph River. Its eastern terminus was Monroe, and the company planned at first to make Monroe an important port by acquiring ships to ply between that port and Buffalo. But in 1849 the Michigan Southern secured a perpetual lease of the famous Erie and Kalamazoo line, connecting Adrian, on the Michigan Southern, with Toledo. Henceforth the Southern began running its trains from Adrian into Toledo over the Erie and Kalamazoo tracks and using that city rather than Monroe as the port at which connections were made with ships to Buffalo. Monroe, much to the chagrin of its citizens, was thus bypassed. Extension of the Southern westward proceeded slowly at first, but reached White Pigeon by 1851. The officers of the Michigan Southern, meanwhile, had acquired stock in other railroads in northern Indiana and Illinois to give their line a route into Chicago. To escape from the necessity of building to the St. Joseph River before veering southward, a four-mile line was built southward from White Pigeon across the Indiana line by a South Bend capitalist who then leased it to the Michigan Southern, and in February, 1852 the first trains were run into Chicago, three months before those of the Michigan Central. The railroad now took the name of Michigan Southern and Northern Indiana.

In the 1850s the Michigan Southern and Northern Indiana built three lines northward from its main line. One of these connected Adrian with Jackson; the second was constructed between Jonesville and Marshall; a third connection linked Toledo with Detroit. Originally built by another company, the Detroit-Toledo line was leased by the Michigan Southern and Northern Indiana in 1856. The Michigan Southern, like the Michigan Central, carried a heavy traffic. A Chicago newspaper reported on June 29, 1854 that 2,000 passengers had arrived on four trains of the Michigan Southern in a single day. In addition to five steamers on Lake Erie, the Southern operated ships from Chicago to Milwaukee and Sheboygan, Wisconsin. It invested heavily in other railroads. In spite of excellent business, the road was in deep financial trouble just prior to the Civil War, due to over-expansion and possibly also fraud, and the value of its stock dropped precipitously.[42]

The state of Michigan never laid rails on its projected northern line. But by 1858 a railroad had been built with private capital to Grand Haven. Its eastern terminus, however, was not on the St. Clair River as the state had planned, but at Detroit. The Detroit and Pontiac Railroad, which had been chartered in 1834, survived the state internal-improvements program, was opened from Detroit to Royal Oak, a distance of thirteen miles, in 1838, but did not reach Pontiac—thirteen miles further—until 1844. The Oakland and Ottawa Railroad Company was chartered in 1848 to build westward from Pontiac to Grand Haven, and in 1855 the two roads were consolidated as the Detroit and Milwaukee Railroad. The Great Western Railway of Canada supplied funds to complete the building of the line. In later years the Great Western became part of the Grand Trunk system, which also ultimately included the Detroit and Milwaukee. The Detroit and Milwaukee was the first railroad to reach Grand Rapids. A line of steamers connected the railroad's western terminus at Grand Haven with Milwaukee. The line was sometimes called the "Emigrant route" because so many foreigners, especially German, used this railroad to reach Wisconsin.[43]

In towns and cities not located on any of the three main lines across Lower Michigan there was intense enthusiasm for railroads in the 1850s. Rallies were held and companies were formed, many of which expired without laying a mile of track. In Paw Paw, for example, a company was formed to build a railroad to connect with the Michigan Central, five miles distant. It was pointed out that whereas the people of Niles, which was on the Michigan Central, could buy flour for $5.50 a barrel, in Paw Paw the charge was $7.00.[44] In Schoolcraft about the same time "railroad fever" was rampant; a public meeting was held and subscriptions were started to form a company, without much success.[45] In spite of opposition by the Michigan Central, which had certain exclusive privileges under its charter, the legislature in 1855 passed a general incorporation law for railroad companies. Under its terms, any group of investors could secure a charter to build and operate a railroad by meeting certain minimum conditions. All new rail-

[42] A. Harlow, *The Road of the Century,* pp. 245-280.

[43] J. T. Percival, "Railroads in Ottawa County," *Mich. Pioneer and Historical Colls.,* IX (1886), 271-277.

[44] T. Brock, "Paw Paw and the Railroads," *Michigan History,* XXXIX (1955), 130-131.

[45] S. B. Smith, "Notes on the Village of Schoolcraft in 1850," *Michigan History,* XL (1956), 146-147.

roads organized under the act were required to install such safety devices as bells on locomotives, a steam whistle to sound before all grade crossings, "stop, look, and listen" signs at the crossings, and fences along the right of way, although no provisions were made to enforce these regulations. Maximum fares for passengers were set at three cents per mile, somewhat above the going rate.[46]

In spite of all the fervor for railroads, investors were hesitant to invest large sums in what still was regarded as a risky venture. The established railroads were making excellent profits, but many doubted that shorter lines would be paying propositions. Schemes to build rail lines into the north country, where population was relatively sparse, were hindered for want of capital. But an inducement to build such lines was provided in 1856 by an act of Congress that offered large grants of public land to the state of Michigan to award railroad companies that would undertake to construct lines into the northern part of the Lower Peninsula and into the Upper Peninsula. Within a year eight new railroad companies had been formed, six of which received land grants, while three existing companies also received grants. Partly because of the economic depression of 1857, however, progress in actual construction was slow. By 1860 only a portion of a line between Saginaw and Flint and another between Owosso and Lansing had been built. There were only a few miles of track laid in the Upper Peninsula.[47]

One of the factors that retarded railroad building in Michigan was the plank-road craze. The abundant timber still standing in most parts of Michigan readily provided the raw material for the building of roads out of sawed plank. Companies were formed to purchase the planks and have a road built, receiving compensation in the form of tolls charged those who used it. To do this it was necessary to obtain, in each case, a charter from the legislature until 1848 when, upon the recommendation of Governor Epaphroditus Ransom, a general plank-road law was passed. It set up the regulations for the formation of plank-road companies, requiring them to build "good, smooth, permanent roads," a minimum of sixteen feet wide, eight feet of which was to be built of three-inch planks. In 1855 the law was amended to permit the use of gravel instead of planks. Two cents per mile was charged for two-horse vehicles and one cent per mile for those drawn by a single horse. Scores of charters had been granted prior to the passage of this law, and more than 200 companies were organized under its

[46] C. Hirschfield, *loc. cit.,* pp. 216-217.
[47] E. A. Calkins, "Railroads of Michigan since 1850," *Michigan History,* XIII (1929), 5-25.

provisions, although only about one-quarter of them actually built roads. Toll houses were erected at intervals along these highways, much in the manner of twentieth-century toll roads.

The plank roads served as feeders for existing rail lines. For example, the state capital, Lansing, which was without railroad service until after 1860, was connected with the railroad at Howell by means of a plank road. An important plank road connected Grand Rapids and Kalamazoo. Both passengers and freight passed over this highway. It was particularly important to Grand Rapids, which did not get a railroad until 1858—twelve years after the Michigan Central reached Kalamazoo. Large amounts of gypsum from the Grand Rapids mines were carried over the plank road for shipment at Kalamazoo. Referring to a stage trip over this road, Mark Twain wrote that it would have been enjoyable had not "some unconscionable scoundrel now and then dropped a plank across the road." This points to the fact that the plank roads when first built were fairly smooth, but soon deteriorated and became rough. Where a rail line was built along their route they quickly disappeared. Some of them, however, continued to operate until the close of the century.

Stagecoach lines already were established over the main roads by the time Michigan became a state. They continued to operate until they were superseded by the railroads. Famous foreign visitors have left records of their experiences riding Michigan stagecoaches. Among these are the French writer on American democracy, Alexis de Tocqueville, and the English authoress Harriet Martineau.[48] The noted "Concord coach" was in general use in Michigan. Along the roads traversed by the stagecoaches were the taverns of pioneer days. Accommodations were crude and often inadequate, but food was abundant and friendliness the rule. Taverns were social centers and places where the latest news was discussed. In the larger towns the taverns were coming to be called "hotels" by 1860.

Improved transportation thus was a crucial factor in bringing Michigan out of the wilderness and connecting it with the outside world by 1860. Steamships, sailing vessels, river boats, railroads, and plank roads all were instrumental in breaking down the isolation of Michigan and facilitating the movement of people and products between the East and the West, as well as within the new state.

---

[48] A. de Tocqueville, *Oeuvres et correspondence inédite,* I, 203ff.; H. Martineau, *Society in America,* I, 245ff.

The communications revolution

The invention of the electric telegraph and the beginnings of telegraphic communication made one of the developments of this period, the revolutionary effect of which is often overlooked. It was on May 24, 1844 that Samuel F. B. Morse flashed across telegraph wires strung between Baltimore and Washington his famous message, "What hath God wrought!" Even after this demonstration the public remained skeptical. To overcome this attitude demonstrations were arranged in various parts of the country. One such was held at Detroit in September, 1845 in a church. At one end of the auditorium an operator clicked out a message; at the other end a recording instrument reproduced the dots and dashes on a roll of paper. Even this demonstration left many unbelieving; they regarded it as a magic show and thought someone had something up his sleeve. But businessmen soon took the electric telegraph seriously and began to invest in the stringing of wires.

The first telegraph wires in Michigan were strung between Detroit and Ypsilanti along the Michigan Central tracks, and the first messages were exchanged between the operators of these two stations on November 30, 1847. The line was built by the Lake Erie and Michigan Telegraph Company, one of two rival companies operating under patents obtained by Samuel F. B. Morse. Building westward continued at a rapid pace, and on April 8, 1848 the first telegraphic greetings were sent from Detroit to Chicago. Meanwhile Detroit had been connected with eastern lines, and on the same day that connections were completed with Chicago a message passed between Detroit and New York. At first the service was unreliable and subject to frequent interruptions. Improvement was slow because of the fierce competition of rival lines. But in 1856 fourteen competing companies were purchased by a group of Rochester capitalists to form the Western Union Telegraph Company. Telegraph wires reached most of the larger Michigan cities by 1860, although it was not until after the Civil War that the telegraph reached the Upper Peninsula.

To a generation that takes instantaneous, worldwide communications for granted it is difficult to comprehend the wonder the electric telegraph created when it was first developed. Michiganians were able to read in their newspapers of events that had happened in the East the day before, something that must have seemed even more miraculous to the people of that time than did the telephone and the radio to those of a later age.[49] Business

[49] R. L. Thompson, *Wiring a Continent; the History of the Telegraph Industry in the United States, 1832-1866.*

firms could exchange messages over thousands of miles within a few minutes. Wherever there was a telegraph station the ticking of a little instrument was a symbol of connection with the outside world.

Great improvements in the postal service also came about during the period from 1835 to 1860. Michigan had 173 post offices in 1835, and by 1837, the mails were being carried over 3,494 miles of post roads in the new state. Stagecoaches, riders, steamships, and railroads all carried the mails. A drastic reduction of postal rates was made in 1845. In 1847 further reductions were ordered, provided the postage was prepaid. Up to this time the postage was paid by the recipient rather than by the sender. Adhesive stamps were introduced the same year. By 1851 letter postage had been reduced to three cents provided the distance carried did not exceed 3,000 miles.

The post office was one of the chief centers of community life. In smaller settlements it was generally situated in a store, and here citizens gathered to talk and gossip while waiting for the arrival and distribution of the mail. The postmaster, who got his job by political appointment of the party in power in Washington, was often a leading citizen—a doctor, lawyer, newspaper publisher, or local merchant. Mail was delivered to homes and business places only in the largest cities, and there was no rural delivery for many years. But, nevertheless, the postal service was of major importance in linking the state together and providing a means of communication with associates or kinfolk far away.[50]

The improvement of postal service and the coming of the telegraph encouraged the establishment of newspapers, although the impetus provided by partisan rivalry was probably an even more potent factor. Most newspapers depended heavily on party subsidies in one form or another. Every leading city had two newspapers, one representing the Democratic persuasion, the other the Whig (after 1854, the Republican) point of view. Editorial columns were filled with vitriolic prose condemning in unmeasured language the members and policies of the opposing party while praising those of the party the newspaper supported.

In Detroit the *Free Press* went all out for the Democratic cause. Its editor after 1853, Wilbur F. Storey, was an intense admirer of Lewis Cass, favored the Kansas-Nebraska law, hated all abolitionists, and denounced the organizers of the Republican party as a "body of unmitigated abolitionists and disunionists."

[50] R. R. Tingley, "Postal Service in Michigan Territory," *Michigan History*, XXXV (1951), 447-460; A. F. Harlow, *Old Post Bags*.

But he was an able newspaper man. He established at the *Free Press* the first real city department, gathered about him a brilliant staff, and published the first Sunday edition. It has been said he had a wider fame and fewer friends than any newspaper man in Michigan before or since.[51] Diametrically opposed to Storey was Joseph Warren of the *Tribune*. Described by his associates as a sedate, gentle, kind-hearted man, he could write with a pen dipped in gall. The *Tribune* was combined with the *Advertiser* in 1858 and became Detroit's leading exponent of the Republican party. James E. Scripps came to Detroit from Chicago in 1859 as business manager of the *Advertiser and Tribune*. In later years he was to become one of the nation's leading newspaper men.

Outside Detroit the rivalry of Democrats with Whigs—later Republicans—was also reflected in rival newspapers. Ann Arbor had its *State Journal* and *True Democrat*, Grand Rapids its *Enquirer* and *Eagle;* Kalamazoo its *Gazette* and *Telegraph;* Hillsdale its *Gazette* and *Whig Standard;* Marshall its *Democratic Expounder* and *Marshall Statesman*. During the 1840s newspapers were established in towns that had not had them previously. The *Northern Advocate* appeared in Flint in 1840; Battle Creek's first newspaper, the *Michigan Tribune,* was launched in 1846; the Coldwater *Sentinel* dates from 1841; the *Western Chronicle* was the ambitious name of a newspaper published in the St. Joseph-county-seat town of Centreville, beginning in 1849. Howell's first newspaper, the Livingston *Courier,* started publication in 1843, the Paw Paw *Free Press* in 1845, the Ypsilanti *Sentinel* in 1843, and the *Eaton Democrat* in 1847. Shortly after the establishment of the state capital at Lansing, a newspaper was started there under the name *Michigan State Journal* (1848).[52]

Many newspapers were shortlived: the *St. Clair Whig* lasted only a single year; the *Western Banner* in Kalamazoo expired within a few months. Some newspapers were published only during a political campaign. The ups and downs of political fortunes and uncertain financial backing caused many casualties in the newspaper field. The average Michigan newspaper of the 1840s and 1850s contained little local news. Its columns were devoted mainly to reprints from eastern and foreign newspapers, poetry, fiction, and national news. Editorials on political subjects were

[51] W. Stocking, "Prominent Newspaper Men in Michigan," *Mich. Pioneer and Historical Colls.,* XXXIX (1915), 153-168; J. E. Walsh, "Radically and Thoroughly Democratic: Wilbur F. Storey and the *Detroit Free Press,* 1853-1861," *Michigan History,* XLVII (1963), 193-226.

[52] D. C. McMurtrie, *Early Printing in Michigan.*

long and acrimonious. The advertisements actually provide a better picture of the community than the news columns. In the larger newspapers telegraphic dispatches were printed, but many of the small papers did not have access to such material. All but a few newspapers were published weekly. Detroit, however, had three dailies by 1850. The Grand Rapids *Eagle* became that city's first daily in 1857. By 1860 a total of eight Michigan newspapers were publishing daily editions; there were three bi-weeklies, one tri-weekly, and 96 weekly newspapers, as well as four religious periodicals and three literary magazines.

The first newspaper in the Upper Peninsula was published in the boom town of Copper Harbor. It was called the *Lake Superior News and Miners' Journal*, and publication started July 11, 1846. In 1847, however, it was moved to Sault Ste. Marie by its owner, John N. Ingersoll. It folded in 1849 or 1850 and was succeeded by the *Lake Superior Journal*, first published at Sault Ste. Marie and generally regarded as the progenitor of the present Marquette *Mining Journal*. "King Strang" published a newspaper on Beaver Island starting in 1850, called the *Northern Islander*.

In addition to newspapers, publications appeared devoted to religion, reform, or other special purposes. At different times during the 'forties and 'fifties, publications advocating the cause of temperance appeared at Adrian, Jackson, Marshall, and Mount Clemens. Several others were founded to cater to readers of literary taste: the Detroit *Evening Spectator and Literary Gazette*, which appeared during 1836 and 1837, and the *Michigan Literary Gem and Parlor Companion*, printed at Kalamazoo about 1841, are examples. There were publications for farmers: *Farmers' Advocate*, published at Kalamazoo in 1841, and *Michigan Farmer and Western Horticulturalist*, issued at Jackson between 1843 and 1847. The *Western Farmer* (which later became the *Michigan Farmer*) began publication at Detroit on January 20, 1841.[53] The first religious periodical in Michigan was the *Michigan Christian Herald*, a Baptist periodical that was started at Detroit in 1842 as a monthly, had a thousand subscribers within a year, and became a weekly in 1845.

Although Michigan had come a long way out of the wilderness by 1860, vast areas of the state were still covered by unbroken forests and isolated hamlets, and a large proportion of the farm homes were often out of touch with the outside world for months at a time—especially during the winter. Rail lines, plank roads, and telegraph wire were remote from many Michigan homes. In spite of improved transportation, probably the great

[53] On the latter, see F. C. Bald, *op. cit.*, pp. 250-251.

majority of Michiganians had horizons that were confined to their own neighborhoods. The world beyond still seemed strange and remote. But it was coming closer.

THE NEW CAPITAL

The constitution of 1835 established the seat of the state government at Detroit but stipulated that in 1847 the legislature was to permanently locate it. In the legislative session of 1847 the question of where the capital should be situated caused a furious controversy. Among the cities that sought to obtain the coveted prize were Detroit, Jackson, Ann Arbor, and Marshall. But there were men in the legislature who believed in the future of the north country and favored a more central location. Furthermore, to choose any one of the principal bidders would antagonize the others. At this juncture, James Seymour, who owned a considerable amount of land in Ingham County, offered to donate 20 acres and to erect buildings as commodious as those used in Detroit if the capital were located there. The site of Lansing was then a wilderness, with no railroads within miles, but it did have the advantage of a central location in the Lower Peninsula. Although some regarded the proposal as a joke, it so appealed to the legislators that they passed a bill, which was signed by the governor on March 16, 1847, accepting the offer. The town to be laid out was to be called "Michigan," although the House had at first approved the name "Aloda." Later, the name Lansing was chosen. On Christmas Day, 1847, a temporary building was completed and the capital was then moved to the new town on the Grand River that was to be its permanent abode.[54]

[54]W. W. Upton, "Locating the capital of the State of Michigan," in *Michigan History*, XXIII (1939), 275-291.

13

MICHIGAN LEADS THE WAY
IN EDUCATION

Throughout the nineteenth century, the Middle West looked to Michigan for leadership in the field of public education. No state so successfully carried out the purpose set forth in the Northwest Ordinance that "schools and the means of education shall forever be encouraged." All the states received munificent grants of land from the federal government for schools, but in Michigan there was better stewardship of these grants than in other states. Elsewhere the funds derived from the lands often were squandered and dissipated, the tracts being sold at low prices to attract settlers. Michigan made mistakes in the management of its land grants for education, but far larger amounts were realized from them here, and they were applied more faithfully to the purpose for which they were intended.

The Catholepistemiad, impractical though it was, had envisioned a comprehensive system of education, reaching from the primary grades to higher education. Michigan's first state constitution, adopted in 1835, also indicated the purpose of establishing a complete system of education, and laws were enacted within two years to implement this purpose. Michigan was the first state to provide for the office of superintendent of public instruction in its constitution and the first to place the proceeds from the sale of section sixteen in each township in a state school fund. During the first quarter-century of its history as a state

Michigan achieved other "firsts" in education. Michigan State Normal School was the first normal school in the West. Michigan Agricultural College was the first state agricultural college in America. And by 1860 the University of Michigan had become the most successful state university in the nation.

FOUNDATIONS

In the constitutional convention of 1835, a committee headed by General Isaac E. Crary of Marshall was appointed to draft an article on education. The article his committee proposed was adopted with little debate. Crary was born in Connecticut in 1804, and was a graduate of Trinity College. He studied law and was admitted to practice. He also had been associated with a Hartford, Connecticut publisher, George D. Prentice, who is reputed to have been a brilliant journalist and a great wit. Apparently Crary had achieved an excellent reputation in his home state before he came to settle in Marshall and practice law in the early 1830s. His title "general" derived from his appointment to that office in the territorial militia. His election as delegate to the constitutional convention indicates that he was highly esteemed by his fellow townsmen. One of these was a home-missionary preacher named John D. Pierce, a fellow New Englander and, like Crary, a man well-educated for his time. The story goes that these two men, sitting under an oak tree, planned Michigan's educational system.[1]

Crary and Pierce were much impressed by a translation of Victor Cousin's report on the Prussian school system. They agreed that Michigan's school system, like Prussia's, should be centralized and should be controlled by a responsible official. Cousin described an educational system that was logical and complete, extending from the lowest grades through a university and co-ordinated by a central body. Curiously enough, this was almost precisely the same sort of system envisioned by Judge Woodward and incorporated into the Catholepistemiad. It was the sort of plan Thomas Jefferson advocated and sought in vain to persuade Virginia to adopt. There is no indication that Crary and Pierce deemed it ironical for a democracy to copy the educational system of an autocracy. It must be remembered that they were concerning themselves at the moment not with what would

[1] Exactly how much each man contributed has been a matter of some controversy. See J. C. Patterson, "Marshall Men and Marshall Measures in State and National History," *Mich. Pioneer and Historical Colls.,* XXXVIII (1912), 220-248. The oak tree still stands.

be taught in the schools, but how the schools would be organized and administered.

Article X of the Constitution of 1835, as drafted by Crary's committee and adopted by the convention, provided for the superintendent of public instruction to be appointed by the governor. The legislature of New York had created the office of state school superintendent in that state as early as 1812, but had abolished it as a separated office in 1821, assigning the duties to the secretary of state. Several other states had also made the secretary of state responsible for schools. Maryland had provided for a state-school officer in 1826, and then had repealed the act in 1828. No other state in the union in 1837 had provided in its constitution for a superintendent of public instruction.[2]

The article included provisions designed to safeguard the lands the federal government would grant the state for education and to prevent the use of the proceeds to be derived from them for other purposes. Schools were to be conducted for at least three months out of the year. The legislature was given the duty of establishing township libraries as soon as circumstances permitted. The article foresaw the foundation of a state university "with such branches as the public convenience may hereafter demand," but it left to the legislature the decisions related to the establishment and government of such a university.

At the conclusion of the convention, the delegates, at Crary's suggestion, adopted a petition requesting that Congress, instead of turning over section sixteen in each township to the township for schools—as had been done in Ohio, Indiana, and Illinois when these states were admitted to the Union—should grant these sections to the state of Michigan, the proceeds to be placed in a state school fund. The interest from this fund was to be distributed among the schools. When the constitution was ratified Crary was elected as Michigan's first member of the national House of Representatives. He was not permitted to take his seat because the border dispute with Ohio delayed the admission of Michigan to the Union. But he was able to exert his influence to persuade Congress to approve the constitutional convention's petition and to grant the sixteenth sections to the state rather than to the townships in which they were located. The act became effective when Michigan was finally admitted. Partly due to this innovation Michigan realized far more income from the sale of these sections than did any other state in the Old Northwest.[3]

[2] E. P. Cubberly, *The History of Education,* pp. 687-688.
[3] For a brief biographical sketch of Crary, see *Mich. Pioneer and Historical Colls.,* V (1884), 382-384.

The total grant of land to Michigan, consisting of section sixteen in each township, amounted to over a million acres. The disposal of the lands and the management of the school fund (called the Primary School Fund) were first entrusted to the superintendent of public instruction. Then in 1842 the sale of the sections was transferred to a state land office. The legislature at first set a minimum price of $8.00 an acre on the school lands, but the depression of the late 'thirties impelled the lawmakers to reduce that figure repeatedly. Some of the proceeds were poorly invested and losses were suffered on this account. By 1850 it had become the practice to "loan" to the state the proceeds from the school lands, in return for which the legislature each year appropriated to the Primary School Fund an amount equal to what the interest would have been if the fund had been invested. Up to the year 1886, by which time about three-quarters of the sections had been sold, the average price realized was $4.58 an acre. This was less than was originally hoped, but it compared very favorably with the average amounts received for school lands in Michigan's neighboring states. The average price received in Illinois was $3.78, in Indiana $3.69, and in Wisconsin less than $2.00.[4]

It had become the practice of Congress to grant to the states, at the time of their admission to the union, other public lands, usually 72 sections, for the support of a university. As early as 1826 Congress had authorized the selection of these lands in Michigan. Accordingly, some of the finest land in the southern counties was reserved from sale. It became the property of the state at the time Michigan was admitted to the Union in 1837. The story of the disposal of these lands resembles that of the school lands: high hopes, then the coming of hard times, constant pressure on the legislature to reduce the price per acre (originally set at $20), and finally the surrender of the lawmakers to this pressure. And as was also true of the school lands, the University lands, while yielding a smaller return than had been expected, still brought much more per acre than the University lands of other states. The average sum received per acre, when the grant was finally completely sold, was almost $12.00—more than twice that received for any other educational grant in the Old Northwest.

In addition to the income derived from the sales of section sixteen in each township and the university lands, Michigan's

[4] G. W. Knight, *History and Management of Land Grants for Education in the Northwest Territory* (*Papers* of the American Historical Association, I, No. 3).

educational system benefitted from other federal land grants. At the time Michigan entered the Union, Congress granted to the state, as was customary, all salt springs and lands adjacent thereto in the state, and no less than 72 sections. There was a proviso that these lands could be leased but not sold; however, their sale was permitted under an act passed in 1847. The legislature, during the years that followed, appropriated the proceeds from 25 of these sections as an endowment for Michigan State Normal School, 25 sections to pay for the erection of the Michigan Asylum at Kalamazoo, and 22 sections to purchase a site and erect buildings for the State Agricultural College. In 1850 a large grant of swamp lands was made to Michigan and other states. In the case of Michigan it has been asserted that these were identified in the spring of the year when many lands were overflowed; at any rate, much excellent land was thus obtained. In 1858 the legislature designated fifty percent of the proceeds from these lands for the Primary School Fund. The remainder was used largely for grants to encourage the building of railroads, but 6,921 acres were given to the Agricultural College. And in 1862 Michigan received an additional 240,000 acres under the terms of the Morrill Act, passed by Congress to encourage education in agriculture and the mechanical arts. The proceeds from the sale of these lands, of course, went to the Agricultural College.

The significance of these federal land grants for education can hardly be overestimated. The development of a public school system would have been greatly retarded without them. Although the amount received each year was pitifully small, it was enough to encourage many districts to establish schools that might otherwise have neglected them for a long time. And without the federal land grants it is almost certain that neither the University of Michigan, Michigan State Normal School, nor Michigan Agriculture College would have been established until much later, if at all. Each was supported in the main by the income from the land grants; it was not until after the Civil War that the University of Michigan received any regular support from the state tax revenues.

JOHN D. PIERCE AND THE MICHIGAN SYSTEM OF EDUCATION

If Isaac E. Crary may be credited with being primarily responsible for laying the foundations of the Michigan system of education, John D. Pierce must receive equal credit for having been the organizer of that system. Crary was absent in Washington as a member of Congress during much of the crucial six-year period following 1835. It was upon the suggestion of Crary, that Governor Mason appointed Pierce in 1836 as first superintendent of public instruction. Pierce is a neglected figure in histories of education in the United States. Historians have stressed the work of Horace Mann as secretary of the State Board of Education in Massachusetts and that of Henry Barnard, who held a similar post in Connecticut. Because Massachusetts and Connecticut were older states, Mann and Barnard undoubtedly had more influence nationally than Pierce did. But Pierce was, nevertheless, the real pioneer in setting up a state system of education. Not only was he the first state-school official appointed on the basis of a constitutional provision, but he also formulated his plan for Michigan's educational system two years before Mann issued his famous first annual report. Pierce started publication of his *Journal of Education* almost a year before Mann published the first issue of his *Common School Journal*.[5]

Born in New Hampshire in 1797, Pierce was taken at the age of two years, following the death of his father, to work on a Massachusetts farm. He got little formal schooling, but somehow acquired a passion for books. A meager inheritance from his grandfather gave him the opportunity to enter Brown University in 1818. Pierce financed much of his education by school teaching and was graduated from Brown in 1822. He then studied theology at Princeton and was licensed to preach as a Congregational minister. After serving for a time as pastor of a church at Sangerfield, New York, he was appointed as a missionary by the American Home Missionary Society. This Society sent many men into the West to bring religion and education to the people on the frontier, and provided financial support for them through contributions of eastern churches. Pierce came to Michigan in 1831 and settled at Marshall, which then contained only two shanties and a partly finished log house. Using this as the center of his activities, he rode horseback to minister to many scattered pioneer communities. When Marshall was visited by the terrible cholera epidemic in 1832, his wife was one of the victims. But Pierce continued his work and saw Marshall become a boom town on the Territorial Road in the period of the great land rush. It was his association with Isaac E. Crary that stimulated his interest in education and led to his appointment as Michigan's first superintendent of public instruction.

[5] R. C. Ford, "The Life and Work of John D. Pierce," *Mich. Pioneer and Historical Colls.*, XXXV (1907), 295-308. See also C. O. Hoyt and R. C. Ford, *John D. Pierce*. E. P. Cubberly, *op. cit.*, devotes several pages to Mann and Barnard but does not mention Pierce.

The constitutional article provided only the framework of a system of education, and it became the responsibility of Pierce to propose to the legislature the steps that should be taken to carry out the provisions of the constitution with respect to education. Before drawing up his plan Pierce made a trip to the East, where he conferred with leaders in the field of education and attended a national education meeting in Worcester, Massachusetts. He also visited Ohio, attending an annual meeting of the College of Professional Teachers, an organization founded in 1831 by teachers of the West. Pierce also carried on an extensive correspondence with educational leaders throughout the nation. He was determined to equip himself with a knowledge of the best educational practices of the day and to become acquainted with the experience of other states before drawing up his plans for Michigan. When the legislature convened in January, 1837, Pierce was ready with his proposals.[6]

On March 18 and 20, 1837 Governor Mason signed three bills that had been passed by the legislature to translate into law the recommendations made by Pierce. These acts achieved many but not all the goals Pierce set. For example, he urged a system of tax-supported public schools in which no primary-school pupil would be required to pay tuition. This was not provided in the acts of 1837, and not until 1869 did the legislature require all public primary schools to be free, although some were free prior to that date. Pierce also proposed that each teacher be required to have had a "regular course of training" and that schools be required to pay teachers a minimum wage in order to be eligible to receive aid from the Primary School Fund. He also suggested the desirability of compulsory education. In this, too, Pierce was far ahead of his time, and the laws enacted by the legislature did not make such provisions.[7]

One of the three bills signed by Governor Mason dealt with the organization of primary schools. It provided for the establishment of school districts in each township. Each district was to have a moderator, a director, and an assessor, and there were to be three school inspectors in each township. The proceeds from the Primary School Fund were to be apportioned among the schools in proportion to the number of pupils between the ages of five and 17 in each. School districts were authorized to lay taxes for the support of schools. Each district that voted a tax

[6] J. D. Pierce, "Origin and Progress of the Michigan School System," *Mich. Pioneer and Historical Colls.*, I (1876), 37-45.

[7] F. W. Shearman, *System of Public Instruction and Primary School Law of Michigan*, pp. 23-37.

for a "suitable library case" and spent $10 a year for the purchase of books was to receive a share in the proceeds from "fines, breaches of the penal laws, and exemption from military duty." Regular reports from each district to the superintendent of public instruction were required. The law did not make it mandatory for schools to be established; the initiative was left to the people of the several townships. In this respect Pierce's plan departed from the plan for the Catholepistemiad, which had placed the entire responsibility for the establishment of schools on a central body. This had proved utterly impractical, as has been noted earlier. The superintendent of public instruction was given the responsibility for taking charge of all school and university lands that had been granted to the state, disposing of these lands according to law, and investing the monies arising from their sale. He was to apportion the proceeds from these funds and to submit an annual report.[8]

The second measure enacted to carry Pierce's plan into execution dealt with the University of Michigan. Its purpose was "to provide the inhabitants of the State with the means of acquiring a thorough knowledge of the various branches of literature, science and the arts." Its government was to be under a Board of Regents consisting of twelve members to be appointed by the governor, with the lieutenant governor, supreme court judges, and the state chancellor as *ex-officio* members. The University was to include three departments: literature, science and the arts; law; and medicine. There was to be an admission fee of $10.00, but tuition was to be free to all residents of the state. The third bill signed by Governor Mason provided for the location of the University of Michigan in Ann Arbor. The incentive for this was a gift of forty acres of land on which the University buildings were to be erected by the Ann Arbor Land Company.

The most unique feature of the law establishing the state university was its provision for branches. The establishment of "such branches as the public convenience may hereafter demand" had been specified in the Constitution of 1835. The idea of branches was strongly advocated by Crary, and Pierce fully concurred. The purposes of the branches appear to have been fourfold. In the first place, each branch was to have a "female department." At that time coeducation beyond the elementary school was generally frowned on, yet it was recognized that a certain amount of advanced schooling for young women was desirable. In actual practice in the branches, young men and women attended the same classes even though the fiction of a separate "female department"

[8] F. W. Shearman, *op. cit.,* pp. 32-33.

was maintained. Secondly, each branch under the original law was to have an agriculture department, though this was later changed to provide for such a department in at least one branch. The great movement for schools to teach agriculture and mechanical arts was to come about twenty years later. That Pierce should have conceived of special education in agriculture at this early date is further evidence of his farsightedness. Actually, however, so far as is known no agriculture department was started in any of the branches. Thirdly, each branch was to serve as a teacher-training school. Pierce placed heavy emphasis on the need for the education of teachers. Finally, the branches were designed to prepare men to enter the University. There were very few preparatory schools in the state and very few young men who were qualified for studies of a college grade. Hence the branches were opened before the University proper in order to provide a student body for the latter. The plan appears to have been for students to undertake some studies at the collegiate level in the branches so that when the University was opened it might have men prepared to enter at the upper class level. The records show that when the University opened in Ann Arbor in 1841 some men already prepared in the branches were admitted as sophomores.

Pierce's plan thus embodied elementary schools to be established in the school districts through local initiative, the state university as the capstone of the system, and the branches as intermediary schools under the control of the University Board of Regents. When Pierce formulated his plan almost all higher education in the nation was provided in church-related colleges. Some state universities had been created, but they had tended to fall prey to sectarian and political rivalries. The predominant institution for secondary education was the private academy, often church-related. In Michigan a few academies had been started during the territorial period, one of these being the Michigan and Huron Institute, chartered in 1833 and opened in Kalamazoo in 1836. Its chief backers were Baptists. The Methodists had also manifested a desire to establish an academy. Pierce himself was closely associated with a project for the establishment of a Presbyterian college in Marshall. But his study of the experience of other states had convinced him by 1837 of the folly of permitting a host of colleges to be chartered, few if any with sufficient resources to provide adequate buildings, equipment, or instructional staff. He concluded that Michigan should concentrate all its resources in the building up of a great state university. He therefore counselled the legislature in his report of

1837 against granting college charters to private institutions. He was willing to permit the denominations to establish academies, but insisted it would be the best policy to confine the power of granting academic degrees to the state university.[9]

THE LITTLE RED SCHOOLHOUSE

The little red schoolhouses are famed in song and story. Just why they were painted red is hard to say; possibly because red paint was cheap and did not show the dirt and wear. Log schoolhouses were the rule at first, but by 1860 they were disappearing from the scene. Most school buildings were inexpensive frame structures, although a few were built of stone and a considerable number of brick.

The severe economic depression that hit Michigan soon after the school system devised by Pierce was established resulted in a retreat from the provisions of the 1837 laws. In 1839 the legislature deprived the school districts of the right to tax, and the expense of maintaining schools over and above the amount received from the Primary School Fund was placed upon the parents of the pupils. The report of the superintendent of public instruction for 1842 shows that only 64% of the districts had maintained a school for three months or more during the year, and that 32% had supported no school at all. The following year the legislature gave the school districts the power to tax at a rate of no more than one mill on each dollar of assessed valuation, beginning in 1845. In the years that followed the maximum was gradually increased, however. By 1850 the sum of $128,189.45 was raised throughout the state by district school taxes, while a total of $32,318.75 was paid by parents in the form of "rate bills," or tuition fees.

By 1860 a total of 4,087 school districts had been formed in Michigan and the number of teachers was 7,921. Even though not all schools were free, 75% of the children between the ages of four and eighteen attended the public schools in 1860. Often, however, the school terms were much shorter than they are today.

In the cities and larger towns additional school districts were formed as the population grew. In 1843 the legislature authorized the creation of "union school districts," which made it possible for municipalities to combine their school districts into a single district. This act also authorized the classification of pupils in

[9] *Ibid.,* p. 32.

such districts "according to their proficiency and advancement in learning." At the time this law was passed Michigan had only two incorporated cities: Detroit and Monroe, and 23 incorporated villages and towns. But the number grew rapidly. Where a union school district was formed, a large "union school" was built, to replace several one-room schools. And in these union schools the students were divided into grades. Detroit organized its schools into a single district in 1842 under a special act passed in that year by the legislature especially for that city.[10] Jonesville was the first town to establish a union school district under the state-wide law of 1843. By 1859 about thirty union school districts had been formed. In some of these an "academic department," or high school, had developed—just how many is not known. Detroit's union school established such an "academic department" in 1848, and this may be said to have been probably the first high school in Michigan. In 1859 the legislature passed an act specifically authorizing any district containing more than 200 children to establish a high school, and vote a tax to support it. The constitutionality of this law was not settled, however, until the supreme court of Michigan handed down its decision in the famous Kalamazoo Case in 1874.[11]

Although the larger towns and cities had graded schools by 1860 the vast majority of schools were still conducted in a single room, where children ranging from five to sixteen or older recited their lessons. Pupils were usually equipped with a spelling book, a reader, an arithmetic text, and a geography book. The prevalent notion was that boys in particular were "a convincing illustration of Calvin's idea of total depravity." Various types of punishment, such as sitting with the girls, standing on one leg, or a thorough lacing with the teacher's beech or birch rod, were in common use to keep the boys in order. Spelling bees, singing schools, and quilting parties were held in the schoolhouse in the evenings, making it a kind of neighborhood center.[12] Teachers in these schools were often poorly prepared, although gifted or "natural" teachers were not uncommon. To many, teaching school was a part-time occupation. Candidates for teaching positions were examined by the inspectors of a school district with such varying standards as may be readily imagined. There was no requirement of advanced training, and most teachers had no more than a common school education. Women came more and more to domi-

---

[10] This law also authorized Detroit to establish free schools.

[11] C. O. Davis, *Michigan's High Schools.*

[12] A. D. VanBuren, "The Log Schoolhouse Era in Michigan . . . ," *Mich. Pioneer and Historical Colls.,* XIV (1889), 283-402.

nate in the teaching profession, the ratio in 1860 being about one man to two women. Men were preferred for the winter term, when the older boys, freed from work on the farm, attended school. School terms were short, often being confined entirely to the winter months.

THE RISE AND FALL OF THE UNIVERSITY BRANCHES

The University Regents held their first meeting in November, 1837. At that time no less than 17 towns applied for the establishment of branches, but only eight were approved. At subsequent meetings the Regents authorized eight more. Out of sixteen authorized, nine were opened, operated for varying lengths of time, and rendered reports. Branches were founded at Pontiac, Monroe, Kalamazoo, Detroit, Niles, White Pigeon, Tecumseh, Ann Arbor, and Romeo. At almost all these places local interest in education had been evidenced by the establishment of an academy, and the branch simply took its place. In Kalamazoo a working arrangement was made with the Trustees of the Kalamazoo Literary Institute (originally called the Michigan and Huron Institute) under which the Institute and the Branch were merged. The course of study in the branches was prescribed by the Regents. Appropriations were made for their support from University funds. The total attendance in all the branches never exceeded 315 for any one year. This number, the enrollment total for 1842-43, included 243 men and 72 women. Because of decreasing revenues the Regents found they could not support the branches and at the same time maintain the University proper. Annual appropriations for the branches were reduced and in 1846 all financial support was withdrawn. Several branches continued to operate thereafter at the expense of the local communities and with tuition fees collected from those in attendance. Most of the branches became private academies with charters from the legislature.

The abandonment of state support for the branches brought considerable protest. In some quarters they were regarded as more useful than the University proper. In an act passed in 1851 reorganizing the University of Michigan, it was made the duty of the Regents, as soon as the University fund would permit, to organize a branch in each judicial circuit of the state and to appropriate not more than $1,500 per year for its support. This was never done, however, presumably because the Regents never thought they had sufficient funds. The attempt made through the branch system to centralize the control and management of the secondary education in the hands of the University Regents thus ended in failure.[13]

THE EVOLUTION OF A STATE UNIVERSITY

The University of Michigan was opened in Ann Arbor in 1841. In that year a main building (named for ex-Governor Mason), four faculty houses, and a president's home were completed. The first faculty consisted of two men who had taught in the branches: the Rev. George P. Williams, professor of mathematics, and the Rev. Joseph Whiting, professor of languages. Six students were enrolled the first day. Only the "literary department" was operated until 1850, when a medical department was opened. The law department came into being in 1859.

During its first decade the University was torn by dissension and beset by problems that threatened its existence. The Regents justified their decision to open the University proper at the cost of continuing to adequately support the branches by calling into question whether it was legal to use funds derived from the federal land grant to support the branches. Nevertheless, their decision was anything but popular. A bitter controversy arose over fraternities in the University. The several religious bodies in the state were insistent on having their "influence" felt. Because the first Board of Regents had not included any clerical members the University was accused by church people of being "ungodly." To meet this criticism the Regents were careful to choose faculty members from different churches. The four faculty houses were designated respectively for the Presbyterian, Methodist, Baptist, and Episcopal professors, and each of the four served successively as president of the University for a one-year period. This deprived the institution of continuing leadership. Enrollment declined in the later 1840s.

When the Constitutional Convention of 1850 met, the University was clearly facing a crisis. To meet the situation the delegates made some drastic changes in the provisions for the University in the new constitution. For one thing, they made the Regents an elective rather than an appointive body. They provided for the selection by the Regents of a president of the University on a permanent basis, and made the president *ex officio* the presiding officer of the Board of Regents. Finally, and most important of all, they made the Regents a body corporate, and gave them complete authority over the University and the expenditure of its

[13] W. F. Dunbar, "The University and Its Branches," *Michigan Alumnus Quarterly Review*, XLVI (July 20, 1940), 303-315.

funds. This was done, in all probability, to get the University "out of politics," and to prevent legislative interference in University affairs. During the decade of the 1850s, the University enjoyed a most remarkable growth and by the end of the decade it had become probably the most successful state university in America. Because of this fact it became almost a University tradition that the success of the institution stemmed directly from the provisions in the Constitution of 1850. The extent to which such a belief may be justified is open to some question; certainly the success of the University in the 1850s was due in no small measure to the quality of the man selected as president, Henry P. Tappan. But the idea that an elected governing board, of which the University president was *ex officio* chairman, and freedom from legislative control were responsible for the growth and prosperity of the University has exerted a powerful influence through the years to perpetuate the system. In the constitution framed in 1961-62, that system was retained almost intact, and it was applied also to the other two largest state universities.

In 1852 the Regents appointed to the presidency of the University Henry Philip Tappan of New York, a Presbyterian minister, a distinguished scholar, and a man with firm ideas of how a university should be built. He was an ardent admirer of the German universities and favored modeling the University of Michigan after them. This meant heavy emphasis on high scholarship. He did not believe that progress lay along the line advocated by some American educators, that of introducing "practical" subjects into the curriculum. Rather, he stressed scholarship and science. He refused to give primary consideration to church connections in appointing faculty members, but based his choices largely on ability and scholarship. He made important additions to the library and built an observatory. Beginning in 1855, civil engineering was taught. Michigan was the first university after Harvard to inaugurate instruction in technical fields. Enrollment in both the medical department and the department of literature, science, and the arts increased rapidly as the University gained confidence and prestige. The law department was opened in 1859 with 92 students enrolled. Under Tappan's leadership the University of Michigan became the leader among state universities in America.

In spite of this, Tappan aroused a great deal of opposition. Some thought his bearing was haughty and aristocratic; because he used the broad "r" of the easterner in his speech he was accused of putting on airs. There was resentment of his fondness for German universities and agitation for more "practical" studies in the curriculum. The farmers of the state were demanding an agricultural college as a separate farmer's college, while Tappan wanted it to be a part of the University. Temperance advocates criticized him for serving wine at his table in the European manner. Tappan seems to have made every effort to avoid criticism from the various denominations and was so "undenominational" that opposition developed to him in his own local Presbyterian church. He was distrusted by rabid antislavery people because he was not an avowed abolitionist. Another of his policies that antagonized certain powerful ecclesiastical organizations was his opposition to the chartering of denominational colleges. Finally in 1863 he was forced to resign, "stung to death by gnats," as an able successor put it.[14]

NEW DEPARTURES

By 1860 Michigan had established two additional state educational institutions: the State Normal School and the Michigan Agricultural College. As early as 1789 American educators had suggested the need for teacher-training courses in existing colleges or in separate schools. Normal schools had been in existence in Europe for over a century. In 1836 the Ohio legislature sent Calvin E. Stowe to visit European, and especially Prussian, schools. Upon his return Stowe published a report that was widely circulated throughout the nation and that contained a full description of the Prussian teachers' seminaries. Horace Mann, Henry Barnard, and John D. Pierce had all strongly emphasized the importance of thorough preparation for teaching. In 1847 Governor Alpheus Felch in his message to the legislature of Michigan proposed the establishment of a normal school. Bills were introduced for the creation of a separate department in the University for the training of teachers, and also for setting up teachers' institutes, but they failed to pass. Superintendent of Public Instruction Ira Mayhew in his 1848 report opposed a single normal school, favoring instead teachers' institutes and the training of teachers in the Union schools. Nevertheless, a bill for the establishment of a separate normal school was introduced by the House Committee on Education, and it became law on March 28, 1849. This law appropriated ten of the 72 sections of salt-spring lands granted to Michigan by Congress for a building fund for the normal school, and another fifteen sections for endowment, the income from which was to pay the salary of instructors in the school. The management of the institution was given to a State Board of Education and thus was entirely separated from the University. The Board was to

[14] C. T. Perry, *Henry Philip Tappan*.

consist of three members appointed by the governor with the approval of the senate, with the lieutenant governor and the superintendent of public instruction serving as *ex officio* members. The Constitution of 1850, however, eliminated the lieutenant governor as an *ex officio* member and provided that the other three members should be elected rather than appointed.

After receiving bids from several communities for the school, the new Board decided to locate it at Ypsilanti. There is no indication that the Board, in choosing the site for the school, felt any concern about the fact that it was located less than a dozen miles from the University. Normal schools were not regarded as being in the same category as colleges and universities. Students with only a common-school education were ordinarily admitted to such schools in the East. A three-story building was erected at a cost of $15,200, and it was dedicated on October 5, 1852. A teacher's institute lasting four weeks was held the same year, but the opening of the first regular term was delayed until March 29, 1853. When Michigan State Normal School was founded, only three states had normal schools, and Michigan was the first state west of the Alleghenies to establish such a school.[15]

While the state normal school was being established, agitation grew for an agricultural college. At that time there was no such thing anywhere in America as a state agricultural college. Farmer's College at College Hill, Ohio, six miles from Cincinnati, seems to have been the first agricultural school bearing the name of college. It was founded in 1833 but soon passed out of existence. But there was a national movement afoot for colleges for farmers, the most important advocate being Jonathan Turner of Illinois. The State Agricultural Society, organized in 1849, demanded that something be done for the education of farmers. The framers of Michigan's second constitution in 1850 empowered the legislature to found a school of agriculture as a branch of the University. But there is evidence that farm leaders wanted a separate college.

Both the University and the new normal school arranged a series of lectures on agriculture and invited the State Agricultural Society to send a committee to inspect the teaching being done. Both were obviously eager to receive the 22 sections of salt-spring lands that the Constitution of 1850 had set aside for an agricultural school. A committee of the Agricultural Society visited both institutions, and its members reported favorably on what they had heard. But they urged that a farm be provided for experimental and demonstration work, and concluded by recommending a separate school. This became the settled policy of the Society.

[15] D. Putnam, *A History of Michigan State Normal School at Ypsilanti.*

A large majority of the farmers in the state became adherents of the Republican Party, which was organized at Jackson in 1854. When the Republicans elected their candidates for governor and the principal state offices, as well as a majority of the legislature, farm leaders redoubled their efforts to secure the establishment of a separate agricultural college. By an act approved on February 12, 1855, the Michigan Agricultural College was created, and its location was designated as a site within ten miles of Lansing. It received a grant of 22 sections of salt-spring lands and a considerable grant of swamp lands located within the sections adjoining the school. A site was selected and a building was completed in 1857. In May of that year instruction began, with an initial enrollment of 81 students. Students worked about four hours per day on the college farm. The first president was Joseph R. Williams of Constantine, and the supervision of the institution was entrusted to the State Board of Education.

For more than a decade agitation continued to have the new agricultural college attached to the University. Letters pro and con appeared in the Detroit newspapers. Farm leaders, however, persisted in favoring an independent status. This was confirmed in 1861 by a law that removed the college from the control of the State Board of Education and placed it under the supervision of a State Board of Agriculture, consisting of six members appointed by the governor.

As early as 1850 the Michigan legislature had asked Congress for a grant of an additional three townships of land for the University, probably with the intent of using the proceeds for teaching agriculture. But the time was not ripe for Congress to take such a step. The father of the movement for land grants for agricultural education was Jonathan B. Turner. A native of Massachusetts, he had been educated at Yale and had been on the faculty of Jacksonville (Illinois) College from 1833 to 1848. In the latter year he became a farmer and fruitgrower, a speaker at farmers' meetings, and an eloquent advocate of agricultural education. The demand for a congressional land grant grew under his leadership to nationwide proportions. A bill proposed by Congressman Justin S. Morrill of Vermont for a land grant to the states for agricultural colleges was passed by Congress in 1859, but President Buchanan vetoed it. Three years later, during the darkest days of the Civil War, a similar measure was enacted and President Lincoln signed it into law on July 2, 1862. The states were to use the proceeds from the grant to promote education for farmers and mechanics. Under the provisions of the Morrill Act Michigan received 240,000 acres of land, and this placed Michigan Agricultural College on a firm financial footing. Only three states—Pennsylvania, Iowa, and Michigan—had founded agricultural colleges before the Morrill Act became law, and of these Michigan was the first.[16]

THE FIRST CHURCH-RELATED COLLEGES

Kalamazoo College was the first denominational college to be established in Michigan. Chartered in 1833 as the Michigan and Huron Institute, it was opened in 1836. Its name was changed soon afterward to the Kalamazoo Literary Institute, and in 1855 it became Kalamazoo College. Members of the Methodist Episcopal church had secured a charter in 1835 for a school at Spring Arbor, but it failed to materialize. Instead, they decided to accept an offer to come to Albion. Here the Wesleyan Seminary —later to become Albion College—opened its doors in 1842. John J. Shipherd, a Congregationalist and founder of Oberlin College in Ohio, came to Michigan in the lush days of the middle 1830s and planned to establish a school in the backwoods on the Grand River near the present site of Lansing. With the coming of hard times his plan went awry, but he returned in 1843 determined to found a college in Eaton County. The following year he brought a colony of settlers to the spot he selected and a school was soon started. It was called Olivet Institute. At first the legislature appears to have been reluctant to grant a charter, possibly due to the reputation Oberlin had of being a hotbed of abolitionism and other reforms that were not yet so popular as they were to become later. Olivet was incorporated as an academy in 1848.

In 1845 Wesleyan Methodists opened a school at Leoni, a few miles east of Jackson, and at about the same time another Methodist denomination—the Methodist Protestants—appear to have opened a "seminary" in the same place. Shortly thereafter the two denominations apparently merged their efforts under the name "Michigan Union College." In 1859 the students and faculty loaded their possessions on wagons and moved to Adrian, where the school was reopened as Adrian College. Members of another small sect, the Freewill Baptists, opened in 1844 a school at Spring Arbor, where the Methodists originally had planned to locate their educational institution. The next year a charter was granted by the legislature under the name Michigan Central College. Although it was at first denied the right to confer degrees, this power was granted in 1850. Five years later, this school was moved

[16] M. Kuhn, *The First Hundred Years.*

to Hillsdale and became Hillsdale College. Michigan Central College was the first institution in Michigan to confer a regular academic degree on a woman.

Up to 1855 none of these five schools, with the exception of Michigan Central College, was given the right to grant degrees by the legislature. Although they occasionally deviated from the policy advocated by John D. Pierce of confining the degree-granting power to the University of Michigan, the lawmakers in the main adhered to it. President Tappan of the University of Michigan strongly favored it. Leading figures in the churches that had established schools sought in vain for college powers. Most of these Protestant leaders supported the newly formed Republican party. Early in 1855, when the Republicans took over the governorship and control of the legislature, friends of the denominational schools flocked to Lansing seeking legislative approval to become colleges. President Tappan contended in vain against them. The Baptists secured an amendment to their 1833 charter, changing the name of their school to Kalamazoo College and giving it the power to grant degrees. A general college law also was enacted, providing that any school that met certain requirements might become a college. The delay in granting college status undoubtedly retarded the development of independent church-related colleges in Michigan, and gave state institutions a head start. This may be a partial explanation of the fact that Michigan in the twentieth century has a far larger proportion of its college students enrolled in tax-supported institutions than most other states have.

The five church-related schools so far mentioned (Kalamazoo College, Albion College, Olivet College, Adrian College, and Hillsdale College) have continued to provide education for Michigan youth to the present day. There were, however, many abortive college enterprises during the period from 1835 to 1860. In 1839 Presbyterians established Marshall College. Prior to his appointment as superintendent of public instruction, John D. Pierce had been an active backer of the movement for a college in Michigan sponsored by the Presbyterian Church. As has been noted, his investigations after he assumed that office led him to oppose the granting of college charters to denominational schools. The adoption of this policy made it necessary for him to oppose the very project he had previously supported. In spite of his opposition, a college charter was obtained, and on the same day a charter giving the right to grant degrees was approved for St. Philip's College, to be situated near Detroit. Marshall College had been given a considerable amount of land, but the decline of land values after

1837 so depleted its resources that the college failed after a few years. St. Philip's was opened and operated for a few years, but its buildings were lost in a fire in 1842 and the college expired with them. The legislature in 1850 once more departed from the policy backed by Pierce and granted two college charters. One of these was to Michigan Central College at Spring Arbor, which, as already mentioned, later was moved and became Hillsdale College. The other was to St. Mark's College at Grand Rapids, an enterprise backed by the Episcopal Church. This institution opened the same year but never offered studies above the preparatory level, expiring after about two and a half years. The United Brethren Church opened a college at Leoni in 1859, using the buildings formerly occupied by the predecessor of Adrian College. This school continued to operate under the name Michigan Union College until 1872.

An unusual school was founded a few miles northeast of Adrian by Mrs. Laura Haviland, a Quaker woman later to achieve widespread fame as a leader of the movement to spirit slaves from the South to freedom in Canada. In 1836 she started "Raisin Institute" as a manual-labor school for dependent children. In 1839 the school was raised to the preparatory level, open to students of both sexes, colored as well as white. Raisin Institute received a charter from the legislature in 1847. It operated somewhat sporadically until 1863, when it was reincorporated as the Raisin Valley Seminary and came under the supervision of the Adrian Quarterly Meeting of the Society of Friends. It continued to operate as an academy until after 1900.

EDUCATION FOR WOMEN

Boys and girls attended primary schools together, and coeducation was actually the rule in most of the academies, although a number of them theoretically segregated the girls into what was usually called a "female department." Michigan Central College was the only institution in Michigan to grant a regular academic degree to a woman prior to the Civil War. Among educational leaders in the state there was considerable support for coeducation, but popular prejudice against it beyond the elementary level is evident. Each of the branches had a "female department," and after the branch system ceased to receive support from the University Regents there was a movement to establish a separate state educational institution for women. An effort was made in 1855 to persuade the legislature to create such a school and to allot it a portion of the swamp lands that had been granted to the state by Congress. This effort failed, probably because opinion was divided between those who favored separate schools for women and those who believed in coeducation. With little hope that women would be admitted to the University, those who were interested in education for women turned to the establishment of non-public seminaries and colleges.

Prior to 1855 a number of female seminaries had been established. An "Association for the promotion of female education" had been incorporated by Detroiters as early as 1830, and separate schools for girls had been chartered in at least five other places by 1855. The founders of the schools for women opened immediately after 1855 probably hoped to secure state aid in the form of a portion of the swamp lands. The Michigan Female College was founded in Lansing by Miss Abigail Rogers in September, 1855, and the following month the Marshall Female Seminary was launched. In 1856 the Michigan Female Seminary was incorporated by members of the Presbyterian church and others in Kalamazoo. In spite of the fact that state aid was not obtained, these institutions performed a useful function. Miss Rogers' college endured until 1871, the buildings originally erected for it being obtained subsequently for a State School for the Blind. The Marshall Female Seminary lasted only four years, but the Michigan Female Seminary in Kalamazoo, which was opened in 1867, continued to operate for forty years. A Catholic seminary for girls was opened at Monroe in 1847. Meanwhile, most of the denominational colleges maintained a "female department" or "female college," some of them granting the degree "Mistress of Arts."

Both men and women students attended Michigan State Normal School from its beginning in 1852. After the Civil War the cause of coeducation triumphed, and women students were admitted to Michigan Agricultural College and the University of Michigan in 1870. The denominational colleges quickly abandoned, in most cases, their separate schools for girls and became coeducational soon thereafter.

Underground railway station, Union City, Michigan

14

POLITICS AND SOCIETY IN
MID-NINETEENTH-CENTURY MICHIGAN

At the time Michigan became a state, the two major political parties in the national arena were the Democrats and the Whigs. Between 1837 and 1854 the Democrats won most of the elections in Michigan. Two minor parties growing out of the struggle against slavery—the Liberty Party and the Free Soil Party—were prominent during the 1840s. Then in 1854 under the oaks at Jackson, the Republican Party of Michigan was formed. It elected its candidate for governor and a majority of both houses of the legislature in the fall elections of that year and was uniformly successful at the polls from then on until long after the Civil war.

During the 1840s and 1850s Michigan, along with the rest of the nation, was reform-minded. Among the reform causes were the antislavery movement, agitation for temperance and for women's rights, and even the complete reorganization of society into communist units. Detroit grappled with urban problems, as did the smaller cities to a lesser degree, and in the cities there were substantial improvements in the facilities for more comfortable living. The majority of the people still lived in the country, however, and Michigan remained a predominantly rural state. The daily newspaper came into prominence and there was a measure of progress in the arts. The number of religious denominations grew, with the churches wielding a powerful influence in public affairs. Most of the reform crusades were led by churchmen. It was a vigorous and growing society; people were "up and coming," anxious to get ahead in the world, supremely confident in the future of their country, and keenly conscious of moral and spiritual values.

DEMOCRATS VERSUS WHIGS

Politics! You could hear men talking politics everywhere—in taverns, in front of the meetinghouses on Sundays, after dinner at harvest time, at camp meetings in summer, around the cracker barrel in the general store in winter—in fact just about anywhere men congregated. And usually they were arguing: not discussing in the manner of polite conversation, but in all seriousness and often with rancor. Government was important, but politics was more than that—it was a sporting interest. A political party was what a major-league baseball or football club is today to many people; you followed it and supported it in the same way. Politics was a great game. Every year there was at least one election and usually there were two or three. Michigan elected its state officials in the odd-numbered years until 1850, in the even-numbered years there were congressmen to elect, and every four years came the most exciting event of them all: the presidential election. Most Michiganians were ardent Jacksonians, and they firmly believed, with Old Hickory, in frequent elections and short terms of office.

For some years prior to Jackson's election to the presidency in 1828, party lines in the nation had been blurred. So vigorous a leader as Jackson was bound to make enemies, and he made them aplenty. They included the remaining New England Federalists, supporters of the United States Bank, anti-Masons, South Carolina nullificationists, Clay men, Calhoun men, and Webster men. Without having anything in common except their dislike of the fiery Andrew, these groups coalesced in the early 1830s under the name of Whig, chosen because the party of that name in England had been opposed to the supporters of the king. The backbone of the early Whig Party in Michigan was a group of three Detroit men who had been appointed to positions in the Territorial government by Jackson's predecessor, President John Quincy Adams: William Woodbridge, Henry S. Chipman, and Thomas Rowland.[1] There was no love lost between Jackson and Adams, and so it was natural that these Adams appointees should lead the fight against "King Andrew."

The Whigs made little headway in Michigan at first. The Democratic candidate for governor in 1835, Stevens T. Mason, was elected, and was re-elected in 1837 with slight opposition. The leg-

[1] For a detailed discussion of political rivalry in this period, see F. B. Streeter, *Political Parties in Michigan, 1837-1860.*

islature contained a large Democratic majority. The Detroit *Free Press*, which began publication in 1831, staunchly supported the Democratic cause, and most of the outstate newspapers were Democratic. But the situation began to change as hard times hit the state. As usual, economic distress was blamed on the party in power. This set the stage for a Whig victory in 1839, when Woodbridge was elected governor. The next year in the famous log-cabin-and-hard-cider campaign Michigan voters gave the Whig candidate for president, William Henry Harrison, a majority. The Whig triumph, however, was short-lived. In Washington Harrison survived his inauguration by scarcely a month, and following his death and the assumption of the presidency by John Tyler, the Whigs divided into snarling factions. Woodbridge resigned as governor to accept election by the legislature to the United States Senate, and this evoked some criticism. In 1841 the Democrats were again triumphant, electing John S. Barry of Constantine as governor on a platform of economy and retrenchment. Barry became known for his insistence on the strictest economy in state government. From 1841 to 1854 the Democrats won every state election, and every legislature had a Democratic majority. The voters also gave a majority to the Democratic candidate for president in 1844, 1848, and 1852.

Whig hopes were kept alive by factions within the Democratic Party. At times the Democrats seemed to dislike each other about as much as they did the Whigs. The first of these groups was headed by John Norvell, the postmaster at Detroit, and consisted largely of federal appointees. The second faction, led by Lucius Lyon of Kalamazoo, Elon Farnsworth of Detroit, and Governor Barry, consisted of the conservatives: men of property who opposed the "extravagances" of the Mason administration and would have preferred to restrict the right to vote to property owners. The "radical" wing of the party was led by Kinsley S. Bingham of Livingston County. He and his followers were critical of banks, corporations, and special privilege groups of any sort. This faction included men of small means, in contrast to the more affluent conservatives. In the later 1840s and early 1850s the radicals came to include a large number of antislavery enthusiasts. Finally, there was a faction of the party that had its strength in the western part of the state and consisted of those who felt that the eastern section received too many favors from state government. Judge Epaphroditus Ransom of Kalamazoo may be regarded as the leader of this faction.

The Whigs might have capitalized on these splits within the Democratic ranks had they not, too, been divided into factions.

The conservative Whigs, led by Woodbridge, resembled in many ways the conservative faction in the Democratic Party. They were monied men, large landowners, and prosperous merchants, most of whom had little time or taste for active political work. The Whig radicals, on the other hand, included a good many younger men, particularly young lawyers, and in the latter part of the period they espoused the antislavery cause.

Besides the two major parties, two minor political organizations deserve mention. They were never successful from a practical standpoint, for they never even came close to winning an election. But the votes polled by the minor parties sometimes drew enough votes from one major party to bring about the success of the other. Their principal achievement, however, was the promotion of the crusade against slavery. The Liberty Party, consisting of avowed abolitionists, was organized in 1840 and managed to poll 294 votes in Michigan that year. The candidate of the party for president, James G. Birney, came to live near Saginaw and became the leader of the Michigan forces. He ran for governor in 1843 and received 2,776 votes, was again a candidate for the presidency in 1844, but shortly thereafter fell ill and was unable to take an active part in political battles. In 1848 the Liberty Party gave way to the Free Soil Party, which was more moderate. It did not advocate outright abolition of slavery, but only opposed its extension into the new western territories. Former President Martin Van Buren, the Free Soil candidate for the presidency in 1848, received over 10,000 votes in Michigan despite the fact that the Democratic candidate was Lewis Cass, a Michigan man.

UNDER THE OAKS

After 1850 the Whig Party rapidly disintegrated. The conservative faction was attracted to the American or "Know Nothing" Party, which had sprung up in opposition to foreigners and Roman Catholics. Whigs blamed their defeats on the solid Democratic vote of the immigrants, many of whom were Catholic. In 1854 the "Know Nothings" ran a few candidates, but demonstrated their greatest strength in the city elections of 1855. They revived their organization in 1856, but it died out soon afterward. The members of the radical faction of the Whigs, in many cases, went over to the Free Soil Party. This party also received adherents from the radical faction of the Democratic Party. In 1849 Whigs and Free Soilers combined forces to support Flavius T. Littlejohn of Allegan for governor, but he was defeated by the Democratic candidate, John S. Barry.

There was some surcease of agitation on the issue of slavery extension after the enactment by Congress of the measures called the Compromise of 1850, which settled the status of slavery in the territories acquired as a result of the Mexican War. But the question was ripped wide open again when in 1854 Congress passed the Kansas-Nebraska Bill, repealing that part of the Missouri Compromise that had prohibited slavery north of the southern boundary of Missouri except in Missouri itself. The new law applied the principle of "popular sovereignty" to this vast western area, opening it to slavery until such time as the states to be carved out of it were ready for admission to the Union; at that time the people of each state would decide whether or not they wanted slavery. The prime supporter of the Kansas-Nebraska Bill was Stephen A. Douglas of Illinois, but it was Lewis Cass of Michigan who was the originator of the principle of popular sovereignty, advocating it in a letter written in December, 1847. Cass wrote:

> . . . it is hardly expedient to call into exercise a doubtful and invidious authority, which questions the intelligence of a respectable portion of our citizens, and whose limitation, whatever it may be, will be rapidly approaching its termination—an authority which would give to Congress despotic power, uncontrolled by the Constitution over most important sections of our common country.[2]

Passage of the Kansas-Nebraska Act brought forth violent protest throughout the North. Meetings were held at which "Free Democrats" and "Free Whigs" joined with Free Soilers to express their outrage at this opening of the West to slavery. Out of these meetings the Republican Party was born.

It is believed that the first of these meetings to form a coalition under the name "Republican" was held at Ripon, Wisconsin on February 28, 1854. In Michigan Free Democrats and Free Whigs held separate protest meetings, and then at a meeting held in Kalamazoo in late June leaders of both groups determined that they would join to form a new political party. A call was sent out for a meeting to be held at Jackson on July 6. About 1,500 persons appeared in response to this call. The throng was so vast that no building in Jackson could accommodate it. Consequently, a speaker's stand was erected "under the oaks" (near the corner of Franklin and Second Sts.) and there the meeting was held. An organization was formed under the name Republican Party, a platform was drawn up and adopted, and candidates for state offices in the fall election were nominated. The question of whether the Republican Party was born at Ripon or at Jackson

[2] Quoted by F. B. Woodford, *Lewis Cass, the Last Jeffersonian*, p. 252.

probably never will be settled. The Ripon meeting preceded the Jackson meeting, but it was hardly more than a local political gathering and only the preliminary steps were taken to form a new party. The assemblage under the oaks at Jackson was the first state-wide Republican meeting; it was there that the first platform was adopted and the first full state ticket was nominated.[3]

The Republican slate was headed by Kinsley S. Bingham, who was nominated for governor. Action on controversial questions other than the extension of slavery was avoided. At the November election Bingham and the entire Republican ticket emerged victorious, and a Republican majority in the legislature was chosen. It was a turning point in Michigan politics. From that day until 1932 Michigan was persistently and overwhelmingly Republican. On relatively few occasions were the Democrats able to win a national or state election. The strength of the Republican Party at the outset came from several sources. The New England element, which was still dominant in the state, regarded the antislavery movement, with which the Republican Party was associated, as a crusade for righteousness. The temperance and women's rights advocates were impatient with the Democrats' failure to enact desired legislation. The Protestant churches, except for the Lutheran groups, were strongly Republican. Many of the foremost Republican leaders were Protestant ministers. The farmers who were seeking the establishment of a separate agricultural college were Republicans. The Democrats relied on Detroit and, to a lesser degree, on other cities for their strength. The foreign element in the population leaned toward the Democrats, a fact that drove many Whigs into the "Know Nothing" Party. When that party fizzled out, probably most of its adherents became Republicans. The election of 1854 was won by the votes of men who were of New England extraction, farmers, members of the Protestant churches, backers of denominational schools, and supporters of such reforms as abolition, prohibition, and women's rights.

POLITICAL LEADERS

Political parties are built more around persons than policies. Behind the election returns are the campaigns, the human relationships, the force of personalities, and the influence of leadership. The foremost name in Michigan politics for a generation was that of Lewis Cass. He served as territorial governor (1813-1831), as secretary of war (1831-1836), as minister to France

[3] F. Curtis, *The Republican Party*; W. Stocking (ed.), *Under the Oaks*

(1836-1842), as regent of the university (1843-1844), as United States senator (1845-1848 and 1849-1857), and as secretary of state under President Buchanan (1857-1860).

Cass endeared himself to the people of Michigan by his deep trust in democracy. Unlike some territorial governors, he rejoiced in the extension of political power to the people. Indeed, this was the fundamental reason for his proposal of the principle of popular sovereignty in 1847 as a means of dealing with the slavery question in the territories to be acquired from Mexico. Some, however, accused him of taking this stand as a means of securing southern support in a bid for the presidency. Actually it probably cost him the election when he ran in 1848. Enough antislavery Democrats, offended by his attitude on slavery extension, voted for the Whig or Free Soil candidate to cost him the election. In Michigan Cass was sufficiently popular to overcome this feeling, and he received the state's electoral votes as well as re-election to the United States Senate by the legislature in 1849 after his failure to win the presidency. But when he sided with Stephen A. Douglas in support of the Kansas-Nebraska Bill he became unpopular in Michigan. The legislature refused to send him back to the Senate in 1857, and his selection as a member of Buchanan's cabinet followed. He resigned from his cabinet post in December, 1860 in protest against Buchanan's failure to take active steps to suppress secession. Returning to Detroit, he supported the Union during the Civil War and lived to see the Union restored. He died on June 17, 1866 at the age of 84.

Party leaders, for the most part, may be found among the men who served as governor or United States senator. Those who served from 1835 to 1860 were as follows:

Governors
Stevens T. Mason, 1835-1839 (Dem.)
William Woodbridge, 1840-1841 (Whig)
James W. Gordon (Acting), 1841 (Whig)
John S. Barry, 1842-1845; 1850-1851 (Dem.)
Alpheus Felch, 1846-1847 (Dem.)
William L. Greenly (Acting), 1847 (Dem.)
Epaphroditus Ransom, 1849-1850 (Dem.)
Robert McClelland, 1851-1853 (Dem.)
Andrew Parsons (Acting), 1853-1855 (Dem.)
Kinsley S. Bingham, 1855-1859 (Rep.)
Moses Wisner, 1859-1861 (Rep.)
United States senators
Lucius Lyon, 1835-1839 (Dem.)

John Norvell, 1835-1841 (Dem.)
Augustus B. Porter, 1839-1845 (Whig)
William Woodbridge, 1841-1847 (Whig)
Lewis Cass, 1845-1848; 1849-1857 (Dem.)
Alpheus Felch, 1847-1853 (Dem.)
Thomas Fitzgerald, 1848-1849 (Dem.)
Charles E. Stuart, 1853-1859 (Dem.)
Zachariah Chandler, 1857-1875. 1879 (Rep.)
Kinsley S. Bingham, 1859-1861 (Rep.)

These eighteen men had certain common characteristics. All but three were born in New York or in one of the New England states. All but two studied and practiced law at some time in their careers. Measured by modern standards all of them were young when they began their public service. Although Woodbridge was sixty at the time he became governor, he had been appointed territorial secretary at the age of thirty-four. Cass became territorial governor when he was thirty-one. Lyon became a United States senator at the age of thirty-five. Mason was acting governor of the territory at the age of nineteen and became governor of the state at twenty-three. Ransom became a justice of the state supreme court when he was thirty-nine, and Felch attained the same position at the age of thirty-six. Only five of the twenty men were Detroiters, and of these, three (Cass, Mason, and Norvell) owed their positions at first to federal appointment. Only Porter and Chandler (each of whom had been mayor of Detroit) attained the position of senator without the prestige of federal favor. It would appear that the citizens of Detroit were handicapped in politics by their residence in that city. It also is apparent that the position of United States senator was more highly regarded than that of governor, since two governors—Woodbridge and Felch—resigned to accept election to the senate.[4] McClelland resigned to become secretary of the interior in the cabinet of President Franklin D. Pierce.

Barry, the favorite of the conservative Democrats, was a merchant in Constantine, a town in St. Joseph county, and was one of the organizers of the Michigan Southern Railroad. Felch, a native of Maine, was a Monroe lawyer. After his retirement from the Senate he practiced law in Ann Arbor, became professor of law at the University of Michigan, and for many years served as president of the Michigan Pioneer and Historical Society. He lived to be 92. Ransom was born in Massachusetts, coming to Michigan in 1834 and making Kalamazoo his home. He was the

---

[4] It must be borne in mind that at this time, and until 1913, United States senators were elected by the legislature, not by popular vote.

first governor to be inaugurated in the new state capital, Lansing, and was known as an ardent advocate of plank roads. After his term as governor he served as regent of the University and one term in the state house of representatives. He moved to Kansas in 1857 and died there in 1859. Robert McClelland was the son of a Pennsylvania physician. He studied law and moved to Monroe in 1833. After the conclusion of his term as secretary of the interior he returned to Michigan. On the eve of the Civil War he counselled moderation and compromise, a policy that was in violent contrast to the views of Republicans such as Senator Chandler and Governor Wisner.[5] Charles E. Stuart, the last Michigan Democrat to serve as United States senator until the election of Woodbridge N. Ferris in 1922, was a Kalamazoo attorney. He was floor leader for Douglas at the Democratic National Convention that met at Charleston in 1860.[6]

Among the Republicans, Zachariah Chandler was destined to be the foremost leader for a quarter of a century after the meeting under the oaks in Jackson. A native of New Hampshire, he came to Detroit in 1833 at the age of twenty, and in the years that followed became a highly successful wholesale dry-goods merchant. He was elected mayor of Detroit after a hotly contested campaign in 1851; the following year he ran for governor of the state on the Whig ticket and was defeated. He was a participant in the historic meeting at Jackson where the Republican party was formed. In 1856 he campaigned actively for the election of John C. Fremont, the Republican candidate for president. Following this the legislature elected him as the successor to Cass in the United States Senate. He held this seat for eighteen years, and was re-elected to it again in 1879, but died the same year. As the crisis of the Union developed in 1860-61, Chandler was a leader among those who opposed any compromise with the South, and his saying "Without a little bloodletting, this Union, in my opinion, would not be worth a rush" became famous. Among the other Whig leaders who joined the Republican party were Jacob M. Howard of Detroit and David Walbridge of Kalamazoo, later to become congressmen. Kinsley S. Bingham, the first Republican to be elected governor, was a New Yorker by birth, and had come to Michigan in 1833, settling on a Livingston

[5] F. D. Williams, "Robert McClelland and the Secession Crisis," *Michigan History,* XLIII (1959), 155-164.
[6] For brief biographical sketches of the governors, see *Messages of the Governors of Michigan,* ed. by G. N. Fuller. On Stuart, see A. McCain, "Charles Edward Stuart of Kalamazoo," *Michigan History,* XLIV, 324-335.

County farm. He held a number of local offices, then was elected
as a Democrat to two terms in Congress in 1846 and 1848.
After serving two terms as governor he was sent to the United
States Senate, but died in 1861 before his term expired. Moses
Wisner, elected governor in 1858, was a Pontiac lawyer. It was
during his administration that the first law was passed requiring
the registration of voters. The embezzlement of a large sum of
money by the state treasurer occurred during Wisner's term,
and this may have been a factor in his decision not to seek a
second term. He died at the age of 46 of typhoid fever while
serving as an officer in the Union army.

A NEW CONSTITUTION

In 1849 the voters of Michigan, by the lopsided margin of
33,193 to 4,095, approved a proposal for the general revision of
the state constitution. Behind this overwhelming desire for a
new constitution was the ferment of Jacksonian democracy.
Michigan's first constitution had been framed before the implica-
tions of Jackson's ideas for state government had been generally
understood. These included the choice of public officials by election rather than by appointment, limitations upon the powers of
the legislature, and opposition to special acts of incorporation.
Michigan was only one of many states that were writing new
constitutions or amending old ones at this time to incorporate
these principles.[7]

The convention called to make a general revision of Michigan's
constitution met at Lansing June 3, 1850 and completed its work
on August 15. It included one hundred delegates, only one of
whom was a native of Michigan. Daniel Goodwin of Wayne
County was chosen as president. The constitution framed by this
convention was submitted to the voters November 5, 1850, and
was ratified by a large margin.

The state's second constitution was more than twice as long
as the first and was much more detailed. It included many restrictions upon the legislature. The lawmakers were prohibited
from passing special acts of incorporation; henceforth all corporations had to be formed under general law, thus assuring that no
group would get special favors. Banking laws could take effect
only after a majority vote of approval by the people; the legislature was forbidden to engage the state in building or financing
internal improvements (a reflection of the antagonisms created

[7] A. R. Richards, "The Traditions of Government in the States," *The
Forty-eight States.*

by the $5,000,000 loan to finance the Internal Improvement program of 1837); salaries of state officials were fixed in the constitution and thus could not be changed by the legislature (the governor was to receive a salary of $1,000 per year). The question of constitutional revision was to be submitted to the people automatically every sixteen years.

Another major change was to make all the principal state officials elective (including the judges). This included the secretary of state, state treasurer, attorney general, auditor general, superintendent of public instruction, regents of the University, and the state board of education—all of which had been appointive up to this time. The terms of members of the state house of representative was extended from one year to two. And henceforth, elections for the chief state officials were to be held in the even-numbered instead of the odd-numbered years, making them come at the same time as national elections and thus paving the way for the long and crowded ballot.

The new constitution altered drastically the judiciary. The county courts were abolished. Instead, the state was divided into eight circuits, each of which was to have a judge elected by the people. The eight circuit judges were to constitute the supreme court, but the legislature was empowered to organize a new supreme court with a chief justice and three associate justices, to be elected by the people.

The article on education stipulated that free schools were to be maintained for at least three months each year beginning five years after the constitution was adopted, but it was not until 1869 that "rate bills" were abolished throughout the state. Not only were the regents of the University made elective, but they also were to constitute a body corporate, were to be free of legislative interference in the supervision of the University, and were to elect a permanent president.

Aliens who had declared their intention to become United States citizens were given the right to vote, as were "civilized" male Indians. An amendment submitted separately, when the people voted on the proposed constitution, would have given Negroes the right to vote, but it was rejected by a margin of 32,000 to 12,000.

The Constitution of 1850 was the fundamental law of the state until January 1, 1909. Between 1850 and 1908, 71 amendments were proposed, of which 38 were adopted. Two attempts at general revision during the period failed. Under the provision in the constitution that the question of general revision must be submitted every sixteen years, the people voted in 1866 for a new constitutional convention. Delegates were elected, met on May 15, 1867, and framed a new document, only to have it rejected by a margin of 110,582 to 71,733. Seven years later the legislature authorized the appointment of a "Constitutional Commission" of eighteen, chosen by the governor to propose a general revision. A revised constitution was drafted, was submitted to the voters on November 4, 1874, and was rejected, 124,034 to 39,285.

THE REFORM CRUSADES

During the 1840s and 1850s a great wave of reforming zeal swept across America. Scholars have traced its beginning to a series of religious revivals in western New York state led by Charles S. Finney in the 1820s.[8] Western New York was peopled largely by New Englanders who had brought their Puritanism along with them. Implicit in Puritanism was the Calvinistic dogma of predestination and the notion that mankind bears the taint of Adam's original sin. The effect of the Finney revivals was to destroy the attitude of resignation towards a wicked world and to substitute for it the view that it is the duty of the Christian to make the world better. The churches had awakened from their lethargy about the beginning of the nineteenth century, and had undertaken through foreign and home missions "to spread the gospel to every creature." But the Finney revivals did something else: they imparted to religion the red hot zeal to change society; not merely to convert the heathen or impart religion to the frontiersmen, but to eradicate evils and injustices in the older parts of the country. This spirit expressed itself in many different ways: the movement for the abolition of slavery, the temperance crusade, the campaign for women's rights, anti-Catholicism, dietary reform, new religions, Utopian socialism, prison reform, new schemes for education, and others. Western New York was the fountainhead of most of these reform movements, and since so many of the people of Michigan had come from western New York, it is not surprising that almost all these manifestations were reflected in Michigan.

In the forefront of the antislavery forces were the Friends or Quakers, but several other religious denominations in Michigan were almost equally vehement against slavery. Abolition societies were formed in the 1830s. The sentiment against slavery found expression in politics during the 1840s in "third parties," an

[8] G. H. Barnes, *The Antislavery Impulse, 1830-1844.*

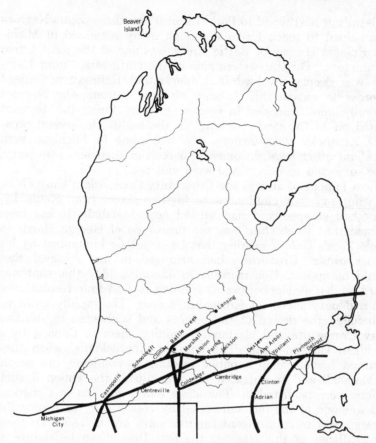

MICHIGAN'S PART IN THE UNDERGROUND RAILWAY

oalesced in 1854 in the Republican party. But many people
ound other ways to aid a cause than voting for polite resolutions
r casting a ballot. There was the "Underground Railroad," an
nformal organization for the assistance of escaped slaves in
eaching free soil. Slaves who escaped across the Ohio River
und their way northward through Indiana or Ohio and were
elcomed by many Michiganians. The Quakers everywhere took
e lead in this work, but others were not lacking to assist them.
n established route ran from Niles through Cassopolis, School-
aft, Climax, Battle Creek, and along the old Territorial Road

to Detroit or northward to Port Huron. From these points Negroes were helped to reach Canada, though many remained in Michigan. Erastus Hussey of Battle Creek was one of the most active "conductors." On the eastern side of the state Mrs. Laura Haviland was deeply involved in Underground Railroad activities.[9] In order to escape the vigilance of slave hunters, the Negroes generally were concealed in houses or barns during the day and carried on to the next "station" in the night. On several occasions Kentucky slave owners, who had come to Michigan with writs and other legal documents to reclaim their slave property, were subjected to delays and even violence.

Most famous of all was the Crosswhite Case. Adam Crosswhite, his wife, and four children were fugitive slaves from Kentucky. They had escaped and had settled near Marshall. It has been claimed that Crosswhite was the prototype of George Harris in *Uncle Tom's Cabin*. Fearing that he might be kidnapped by his former owner, Crosswhite had arranged to fire a signal shot should he appear. One morning in January, 1847 this shot was heard, and the neighbors came running to find four Kentuckians and a deputy sheriff at Crosswhite's door. The rapidly gathered mob foiled the design of the owners and succeeded in spiriting away Crosswhite and his family, sending them to Canada by a Michigan Central train. The enraged Kentuckians, when they returned home, called a public meeting to condemn the people of Marshall and to threaten the breakup of the Union if such actions were persisted in. The affair found an echo in Congress, and was one of the incidents cited by Henry Clay to justify the passage of a more stringent fugitive slave law in 1850. To meet the challenge of this measure the first Republican legislature of Michigan passed in February, 1855 a strong "personal liberty law," going to the very limit of every constitutional device to prevent the recovery of fugitive slaves in Michigan. State and local officials were forbidden to co-operate with federal marshals in the recovery of slave property.[10]

The temperance crusade was led by many of the same people who were engaged in antislavery activities. For Michigan people slavery was far away, while the evils of heavy drinking and drunkenness were everywhere in evidence. Since early Territorial days

---

[9] M. M. Danforth, *A Quaker Pioneer: Laura Haviland, Superintendent of the Underground.*

[10] C. Barnes, "Battle Creek as a Station on the Underground Railroad," *Mich. Pioneer and Historical Colls.*, XXXVIII (1912), 279-285; M. Aiken "The Underground Railroad," *Michigan History*, VI (1922), 597-610; W Hobart, "The Crosswhite Case," *Mich. Pioneer and Historical Colls.* XXXVIII (1912), 257-278.

certain restrictions had been placed on the liquor traffic. The sale or gift of intoxicating liquor to Indians was prohibited by a law of the Northwest Territory passed in 1790 and by an act approved by the governor and judges of Michigan Territory in 1812. The sale of liquor to minors, servants, soldiers, prisoners, and anyone on Sundays was forbidden. Another type of restriction was the requirement that vendors of intoxicating liquors obtain a license. In 1845 the legislature empowered any township or city to refuse to issue such licenses, and the Constitution of 1850 banned licenses altogether. But the net result was only to leave the sale of liquor unregulated. "Demon rum" was also attacked by means of "moral suasion." Societies were formed to promote the cause of temperance, first local, then state-wide, and in 1826 the American Temperance Society was established on a national basis. The Michigan Temperance Society was formed in 1833, and had many branches. At first the temperance movement stressed moderation. Since this effort brought no concrete results, abstinence from "ardent spirits" was advocated. The drinking of beer and wine rather than whisky, rum, and brandy was encouraged. But this policy was condemned as undemocratic. Whisky was cheap, but beer and wine were relatively expensive at that time. So finally the temperance forces were driven to the advocacy of total abstinence.

About 1840 the "Washingtonian movement" was started by a group of reformed drunkards in Baltimore, and it rapidly spread to the West. Some of these ex-tipplers developed mighty oratorical powers. They held meetings or attended them, told their experiences "before and after," and urged everyone to sign a pledge to abstain from all drinking. The Washingtonian meetings were characterized by lusty singing, excited oratory, and pledge-signing. One writer has left us a vivid picture of these temperance meetings. Augustus Littlejohn of Allegan, brother of the Free Soil candidate for governor in 1849, conducted a series of meetings in Kalamazoo County in 1844. Littlejohn is described as a man of medium height, well-proportioned, "straight as a Choctaw," with a face of "clear intellectual cast and a keen black eye." We are told that his voice was "strong and splendidly modulated to express feelings of pathos or to emphasize a point." In one town the meetings were held every evening and a part of each day for two weeks. Crowds came from miles around. Littlejohn organized his work carefully, put great emphasis on the singing of temperance songs, drilling a choir an hour before each meeting, and then lectured so as to entertain as well as persuade. He practically forced the preachers of the community to attend. He put

on a good show. Sometimes he included a description of the
Battle of Bunker Hill or Waterloo, climaxing the latter description by kneeling at the pulpit (his meetings always were held
in churches) and imitating Wellington dramatically: "Oh that
night or Blücher would come." One wonders whether the cause
of temperance or the show really brought the crowds. At any
rate, we are told, the saloonkeepers bent every effort to bring
disrepute on Littlejohn and his cause, without success, of course.
Such meetings were held in Battle Creek, Marshall, and other
parts of the state, and the people came to be sold on the temperance cause even though they did not stop drinking.[11]

Soon the temperance crusade turned from "moral suasion"
and pledge-signing to prohibition as the answer to the liquor
problem. The movement for prohibition started in Maine, with
Neal Dow as its champion. As early as 1846 a prohibition law
was passed in Maine, but it proved to be defective. Then in 1851
the legislature of that state passed a prohibitory act that became
a model for other states to the extent that prohibition acts came to
be known as "Maine laws." This act prohibited the manufacture,
sale, or keeping for sale of intoxicating liquors and set heavy
penalties for violations. Minnesota, Rhode Island, Massachusetts,
and Vermont enacted prohibition laws of this kind in 1852. In
Michigan the legislature adopted a prohibition law in 1853, but
provided that it should go into effect only upon approval by the
voters in a popular referendum. This approval was given by a
substantial majority, but the state supreme court declared in
1854 that the legislature did not have the right to make the law
dependent on a popular referendum and declared it, for that
reason, to be invalid. The first Republican legislature in 1855,
however, passed an acceptable law. After this the temperance
forces rested on their oars, thinking that the battle had been
won. They soon found that it was one thing to pass a law and
quite another to enforce it. Loopholes were discovered and soon
liquor was being sold openly. In 1857 Detroit is reported to
have had 420 saloons, 56 hotel and tavern bars, 23 breweries, and
six distilleries. The prohibition law remained on the statute books
until 1875, but for many years prior to that date it was in reality
a dead letter.[12]

---

[11] A. D. P. Van Buren, "Temperance in Pioneer Days," *Mich. Pioneer
and Historical Colls.,* V (1882), 426-433; and "Our Temperance Conflict,"
op. cit., XIII (1888), 388-407.
[12] F. B. Streeter, "History of Prohibition Legislation in Michigan," *Mich.
History,* II (1917), 289-309; J. Fitzgibbon, "King Alcohol, His Rise, Reign,
and Fall in Michigan," *Mich. History,* II (1917), 737-781.

The reform crusade of the 1840s and 1850s gave rise to several new religious denominations, among them the Spiritualists, Seventh Day Adventists, and Mormons. Battle Creek had by 1860 become the foremost center of the Seventh Day Adventists. An offshoot of the Mormon church also grew up in Michigan. The founder of Mormonism was Joseph Smith. Following their beginnings in western New York, the Mormons moved to Ohio, then to Missouri, then back to Illinois. Their city of Nauvoo in southern Illinois was a community of considerable size and importance. But claims that Smith practiced polygamy brought down on his head general condemnation, and in 1844 Joseph and his brother Hyrum were murdered by an angry mob. After Smith's death most of the Mormons accepted the leadership of Brigham Young, who in 1846-47, led them to Utah. But not all the Mormons followed Young. One relatively small group accepted the leadership of James J. Strang and settled in Voree, Wisconsin. Sufficient lands were not available for the entire group, and Strang began to look around for greener pastures and more acres. His attention was drawn to the Beaver Islands, which lie in the northern part of Lake Michigan and are a part of the state of Michigan. There are twelve of these islands, the largest being twelve miles long and six miles wide. The only inhabitants at the time were a few Irish fishermen. Here was an ideal spot for his people, Strang believed, and in 1848 and 1849 they began to arrive in large numbers.

Strang, like Joseph Smith, was favored with divine revelations, so he claimed. In accordance with commands he said he received in one of these revelations, Strang had himself crowned as "King James, Viceregent of God on earth." At first he was not a polygamist, but he dutifully obeyed another revelation, and in the end took unto himself additional wives. Although "plural marriage" was permitted, the code of the community was very strict regarding immoral conduct, drinking, and profanity. Strang absolutely dominated the settlement. But he made enemies, and on one occasion he was taken to Detroit for trial in federal district court. He was acquitted of the charges against him and returned in triumph. Then he ordered his followers to elect him to the state legislature. In 1852 he went to Lansing and was highly regarded by his fellow legislators. Both Whigs and Democrats courted his favor, for it was said that he could control about 2,500 votes. His downfall was the result of the enmities and jealousies that always result from one-man rule. On June 16, 1856 he was assassinated. His people, left leaderless, were attacked by a mob of fishermen from the mainland, their houses were looted, and they were forced to flee for their lives.[13] A remnant remained true to the faith. The 1936 census of religious bodies showed fifteen Strangites remaining in Michigan.

While some men and women seemed to believe that the abolition of slavery, prohibition, or a new church might bring the millennium, others embraced the ideas of communitarianism. Inspired by the theories of François Fourier, Robert Owen, or one of the other "Utopian Socialists," they believed that a better society could emerge if people were organized into communities where the means of production were owned, managed, and utilized in common. About a hundred such communities appeared in the United States during the first sixty years of the nineteenth century, a large proportion during the great reform era of the 1840s and 1850s. Among the more famous were the Brook Farm project in New England, the New Harmony community of Owenites in Indiana, and the Oneida community in New York. Only one of these, curiously enough, seems to have been organized before 1860 in Michigan. It was called Alphadelphia, was located near Galesburg, and was founded on the ideas of Fourier. A German, Dr. H. R. Schetterly, was the leading spirit in the enterprise. The group purchased 3,000 acres of land and erected a large "mansion" where the members, each of whom followed his own trade and shared with the others the fruits of his labors, were housed. At one time there were about three hundred members and the property was valued in 1846 at $43,897.21. Internal dissension arose, as was usual in such projects, and the members began to drift away after two or three years. In 1848 the project was abandoned and the property was divided. The impetus behind such projects seems to have been a feeling on the part of Americans that here a new society was being built and that it ought to be built on a new and better pattern.[14] One contemporary of the Alphadelphia experiment who lived in nearby Galesburg expressed the opinion that the pioneers were accustomed to working together, that none were rich and none were poor; hence that they did not view the communitarian principle as foreign to their nature.[15]

13 M. M. Quaife, *The Kingdom of St. James*; O. W. Riegel, *Crown of Glory.*

14 A. E. Bestor, Jr., "Patent-office Models of the Good Society: Some Relationships Between Social Reform and Western Expansion," *American Historical Review,* LVIII (1953), 505-527. See also his *Backwoods Utopias*

15 A. D. P. Van Buren, quoted in S. Durant, *History of Kalamazoo County,* p. 370. Several other communitarian projects were launched in Michigan after 1860. The *Ora Labora* community existed in the thumb area between 1862 and 1868; the Hiawatha Association maintained a com

The crusade for women's rights, inaugurated at the Seneca Falls Convention in New York in 1848, was considered to be among the most radical of the reform movements of the time. Two years before the Seneca Falls Convention one of the leaders of the movement, Ernestine L. Rose, addressed the Michigan legislature in an appeal for women's rights. In 1849 a senate committee headed by Rix Robinson of Grand Haven reported a resolution in favor of a women's suffrage amendment, but it was ridiculed by other lawmakers. At the time, women had virtually no rights before the law. The Michigan Constitution of 1850 gave women property rights but not the ballot. Another phase of the women's rights movement aimed at greater educational opportunities for women. The conflict between those who favored coeducation and those who thought there should be separate schools and colleges for women already has been described. The opening of the University of Michigan to women students in 1870 was a landmark in the women's rights struggle. The incentive for this came largely from the labors of Lucinda Hinsdale Stone of Kalamazoo, who had conducted a successful female college in connection with Kalamazoo College. She also had been a leader in the formation of the Ladies' Library Association in Kalamazoo in 1852, which was the first women's club in Michigan and the third oldest in the United States. In later years Mrs. Stone came to be known as the "mother of women's clubs" in Michigan.[16]

The great reform crusades of the 1840s and 1850s reached their climax in the Civil War, which, at first a war to save the Union, later became also a crusade against slavery. But once the war was over, the zeal for reform faded. It was not until the first two decades of the twentieth century that another wave of enthusiasm for reform became widespread, although proposed political and economic reform attracted considerable attention after 1873.

THE AMENITIES OF CITY LIFE

Detroit was not in the front rank of American cities in 1860, but it was a metropolitan center of importance in the Middle

munity near Manistique in the 1890s, and the Sunrise Co-operative Farm Community existed in the Saginaw Valley, 1933-1936. See C. Wittke, *"Ora Labora,* a German Methodist Utopia," *Ohio Historical Quarterly,* LXVII (1958), 129-140; D. C. Byers, "Utopia in Upper Michigan," *Michigan Alumnus Quarterly Review,* LXIII (1957), 168-174; J. J. Cohen, *In Quest of Heaven.*

[16] C. R. Starring, "Lucinda Hinsdale Stone: a Pioneer in the Education of Women in Michigan," *Michigan History,* XLII (1958), 85-97.

West. Trade and manufacturing flourished and the population more than doubled in the 1850s, rising from 21,019 in 1850 to 45,619 in 1860. Such an urban center developed refinements and cultural advantages not enjoyed by those who lived outside. The manufacture of illuminating gas was begun on a small scale in 1849. By 1851 gas lights illuminated the principal streets, and gradually in business places, hotels, and the homes of well-to-do citizens gas lights replaced candles. Kerosene lamps were beginning to appear by 1861, replacing whale-oil lamps and candles in the homes of persons of moderate means. The sewing machine, which was coming into use about 1860, lightened household tasks. Even before the end of the Territorial period a water system was in use, the water being conveyed through wooden pipes made by hollowed-out tamarack logs. By 1839 a reservoir holding 422,000 gallons was needed to supply Detroit's needs. The open well and the pump were gradually outmoded. The use of stoves instead of fireplaces for heating was greatly expanded. In the early 1830s, the manufacture of stoves began in Detroit, and in time the Michigan metropolis became the chief center of the stove industry in the United States. The bathtub was another household accessory that many of the wealthier Detroiters were installing. Ice for refrigeration must have been used rather extensively, for there were no less than 23 ice dealers by 1860.

Along with these improvements in material comforts was a growing interest in cultural, religious, literary, and social affairs. The German element took the leadership in music. The Harmonie Society, a singing organization incorporated in 1852, was primarily a German group, although its membership included non-Germans. Other choral societies had been formed by 1860. The city was visited by musical artists of note, including Theresa Parodi and Adelina Patti. Many bands were formed. There was also a lively interest in the theater. Dramatic productions were presented in the City Hall in 1848, and in the following year the Metropolitan Theater was completed. Traveling players visited the city, although they came in larger numbers after 1865 than in the prewar era. The theater was frowned on by most Protestant churches, a fact that limited its patronage.[17]

Among the portrait painters in Detroit were J. M. Stanley and Alvah Bradish, both of whom were in great demand to reproduce the likenesses of such bigwigs as Governor Mason, John Biddle, Senator Cass, and President Tappan. At an 1853 art exhibition 419 paintings, 153 engravings, 42 statuaries, and

[17] M. O. Kistler, "The German Theater in Detroit," *Mich. History*, XLVII (1963), 289-301.

many other art objects owned by artists and private citizens
were shown.

For public meetings Detroit boasted at least two halls capable
of seating a thousand persons and several with a smaller capacity. Here were heard debates, concerts, and political oratory.
Throughout the period the hotel or tavern, with its ever-present
bar, was a favorite informal meeting place for the male element
of the population. Although fraternal orders were to attain their
greatest popularity after the Civil War, Detroit had several
Masonic lodges and at least one Odd Fellow lodge before 1860.

One of the earliest concerns of Detroiters was the prevention
and fighting of fires. Early regulations took the form of requiring
each shopkeeper and householder to provide and have in readi-
ness buckets, ladders, and kegs or barrels of water, and to turn
out to form a bucket brigade from the river to the scene of any
conflagration. In 1815 the city bought battering rams and fire
hooks to be used in tearing down burning buildings so as to
prevent the spread of fire. A private fire company had been
organized and a crude fire engine had been obtained by 1820.
By 1837 there were four fire companies; two years later a large
hall was erected for them, with rooms for the city council and
for public meetings.

In Detroit, as in other cities, the fire companies were social
and political groups. It became the fashion to visit other cities
and to receive visiting firemen in gala fashion. In 1845 the Ithaca
fire laddies were treated to a torchlight procession and a banquet
on the occasion of their visit to Detroit. At an annual review
and parade the engines were gaily decorated and polished to the
highest brilliance, the firemen decked themselves out in their
stiff leather helmets, red shirts, and black trousers, and there
was a contest to determine which company could throw the
largest stream of water highest or furthest. Between the companies competition was fierce. Sometimes, lacking a real fire,
some rogue would light a bonfire in order to start a race between
the companies to see which could arrive at the scene of the blaze
first. The firemen were a closely knit group and wielded a lot of
political influence. In some instances the rowdy element made
the annual firemen's ball a "rout." When the members of a fire
company reached a conflagration before their hose cart, they
often threw a barrel over the hydrant to prevent a rival company
from getting water, unless, that is, the rival laddies put up a
scrap to attain their end. It was the custom for citizens whose
property had been saved to serve refreshments after the fire.
Rivalries became so intense as to become a nuisance, and some-

thing had to be done about it. In 1860 two steam fire engines were purchased by the city and a paid fire department was organized.

The organization of a police force in the modern sense did not come about in Detroit until the early 1860s. There was a marshal as early as 1802 and whenever an epidemic of thievery or disorder occurred the merchants and other citizens subscribed funds to pay a night watchman.

The life of the city was punctuated by many events of general interest during these years. At least two presidents of the United States—Van Buren and Fillmore—paid the city a visit and were, of course, received with much fanfare. Elaborate public funerals for prominent citizens were held. In 1845 a public funeral for Andrew Jackson was held in Detroit, even though the former president had died and was buried at his home near Nashville, Tennessee. In 1849 another cholera epidemic hit the city, though it was less severe than the ones in the 1830s. In the early 1850s the railroad conspiracy trials were the sensation of the hour.[18]

In the smaller cities of the state—Grand Rapids, Jackson, Kalamazoo, Marshall, Battle Creek, Adrian, Monroe, and Saginaw—life took on a somewhat similar pattern but was affected to a greater degree by the rural environment in which they existed. The files of the Kalamazoo *Gazette* for 1854 reflect the interests and concerns of the townspeople of this period. The columns of the paper indicate great interest in prohibition and the slavery issue. A new female seminary was projected. A cyclone leveled several buildings. Four circuses and an "Uncle Tom's Cabin" troupe visited the town that year. The Ladies' Library celebrated its second anniversary. The ninth annual county fair was a huge success. The state census reported the population of the town to be about 3,000. A total enrollment of 962 in the public schools was reported. A plowing match, conducted by the County Agricultural Society, was an outstanding event of the year. A local artist was reported to have painted the portraits of two leading citizens. Three fire companies were supported, and Company No. 2 threw a stream of water 200 feet over the Congregational Church steeple. A big Fourth of July celebration was held. Sunday trains on the railroad were discontinued at the request of the churches. A stage line to Three Rivers was advertised. The Kalamazoo Brass Band, en route to Allegan on its bandwagon, had an accident when the bandwagon ran off the plank road and overturned. Lucy Stone, champion of women's rights, Bayard Taylor, and Horace Greeley were announced as

[18] S. Farmer, *The History of Detroit and Michigan.*

speakers on the lyceum course. A doctor was killed when his horse ran away and threw him from his buggy. A new factory to manufacture sash, doors, and blinds was launched. Several "forty-niners" returned from California. Two new hotels were opened.

RURAL LIFE

But we must not forget the people who lived in the country, for they were more numerous than those who lived in cities. Detroit, the state's largest city, contained 26% of the total population in 1950, but a century earlier it accounted for only 7% of the total for the state. On the farm the rhythm of the seasons and the vagaries of the weather were prime determinants. Each season brought with it a new set of duties for the farmer and his wife, new opportunities for fun to the youngsters, a different set of diseases and ailments to combat, and a new assortment of foods for the table. Spring meant plowing and sowing to the farmer, housecleaning and fresh vegetables for the kitchen to his wife, "school's out" and fishing to the boys, unless they happened to be unfortunate enough to catch the chicken pox, mumps, measles, or whooping cough. In summer came the haying and harvesting, the hardest work of the year. Usually, however, the Fourth of July was taken off as a pleasant interruption, and the whole family climbed aboard a wagon for a trip to a nearby town where political oratory, fireworks, greased-pig and pie-eating contests, and a barbecue commemorated the late unpleasantness with John Bull. Summer had its delights as well as its hard work. Late June was strawberry time, July brought raspberries, and about the first of August that most succulent of all American delicacies, the roasted ear of corn, began to appear on the farmer's table. Watermelons and wild berries were not far behind, only sometimes these were not eaten at the table. All this was delightful if no one in the house got the "summer complaint," the fever and ague, or one of the other common summer diseases. At least one should be well enough in August to go to camp meeting and visit one's neighbors.

Then came the autumn, with its crisp morning air, the haze of eventide, and the glory of the colors on the foliage of the trees. Now the corn was to be cut, shocked, and husked, the potatoes, beans, pumpkins, squash, and cabbage harvested and stored away in the cellar, apples picked, and cider and apple butter made. All through the summer and fall the housewife made preserves, jellies, and jams, dried apples and peaches, and cared for the vegetable garden. If she had an eye for beauty she

Old mill near Howell, Michigan

would also find time to grow some flowers. In the fall the younger contingent of the family made off for school, usually walking from one to four miles morning and night and carrying lunch in a pail. Election day and Thanksgiving were holidays universally observed. Finally winter came, with bitter cold and drifting snow often isolating the farmstead for weeks. But with plenty of potatoes, meat, vegetables, and other foodstuffs on hand there was no need to worry about provender. The farmer kept busy tending his livestock and cutting wood. If he was a wise and careful man he would have at least one and usually two winters' supply of wood on hand, neatly corded near the kitchen door. When the snow came the sleighs were brought out and the family could be carried to church or to a neighbor's house in brave fashion. Your appreciation of the snow varied in direct ratio to your age, but there was no escaping it for anyone, as there is now, by running off to a warmer clime.

Except in the north country, rural areas were not so isolated as they had been in the Territorial period. The railroads, plank roads, and telegraph lines connected the hinterland with the outside world. The farmer did not get a daily paper nor was his mail delivered. Still, he had neighbors not far away and visiting was much in vogue in this pre-movie, pre-radio, pre-TV, and pre-automobile age. The homes of the less strictly religious folk resounded to the music of the fiddle of an evening. While the young folks danced the older ones talked endlessly of crops, politics, or neighborhood events. Revival meetings in the school-house or church, spelling bees, and singing schools were occasions for community gatherings.

A tiny village with two or three stores, a church, a school, a sawmill, a gristmill, and a post office was usually found in each township. In cases where a railroad was built through the village, there were high hopes for growth. A modest hotel would be built, and certain types of specialty stores would appear. Those towns not so fortunate grew less vigorously.

THE CHURCH

A much larger proportion of the people today are church members than in the pre-Civil War period. But even though membership was smaller, the churches exercised a great deal of influence in political and social matters. The Protestant churches of the mid-nineteenth century were more frequently meeting-houses than sanctuaries. Women found an outlet for their interests mainly through church work. Reform movements, social improvement, charity, and relief of poverty largely centered around the church and its agencies. Theological questions were debated with vigor. The several denominations continued to split into new divisions. The Methodist Protestants and the Wesleyan Methodists split away from the Methodist Episcopal Church. The Free-will Baptists separated from the regular Baptists. But the established denominations continued to enjoy a healthy growth in numbers. The Roman Catholics established a separate diocese in the Upper Peninsula in 1857. In the same year the Detroit Conference was separated from the Michigan Conference of the Methodist Episcopal Church. In many towns pretentious church structures were erected, but in rural areas church facilities were modest. Whether their buildings were ornate or simple, the churches were vital and dynamic. They did not hesitate to excommunicate wayward members. They were the centers from which many of the reform movements drew their strength and support. The crusade against slavery was essentially a moral crusade. The Civil War came for several reasons, but the resentment of southern folk against the preachment of the northerners that slavery was evil was certainly one of its major causes.[19]

[19] E. H. Pilcher, *History of Protestantism in Michigan.*

15

A NEW BIRTH OF FREEDOM:
MICHIGAN AND THE CIVIL WAR

The Civil War brought no sharp break in the continuity of Michigan history, but it was such a momentous episode in the lives of the people of the time that afterward they tended to regard it as the dividing point in all their experiences. As Bruce Catton has remarked, the Civil War is even today to most Americans "*the* war." It was punctuated by idealism, high adventure, trial, and tragedy. Afterward, as the veterans grew older they tended to forget the wounds and hardships they had suffered and to remember their service in the Union army or navy as the greatest adventure of their life. Seen in the retrospect of a century, however, the element of tragedy predominates. It was the one major instance in American history in which the usual democratic pattern of settling controversy by compromise and accommodation utterly failed.

Michigan contributed over ninety thousand men to the Union forces. On the home front life was disrupted, though not so seriously as in either World War I or World War II, for the Civil War was not a "total war." The chief problem was the shortage of labor. The farmers received high prices for their products but had to pay much more for what they bought. Labor was caught in the squeeze of prices that rose faster than wages. The war first depressed, then vastly stimulated Michigan mining. Lumbering and railroad building continued. Women did what they could to alleviate the suffering of men at the front by gathering and shipping food and clothing and by helping to supply the needs of the hospitals. To the people of Michigan it was primarily a war to restore the Union. There was strong anti-slavery sentiment in Michigan, but it is doubtful whether the majority of the men who fought were greatly interested in freeing the slaves. At one stage in the war there were even anti-Negro riots in Detroit.

Michigan gave Lincoln a thumping majority in 1860 and stood behind him throughout the war. At its close, due at least in some degree to the influence of Senator Zachariah Chandler, the Republican Party in Michigan supported the radicals in Congress who were bent on a policy of revenge toward the South. The high idealism with which the war had begun was forgotten during the Reconstruction, as were the words of Lincoln urging malice toward none and charity for all.

The road to disunion

When Congress passed the Kansas-Nebraska Act in 1854, opening to slavery immense regions in which it previously had been prohibited, the nation started down the road to disunion. In the years that followed, the Kansas troubles, the Dred Scott decision, and John Brown's raid further heightened sectional animosity. Henry Clay, the great compromiser, was dead; so was Daniel Webster, who in 1850 had alienated his New England followers by coming out for compromise. Extremists in both sections—abolitionists in the North and secessionists in the South—were attracting more followers, although even in 1860 they were still very much in the minority. Most people seemed to believe that somehow a peaceful solution would be found. President James Buchanan and his cabinet were middle-of-the-road men, sincerely attached to the Union, yet disposed to lean over backwards in order to pacify the South.

Already the leading Protestant churches had broken into northern and southern factions. Many professional and business organizations had done the same. The Whig Party was dead; in its place was the Republican Party, a purely sectional aggregation of former Whigs and Democrats. By 1860 one major organization remained to hold together the North and the South: the Democratic Party. If it could decide on a candidate acceptable to both sections, the Union might still continue.

Delegates to the Democratic National Convention assembled in Charleston, South Carolina in late April, 1860. It soon became

apparent that they were sharply divided. The southerners not
only demanded that their right to carry slaves into the territories
be respected, but also that federal laws be passed to secure them
the possession of their slave property there. Northern Democrats
were not willing to go so far. Their champion was Stephen A.
Douglas of Illinois. While he upheld the right of southerners to
take their slaves into the territories, he asserted at the same time
that slavery could not exist without legal protection, which the
territorial legislatures might provide or withhold as they saw fit.
A compromise was sought but none could be found. The floor
leader for Douglas' forces was Charles E. Stuart of Kalamazoo,
Michigan, and according to Avery Craven, an authority on the
Civil War, it was Stuart's speech that made the southern delegates decide to withdraw from the convention. It then adjourned to meet later in Baltimore. When the convention met
again in June the deadlock continued. Finally the southern
delegates once more withdrew and the remaining delegates then
gave the nomination to Douglas. The southern Democrats who
had withdrawn nominated John C. Breckenridge of Kentucky
and confirmed this action a few days later at a convention held
in Richmond, Virginia. The Democratic Party was thus split
asunder.

Before the Democrats had reassembled at Baltimore the Republican National Convention had met and named its candidates.
The Republicans held their convention at Chicago starting May
16 in an immense auditorium called the Wigwam that had just
been built on the lake shore. They demonstrated intense enthusiasm, for they scented victory. The foremost candidate for
the presidential nomination was William H. Seward of New
York. Seward had the complete support of the Michigan delegation. There seem to have been several reasons for Seward's
popularity in Michigan. He was a close friend of Senator Zachariah Chandler, for one thing. His firm attitude on slavery was
popular. He had become known a decade earlier as the defense
attorney for the men arrested in the famous "railroad conspiracy."
And he was from New York, the state in which more than a
quarter of the people of Michigan in 1860 had been born. Trains
carrying New York delegates were greeted with cheers for Seward
at every stop as they crossed Michigan. In Chicago there was
great excitement and a mad scramble to secure space in the
Wigwam, which was built to seat 10,000 and was decorated with
evergreen boughs brought from northern Michigan. Although
Seward was in the lead, he had his enemies, including the influential Horace Greeley, and other states had their favorite

sons. The opponents of Seward were able to prevent his nomination on the first or second ballot. The strongest of the other candidates was Abraham Lincoln of Illinois, and on the third ballot he was nominated. The Michigan delegates swallowed their disappointment and pledged their support to the "rail splitter." Austin Blair, who had been nominated by the Republicans as their candidate for governor, told the convention that Michigan would give Lincoln a 25,000 majority.

The campaign in Michigan was a lively one. Lincoln did not visit the state during the campaign, but Seward spoke in his behalf. In October Douglas appeared at Democratic rallies all across the Lower Peninsula.[1] Newspapers were, as usual, divided between those supporting the Democrats and those backing the Republicans, but whichever side they took it was strong and positive. None were neutral. Political clubs such as the "Wide Awakes" and the "Invincibles" whooped it up for their favorites. Although the contest in Michigan was clearly between the Republicans and the Douglas Democrats, Breckenridge had a few supporters. A small number also worked in behalf of John Bell, who had been nominated by a group of former Whigs on a compromise platform as the candidate of the Constitutional Union Party. The Democrats sought to gain strength by trotting out as their candidate for governor John C. Barry of Constantine, who had been elected to the office three times before. But their efforts were in vain. When the ballots were counted Lincoln and Blair had won a clear victory in Michigan. Lincoln received 87,457 votes to 66,163 for Douglas. Breckenridge was given 805 and Bell received 373. Blair polled a few more votes than did Lincoln, defeating Barry by a margin of 87,806 to 67,221.[2] The Democrats were able to place only two members in the state senate and ten representatives in the house. All four congressmen elected were Republicans.

In the nation as a whole the Republicans also won a decisive victory. Lincoln received 1,800,000 popular votes to 1,300,000 for Douglas, and even though his popular vote was less than the combined popular vote of his three opponents, he received 180 electoral votes to 123 for Douglas, Breckenridge, and Bell combined. Unfortunately, Lincoln did not say immediately after th

[1] T. M. Collier, "William H. Seward in the Campaign of 1860," *Michigan History,* XIX (1935), 91-106; A. S. Brown, "Southwestern Michigan i the Campaign of 1860," *Michigan Heritage,* II (1960), 67-75; F. Streete *op. cit.,* pp. 273-292.

[2] These figures do not include returns from Houghton or Marquet counties. See Streeter, *op. cit.,* p. 292.

election some of the reassuring things he did say in his inaugural the following March, perhaps out of concern for radicals within his own party. Less than seven weeks after the election a convention of delegates in South Carolina unanimously voted for the secession of that state from the Union, and before Lincoln was inaugurated, the rest of the Deep South had followed South Carolina's lead.

THE COMING OF THE WAR

During the four months that elapsed between the election of Lincoln and his inauguration as President, sincere efforts were made to discover some compromise. President Buchanan, although he held that the southern states did not have the right to secede from the Union, concluded there was nothing he could do within the limits of the Constitution to prevent them from doing so. His indecisive policy was no doubt induced also by his recognition of the fact that he would soon be superseded as President by Lincoln. Lewis Cass of Michigan, Buchanan's secretary of state, resigned in disgust and returned to Detroit, where he staunchly upheld the Union cause. Lincoln gave little indication during these critical months of what his policy would be, and it is probable that he did not know himself for some time. The Republican Party was split between those who were receptive to some sort of compromise that would guarantee slavery in the states where it already was established as a gesture of conciliation to the South, and those who were opposed to any compromise. This also no doubt played its part in causing Lincoln to hesitate to take a positive stand. During the interim efforts to discover a satisfactory compromise included the holding of the so-called Washington Peace Conference, over which former president John Tyler presided. But it failed, chiefly because the majority of the Republicans were unwilling to barter away what they had won in the election.

Michigan's Republican leaders were opposed to compromise. Retiring Governor Moses Wisner, in his farewell address on January 1, 1861, said, "This is no time for timid and vacillating counsels when the cry of treason and rebellion is ringing in our ears. . . ." And the incoming governor, Austin Blair, was equally positive in his stand that stern measures were called for. He warned in his inaugural address that the Union "must be preserved and the laws must be enforced in all parts of it at whatever cost," adding that "secession is revolution and revolution in the overt act is treason and must be treated as such." The legislature, heeding his recommendation, passed a resolution pledging the military power and the material resources of Michigan to the support of the United States government. In Washington Senator Zachariah Chandler was in the forefront of those who opposed any compromise; it was in February that he wrote his famous opinion that "without a little bloodletting this Union will not, in my estimation, be worth a rush."

Lincoln's inaugural address was conciliatory, but it contained a hint of how the new President planned to deal with secession. He pleaded with the South to remember all the Union had meant, and assured southerners of his determination not to disturb the institution of slavery where it already existed. But he warned that he would "hold, possess, and occupy, the property and places belonging to the Government. . . ." The Confederate states had already taken over most of the federal forts, navy yards, and custom houses within their borders when Lincoln spoke these words. Fort Pickens and Fort Sumter, however, remained in federal hands. It was Lincoln's announced plan to bring supplies into Fort Sumter that precipitated the crisis. There can be little question that Lincoln understood this probably would be resisted, but he could accept no alternative. When Lincoln's decision was made known in South Carolina, a demand was sent to Major Robert Anderson that the fort be evacuated. Anderson agreed to evacuate by April 15 if he did not receive other orders or relief in the meantime. This was not accepted, and at 4:30 a.m. on April 12 the bombardment of the fort began.

The three-month mirage

Three days after the firing on Fort Sumter President Lincoln issued his call to the states to furnish 75,000 men for three-months' duty to suppress "combinations" in seven states opposing the laws. The brief term of service the President stipulated helped support a widespread belief in the North that a show of force would compel the southern states to return to the Union. That belief persisted until July 17, 1861, when the Union army in the first major battle of the Civil War suffered a crushing and humiliating defeat. This battle, the first battle of Bull Run, rudely shattered the mirage of an easy victory.

Governor Blair was at his home in Jackson when he received Lincoln's telegram requesting Michigan to furnish one regiment of ten companies (800-1,000 men) as its quota of the 75,000 volunteers. The governor at once went to Detroit where he took counsel with Adjutant General John Robertson, civil officials and men with military experience on how Michigan could meet its obligation. It would be necessary not only to enlist the volunteers, but also to arm, clothe, and equip them. There were no funds available in the state treasury for this purpose. Governor Blair had already called the legislature into special session on May 7, but that was too long to wait. Accordingly, an effort was launched to raise $100,000 by private subscription as a loan to the state. The sum of $81,020 was obtained in this manner.[3] On April 16 Blair issued his call for ninety-day volunteers, and the Adjutant General was instructed to accept the first ten uniformed militia companies that offered their services. There were at the time a total of 28 companies with a strength of 1,241 officers and men in the state militia. But these companies were really local rather than state organizations. The state had spent less than $3,000 a year for military purposes. Actually the militia companies, with such high-sounding names as the Detroit Light Guard, Michigan Hussars, Coldwater Cadets, Flint Union Greys, and Hudson Artillery, were more social than military organizations. Before the war they often took part in parades and drills, frequently visiting other cities and towns. When the call to arms came, however, they responded with zest and enthusiasm. Within their ranks were a number of West Point graduates and veterans of the Mexican War. These men formed the backbone of the state's initial military effort.[4]

In addition to the men belonging to these military organizations hundreds of others hurried to volunteer. While volunteers were being recruited and drilled, citizenry all over the state held mass meetings to show their support for the Union cause. In Detroit a flag-raising ceremony on April 18 and a meeting three days later at which the oath of allegiance was administered to all civil and military officials were occasions for an outpouring of public sentiment in behalf of the Union. At a mass meeting held in Kalamazoo on April 16, members of both political parties voted unanimously that the rebellion must be resisted and put down by force of arms. By the end of that day 45 men had enlisted, the first being a 17-year-old youth named William Shakespeare.

The general order forming the First Michigan Infantry Regiment was issued on April 24. The Detroit Light Guard was to constitute Company A, while the other companies were to be made up of the Jackson Greys, Coldwater Cadets, Manchester Union Guard, Steuben Guard (Ann Arbor), Ypsilanti Light Guard, Marshall Light Guard, and the Hardee Cadets (Adrian). Older

[3] J. Robertson, *Michigan in the War*, pp. 17-21.
[4] F. Woodford, *Father Abraham's Children*, pp. 17-24.

members of these organizations, in many cases, resigned, and the ranks were filled with younger volunteers. The regimental officers were named in the April 24 order. Commander was to be Colonel Orlando Willcox of Detroit, a graduate of West Point who had seen service in the Mexican War and on the western plains. By April 29 all ten companies of the regiment had arrived at Fort Wayne in Detroit. Experienced military officers at once started an intensive training of the men in military discipline, use of fire arms, drill, and battle formations. Friends and relatives were allowed to visit the fort and witnessed frequent drills and parades. On May 1 the men were formally inducted into the federal service, and on the same day the first consignment of rifles arrived. Soon afterward uniforms were provided. The flamboyant uniforms of the individual companies had to be discarded and shipped home. An impressive ceremony was held in the heart of Detroit on Campus Martius May 11, when the ladies of the city presented the regiment with its colors. Two days afterward two steamships drew alongside the fort, and the men of the First Regiment, numbering 789, went aboard to begin the first leg of their journey to Washington.

At Cleveland the regiment was transferred to railroad cars. In that city and at others along the way large crowds greeted the Michigan recruits. Delegations brought good things to eat, and pretty girls bestowed locks of their hair and an occasional kiss upon the gallant Michiganians. It was at ten o'clock on the evening of May 16 that the regiment arrived in Washington—one month and one day after Lincoln's call for troops. It was the first regiment from the area west of the Alleghenies to reach the national capital and its arrival reassured the President that the western states would remain loyal. He is said to have exclaimed "Thank God for Michigan."[5]

The First Michigan received its first assignment on May 23 It was ordered to cross the Potomac and to occupy the town o Alexandria. A company of New York Zouaves were sent by wate to arrive at the same time as the Michigan troops marched in No organized resistance was encountered but the commander c the Zouaves, 24-year-old Elmer Ellsworth, was killed by th proprietor of a hotel, a rabid southern supporter, after Ellswort had hauled down the Confederate flag that flew atop the build ing. Back in Michigan Willcox's "victory" was roundly cheere and was taken as further confirmation of the belief that th rebellion would be easily suppressed.

[5] *Ibid.*, pp. 25-30.

The First Michigan included only a few of the men who clamored to get into the fight. The Second Michigan Infantry Regiment was formed under an order of Adjutant General John Robertson dated April 25, 1861. It consisted of uniformed militia companies except for those comprised of Kalamazoo and Niles volunteers. The Regiment was called into service for three months, but on May 3 President Lincoln, in calling for 42,000 more recruits, changed the term to three years. Accordingly, the men in the Second Michigan Infantry were re-enlisted for the longer period, those not willing to do so being allowed to withdraw. Men in this regiment came from Battle Creek, Flint, Niles, Kalamazoo, Constantine, Hudson, and Detroit. Throughout the war companies were made up of friends and neighbors from the same community, a practice abandoned in later conflicts. The Third Infantry Regiment was mustered into state service May 21, and into federal service June 10. It consisted largely of men from Grand Rapids, Lansing, and Muskegon. The Fourth Infantry Regiment, largely recruited from communities in Monroe, Lenawee, Hillsdale, Washtenaw, and Branch counties, was mustered into the United States service June 20. The companies of the Second Regiment, like those of the First, were assembled at Fort Wayne in Detroit before starting for the East. The Third and Fourth were transported directly to Washington from their points of "rendezvous" at Grand Rapids and Adrian, respectively. The period of training for the men in these regiments was very brief; all three had arrived in Washington by June 25.

And now throughout the North the cry was "On to Richmond!" With 80,000 troops in the vicinity of Washington an insistent demand for action was heard. General Winfield Scott, the nation's highest ranking military officer, advised delay until the troops could be better trained, but his caution was attributed to his advanced age. President Lincoln, reasoning that Union troops were probably as well prepared as the Confederates, ordered General Irvin McDowell to strike a blow. The result was the Battle of Bull Run, fought on July 21. The First Michigan was in the thick of the fight. Six of its members were killed in battle, 37 were wounded, and 70 were reported captured or missing. Its commanding officer, Colonel Willcox, suffered a severe wound and was taken prisoner. Although the Union forces were at first successful, the Confederates counterattacked, and the Union retreat turned into a rout. The Second and Third Michigan Infantry Regiments were not in the battle but helped cover the retreat. Members of Congress, including Michigan's Senator Zachariah Chandler, who had come out in carriages to watch the

battle, scurried back to Washington. The illusion that the business
of suppressing the secessionists would be something in the nature
of a summer lark was shattered. It was a testing time for the
people of the North. No attempt was made to minimize the loss.
There were voices of despair, but the great majority of the people
simply accepted the hard fact that the task ahead was likely to
be long and difficult. Now it was in the South that overconfidence
was manifested. Seen in retrospect, the defeat at Bull Run was
salutary to the Union cause.

THOSE WHO FOUGHT

More than 90,000 Michigan men served in the Union army
and navy during the Civil War.[6] This was approximately 23%
of the male population according to the census of 1860. Included
were 1,661 Negroes, of whom about one-quarter came from Canada. A colored Infantry Regiment was raised in 1863. Michigan
troops also included 145 Indians. Many who were not United
States citizens fought for the Union cause. The Michigan con-
tingents included 3,929 Irishmen, 4,872 Germans, and 3,761 Englishmen. Michigan, which ranked tenth among the northern states
in population, ranked eighth in the number of troops furnished.
Michigan raised thirty regiments of infantry, eleven of cavalry,
one of engineers, one of artillery, and one of sharp-shooters. An
estimated 483 men from Michigan served in the navy. The number
of Michigan regiments was relatively small in proportion to the
total number who served as compared with other states. This
is accounted for by the practice in Michigan of keeping its regiments intact by filling those whose ranks became depleted with
fresh recruits rather than organizing the latter into new regiments.[7]

Enthusiasm for the cause and a yen for adventure characterized
the early volunteers. As the war advanced it became more difficult
to supply the needed manpower. Various methods were employed
to encourage enlistments. The legislature authorized townships to
raise by taxation funds to pay $15 per month to each family whose
breadwinner had gone to war. Individuals, local governmental
units, and finally the state paid bounties to volunteers. Although
Congress enacted a draft law in 1863, only 4,281 Michigan men

[6] Computations of the exact number vary. The War Department in 1865
reported the number to be 90,048. The State Adjutant General in 1882
computed 90,747, but stated this total did not include Michigan men enlisted in the regiments of other states.

[7] Woodford, *op. cit.,* p. 251. See also Robertson, *op. cit.*

were actually inducted by conscription. There was a great deal of social pressure on able-bodied men to enlist. The practice of raising companies consisting largely of men living in the same community encouraged friends to enlist together. It was possible for a draftee to hire a substitute or obtain exemption by a payment of $300, but relatively few took advantage of this undemocratic feature of Civil War conscription.

Of those who went to war about one out of seven did not return. Michigan men who died in service numbered 13,985. Among the enlisted men nearly three times as many died of disease as were killed in action or died from wounds. Most of the military hospitals were hardly better than pesthouses; physicians and surgeons were too few, and they had no knowledge of the importance of sanitation and antiseptics. Losses among officers tell a different story: 262 were killed in action or died of wounds, while only 96 died of disease. Whether this difference was due to better food, better living conditions, or better care is hard to tell.

Michigan men served in every section of the front and on the sea. We hear of them in the Peninsular campaign, at Antietam, Shiloh, Fredericksburg, Chancellorsville, Gettysburg, Vicksburg, on the Mississippi, on the "March through Georgia," around Richmond, and at Appomattox. They took part in more than eight hundred battles and skirmishes. Hundreds of examples of individual heroism can be found in the records of these engagements.

Michigan regiments played a crucial role in some of the war's major battles. The 24th Michigan Infantry, part of the famed Iron Brigade, was in the thick of the first day's fighting at Gettysburg. By staving off an overwhelmingly superior Confederate force, the Iron Brigade gave the Union commander, General George Meade, time to bring up the rest of his army and to occupy those positions that the picked men of General Robert E. Lee's Army of Northern Virginia were to assault in vain on the third and decisive day of the great battle. The 24th Michigan suffered 80% casualties in this engagement, a higher rate than any of the 400 Union regiments that took part in the three-day struggle. The First, Fifth, Sixth, and Seventh Michigan Cavalry regiments also had an important part in the Union victory at Gettysburg. They constituted the Michigan Cavalry Brigade commanded by General George A. Custer, of Monroe, Michigan, as dashing and flamboyant a figure as the war produced. He was only two years out of West Point and 24 years old when destiny assigned him to meet in combat the Confederate cavalry general Jeb Stuart, an equally picturesque figure. Stuart had failed in his major responsibility of keeping General Lee informed as to the location and movements of the

Union army, and hoped to retrieve his failure by assaulting the rear of Meade's army at the moment of Pickett's charge, thus assuring the South a great victory. In this design he was foiled by General Custer and his Michigan cavalrymen. A cavalry charge launched by Stuart in the classic manner was turned back by the sabers of Custer's horsemen, and Meade's army was thus shielded and assured of victory in the greatest battle of the war.

The year before, on the bloody battlefield of Antietam, 350 Michigan men were killed, wounded, or missing. General Israel B. Richardson of Pontiac, who had entered the service as commander of the Second Michigan Infantry and had been promoted to the rank of major general just before Antietam, was killed while leading a charge in Bloody Lane. The Seventh Michigan Infantry was part of the brigade that crossed the Rappahannock under fire at the start of the Battle of Fredericksburg in December, 1862. Michigan regiments also took part in the western battles of 1862. The Twelfth Michigan, commanded by Colonel Francis Quinn of Niles, fought in the bloody battle of Shiloh. The Third Cavalry and Fifteenth Infantry were commended by General William Rosecrans for their courage, efficiency, and gallantry in the Iuka-Corinth campaign. Michigan cavalry, infantry, engineers, mechanics, and artillery helped turn back the Confederate invasion of Kentucky at the Battle of Perryville. And late in December six Michigan infantry regiments and one cavalry regiment saw action in the Battle of Murfreesboro, where the casualties amounted to nearly one-third of those engaged on both sides.

In July, 1863, while Michigan soldiers were fighting at Gettysburg, others were with General Grant in the siege of Vicksburg. Seven Michigan regiments had arrived to strengthen Grant's forces prior to the start of the 45-day siege. The following September eight Michigan regiments, together with units of Michigan's First Light Artillery and First Engineers and Mechanics, took part in the fierce fighting at Chickamauga. Battery A, First Michigan Light Artillery, a unit organized at Coldwater, suffered frightful losses and its commander, George W. Van Pelt of Coldwater, was killed in a Confederate attack that overran the battery. Eight Michigan regiments helped win the Battle of Chattanooga and to retrieve the loss suffered at Chickamauga.

Viewing the war in retrospect, it is apparent that Gettysburg and Vicksburg were the turning points, but this was far from being apparent at the time. In many respects the darkest days of the war for the Union cause came in 1864. Heavy casualties necessitated a call for more men. General Sherman's army, which included fifteen Michigan regiments, battled it out with the Confederates in Georgia, finally capturing Atlanta and then marching across Georgia to the sea in one of the dramatic exploits of the war. The heaviest losses occurred in the Battles of the Wilderness in the East, where General Grant gradually pushed the Confederates under Lee into Richmond and Petersburg. At Spotsylvania, the Seventeenth Michigan Infantry lost 190 out of 225 men in a single attack. Once the Confederates threw up their defenses around the Confederate capital and Petersburg, the Union advance was stalled. At one juncture, a tunnel was dug underneath the Confederate works, four tons of powder were exploded, and Union soldiers rushed forward. The attack, which was poorly organized and ended in dismal failure, was made by a force that included six regiments of Michigan infantry. Enemy artillery slaughtered scores of men in the "crater" formed by the explosion. But in the cavalry battles around Richmond that summer the Confederacy lost its most colorful and romantic figure, General Jeb Stuart. At a place called Yellow Tavern a bullet fired by a Michigan trooper named John A. Huff, who had enlisted at Pontiac February 10, 1864 and was serving in the Fifth Michigan Cavalry, ended Stuart's life only one day over three months from the date Huff enlisted.

The collapse of the Confederacy quickly followed the surrender of General Lee to General Grant at Appomattox on April 9, 1865. Even so, there were Michigan soldiers who gave their lives afterward in the fighting in South Carolina before Johnson surrendered to Sherman on April 26. The Fourth Michigan Calvary, which had left Michigan in September, 1862 under the command of Colonel Robert H. G. Minty of Detroit, after distinguishing itself in many of the battles fought in the West, found itself at the close of the war in the Deep South. Colonel Benjamin D. Prichard of Allegan had become its commander. Shortly after the regiment had occupied Macon, Georgia, Prichard learned that Confederate President Jefferson Davis, after fleeing from Richmond, had traveled southward and was somewhere in south central Georgia. On May 7 Prichard entered Irwinville about one o'clock in the morning in search of Davis. There he received information that the Confederate leader and his party were camped about a mile and a half away. The place was located and surrounded. Davis, attempting to flee, reached for a coat to put over his shoulders and by mistake took his wife's coat. This is what gave rise to the story that when captured Davis was dressed in women's clothing. Prichard delivered his famous prisoner to Fortress Monroe, Virginia.[8]

[8] A convenient source of information concerning the record of Michigan soldiers in the Civil War is Robertson, *op. cit.* This work contains a brief

A SOLDIER'S LIFE

From the hundreds of letters and diaries that have been preserved, a great deal of information is available on what life was like for a Michigan soldier during the Civil War.[9] In the early months of the war men entered the service lightheartedly, with no conception of what the life of a soldier would be like. Letters home reflect the disillusionment that came with endless drilling, long marches, poor food, bad weather, the tedium of life in the camps during winter, and sickness. The men were impatient to get on with the fighting, and the imminence of action, even though it entailed danger, was viewed with relief. As the going got rougher, there were desertions and "bounty jumping." The sizable bounties offered to volunteers tempted men already in the ranks to desert, return home, and re-enlist. Of course some were caught and punished, but this did not deter others from trying. Many Michigan men were captured and imprisoned at Richmond, Andersonville, or one of the other Confederate prisons where lack of good food, poor sanitation, and disease took many lives. Accounts written after the war recall attempts to escape, sometimes successful, sometimes not.[10]

The ranks of Michigan soldiers included at least one woman. She was Sarah Emma Edmonds, who enlisted at Flint in 1861 disguised as a man under the name of Franklin Thompson. For some years she had masqueraded as a man, and at the time of

history of each regiment and the roster of officers. A history of each of the Michigan regiments, with a roster of privates as well as officers, was published by the Michigan Adjutant General's Office under the general title *Record of Service of Michigan Volunteers in the Civil War, 1861-1865.* Any citizen may obtain photostats of the military record of a soldier by securing application blanks from the General Services Administration, Washington, D. C., filling out the same, and sending them back with $1.00. General histories of Michigan in the Civil War include F. Woodford, *op. cit.;* F. D. Williams, *Michigan Soldiers in the Civil War;* P. P. Mason and P. J. Pentecost, *From Bull Run to Appomattox.* There are many works on individual regiments. Among these are D. L. Smith, *The Twenty-fourth Michigan of the Iron Brigade;* C. W. Owen, *The First Michigan Infantry;* J. G. Vale, *Minty and the Cavalry;* J. H. Kidd, *Personal Recollections of a Cavalryman;* B. M. Cutcheon, *The Story of the Twentieth Michigan Infantry.* For further sources, consult G. S. May, *A Bibliography of Printed Sources on Michigan and the Civil War.*

[9] I. C. Brown's *Michigan Men in the Civil War* contains a list of manuscript materials available in the University of Michigan Collections.

[10] See D. Arnold, *A Kalamazoo Volunteer in the Civil War;* A. S. Brown, (ed.), *A Soldier's Life;* A. Williams, *From the Cannon's Mouth;* W. Gardner, "Civil War Letters," *Michigan History,* I (1917), 3-18; R. Kirk, "A Michigan Soldier's Diary, 1863," *Michigan History,* XXVIII (1944), 231-245.

her enlistment was working as a Bible salesman. She took part in several battles and skirmishes as a member of the Second Michigan Infantry. Probably because of poor health she deserted in April, 1863. Her identity was finally revealed in 1882 when she applied for a pension, although there is some evidence that while she was still in the army some of her fellow soldiers knew her secret. She wrote a book describing her adventures entitled *Nurse and Spy in the Union Army*. It is a collection of tall tales that stretch the credulity of the reader. A special congressional committee examined her claim for a pension. She was granted an honorable discharge back-dated to April 19, 1863, and was granted a pension. After the war she married and bore three children. She was accepted into membership in the Grand Army of the Republic—the only woman ever received into full membership by that organization. She died in Texas in 1898.[11]

A total of 181 soldiers of the Jewish faith served in Michigan regiments during the war. This was a remarkable number when it is noted that there were only about 150 Jewish families in Michigan when the war began. The Jewish Civil War soldiers included 11 commissioned officers, and 38 died of disease or were killed in action.[12] The number of Negro soldiers from Michigan who were in the Union army (1,661) is surprisingly large in proportion to the Negro population of the state, even though about a quarter of these came over from Canada to enlist. In contrast, the number of Indians from Michigan who were soldiers (145) was small. There appears to have been some reluctance to enlist Indians because of the fear that they would not be adaptable to "civilized" warfare.[13] The state's foreign population bore its full share of the burden of war. The percentage of Germans and Irish from Michigan in the Union forces was larger than that of the native-born.

A yearning for home was a common experience of men at the front. The great adventure had dimmed, and life back in Michigan that had seemed dull when the excitement of war was new now took on an aura of glamor. This is reflected not only in the letters the soldiers wrote home, but also in the songs they sang. Shortly after the Battle of Fredericksburg a Detroit woman, Winifred Lee Brent, composed words for a song to be sung to the old German tune "O Tannenbaum," which also was used for the song "Maryland, my Maryland." The verses to the song were first printed on a

---

[11] B. Fladeland, "Alias Franklin Thompson," *Michigan History*, XLII (1958), 435-462; "New Light on Sarah Emma Edmonds, Alias Frank Thompson," *ibid.*, XLVII (1963), 357-363.
[12] I. I. Katz, *The Jewish Soldier from Michigan in the Civil War*.
[13] Woodford, *op. cit.*, p. 252.

leaflet, then printed in the *Detroit Tribune* and later reprinted and published for the army at the front. The song became immensely popular both in Michigan and among the state's soldiers in the various sectors of the war. The first verse provided a nostalgic introduction:

> Home of my heart, I sing to thee!
> Michigan, my Michigan.
> Thy lake-bound shores I long to see,
> Michigan, my Michigan.
> From Saginaw's tall whispering pines
> To Lake Superior's farthest mines,
> Fair in the light of memory shines,
> Michigan, my Michigan.

There were ten verses in all, many of which centered around famous battles of the war.

> Dark rolled the Rappahannock's flood,
> Michigan, my Michigan.
> The tide was crimsoned with thy blood,
> Michigan, my Michigan.
> Although for us the day was lost,
> Still it shall be our proudest boast,
> At Fredericksburg the Seventh crossed,
> Michigan, my Michigan.[14]

THE HOME FRONT

In Michigan life went on much as usual during the war. New railroads were built, lumbering operations were continued, and manufacturing and mining developed rapidly in spite of the shortage of labor. The farmers went on about their daily tasks, working overtime and enlisting the aid of older men, boys, women, and new kinds of farm machinery. Prices rose rapidly, wages more slowly, a fact that encouraged the spread of organized labor. Capitalists dealt with sums that would have been thought fantastic a

[14] Michigan has no official state song, but "Michigan, my Michigan," to the tune of "O Tannenbaum," is the one most widely sung. In 1902 the poet Douglas McCulloch composed new words that could be sung to the familiar tune, and these are the ones most generally used today. A different tune was widely promoted, but never attained the popularity of "O Tannenbaum," partly because its range was too great. See *Mich. Pioneer and Historical Colls.*, XXXV (1907), 155-170 for the story of the original song and a copy of all its verses. For music and words of the new version, see the *Golden Book of Song*.

few years before. Industrialists stepped up production and made fabulous profits. Business after the war never reverted to the leisurely pace of the years before 1861.

Women were busy preparing bandages and clothing for soldiers, organizing themselves for that purpose into "Soldiers' Aid Societies."[15] These activities, together with recruiting, kept the war constantly before the people. Newspapers were read avidly, and the number of dailies increased. Probably thousands of people first acquired the habit of reading a daily newspaper during the war.

The war proved to be a great impetus to the use of labor-saving machinery on the farm. The demand for reapers and mowers was so great that at times it could not be met. Improved harrows, wheat drills, gang plows, horse rakes, cultivators, threshing machines, and stump lifters helped alleviate the lack of male labor. It became a familiar sight to see women working in the fields. In spite of the shortage of workers, the war brought prosperity to Michigan farmers such as they had never known before. Bumper crops enabled them to send large shipments of wheat, corn, oats, and rye to feed the Union armies. The price of wheat had reached $1.84 a bushel by 1864. One of the most spectacular wartime agricultural developments in Michigan was the enormous increase in the production of hops. A heavy tax on whisky and a growing taste for lager beer heightened the demand for hops, a major ingredient in the brewing of beer. A series of crop failures in New York, the leading producer of hops, further stimulated the growth of hops in Michigan. The cutoff in supplies of southern cotton increased the demand for wool, while the loss of Louisiana cane sugar stimulated the growth of corn sorghum for molasses. The production of butter and cheese in creameries was another outgrowth of the war.[16]

One method by which the labor-shortage problem was solved was bringing in immigrants. The population of the state increased by 435,169 during the decade of the 'sixties, and it is estimated that at least 90,000 of that number were foreign immigrants.[17] The newcomers not only found employment on the farms but also in lumbering, mining, and railroad building. During the first two years of the war the number of foreign immigrants declined. The passage of the Homestead Act of 1862 helped to reverse the trend, and in 1864 Congress passed a contract labor law, permitting

[15] Michigan Civil War Centennial Observance Commission, *Michigan Women in the Civil War*.

[16] R. H. Sewell, "Michigan Farmers and the Civil War," *Michigan History*, XLIV (1960), 353-374.

[17] *Ibid.*, 357.

immigrants to be brought to the United States under contract to labor for the person or persons who paid for their passage. By 1863 the number of newcomers was above the level of 1860, and it continued to increase during the next two years.

During the first year of the war the copper-mining industry in Michigan was beset by several difficult problems. The price of the metal had dropped to 17¢ a pound; 20¢ was considered a fair price. The domestic market was disorganized and Confederate privateers threatened to cut off the foreign market. But recovery came fast. As government orders for brass buttons, copper canteens, bronze cannon, and naval equipment began to accumulate, prices rose. They were up to 46.3¢ a pound by 1864. Producing mines paid their owners fabulous profits. New discoveries were made during the war that led to the formation of the Calumet and Hecla Mining Company and others. The number of companies increased from sixteen in 1860 to 36 in 1865. Oddly enough, production did not keep pace with higher prices; in fact, it fell by a million and a half pounds in 1862, another half-million in 1863, and still another half-million in 1864. The reason seems to be that the scarce labor supply was being diverted to the development of new mines that had not yet come into full production.[18] The labor shortage was so acute that mine-owners contributed a pool of $90,000 for a young Swedish engineer who promised to go to Europe and bring back workers. The workers were to be divided among the contributors, and deductions from their wages were to reimburse their employers. The young Swede, named Silverspar, managed to get well over a hundred Swedes, Norwegians, and Finns as far as Detroit, but on the ship en route to the Upper Peninsula an army recruiter got some of them away from him. It was rumored that some of the men were long-term prisoners in Sweden whose release for immigration to America had been secured from the Swedish government.[19] In spite of the falloff in production, 70% of the nation's copper during the Civil War came from Michigan.[20]

The iron-ore industry, like the copper-mining industry, had a lean year in 1861. Production at all the mines declined drastically. This may have been due partly to labor shortage, but it is also attributed to the fact that Cleveland, the main market for Michigan ore, had a large surplus on hand at the beginning of the year and buyers ceased purchasing additional supplies due to the uncertain-

---

[18] W. B. Gates, *Michigan Copper and Boston Dollars,* pp. 15-18.
[19] A. B. Lindley, "The Copper Tariff of 1869," *Michigan History,* XXXV (1951), 4-5.
[20] Gates, *op. cit.,* p. 18.

ties at the beginning of the war. Recovery in iron production, however, was even more rapid than in copper. In 1862 the leading mines (the Jackson, Cleveland, and Lake Superior mines) produced more ore than in any previous year.[21] Production increased thereafter, stimulated by wartime demand.

The lumber industry was hit even harder at the opening of the war than iron and copper mining. The market was glutted at the outbreak of hostilities. The war emergency made it difficult for the lumbermen to secure capital with which to conduct their business.[22] Nor did the lumber business fully recover until after the war. Labor shortage was acute, and higher wages had to be paid to workmen. The price of lumber went up, however, almost doubling by 1865. Henry H. Crapo, a Flint lumberman (later to become governor of Michigan), was able in 1863, for the first time in his career, to build up a substantial and uncommitted cash balance. In part this was due to his ability to supply seasoned lumber for the construction of salt vats and salt works in nearby Saginaw.[23]

The state legislature in 1859 considered a bill introduced by Senator James Birney of Saginaw to pay a bounty of 10¢ a barrel for the production of salt. The proposal was subjected to ridicule, apparently because the lawmakers did not believe salt could be produced in Michigan. An anonymous joker suggested an amendment to make the bounty 10¢ *a bushel*, and the bill was passed and signed by the governor in that form. A company of investors promptly bored a well in East Saginaw, erected the necessary facilities for evaporating the brine, produced 10,772 barrels of five bushels each the first year, and tripled their production the following year (July 1, 1861-June 30, 1862). The legislature hastened to repeal the bounty law. Cordwood was used to evaporate the brine. The business was not profitable after the cancellation of the state bounty, until the sawmills began using scrap lumber as fuel to evaporate the brine.[24] Then production increased at a rapid rate. By 1880 Michigan was supplying half the salt of the nation.

Railroad building slackened during the war but did not stop. In the Upper Peninsula a line from Escanaba to Negaunee was built between 1862 and 1864. A twenty-mile stretch of the railroad from Marquette to Ontonagon was completed in 1865. In the

[21] H. Brinks, "The Effect of the Civil War in 1861 on Michigan Lumbering and Mining Industries," *Michigan History*, XLIV (1960), 103-105.

[22] *Ibid.*, p. 106.

[23] M. D. Lewis, *Lumberman from Flint*, p. 122.

[24] W. L. Webber, "Discovery and Development of the Salt Interest in the Saginaw Valley," *Mich. Pioneer and Historical Colls.*, III (1881), 13-23.

Lower Peninsula, towns and cities voted funds to attract railroads. In 1863 the legislature passed the first act empowering a municipality to use public credit for grants to a railroad. Twelve other such acts were passed in 1864 and eight more in 1865. So general was the belief that the growth and prosperity of a town depended on a railroad that citizens were willing to pledge thousands of dollars to induce the railroad builders to extend lines to their community. In the Lower Peninsula a railroad northward from Jackson to Mason was built during the Civil War. The Flint and Pere Marquette Railroad, connecting Saginaw and Flint, was completed in 1862. In 1863-64 Henry H. Crapo headed a company that built another line connecting Flint with the Detroit and Milwaukee Railroad. In spite of a delay in construction due to a strike of workmen, the line was completed by November 1, 1864.

The Civil War stimulated manufacturing in Michigan. Between 1860 and 1870 the number of manufacturing establishments increased by 174% and the amount of capital invested by 201%.[25] In Detroit the Michigan Car Company, the Detroit Bridge and Iron Works, the Detroit Safe Company, and the E. T. Barnum Wire and Iron Works were among the plants started during the war. In 1864-65 the Detroit Board of Trade built a large new structure. A law passed by the legislature in 1863 permitted the manufacture of beer in spite of the 1855 prohibition law, and this legislation resulted in the launching of many breweries. Following the passage of the National Bank Law by Congress in 1863, national banks were founded in several Michigan cities, the first being the First National Bank of Kalamazoo. Three national banks had been launched in Detroit by the end of the war. The accumulation of capital in the rich agricultural counties of southern Michigan as a result of high prices for farm products helped finance the establishment of factories in the cities and towns of the area.

One of the annoying features of wartime life was the scarcity of small change. When the government ceased to redeem its paper currency in gold or silver, individuals and banks hoarded the coins that had been in circulation. At first postage stamps were used for change, but the gummed backs were a nuisance and ungummed stamps were substituted. Finally came the issue of "shin plaster" paper, so called because its size was only two by three inches. It was issued in denominations of 5, 10, 25, and 50¢.

Michigan remained overwhelmingly loyal to the Union cause throughout the war. There was little trouble with "copper-heads." Politically, the Democrats, while making gains during the war, were

[25] S. Glazer, "The Beginnings of the Economic Revolution in Michigan," *Michigan History*, XXXIV (1950), 194.

unable to score any major victories. Governor Blair was re-elected in 1862, with a majority reduced from 20,000 to 6,000. Two of the six congressmen elected from Michigan that year were Democrats. In the presidential election of 1864 Lincoln's margin of victory over his Democratic opponent, General George B. McClellan, in the civilian vote was less than 11,000, whereas in 1860 he had won by almost 24,000. However, Michigan soldiers, permitted to cast absentee ballots by special act of the legislature, supported Lincoln, 9,402 to 2,959. The Republicans nominated Henry H. Crapo of Flint as their candidate for governor in 1864. His majority over the Democratic candidate, counting the soldier vote, was over 17,000. He was the first of the "lumber barons" to serve as the state's chief executive. Only one Democratic congressman was elected in 1864. Jacob M. Howard and Zachariah Chandler were Michigan's two United States senators during the war; both were Republicans.

Michigan's wartime governor, Austin Blair, was a native of New York and was but 43 years of age when he became chief executive. He supported the Lincoln administration vigorously, and his energy and foresight did much to keep Michigan in the forefront of the loyal states. He spared no effort to provide the needed supplies and equipment for Michigan soldiers enlisting in the army. He spent his own funds in behalf of the cause and left the capital a poorer man than when he entered upon the duties of his office. A bronze statue of Blair was later erected at the chief entrance to the Capitol in Lansing, a merited tribute to a great leader.

There was much activity on the home front on behalf of the soldiers and sailors from the state. A "Michigan Soldiers' Relief Association" was formed in Washington, D. C. to take care of the emergency needs of Michigan troops in the Army of the Potomac. Contributions of money, clothing, and hospital stores were made by the people back home and forwarded to the national capital. Among the services of this organization was the maintenance of a hostel in Washington, which went under the inelegant name of the "Michigan Soup House" and provided food and lodging for soldiers on leave. Back in Michigan the "Michigan Soldiers' Relief Association" was formed in April, 1862. This organization collected and sent to the front hundreds of boxes and barrels filled with food and clothing for Michigan soldiers, including such items as socks, underwear, handkerchiefs, canned fruit, pickles, jellies, and wines. Newspapers, books, needles, pins, thread, and other items the people back in Michigan thought the soldiers might need were included. The army maintained hospitals for sick and wounded soldiers and each regiment had its surgeon. The United States Sanitary Commission was formed to assist the government in this work. A Michigan branch of the Sanitary Commission was formed in Detroit in November, 1861, known as the Michigan Soldiers' Aid Society. In various towns Ladies' Soldiers' Aid Societies were active. The one in Kalamazoo staged a big "Sanitary Fair" in the fall of 1864. A state fair was held in Kalamazoo both in 1863 and 1864, and it was in connection with this event in 1864 that the ladies of Kalamazoo originated a plan to enlist state-wide support for the various soldiers' aid societies. Merchandise, produce, farm animals, and implements were contributed and sold for the benefit of the cause. The torn and battle-scarred flags of Michigan regiments were displayed, and Governor Blair gave the opening address. Over $9,000 was raised. The United States Christian Commission was another wartime organization that received help from Michigan. Bibles and religious literature were collected and sent to the front; "delegates," mostly ministers, volunteered to serve in the army hospitals for a period of six weeks to comfort the sick and dying.[26]

The firm support the people of Michigan gave the Lincoln administration was based primarily on a determination that the Union must be restored. There appears to have been little enthusiasm for freeing the slaves among most of the civilians and soldiers at the outset of the war. Lincoln's primary object in the early months of the war was to keep the border slave states in the Union, and to promote this he steadfastly refused to make the war into a crusade against slavery. When the President revoked an order by General John C. Fremont freeing the slaves in Missouri, he was subjected to a torrent of criticism. One of his most vitriolic critics was Michigan's Senator Zachariah Chandler. About the same time, Colonel Frederick Curtenius of Kalamazoo, commanding officer of the Sixth Michigan Infantry, chose to resign his commission rather than obey an order to return escaped slaves in Louisiana. His action was upheld by a resolution passed by the Michigan legislature. When Lincoln issued his Emancipation Proclamation it was received with acclaim in Michigan. In Detroit meetings to celebrate the event were held in the Negro churches and were well-attended.

Although a large majority of the people of the state were steadfast in their zeal for the Union cause, grumblers, dissenters, and defeatists were not lacking. A rally held in Detroit on July 15, 1862 following Lincoln's call for 300,000 more men, was broken up by hecklers and rowdies. The following March, when the national draft was announced, uneasiness was prevalent in Detroit as a

[26] J. Robertson, *op. cit.*, pp. 123-134; W. Q. Maxwell, *Lincoln's Fifth Wheel . . . , passim.*

result of several strikes. The resentment and the aroused passions of the populace triggered a tragic race riot. The central figure of the trouble was a Negro named William Faulkner, who was accused of assaulting a white child. It was later proved that the charge was completely false. But his trial aroused great excitement. A howling mob threatened him; a guard fired into the mob, a bystander was killed, and the riot began. Before it was over fire had destroyed between 30 and 35 buildings, an estimated 200 Negroes were homeless, and two people had been killed. Soldiers from Fort Wayne were called out to suppress the disorder. The city quieted down quickly afterward, and there were many expressions of shame and regret over the affair. When the little girls who accused Faulkner admitted they had fabricated the tale, he was pardoned, returned to Detroit, and was helped to establish himself in the produce business.[27]

Detroit was also the center of a plot to free Confederate prisoners held in the cities of the northwest and to provide them with arms to cause trouble in the area. Involved were Confederate spies and sympathizers from Canada. The ringleaders boarded the vessel *Philo Parsons* at Detroit on September 19, 1864. More men were taken aboard when the ship stopped at Amherstberg on the Canadian side of the river. The conspirators seized the vessel once it left Amherstberg, locking up its officers in the cabin. The plan was to capture the U.S.S. *Michigan*, which lay off Sandusky guarding the prison camp on Johnson's Island. They did not know that Lt. Col. Bennett H. Hill, acting assistant provost marshal general in charge of the Detroit district, had gotten wind of the plot and had carefully prepared to foil it. The conspirators on the *Philo Parsons* realized something was wrong only when they failed to get the prearranged signal from the U.S.S. *Michigan*, which their fellow operatives were supposed to have seized. The *Philo Parsons* thereupon put back to Canada, where she was abandoned by her thwarted mutineers. Several of the plotters were arrested, but they escaped from jail.[28]

On April 3, 1865 news came to Michigan that the Confederate capital, Richmond, had fallen. The people were delirious with joy. Everywhere there were processions, bonfires, shouting, singing, and fireworks. A few days later the telegraph brought word of the surrender of Lee at Appomattox and the celebrations were resumed with even greater enthusiasm. Then on April 15 came the tragic news of Lincoln's assassination, and joy was turned into profound sorrow. It seemed almost unbelievable that "Father Abraham" was

[27] Woodford, *op. cit.*, pp. 63-70.
[28] H. Hatcher, *Lake Erie.*

dead. In the excited temper of the time the blame for Lincoln's assassination was laid at the door of the southerners. It was universally believed that the highest officials of the Confederacy were involved, though subsequently this was proved false. But the popular idea persisted and had much to do with the "tragic era" that followed.

THE SEQUEL

Soon after the fighting was over the mustering-out process began, but not until after the grand parade in Washington in which the armies of Grant and Sherman marched in triumph in a never-to-be-forgotten procession. One by one the various regiments were then brought back to their home states and dispersed. Among the survivors were men who had suffered severe hardships in southern prisons and prison camps. Some 423 Michigan men, most of them recently released from southern prisons, were assembled at Vicksburg, Mississippi on April 24, 1865, where they were crowded aboard the steamer *Sultana* for transportation northward. About 1:00 a.m. on April 27, after the ship had left Memphis, Tennessee, one of her boilers burst and there was a terrible explosion. A total of 1,238 were burned to death or drowned in this frightful and tragic disaster; of these, 1,101 were returning soldiers, many from Michigan.[29]

Most of the veterans quickly resumed their places in society, though a few remained in the army. Among these was a young recruit from Galesburg, William Rufus Shafter, who was to command the American army in Cuba during the Spanish-American War over thirty years later. It was natural that the returned veterans should form an organization to promote their interests. The Grand Army of the Republic was formed in 1866, and a Michigan chapter was organized the following year. But it was not until 1878 that the Michigan Department of the G.A.R. was permanently established. The organization reached its highest point in membership in Michigan in 1893 when more than 21,000 men were enrolled in its local "camps." The G.A.R. became a powerful pressure group. It fought successfully for pensions and other benefits for the veterans. Most of its members were strong Republicans, and they helped keep Michigan in the Republican column consistently. For many years the various Michigan regiments held annual reunions, where veterans met to exchange yarns, to march once more shoulder to shoulder, and to pose for photographers. Orlando Le

[29] C. D. Berry, *Loss of the "Sultana" and Reminiscences of Survivors.*

Valley of Caro was the last Department Commander of the Michigan G.A.R. and the last surviving Civil War veteran in the state. He died in 1948 at the age of 107.

The legislature of Michigan after the war appropriated considerable amounts to erect monuments to Michigan's fallen soldiers on national battlefields and in national cemeteries. Voluntary subscriptions by Michigan citizens provided for the erection in Detroit of a monument to Michigan soldiers and sailors in the Civil War at a cost of over $70,000. Almost every city and town also erected a monument to its Civil War dead. The demand for these monuments became so great that they were turned out in a uniform design by manufacturers.

Harper Hospital in Detroit dates its origin to the Civil War. In 1863 citizens of Michigan sought support from the government to locate a hospital for sick and wounded soldiers in the state. One purpose of this was to reduce the travel of parents and friends who were anxious to visit hospitalized soldiers. Walter Harper, a native of Ireland and a wealthy citizen of Detroit, donated a thousand acres of land and other property to establish a hospital. The trustees of this property offered the use of the land to the government, and a military hospital was completed on the site October 12, 1864. After the war it was turned over to the Harper Hospital Board of Trustees, and on January 1, 1866 it accepted its first civilian patients. As one writer has stated,

> Thus a great modern institution of healing has arisen on the foundations of a Civil War hospital, a finer memorial undoubtedly than the statues and monuments of cast iron and sculptured stone which stand in scores of municipal parks and courthouse plazas across Michigan.[30]

The postwar period was marked by great bitterness as the radical Republicans in Congress pressed for military occupation of the South and the imposition of Negro suffrage. Among the ringleaders of the radicals, none was more vociferous than Senator Zachariah Chandler of Michigan. There is little evidence that Chandler had any sincere solicitude for the bewildered former slaves of the South, but he saw in Negro suffrage a means whereby the Republican Party could remain in power. The southerners used poor judgment immediately after the war in passing the notorious "black codes" that many northerners believed imposed slavery in another form. Race riots intensified fears that the South would snatch away the fruits of victory. Andrew Johnson, who succeeded Lincoln as President, favored a moderate and conciliatory policy,

[30] Woodford, *op. cit.,* p. 213.

but the triumph of the congressional radicals in the elections of 1866 spelled defeat for him. In Michigan Governor Crapo staunchly supported the radical program in Congress. His re-election in 1866 by the largest majority ever given to a gubernatorial candidate up to that time indicates that Michigan voters generally approved the radical program. All six of the Michigan congressmen elected that year were Republicans.

Although Michigan's representatives and senators in Congress were advocating Negro suffrage in the South, the people of Michigan made no move to enfranchise their own Negro citizens. The Constitution of 1850 restricted the franchise to white males. In 1866 the calling of a convention for the revision of the constitution was approved by a popular vote. After extended debate the delegates decided to remove the obstacles to Negro voting in the proposed new constitution. But the next year voters rejected the new constitution, and thus continued the ban on Negro voting. In 1870, however, the legislature ratified the Fifteenth Amendment to the United States Constitution, which prohibited any state from denying the right to vote because of race, color, or previous condition of servitude. The Michigan constitution was then amended to permit Negro suffrage, and on November 8 of that year Negroes cast their votes for the first time in Michigan's history.[31]

For many years Civil War passions were kept alive by politicians in quest of votes who "waved the bloody shirt" to remind voters that the Republican Party had saved the Union. In Coldwater one Republican orator, Ben Butler, cried, "Show me a Democrat and I'll show you a rebel." No doubt this strategy was effective, but as the war receded other issues gradually replaced the "bloody shirt."

The triumph of the federal forces in the Civil War made possible the restoration of the Union and the abolition of slavery. But it did not settle the problem of federal-state relations. Nor did it solve the problem of race relations.

[31] J. C. Dancy, "The Negro People in Michigan," *Michigan Histor*: **XXIV** (1940), 221-240.

16

THE HEYDAY OF THE LUMBERMEN

The economy of Michigan was dominated from 1860 to 1900 by the harvesting, sawing, and marketing of lumber, chiefly white pine. Thousands of men found employment in the industry, fortunes were made from it, and it made a major contribution to the establishment of farms, towns, and cities in the prairie states.

The trees, their size, number, and varieties were a matter of vital importance to the early settlers of Michigan. They were used to mark trails, to judge the quality of the soil, and to build homes, barns, and fences. They provided fuel over the long winters. In course of time, log shelters gave way to buildings constructed from sawed lumber. The sawmill appears early in the history of Michigan towns. In the 1840s the export of lumber began, first to the East, then to other parts of the nation. The period from 1860 to 1900 was the heyday of the lumbermen in Michigan. Almost every young man with energy spent a winter or two in a logging camp, towns sprang up like mushrooms in the north country, sawmills were built, immigrants flocked into the state, and over-optimistic dreams of the future were common. Railroads were extended into the North. Grand Rapids, located near vast supplies of lumber, became the nation's furniture capital. In 1890 there were 1,957 sawmills that sawed some four and a half billion board feet of lumber.[1] The salt industry grew up as an adjunct of the sawmills. The supply of timber was so vast that much good timber was wasted. But by 1900 the remaining stands of virgin pine were becoming scarce. Gradually cutting declined and the sawmills were dismantled.

Although the boom days of lumbering are long since past, there were still in Michigan in 1958 1,224 establishments employing 11,374 workers engaged in the manufacture of lumber and wood products. Many other workers were engaged in cutting and replanting trees. The yearly cut of lumber today is only one-sixth of what it was in 1910, but the production of wood pulp has increased fourfold in the same period. More than half the area of Michigan is still covered by forests. Michigan produces 95% of the world's supply of birds-eye maple. Some 13,000 growers are engaged in the production of Christmas trees. And the forests are vitally important for recreation, both to the people of Michigan and to the thousands of vacationers who come to the state.

BEGINNINGS

If we search for beginnings we must go back to the French period, for the French felled trees to construct forts and missions. They even built windmills to provide power for sawing the lumber they needed. When the British came they cut and sent down the St. Lawrence huge oak logs to be used for constructing the stout beams and masts of the British men-of-war and merchantmen. After the War of 1812 the Americans cut these timbers to build ships to be used on the Great Lakes. For these purposes hardwoods were used.

It was not the hardwood trees that grew in the southern part of the state that built the lumber industry, however. This beech, oak, hickory, sugar maple, and ash was of only limited usefulness. North of the forty-third parallel the softwoods predominated. Here were the white pine, the Norway pine, the jack pine, as well as the less valuable spruce, white cedar, tamarack, and hemlock. The pines were most highly prized. Pine was king in the heyday of the lumbermen. The best of the white pines were called "cork pines." White pine, which once covered hundreds of square miles of Michigan's surface, is now almost extinct. A few specimens are preserved in the Hartwick Pines State Park near Gaylord.

[1] A board foot of lumber is a piece of wood one foot long, one foot wide, and one inch thick.

The first sawmills were being set up in Detroit, Port Huron, Flint, Grand Rapids, and Muskegon in the early 1830s. The first such mills used water power, but the first steam sawmill dates back to 1834. These early mills served a local market, but they mark the beginning of what was destined to be one of Michigan's great boom industries.

THE SAGINAW COUNTRY

The first region in which large-scale exploitation of Michigan's pine forests was undertaken was the Saginaw Country. Here was an area of more than 3,000,000 acres covered with white pine of size and quality nowhere excelled. Since the earliest markets outside the state for Michigan lumber were in the East, the location of the outlet for the lumber of the Saginaw Country on the east side of the Lower Peninsula was an advantage, being closer to the eastern markets. But the key to the early exploitation of this particular segment of Michigan's pine forests was the fact that it was threaded by a large number of rivers that could be used to float the logs to the sawmills. The Cass, Flint, Shiawassee, Bad, Tittabawassee, Chippewa Rivers, and several others which converged to form the Saginaw River, had a total length of 864 miles for log driving. Until the development of the logging railroads many years later, the only method of transporting the logs from the forests where they were cut to the sawmills was to float them down the rivers.[2] By 1854 there were 29 mills in the Saginaw Valley with a capacity of 100,000,000 board feet per year.

Lake steamers, boats on the New York and Ohio canals, and later the railroads provided cheap and ready transportation for the Saginaw pine lumber. Farmers building homes on the prairies received it joyfully when they had become sufficiently prosperous to advance beyond the sod-house stage. There was no timber on the vast and fertile prairies of mid-America, and so, with the increase in population, this region became a ready market.

Methods and tools peculiar to the logging business had developed over a period of time in Maine, which had long been the source of prime lumber and the home of the lumberjack. The tools, techniques, and personnel of the Maine lumber camps were moved bodily, in some instances, to Saginaw. For the next

[2] W. G. Rector, *Transportation in the Lake States Lumber Industry,* p. 48.

generation or two the lumberman was at home in Michigan. While the Saginaw Country was still booming, he moved northward to the Au Sable and westward to the Grand River valley, then northward along the west coast of the Lower Peninsula. In the 1880s large-scale lumbering began in the Upper Peninsula. By the turn of the century the lumbermen were leaving Michigan, headed for the forests of Oregon, Washington, and the Canadian Northwest.

The town of Saginaw became a trading center and the site of several of the sawmills of the Saginaw Country. Located about twenty miles up the Saginaw River from its outlet into Saginaw Bay, the town traced its beginnings to a fur-trading post established by Louis Campau in 1816. Beginning in the 1850s and continuing for a generation, lumber was the lifeblood of Saginaw. Although the risks were great and many operators suffered losses, under the right combination of capital, management, and luck, enormous fortunes were made. The lumberjacks made it a lively place when they came in the spring. Fabulous stories are told of their roistering. One of the colorful figures of these days in Saginaw was "Little Jake" Seligman, clothing merchant, banker, real-estate dealer, and operator of the horse-drawn street railway cars. To attract crowds Seligman would often scatter coins into the streets from the upper story of his store. He hired bands to march through the town. When the lumberjacks came in droves, Seligman would toss them vests, promising to provide matching coats and trousers for those who caught the vests. He kept his promise, but in the process the vests were usually torn to shreds, and the captor who claimed a free coat and pants had to pay a fancy price for a matching vest. Later Seligman had workmen erect a statue of himself above a four-faced clock atop the Tower Building.[3]

LUMBERING IN WESTERN MICHIGAN

On the western side of the Lower Peninsula the first sawmills were built at Grand Rapids (1832) and Muskegon (1837). Others soon followed and by 1860 there were mills at the mouths of most of the larger rivers flowing into Lake Michigan to the north of Muskegon. The richest drives came down the Muskegon, the Manistee, and the Boardman. Towns that later developed in many instances into cities grew up at the mouths of these rivers. A few, like Singapore at the mouth of the Kalamazoo, failed to survive the great days of lumbering and became "ghost towns."

[3] *Michigan, a Guide to the Wolverine State*, p. 369.

The work of cutting the timber was done in the winter because only then was it possible to transport the logs economically to the banks of streams. This was done by the use of huge bobsleds. The logs were piled along the banks of the rivers twenty to thirty feet high. Each log was marked on both ends with the initial or sign of the man or the firm to which it belonged. Many of these log-marks resemble the brands devised by Texans to identify cattle.[4] As soon as the ice melted off the surface of the rivers in the spring, and while the stream was still flooded, the rivermen took over the task of getting the logs downstream. This was difficult and perilous business. The first operation consisted of dislodging the "key" log so as to bring the whole pile rolling and plunging into the river. Then the problem was to prevent jams from forming, and if they did form, to break them up. If there were falls, dams, or rapids on the way, a new problem was presented. A sluiceway was built around such obstacles to get the logs through. If water was low a dam was necessary to back up the water enough to float the logs. The riverman, with his heavy spiked boots, worked night and day until the drive was over. His was a special profession and he was generally reputed to be the toughest man in the business.[5]

The business of running logs downstream was known as "booming." On some rivers "boom" companies were formed and by lobbying in Lansing some of them obtained exclusive rights to boom lumber on a certain river for an established price. Such companies could then afford to invest capital in making the river more usable for their purposes: removing obstacles, building dams and sluiceways, and so on. When the logs reached the river's mouth where the mills were, they were sorted according to the marks on them, then fastened together to form rafts for storage until the mills could use them.

A new era in the lumbering business began in 1876 when the first logging railroad was constructed. Winfield Scott Gerrish, a native of Maine who started logging on the Muskegon River at the age of eighteen, visited the Centennial Exposition at Philadelphia in 1876, where he saw on exhibit a small Baldwin locomotive. It occurred to him that such a locomotive could be used to pull flat cars loaded with logs from the woods to the banks of the rivers. This would enable the lumbermen to extend their

[4] C. Allen (ed.), *Michigan Log-Marks*.

[5] S. E. White's *The Riverman* is a novel that vividly portrays this phase of lumbering. White wrote several other novels about the lumbermen, including *The Blazed Trail*. Other novels dealing with lumbering are E. hwing's *The Red Keggers*, H. Titus's *Timber*, and J. O. Curwood's *The ilent Men*. White, Titus, and Curwood were all Michigan natives.

operations several miles from the rivers, further than it was practical to haul logs by bobsled. Returning to Michigan, he organized the Lake George and Muskegon Railroad, built a six-mile rail line from his holdings to the Muskegon River, secured a locomotive and, amidst the hoots of derision from lumbermen, started operations. The experiment proved a great success. In 1882, 32 of these narrow-gauge logging railroads were built in Michigan and by 1889 a total of 89 were in operation. By this means, enormous stands of pine, previously too remote to be harvested profitably, were attacked by the lumbermen. The logging railroads not only opened immense new areas but also made year-round cutting possible.[6]

The advance of the lumberman was never on a straight line. For instance, Van Buren County, located in the second tier of counties north of the Indiana border, was heavily forested and contained both soft- and hardwood trees in abundance. Yet this county was scarcely touched by the lumbermen prior to 1870 because of lack of transportation facilities.

On to the Upper Peninsula

The first sawmill in the Upper Peninsula was built at Sault Ste. Marie in 1822; others were built on the Lake Michigan side in the 1830s, but only to supply local needs. The great migration of the lumbermen to the Upper Peninsula began in the 1880s, when lumbering in the Lower Peninsula was still big business. The chief rivers utilized by the lumbermen were the Tahquamenon and the Ontonagon flowing into Lake Superior, and the Escanaba and Menominee emptying into Lake Michigan.[7] The original forests in the Upper Peninsula covered some ten million acres, a little less than half being hardwood. There were even larger areas in this region than in the Lower Peninsula that were not penetrated by navigable rivers, and hence a larger proportion of the logs had to be transported by railroads. Lumbering in its later stages in Michigan became more and more a big business, as extensive wealth or credit was required to finance a lumbering operation. The small operator found himself unable to bid against the big firms for stumpage.[8]

Lumber production in Michigan hit its highest point in 1888,

[6] R. H. Maybee, *Michigan's White Pine Era, 1840-1900*, pp. 37-43. See filmstrip on lumbering in Michigan, prepared by the Michigan Historical Commission.

[7] W. D. Hulbert, *White Pine Days on the Tahquamenon.*

[8] W. G. Rector, *op. cit.*, pp. 48-49, 53, 59.

when 4,292,000,000 board feet were sawed. Although the annual output declined steadily thereafter, Michigan was still ahead of every other state in 1900. Lumbering on the Menominee reached its zenith in 1889, but in 1915 there were still 140 operators in the Upper Peninsula. At present almost all the merchantable lumber left in Michigan is in this area.

THE LOGGING CAMP

A logging camp in Mecosta County in the 1870s may be regarded as fairly typical. It was directed by two men and was located in the middle of a 240-acre forest area. The camp consisted of six buildings accommodating 70 men, 20 teams of horses, and seven yoke of oxen. The cook shanty, always the central building in a camp, was 20 by 52 feet in size, one story high, and consisted of a kitchen and a dining room. The latter contained two long tables covered by oilcloth, where 42 men could be fed at one time. The staples consisted of potatoes, beans, pork, bread, molasses, and strong tea. These could be found on the table in some form three times a day. Five barrels of flour, five barrels of pork, and fifteen to twenty bushels of potatoes were used each week. An alarm clock set three-quarters of an hour fast went off at 4:00 a.m. The teamsters were out first, and were off to work long before daylight, making one trip to the river, a distance of two miles, before breakfast. They made five trips a day. When that was done, they unhitched and did no more, even though it might be some time before sundown. The horses were given loving care and were not overworked. The bunkhouse was a building 26 by 36 feet, one and a half stories high. It contained eighteen bunks on the first floor and fourteen on the second, each accommodating two men. The bunks were made of boards, and were "double-deckers"; each was supplied with a straw tick and blankets. For heat there was a large box stove, and for light, kerosene lamps. In the evening there was card playing, storytelling, and tall talk. There was no drinking of intoxicating liquors in this camp or in others; that was left for the end of the season when the boys "went to town." The other buildings consisted of a barn, a granary, a blacksmith and carpentry shop, and a store where a contractor sold tobacco, clothing, and odds and ends. This camp turned into the river in a single season 4½ million feet of timber. In addition to this the workers had cut another million feet that were rejected by the scaler for some defect. The chronicler states that the labor on this million feet was all lost. One is tempted to ask, "What about the trees?"[9]

Most lumber camps were intended to be merely temporary. In the later years of the lumber era there are instances of towns being built by the operators. One such was Deward in Kalkaska County, named for a famous lumberman, David Ward. When he died in 1900 it was found that under the terms of his will his estate had to be settled within twelve years. The executors decided to clear a tract of timberland consisting of 90,000 acres within that period. They built the town of Deward in the heart of the forest, had a huge mill constructed, and started operations in September, 1901. Cottages were built for the workmen and their families. There was a company store, a schoolhouse, a church, and a community hall, but no saloons. At its height Deward had 800 inhabitants. But in 1912 the job was done, the mill was dismantled and hauled away, and gradually the people moved elsewhere. Deward became a ghost town.[10]

THE LUMBERJACK

The personnel of the lumber camp varied. There were always Irishmen, and in later years a large number of Swedes, Finns, and Norwegians. A Swede named Louis Sands brought Swedes, called "Sandies," into Michigan by the boatloads and trainloads. Hundreds of young men from southern Michigan farms spent one or more winters in the camps. Many of the lumberjacks were Yankees who had come to Michigan from the Maine woods. There were also French-Canadians, many of them also veterans of the lumber camps of Maine and Quebec. Whoever they were and wherever they came from, they were a hardy, tough lot, capable of gargantuan labors and filled to the brim with the zest for living.

The lumberjacks, unlike the cowboys and the voyageurs, did not sing while working. The reason is obvious to anyone who has ever been at the business end of an axe or a crosscut saw. But in the bunkhouse in the evening they sang interminable ballads, most of them with a sad ending. Two of these, "The Jam of Garry's Rock" and "The Red-light Saloon," were sung in log-

[9] *Mecosta County Album,* p. 572ff. A reconstruction of a lumber camp may be seen at Hartwick Pines State Park.

[10] C. A. Leech, "Deward; a Lumberman's Ghost Town," *Michigan History,* XXVIII (1944), 5-19. See also F. E. Lewis, "Frederic: a Typical Logging Village in the Twilight of the Lumbering Era," in *Michigan History,* XXXII (1948), 321-339 and XXXIV (1950), 35-49.

ging camps from coast to coast. These and others emphasized the story, not the music. Indeed, the lumberjacks rendered these ballads to almost any tune, or to no tune at all. One author states that the singers were of two principal schools, wailers and bull roarers.[11]

When the hard winter's work was over and the lumberjacks arrived at the nearest town, they let loose with unrestrained merrymaking. Fighting, with no holds barred, appears to have been their favorite sport. There were legendary battlers, such as the muscular Silver Jack, who, it was told, once felled an ox with his fist and could twist horseshoes at will with his bare hands. Then there was Joe Fournier, a French Canadian, whose specialty was butting with his head his opponent or an oak bar or anything else in his way.[12] In the Upper Peninsula the most notorious town in the lumbering era was Seney. The accounts of the wickedness of Seney in its prime are legendary and no doubt highly exaggerated, but it was a rough place.

There is a wealth of folklore about the lumberjack. Of a somewhat different character, however, is the mythology of Paul Bunyan. Where and when it arose is not known. Some trace it back to a figure who appeared during the Canadian rebellion of 1837, a "mighty-muscled, bellicose, bearded giant" who "raged among the Queen's troops like Sampson among the Philistines." But the myth is usually traced back to the Saginaw Country. Paul was the super-logger of them all, and as stories were told of his exploits, they gained by accretion. Paul Bunyan and his blue ox, which measured 42 axe handles and a plug of chewing tobacco between the horns, became so well-known that they have become the symbols of countless establishments dedicated to extracting dollars from the pockets of tourists. Paul Bunyan is not an authentic folk hero; rather he is a product of popular mythology, with a strong infusion of commercialism.[13]

Remembered through folklore and mythology, his drinking, fighting, and wenching exploited by sensation-mongers, the real lumberjack has become difficult to distinguish. There can be little doubt that the sort of lumberjacks that are the best-known were far from typical. A great many and probably the majority of the lumberjacks were honest, law-abiding citizens who were as

[11] S. Holbrook, *Holy Old Mackinaw, a Natural History of the American Lumberjack.* This book is also available in paperback under the title *American Lumberjacks.* E. M. Beck has collected many of these ballads. See his *Songs of the Michigan Lumberjacks* and *Lore of the Lumber Camps.*

[12] Holbrook, *op. cit.*

[13] Holbrook, *ibid.,* traces the myth at some length. See also J. Stevens, *The Saginaw Paul Bunyan.*

moderate in their habits as most men are. Most of the men from the farms of southern Michigan, after a winter in the North, returned to their homes in the spring and put away their winter's earnings to start a career or a family.[14]

THE TOOLS AND MILLS

Numerous inventions and improvements resulted in much speedier production of lumber in Michigan than in Maine. Until the 1870s trees were felled by the use of the single-bitted axe, though the crosscut saw was employed to cut the logs into sixteen-foot lengths. It was only when manufacturers produced crosscut saws of improved design and strength that they were used to cut standing timber. In the mills a major advance was achieved when the circular saw was introduced about 1850. The first circular saw in the United States is said to have been produced about 1814 by Benjamin Cummins, who later came to Michigan and who was buried in the Richland cemetery, Richland, Michigan. Two men, one from Kalamazoo and the other from Muskegon, perfected a device for the more efficient handling of logs in the mills. Another idea that paid big dividends was to shoot steam into the millponds to prevent the formation of ice, so that logs stored in the ponds could be used throughout the winter. Logging in the summer was facilitated by the invention of the "big wheels" attached to carts for the hauling of logs so as to clear the stumps. They were invented and produced at Manistee for many years by Sylas Overpack and Sons. Several towns in northern Michigan have "big wheels" on exhibit.

The sawmills were usually two-story buildings made of wood and located close to a river or lake. The power plant was situated in a frame lean-to attached to the mill. There were some huge mills, but far more were relatively small. Improved machinery greatly increased production even in the smaller mills; in the 1850s they cut about 3,000,000 board feet annually, while three years later they were producing from 10,000,000 to 20,000,000 feet. One of the constant menaces to the mills was fire, and many of them burned down.

THE LUMBER BARONS

Just as it is a mistake to assume that all lumberjacks resembled those about whom the tall stories were told, so it is a

14 J. I. Bellaire, "Michigan's Lumberjacks," *Michigan History,* XXV (1942), 173-180; G. B. Engberg, "Who Were the Lumberjacks?" *ibid.* XXXII (1948), 238-246.

mistake to assume that all those who invested in timber and sawmills became fabulously rich. There were thousands of small operators; there were many who made only modest profits, and there were those who failed altogether. To make money in logging and lumber manufacture required all those qualities that success in any business enterprise demands. Another myth is that the men who made good in the industry were uniformly crooked and dishonest. One competent historian of the Saginaw area concluded that the lumbermen were as honest and straightforward as any group of businessmen. Great opportunities for wealth were available to the man who worked hard and used his head; it was not necessary to resort to shady dealing, though many unquestionably did.

The success of an investor in Michigan pinelands began with the selection of the best available tracts. Notes of government surveyors included information concerning topography, vegetation, and forests, sometimes giving hints of the quality of the timber. But more data than this were desirable. To obtain this information lumbermen engaged "timber cruisers," who were expert judges of pine and roamed the forests looking for it. They climbed tall trees to get a look at large areas, then made on-the-spot inspections. When they located a choice tract they hurried to the land office to reserve it for their employers. On occasion there were races between rival cruisers to arrive first.

A considerable amount of the land obtained for logging was purchased from the United States government at $1.25 an acre, the minimum price. After the Homestead Act was passed in 1862 lumbermen hired men to enter claims to 160 acres each, which were made available without cost under the law to bona fide settlers. Some token of settlement was maintained long enough to allow the timber to be cut. Millions of acres of land were given to railroad companies to induce them to build lines into the northern country, and lumbermen often bought tracts from these companies, or from the company that received 750,000 acres for building the Soo Canal. In other cases purchases were made from the state. Millions of acres of "swamp lands" granted to the state by the federal government were sold to the lumbermen for a small amount or given outright as a reward for building roads. Operators often did not confine their cutting to the area they had purchased. There was the practice of "logging a round forty," which meant buying forty acres and then cutting the timber around it in all directions far beyond the boundaries of the area to which title had been secured.

Whether through honest or dishonest means, or both, a sizable number of men became rich through profits from lumber. By the 1890s almost every town or city in Michigan had wealthy citizens whose fortune had been made in lumber. Such men built huge, imposing residences, replete with all the scrollwork and decoration characteristic of mansions in the "gay nineties." The first to become prominent in Saginaw were Maine lumbermen who sought and found opportunities for money-making in the West: the Eddys, the Murphys, the Dorrs, and the Leadbetters. Because some of them took the law into their own hands, wealthy lumbermen have been called the "lumber barons." Most of them carved success out of hard work, but once they had made their fortune they were fond of living in an ostentatious style. Each tried to outdo the other in the scale and magnificence of the homes they built. One of them built a fence of brick and concrete studded with some 15,000 champagne, wine, and whisky bottles. Portions of this may still be seen near the town of Waters, north of Grayling. Many of these mansions, far from handsome by any standard and much too large for modern living, have been torn down.

At least one of the lumber barons used his wealth to endow a college. The most liberal donor to Alma College in its first half-century was a local lumberman named Ammi Wright. The lumber barons were fond of seeing their names inscribed on lake boats, but most of all they coveted political preferment. The lumbermen liked to mix "pine and politics." Among them was Henry H. Crapo of Flint, who served as governor from 1865 to 1869. Coming to Michigan in 1856 with very little capital, he made a fortune from lumbering within a decade, but worked so hard doing it that he died prematurely.[15] Russell A. Alger, a wealthy Detroiter who gained much of his fortune from lumber after winning distinction as a cavalry officer in the Civil War, served as governor, United States senator, and secretary of war in President McKinley's cabinet. He was even considered as a presidential candidate in 1888. Francis B. Stockbridge of Kalamazoo, another man who made a fortune out of lumber, gained appointment to the United States Senate. He was the moving spirit in the construction of the Grand Hotel on Mackinac Island. Thomas W. Ferry of Grand Haven also represented Michigan in the United States Senate. There are but a few examples of how pine and politics mixed. Many other lumbermen served in the lower house of Congress or in the state legislature. David H. Jerome and Aaron T. Bliss, like Crapo and Alger, were lumberman-governors.

[15] M. D. Lewis, *Lumberman from Flint.*

WASTE AND FIRE

Waste in the harvesting and sawing of lumber was enormous. Woodsmen were paid so much per stump, so they cut everything in sight, providing, of course, it was pine. Scalers so often rejected the logs for some minor defect that billions of board feet of fine lumber were left to rot in the woods. No attempt was made to conserve the uncut trees or to replant: the supply of pine seemed inexhaustible. Most destructive of all were the fires that periodically raged in the northland destroying huge tracts of forest. Even though the trees were only slightly scorched the lumberman passed them by. The charcoal dulled the saws in the mills!

Most disastrous of all these fires was the great conflagration that swept the north country in the fall of 1871. The summer had been hot and dry. In the cut-over areas brush (called "slashings") was like tinder. Mills, houses, and stores in the lumber towns were all made of wood; even the sidewalks were built with boards. On Sunday, October 8, the famous Chicago fire broke out. The flames roared out of control for 48 hours and subsided only when most of the city had been wiped out. As the fire raged in Chicago a southwest gale of tornado proportions sprang up. Some contemporaries believed it carried sparks from the Chicago fire across Lake Michigan. At any rate, fires sprang up along the whole west coast of the Lower Peninsula. The city of Holland was totally destroyed in two hours. Farther north, the same fate came to Manistee. The flames spread with lightning-like rapidity eastward across the state clear to Port Huron, carrying everything before them. The people of Michigan, just preparing to raise a relief fund for Chicago sufferers, were now forced to provide succor for their own citizens. Half a million dollars was raised, over a thousand dwellings were built, and food and clothing were distributed. The loss in standing timber was simply incalculable.

Exactly a decade later another disastrous forest fire broke out, though it was largely confined to counties in the Thumb area. Small fires burning in Lapeer, Tuscola, and Huron Counties spread suddenly when a gale from the southwest arose on September 5. Residents fled their homes, some taking refuge in Lake Huron. A total of 125 lives were lost and thousands were left homeless. This time Michigan received help from the newly organized American Red Cross. It was the first disaster-relief project of the Red Cross, and was directed by Clara Barton from her home in Dansville, New York. Lesser fires broke out frequently in the years that followed; a dense pall of smoke often was carried far to the south of the fires in late summer and autumn.[16]

HARDWOODS AND FURNITURE

The professional lumberjack of song and story was interested only in pine. Yet most of the trees south of a line running from Grand Rapids through Port Huron were hardwoods. Pioneers slashed and burned them to clear the land. Thousands of trees were cut to be burned in kilns to produce charcoal, for which there was a heavy demand in the manufacture of iron in the nineteenth century. The choicest hardwoods were sawed into lumber for flooring, veneer, and furniture-making. The hardwood belt extends down into Indiana and Ohio. Grand Rapids, which became the furniture capital of the world in the period after the Civil War, was not located in the center of the hardwood belt, but rather on the northern edge of it. It seems to have possessed no particular advantages for furniture manufacturing, and had the disadvantage of lacking for some years adequate rail service. The development of Grand Rapids as a great furniture center appears to have been due to the business acumen of the men who located there, their inventiveness, and the skilled craftsmen they attracted. Among the pioneers in the industry were William Haldane, A.B. and George Pullman, C. C. Comstock, Elias Matter, and William Widdicomb. Deserving special mention are A. D. Linn and Z. Clark Thwing, the men who invented the dry kiln process for seasoning lumber. Prior to this development furniture manufacturers had been forced to invest money in enough lumber to supply them for three or four years, since furniture would not hold together if any sap was left in the wood. Perhaps most important of all the Grand Rapids furniture manufacturers were Julius Berkey and George W. Gay. These two men joined forces in 1867 and soon developed a manufacturing plant of immense size. They engaged the very best craftsmen, opened a showroom in New York, later established the semi-annual furniture show in Grand Rapids that became an institution, introduced extensive improvements in machinery, and stimulated by their efforts other manufacturers in the city. By the close of the century every conceivable kind of furniture was made in Grand Rapids.

Encouraged by the success of the Grand Rapids manufacturers, capital in other cities found its way into the establishment of furniture plants. Detroit had twenty furniture factories in 1890.

[16] S. Holbrook, *Burning an Empire: The Story of American Forest Fires.*

Among the other cities and towns where furniture was made were Owosso, Muskegon, Big Rapids, Manistee, Saginaw, Holland, Allegan, Sturgis, Niles, Ann Arbor, Buchanan, and Grand Ledge. About the time of World War I, however, plants for the mass production of furniture began to move to the south. By the mid-twentieth century furniture making was no longer the leading Grand Rapids industry. As of 1958 there were still 398 establishments in Michigan making furniture and fixtures, though many of these specialized in metal furniture.

SALT AND LUMBER

The beginnings of large-scale salt production in Michigan have been related above. It was during the Civil War that the industry got its start. The idea of using the scrap wood left over from lumber sawing as fuel to evaporate brine was the key to the rapid growth of salt production. Shortly the Saginaw Valley was bristling with salt wells, and the west Michigan sawmill operators also got into business. By using the exhaust steam from the sawmills to evaporate the brine, the cost of production in 1879 had been brought down to 40¢ a barrel. The next year Michigan produced nearly 2,500,000 barrels, 42% of the nation's output. On the western side of the state, salt was produced at Frankfort, Ludington, and Manistee. When the lumber business faded out, the manufacture of salt became even more important, especially at Manistee.

In the eastern part of the Lower Peninsula salt-making moved southward from the Saginaw Valley along the Detroit and St. Clair Rivers. For many years it had been known that a deep vein of rock salt underlay the soil in the vicinity of Detroit, but the first use of the resource was made when a well was sunk near Wyandotte to provide salt for making the soda ash used in the manufacture of glass. At first, water was forced through the rock formations and a strong brine was brought to the surface. This was the start of the alkali industry in this region. In 1910 a deep shaft was sunk and the mining of rock salt was begun.

Michigan became the nation's leading producer of salt, but the byproducts and auxiliary enterprises of the salt industry came to overshadow the original business. Sodium carbonates obtained from salt are used extensively in a wide variety of manufactures, such as soap, paints, and varnishes. The early method of making soda ash from salt was expensive, but when the new "solvay process" came into use, production was greatly increased.

Such commodities as bicarbonate of soda and caustic soda were made in the Detroit region.[17]

Among the products secured from Michigan brines are bromine, calcium chloride, and magnesium. All of these have found a vastly increased field of use through the magic of chemistry. The largest organization turning out these materials and many other chemicals and dyes similarly derived is the Dow Chemical Company of Midland. This giant industry is the direct outgrowth of the salt wells sunk by the numerous sawmills that were built on the Tittabawassee River at Midland when pine lumber was being produced. By 1888 Midland had become the largest producer of bromine in the world. Two years later Herbert H. Dow, a native of Ohio and a chemist with a degree from the Case School of Applied Science in Cleveland, came to Midland, where he organized the company that now bears his name. This company makes more than four hundred products from brines pumped from the earth in Michigan. It has plants in several other Michigan cities, including Ludington, Marquette, and Mount Pleasant, as well as in other states. Thus, where the hardy woodsman swung his axe and the transient sawmill briefly had its day, new resources have been found to meet man's many needs.[18]

LUMBER AND THE RAILROADS

While the production of pine lumber was at its height in Michigan during the four decades after 1860, the railroad network of the state was being constructed. On the eve of the Civil War Michigan had less than eight hundred miles of railway tracks, consisting principally of three lines crossing the southern part of the Lower Peninsula. By 1900 the state had 7,945 miles of main-line track, 2,903 miles of other tracks and yard tracks, or a total of 10,848 miles. During the first two decades of the twentieth century additional tracks were laid both by the steam-railroad companies and by electric interurban companies. Thereafter, as automotive vehicles and airplanes broke the rail monopoly in transportation, mileage began to decline. By 1950 it was well below the figure for 1900, though the railroads continued to serve a vital function in the transportation of goods and people.

The fact that the major rail network of Michigan came into being during the heyday of lumbering is significant. Many lines

[17] A. Pound, *Salt of the Earth, the Story of Captain J. B. Ford and the Michigan Alkali Company.*

[18] M. Campbell and H. Hatton, *Herbert H. Dow, Pioneer in Creative Chemistry.*

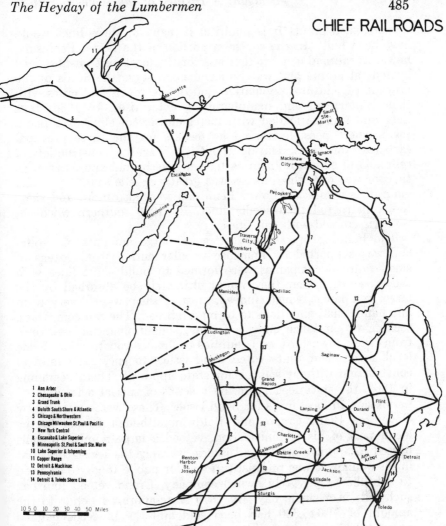

CHIEF RAILROADS

1 Ann Arbor
2 Chesapeake & Ohio
3 Grand Trunk
4 Duluth South Shore & Atlantic
5 Chicago & Northwestern
6 Chicago Milwaukee St.Paul & Pacific
7 New York Central
8 Escanaba & Lake Superior
9 Minneapolis St.Paul & Sault Ste. Marie
10 Lake Superior & Ishpeming
11 Copper Range
12 Detroit & Mackinac
13 Pennsylvania
14 Detroit & Toledo Shore Line

10 5 0   10   20   30   40   50 Miles

were built into areas where lumbering was in progress and where
lumber towns had sprung up with the expectation that after the
pine was gone the country would fill up with settlers. This hope
was not fulfilled, largely due to the sandy soils that underlay
the pine. As will be indicated, the railroads were compelled to
search for other means of stimulating traffic on the lines that
originally had been built for the lumbermen.

The construction of rail lines reaching into the northern part
of the Lower Peninsula and into the Upper Peninsula was vastly
stimulated by federal subsidies in the form of land grants. Indeed,

without such grants it is doubtful if many of these lines would have been built. In the southern portion of the Lower Peninsula, however, railroad construction was for the most part unsubsidized by federal grants and was undertaken to serve the needs of the growing agricultural population and of the towns and cities with their commercial and manufacturing enterprises. In 1860 stage lines and wagons loaded with merchandise, traveling over plank roads where possible, served as feeders for the three principal east-west rail lines. During the Civil War the construction of railroads to supplant them as feeders was begun, and as soon as the war was over this process was greatly speeded up. Additional main lines across the Lower Peninsula were also built, and they, too, constructed their feeder lines. By 1900 southern Michigan was crisscrossed with rail lines.

The building of railroads attracted large amounts of capital and was supported by immense popular enthusiasm. Dozens of small railroad companies were formed to build short lines with the expectation that they would ultimately be absorbed by the larger companies, which, indeed, most of them were. Every town and hamlet had ambitions to be on a railroad. The rail companies, seeking to capitalize on this feeling, sought financial assistance from cities, townships, and counties to finance construction. Some local government units voted bond issues to encourage railroad construction without waiting for state approval. Then, beginning in 1863, the state legislature, by a series of special acts, granted permission to local units for bond issues. These were approved by Governors Blair, Crapo, and Baldwin, although Crapo, in the latter part of his administration, vetoed a large number of bills passed to approve local bond issues, warning the legislature that in his opinion it was unconstitutional for public funds to be used to subsidize a privately owned company. Crapo vetoed fourteen such bills in a single day. By 1870 state-approved bonds to the amount of $1,646,300 had been sold and the proceeds handed over to the railroads. Additional bonds with a face value of more than twice this sum had been issued and deposited with the state treasurer but had not yet been delivered to the railroad companies. In April, 1870 the state supreme court declared one of the acts that had been passed by the legislature to approve such a bond issue to be unconstitutional, and this decision in effect made all the bonds so issued valueless. The railroads sought in vain to secure a constitutional amendment to validate the bonds, but it was voted down by the people. In the end, after long litigation some of the bondholders were able to collect by

"Side-winder": Shay logging locomotive of the 1880s

turning their bonds over to non-residents of the state who then brought suit in federal courts.[19]

Each of the three rail lines that spanned Lower Michigan in 1860 built branches and feeders after the Civil War and also purchased or leased lines that had been built by small companies. The Michigan Southern, with its eastern termini at Monroe and Toledo, Ohio, ran through the southernmost tier of counties, then, west of White Pigeon, veered southward into Indiana to reach Chicago. This line built or otherwise acquired lines reaching northward from Hillsdale to Lansing, from Hillsdale to Ypsilanti, from Jonesville to Marshall, from Adrian to Jackson, and from White Pigeon to Grand Rapids. The Michigan Central's main line extended westward from Detroit through Ann Arbor, Jackson, Battle Creek and Kalamazoo, then veered southward to Niles and Chicago. Fiercely competitive for many years with the Michigan Southern, the Central secured branch and feeder lines from Jackson northward to Lansing, Saginaw, and Mackinaw City (which was reached in 1881); from Detroit northward to

[19] H. M. Utley and B. M. Cutcheon, *Michigan as a Province, Territory, and State*, IV, 52-58.

Bay City; from Jackson northwestward to Grand Rapids; from Kalamazoo westward to South Haven; and from Battle Creek southward to Sturgis. The Central also built in the 1870s an "Air Line" on a shorter and more direct route between two points on its main line, Jackson and Niles. The Detroit and Milwaukee, which had its western Michigan termini in Grand Haven and Muskegon, also built branches running northward to Bay City and the Thumb area, a parallel line running slightly to the north of the main line, and a branch southward to Jackson. This railroad subsequently merged with the Grand Trunk lines.

Other major railroad lines were being constructed across Lower Michigan in the 1870s and 1880s. The Peninsular Railroad was built from Chicago, entering Michigan through Cass County and following a diagonal line northeastward to Lansing. There it was connected with another line from Port Huron, and in 1871 the two were combined and acquired by the Grand Trunk. The Ann Arbor Railroad had its origin in 1869 when building was started on a line that ultimately ran from Toledo, Ohio, northwesterly across Lower Michigan to Frankfort far to the north. Still another east-west line was constructed from Saginaw west to Ludington on Lake Michigan. This became part of the Pere Marquette System.

The Pere Marquette was a consolidation, formed in 1900, of more than a hundred different railroad companies. These had previously been merged into three main groups. The original Flint and Pere Marquette Railroad was opened in 1863, connecting Saginaw and Flint. During the next 37 years this railroad acquired many independent lines, secured connections with Detroit, Monroe, and Toledo, and built the line from Saginaw to Ludington mentioned earlier. The second main constituent of the Pere Marquette was the Chicago and West Michigan, which had built or acquired a line running northward through towns and cities in western Michigan to Grand Rapids, Traverse City, and Petósky, with numerous branches reaching out to Muskegon, Pentwater, Allegan, and other cities. The third main constituent of the Pere Marquette was a line connecting Detroit and Grand Rapids through Lansing, which also owned a line connecting Grand Rapids and Saginaw.

As has been noted in an earlier chapter, Congress in 1856 passed a measure that granted to the states millions of acres of public lands to be doled out to the railroads at a rate of three sections on each side of the tracks for every mile constructed, provided that at least twenty miles were built within the period of one year. So many scandals and shady transactions resulted that in 1872 further aid was withdrawn but not before more than 3,000,000 acres had been granted to Michigan railroads. In addition to these lands the state of Michigan granted to the railroads 1,659,509 acres of "swamp lands" that had been donated by the federal government to the state.

The amounts obtained by the railroads from these land grants by no means paid for the cost of construction, but they were sufficient to attract capital from domestic and foreign sources to do so. The lands were generally awarded to induce railroads to build into sparsely settled areas; thus in Michigan most of the land grants were made to railroad companies that built lines into the northern part of the Lower Peninsula and into the Upper Peninsula. It is a common misconception that these land grants were outright gifts. Under the terms of the grants, the land-grant railroads were obligated to carry government property and personnel at approximately half-price. It has been estimated that in the period since these railroads were built the saving to the government by these reduced rates amounts to over ten times the original value of the lands granted.[20] One writer sums up the "railroad land-grant legend" in these words:

> The net result of the treatment of the land-grant transaction as a whole is to present to the student a picture of a wastrel Uncle Sam scattering his substance with reckless extravagance, instead of the more nearly correct picture of a canny landowner using part of his holdings to increase immeasurably the value of the rest, not as a gift but on terms which constituted a bargain shrewder than he realized.[21]

In the Lower Peninsula land grants were made to a number of railroads that built lines into the north. The companies that merged into the Pere Marquette system in 1900 received land grants for building the line from Saginaw to Ludington and the line northward from Grand Rapids. The largest single land grant in the Lower Peninsula was made to the Grand Rapids and Indiana Railroad for building a line northward from Sturgis to Mackinaw City, which was completed in 1882. The Michigan Central was another major recipient, being granted over 721,000 acres to build its tracks northward from Jackson to Mackinaw City. A small amount was granted to the Grand Trunk for building its northern lines. But it should be noted that not all

[20] A. Roob, *Everyman's Almanac,* p. 29.
[21] R. S. Henry, "The Railroad Land Grant Legend in American History Texts," *The Public Lands,* ed. by V. Carstensen, p. 135.

railroads built into the north received grants. Neither the Ann Arbor, whose line from Toledo to Frankfort has already been mentioned, nor the Detroit and Mackinac, which constructed a line northward from Bay City to Cheboygan, received land grants.[22]

Not all the railroads built during this period were gobbled up by the big companies. There were dozens of short lines that were operated independently. Many such companies had grandiose ideas of becoming through lines. One such, the Toledo and South Haven, meandered through Van Buren County from South Haven to Lawton, eventually reached Kalamazoo, but never got any further.[23] The Manistee and Northeastern and the East Jordan and Southern are examples of independent lines in the north. Literally hundreds of railroad companies, formed with great expectations, never laid any track at all.

As lumbering declined after 1900 the railroads that had been built into the northern part of the Lower Peninsula suffered a serious decline in passenger and freight traffic. They sought to meet this challenge in a number of ways. In co-operation with lumber companies that had cut-over lands for sale and with local development associations, the railroads sought to lure farmers into the area by offering land at low prices. At first some measure of success was achieved, but it was quickly demonstrated that the sandy soils could not compete with the rich prairie lands in the states further west. Some townships in northern Michigan where almost every section had three or four farms in 1890 are completely overgrown with brush and trees. Scores of abandoned farm buildings may still be seen.[24]

Another device used by the railroads to obtain business as lumbering dwindled was the promotion of northern Michigan as a resort area. The Grand Rapids and Indiana Railroad called itself "the fishing line" and widely advertised the attractiveness of northern Michigan for the angler and hunter. This railroad, as well as the Michigan Central and the Pere Marquette, built huge resort hotels at such places as Petosky, Harbor Springs, and Charlevoix. The largest of all, the Grand Hotel on Mackinac Island, was financed by the Grand Rapids and Indiana and the

[22] A. Calkins, "Railroads of Michigan Since 1850," *Michigan History*, XIII (1929), 5-26.

[23] T. D. Brock, "Paw Paw Versus the Railroads," *Michigan History*, XXXIX (1955), 129-183.

[24] L. Alilunas, "Michigan's Cut-over Canaan," *Michigan History*, XXVI (1942), 188-201.

Michigan Central Railroad engine, at Kalamazoo, 1874-88

Michigan Central Railroads and the Detroit and Cleveland Navigation Company. It was opened on July 10, 1887, with Chauncey Depew presiding at the opening dinner. The Grand Hotel quickly became the most fashionable resort in the Middle West. Mackinac Island had been known for many years for its pleasant summer climate and its clear air, which was especially attractive to sufferers from hay fever. Summer visitors had been coming before 1850. Numerous northern Michigan cities and towns, once centers of the lumber industry, were in process of becoming resort towns by 1900. In 1875 the Bay View Assembly, modeled after the original Chautauqua at Lake Chautauqua New York, was organized. This provided an educational and cultural program to supplement the health and recreation attractions of northern Michigan. Bay View Assembly was formed principally by Methodists. Other religious groups established camps and colonies for summer visitors to Michigan's north country.

The summer resorts provided increased traffic for the railroads, even though many of the visitors came by steamship. But this traffic was confined largely to the three summer months. The railroads could hardly operate profitably with heavy business only a quarter of the year, and relatively little for the remainder. There were numerous bankruptcies. The Pere Marquette was in chronic financial trouble. Some lines were abandoned. The railroads next turned to consolidation with larger systems, to which they were valuable as feeders. The merger of three different groups of railroads into the Pere Marquette system in 1900 was a first step in this direction. Ultimately the Pere Marquette itself was merged with the Chesapeake and Ohio. The Grand Rapids and Indiana was acquired by the Pennsylvania Railroad. The Ann Arbor formed an alliance with the Wabash. The Grand Trunk became part of the Canadian National Railway. And both the Michigan Southern and the Michigan Central merged with the New York Central Railroad.

The Great Lakes and their connecting rivers on three sides of the Lower Peninsula constituted serious barriers to through railroad traffic. This handicap was overcome to some degree by the railroad companies through the construction of tunnels and car ferries. Prior to the Civil War passengers and freight reached Detroit by steamboat or sailing vessel, from whence they were transferred to railroad trains running westward. The Michigan Central reached Chicago by running its lines around the southern tip of Lake Michigan. Goods and passengers on trains to Grand Haven and Muskegon were transferred to ships crossing Lake Michigan to Milwaukee. The first rail line across southern Canada reached Windsor, across the Detroit River from Detroit, in 1854. Ferries were put into service to transport passengers and freight across the river. In 1867 a ferry, the *Great Western*, capable of carrying twelve railroad cars, was put into service. Thenceforth passengers could remain in railroad coaches while crossing the river, and freight could be transferred without the labor and expense of handling on both sides of the river. In 1872 the Grand Trunk placed into service a similar but larger car ferry between Port Huron and Sarnia, Ontario. In 1887 railroad companies operating lines in the Lower and Upper Peninsulas formed an association that ordered a car ferry built to transport cars across the Straits of Mackinac between Mackinaw City and St. Ignace. It was placed in service the following year and was so constructed as to be able to operate the year around.

Up to this time car ferries had operated only across rivers or narrow bodies of water. The first car ferry in the world to navigate open waters was placed in service by the Toledo, Ann Arbor, and North Michigan (later called simply the Ann Arbor Railroad) on November 24, 1892. It operated between Frankfort, Michigan and Kewaunee, Wisconsin.[25] The Ann Arbor later operated ferries to Manitowoc, Wisconsin, and to Menominee and Manistique, Michigan. The success of these ferries induced other railroads to use the same method of promoting through traffic by securing a connecting link with western railroads having termini on the Wisconsin side of Lake Michigan. The Pere Marquette's first car ferry between Ludington and Manitowoc crossed Lake Michigan February 16-17, 1897. Subsequently, car ferries were put into service between Ludington and both Milwaukee and Kewaunee on the Wisconsin side. In 1903 the Grand Trunk began operating car ferries between Grand Haven and Milwaukee. The car ferries did much to promote railroad traffic; in later years they also became carriers of automobiles.[26] In 1891 the Grand Trunk completed a tunnel under the St. Clair River between Port Huron and Sarnia, replacing the car ferry. And in 1910 after several futile attempts a railroad tunnel under the Detroit River was completed, making it possible to run through trains from Chicago to New York by way of Detroit.

Almost 2,000 miles of railroad were constructed in the Upper Peninsula. An account of this will be found in the next chapter.

IN RETROSPECT

The cutting of timber began with the coming of the French to Michigan and is still going on. Although far from exhausted, Michigan's forest resources are only a fraction of what they once were. They have been wastefully exploited and plundered. Conservation and replanting are only a recent development, but considerable strides have been made through efforts to prevent or control forest fires and through the planting of millions of seedlings. The cut-over areas of northern Michigan, however, still have serious economic problems. These problems are similar to those of the cut-over areas of Wisconsin and Minnesota. In the Upper Peninsula mining took up the slack when the lumbermen left, but, as will be related in the next chapter, that has declined in recent years. The tourist and vacation business is now the major industry of northern Michigan, and the development of winter-sports areas has done something to provide income for the area during the nine months between one summer and the next. In retrospect it appears regrettable that the exploitation of

[25] Although the railroad company lists the Michigan terminus as Frankfort, the ferries actually dock at Elberta, across a small lake from the City of Frankfort.

[26] G. W. Hilton, *The Great Lakes Car Ferries*.

Michigan's timber resources did not proceed in a slower manner, and that some degree of regulation and control of timber harvesting was not instituted before it was too late. In the twentieth century the people of Michigan have become much more aware of the value of their natural resources and have taken steps to preserve and renew them so far as it is possible to do so.

Ore boat

17

THE UPPER PENINSULA, 1865-1960

Lumbering and mining brought prosperity to the Upper Peninsula in the generation following the Civil War. The population grew rapidly, cities sprang up, railroads were built, and those who remembered how reluctant Michiganians were to accept this region in exchange for the Toledo strip at the time Michigan attained statehood had to admit that it was, after all, a good bargain. But by 1910 the lumbermen were beginning to move on. Copper production reached its height during World War I and then began to decline. After 1900 Minnesota was producing more iron than Michigan. The depression of the 1930s hit the Upper Peninsula hard, as mines were closed and businesses collapsed. The growth of the tourist and vacation business, which the coming of the automobile greatly stimulated, was of some help, but it was a seasonal industry. In the 1940s and 1950s iron production declined still further. Some industry appeared and agriculture on a limited scale continued to provide some employment. The building of the Mackinac Bridge was expected to contribute to the recovery of the economy of the Upper Peninsula, but the first five or six years during which it was used did not substantiate any expectation that it would provide a solution to the region's problems. More hope was found in the concerted efforts by the people of the region, by experts on economic development, and by citizens of the Lower Peninsula to find ways and means to make this beautiful part of the state more prosperous.

BOOM YEARS IN THE COPPER COUNTRY

The rush to Michigan's Copper Country that began in 1844 was the first major mining boom in the United States. Hundreds came to get rich quick, and excitement was intense. As has been related in an earlier chapter, few individuals, equipped only with hand tools, made any great amount of money out of the copper boom. Capital was needed to sink shafts, to provide machinery, and to conduct the business on a large and profitable scale. This was provided largely by Bostonians, and in due course they reaped fabulous profits from Michigan copper. Most of their earnings were reinvested in the 1850s and 1860s. There was a brief period of depression in the Copper Country after the Civil War. But production soon increased again. From less than 25,-000,000 pounds in 1872, mine output rose steadily to over 233,-000,000 pounds in 1908. Thereafter a decline set in until the coming of World War I. Production reached an all-time high of 266,839,000 pounds in 1916, with an estimated value of $76,-080,000. From 1847 to 1887 Michigan produced more copper than any other state. Montana, and later Arizona, took the lead after 1887 even though Michigan production continued to increase for more than two decades thereafter.

The mines near the tip of the Keweenaw Peninsula around Copper Harbor and Eagle Harbor were the first to be opened. By 1867 they were largely worked out. The famous Cliff Mine closed down that year, although it was reopened later. Copper Harbor became almost a ghost town, and Eagle Harbor's population declined. The second major copper area around Ontonagon, the exploitation of which started about the same time as Copper Harbor, was productive somewhat longer, but by 1890 its fissure veins were almost exhausted. It was the third area, that around Portage Lake in the middle of the Keweenaw Peninsula, that continued longest to be a heavy producer. It was here that the Calumet and Hecla Company originated. Edwin J. Hulbert, who formed the Calumet Mining Company in 1861 and opened the Hecla mine in 1866, failed to manage the enterprise successfully. He was replaced in 1867 by Alexander Agassiz, son of the famous naturalist, Louis Agassiz, under whose direction the Calumet and Hecla mines were combined in 1871. The Calumet and Hecla Corporation also operated the Pewabic, Quincy, Osceola, Franklin, and Allouez mines.

Enormous profits were made by the Boston investors who owned the Calumet and Hecla and other mining companies

Dividend payments between 1885 and 1904 totalled $90,316,000, and between 1905 and 1918 the amount rose to $146,312,000. During World War I profits made by Michigan copper companies ranged from 16% to 31%. Even larger sums were realized from the appreciation of the price of stocks.[1] Calumet and Hecla stock, which at one time sold for $1.00 a share, brought $1,000 a share in 1907. As late as 1923 Calumet and Hecla paid a 700% stock dividend.

But it would be a mistake to assume that only a few lucky investors profited from the sustained boom in Michigan's Copper Country. The number employed by the mining companies increased from 4,188 in 1870 to 21,014 in 1907. Many thousand more people in the area earned their living as merchants, farmers, clerks, manufacturers, or in the professions that depended indirectly on copper mining. Houghton County, which had a population of 9,234 (including 279 Indians) in 1860, had grown to 88,098 by 1910.

Several flourishing cities grew up in the Copper Country. Oldest of these was Houghton, named for the first state geologist, Douglas Houghton, whose report attracted prospectors to the area. The famous Quincy mine, located near Hancock, was for years its major industry. Brass foundries and factories where mining machinery was manufactured grew up. The Finns, who came to the Copper Country in large numbers, founded Suomi College as a cultural center in 1899 at Hancock. Native red sandstone was the basic building material used in both Hancock and Houghton, giving the cities a unique appearance.

Through the efforts of Jay Hubbell, a resident of Houghton, the state legislature established the Michigan School of Mines in 1885. Hubbell donated the land for the first building, which was named in his honor. Classes started in 1886. By 1897 the school had attained the status of a college and was renamed the Michigan College of Mines. Enrollment increased to 266 and the faculty numbered thirty members by 1909. The college provided courses in metallurgy and mining engineering, and was an asset of considerable importance to the Copper Country.

Other sizable towns and cities grew up. Calumet was founded when the Calumet and Hecla Company built a town near its mine. Nearby Laurium had a population of 8,537 in 1910. Lake Linden grew up near the stamping mills of Calumet and Hecla. Schools and churches were built, and newspapers were established. Houghton County in 1910 had nine weekly newspapers,

[1] W. B. Gates, *Michigan Copper and Boston Dollars*, p. 116.

five dailies, one tri-weekly, three monthlies, and two quarterly publications. The number included an Italian daily, and publications in Slavonic, Finnish, and Swedish. There was an amazing amount of enthusiasm for the theater in the Copper Country. Calumet, Lake Linden, Laurium, Hancock, and Houghton all had their opera houses or theaters. For the opening performance in the Kerredge Theater at Hancock in 1902 box seats sold for $40 and seats in the orchestra section for $10. First-class theatrical troupes played the theaters in the Copper Country between 1900 and 1917. Among the artists and actors who appeared on their stages were Fritz Kreisler, Maude Adams, Sarah Bernhardt, and Alma Gluck.[2]

For six years following the Civil War Michigan copper companies were operating unprofitably, mainly due to the exhaustion of the older mines. Congress imposed a protective tariff of 5¢ a pound on copper in 1869. By that time Calumet and Hecla was the dominating company in Michigan copper mining. While Michigan produced far more copper than any other state, Calumet and Hecla mined more than half the copper output of the state. In 1870 all the mining and smelting companies in the United States formed a "pool," the purpose of which was to export and to sell on the world market enough copper to keep up domestic prices. The tariff and the pool enabled the companies to operate profitably and to make many technological improvements. Shafts were sunk deeper to reach the rich conglomerate lode, and air drills and high explosives were introduced. Between 1860 and 1880 the output of refined copper per worker tripled. Local railroads were built to move the copper. In 1873 the Portage Lake and Lake Superior Ship Canal was completed, permitting vessels to pass through the Keweenaw Peninsula. The federal government provided a land grant of 450,000 acres to finance this project—more than half the amount granted to build the Soo Canal two decades earlier. By 1884 the Copper Country was linked with Chicago by rail.

One of the great mines of the Copper Country, nicknamed "Old Reliable," was the Quincy, located just north of Hancock. Prior to the time it was shut down in 1931 during the great depression, it had produced continuously for 83 years; it was reopened in 1937 and once more produced copper until 1945. By that time it had paid its stockholders more than $27,000,000 in dividends. It reached 6,400 feet straight down into the earth.

[2] W. F. Dunbar, "The Opera House as a Social Institution in Michigan," *Michigan History,* XXVII (1943), 661-672.

had 91 levels, and hundreds of miles of underground railroad tracks.[3]

By 1904 in spite of consolidations there were still nineteen producing companies in the Copper Country. The stock of nine of these, however, was held by the Copper Range Consolidated Company, while four others were controlled by another holding company. These together with Calumet and Hecla and the Quincy Mining Company produced 95% of the state's output. Furthermore, these companies had obtained control of smelting operations. One of them was also engaged in copper manufacture, and some of them invested heavily in timber and sawmills. All of them owned short railroads and the Calumet and Hecla had a fleet of lake vessels. In the years immediately following the turn of the century copper prices were high, large profits were earned, and shares of the companies skyrocketed on the stock market. Low-cost mining fields in the West were hurting Michigan's competitive position, but this was partially offset by speeding up technological change.

The proportion of foreign-born in the Copper Country during these years was very large. Over 56% of the population of Houghton County in 1870 was foreign-born. From the beginning the Cornishmen were the backbone of the underground work force and supervisors of both underground and surface operations. These "Cousin Jacks" brought to America the traditions of generations of miners in England. One author says they had the "mathematics of a mole" and they were widely credited with having a nose for ore. Their "pasties" consisted of a mixture of meat, potatoes, and vegetables (always including turnips) enclosed in a crust, so that they could be carried down into the mines and supply a warm meal.[4] The Irish, nicknamed "Micks," were about as numerous in the Copper Country as the Cousin Jacks. And there was a traditional rivalry between the two. In a battle between Cornishmen and Irish in Ontonagon, the outnumbered Irish fled to the second story of a local saloon, whereupon the Cornishmen promptly set it afire. In the melee the saloon owner felled a Cornishman from behind with an axe. When word reached the Portage Lake region that the Ontonagon Irish were outnumbered, about 400 Irishmen prepared to march overland to re-enforce their countrymen. Wiser heads finally called a halt to the plan, but the word that the "Micks" were

[3] W. H. Pyne, "Quincy Mine: The Old Reliable," *Michigan History,* XLI (1957), 219-242.

[4] J. Fisher, "Michigan's Cornish People," *Michigan History,* XXIX (1945), 376-385.

coming got to Ontonagon, and Cornishmen by the dozens immediately took passage on a steamer that was about to depart to escape the wrath of the Irish.[5] Germans, Canadians, and Scandinavians also were numerous in the Copper Country. In the 1890s immigration to Houghton County underwent a considerable change; non-English-speaking newcomers began to predominate, especially those coming from Finland, Austria-Hungary, and Italy.

The copper companies by 1900 had come to own the land on which the miners lived, and in some cases the houses as well. Schools, hospitals, churches, libraries, and health insurance were subsidized by the companies. The earliest strike occurred in 1872, and labor troubles were common thereafter. The companies staunchly resisted labor organizations, but by 1911 many of the miners had joined the Western Federation of Miners, which became affiliated with the American Federation of Labor in that year. A strike began July 22, 1913. The workers demanded an eight-hour day, improvement of working conditions, minimum pay of $3.50 a day, and recognition of the Union. A "Citizens Alliance" was formed to maintain order, but the sheriff of Houghton County appealed to Governor Woodbridge N. Ferris for help, and the state militia was sent to the Copper Country. Efforts at negotiation failed because the operators refused to recognize the Union. A tragic incident occurred during the strike when someone cried "Fire" in a crowded hall at Calumet that was filled with miners and their families attending a Christmas party. In the rush for exits 73 women and children were trampled to death. The strike lasted until April 14, 1914. The miners won an eight-hour day, a minimum wage of $3, and certain other benefits, but the operators successfully resisted a recognition of the Union. World War I broke out later in 1914, and during that conflict copper production soared to new heights, but thereafter a steady decline set in.[6]

IRON FOR AN EXPANDING NATION

During the half-century that followed the Civil War the United States experienced its greatest period of expansion. Railroads spanned the continent and threaded their way to almost every town and hamlet. Iron ships were built to ply the Great Lakes and the oceans. Manufacturing grew under the wing of pro-

[5] Pyne, *op. cit.,* pp. 228-29.
[6] W. A. Sullivan, "The 1913 Revolt of the Michigan Copper Miners," *Michigan History,* XLIII (1949), 294-314.

tective tariffs, requiring thousands of factories to be built and equipped. Skyscrapers arose in the cities. Much of this expansion in transportation and industry depended on iron and steel. Michigan was the leading producer of iron ore until 1900, when the output of the great Mesabi Range in Minnesota began to outstrip that of Michigan mines. But Michigan's iron production continued to increase rapidly, reaching its height in 1920.

In 1865 the tonnage of iron ore passing through the Sault locks was 236,208, all of it from the Marquette Range in Michigan. Half a century later in 1905 ore tonnage was 34,353,456, of which something over 12,000,000 tons came from Michigan mines. In 1916 over 18,000,000 tons of Michigan ore were shipped.

The great increase of ore production in Michigan was made possible by the discovery and exploitation of two additional iron ranges. Government surveyors had reported traces of iron ore in the Ironwood area and near the Menominee River in 1850 and 1851. Lack of transportation facilities was the main factor in retarding the start of mining in these areas. With the coming of the Chicago and Northwestern Railway the Breen and Vulcan mines near Iron Mountain shipped their first ore in 1877, while the mines around Crystal Falls began production in 1882. Between 1877 and 1955 the Menominee Range alone produced 253,000,000 tons of ore.[7]

In 1871 Raphael Pumpelly, a Harvard geology professor, after studying the original survey notes of William A. Burt, found traces of iron ore between the Montreal River and Lake Gogebic in the extreme western part of the Upper Peninsula. With the financial aid of Alexander Agassiz and Quincy Shaw, a Boston capitalist, he purchased five miles of what came to be called the Gogebic Range. The Colby Mine, first to produce in this area, was the result of the discovery of a lump of rock in 1873 by N. D. Moore, who was exploring for timber. This mine, located at Bessemer, started shipping ore after the completion of a railroad into the district in 1884. Other mines were opened in rapid succession. The Gogebic Range proved to be an even greater producer than the Marquette and the Menominee Ranges. From 1884 to 1955 over 294,000,000 tons of ore were shipped from its mines. The Marquette range produced 283,000,000 tons from 1849 to 1955.[8]

The earliest producing iron mines in the Upper Peninsula were

[7] The Vulcan mine near Norway, no longer in production, is open to visitors and is a prime tourist attraction.

[8] C. L. Cobb, "Ho! Gogebic County," *Michigan History,* VI (1922), 328-45; P. P. Mason, *Iron Ore Mining in Michigan Past and Present,* p. 5.

the Jackson mine at Negaunee and the National mine at Ishpeming, three miles away. After 1865, however, many additional
mines were opened in the Marquette range. Several towns take
their names from these mines. The Republic mine produced ore
that was 88% pure iron oxide. Opened in 1871, it continued to,
produce until 1927. The Champion mine was worked from 1867
to 1910, and the Michigamme mine from 1872 to 1905. There
were many other smaller mines. In the Menominee range scores
of mines, large and small, were opened, worked for various
periods of time, and then abandoned. Among the more famous
was the Vulcan mine near Norway, opened in 1877 and worked
until 1946. Iron Mountain grew up around the Chapin mine.
Other heavy producers around Iron Mountain were the Pewabic,
Ludington, Hewitt, Indiana, Calumet, Cornell, Garfield, and Hancock mines. Crystal Falls, so named for its location near a cascade
on the Paint River, grew up around the Bristol mine, opened in
1882. Iron River and its sister city, Stambaugh, were the last of
the large communities in the Menominee range to be developed.
The largest producer in this area is the Caspian mine. A large
number of Finnish immigrants who came in the 1890s settled
in the Crystal Falls—Iron River area. In the Gogebic range
twelve mines were opened between 1884 and 1887, and twenty
others up to 1925. Ironwood is the principal city in the Gogebic
range. The site of the city was platted by a railroad company
in 1885. Other towns and cities that grew up around mines in
the Gogebic range were Wakefield, Ramsay, and Bessemer. The
Norrie-Aurora-Pabst mine at Ironwood outproduced any other
mine in the Upper Peninsula. The Chapin at Iron Mountain in
the Menominee range was the second largest producer.

As has been noted in an earlier chapter, over 25 forges were
built in the Upper Peninsula during the nineteenth century to
process the iron ore. The early forges brought lumps of iron ore
to a high degree of heat, and they were then "wrought" into iron
"blooms" through a process of hammering. Vast amounts of hardwood were required to make the charcoal used in these forges.
Fortunately, there were large stands of hardwood as well as pine
in the Upper Peninsula. Limestone, another essential material in
the process, was readily available in abundant quantities. An
immense quantity of hardwood was required to produce the
amount of charcoal needed to operate these forges. It was estimated in 1903 that the furnaces of the Upper Peninsula consumed so much charcoal that thirty acres of hardwood per day
had to be cut to supply the kilns.[9] By that time the supply

[9] Mason, *op. cit.*, p. 8.

of hardwood was beginning to be exhausted; furthermore, the process was too expensive. It was more profitable to ship the ore in the big ore carriers that were being built and to smelt it with coke in furnaces on Lake Erie and at the southern end of Lake Michigan. One by one the charcoal kilns and blast furnaces in the Upper Peninsula were abandoned until none were in use.

Some idea of this extinct industry in the Upper Peninsula may be gained by visiting the "ghost town" of Fayette, located on the Garden Peninsula, which juts down into Lake Michigan from the Upper Peninsula. The Jackson Iron Company, which developed the first iron mine of the Upper Peninsula, purchased the site of Fayette and some 16,000 acres of hardwood forest located nearby in 1864. Charcoal kilns and smelting furnaces were constructed. Limestone at the site provided the flux needed in the smelting process. A narrow gauge railroad brought the wood to the kilns. Docks were built. By 1869 there were a store, office building, carpenter and blacksmith shops, and over forty houses. Subsequently a hotel, a post office, and even an opera house were built. The iron ore used in the furnaces was shipped from Negaunee to Escanaba by rail and from there to Fayette by scows towed by tugs. The hardwood supply of the Garden Peninsula was the key to the prosperity of this boom town, and when it was gone Fayette—after a brief interlude during which it was a resort town—was abandoned. Many of its buildings and the remains of its kilns and furnaces may still be seen. The site has been acquired by the Conservation Department for a State Park.[10]

During the half-century following the Civil War improvements in the methods of mining iron matched those in copper mining. In the early years until the 1870s the production of iron ore was really a quarrying operation. The overburden of trees, sod, and soil was removed, and the iron ore that lay underneath was then broken up and carried away. When the surface ore had been secured, shafts were sunk adjacent to the ore bodies and horizontal tunnels were cut into the ore beds. Miners descended into the shafts by wooden ladders and the ore was brought to the surface by bucket hoists. But by 1900 steam-powered machinery was being used in the mines. Elevators or "cages" took miners underground and later brought them back to the surface. Ore was hoisted by machinery, which also operated the pumps required to remove water from the mines. Electrical power and lighting were introduced around 1895. Dynamite replaced black blasting powder; diamond drills revolutionized the discovery of new

[10] C. Dunathan, "Fayette," *Michigan History*, **XLI** (1957), 204-208.

lodes, while power drills and electric cap lamps represent other improvements. Hard-toed boots, safety hats, and shatter-proof glasses became standard equipment for the miner.

Excitement swept the Upper Peninsula periodically when rumors spread that silver and gold had been found. As early as 1846 a visitor to Michigan's copper mines reported abundant signs of silver. Small nuggets of silver were found occasionally, the miners usually pocketing them as a bonus. A small amount of silver was obtained by the mining companies; in 1887 it was reported that $3,500,000 worth of silver had been produced by Upper Peninsula mines. As recently as 1939 Michigan produced 101,878 fine ounces of silver. Discoveries of gold occurred chiefly in the Marquette Iron Range. Several mines were opened, the most promising being the Ropes mine near Ishpeming. First worked in 1883, this mine was reopened briefly in 1933. But in no case has gold production over any considerable period of time equalled the costs of mining.[11]

As shafts were sunk deeper and as the tunnels or "drifts" were extended further, the iron-mining companies required large amounts of timbers to support the overhang. For this reason, and also to obtain hardwood for charcoal, they acquired in many cases large tracts of timber. Of critical importance in mining and lumbering was transportation, and the mining companies thus built railroads and ore carriers. All this required large amounts of capital, and as a consequence, the smaller operators were gradually squeezed out as large, integrated companies took their place.

THE DEVELOPMENT OF TRANSPORTATION FACILITIES

The growth and prosperity of the Upper Peninsula in the half-century after the Civil War was made possible to a large degree by a beneficent government in Washington. As mentioned earlier, the copper tariff was an important factor in keeping up the price of copper, enabling the companies to make large profits, and indirectly bringing lush times to the Copper Country of Michigan. A tariff placed upon iron in 1880 had a similar effect on the iron-mining industry. Of equal or greater importance was the contribution of the federal government in providing transportation facilities. A grant of 750,000 acres of public land made possible the Soo Canal. The United States government also built the new and larger Weitzel lock. In 1881 when this lock was opened, the

[11] L. A. Chase, "Silver and Gold in Michigan," *Michigan History,* XXX (1946), 255-262.

Soo Canal was turned over by Michigan to the United States and thenceforth the locks were operated toll-free at public expense. The Poe Lock replaced the old state locks in 1896. Meanwhile, another grant of 450,000 acres of public land had been made to build the canal across the Keweenaw Peninsula. Federal land grants also made a major contribution to railroad building in the Upper Peninsula. Over 60% of the 5,505,336 acres of public lands granted to encourage railroad building in Michigan went to Upper Peninsula lines.

The year 1855 marked the completion of the Soo Canal, and on August 17 of that year the Brig *Columbia*, laden with ore from Marquette, was the first ore ship to pass through the locks. The same year a twenty-mile railroad connecting the iron mines at Negaunee with Marquette was completed. It was conceived and carried to completion by Heman D. Ely,[12] and was the first Upper Peninsula railroad. Cars were at first hauled by mules, but a steam locomotive was put in use in 1857. During the Civil War a company was formed to connect this railroad with a line to the Bay de Noquet on Lake Michigan. Construction was completed in 1864 from Escanaba on Bay de Noquet to Negaunee and from there by the twenty-mile line constructed earlier to Marquette. The iron from the mines around Negaunee and Ishpeming could now be shipped either north to Marquette on Lake Superior or south to Escanaba on Lake Michigan.[13]

Under the impetus of munificent land grants, railroad construction in the Upper Peninsula proceeded rapidly during the years after the Civil War. One line was built westward from Marquette and reached Michigamme in 1865. By 1883 this line had been extended to Houghton. A railroad connecting Marquette with St. Ignace was completed in 1881, and a branch linked this road with Sault Ste. Marie in 1887. Connections between this railroad and the two railroads reaching Mackinaw City from the south—the Michigan Central and the Grand Rapids and Indiana —were made by means of steamers. A car ferry placed in use in 1888 and operated jointly by the three railroads reaching the Straits made it possible to transport freight and passenger cars across the Straits and thus provided a link by rail between the Lower and Upper Peninsulas. Passengers could entrain at Marquette or Sault Ste. Marie and travel directly to Detroit or Grand Rapids. Freight shipments could be made without load-

[12] "Historical Address, Delivered July Fourth, 1876, by the Hon. S. P. Ely of Marquette," *Mich. Pioneer and Historical Colls.*, VII (1884), 168.
[13] E. A. Calkins, "The Railroads of Michigan Since 1850," *Michigan History*, XIII (1929), 8-10.

Train carriers on the Great Lakes (Ludington, Michigan)

ing and unloading at the Straits. On the western side of the Upper Peninsula, copper companies built short railroads, one connecting Calumet with Hancock. A land-grant railroad was built southward from Ontonagon to the Wisconsin state line, where it formed a connection with one of the railroads being built northward through Wisconsin. In 1872 the Chicago and Northwestern Railroad reached Escanaba from Chicago. By using the line already built between Escanaba and Marquette, Marquette had direct rail connections with Chicago. A branch from Escanaba was built into the Menominee Range, reaching Quinnesec in 1877 and Iron Mountain in 1880.

Through the process of consolidation the railroads of the Upper Peninsula were brought together into four main systems. The Duluth, South Shore, and Atlantic (recently acquired by the Soo Line) stretches across the northern edge of the peninsula, extending from St. Ignace and Sault Ste. Marie in the east, through Marquette to Houghton and westward to Duluth and Superior, Wisconsin. Paralleling it along the Lake Michigan shore, the Soo Line connects Sault Ste. Marie with Manistique and extends westward to Minneapolis and St. Paul, with a branch extending southward to Chicago. From the latter city two main lines were built northward through Wisconsin into the copper and iron ranges of northern Michigan: the Chicago and Northwestern and the Chicago, Milwaukee, and St. Paul.

Railroads were indispensable in getting the ore from the mines to ports, and in bringing merchandise into and out of the mining and lumbering towns and cities. To a limited extent they were used for the shipment of ores directly to the smelting plants. But the most economical and practical way to ship the ores was by water. When ships first loaded iron ore most of the work had to be done by hand. Ore was loaded in barrels and put aboard the vessels. Later, wheelbarrows were used to carry the ore onto the docks, where it was dumped into the holds of vessels. When the ore reached its destination, it had to be shoveled into buckets that were hoisted and dumped on shore. In 1859 the first modern dock was built at Marquette by the Cleveland Iron Company. Other huge docks were built at Escanaba for the Menominee Range, and at Ashland, Wisconsin for the Gogebic Range.

Schooners and other sailing vessels were first used to transport the ore, but steamships soon took their place. In 1869 the first bulk freighter, the *R. J. Hackett*, was launched. Built of wood, it was 211 feet long, had a 33-foot beam, and a capacity of 1,200 tons. In 1882 the *Onoko* was built, the first iron-hulled steamer. It had a gross tonnage of 2,164. The first steel ship built for service on the Great Lakes was the *Spokane*, launched in 1886. She was 249½ feet in length. Two years later Alexander McDougall of Duluth, Minnesota designed the famous "whaleback" for carrying ore. Built especially to withstand the storms of the Great Lakes the "whaleback" resembled a huge floating cigar. Many ships of this design were built, and were in use for years. Later improvements in design brought the abandonment of the whaleback. Length and capacity of the ships were steadily increased. The year 1906 saw the advent of 600-foot vessels. It was not until 1952 that the first 700-footer was launched. The profitable operation of such immense ore-carriers required that they be held in port as short a time as possible. Loading could be accomplished quickly but unloading was a slower process until 1899, when Robert Aspin designed and built the first unloaders. They made it possible to remove the ore from the largest carriers within a few hours.[14]

Ownership and operation of the giant ore carriers came largely

---

[14] W. Havighurst, *Vein of Iron; the Pickands Mather Story*, pp. 95f.; M. M. Quaife, *Lake Michigan*, p. 167; Havighurst, *Long Ships Passing*; G. A. Cuthbertson, *Freshwater: A History of the Great Lakes.*

into the hands of the companies that owned the mines. In the
early years when small companies were the rule, owners had to
pay the going price for the transportation of their ore. One of
these was the Cleveland Iron Company, organized in 1847 by 11
Cleveland men, including a young lawyer named Samuel L.
Mather. By 1869 Mather had become president of the company,
a position he held until 1890. In 1872 the Cleveland Iron Company acquired a controlling interest in a fleet of steamers and
schooners owned by the Cleveland Transportation Company. In
1891 a merger was formed with the Iron Cliffs Company, which
had been organized in 1864 by Samuel J. Tilden of New York and
William B. Ogden of Chicago. This was the origin of the great
Cleveland-Cliffs Mining Company. This company not only owned
a fleet of ore carriers, but it also built railroads and conducted
logging operations on a huge scale. Carefully eliminating waste, it
used forest products for the manufacture of veneer, wooden-
ware, and pulp as well as lumber. In 1903 Cleveland-Cliffs purchased the Jackson Mining Company, originally formed in 1844
and the oldest iron-mining company in the Upper Peninsula.[15]

Another of the major iron companies came into being in 1883
when Samuel Mather, eldest son of Samuel L. Mather, joined
forces with James Pickands, a Marquette merchant, and Jay
Morse, an agent for iron companies, to form Pickands, Mather and
Company. Extending their operations into the Menominee and
Gogebic ranges, Pickands Mather, by the time of World War I, had
become the second largest producer of iron ore in the United
States. Like Cleveland-Cliffs, Pickands Mather became a heavy
investor in ore carriers. By 1913 Pickands Mather was the second
largest fleet operator on the Great Lakes.[16] A third major com-
pany, the M. A. Hanna Company, was formed in 1885, also by
Cleveland men, and came to own a complex of iron mines, coal
mines, and carriers. After the formation of the United States Steel
Company in 1901, this enormous corporation dominated the
Mesabi Range in Minnesota and also owned a fleet of carriers.[17]

AGRICULTURE

In the early days of mining in the Upper Peninsula, food
in large amounts had to be brought into the mining towns.
The problem of maintaining local food supplies was always a serious one. It was soon discovered that most grains except corn could

15 H. Hatcher, *A Century of Iron and Men.*
16 Havighurst, *Vein of Iron,* pp. 90-99.
17 S. H. Holbrook, *Iron Brew.*

be grown. Around the mining camps, as the trees were cleared away, gardens and farms began to appear. But it was years before local supplies of foodstuffs were adequate. Upbound vessels from lower-lake ports brought provisions of all kinds, and even feed for livestock. Oxen, cattle, and horses were brought in, and in the days before docks were available, they were put overboard to swim for shore.[18]

As the timber was removed, farmers moved in. But the cold climate and the thin and sandy soils in many parts of the peninsula prevented it from becoming a flourishing agricultural area. In the eastern portion there were large swamp areas. Nevertheless, the land in general was better for farming in the eastern part of the peninsula than in the western part. The better farming areas were found in Chippewa, Delta, and Menominee Counties. Hay and potatoes were the best crops. Abundant pasturage encouraged the growth of livestock. A considerable amount of the population growth in the fifteen counties of the Upper Peninsula from 180,523 in 1890 to 332,556 in 1920 was due to the expansion of agriculture. The number of farms doubled between 1900 and 1920, increasing from 6,102 to 12,315. By 1920 about one-tenth of the 10,000,000 acres of the Upper Peninsula were under cultivation.

THE BEGINNINGS OF THE VACATION INDUSTRY

A traveler on a Great Lakes ship in 1855 wrote in regard to a stop at Detroit: "We have a large accession of excursionists at this point; indeed, our number is more than doubled. Among the number are some elegant looking ladies and fine-looking men. The *North Star* has just come down from an excursion trip. And she is landing amid strains of music and shouts of excursionists." As early as 1842 a prominent Cincinnati physician was directing attention to the Great Lakes area for its beneficial effects on health. After expatiating at some length on the excellence of the climate, Dr. Daniel Drake wrote that the traveler on the Great Lakes "has then escaped from the region of miasmas, mosquitoes, congestive fevers, calomel, intermittent ague, cakes, liver diseases, jaundice, cholera morbus, dyspepsia, blue devils, and duns, on the whole of which he looks back with gay indifference, if not a feeling of good-natured contempt." The physician then contrasts the typical eastern watering place where the eye "wanders over the comingled dlers, gamblers, coquettes, and dandies," to the experience of seeing the "hourly unfolding of fresh aspects of nature." After calling

[18] L. A. Chase, "Michigan's Upper Peninsula," *Michigan History*, XX 1936), 327ff.

attention to the historic places on the Great Lakes, he continues, "But a different inhabitant, of more interest . . . to the dyspeptic and the gourmand, is the celebrated whitefish . . . . Its flesh, which in the cold and clear waters of the lake, organized and imbued with life, is liable but to this objection—that he who tastes it once will thenceforth be unable to relish that of any other fish," but he cautions against eating too much trout, which "is said to produce drowsiness." One of those who took Dr. Drake's advice was Horace Mann, the famous eastern educator. Writing from Mackinac Island in 1857 Mann attests to the joys of a summer vacation in Michigan: "I never breathed such air before, and this must be some that was clear out of Eden, and did not get cursed. I sleep every night under sheet, blanket, and coverlet, and no day is too warm for smart walking and vigorous bowling. The children are crazy with animal spirits."[19]

Mackinac Island was probably Michigan's first mecca for tourists and vacationists. Among those who visited this historic spot in the 1830s and 1840s were the English writer Harriet Martineau, Prince de Joinville, son of King Louis Philippe of France, and the American writers Margaret Fuller and William Cullen Bryant. In 1871 three of the buildings constructed by the American Fur Company were linked to form a hotel, the John Jacob Astor House, to accommodate tourists. The construction of the Grand Hotel in 1887 by two railroads and a steamship company has been noted earlier.

In the Upper Peninsula Marquette was becoming noted as a tourist and resort center as early as 1857. Among the prominent personages to visit the city were Robert Dollar, Andrew Carnegie, and Mrs. Abraham Lincoln. By 1860 Marquette had a three-story frame hotel located in a grove of pines and maples with an excellent view of the harbor, built especially for vacationists. It had over a hundred family rooms and a dining hall to seat 125. There were croquet courts, arbors, swings, rustic benches, and a bandstand, as well as a dock where sailboats and rowboats could be moored. Wealthy people from Pittsburgh, New York, Chicago, and Detroit came here to spend the summers. The Northwestern Hotel, as it was called, attracted many visitors from Boston and New York who had financial interests in the iron mines and furnaces of the Marquette Range. Another four-story resort hotel, the Mesnard, was built in 1883. In 1896 an enormous hostelry called Hotel Superior was opened with a grand ball. Furnished in flamboyant willow and golden-oak furniture, it was designed to cater to the

[19] D. Drake, *Discourses on Northern Lakes and Southern Invalids,* quoted in J. A. Fleet, *Old and New Mackinac,* pp. 157-163.

summer-cruise tourists on Great Lakes passenger steamers.[20]

Other cities in the Upper Peninsula also were summer resorts. Among these were Hancock, St. Ignace, and Sault Ste. Marie. A brochure published in 1895 mentions the "weary sameness" of eastern mountain and beach resorts and contrasts this with the natural beauties, the pure air, and the excellent fishing and hunting in the Lake Superior country.[21] Guidebooks were published to direct the tourist to northern resorts.[22] At first the tourist and resort business was merely incidental to the much more important mining, lumber, and farming industries. But in 1912 the Grand Rapids *Press* proclaimed in a full-page story that "resorters bring prosperity." The story stated that railroads and steamships were among the chief benefactors, but even the small resort operator was grateful for the substantial supplement to his income from farming attributable to the resorters.[23]

As the twentieth century entered its second decade, leaders in the Upper Peninsula were becoming conscious that the great days of lumbering were about over. Rocky Mountain copper mines and Minnesota iron mines were out-producing Michigan mines. On February 22, 1911 some 240 delegates from the fifteen Upper Peninsula counties met to organize a co-operative organization to deal with their economic problems. The aim of the organization, as expressed in its preamble, was "to endeavor to bring about the wise use of land and water resources of the Upper Peninsula of Michigan that they might better administer to the economy of our people." Financed by contributions from transportation companies, mining firms, businessmen, and local goverment units, the Bureau issued brochures setting forth the agricultural opportunities of the Upper Peninsula. It also began to extol the recreational attractions of the region and to support the building of highways.

THE PEOPLE

The development of the Upper Peninsula was due as much to its people as to its resources. Even before the Civil War large numbers of immigrants were coming to the Upper Peninsula from Europe. The first Cornishmen arrived in 1844 to work in the copper mines of Keweenaw County. After the Civil War they came in ever increasing numbers. Their speech and manners made them

[20] *Marquette Centennial.*

[21] *The Tourist and Investor. An Illustrated Guide to the Lake Superior District* (1895).

[22] *The Standard Guide. Mackinac Island and Northern Lake Resorts* (1904).

[23] Grand Rapids *Press,* July 1, 1912.

a distinctive group. They were interested only in mining. Rugged and rough, they made excellent citizens. They were known for their love of singing, their humor, and their fondness for sports such as wrestling matches. Through their organization, the Order of the Sons of St. George, the Cornish kept in touch with the old world.[24]

Among the immigrants brought in during the Civil War the Swedes were especially numerous. They came in large numbers to Houghton County and to the iron ranges. The Norwegians also came into the lumber and mining areas, predominating around Ishpeming during the 1870-1880 decade. The town of Norway in the Menominee Range symbolizes the large number of Norwegians there.

The Finns began to arrive about 1870. The great influx did not occur, however, until about the turn of the century. The Finnish pioneers were employed extensively as blacksmiths, carpenters, and skilled yardsmen around the mines. Most of them were mainly interested in acquiring land, and their chief contribution has been their work as pioneer farmers in this rugged land. The Finnish immigrants were usually literate and very intelligent. They established not only their own school at Hancock, but also their own newspapers and their own churches—the Finnish Evangelical Lutheran Church, the Apostolic Lutheran Church in America, and the National Finnish Lutheran Church. Many of them brought over liberal or radical ideas. One of their most notable achievements was the successful operation of consumer co-operatives on a large scale. Nowhere else in America has this movement been so successful.[25] The Finns settled mainly in the western part of the Upper Peninsula.

The Copper Country, as already indicated, attracted a number of other nationalities: Irish, Germans, and—in the later years—Italians. Another sizable element in the population of the Upper Peninsula were the French Canadians. Some were descendants of the early French fur traders; others were immigrants from Canada who came later. They were employed extensively in lumbering and many of them were fishermen and part-time farmers. They tended to avoid the mining areas. As late as 1930 about one-quarter of the population of the Upper Peninsula was foreign-born.

[24] J. E. Jopling, "Cornish Miners of The Upper Peninsula," *Michigan History*, XII (1928), 554-567.

[25] J. Wargelin, "The Finns in Michigan," *Michigan History*, XXIV (1940), 179-204; L. C. Kercher, V. W. Kebker, and W. C. Leland Jr., *Consumers' Co-operatives in the North Central States*.

THE COUNTIES

The counties of the Upper Peninsula were laid out and organized by legislative act as settlement advanced. Michilimackinac County, created in 1818, at first included most of what is now the Upper Peninsula. At the request of residents of Sault Ste. Marie a second county, Chippewa, was organized in 1826. In 1843 these two counties were reduced in size and four new counties were organized: Delta, Marquette, Ontonagon, and Schoolcraft. The rush to the Copper Country led to the organization of Houghton County in 1845, from which Keweenaw County was separated in 1861.

A resident of that part of Delta County in the region of the Menominee River, Asa Bangs, appeared in Lansing in 1861 and persuaded the legislature to organize the region into a new county to be named Bleeker. The name was that of Bang's wife before her marriage. When word got back to the residents of the area of what had been done, they were so incensed that they refused to go ahead with the formation of a county government. In 1863 they persuaded the lawmakers to change the name to Menominee. In 1867 the legislature provided that the region around Ishpeming was to be set apart from Marquette County as Washington County. Marquette citizens brought suit to nullify the action, and their efforts met with success when the state supreme court declared the act unconstitutional. Thus Michigan missed having a county named for the first President.

In the 1870s and 1880s the growth of population in the Upper Peninsula led to the organization of additional counties, formed by reducing the size of those already in existence. Two of the new counties, Alger and Luce, were named for governors of the state. Baraga honored the name of the great Catholic missionary and bishop of the Upper Peninsula. Gogebic and Iron Counties were created to meet the governmental needs of the increasing population of the iron ranges. Isle Royale County was created in 1875, but sixteen years later it was disorganized and became attached to Keweenaw County. The last of Michigan's 83 counties to be organized was Dickinson. It was established in 1891 by what had become a rarity in Michigan: a legislature controlled by the Democratic party. It was named for Don M. Dickinson, a prominent Michigan Democrat who had been a member of the cabinet of President Grover Cleveland during his first administration.[26]

[26] W. L. Jenks, "The History and Meaning of County Names in Michigan," *Mich. Pioneer and Historical Colls.*, XXXVIII (1912), 439-478.

ECONOMIC PROBLEMS SINCE *1918*

Wartime demand for minerals and agricultural products between 1914 and 1918 brought considerable prosperity to the Upper Peninsula. But after the close of the war a long period of economic decline set in. Four decades later no satisfactory answer had yet been found for these problems.

The decline that became evident in the 1920s was due to a combination of circumstances. The stands of virgin pine, the harvesting and sawing of which had for a generation been a major component in the economy of the area, were now gone, and logging was reduced to small-scale operations. Farmers all over the nation suffered from adverse conditions in the 1920s, and those in northern Michigan were particularly hard hit. With the end of World War I came a sharp decline in the demand abroad for American agricultural products. Prices declined and surpluses began to accumulate. Farmers in the Upper Peninsula, tilling soils far less fertile than those of the prairie states, could not compete successfully in such a situation. Some left to find jobs in the cities down below, but most of them hung on, hoping for better days. There was actually a small increase in the number of farms in the Upper Peninsula between 1920 and 1930, but much less than in the preceding two decades. It is probable that many workers formerly employed in logging and mining and now thrown out of work in those industries were hoping to earn a living on the land. While the population of the state as a whole increased by almost 1,200,000 between 1920 and 1930, that of the Upper Peninsula declined from 332,556 to 318,675. Iron mining reached a peak production of 18,993,000 tons in 1920, dropped to less than one-quarter of that amount in 1921, then leveled off to an average of about 15,000,000 tons annually during the remainder of the decade. But mechanization made it possible to produce the iron with less manpower, and as a result hundreds of iron miners were left without jobs.

Even more serious was the decline in copper mining. Prices of copper declined sharply in the 1920s, and as a consequence only the richest lodes could be mined profitably. For half a century after the production of Michigan copper had begun it enjoyed a marked advantage by virtue of the fact that the rock contained copper in its pure state. This advantage was partly overcome when the Bessemer process was adapted to convert the sulphide ores of the western mines. The Arizona and Montana mining companies also benefited from the value of silver and gold mined as a byproduct. These factors had been operative for some years before 1920. But lower labor costs in Michigan helped compensate for the difference until about the time of World War I, due to the abundance of immigrant workers who were willing to work for lower wages than western miners received. Labor costs of Michigan copper mining companies in the 1920s increased by about 50%, and the passage of restrictive immigration acts cut off the supply of cheap immigrant labor. Meanwhile, copper prices in the 1920s averaged about 10% below those of the prewar period. As a consequence, production declined from the peak of 267,-000,000 pounds in 1917 to 92,000,000 pounds in 1921. There was some improvement after that, but in no year did the output reach more than 83% of the 1905-1912 average. Employment dropped faster than production, because fewer workers were required for selected mining. In 1909 copper mining had provided employment for 19,000 workers; the number was down to 12,200 in 1919 and declined still further to 7,800 in 1929.[27]

The depression decade of the 1930s intensified the difficulties already in evidence during the preceding decade. In spite of agreements among the copper companies to control production, the price of copper declined to a low point of 5.6¢ per pound in 1932. In 1929 it had been 18.1¢ per pound. Of the six companies that had been operating in 1929 four were completely shut down by 1933. Almost 6,000 miners lost their jobs. Between 1910 and 1940 Houghton County lost almost half its population. Two-thirds of the families in Keweenaw County and more than one-third of those in Houghton County were on relief in 1934, as compared with 12.2% in the state as a whole. Iron mining was also hit hard by the great depression of the 1930s, though not so badly as copper mining. Production, which had been at an annual level of about 15,000,000 tons in the 1920s, was down to 1,000,000 tons in 1932. By 1939, however, it was back up to around 11,000,000 tons. One casualty of the depression was the fabulously rich Chapin Mine near Iron Mountain, which had produced continuously since 1880. It was closed in 1934. The distress in the mining areas had a tendency to drive people back to the land, and there was a rather significant increase in the number of Upper Peninsula farms between 1930 and 1935. Because of the effects of the depression elsewhere, there was little opportunity to find employment by leaving the region. The population of the Upper Peninsula increased slightly during the decade, as it did in the Lower Peninsula.

But during the decade of the 1940s, while the population of the state as a whole increased by 20%, that of the Upper Pen-

27 W. B. Gates, *op. cit.*, p. 145.

insula decreased by more than 20,000. War production and the postwar boom created a demand for labor, and encouraged an exodus from the Upper Peninsula. World War II, like World War I, tended to stimulate both iron and copper production. But the output of Michigan mines failed to reach the high levels of World War I, and higher copper production was made possible only through the premium price set by the government on Lake copper to compensate for the higher costs in that area. After the war Calumet and Hecla was the only significant miner of copper in Michigan, and even its mines were closed for several months in 1949 when copper prices slumped. Iron production after the war averaged about 11,000,000 tons annually during the remainder of the decade. The problem of farm surpluses reappeared after the war, and the marginal farming of the Upper Peninsula became even less profitable.

IN SEARCH OF A SOLUTION

By 1950 concern for the economic future of the Upper Peninsula was becoming serious, and a variety of efforts were made to discover means of improving the situation. The one bright prospect was provided by the vigorous growth of the tourist and vacation industry. With the growth in the number of automobiles and improved highways, both Michiganians and those from other states were discovering the attractions of northern Michigan for those seeking recreation. In 1924 the State Highway Department had placed in operation automobile ferries across the Straits of Mackinac, greatly improving the facilities formerly provided only by the railroad car ferries for crossing the Straits. In order to promote the tourist and vacation industry the legislature in 1932 allocated 25% of the proceeds from the gasoline tax to the building of Upper Peninsula highways and 25% for highways in the northern half of the Lower Peninsula. This made it possible to build good roads in these areas, even though they were sparsely populated. With the advent of the automobile, the huge resort hotels became less popular, and one by one they disappeared. But tourist homes, lodges, and motels took their place. Restaurants, amusement places, and recreational facilities were provided to serve the tourist. Thousands of people in the Upper Peninsula found employment in this way, and by 1950 it was calculated that the tourists spent $50,000,000 annually in the Upper Peninsula alone.

Summer attractions were supplemented by winter sports, which brought more and more people to the area. A group of Norwegians in Ishpeming formed the first ski club in Michigan in 1888, and in 1905 Ishpeming was instrumental in forming a national ski association. Skiing enthusiasts from the Middle West gathered there annually after 1905 for the winter ski tournament. A ski jump with a vertical height of 280 feet and a length of 860 feet was built in 1925. Iron Mountain and other Upper Peninsula cities also provided ski jumps and other facilities for winter sports. Meanwhile, the Conservation Department established in 1921 began its work of preserving the natural resources of the area and the establishment of state parks. The magnificent Porcupine Mountain State Park in Gogebic and Ontonagon Counties, containing 58,046 acres, was established in 1944, and is the largest state park in Michigan.

For many years the possibility of building a bridge across the Straits of Mackinac had been considered. Engineers had doubted that the underwater rock was solid enough to support the weight of a bridge. But in 1951 after further studies it was concluded that the difficulties could be overcome and that the bridge could be built. These studies were conducted under the supervision of a seven-member Mackinac Bridge Authority, headed by Prentiss Brown of St. Ignace and created by the legislature in 1950. After finding that the bridge was feasible from an engineering standpoint, the Authority undertook cost studies and made careful estimates of the traffic that might use the bridge during the years following its completion. It was found that construction would cost nearly $80,000,000. The Authority determined that the bridge would be financed by the issuance of revenue bonds secured by the tolls to be collected. To make the bonds more attractive the legislature in 1954 obligated the state to pay to the Authority $417,000 per year to cover the maintenance costs, leaving the tolls intact to pay the interest and principal on the bonds as they came due. Bonds in the amount of $99,800,000 were sold at $99,000,000, drawing interest at 4.26%. The bond issue produced funds to build the bridge and to pay interest charges during construction. It was calculated that the bonds could be retired in forty years, at which time the bridge was to become the property of the state.

Designer of the bridge was David B. Steinman of New York. Constructed between 1954 and 1957, it has a center span of 3,800 feet hanging between 552-foot towers, second in length only to the Golden Gate bridge. Total length is 26,444 feet. It carries four lanes for traffic. Height above the water at the center is 148 feet, sufficient to allow the largest ships to pass underneath. The structure was opened in November, 1957, in time for use by the annual army of deer hunters moving to the Upper Peninsula. With the opening of the bridge, the state-owned auto ferries were discontinued and sold.[28]

The Mackinac Bridge helped establish closer links between the Lower Peninsula and the Upper Peninsula; it also promoted tourism and vacationing in the Upper Peninsula. But it performed no miracle for the people of the region and provided no automatic solution for their economic problems. In 1953 businessmen in both peninsulas engaged a New York engineering firm to make a study of the economic and industrial resources of the area. This report, made by Ebasco Services, Inc., cited assets that included vast hardwood timber areas that could invite wood-using industries, copper and iron reserves, abundant industrial water supplies, agricultural lands suitable for hay, potatoes, strawberries and other crops, great areas of lakes and streams that make unsurpassed recreational facilities, and a large labor pool made up of people adaptable to new methods, having excellent attitudes toward their jobs, and a high productive rate. Among the liabilities cited were an attitude of defeatism by those who longed for the "good old days" of mining and lumbering, belief elsewhere that the Upper Peninsula has a climate too harsh for year-round industry, and some shortage of electricity and natural gas for expanding industry.[29]

One of the difficulties encountered in trying to locate new manufacturing industry in the Upper Peninsula is the remoteness of the region from the large markets of the nation. But the presence of rich natural resources, especially wood, and the abundance of water, so important in certain types of manufacturing, as well as the large pool of labor stand to overcome the obstacle of remoteness from markets. In 1959 total employment in manufacturing in the Upper Peninsula stood at 35,500.

In the 1950s there were encouraging developments in mining. A process called beneficiation was discovered by which jasper, a low-grade ore that in earlier years was unprofitable to mine, could be made into a salable product. On all three Michigan iron ranges there are huge quantities of jasper or hematite ore; rough estimates run as high as five billion tons. A pilot operation began at the Humboldt Mine near Ishpeming in 1954, and the process was started at Eagle Mills in 1956. The low-grade ore must first be crushed finely before iron minerals can be liberated. The concentration of the iron can be achieved by specific gravity, surface

[28] D. B. Steinman, *Miracle Bridge at Mackinac*; P. Brown, *The Mackinac Bridge Story.*
[29] Detroit *Free Press,* June 28, 1953.

chemistry, or by magnetic separation. The latter process, which is most efficient, cannot be used with most Michigan low-grade ores without an intermediary process, however, because they are not of the magnetic type. The high-grade concentrate, after it is obtained, is made into tiny pellets. The basic problem is the cost factor. The key to the future is the hope that technologists can find a way to keep the combined cost of mining and beneficiation competitive with that of high-grade natural ore. In 1964, about 200 million dollars worth of iron ore was produced in the Upper Peninsula.

During the decade of the 'fifties the outlook for future copper production in the Upper Peninsula also brightened somewhat. Following World War II, the Reconstruction Finance Corporation loaned the Copper Range Company $56,000,000 to put the abandoned White Pine mine, located nineteen miles from Ontonagon, back into production and guaranteed the price of the copper it would produce. A new mining village was laid out and built with homes, schools, and churches. The mine began to produce in the 1950s. Two additional deposits discovered in the same vicinity are believed to be sufficient for forty years of mining. In 1959 nine mines were operating and two companies were reclaiming copper from the tailings of older mines. From 1955 to 1960 the annual output of copper in the Upper Peninsula averaged 114,000,000 pounds.

There were other encouraging developments. Following the completion of the Mackinac Bridge, a span across the St. Mary's River connecting Sault Ste. Marie, Michigan and the Ontario city of the same name was projected. A bonding unit called the International Bridge Authority was formed and the cost was shared between the United States and Canada. The bridge is three miles long, cost $20,000,000, and was opened late in 1962. The completion of this bridge was expected to still further increase the tourist and vacation business of the Upper Peninsula. One estimate was that tourism would increase 34% during the 1960s.[30] An important prerequisite for the growth of tourism is the continued development of parks and recreation areas. In 1962 a bill was proposed in Congress by Michigan Senators Philip Hart and Patrick McNamara to develop 67,000 acres of scenic and historic Lake Superior shoreline between Grand Marais and Munising into a National Lakeshore area.

As the population of the nation grows by leaps and bounds more and more land and water will be needed for recreational uses. The Upper Peninsula of Michigan affords one of the largest

[30] W. P. Stassman, *Economic Growth in Michigan.*

areas of unspoiled natural beauty in the eastern part of the nation. Much as they would like to have more industry and more employment opportunities, the people of the Upper Peninsula want that natural beauty to remain unspoiled. And their wish is shared by all Michiganians who at one time or another have visited the Upper Peninsula and have enjoyed what is truly one of nature's wonderlands.

Zachariah Chandler

18

CITADEL OF REPUBLICANISM

F rom the organization of the Republican Party at Jackson in 1854 until 1932 Michigan was almost a one-party state. At 34 of the 38 biennial elections from 1854 through 1930 the Republican candidate for governor was elected. In all but two of the presidential elections held in this 76-year period, Michigan gave its entire electoral vote to the Republican candidate. The only Democrat to be elected to the United States Senate during this time was Woodbridge N. Ferris, chosen in 1922 not because of his party affiliation but rather because of his great personal popularity with the voters. Throughout the period the Republicans elected a heavy majority of Michigan's members of the national House of Representatives. With few exceptions the G.O.P. controlled both houses of the state legislature, and in the legislature elected in 1924 there was not a single Democrat in either house.

Why did the g.o.p. dominate Michigan for 78 years?

There seems to be no single reason for this long Republican dominance in Michigan. In the beginning the strong antislavery sentiment, which contributed to the strength of the Republican Party, was unquestionably due to the predominance of New England stock in the state's population. Another factor that probably contributed to Republican strength was the slow growth of cities in Michigan until about 1910. The predominantly rural population seems to have had a preference for the Republican Party. Neither agrarian discontent nor industrial unrest appeared in such serious form in Michigan as in many other states of the Middle West. Lumber, iron, copper, and certain other industries relied heavily on a protective tariff, which the Republicans generally favored. The Republicans so dominated Michigan politics that any young man seeking political office had no choice but to join the ranks of the G.O.P.

Even after Detroit, Flint, and other cities began their period of rapid growth around 1910 Republican strength was relatively unaffected. Indeed, during the 1920s the G.O.P. appeared to be stronger than ever. Although careful studies have yet to be made, it may be suggested that the large numbers of foreign-born workers who flocked to these cities to work in the automobile plants tended to be politically impotent until the coming of the great depression of the 1930s. They came, as most immigrants did, seeking greater economic opportunity. The largest numbers came from southern and eastern Europe and had had little or no experience in democracy. Their assimilation was much slower than that of the Germans, Irish, English, and Dutch who had come in the nineteenth century. The political impact of these newcomers thus was not felt until the 1930s, when loss of jobs and hard times drove them to seek the solution to their distresses by political action. Until 1928, the Republican Party attracted a large part of the urban as well as the rural vote.[1]

The most serious threat to Republican dominance down to 1932 came not from the Democratic Party but rather from splits within the Republican ranks. There were sizable defections in the late 1870s to the Greenback Party. The Populist movement of the 1890s attracted considerable support. Most serious was the split that took place in 1912, when supporters of Theodore Roosevelt deserted the Republican ranks and organized the Progressive Party. It was mainly during these periods of factionalism within the Republican ranks that the Democrats were able to take advantage of the splits and win an election.

ZACH CHANDLER AND HIS TIME

During the Civil War United States senator Zachariah Chandler became the leading figure of the Republican Party in Michigan. Though his leadership was challenged from time to time, he

---

[1] Degler, Carl N., "American Political Parties and the Rise of the Cities," *Journal of American History,* II (June, 1964), 41-59.

continued to dominate the party in the state until his death in 1879. As has been indicated earlier, he ardently opposed any compromise with the South on the eve of the Civil War, was a leader of the "Republican Radicals" who were critical of Lincoln during the conflict, and became one of the best-known advocates of a harsh Reconstruction policy after 1865. Chandler was re-elected to the Senate by the Michigan legislature with little opposition in 1863 and 1869. During this period he invariably returned to Michigan to support his party in the campaigns, and became without doubt the best-known political figure in the state.[1]

Until 1870 there was no serious threat to Republican dominance in Michigan. Henry P. Baldwin, a Detroit merchant and banker, was elected governor to succeed Henry H. Crapo in 1868 by a majority of 30,851. He was re-elected in 1870, however, by a plurality of only 16,085. In 1872 there was a split within the Republican Party in the nation, principally as a result of growing sentiment against the radical policy of Reconstruction and the scandals of the Grant administration. A group known as the Liberal Republicans nominated the New York editor Horace Greeley for the presidency, and the Democrats endorsed his candidacy. In Michigan, Liberal Republicans nominated the state's Civil War governor, Austin Blair, as their candidate for governor, and the Democrats also named him. In the fall elections, however, Greeley was snowed under, and the regular Republican candidate for governor, John J. Bagley, was elected by a plurality of 56,644.

Bagley, like Crapo and Baldwin, was a wealthy businessman, deriving his fortune from tobacco manufacturing, insurance, and banking in Detroit. During 1873 and 1874 public sentiment against the "moneyed class" grew rapidly. A severe economic depression hit the nation in 1873, and the invariable habit of the electorate to blame hard times on the party in power asserted itself once again. Even before the depression there had been protests against the retirement of the "greenbacks," paper currency issued by the government during the Civil War. The depression brought a demand for the issuance of more paper money, a move Senator Chandler strongly opposed. Congress passed an act providing for a modest expansion of the greenbacks but it was vetoed by President Grant. The Patrons of Husbandry, a farmers' organization better known as the Grange, was organized in Michigan in 1872, and many Grangers were also Greenbackers. To complicate matters still further for the Republicans, the liquor interests in the state, demanding the repeal of Michigan's prohibition law, formed an alliance with the Democratic Party. All these factors resulted in sharp reverses for Michigan Republicanism in the 1874 fall elections. Bagley was re-elected governor but his margin of victory was less than 6,000 votes. Democrats captured three of the state's nine congressional seats, and in the state legislature the Republican majority was reduced to ten.

Senator Chandler's third term expired in 1875. Most of the Republicans in the legislature favored re-electing him, but six members of the party formed a coalition with the Democrats to defeat him. In his place the legislature chose Isaac P. Christiancy, a member of the state supreme court, who was a nominal Republican but had favored the Democrats on certain matters. Following his defeat Chandler was appointed secretary of the interior by President Grant. In this office Chandler served with considerable distinction. One writer summarizes Chandler's service thus: "Taking office in October, 1875, Chandler overhauled the malodorous Indian and Patent bureaus and built up the morale of the entire department. He stopped one glaring fraud in the Land Office and conspicuously refused a bribe in a case on appeal which was given wide publicity at a time when charges of fraud and bribery were hanging over the Republicans in the election of 1876."[2] This gave Chandler prestige as national chairman of the Republican Party in the elections of 1876. That was the famous disputed election in which Samuel Tilden, the Democratic candidate for President, at first appeared to have defeated the Republican candidate, Rutherford B. Hayes. Chandler, as national chairman, however, refused to give up. It was his dogged determination more than anything else that maintained the fight to win the disputed electoral votes. In the end Hayes was declared elected by a single electoral vote.

Michigan in the 1876 election gave Hayes a plurality of more than 25,000 votes. The Republican candidate for governor, Adrian lawyer Charles M. Croswell, was elected with a plurality of over 33,000 votes. The result may be attributed to the recovery of the economy and returning prosperity in the state. The Republicans scored an even more decisive victory in the 1878 fall elections. Croswell won re-election by a decisive majority, every congressional seat was captured by the Republicans, and they also won a large majority in the legislature. Senator Christiancy, because of failing health, resigned his seat in January, 1879, and Chandler was chosen by the legislature to fill the unexpired term. The latter resumed his old seat in the Senate on February 22. There seemed

[2] H. H. Dunham, "Some Crucial Years of the General Land Office, 1875-1890," *Agricultural History*, XI (1937), reprinted in V. Carstensen, (ed.), *The Public Lands*, p. 192; *Zachariah Chandler: An Outline Sketch of His Life and Public Services*, published by *Detroit Post and Tribune*.

to be no diminution of the old senator's vigor. But on the morning of November 1, 1879, he was found dead in bed at a hotel in Chicago, where he had gone to deliver a political address the night before. With his death an era of Michigan politics came to an end.[3]

PINE, POLITICS, AND POPULISM, 1880-1896

It was a long time before any political leader could dominate Michigan Republicanism as "Old Zach" had for more than two decades. During the sixteen years following Chandler's death the power in Michigan Republican circles lay with successful businessmen and the lawyer-politicians allied with them. Wealthy lumbermen were particularly prominent. David H. Jerome, elected governor in 1880, made his fortune in lumbering in the Saginaw Valley. So did Russell A. Alger, who was the successful Republican candidate for governor in 1884. In the United States Senate Thomas W. Ferry of Grand Haven, former Governor Henry P. Baldwin of Detroit, and Francis B. Stockbridge of Kalamazoo, who represented Michigan during this period, were all wealthy lumbermen. James McMillan of Detroit, who became the most prominent Republican leader in the early 1890s, was a Detroit manufacturer.

The G.O.P. did not enjoy the unbroken successes during this period that had been characteristic of the Chandler era. The campaign technique of reviving Civil War issues by "waving the bloody shirt" was wearing thin, and new issues began to emerge, such as the currency and the tariff. In 1882 the Greenbackers and the Democrats formed a "Fusion ticket" and nominated Josiah W. Begole, a Flint farmer, as their candidate for governor. In the election Begole won by the slim margin of 4,572 out of over 300,-000 votes cast. It was the first break in the series of victories won by the Republicans in gubernatorial contests since 1854. Two years later Begole was defeated for re-election by Russell A. Alger, the Republican candidate, by only 4,000 votes. The following spring the Fusionists were able to defeat Supreme Court Justice Thomas M. Cooley, the most notable jurist Michigan has produced, who was running for re-election as the Republican candidate.

Their defeat in the race for governor in 1882, their narrow victory in 1884, and the defeat of Cooley in 1885 convinced the Republican leaders that new tactics were required. Alger refused to accept renomination, and the Republicans turned to a Branch

[3] H. M. Dilla, *The Politics of Michigan, 1865-1878.*

County farmer, Cyrus G. Luce, in an obvious attempt to win the favor of those who had become critical of the lumber barons. Luce won by a margin of about 7,000 votes in the 1886 election and was re-elected by a slightly larger margin in 1888. A factor of considerable importance in these close elections was the Prohibition Party, which had been organized in 1869. In 1886 that party's candidate for governor polled 25,179 votes. The Republican leaders, regaining their confidence following the two successful campaigns of Luce, nominated for governor in 1890 James M. Turner, a wealthy Lansing railroad man. Party nominations were made in state conventions, which the lumber and railroad barons and their allies could usually control. There was strong support in the Republican ranks for the nomination of John T. Rich, a Lapeer County farmer but the G.O.P. convention rejected him in favor of Turner. The Democrats, sensing their opportunity, chose Edwin B. Winans, a Livingston County farmer, as their candidate. By this time the Greenback movement had faded away. Falling prices and bad seasons, however, had stirred new discontent among the farmers of the South and West, resulting in the growth of the Populist movement. This movement represented a wide range of reforms, including the expansion of the currency through the free and unlimited coinage of silver at a ratio to gold of sixteen to one. The extent of dissatisfaction in Michigan with the ruling clique in the Republican Party was demonstrated in the fall election of 1890, when Winans won the governorship by a margin of 11,520 votes. Even more of an upset was scored when the Democrats elected a majority of the state house of representatives and, through a clever bit of chicanery, also got control of the state senate.

In spite of these setbacks, the Republicans could point with pride to the fact that never once since 1852 had Michigan given a single electoral vote to the Democratic candidate for President. Then, as now, in all states the presidential electors of each party were voted on as a group, and hence the entire electoral vote of the state went to the candidate whose electors received the largest vote, regardless of the size of the opposition. In 1891 Democrats in the Michigan legislature passed an act, however, which provided that each congressional district should choose one elector and that two electors should be chosen by the state at large. The purpose of this was to give the Democratic candidate for President some portion of Michigan's vote. Thus in the 1892 presidential election for the first and only time in its history the state's electoral vote was split. Grover Cleveland, the successful Democratic candidate, received five of Michigan's electoral votes, while

Benjamin Harrison, the Republican nominee, received the remaining nine. When Republicans resumed control of the legislature in 1893 they promptly repealed this law. It is worthy of note that some critics of the electoral system in the 1960s were suggesting a reform that would closely resemble the system Michigan used in 1892.

Having learned their lesson, the Republican leaders gave the gubernatorial nomination in 1892 to Rich, who was elected in November and re-elected two years later. It was during Rich's term that the Panic of 1893 shattered the nation's economy, and brought in its train widespread bankruptcies, unemployment, falling prices, and general distress. The Populists, who had polled a million votes in 1892 for their presidential candidate, were now functioning as a vigorous political party in Michigan and elsewhere. They called for "free silver" along with public ownership of the railroads, a graduated income tax, direct election of United States senators, and women's suffrage as remedies for the nation's ills. Democratic President Grover Cleveland, however, staunchly upheld the gold standard and even persuaded Congress to repeal an act passed earlier for increased silver coinage. In the state elections in Michigan in 1894 Democrats, Populists, and Prohibitionists all had candidates in the field. The fact that the Republican candidate, John T. Rich, was himself a farmer and sympathetic to the needs of the farmers, together with the division among his opposition, made possible his re-election. With a Democratic President in Washington, however, Michigan Democrats won rewards for political service. Don M. Dickinson of Detroit was chosen postmaster general in the cabinet and four prominent Michigan Democrats received appointments to diplomatic and consular posts.[4]

PINGREE: PRECURSOR OF PROGRESSIVISM

The election of 1896 followed one of the most bitterly contested political campaigns in American history. The Democratic Party, strongly affected by agrarian discontent in the South and West, repudiated its own President, Grover Cleveland, and adopted a platform favoring "free silver." William Jennings Bryan electrified the Democratic National Convention with his "Cross of Gold"

[4] H. M. Utley and B. M. Cutcheon, *Michigan as a Province, Territory and State*, IV, 217-218. See also E. D. Babst and L. G. Vander Velde, (eds.), *Michigan and the Cleveland Era*; J. W. Lederle and R. F. Aid, 'Michigan State Party Chairmen: 1882-1956," *Michigan History*, XLI (1957), 257-268.

speech and was nominated for the presidency. This youthful and eloquent Nebraskan so thoroughly alarmed the powerful business, corporate, and financial leaders of the nation that they left no stone unturned to bring about his defeat. The Republicans nominated William McKinley as their presidential candidate. McKinley, known as an advocate of protective tariffs, tried to soft-pedal the currency issue but was unable to do so. The fear of Bryan and "free silver" was shared by the Michigan businessmen and other conservative-minded Michiganians. Their determination to defeat Bryan and elect McKinley was a primary factor in their selection of Detroit Mayor Hazen S. Pingree as the Republican candidate for governor in 1896.

Pingree, a native of Maine, was a successful and wealthy Detroit shoe manufacturer in 1889, when he was nominated by the Republicans to run for mayor of the city. Detroit's voters had generally given the Democratic candidates a majority, in spite of Republican dominance in the state as a whole. A group of influential businessmen, hoping to break the Democratic hold on Detroit, persuaded Pingree to run. Since he was a man of wealth, they expected him to support the business interests. But following his election, he launched a reform program that quickly alienated his wealthy backers. He attacked the city's assessments, which were far higher in proportion on homes than on factories, downtown business buildings, and vacant lots owned by real-estate speculators. He attacked the gas company, proving its rates were almost twice as high as those in other cities, and he condemned the street railway company for failing to electrify its line and paying the city nothing for its franchise. Stockholders in the corporations involved violently attacked the mayor. They avoided him socially, the newspapers turned against him, and even the banks refused to do business with him. In spite of this, and perhaps in part because of it, he was immensely popular with the people. They lined up in front of the City Hall to read his statements that the newspapers refused to print. When the Panic of 1893 hit Detroit Pingree permitted the unemployed to use vacant city land to plant gardens and grow their own food. He sold his riding horse at auction to provide seed. The potato patches that sprang up as a result gave him the nickname "Potato Pingree." Three times Pingree was elected mayor of Detroit, winning 67% of the vote in the third election in spite of all the opposition to him. He succeeded in getting the gas company to lower its rates and established a municipal lighting plant. He persuaded a group to build a rival streetcar line and charge lower fares.

Pingree found that some of the changes he wished to make in

Detroit were blocked by state law. This may have been one factor in arousing his interest in state politics. He was a candidate for the Republican nomination for governor in the Republican state convention of 1892, but was defeated through the influence of party leaders such as Senator James McMillan, who shared the dislike for Pingree that was so intense among the conservative business community. In 1894 Pingree withdrew his name from consideration at the last moment, but in 1896 he traveled all over the state seeking support for the nomination. Perhaps the party leaders could have blocked his nomination in 1896 as they had in 1892 and 1894, but this time there was a new factor at work. McMillan and his supporters were far more interested in defeating Bryan and electing McKinley President than they were in the governorship of Michigan. To be sure, they hated Pingree, but they saw in his great popularity with the people a means whereby the end they sought could be achieved. With Pingree's name on the Republican ballot as candidate for governor, enough support might be given to the G.O.P. to carry McKinley to victory, too. They foresaw that the state senate, which was sure to be dominated by Republican conservatives, would be able to call a halt to any dangerous reforms Pingree might try to bring about in Lansing. Furthermore, with Pingree in Lansing, he would be out of their hair in Detroit!

The plan worked perfectly. McKinley won Michigan's electoral vote by a majority of 56,000. Pingree's majority was over 83,000. And as the Republican bosses had anticipated, the state senate was able to block a large part of Pingree's program. For a while the new governor continued to hold his position as mayor of Detroit, but when the state supreme court ruled he could not hold the two offices at the same time, he resigned as mayor. He never moved to Lansing, but retained his home and office in Detroit, regularly spending weekends there. Regarding Detroit as the business center of the state, he even suggested that the capital be moved there. Many of the reforms Pingree advocated were completely disregarded, others were killed at some stage in the legislative process.

Governor Pingree fought hardest, as governor, to compel the state's railroad corporations to pay a fair tax on the value of their properties. At least four governors since 1877 had urged the legislature to impose such a tax, but "the immortal nineteen" senators had been able to prevent any bills increasing railroad taxes from becoming law. In the first legislature during the Pingree administration a bill was introduced by a Detroit legislator, John Atkinson, to set up a commission to assess the property of the railroads, to levy a tax thereon, and to pay the sum so raised into the primary school fund. The house passed the bill, but the "immortal nineteen" killed it in the senate. In 1898 Pingree was. re-elected by a large majority, and again recommended the railroad tax measure to the legislature. This time both houses passed the bill, but the state supreme court quickly declared it unconstitutional. Pingree then asked the legislature to approve a constitutional amendment that would legalize the Atkinson bill. The senate refused to approve such a resolution in both the regular session and in a special session called by the governor, but finally accepted it when Pingree called a second special session. The proposed amendment was approved by a popular vote in the November, 1900 elections. Desiring to see his favorite measure become law before his retirement from office January 1, 1901, Governor Pingree called another special legislative session to re-enact the Atkinson bill. As a final gesture of defiance the senate refused to give the governor that much satisfaction. However, the following May after Pingree's successor, Governor Aaron T. Bliss, had taken office, the bill became law.

It was during Pingree's first term that the Spanish-American War took place. Pingree was opposed to the war, but after it was declared he left no stone unturned to see to it that Michigan volunteers were well cared for. He set up a military camp at Island Lake and lived there with Michigan troops. When they left for southern camps he made sure that the men had well-fitted shoes. He sent special trains to return the sick and wounded from southern and eastern hospitals. He was proud of the fact that Michigan was the only state that had two regiments in the Cuban campaign.[5]

Two Michigan men played major roles in the Spanish-American War. One was General William R. Shafter, a native of Galesburg, who was commander of the American forces in Cuba. He had won distinction as a volunteer during the Civil War, later receiving the Congressional Medal of Honor for his bravery. He chose the army for a career and during the Indian wars on the western plains had won the nickname "Pecos Bill." At the time the Spanish-American War broke out he was 63 years of age, weighed upwards of three hundred pounds, and during the entire Cuban campaign suffered from illness. Nevertheless he conducted the campaign with considerable competence. Newspaper men gave the headlines to the dashing young Theodore Roosevelt and his Rough Riders rather than to Shafter, partly because Shafter refused to reveal his plans

[5] C. R. Starring, "Hazen S. Pingree, Another Forgotten Eagle," *Michigan History*, XXXII (1948), 129-149.

to them. Less than a month after Shafter and his force landed in Cuba the chief Spanish stronghold, Santiago, surrendered.[6]

While one Michiganian commanded the Cuban expeditionary force, another served as secretary of war. Former Governor Russell A. Alger had been appointed to this cabinet position by President McKinley. The inefficiency of his department was subjected to bitter criticism. At the embarkation point at Tampa, Florida, the soldiers were issued wool uniforms for a campaign in the tropics. Mess pans were those left over from the Civil War. Instead of modern rifles the troops were issued old Springfields. Food was wretched; the canned meat was so bad that it was popularly referred to as "embalmed beef." Medical supplies were totally inadequate. For all this, Alger received the blame, and he finally resigned in order to save the McKinley administration from embarrassment. Yet it is doubtful that Alger was really at fault so much as the spoils system, under which the personnel of the War Department over the years had come to consist of men who obtained their positions because of political services rendered rather than for any competence they might possess for the jobs to which they were assigned. Governor Pingree rose to the secretary's defense and joined in the public welcome for him when he returned to Detroit.

The last year of Pingree's administration was marred by a scandal involving a member of his staff. The Henderson-Ames Company of Kalamazoo, through the connivance of certain state officials, was able to buy a stock of unused uniforms at salvage prices and after minor alterations to sell them back to the state at the full price. Five company officials confessed their complicity and made restitution. Several state officials were sentenced to prison terms. A trusted adviser of Pingree was accused of being a part of the conspiracy but was acquitted. The governor thought the company officials had been treated more leniently than the state officials involved, and pardoned two of the latter, an act for which he was sharply criticized. It his farewell address Pingree said, "I am satified that I could have had the praise and support of the best 'citizens' and our 'best society,' and of the press of the state generally, if I had upheld those who have for years attempted to control legislation in their own interests, to the end that they might be relieved from sharing equally with the poor and lowly the burden of taxation."[7]

Hazen S. Pingree has received less attention than he merits in

[6] C. D. Rhodes, "William Rufus Shafter," *Michigan History,* XVI (1932), 375-383.

[7] G. N. Fuller (ed.), *Messages of the Governors of Michigan,* IV, 310.

writings that deal with the progressive movement that swept the United States during the first two decades of the twentieth century. Pingree advocated many if not most of the reforms associated with this movement in advance of most of the better-known progressive leaders. He favored the direct primary, popular election of United States senators, a graduated income tax, and more stringent regulation of big business. To be sure, some of these reforms had been demanded by the Populists in the early 1890s, but it was quite another thing for them to be advocated by a Republican governor who was also a successful businessman. Pingree was a prophet before his time. The progressive movement had not yet gathered sufficient force to enlist the public support that was necessary if the reform programs it stood for were to gain acceptance. Perhaps another explanation for the minor position given Pingree in most histories of progressivism is that he did not stand preeminently for a single reform measure, as did Robert M. LaFollette in his long fight for the direct primary in Wisconsin.

Pingree did not live long after retiring from office. He left on a trip to Europe shortly after his second term was finished, and died suddenly in a London hotel June 18, 1901. His body was returned to Detroit, where friends and enemies joined to extol his sterling character.

THE PROGRESSIVE MOVEMENT

The presidential election of 1900 saw President William Mc-Kinley pitted once more against his Democratic opponent of 1896, William Jennings Bryan. But the issues involved were not the same. Byran's advocacy of free silver now had little appeal, for new sources of gold had been found and silver was no longer as cheap in relation to gold as it had been in 1896. Besides, prosperity had tended to erase the demand for change. Bryan and the Democrats shifted their appeal to those who had opposed the acquisition of the Philippine Islands by the McKinley administration at the close of the Spanish-American War. However, the distrust of Bryan's currency ideas by conservatives was still a potent factor in the campaign, and his second defeat was actually no proof that the country favored the United States acquiring territory on the opposite side of the earth.

In Michigan McKinley received over 58% of the popular vote. Sensing victory and longing for someone in the governor's chair at Lansing less rambunctious and more conservative than Pingree, the Republican leaders persuaded the state convention to nominate a rich Saginaw lumberman and banker, Aaron T. Bliss, for governor. He was swept into office by a majority almost as large as McKinley's. However, Bliss in his inaugural came out in favor of Pingree's pet railroad tax measure, and the legislature proceeded to enact it. One may assume that the bill was no more palatable to the conservatives than it had been when Pingree advocated it, but conservative leaders were sensing that certain concessions to public demand must be made. It was this strategy of bending with the wind that enabled the conservatives to retain their hold on the state government during the next decade. Bliss was re-elected in 1902. His successor, Fred M. Warner, was a successful farmer and businessman possessed of a considerable amount of political wisdom. He was re-elected in 1906 and again in 1908, the first three-term Michigan governor in Republican history. Warner was by instinct a conservative, and his supporters held the same political philosophy. But both Bliss and Warner advocated reforms they believed the people demanded. No doubt, too, the Republican cause in Michigan and the concessions the governors and legislators made to the demand for reform were promoted by the popularity of President Theodore Roosevelt. Taking over the presidency following the assassination and death of President McKinley, Roosevelt spoke loudly for progressive measures, though in practice he was far from being a radical.

Articles in popular magazines, novels, and scholarly works by the so-called "muckrakers," beginning about 1902, provided detailed and sometimes lurid accounts of political malfeasance, frenzied quest for wealth, and disregard of the public welfare by big business. Such articles revealed sordid conditions in city slums and graft in city and state governments. The muckrakers played a major role in bringing about an insistent public demand for reforms. In different parts of the nation leaders appeared to champion one or another of dozens of different reform proposals. Thus arose what is called the progressive movement. Each of the two major political parties had its progressive wing, opposed by the conservatives or "stalwarts" within the party. The demanded reforms related to every level of government from local to national. In general they may be grouped under three major headings: first, those reforms like the initiative, referendum, recall, direct primary, women's suffrage, and the direct election of United States senators which were designed to make government more democratic and closer to the people; second, regulation and control over big business through such reforms as railroad-rate controls, antitrust laws, a graduated income tax, and pure-food-and-drug laws; third, social reforms, including such proposals as workmen's compensation, limitation of the hours of labor for women and children, mothers' pensions, and prohibition of the manufacture and sale of intoxicating liquors. The movement resulted, by 1920 in four amendments to the United States Constitution and many laws enacted by Congress as well as important changes and modifications in government at the local and state levels.

In Michigan the nomination of state officials by primary elections rather than by state conventions was advocated when it was rumored that $750,000 had been spent in the 1900 Republican convention by those who sought the gubernatorial nomination. Sensing public demand, Governor Bliss, who had won the nomination at the convention where so much money was passed, came out in favor of the primary. In 1903 the legislature authorized primaries in three of the larger counties. A general primary law was passed in 1905, but it proved unworkable. By this time agitation for a general revision of the state constitution had gained momentum. This, too, was supported by Bliss and by his successor, Governor Warner. The voters in 1906 approved the calling of a constitutional convention. The delegates elected to the convention met on October 22, 1907, and finished their work on February 21, 1908. All but eight of the delegates were Republicans.

Conservative leaders, who predominated in the convention, made just enough concessions to the adherents to the progressive movement to assure popular ratification. The Constitution of 1908 was largely a rewrite and reorganization of the Constitution of 1850. Woman suffrage was turned down, but women taxpayers were allowed to vote on bond issues. The initiative and referendum were rejected, though the legislature was allowed to refer a measure to a popular vote. Cities were given the right to home rule and were authorized to own and operate public utilities. Juvenile offenders were placed under the jurisdiction of the probate court. And the legislature was given the power to pass laws limiting the hours of labor for women and children in factories and the conditions under which they worked. There were other minor changes. In the November, 1908 election the voters endorsed the new constitution and it went into effect the following year.

Meanwhile, the state legislature, with the astute support of Governor Warner, was enacting a considerable body of progressive legislation. Taxes on telegraph and telephone companies were increased, the receipts being added to the primary-school fund. Laws were passed regulating insurance companies, providing for food inspection, requiring safety measures in factories, and limiting the hours of labor for employees under eighteen years of age to ten hours a day or 54 a week. In 1909 the legislature finally passed a workable primary law, under which the voters in each party were given the opportunity to nominate their candidates for public office. There were allegations, however, of poor management and corruption in the administration. Warner had been elected to his third term in 1908 by a thin margin. And even though the governor boasted of the reforms made during his administration, the progressives were far from satisfied.

It was at this juncture that a new political figure rose to prominence in Michigan: Chase Salmon Osborn. He first became known as an ardent advocate of conservation. As state game warden from 1894 to 1899 he had fought for enforcement of conservation laws and additional legislation for the protection of game birds and wild animals. He was an admirer of Governor Pingree, who had appointed him state railroad commissioner. In that position he had induced the legislature to reduce passenger fares and inaugurated a program of grade separation. In 1908 he had been appointed a regent of the University of Michigan. His profession was journalism. Prior to 1900 he edited a Sault Ste. Marie newspaper, and although he sold this paper that year he continued to live in the Upper Peninsula and to be one of its most enthusiastic boosters. He had sought the Republican nomination as governor at the end of Pingree's term, but found himself pitted against men who had far more money to influence votes than he did. He concluded that a man in politics must be wealthy or else be at the mercy of the bosses. Consequently he proceeded to accumulate a fortune. Most of it was gained by the discovery of iron deposits in the Upper Peninsula that he sold to mining companies.[8]

By 1910, Osborn was ready to make his second bid for the Republican gubernatorial nomination. But this time his success or failure depended not on the party bosses but on the people, because of the primary law the legislature had passed in 1909. Osborn started early and worked hard to win the nomination. His campaign manager was Frank Knox, to whom he had sold the *Sault Ste. Marie News* in 1900. Osborn traveled to every corner of the state seeking support, using what was then the novel method of traveling by automobile. He repudiated Warner, spoke of the scandals of the government in Lansing, promised to wipe out the state deficit and inaugurate an economical, efficient administration of state affairs, and committed himself to serving only one term in order that he might devote his full time to the duties of governor instead of taking time to run for re-election. In the September primary Osborn outdistanced two opponents for

[8] R. M. Warner, *Chase Salmon Osborn, 1860-1949.*

the G.O.P. nomination. His margin of victory in November over his Democratic opponent was only 43,033 votes, chiefly because Republican conservatives refused him their support.[9] In the Republican primary in 1910 the progressives scored another victory by defeating the conservative United States senator Julius Caesar Burrows and nominating in his place the progressive Charles E. Townsend.[10]

During Governor Osborn's term, from January 1, 1911 to December 31, 1912, the progressive movement gathered force and momentum. The governor persuaded the legislature to enact a law prohibiting distillers, brewers, or wholesalers from owning saloons. One of the major achievements of his administration was a workmen's compensation law. Under the old English common law, an employer was not responsible for an injury suffered by an employee on the job if it could be proved (as it usually could) that he or a fellow-employee had been negligent. Under the new law there was no such escape for employer liability in such cases. Osborn practiced strict economy in state government, discharging many employees in the process, but leaving office with a large surplus in the treasury.[11] Osborn, like Pingree, battled with the conservative senate over appointments and other matters. He called the legislature back for special sessions, as Pingree had done, when it failed to carry out his recommendations. Besides the measures already mentioned, Osborn emerged from these fights with the legislature with laws giving more powers to the state tax commission and regulating railroads, express companies, telephone companies, banks, insurance, and saloons. In cases where he was turned down, such as on his proposals for the initiative, referendum, and recall, he planted the seeds that were to bring a

[9] R. M. Warner, "Chase S. Osborn's 1910 Primary Election Campaign," *Michigan History,* XLIII (1959), 349-384.

[10] Though United States senators were nominated in the primaries in Michigan beginning in 1910, the legislature continued to elect the senators until after the ratification of the 17th amendment to the U.S. Constitution in 1913 which stipulated that they must be popularly elected. The first popular election of a United States senator in Michigan occurred in 1916.

[11] In accordance with his policy of economy, Osborn in 1911 vetoed a bill appropriating state funds to the Michigan Pioneer and Historical Society. Since the inception of the Society in 1874, the state had provided annually a sum varying from $500 to $4,000 to publish an annual volume of historical materials. In 1913, during Governor Ferris' term, the legislature passed an act creating the Michigan Historical Commission as an official state body. Apparently there had been some question whether the Society, as a private organization, could legally receive state funds. The Pioneer and Historical Society continued as an independent organization, later changing its name to the Historical Society of Michigan.

harvest of reform after his term had ended. He persuaded the lawmakers to submit to the people a constitutional amendment providing for woman suffrage; but in the November, 1912 election the amendment was defeated by a close vote: 248,135 to 247,375.

While Governor Osborn was battling for progressive reform in Michigan, progressive sentiment throughout the nation was turning against President William Howard Taft, who had been nominated by the Republicans for the presidency in 1908 upon the recommendation of retiring President Theodore Roosevelt and had been elected over William Jennings Bryan. Taft continued Roosevelt's progressive program in several respects, such as prosecuting trusts, but he lacked the Rough Rider's flair for publicity. Taft's approval of the Payne-Aldrich tariff, which raised rates of import duties to new highs, deeply offended the progressives, as did his handling of conservation. Robert M. La Follette of Wisconsin emerged as the leader of the progressive forces while former President Roosevelt was in Africa on a lion-hunt, but when Roosevelt returned he took the leadership from La Follette and after some hesitation announced that his hat was in the ring for the Republican nomination in 1912. Republicans split down the middle between Roosevelt and Taft, and a spirited contest ensued for delegates to the Republican National Convention. In the few states where presidential primaries had been adopted, the voters showed their preference for Roosevelt.

Governor Osborn, an enthusiastic supporter of Roosevelt, tried to induce the state legislature in the spring of 1912 to approve a presidential preferential primary in Michigan. A bill providing for such a primary was passed, but failed in the senate to get the two-thirds majority required for immediate passage and thus the law did not become effective until too late to affect the 1912 nominations.[12] The Republican state convention was held in Bay City on April 11, 1912. It was calculated that the twelve delegates to the national convention to be chosen by congressional district caucuses at the convention would be evenly divided between Roosevelt and Taft supporters. The fight centered upon the six delegates to be chosen by the convention at large. Frank Knox, chairman of the Republican State Central Committee, which had charge of arrangements for the state convention, was a Roosevelt

---

[12] A presidential preferential primary is one in which the voters in each party indicate their preference for the condidate to be nominated by the party's national convention. The law passed in 1912 was repealed in 1931. Delegates to national conventions in Michigan are chosen in this manner: two delegates are chosen by the delegates to the state convention from each congressional district, and the balance are elected by the state convention at large.

man, but Paul King, the secretary, and a majority of the committee members were for Taft. Two delegations from both Wayne and Calhoun Counties—one for Taft and the other for Roosevelt—claimed seats in the convention. The Taft majority on the state central committee sought to seat the Taft delegates from these counties and to exclude the Roosevelt delegates. Within the hall disorder was rampant and there were several fist fights. Police finally restored order, but in the meantime the Roosevelt delegates got into the hall, held a meeting in one corner and chose six Roosevelt delegates to the national convention. The remaining members, of course, chose six Taft delegates. Unfortunately, the Roosevelt convention held in the corner failed to name a secretary, so there was no official record of its proceedings.

The Republican National Committee, which had charge of arrangements for the Republican national convention in Chicago, was Taft-dominated. There were several contested delegations, including Michigan's, but all the Taft delegations were seated temporarily and the convention was then allowed to decide which delegation in each case should receive permanent seats. When the Michigan case came before the convention, the lack of an official record of the selection of the Roosevelt delegates proved fatal. The Taft delegates retained their seats, and Taft won nomination for a second term. The Roosevelt delegates at once withdrew to a separate hall, claimed the nomination had been stolen for Taft, and proceeded to organize a new political party: the Progressive Party. Roosevelt was promptly nominated for the presidency. The Democrats held their national convention at Baltimore and after 46 ballots nominated Woodrow Wilson as their candidate. Both Roosevelt and Wilson were progressives, although there were sharp differences between their points of view.

In Michigan the Progressives organized to back Roosevelt in the fall elections and nominated a state ticket headed by Lucius Whitney Watkins for governor. The Republicans nominated Amos S. Musselman for governor, while the Democrats chose Woodbridge N. Ferris.

The latter had become widely and favorably known in Michigan as head of Ferris Institute, which he had founded in Big Rapids in 1884. It was a school where practical subjects were emphasized and where students with small means could get an education. Ferris and his wife took a deep personal interest in each student, and over the years made many fast friends. Ferris had "a wiry physical organism, an active, inquiring mind, a quick temper, a boy's love of fun, an enthusiasm for great deeds and great men, and a wholesome fear of moral baseness."[13]

It was the split within the Republican ranks that gave the election to Ferris, who was every inch a progressive. Musselman and Watkins polled a total of 322,872 votes, but neither won as many votes as did Ferris (194,017). Nationally, the same split resulted in the election of Wilson to the presidency. In Michigan, however, Roosevelt received the plurality of the popular vote and the entire electoral vote of the state. Wilson polled fewer votes than did Taft. Thus, while the 1912 election indicates the strength of the progressive movement, it also illustrates the continuing Republican preference of the Michigan electorate. The election of Ferris was clearly the result of personal popularity rather than party affiliation. Osborn took no part in the campaign, being out of the country on a world tour.

The progressive movement in Michigan reached its height during the Ferris adminstrations. The initiative, referendum, and recall were added to the constitution by amendment. During Ferris' second term a prohibition amendment was added to the constitution (1916).[14] Other progressive reforms were adopted through a legislative coalition of Democrats and Progressives.

The Progressive Party was shortlived. In 1914 many Progressives either returned to the Republican party or went over to the Democrats. Former Governor Osborn was nominated by the Republicans, but Ferris won re-election in 1914. The Progressive candidate polled a relatively small vote. The demise of the Progressive Party came as the major parties accepted the progressive reform program. While Ferris was pushing through a progressive program in Michigan President Wilson succeeded in persuading Congress to adopt one of the most extensive series of reform measures in American history. By 1916 the progressive movement had about run its course. Wilson was re-elected President by the narrowest of margins over the Republican candidate, Charles Evans Hughes. Michigan returned to its normal Republican preferences, giving Hughes its electoral vote and choosing the Republican candidate for governor, Albert E. Sleeper of Bad Axe.

The attention of the people of Michigan and the rest of the nation was being diverted to the war in Europe by 1916. In spite of the efforts of President Wilson to keep the nation out of this conflict, the use of submarines by the Germans to stop the flow

---

[13] For a biographical sketch of Ferris, see G. N. Fuller, *op. cit.*, IV, 639.

[14] The amendment was implemented by a law passed in 1917, and Michigan "went dry" in 1918, more than a year before national prohibition became effective.

of foodstuffs and arms to the allies from the United States eventually engulfed this country in the war. In a sense, World War I was the culmination of the crusading zeal inspired by the Progressive movement, even though a number of leading progressives in Congress voted against war. Wilson's appeal for a war "to save the world for democracy" and "a war to end war" fired the same spirit of human betterment that had been characteristic of progressivism. But the war diverted attention from domestic reform. And Wilson's handling of the Treaty of Versailles and the League of Nations, in seeking to win Senate approval, alienated many of his followers. The refusal of the Senate to ratify the Treaty of Versailles was profoundly disillusioning to those who had been caught up in "the great crusade," and after the war the nation was in the mood for "normalcy."

THE TWILIGHT OF REPUBLICAN DOMINANCE IN MICHIGAN

From 1916 until 1932 the Republican party won elections as handily in Michigan as it had before the days of the progressive movement. The 1918 campaign centered around a contest for a seat in the United States Senate. Truman Newberry, a wealthy Detroiter who had been associated with the progressive movement, won the Republican nomination in a spirited primary contest with former governor Chase S. Osborn and Henry Ford. Ford also ran in the Democratic primary and won nomination. In the November election he was defeated by Newberry. However, the latter and his supporters spent large sums in winning the primary, and he was accused of having exceeded the limit set by the national Corrupt Practices Act. The case was carried to the United States Supreme Court, which ruled, in a five-to-four decision, that Congress had no power to limit the amount spent in primary elections. Newberry accordingly was admitted to the Senate, but the affair caused so much criticism that he resigned in 1922 to save his party embarrassment. James Couzens, a former associate in the Ford Motor Company, was appointed to fill out Newberry's term. Couzens was distinctly an independent in politics, and generally favored progressive policies. Former Governor Ferris was elected to Michigan's other senate seat in 1922, and served until his death in 1928. Ferris's election represented the only major Democratic victory in Michigan between 1916 and 1932. Following Ferris's death, Arthur H. Vandenberg of Grand Rapids was appointed to serve in his place, and in November, 1928 Vandenberg was elected to fill the remainder of the unexpired term. Both

Couzens and Vandenberg were re-elected and served until they died, Couzens in 1936 and Vandenberg in 1951.

The dominant figure in the Republican party in Michigan from 1920 to 1926 was Alex J. Groesbeck, a Detroit lawyer. He was a native of Michigan and was of Dutch-French ancestry.[15] He had been attorney general during Governor Sleeper's two terms, and in that position attracted a great deal of public attention through a series of investigations which revealed prison labor being employed by private contractors, rampant vice and lawless conditions in Hamtramck, and lamentable conditions in the State Industrial Home for Girls in Adrian. Although he was opposed by Governor Sleeper, he won the Republican nomination for governor in 1920 and was elected by more than a two-to-one margin.

As governor, Groesbeck is chiefly known for his reforms in the state administration carried out to introduce greater efficiency. Following Groesbeck's recommendation, the legislature created the State Administrative Board, consisting of the principal elected state officials. It performed three major functions: (1) it drew up a budget for the guidance of the legislature in making appropriations—the first state budget in Michigan's history; (2) it set up a centralized purchasing system, so that the state could buy materials needed at wholesale prices; (3) it devised a uniform accounting system for all state agencies. Groesbeck was re-elected in 1922 and again in 1924, serving a total of three terms, the third Michigan governor to do so. In 1924 the Republican party under Groesbeck's leadership was so strong that it captured every one of the 100 seats in the state house of representatives and also every one of the 32 senate seats. Groesbeck brought about the reduction in the number of state agencies (boards, commissions, and departments) from 98 to 65. He carefully administered the expenditure of $50,000,000 that had been authorized by a vote of the people for highways. It was during his administration that the state highway department began the operation of automobile ferries at the Straits of Mackinac (1924). Groesbeck never married, and had no family to divert him from his habit of spending long hours in the governor's office. Personally, the governor was neither amiable nor possessed of those qualities that are regarded as typical of politicians. But he ran Michigan's government with the competence of a business executive, and he was respected if not liked. During the latter part of his administration opposition to him began to accumulate on the ground that his

[15] Governor David H. Jerome, who served from 1881 to 1883, was Michigan's first native-born governor; Groesbeck was the second.

penchant for strong government had led him to become something of a dictator. After his retirement from the office of governor at the end of 1926 he returned to the practice of law in Detroit. He lived until 1953; although he sought the Republican nomination for governor in 1930 and again in 1934, he met defeat on both occasions.[16]

The reforms in state government brought about during the Groesbeck administration did not represent any continuation of the mainstream of the progressive movement. Groesbeck did not champion measures designed to make the government of Michigan more democratic. Nor was he interested in a more stringent regulation of business or in social reform. Rather it was administrative efficiency that he sought and, to a considerable extent, attained. His successor as governor, Fred W. Green of Ionia, was a political enemy of Groesbeck, and showed little interest in or concern for any sort of reform. State government under Green (who served two terms from 1927 to 1931) became the same sort of holding operation that characterized the Coolidge administration in Washington.[17]

The stock market crash of October, 1929 ushered in the Great Depression of the 1930s, but the full effect of the economic collapse had not been felt at the time of the November election in 1930. The Republican nominee, Wilber M. Brucker, had been attorney general during the second Green administration. He was elected over the perennial Democratic candidate, William Comstock, but his majority was smaller than that of any gubernatorial winner since 1918. During his term of office the depression deepened, and in 1932 a sweeping Democratic victory marked the close of the long period of Republican dominance. After 78 years the Republican citadel had fallen.

[16] F. B. Woodford, *Alex J. Groesbeck, Portrait of a Public Man.*
[17] Governor Green had been head of an Ionia firm that had employed prison labor under contract. He originated the tradition of making Governor's Day at the Ionia Free Fair a major political occasion.

THE TWENTIETH CENTURY

Soon after the turn of the century a lively ditty entitled "My Merry Oldsmobile" became popular all over the nation. This is worth mentioning in a history of Michigan, for it marked the beginning of the popularization of automobiles. The production of automotive vehicles was to become, within a few years after the beginning of the twentieth century, Michigan's dominant industry. It did more than anything else to transform Michigan from an agricultural state to an industrial state.

Along with automobile manufacturing, other new industries appeared. Huge numbers of immigrants came to the burgeoning cities from eastern and southern Europe, and others came from the southern states. There was a mass migration from the farms and small towns to the cities. Agriculture became mechanized and specialized. Lumbering, past its peak by 1900, became a minor industry, while copper and iron mining—after a brief spurt— declined. Michigan turned from an extracting economy to a processing economy. And the tourist and vacation industry became a major asset to the state.

These economic shifts were accompanied by a growth of social consciousness, a wider dissemination of knowledge, and a broader spread of culture. Life became infinitely more complex. A people who at the dawn of the century knew little and cared less about affairs outside the United States, were compelled by the force of circumstances to take a world view of their fortunes and the destinies of their children. For better or for worse, Michigan was drawn into the fast-moving current of world affairs.

Expressway Interchange at Grand Rapids, Michigan

Ford Quadricycle, 1896

19

MICHIGAN
AND THE AUTOMOBILE AGE

The coming of the automobile affected the daily life of twentieth-century Americans to a greater degree than any of the other technological developments brought about by inventors and scientists. It was not so much the speed of the automobile as its flexibility that marks its chief significance in the history of transportation. The impact of the automobile on the nation's economy was due not only to the amount of capital and the number of workers involved in its manufacture, but also to the many service occupations it spawned: filling stations, repair garages, motels, and wayside inns, to mention a few. The success of passenger cars powered with gasoline motors prepared the way for trucks, buses, and tractors. The customs and mores of the American people were changed almost as much as their economy by the coming of the automobile. Courtship, for instance, was never quite the same as in horse-and-buggy days. The growth of cities and suburban developments around cities was heavily influenced by the coming of the automobile. And the life of the farmer was revolutionized by automotive vehicles as much as that of the city dweller or suburbanite.[1]

All this is particularly pertinent to Michigan history, since it was Michigan that became the center of automotive manufac-

[1] F. L. Allen, *The Big Change.*

turing in the world. While cities like Flint, Lansing, Saginaw, Jackson, and Muskegon grew lustily as automobile towns, it was Detroit and its environs that became the focus of the industry. Just why it happened that way is not altogether clear. No doubt the location of Detroit near the source of raw materials and close to major markets had something to do with its becoming the center of automotive manufacturing, but other cities such as Toledo, Cleveland, Chicago, or Indianapolis are almost if not quite as advantageously situated. It may be significant that Detroit in the pre-automobile age was a center of wagon and buggy manufacturing. Flint was also quite a buggy- and cart-manufacturing center, but so was Kalamazoo; and while Flint became an important automobile manufacturing city, Kalamazoo never did. Three of the automobile pioneers were Detroiters, and they were at the same time excellent businessmen. There was a great deal of capital in Detroit, gained largely from lumbering and mining, which its owners were willing to invest in automobile-manufacturing facilities. It was difficult to persuade Eastern bankers to invest in what was regarded as a risky enterprise in the early years. These appear to be some of the reasons that Detroit and Michigan early became the focal area for automotive development and production.

The story of the automotive industry, like that of the railroads and other great enterprises, catapults the historian into an intricate maze of corporate organizations, combinations, stock manipulations, and finance. Names once important drop out of the story and new ones appear. David Buick, whose name is perpetuated in the Buick automobile, was no longer associated with the Buick Motor Car Company after 1909; he lost his money in oil speculation and died poor and obscure in 1929. Louis Chevrolet never had much to do with the production of cars bearing his name—another "forgotten man" in automobile history. At one time William C. Durant was the greatest name in the automobile world, but long before his death he had ceased to have any connection with the industry. On the other hand, R. E. Olds and Henry Ford continued to be active in the industry for over half a century. The evolution of the automotive industry may be divided into periods of varying length, each representing a phase in that evolution, though with a considerable amount of overlapping.

THE AGE OF INVENTION, 1892-1900

The automobile, like the steam engine and other great discoveries, cannot be said to have been invented by any one individual.

The principle of combustion within a closed cylinder was fore-shadowed as early as 1678 in a gunpowder engine developed by Abbé Jean Heautefeuille in France. Another Frenchman, Nicholas Cougat, was building successful steam carriages in 1770. Jean Joseph Lenoir, a Belgian machinist, invented the first successful gas engine and built a "road wagon" powered by it in 1860. In the 1870s and 1880s three Germans—Nicholas August Otto, Gottlieb Daimler, and Karl Benz—developed the internal-combustion engine. In the United States an Englishman living in Boston, George Bradley Brayton, produced in 1872 a gas engine supposedly adaptable to liquid hydrocarbon fuels. George P. Selden, a shrewd patent lawyer, worked on an engine incorporating the principles developed by Brayton, and applied for a patent on it in 1879. He made frequent amendments to the patent application in the years that followed, many incorporating discoveries made by others. The Selden patent was not finally granted until 1895. Under American law it had 17 years to run.

The first Americans to build a practical motor car powered by gasoline were probably Charles E. Duryea and his brother Frank, of Springfield, Massachusetts. The date was 1892. Another successful gasoline automobile was built by Elwood Haynes, superintendent of a gas company in Kokomo, Indiana. It made its first run July 4, 1894. By this time tinkerers and machinists all over the country were attempting to contrive "horseless carriages." Ransom E. Olds of Lansing, Michigan, built a gasoline automobile in 1895 but did not operate it until the following year. Charles B. King of Detroit publicly tested a machine he had built on March 6, 1896. Henry Ford, another Detroiter, made the first run with a carriage powered by a four-cycle engine he had built in June, 1896. And Alexander Winton of Ohio demonstrated his first car the following September. These are some of the leading inventors and pioneers of the automobile industry, although many others might be mentioned and many have been forgotten. They were all local mechanics, obscure and possessed of only meager educational training. Winton was a bicycle repairman, Ford was a mechanic in an electric-power house, and Haynes was a superintendent of a gas company.

Henry Ford was born on a farm in Wayne County in 1863. From his earliest years he was fond of tinkering with machines and tools, and at the age of sixteen he went to Detroit to learn the trade of machinists. When he was 24 he returned to the farm and operated a sawmill as a sideline. About this time he worked on a road carriage powered by a steam engine. After two years he again moved to Detroit and became an engineer in the Detroit Edison plant. Back of his small house on Bagley Avenue there was a small brick shed, and here he went to work experimenting with gas engines. The car he drove in 1896 was a small, one-seated affair, with a two-cylinder engine and wheels and tires resembling those of a bicycle. In 1899 the Detroit Automobile Company was formed, with Ford as chief engineer at a salary of $100 a month.[2]

Ransom E. Olds, another Michigan automotive pioneer, was born in Ohio. He came with his parents to Lansing in 1880 at the age of sixteen. His father was a manufacturer of steam engines and pumping machinery for windmills. Olds worked in his father's factory, subsequently became a partner, and later the full owner of the enterprise. After hours he devoted his thought and mechanical skill to the problem of power-propelled vehicles for use on the road. As early as 1886 he produced a steam-powered car. Later he turned to working on gasoline-driven cars. Following the successful demonstration of the car he had built, the Olds Motor Vehicle Company was organized with capitalization of $50,000, furnished by Lansing investors. Six vehicles were built in 1897. Desiring to expand his operation, Olds sought additional capital from New York bankers and was turned down. But he found an "angel" in the person of Samuel L. Smith, a wealthy Detroiter who, having made his fortune in lumbering, furnished funds with which to organize in Detroit the Olds Motor Works in 1899 with a capitalization of $350,000. A plant was built and cars were turned out to sell for $1,250. Few were sold, however, and Olds then turned his ingenuity to the development of a smaller, cheaper vehicle.[3]

Meanwhile, other inventors were starting to manufacture cars. Alexander Winton of Cleveland was the first to market an internal-combustion-motor vehicle. In Kokomo, Indiana, Elmer Apperson was manufacturing the car invented by Elwood Haynes, and the Duryea brothers started to make cars at Chicopee, Massachusetts. These early cars were fabricated by using materials designed for other purposes: bicycle wheels and tubing, carriage seats and springs, and parts for windmills, for example. The early manufacturers tried to popularize the automobile by staging races. The first automobile race in America was held in 1895 under the aus-

[2] There are many biographies of Ford. Among the better ones are A. Nevins, *Ford, Expansion and Challenge* and *Ford: The Times, the Man, and the Company;* W. C. Richards, *The Last Billionaire;* R. Burlingame, *Henry Ford, a Great Life in Brief;* W. A. Simonds, *Henry Ford: His Life, His Work, His Genius;* K. T. Sward, *The Legend of Henry Ford.*

[3] For a more complete discussion of Olds, see D. Yarnell, *Auto Pioneering;* G. Niemeyer, *The Automotive Career of Ransom E. Olds.*

First U. S. automobile: Duryea "Gas Buggy," 1893

pices of the Chicago *Times-Herald* and was won by Duryea. The car he drove in that famous race has been preserved in the Smithsonian Institute in Washington. The people who bought these first cars may be classed as enthusiasts interested in an automobile as a means of display or as a fascinating hobby. A good example of this was Walter P. Chrysler, an Iowa railroad man, who had a car shipped to his home town by railroad and delivered to his barn by a drayman. For weeks Chrysler made no attempt to drive the car, but with burning curiosity proceeded to take it apart and reassemble it.

The first automobiles were built and sold at a time when a bicycle craze was sweeping the nation. Millions of "wheels," as they were called, were sold. Bicycle clubs sprang up, and a Michigan man, Horatio S. Earle, became president of a national association called the League of American Wheelmen. The popularity of bicycling probably carried over to automobiles, and, as will be noted later, the bicycle enthusiasts were the first advocates of improved roads. The gasoline-powered cars by no means had the automotive field to themselves. Steam-powered cars seemed at first to have greater potential than those using gasoline as fuel. As late as 1905 over 7% of the cars manufactured in the United States were steam-powered. Between 1895 and 1900, however, the electrics enjoyed tremendous popularity. They were propelled by electric current from batteries which had to be recharged frequently. Hansom cabs, electrically propelled, were placed in service in New York in January, 1897. A syndicate headed by

William C. Whitney, a New York financier, quickly got control of the New York company that operated these cabs. This company also obtained franchises in other cities and acquired manufacturing facilities. The resources of this syndicate in 1899 were over $100,-000,000. The same syndicate late in 1899 purchased from George P. Selden his patent rights on a gasoline-powered automobile, with the right to issue sublicenses to other manufacturers. Selden received $10,000 plus a royalty of $15 on each vehicle manufactured.[4] This gave the Whitney syndicate the power to demand that every manufacturer of gasoline automobiles secure a license from the syndicate. Had it not been for this, the syndicate would have shriveled and died. For the electric car enjoyed but a brief period of popularity. A few wealthy people bought electrics, but the necessity for frequent battery-charging and other handicaps made electric cabs impractical. And the vast improvements in the construction and performance of gasoline engines, which included sturdier cylinder castings, better coils and improved spark plugs, made possible the ascendancy of gasoline powered vehicles over electric cars.

THE MERRY OLDSMOBILE, 1900-1904

When higher-priced models failed to sell, R. E. Olds designed the "curved dash" Oldsmobile, weighing only 580 pounds and selling for about $650. In 1900 the Olds Motor Works sold 1,400 of these cars, and by 1904 annual production was up to 4,000. The Olds was the first cheap car on the market, the pioneer in the lightweight field. In spite of the car's low price the company made excellent profits, paying 105% cash dividends during the first two years. The automobile was still very much of a novelty, not reliable enough for business use, but very much the thing to impress your friends and attract attention. It checked the bicycle craze and attracted numerous investors and speculators into the auto manufacturing field. Just about everyone was humming the song that told of "My Merry Oldsmobile."

Henry Ford was less successful in these years. He broke with other stockholders in the Detroit Automobile Company and withdrew from it to form the Ford Motor Company in 1903. The early stockholders in this concern included the later famous Dodge brothers, John and Horace, Horace H. Rackham, and Alexander Malcolmson. The latter, a Detroit coal dealer, must

[4] W. Greenleaf, *Monopoly on Wheels: Henry Ford and the Selden Patent,* pp. 35ff.

have had reservations with regard to Ford's ability as a businessman, and made it a condition of his participation in the enterprise that Ford take into the firm a promising young Canadian-
born employee of Malcolmson, James Couzens.[5] During this period
Ford was constantly experimenting, and participated in frequent
automobile races as a means of publicizing his car. Manufacturing
was on a very small scale.

When Ford withdrew from the Detroit Automobile Company,
it was reorganized as the Cadillac Automotive Company, its leading figures being Henry M. Leland and William E. Metzger.
Leland had been manufacturing parts for cars for some time and
later he was to make a significant contribution to the industry
with his idea of interchangeable parts. Metzger had been a bicycle
dealer in Detroit and had carried steam cars as a sideline. The
first Cadillac, put out in 1902, was a one-cylinder contraption
that is said to have made a terrific racket.

In 1903 the Packard Motor Car Company moved to Detroit.
The first Packard was turned out by two sons of a hardware
merchant in Warren, Ohio, in 1899. The move to Detroit was
motivated by the availability of capital there. Henry B. Joy,
Russell A. Alger, and Truman Newberry were among the wealthy
Detroiters who provided $400,000 in capital stock for Packard.
About 200 cars were produced in 1904. In Flint, David Buick, a
manufacturer of plumbing fixtures, designed a car and organized
a company to build it. He soon lost control of the venture, however, and all rights owned by it were purchased by the Durant-
Dort Carriage Company in 1905. Benjamin Briscoe, who had
been associated with Buick, joined forces in 1904 with J. D. Maxwell, who had served an apprenticeship in the Olds Works, to
form the Maxwell-Briscoe Company in 1904.

These are but a few of the hundreds of individuals and companies manufacturing cars in this period. Some cars were turned
out by mechanics and small firms, and not a few were faulty and
difficult or impossible to operate practically. George H. Day, who
was connected with the Whitney syndicate, saw in the Selden
patent rights, which the syndicate owned, a tool by which fly-
by-night, back-yard auto assemblers might be restricted or suppressed. In 1900 the syndicate won a preliminary round in the
fight over the validity of the Selden patent, and in 1902 Henry
B. Joy of Packard and Frederic L. Smith of Olds took the leadership in coming to terms with the syndicate. It was agreed that
an organization called the Association of Licensed Automobile

[5] The best biography of Couzens is H. Barnard, *Independent Man: The
Life of Senator James Couzens.*

Manufacturers would be formed, and that a total royalty of 1¼%
would be paid on each vehicle manufactured. Ten firms, including Olds and Packard, formed the Association. Standards were
set for the admission of other applicants. Many were denied licenses; one of these was the Ford Motor Company. Some 27
companies had been granted licenses by 1903, but over 100 others
had refused to apply or had been denied licenses. Suits were
begun to prosecute those who continued to operate without a
license.

THE AGE OF THE BIG CAR, 1904-1908

The American League of Automobile Manufacturers' policy
had the effect of encouraging the restricted production of luxury
cars for a limited market. The noisy and unreliable gasoline
buggies produced in the early years of the industry had little
appeal to people of wealth, who preferred fine carriages and spirited horses or electrics. But by 1904 gasoline cars were becoming
more dependable and more fashionable. It became the custom now
for families of social standing to have an automobile. Between
1904 and 1908 the greatest success in the business was achieved
by concerns manufacturing the heavier and higher-priced cars. The
promoters abandoned the one-cylinder car and in 1905 turned to
four-cylinder engines. Parts were standardized; a great stir was
made in England when Henry M. Leland assembled the parts of
cars shipped there using only a screwdriver and wrench. Cadillac
was the first to use precision gauges perfected by Johansson and
the first to use the magneto instead of dry batteries for ignition.
But by 1908 it was Buick that led the other companies in production. The Buick acquired an enviable reputation for sturdiness
and dependability. It sold for about $2,000, rather less than the
Cadillac or Packard.

Other firms also enjoyed a healthy growth. Olds withdrew
from the Olds Motor Works, returned to Lansing, and formed
the Reo Motor Car Company in August, 1904. Reo, like
Cadillac, Packard, and Buick, was in the highprice class.
Two new firms established in Detroit during 1908 and early
1909 were to have a long history: Hudson and Hupp. The cars
of this period introduced many new features: demountable
tire rims date from 1904; tire chains, ignition locks, and the
spare wheel appeared in 1905; front bumpers came in 1906; left-
hand steering, motor-driven horns, and baked-enamel finishes
date back to 1908. Installment buying of cars started in 1905. In

1907 Glencoe, Illinois, built bumps into its streets to discourage speeding.

By 1909 there were 265 establishments making motor cars and twice as many manufacturing parts. About 65,000 cars were manufactured in 1908, the average selling price being about $2,000, a sum far beyond the means of middle-class families. There were, however, a number of "motor buggies"—produced in this period by midwest manufacturers for small town doctors, farmers, and traveling salesmen—that sold for between $250 and $750. Most of the individuals and firms assembling such cars were unlicensed by the Association of Licensed Automobile Manufacturers. The A.L.A.M. sought through advertising to discourage the purchase of unlicensed cars, but never with complete success. By 1908 the time was ripe for large-scale production of small, cheap cars. And it was Henry Ford who grasped this fact and capitalized on it.[6]

THE GOLDEN AGE OF THE MODEL T, 1908-1917

The first Model T Ford was produced at the Ford Highland Park plant in 1908. It continued to be manufactured with relatively little change until May 31, 1927, by which time an amazing total of 15,007,033 had been turned out. No other motor car in automobile history enjoyed such phenomenal success. Until about the time the United States entered World War I (1917) the Model T dominated the low-cost field. After that it had important competitors. Even so, the peak year of Model T production was 1923, when 2,011,125 of these cars were manufactured, a record for a single company not exceeded for 32 years. But it was in the decade after 1908 that the Model T really captured the imagination of the American people and catapulted Henry Ford to fame.

From 1903, when the Ford Motor Company was formed, until 1908, Ford was constantly experimenting with new models. The

[6] Among the best general histories of the automobile industry are R. Cleveland and S. T. Williamson, *The Road Is Yours: The Story of the Automobile and the Men Behind It*; M. Denison, *The Power To Go: The Story of the Automobile Industry*; C. B. Glasscock, *Motor History of America, or, The Gasoline Age; the Story of the Men Who Made It*; Automobile Manufacturers Assoc., Inc. (comps.), *Automobiles of America: Milestones, Pioneer Roll-call, Highlights. Automobile Facts and Figures,* compiled annually by the Automobile Manufacturers Association, is a valuable source of reference. A pamphlet entitled *Tallyho*, compiled by H. N. Rogan and published by the Automobile Club of Michigan, lists some 2,500 names of cars manufactured between 1895 and 1945.

original Model A, first to be produced, sold for $850 to $950. Next came the Model B, the first four-cylinder Ford, which sold for $2,000. There were also Models F and K. But the real progenitor of the Model T was the Model N, a good, solid little car with a four-cylinder vertical engine that produced fifteen horsepower and could travel 45 miles an hour. The price was $600. Models R and S were deluxe editions of Model N. Within the Ford organization there was spirited controversy over the wisdom of concentrating on the low-cost models. Alexander Malcolmson, the largest stockholder, favored the big car, but he was overruled and withdrew from the company. By this time Ford had gathered together a remarkably able group of men in his organization, men who contributed much to his success. Besides Couzens, who proved to be a financial and sales genius, there were C. Harold Wills, chief engineer, Walter Flanders, who devised production methods, and Charles Sorenson, a master mechanic.[7]

Work on the Model T began in 1907. Sorenson worked closely with Ford in designing the experimental car. Unlike most other cars, it was built with a left-hand drive. The cylinder engine block was cast in one piece instead of in separate sections, the cylinder head was removable, and the magneto was built into the flywheel.

The 1909 Model T touring car, introduced in October, 1908, sold at $850. The price rose to $950 in 1910, then went down every year until 1916, when the touring car sold for $360. This low price was made possible by economy in production. At the Highland Park plant the introduction of the moving assembly line, an idea originated by Sorenson, not only made it possible to turn out enormous numbers of cars at a low price, but also marks the birth of modern mass production. The advantages and economies of the moving assembly line were soon adapted to the manufacture of other products. It was made possible, of course, by the use of interchangeable parts, an idea that Henry M. Leland had introduced into automobile manufacture. The birth of mass production methods in the Ford plant in 1908 is even more important and significant in the history of the twentieth century than the Model T itself. It would not be too much to say it was the basis of the "affluent society" of the mid-century.

There were other reasons for the success of the Model T. Its price put it within reach of all but the poorest families; it literally put America on wheels. It was built with simplicity and was so easy to repair that almost anyone could fix something that went wrong with a pair of plyers and a screwdriver. Spare parts were made available to dealers everywhere. And the little car never

[7] C. E. Sorenson, *My Forty Years with Ford,* pp. 13-131.

wore out, it seemed. There was nothing fancy about the Model T: it was built not for faddists or for display but for practical use. Ford never would tolerate using any other color than black. In the course of time the Model Ts developed rattles, which gave rise to the popular idea that they were made from tin. Hence the nickname: Tin Lizzie. The Model T became a national institution, and countless stories sprang up about it, usually related to its supposedly tin construction, its durability, its rattles, and dependability. For instance, it was said that during a tornado the tin roof was blown off an Illinois farmer's barn. As a joke, he boxed up the mangled tin and shipped it to the Ford factory. In due course he received a polite letter stating that his Ford was pretty badly damaged but that it could be repaired, and that it would be returned in running order shortly.[8]

In spite of the low selling price of the Model T, the Ford Motor Company made huge profits. In 1919 when Ford bought out the other stockholders and secured exclusive control of the company the Dodge brothers, who originally invested $10,000 were paid $25,000,000 in addition to the $10,000,000 in dividends they had received. James Couzens, who had invested $2,500 originally, received over $29,000,000. The six stockholders who sold out in 1919 had originally put up $33,100, and they or their estates received a total of $105,000,000 in addition to dividends, which had totaled some $30,000,000.

Henry Ford and his company got much favorable publicity as a result of a protracted battle with the holder of the Selden patent. It will be recalled that Ford in the beginning had sought a license from the Association of Licensed Automobile Manufacturers, which had been set up by the Whitney Syndicate, and was turned down. Suit was begun against Ford for infringement of patent rights on October 22, 1903. The fight dragged on until the final court decision, January 9, 1911. The A.L.A.M. offered Ford a license in 1904, but Ford refused. During part of the period of over seven years during which the legal battle was waged, other unlicensed manufacturers joined Ford in the fight, but after a U.S. district court upheld the patent right in 1909, most of them capitulated and Ford stood virtually alone. The Ford Motor Company did not conceal its fight against the Selden patent holders, but rather advertised its stand. At the time, the American people had become aroused by the menace of great trusts, and the popular conception—not altogether unfounded—was that the

[8] P. V. Stern, *Tin Lizzie, the Story of the Fabulous Model T Ford*; W. J. Trepagnier, "The Tin Lizzie," *Motor News* (May 1959), 12ff.; F. Clymer, *Henry Ford's Wonderful Model T, 1908-1927.*

Model T Ford, 1908

Selden patent holders were trying to control the entire automobile industry. This resulted in widespread support and applause for the stand Ford was taking. In fact, the fight was of considerable consequence in publicizing the Ford car and stimulating sales. The final decision was a victory for Ford. The court upheld Ford's contention that the original Selden car was utterly impractical, and that his patent rights incorporated many features that were common knowledge and not Selden's invention at all.[9]

Even with all the publicity he received in connection with the Selden patent case, Henry Ford was little known as late as 1913. His name was not included in the edition of *Who's Who in America* of that year, even though it did list Henry J. Ford, a university professor, and Henry P. Ford, an ex-major of Pittsburg. Two events of 1914 and 1915, however, brought Ford very much into the public eye. On January 5, 1914 he announced that henceforth he would pay a minimum wage of $5.00 per day to his employees. At a time when the going rate was $2.00 to $3.00 a day, such a wage was regarded as fantastic. Couzens' biographer claims the idea originated with Couzens, not Ford;[10] Sorenson denies this and asserts that Ford had made the decision even before Couzens knew about it.[11] There is some question as to whether the plan was designed for publicity purposes or was the result of a com-

[9] W. Greenleaf, *op. cit.*
[10] H. Barnard, *op. cit.*
[11] C. E. Sorenson, *op. cit.*, p. 132. See p. 578 below.

prehension of the fact that if the mass market for cars was to continue to grow, workers must be paid good wages. Whatever its origin and its purpose, the announcement received worldwide attention.

If the $5.00 minimum wage may be regarded as an indication of Ford's good judgment, as much cannot be said for another of his ideas that came to light in 1915. A woman with a Hungarian background, Madame Rosika Schwimmer, convinced Ford and his wife to finance a "peace ship" to carry a delegation to Europe for the purpose of enlisting public sentiment to end World War I. Ford himself accompanied the party to Norway, but promptly returned already sensing the futility of the effort. The expedition, of course, came to naught, and in fact no informed person ever gave it a chance to succeed.[12]

The Ford enterprises grew in number as production mounted. Ore and timber lands, coal fields, foundries, glass factories, steel plants, coke ovens, and even a railroad were acquired. Ford pioneered in the cultivation of soy beans, from which panels, knobs, and horn buttons were made. Ford once declared that history is bunk, but he developed a keen interest in collecting early Americana. Out of this the Ford Museum and Greenfield Village near Dearborn originated.

Although the spectacular success of the Model T is the most outstanding fact of this period, other companies making cheap cars were enjoying considerable growth. The Maxwell enjoyed a wide popularity during the war years, 1914-1917. The Dodge brothers, originally associated with Ford, began to produce cars bearing their name in 1914. The early Dodge, though not easy to ride in, became well known for its ability to take unlimited punishment. Dodge pioneered in the use of all-steel bodies. Hudson organized a division in 1917 to make the Essex, a popular low-priced car. Most successful, however, was Chevrolet, which in 1917 made well over 100,000 cars. From 1910 to 1914 production of all cars rose from 181,000 to 548,000. The war boom served to stimulate car manufacture; in 1916, 1,617,000 cars were manufactured. There were in 1917 no less than 184 companies making passenger cars; 145 others made trucks and delivery cars. There were still ten makers of electrical cars. About 25% of all cars by 1917 were made in Michigan. Among the cars then being sold were the Chalmers, Columbia, Detroiter, Downing, Harroun, King, Leslie, Liberty, Princess, Regal, Ross, Saxon, and Scripps-Booth—all made in Detroit; the Dort and Paterson of Flint; the Austin

[12] M. Sullivan, *Our Times*, IV, 5ff.

of Grand Rapids; and the Brixcoe, Hackett, Hollier, Jackson, and Handley—all of Jackson. Grand Haven, Pontiac, Lansing, and Kalamazoo also had auto factories.

THE PERIOD OF MERGERS, 1917-1921

The growth of General Motors is the outstanding feature of the period from 1917-1921 in the automobile industry, and its creator, William Crapo Durant, is the central personality. At one time Durant's fortune was estimated to amount to $120,000,-000. When he filed a petition in bankruptcy in 1936, he listed his assets as $250 in clothing. At the height of his activity his New York broker's annual commission was $6,000,000. His death in 1939 brought to an end one of the most amazing careers in American business history. Born in Boston, he was a grandson of Henry H. Crapo, Michigan governor, 1865-1869. He came to Flint with his parents as a boy, quit school at 17, and with borrowed money joined a hardware clerk named J. Dallas Dort in buying a carriage factory in Coldwater for $2,000. This was the origin of the Durant-Dort Carriage Company. It developed into a concern having fourteen plants and making 150,000 carriages annually. In 1904 Durant bought out a firm that made the Buick car, and by 1908 had made Buick into the largest-selling car in the country. For Durant the sky was the limit. He appears to have sought to get control of the entire automobile industry. Ford offered to sell out for $8,000,000 but Durant couldn't borrow that much money. He nevertheless organized the General Motors Company on September 16, 1908. It was a holding company, not an operating concern. By 1910 Durant had brought under the General Motors wing Cadillac, Oakland, Oldsmobile, and several parts-manufacturing companies, as well as Buick. Conservative investors called this "Durant's Folly," but changed their minds when a profit of $10,500,000 showed up on the books at the end of the year. But a depression hit the country, General Motors stock listed at $100 a share slipped to $24, and the eastern bankers who held the large blocks of G. M. stock shunted Durant to the sidelines.

But not for long. Durant now shifted his attention to Chevrolet, and in a little over a year had gathered assets of $94,000,000. With this stake and using borrowed funds, he began buying General Motors stock until he could claim virtual control. Once more in the driver's seat, Durant now reorganized General Motors as the General Motors Corporation under the laws of Delaware. And once more he began plunging, buying up automobile companies, parts manufacturers, body plants, truck factories, and even a company that made incandescent electric light bulbs! Among those acquired were Fisher Body and Oakland. Pierre S. du Pont, the armament manufacturer, now began buying G. M. stock, driving the price up at one stage to $400 a share. Sales amounted to $270,000,000 in 1918; they were to reach the billion-dollar mark in 1926. General Motors was on the way to becoming the world's largest business corporation.

In 1921 a brief but severe business depression hit the country. In spite of ominous signs Durant continued to plunge. By getting General Motors into the tractor business he lost millions of dollars. There were other examples of bad business judgment. When G. M. stock began to decline he tried vainly to bolster it by buying shares with his own funds. Durant had got General Motors into a hole from which it could be rescued only with the vast resources of J. P. Morgan. And so before the end of the year Durant was again squeezed out of G. M. He now organized Durant Motors, acquired several other firms, and started producing a new line of cars. They did not catch the public fancy as he hoped, and the depression of the 1930s wiped out his company and most of his fortune.[13]

Largely as a result of William C. Durant's genius Flint was transformed from a small northern Michigan town that had had its greatest days in the lumber era into a huge, overgrown industrial city. Flint's population more than doubled between 1910 and 1920, and in the latter year more than half its people were the foreign-born who had come to work in its auto plants.

Durant had a talent for locating able men and attracting them to the company. But he often disregarded their counsel when he got a new idea. Among those who broke away from G. M. to form their own companies were Walter P. Chrysler and Charles Nash. Another man who joined General Motors while Durant was at the helm was Charles F. Kettering. Unlike most men in the industry, Kettering had an academic degree. He established the Dayton Engineering Laboratories Company, Delco, as it was called, and here he perfected the self-starter for cars. Cadillac was the first to use it, but it was quickly adopted by other manufacturers. Kettering was for years the most consistent inventor in the industry; ethyl and high-octane gasoline are among his contributions to the automobile age.

The increase in the number of automobiles gave rise to a demand for improved roads. In 1919 the people of Michigan

[13] A. Pound, *The Turning Wheel; the Story of General Motors Through Twenty-five Years.*

approved a state bond issue in the amount of $50,000,000 to build better highways. Back of this decision was the experience of a quarter of a century in providing improved roads. After the disappearance of the plank roads, cities and villages maintained their own streets, while the township was the unit for rural road maintenance. In 1893 the legislature passed an act permitting counties to take over this function if the voters of the county approved, but only eighteen counties had taken advantage of the law by 1905. As has been noted, the bicyclists were the pioneer enthusiasts for good roads. The national president of the League of American Wheelmen in 1901—Horatio S. Earle—was also a member of the state senate, where he sponsored a resolution calling for a committee to report on improving highways. He became so prominent in the cause of better highways that he won the nickname "Good-Roads Earle." Under the provision of the Constitution of 1850 prohibiting the state from engaging in internal improvements, the state was without authority for getting into the road-building business. Earle campaigned successfully for the exemption of "public wagon roads" from this prohibition, and an amendment making this change was adopted by the voters in April, 1905. The legislature at once established a State Highway Department, and Governor Warner appointed Earle as the first state highway commissioner. The same act provided "rewards" ranging from $250 to $1,000 per mile to townships and counties for building roads that met certain minimum standards. Up to the time of the repeal of this act in 1925 some $25,000,000 had been paid out by the state in reward money. Funds were derived from the sale of auto licenses. The Highway Commissioner continued to be appointed by the governor until 1913, when an act making the office an elective one was passed. By 1961-62, when a new constitution was drafted, Michigan was the only state to choose its chief highway officer by election; under the new constitution the highway commissioner is appointed by a bipartisan board.

In 1913 the legislature provided for the laying out of some 3,000 miles of state-trunk lines, and these were numbered with the prefix "M." In 1916 the federal government provided funds for main-road construction, and the "U.S." highways came into being. Even with this help, progress in road building was slow. Drivers found that good roads through certain townships or counties in many cases led into miserable roads in the adjoining unit. These conditions paved the way for popular approval of the $50,000,000 bond issue in 1919. During the next five years hundreds of miles of graded gravel roads and some concrete roads were built.[14] Adding federal and county appropriations, the total available was $81,000,000, all of which had been expended by 1924. Good roads whetted the public appetite for larger and faster cars, and probably were one factor in the decline of the Model T.

THE BOOM YEARS, 1921-1930

The business depression of 1921 was followed by an era of sustained prosperity, which the automobile industry did much to support. Thousands of workers were employed and millions of dollars were invested in automobile manufacturing. The production of raw materials needed—steel, wood, glass, and rubber— was stimulated. The road-building business absorbed manpower and capital, too, as did the petroleum industry. The roadside inn, which had flourished in stagecoach days and had disappeared when the railroads came, was reborn. The resort business in Michigan began to undergo a marked change: large, ornate resort hotels lost patrons, while tourist homes and tourist lodges gained favor.

Production of passenger automobiles reached a peak of 4,455,178 units in 1929. But this does not tell the whole story of the industry. For in the 1920s the production of trucks, tractors, and buses became a major segment of the business. Total production of passenger cars, trucks, and buses in 1929 was 5,337,087, a mark that was to stand for twenty years. R. E. Olds was a pioneer in truck manufacture; for many years the "Reo Speed Wagon" was almost in a class by itself. These were light trucks. After World War I, however, the use of trucks for carrying freight began, and larger vehicles were required and made. The first buses were often improvised by rebuilding a large touring car or by putting side seats in a Reo Speed Wagon. The first ones were operated, usually, by some local mechanic or other enterpriser and ran through towns having poor rail service or none at all. The railroads had a reputation for following a "public be damned" policy. The electric interurbans had already robbed them of some of their local traffic in passengers, but they still enjoyed a virtual monopoly of through passenger business and, what was more valuable, freight, express, and mail carrying. The Pere Marquette Railroad, which had undergone numerous financial reorganizations, was famous for unreliable service. There was novelty in 'riding the bus," fares were low, and bus stations were located

[14] The first mile of concrete road in the United States was laid on Woodward Avenue in Detroit between Six Mile Road and Seven Mile Road in 1909.

nearer to the centers of villages and cities than were railroad depots.

The motorbus business grew by leaps and bounds. Soon special concerns were organized especially to make bus bodies and motors. Lines were extended so that not only local but also through traffic was attracted. State control was instituted in 1923, forcing operators to follow prescribed routes and to maintain schedules. By 1929 a total of 164 companies were operating 1,500 intercity buses in Michigan. Increased regulation and higher standards imposed by the state, however, gradually drove out the small operators and forced consolidation into major corporations such as Greyhound.

The major railroads were not hurt much by the buses and trucks until the depression of the 1930s. Local passenger business was unprofitable to them anyway. The most spectacular casualties resulting from the increased number of passenger cars, buses, and trucks, were the trolley cars and interurban lines. Historically, the interurban era bears somewhat the same relation to motor traffic as the plank roads did to the railroads. Electric trolley cars first appeared in Port Huron in 1886, and within a decade every sizable city had them. The first interurban line in Michigan connected Ann Arbor and Ypsilanti in 1890. It was heavily patronized by University of Michigan swains dating Ypsilanti coeds. The Ypsi-Ann was so successful that it quickly attracted the attention of investors. Detroit interests acquired the line in 1898 and began to build extensions to Detroit on the east and Jackson on the west. The Detroit United Lines grew like a mushroom from this small beginning. By 1907 this company had interurban lines radiating from Detroit to Port Huron, Toledo, Flint, Saginaw, Pontiac, and Jackson. For several years Detroit was the most important nucleus of interurban lines in the nation, a position later taken by Indianapolis. To the west of Jackson the Michigan United Traction Company acquired lines to Kalamazoo and Lansing. As early as 1899 an electric interurban connected Grand Rapids with Grand Haven and Muskegon; later, other lines ran from the furniture city to Holland and Kalamazoo.

Most of the business of the interurban lines consisted of passenger traffic, although some light freight and fast express were carried. Much of the passenger travel was for short distances. Though "limited" and "express" cars made no local stops, most cars stopped at every crossroads to receive or discharge passengers. Some cars had parlor-car sections. Power was obtained from a cable stretched above the track from poles, or from an elevated third rail. Where the latter was used, great care had to be taken to fence off the tracks, since it was sure death to touch the third rail. The interurban served a real need. It brought small towns into easier reach of the cities and provided frequent service. In many cases the interurban tracks ran alongside the highways, although some lines had their own right of way. The heyday of the interurban was from 1900 to 1920. By 1914 almost 900 miles of lines were in operation, and literally hundreds of schemes were being proposed for additional lines.[15] By 1919 over a

[15] The number of projected interurbans may be judged by consulting the excellent history of "The Electric Interurban Railway in Kalamazoo

thousand miles of track were in use and eighteen companies with an investment of close to $140,000,000 were operating in Michigan.

The decline of the interurban was even more rapid than its rise. By 1924 ten out of the 17 companies in the state were operating in the red. One by one the roads went into receivership, the tracks were torn up, and the cars were junked. The last interurban in Michigan was the line running into Benton Harbor and St. Joseph from South Bend; it was abandoned in 1934. The interurban disappeared in Michigan somewhat earlier than elsewhere. An electric interurban was still operating between South Bend, Michigan City, and Chicago in 1965. The demise of the interurban was clearly the result of the great increase in passenger automobiles and the greater economy and flexibility of the motorbus. The motorbus not only replaced the interurban, it also superseded the trolley car. Trolley cars were replaced by buses on streets of most cities during the 1930s, although in Detroit they continued to operate for some years longer.

In the automobile industry there were many improvements in passenger cars during the 1920s. The larger "balloon" tires gave a better ride. Closed cars (sedans and coupes) generally replaced the open cars (touring cars and roadsters) after Hudson in 1922 came out with a closed car selling for only 6% more than open cars. By 1925 more than half the cars sold were closed cars.

It was on June 6, 1925 that the Chrysler Corporation—destined to become one of the "big three" in the industry—came into being. Walter P. Chrysler, its founder, had been associated with Durant for a time. In 1921 he had joined the Maxwell Company. Maxwell had absorbed the Chalmers Company, one of the pioneer manufacturing firms, and Chrysler, in turn, absorbed Maxwell. After 1925 the Chrysler sixes and eights replaced the Maxwell and Chalmers. Chrysler introduced hydraulic four-wheel brakes and a streamlined body design. In 1928 Dodge Brothers Inc. was purchased by Chrysler, which continued to manufacture a car bearing the Dodge name.

THE DEPRESSION YEARS, 1930-1940

The depression of the 1930s dealt a heavy blow to the automobile industry. Practically all Americans suffered a severe decrease in income and millions were unemployed; in such conditions

County" by Rodney Lenderink (*Michigan History,* XLIII [1959], 43-93) For the whole story of the interurban railway in Michigan, see *Electric Railways of Michigan;* G. W. Hilton and J. F. Due, *The Electric Interurban Railways in America.*

one could make the old car do. Total production of passenger cars, trucks, and buses, which hit a peak of 5,337,087 units in 1929, declined steadily to a low of 1,331,860 in 1932. It then increased each year until 1937, when 4,820,219 units were manufactured, only to decline again as a result of the recession in 1938. It was up again to 4,472,286 in 1940, the year the automobile industry began to turn to defense production.

The major automobile companies—General Motors, Ford, and Chrysler—successfully weathered the storms of depression and labor troubles that came in the 1930s. General Motors had the largest production, but Chrysler made the biggest gains. There was a flurry of interest in the small car field during the 'thirties, and a little car called the Austin was quite a fad for a few months, but it failed to attract enough buyers to prosper. The quality, power, and general appearance of cars in the 1930s steadily improved. Streamlining, higher-powered engines, and more luxurious appointments were notable. The continuing improvement of highways encouraged interstate touring. The auto-trailer made its appearance. In spite of the hard times, the tourist and vacation business in Michigan enjoyed a healthy growth.

The depression years brought a crisis in labor relations for the automobile industry. Several factors had prevented organized labor from becoming an effective force in the automobile plants prior to this time. The American Federation of Labor was organized on a craft basis; in the auto plants there were dozens of different crafts. This made it difficult for workers to speak with one voice. Another factor discouraging labor organization was the rapid turnover. Excellent wages were paid on an hourly or daily basis by the auto plants, higher than were paid in other industries. Annual wages, however, were never good because of extended layoffs during model changes. In 1933 Congress passed the National Industrial Recovery Act, containing a section recognizing the right of labor to organize and to bargain collectively. The act permitted producers in an industry to enter into agreements to limit production and eliminate price-cutting. Ford refused to enter into such an agreement in the auto industry. The other major companies became members of the "N.R.A.," as it was called, and met the labor provisions of the law by forming company unions. In 1935 the Supreme Court declared the National Industrial Recovery Act unconstitutional, but Congress quickly re-enacted its labor provisions by passing the Wagner Act.

Meanwhile, within the ranks of organized labor a movement toward "industrial unions," comprising all workers—skilled and unskilled—in a given industry was under way. The workers in the mining and clothing industries were the first to form such unions. Between 1933 and 1935 there was a 132% increase in the membership of the industrial unions, while the craft unions grew by only 13%. Out of this movement came the United Automobile Workers of America (U.A.W.), organized in 1935. At first the industrial unions were represented within the American Federation of Labor by the Committee of Industrial Organizations (C. I. O.), but in 1936 the Executive Committee of the A. F. of L. voted to exclude these unions from the A. F. of L. The industrial unions then formed the *Congress* of Industrial Organizations and the two federations remained separate until 1955. Shortly after the break, in September, 1936, the U. A. W. joined the C. I. O. The first president of the U. A. W. was Homer Martin, a former minister.

The U. A. W. lost no time in moving toward its objectives. Its leaders decided to tackle General Motors, the biggest firm in the business. Among the grievances it cited were the speed-up of assembly lines, low wages, insecurity, degrading working conditions, and denial of individual rights. In reply to these charges Alfred P. Sloan, president of General Motors, claimed that G. M. was paying the highest wages in history, even though the purchasing power of the dollar was greater than at any time since 1929. He stated that the corporation's policy was to bargain collectively with any group selected by the workers, but that it would not recognize any group as the sole representative. On New Year's eve, December 31, 1936, workers on the night shift at Fisher Body Plant Number One in Flint heard that dies were being transported out of Flint to other cities where unions were weaker. A spontaneous sit-down strike began, and it quickly spread to other G. M. plants in the city.

The sit-down strike was not unprecedented. There had been one in 1934 at the Goodyear plant in Akron, Ohio. The essential reason for the sit-down rather than the walk-out was to prevent management from bringing in strikebreakers. The Flint sit-downs set a pattern; there were many strikes in 1937 and one out of ten was a sit-down. General Motors at once declared the workers were occupying the plants illegally and asked the Genesee County Circuit Court for an injunction ordering the men to leave the premises. On January 2, 1937 Judge Edward S. Black issued a sweeping injunction directing the sheriff to eject the men from the plants. The workers ignored the injunction, and weakened the position of G. M. by proving that Judge Black held 3,665 shares of G. M. stock. At the plant gates disturbances arose and in one melee, twelve policemen and sixteen strikers were injured.

Frank Murphy, a Democrat, took office as governor of Michigan on January 1, 1937. He was under immense pressure to call out the state militia and carry out the orders of the court. Recognizing the tenseness of the situation in Flint and fearing that if he were to attempt to have the men forcibly ejected from the plants there would be bloodshed, which could embitter labor-management relations for years, Murphy finally decided to send the militia to Flint to keep order but not to evacuate the plants. Meanwhile he sought to effect a truce between the parties. An agreement for a truce was worked out, but the Union claimed that a statement issued by William S. Knudsen, G. M. vice-president, indicated bad faith on the part of the corporation, and the sit-downs continued. General Motors adamantly refused to negotiate with the U.A.W. unless the plants were evacuated first. It was only an indirect hint that President Franklin D. Roosevelt wanted the two parties to negotiate that finally brought them together. An agreement on February 11 finally brought about the end of the sit-down strike. On March 12 a final agreement was reached. Both sides made concessions, and the settlement was in the nature of a compromise. On the crucial question of union recognition, G.M. agreed to recognize the U.A.W. as a bargaining agent only of those workers who belonged to it, but pledged that there would be no negotiations with any other organization for six months without the express permission of Governor Murphy. The technique of the sit-down strike was dealt a death blow by a Supreme Court decision in 1939 declaring that a company was not required under the National Labor Relations Act to rehire employees who had engaged in such a strike.[16]

Following the strike against General Motors, the U.A.W. turned to Chrysler, which quickly recognized the union. Ford, however, held out much longer. In an incident that occurred on May 26, 1937, several union officers were beaten and mauled near the River Rouge plant. Ford used a strongarm squad under the leadership of Harry Bennett to root out union men from his factories. A decision of the Supreme Court upholding the powers of the National Labor Relations Board under the Wagner Act handed down in 1941, however, forced Ford to capitulate. An election was held in the Ford plants, resulting in the selection of the U.A.W. as their bargaining agent by 70% of the workers. Ford now gave the union all it asked and more. He agreed to the closed

[16] T. A. Karman, "The Flint Sitdown Strike," *Michigan History,* XLVI (1962), 97-125 and 223-250.

shop and the check-off, which had not been included in the other contracts. This brought the period of acute labor troubles to an end; although there were to be disputes and strikes in the years that followed, the auto companies never again challenged the right of the U.A.W. to negotiate labor contracts.

THE WAR-PRODUCTION YEARS, 1939-1945

When war broke out in Europe in 1939 the United States almost at once started on a program of preparedness. Large amounts of war materials were produced not only for United States forces but also for those of Great Britain and France. After the fall of France in the summer of 1940, President Roosevelt gambled on sending war materials to Britain; had the gamble failed, that material might have fallen to Hitler. Under the Lend-lease Act, the President was empowered to send materials of war to any nation the defense of which he considered vital to the defense of the United States. It was during this period that the United States was called the "Arsenal of Democracy," and this designation came to be applied particularly to Detroit. The government turned to the automobile industry for aircraft, tanks, guns, and other materials to feed the maw of Mars. The workers in the auto plants had the required skills; furthermore, Michigan had become the home of mass-production techniques.

Shortly after the Japanese attack on Pearl Harbor and the entrance of the United States into the war, the automobile industry was recruited in toto for war production. On February 10, 1942 automobile production for civilian use ceased altogether. Tires and gasoline were rationed. Once-busy highways were almost deserted except for huge trucks, buses, and cars on essential missions. Most people were able to keep their cars running, however, and replacement parts continued to be manufactured. Citizens "hoarded" their gasoline coupons to enable them to go on short trips. Somehow the army of deer hunters always managed to make the northward trek in November.

From September 1, 1939 to VJ Day in 1945 the automobile industry delivered to the government almost $50,000,000,000 worth of war materials. Thirty-nine percent of this output consisted of aircraft and aircraft parts. About 30% was comprised of military vehicles and parts. Another 13% went for tank production. Marine equipment, guns, artillery, and ammunition were among the other major items. Almost 4,000,000 engines of various types were made. Tank production, armored cars, and other combat vehicles totaled almost 200,000. Because Michigan was the hub of the automobile industry the greater share of the frenzied war production was accomplished in this state. Michigan supplied more munitions than any other state. The sprawling Willow Run bomber plant built by Ford (with government subsidy) at a cost of $100,000,000 and finished in mid-1942 provided employment for 42,000 people. It built 8,685 huge B-24 bombers, more aircraft than were produced at any other plant in the nation. The Chrysler Tank Arsenal in Detroit and the General Motor Tank Arsenal at Flint were gigantic war plants. War materials were also turned out in scores of smaller factories scattered over the state in such places as Grand Rapids, Kalamazoo, Bay City, and Iron Mountain.

One of the difficult problems was to find enough labor. With 613,542 Michigan men and women in the armed services, the pool of skilled and unskilled workers was drained. Wherever possible, machines were designed to do the work. Thousands of women were employed to fill jobs formerly held by men. There was a great influx of population from the rural areas of Michigan and surrounding states to the war-production cities, and many thousands came to Michigan from the South. The increase in the number of Negroes caused problems in Detroit; on June 20, 1943 fights and riots began on a large scale, and it was necessary to call in army units to restore order. There was extensive bloodshed and property loss.

There were still over 25,000,000 cars on the road in 1945, only 4,000,000 less than in 1941. But a great many of them were decrepit and ready for the junkpile. During the war workers had earned high wages and because of rationing they were unable to spend their earnings except for essentials. Accordingly, when the war ended there was a pent-up demand for cars that took years to fill.

THE BOOM YEARS, 1945-1955

Advance planning helped to speed the reconversion of war plants to civilian production. War production was cut back after the surrender of Germany in the spring of 1945, and substantial progress was made toward reconversion during the summer. One company turned out several hundred cars before Japan surrendered. When the Japanese capitulated in August, war contracts were canceled and reconversion began in earnest. By the end of 1945, 75,000 cars had been built, enough to supply about two to each of the 33,000 dealers in the nation.

The postwar cars were wide and long, with smooth lines. Their engines were more powerful than ever. They were more comfortable because passengers were moved forward and a lower center of gravity was attained. Like everything else, the new cars were more expensive: the Chevrolet, which sold for $745 in 1939, was priced at $1,439 in 1948. The Big Three maintained their dominance in the industry. For a short time after the war Henry M. Kaiser created a sensation with a new line of cars, but subsequently he moved out of the auto-manufacturing business.

Production in 1949 totaled 6,253,651 passenger cars, trucks, and buses, exceeding for the first time the prewar peak year, 1929. In 1950 the total was 8,003,056. For the next four years there was some slackening off. But a new factor entered the picture just at this time. The fall of Czechoslovakia to the Communists, the Communist take-over in China, and finally the Korean conflict, which broke out in 1950, roused the United States to the necessity for rearmament. The magnificent war machine built up between 1941 and 1945 had been permitted to deteriorate; now world conditions demanded that a new and stronger American defense force be called into being. Congress not only appropriated vast sums for United States rearmament, but also authorized military aid to other non-Communist nations. Once more, as in 1940, the nation turned to the automobile industry for defense and war materials. Just as the demand for civilian cars had about been met, the automobile industry got this new shot in the arm. New plants were built, new equipment was purchased, and employment zoomed to new high levels. In 1955 a new all-time high of 9,169,276 vehicles were manufactured. To supply the needed workers, the inflow of people from other states, which had started during the war years, continued at a rapid rate. Between 1940 and 1955 only two or three states exceeded Michigan in the rate of population growth.

PROBLEMS AND READJUSTMENTS, 1955-1963

Employment in the automobile industry in Michigan declined sharply in the years after 1955. For this there was a variety of causes. When the emphasis in defense shifted to rockets, missiles, and spacecraft most prime government contracts went to other states. For a time Michigan received almost no defense contracts, although there was an encouraging upturn in 1962. It was estimated that between 125,000 and 150,000 jobs were lost after 1953 as a consequence of the awarding of defense contracts to firms in other states. Related to this is the fact that Michigan lagged in the industrial research so essential to this field. The big boom, lasting from 1940 to 1955, had absorbed the energies of Michigan industrial leaders. They did not look far enough to the future.

A second factor in the loss of employment in the auto industry was decentralization. Actually this had been going on for some time. In the 1930s Michigan had accounted for over 60% of all automotive employment. By 1958 this state had only about 47% of the nation's employment in the industry. Assembly plants were moved elsewhere to be closer to major markets. It is a moot question whether this movement outside Michigan was induced to any appreciable extent by the relatively high taxes Michigan levied on corporate business.

Also contributing to the decline of employment in the automobile industry was automation, the installation of machinery and devices that reduced the amount of manpower needed to produce a car. Immense sums were spent by the auto companies in 1955 and 1956 for automation. It was estimated that 130,000 additional workers would have been needed in 1958 if productivity had been at the 1948 level. Other factors that also caused unemployment in the industry were the 1958 recession and the competition of the foreign car. Employment in Michigan auto plants, which stood at 503,000 in 1953, had dropped to 293,000 in 1958.

The result of this on the state as a whole was catastrophic. Michigan had come to be so heavily dependent on automobile manufacturing that it has been called (but not accurately) a "one industry state." The sustained boom over a fifteen-year period brought a huge influx of workers, and when employment in the auto industry was cut almost in half, the unemployment rate in the state, and especially in the Detroit area, far exceeded the national averages. Out-of-work people bought less and therefore the revenues from the state sales tax, chief source of revenues for the state government and an important source for local government and schools, declined sharply. Relief costs, of course, skyrocketed. Meanwhile the children of the people who came to Michigan in the boom years were knocking at the doors of the schools and colleges, and soon heavier expenditures for education were required. Thus the decline of employment in the auto industry became a matter of deep concern to all the people in Michigan.

Car production in 1962-64 set records, and a number of sizable defense contracts were awarded to Michigan firms. These were encouraging signs. But the experience of the state in the years after 1955 indicated a need for greater industry diversification. The automobile industry would continue to be a major element in the Michigan economy, but those who looked to the future were recommending that efforts be made to secure a greater variety of industries. Michigan's abundant water resources, its ports on the Great Lakes accessible to world markets by the St. Lawrence Seaway, and the prospect for increased world trade in the years ahead seemed to offer promise for the state's economic future.[17]

Mass production in American industry largely stemmed from the automobile manufacturing plants. And the sharing of larger amounts of profits earned with workers goes back to the $5.00 per day minimum wage announced by Ford in 1914. This makes the origin of this policy of special interest to the historian. The plan was not an offhand order of a benevolent dictator. It was carefully worked out by James Couzens, Norval Hawkins, and Dean Marquis, the latter an Episcopal dean who was in charge of personnel. The incentive for the action was a letter received from an unknown person suggesting the division of the exorbitant profits being made by Ford with the laborers who made them possible. Couzens got the letter. At that time, labor was getting $2.60 for a ten-hour day. The human relations problems incident to the hiring and firing of some 15,000 employees made things rather difficult for Couzens, Hawkins, and Marquis, and the plan was the work of these three. It was designed to secure the best laborers in the district, to put the company on a year-round production schedule, and alleviate the misery resulting from periodic hiring and firing. Couzens appears to have been the one who sold the idea to Ford. Ford apparently seized upon the idea because of its publicity value. It may have been he who suggested the exact figure: $5.00.[18]

[17] W. Haber, E. C. McKean, and H. C. Taylor, *The Michigan Economy Its Potentials and Its Problems.*

[18] Clarence J. Huddleston to the author, November 4, 1965. Huddleston was a member of the law firm of Anderson, Wilcox and Lacey. Anderson was counsel to the Ford Motor Company and a director for many years.

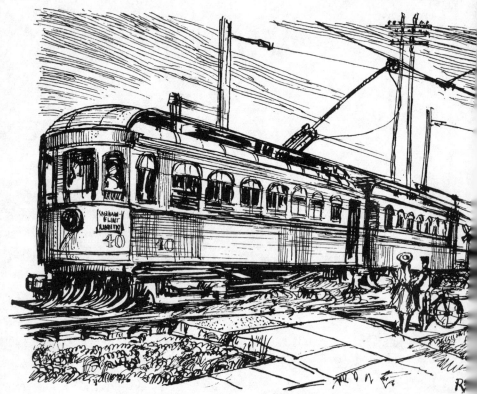

Interurban railway, 1914

20

THE SPEEDING TEMPO OF
URBANIZATION

The movement from the farms to urban centers has been one of the most important changes in American life in the century since the Civil War. The trend was nation-wide. In Michigan the movement to the cities was slower than in the other states of the Great Lakes region until about the turn of the century. Then it proceeded more rapidly than in Michigan's neighboring states. During the Great Depression of the 1930s there was a slight reversal of the trend, but in the war years and post-war period it was renewed. The 1950s were characterized by a spilling over of the urban population into fringe areas around the cities. With more automobiles and better highways, many people lived even beyond the suburbs and worked in the cities. The decade of the 'fifties witnessed a decrease in the population of central cities but an enormous growth of the fringe areas.

Michigan cities, like those in other states, developed individual characteristics. Detroit, Flint, Dearborn, Jackson, Pontiac, and others came to be dominated by the automobile industry; Battle Creek became the food-cereal city, Grand Rapids the furniture city, Kalamazoo the paper city.

In Michigan, as elsewhere, the growth of cities and urban areas brought a multitude of problems. Thousands of families accustomed to rural life had to adjust to urban living. Immigrants by the thousands flocked to Michigan cities, and there was a large influx of both whites and Negroes from the South. Every city had to cope with crime and delinquency, public-health problems, the need for recreational facilities, and dozens of other problems. The coming of the automobile brought traffic and parking problems, made possible surburban shopping centers, and led to conflict between the central cities and the areas outside the city limits.

THE URBAN URGE

Farmer Jones, who lived on a farmstead of 160 acres in southern Michigan in 1860, had five sons and three daughters, not an unusually large family for the time. One son and two daughters were married and lived on nearby farms acquired by borrowing and with parental help. Three of the sons were old enough to join in the fight to save the Union; all were fortunate enough to survive. One of them stayed in the army after the war, later helped build the Union Pacific Railroad, and wound up with a cattle ranch in Wyoming. The married son came back home, but found farming a dull routine after the excitement of the war and moved to Jackson to work in a factory. The other war veteran, after a brief sojourn at home, went to Chicago to seek fame and fortune, finally becoming a wealthy broker. One of the younger boys went to the Agricultural College, married, and homesteaded in Nebraska. The other stayed at home and when Farmer Jones ended his mortal days, this son inherited the old homestead. One daughter never married; she taught school for years and finally retired in a cozy little house in a nearby town. The other two daughters found husbands, one of them a village lawyer who later moved to Detroit, the other an ambitious young farm lad who was lured to North Dakota in the boom period of the 1880s.

Farmer Jones and his progeny are purely imaginary beings, but what has been related is typical of many Michigan family histories in the post-Civil War period. Greater opportunity beckoned some westward, others flocked to the growing cities in order to make the big money they had read and heard about. Farm population in southern Michigan grew very little, while the cities became steadily larger. By 1910 the percentage of the population living in incorporated villages and cities of over 2,000 population was 47.2%, as compared with 52.7% for all the states of the Great Lakes Area (Ohio, Indiana, Illinois, Wisconsin, and Michigan). Thus until 1910 urbanization had proceeded somewhat more slowly in Michigan than in adjacent states. By 1930, however, 68.2% of Michigan's people were living in urban areas (places of over 2,500), while the average for the Great Lakes states was 66.4% and the national average was 56.2%. The 1960 census classified 73.4% of Michigan's population as urban. Comparable figures for Wisconsin were 63.1%, for Indiana, 62.4%, for Ohio, 73.4%, and for Illinois, 80.7%, with the national average 69.9%. Thus the urban population of Michigan constituted a larger percentage of the total in Michigan than in the nation as a whole, was equal to that of Ohio, and was exceeded in the Great Lakes area only by Illinois.

The changes in the pattern of living wrought by this move to the cities was profound. Gone was the independence that came from producing a large part of the family's needs without relying on other sources. Gone was the contact with the land and growing things. Gone, too, was the simple neighborliness of rural life. But there were compensations. No longer were the vagaries of the weather—rain, snow, hail, cold, heat, and drought—the masters of one's fortunes. In most cases the toil was lighter. There were the conveniences of electricity, running water, and gas. There were libraries, colleges, theaters, museums, and the thrill of watching the crowd and being one with it. But all too often in depression years the breadwinner might find himself without a job and with no neighbors to help him. In such times he might drift back to the farm for a time, but usually pride and the fascination of urban living caused him to hang on even while envying the bountiful tables and warm clothing of his relatives in the country. After the 1930s social security, unemployment compensation, and other types of aid made it easier for the urban family to meet the problems of unemployment and old age.

DETROIT BEFORE THE AUTOMOBILE AGE

Among Michigan cities, Detroit has always been in a class by itself. As early as 1870 it had almost five times as many people as Grand Rapids, the state's second largest city. By 1940 it had almost ten times as many. In 1960 the population of Detroit constituted almost one-quarter of the state's total. In the Middle West, Chicago is the only other city that contains such a large percentage of the population of the state in which it is situated. Detroit was the fifteenth city in size in the United States in 1860, seventeenth in 1870 and 1880, and thirteenth in 1900. In 1910 it stood ninth and in 1920, fourth. Thus, while Detroit was the Michigan metropolis from the beginning, it became one of the major cities in the nation only after the coming of the automobile.

Detroit grew in size from about 45,000 in 1860 to 285,704 in 1900. Much of this increase was the result of the development of manufacturing industries. The easy availability of iron, copper, lead, wood, and other raw materials had much to do with the location of important manufactures. Boxes and barrels for shipping were cheap at Detroit; coal had to be shipped a relatively short distance; railroad and water transport facilities were excellent. By 1880 it was estimated that almost $16,000,000 was invested in manufacturing plants, and that the annual product was worth $35,000,000. Iron and steel industries were the most important Detroit industries in the 1880s. The largest factory for the manufacture of railroad cars and car wheels in the nation was located at Detroit. Immense stove factories, notably the Detroit Stove Company, the Peninsular Stove Company, and the Michigan Stove Company, were front-rank industries. Parke, Davis and Company, famed maker of pharmaceuticals, had its beginning in Detroit in 1867. The manufacture of chewing tobacco and cigars was carried on by over sixty establishments in 1880, and the city was one of the largest manufacturers of chewing tobacco in the country. The shoe factory in which Hazen S. Pingree made his fortune was the largest of its kind west of New York. D. M. Ferry and Company was the leading concern in the growing and distribution of seeds. The 919 manufacturing establishments in Detroit in 1880 employed some 16,000 persons.[1]

Detroit was an important port city; nearly 6,000 vessels tied up in the year 1880. More and more railroads entered the city. Connection with the East had been made when the Great Western Railway of Canada reached Windsor, across the Detroit River, in 1854. At first, goods and passengers had to be transferred to ferries to reach Detroit, but in 1867 the first railroad car ferry went into service, making it possible for railroad cars to be ferried across the river.[2] In 1870 15,000 passenger cars and 400,000 freight cars were ferried across the river. The amount of traffic and the delay occasioned by the ferrying gave rise to proposals for a bridge, but the river shippers protested effectively against any bridge that was not a clear span from shore to shore, which seemed an impossible undertaking. A tunnel under the river was started, but after 135 feet of it had been completed an accident occurred that caused the work to be suspended. It was not until 1910 that the Michigan Central Railroad completed a tunnel under the river for railroad traffic.

Wholesale and retail trade, of course, was a source of employ-

[1] *Compendium of the Tenth Census.*
[2] G. W. Hilton, *The Great Lakes Car Ferries,* pp. 3-53.

ment and profit to many Detroiters. There were many residents of the city who made fortunes in lumbering operations, water transport, and railroads. They built palatial homes along East Jefferson Avenue and West Fort Street. Among these were many who were successful in politics as well as business: Senators Mc-Millan, Chandler, and Palmer; Governors Baldwin, and Alger; and others whose political conquests were confined to municipal office. Here also lived the Newberrys, Joys, and others whose homes were built on a magnificent scale, but often in lamentably poor taste. There were broad grassed areas, an abundance of stately trees, statuaries, and fountains. Such men as these were patrons of the city's cultural activities. There was no stigma attached to wealth in those days; the rich were admired and emulated in an age when opportunity aplenty beckoned every boy of energy and ambition who wanted money and would work hard to get it.

In far less pretentious homes lived the workers who toiled ten to twelve hours a day for meager wages, hoping and expecting that someday they would become owners and operators. Immigration from abroad and the influx to the city from the rural areas and small towns furnished an abundant supply of labor. In 1850 over half the population of Detroit had been foreign-born; the proportion by 1880 was only a little over one-third. The largest number of foreign-born had come from Great Britain and Canada; more than a third were born in Germany. Nationality groups that later were to be represented by large numbers in Detroit were relatively small in 1880: there were only 1,771 Poles, 127 Italians, and 64 Hungarians. Only 2,821 Negroes were enumerated as residents of Detroit in 1880. The tendency of foreign peoples to settle together in certain areas was already notable; the Germans, for instance, predominated in the fourth and seventh wards, while the Irish were in the majority in the eighth ward.

There was excitement aplenty in urban life in this pre-automobile age. Among the notable events in Detroit were the visit of President and Mrs. Hayes in 1879, lively scenes at elections, the horse cars, the unveiling of the Soldiers' Monument in Campus Martius, fires, storms, the introduction of the telephone, and the opening of Belle Isle as a park, following its purchase by the city council in 1878. The theaters, art galleries, churches, schools, and the public library were the centers of the city's cultural life.

Public utilities were being developed rapidly. By 1886 approximately one-fifth of the families had running water in the home, obtained from the city waterworks. A police force of 267 men maintained law and order. The old volunteer fire companies had given way to professional firefighters equipped with horse-drawn steam pumpers, housed in nineteen engine houses. After 1870 alarms could be turned in by means of an electric telegraph system; by 1886 there were 188 alarm boxes at strategic points in the city. Streets were lighted by gas as early as 1851. In the 1870s naphtha lamps for a time replaced gas lights. Gas lights were used privately at first only in stores and factories, but by the 1890s they were becoming common in the wealthier homes. The first incandescent electric lights were installed in a dry-goods store in 1883. The following year a contract was made with a private company to illuminate the streets with electric lights. Residential lighting in all but the wealthier homes was by kerosene lamps.[3]

Some of the streets were paved with stone in 1865. During the early 1870s wood pavements were much in vogue. They had the advantage of being less noisy and smoother than the cobblestone pavements. Pavements were swept at public expense as early as 1882. The first street railways date from 1863, the cars being drawn by horses. An epidemic of horse disease disrupted the city's transport system in the 1870s. Electrification came in the 1890s. The streetcars were operated by the Detroit City Railway Company and several smaller competing concerns, but most of the lines were controlled by a small group of capitalists.

Employees working twelve to fourteen hours per day for a wage of $1.50 already were disgruntled when the arbitrary dismissal of several men in 1891 resulted in a strike. The people of the city were antagonized by the company, but the owners expected Mayor Hazen S. Pingree to take prompt action against the strikers. Instead he advised the company officials to arbitrate and refused to ask the governor to call out the militia as they demanded. A little later Pingree vetoed the grant of a new franchise to the Detroit Citizens' Street Railway Company, which had acquired the properties of the old and hated company and which included among its stockholders several of Detroit's foremost citizens. Pingree claimed the same old gang was in control. Then followed the organization of a competing company and its blessing by Pingree. When this company sold out to the older concern, the mayor's rage knew no bounds. What "Ping" wanted was municipal ownership; he already had succeeded in persuading the city council to establish a municipal lighting plant. Not until 1922, however, did the city actually acquire ownership of the street railway system.

Communication with the outside world by means of the telegraph was enjoyed before the Civil War. In addition to applying

[3] S. Farmer, *The History of Detroit and Michigan.*

the principle of the telegraph to fire alarms, signal boxes were installed beginning in 1875 for messenger and police calls and for burglar alarms. In 1877 the telephone came to Detroit, business houses being the first subscribers. In 1893 long-distance service to Chicago and New York became available.

OTHER CITIES BEFORE 1900

There were 25 other Michigan cities in 1880 having a population of 4,000 or more. The largest of these was Grand Rapids. In 1880 it had a population of 32,016; by 1900 it had grown to 87,565, about one-third the size of Detroit. The chief industry was the manufacture of furniture, but the city also was a major wholesale-trade center. Grand Rapids owed much to lumbering. Other cities that had grown up as a result of sawmills and as supply centers of goods and services required by loggers, sawyers, rivermen, and others engaged in the lumber business were Alpena, Bay City, Saginaw, East Saginaw, Flint, Port Huron, Ludington, Manistee, Grand Haven, Muskegon, and West Bay City. Ishpeming and Marquette were mining towns. The other cities of 4,000 and over were trading centers for farm areas with a variety of relatively small manufactures: Adrian, Battle Creek, Coldwater, Ionia, Jackson, Kalamazoo, Monroe, Niles, Pontiac, and Ypsilanti. Lansing, the state capital, had a population of 8,319; Ann Arbor, seat of the University of Michigan, was about the same size.

Typical urban problems such as supplying water for domestic use, fire fighting, police protection, sewage disposal, transportation, and public health were important concerns of these cities. In Grand Rapids a private company was incorporated in 1849 to supply water for the city. A rival concern began operations in 1854. The two were merged in 1870, but disastrous fires in that year caused citizens to clamor for a more abundant supply of water. Another conflagration in 1873 intensified the demand, and the following year the city laid 11 miles of water mains. Wooden pipes, prepared by boring out the centers of logs, binding them with hoop iron, and covering them with asphalt, were installed. The private company continued to supply water to the city until 1920 when it was purchased by the city. Volunteer fire companies, subsidized by the city and knee-deep in politics, carried the responsibility for fire fighting until about 1875. As early as 1865 a small fire engine was acquired. Until 1871 there was no professional police force, the merchants and householders uniting to hire night watchmen and the city appointing constables to make arrests. The first police force consisted of a chief and eight patrolmen.

Horse-drawn streetcar, Grand Rapids, early 1900s

Horse-drawn street cars appeared in 1865, with a flock of competing companies. The first improvement was the cable car, pulled by imported hemp rope, with the power supplied by central stations. Each car had a bell attached to its rear axle, which clanged each time the wheel went round. Electrification of the street railway system was an event of 1892. The first gas company was started in 1856. Gas lamps were installed by the city; the first gas stoves were used in 1880. The brothers W. A. and J. B. Foote were pioneers in high-voltage transmission of electric power. They built the Rogers dam near Stanwood in 1905, the Croton dam on the Muskegon in 1911, and others. These developments laid the foundations for the Consumers Power Company. Telephone service in the Kent County metropolis was inaugurated in 1877; by 1883 there were 530 subscribers.

Alongside these enterprises catering to the physical needs of the people, cultural institutions developed. The City Library Association came into being in 1860 and the Grand Rapids Public Library opened its doors two years later with 4,045 books on its shelves. John Ball Park was deeded to the city in 1869. By 1867 there were two scientific societies in Grand Rapids. The Young Women's Christian Association was formed in 1900. Schools, theaters, churches, and dozens of societies and clubs also contributed to the city's cultural life.[4]

The smaller cities, during the years between 1865 and 1900, were building up civic institutions and enterprises similar to those in Detroit and Grand Rapids. But there were few places of sufficient size to develop truly urban conditions. Outside Detroit, Grand Rapids, the lumber towns, and a few trading centers, the people lived mainly in rural areas and small towns.[5]

MICHIGAN BECOMES AN URBAN STATE

In the twentieth century, cities in Michigan experienced a phenomenal increase in size and numbers. As has been noted, the Wolverine State by 1950 had a larger proportion of its population living in cities than any of its neighbors except Illinois. Detroit grew from 285,704 in 1900 to 1,838,517 in 1950. Outstate cities like Flint, Pontiac, and Ann Arbor also burgeoned. There had been only three cities in the state with more than 50,000 inhabitants in 1910; by 1950 there were ten, and by 1960 there were 17. In 1910 there were six cities in Michigan with populations ranging from 25,000 to 50,000; in 1950 there were ten, and by 1960 there were twenty.

The development of the automobile industry accounts for much of this urban development, though not all of it. Several cities outside Detroit owe their growth principally to automotive manufacturing, notably Flint, Pontiac, Lansing, and Muskegon. But it was in Detroit and the area around that city that the automotive industry promoted the largest urban growth. Detroit itself, which had been only about three times larger than Grand Rapids in 1900, had become almost ten times as large by 1950. Around the central city grew up dozens of suburban communities, which in due course formed satellite cities. Of the 37 Michigan cities having a population of above 25,000 in 1960, no less than 22 may be considered within the Detroit urban complex. About one-half of the entire population of Michigan is in the Detroit area.

Another notable feature of urban growth in the state is that it took place to a very large extent in the southern half of the Lower Peninsula. None of the 37 cities over 25,000 in 1960 were

[4] W. J. Etten (comp. and ed.), *A Citizen's History of Grand Rapids, Michigan*. . . .

[5] For information on other Michigan cities, see C. Crow, *The City of Flint Grows Up*; W. F. Dunbar, *Kalamazoo and How It Grew*; B. Darling, *City in the Forest: The Story of Lansing*; F. C. Hanna, *Sand, Sawdust, and Saw Logs: Lumber Days in Ludington*; O. W. Stephenson, *Ann Arbor: The First Hundred Years*; *Michigan, a Guide to the Wolverine State*.

north of Muskegon. Marquette, largest city in the Upper Peninsula, had a 1960 population of 19,824; Sault Ste. Marie, Escanaba, and Menominee were the only other Upper Peninsula cities having more than 10,000 people. Several cities in the Upper Peninsula experienced population losses, notably the Copper Country cities of Houghton and Hancock.

The development of suburban or fringe areas around the cities was another important development. It became practicable for city-dwellers to move outward with the coming of the electric trolley car and the electric interurban in the 1890s. With the coming of the automobile, suburban development swelled to major proportions. Real-estate dealers acquired land adjacent to all the major cities, platted lots, laid out streets, brought in utilities where possible, and enticed city dwellers who hankered after more space and purer air to make purchases. This movement to the suburbs did not begin to prevent city growth, however, until the 1950s. The impact of the exodus from the central city was clearly demonstrated by the 1960 census. Several major cities, including Detroit, lost population in the decade of the 1950s. Not only people but manufacturing industries and retail stores began to move out; suburban shopping centers sprang up around all the cities in the 1950s. Downtown stores were left vacant. As those able to pay for suburban homes moved out of the city, their homes were taken over by poorer people, less able to maintain them in good condition. The decay of cities at the center became a common phenomenon in the 1950s. Among other results was a decline in the assessed valuation of properties and diminishing tax revenues for the cities. City governing bodies began to take action to solve the problem. Urban renewal projects were inaugurated with federal aid. Kalamazoo transformed three blocks of its downtown streets into the first permanent pedestrian mall in the nation. Detroit built a huge downtown civic center to restore vitality. Parking lots and parking ramps were provided for parking. But there remained a question as to the future of the central cores of the cities.[6]

The evolution of fringe areas around the cities posed many other problems. As suburban communities grew, the need was felt for municipal services: water supplies, storm and sanitary sewers, fire and police protection. In some cases these problems were met by annexation to the central city; both Grand Rapids and Kalamazoo succeeded in consummating extensive annexations in the 1950s. But in many cases people in the fringe areas resisted annexation; under Michigan law their consent was necessary. Another solution

[6] S. T. Kimball, *The New Social Frontier: The Fringe.*

was to purchase municipal services from the central city; for example, Detroit provided water under contract for large portions of its fringe areas. Still another answer was the incorporation of new cities around the older cities, or even, as in the case of Hamtramck, within the older city. Sometimes, as in the case of Warren in Macomb County and Portage in Kalamazoo County, entire townships were incorporated as cities. Allen Park, Garden City, Hazel Park, Lincoln Park, Roseville, and Livonia are a few of the new cities that were established adjacent to Detroit. Wyoming is a sizable city in the fringe area around Grand Rapids.

The availability of fast transportation was the key to the development of the suburban fringe. Until after World War II mass transit was utilized to a large extent to bring workers and shoppers downtown and to return them to their homes. The trolley car began to give way to the motor bus as the backbone of mass transit about 1930. One by one the street railway systems were abandoned and buses were substituted. Heavy patronage made it possible to provide transportation at a small price. But the rapid increase in the number of passenger automobiles began to hurt mass transit systems about 1948. More and more people preferred driving their own cars downtown to taking a bus. By 1960 a number of the smaller cities like Benton Harbor and Ann Arbor had no bus transportation at all. Elsewhere mass transit was in trouble; fares were raised as patronage declined, and this in turn resulted in further declines. As auto traffic increased downtown streets became so congested that major cities were compelled to spend millions of dollars to provide wider thoroughfares. And downtown parking became a problem of major proportions.

As cities and their suburban fringes grew, sharp conflicts of interest developed between the urban communities on the one side and the rural areas and small towns on the other. The state legislature, a majority of the members of which represented rural Michigan, the small towns and small cities, refused to reapportion the seats in the state senate and house of representatives to give the larger cities the increased representation to which their population entitled them. And when reapportionment did come it went only part way toward giving the cities their fair share of legislators. The voters approved in 1952 an amendment to the state constitution that apportioned the house of representatives to a large extent on the basis of population, but gave the sparsely populated areas of the state far more than their share of senate seats. The intervention of the federal courts in legislative apportionment and the framing of a new state constitution in 1962-63 brought the issue sharply to public attention. There were other matters on which urban and nonurban interests clashed. Among these were the proposal to allow cities to tax nonresidents who worked within the city, several different proposals to facilitate the annexation of adjacent areas to cities, and the allocation of state-aid funds. Immensely complicating the conflict of urban and nonurban areas was the fact that in politics the Detroit area and to a lesser degree the Flint area were strongly Democratic, while the outstate areas were normally Republican in their preferences. Also, there was strong outstate antagonism toward the strong role played by organized labor in the Detroit area and in the Democratic Party. Thus the urban and nonurban conflict had political and social overtones.

Of the cities that owe their growth largely to the automotive industry, none outside Detroit could match Flint. The increase of its population from 1900 to 1930 was twelvefold: from 13,103 to 156,492. Once a sleepy ex-lumber town, Flint developed in three decades into a booming industrial city. The great Buick and Chevrolet plants, the AC Spark Plug factory, and the Fisher Body Works employed thousands of workers. In 1961 General Motors paid almost $500,000,000 to its employees and suppliers in Flint. Saginaw, like Flint a former lumber town, also felt the impact of the automobile age. The largest gray-iron foundry in the world, an extensive Chevrolet plant, huge bean-storage elevators, and sugar refineries are features of Saginaw's economy. Lansing's growth since 1900 has been due more to the genius and enterprise of R. E. Olds and General Motors than to the fact that it is the state capital. In 1963 there were 209 industries in Lansing; only 11% of the people were employed by state, local, or federal government, while 65% worked in manufacturing, business, and service trades. Jackson has almost tripled in size since 1900. It had the misfortune to be the home of many automobile plants that turned out to be "duds." The Jackson, the Imperial, the Clark-Carter, the Cutting, the Briscoe, and the Earl are a few of the cars once made in Jackson. But industries supplying automotive plants proved to be more successful. Goodyear Tire and Rubber Company built a major plant in Jackson, as did the Dow Chemical Company. Plants supplying automobile engines and parts contributed heavily to the growth of Muskegon, but after the Great Depression a more diversified industrial economy developed. Office equipment and sporting goods are among the products made there. Muskegon had a major refrigerator-manufacturing plant, but like a number of other Michigan industries, it was induced to move to a southern state by the prospect of lower labor costs.

Grand Rapids continues to be known as the "furniture city,"

and a considerable amount of high-grade furniture is still manufactured there. But the industrial character of the state's second city has undergone a major change since 1920. The companies making less expensive, mass-produced furniture have largely moved to locations in the South. Furniture making no longer is the backbone of the Grand Rapids economy. Such products as refrigerators and other household appliances, paper products, seating, machinery, and machine tools are much more important. The Lear Siegler Corporation in Grand Rapids is a major producer of aircraft and electronic equipment. In the 1960s a major airport was built near Grand Rapids, and a major redevelopment of the downtown area was started. Grand Rapids, with its many large hotels and its huge convention hall (built at low cost during the Great Depression), is a major convention center.

Battle Creek won distinctive fame in the twentieth century as a producer of cereal foods. This industry grew indirectly from the Western Health Reform Institute, founded there in 1866. A decade later under the direction of Dr. John Kellogg the famous Battle Creek Sanitarium was founded. The importance of diet in the cure of human ailments was emphasized and meat-eating was frowned upon. Hence the effort to provide cereal foods with eye and taste appeal. A former patient in the sanitarium, C. W. Post, concocted a preparation made from molasses and bran called Postum that served as a substitute for coffee. This product was marketed in 1895, and later Grape Nuts was added to the line. In 1899 William K. Kellogg, a brother of Dr. John Kellogg who had been the latter's aide, began manufacturing food cereals. W. K. Kellogg built the business largely through advertising, and Kellogg's Corn Flakes became known the world over. The success of Kellogg and Post brought dozens of competitors into the business, but they were mostly short-lived. General Foods (which bought the Post cereal business), Kellogg, and Purina-Ralston provide a major part of Battle Creek's employment. The Battle Creek Sanitarium, closed after the passing of Dr. Kellogg, has been used to house federal-government agencies. Battle Creek was long the home of a large manufacturer of farm equipment, the Oliver Company. It also attracted a number of other firms making a variety of products.[7]

Kalamazoo developed as a city of diversified industries, the most important of which was the manufacture of paper and paper products. The Kalamazoo Paper Company was established in 1867. Between 1890 and 1915 many other paper mills and plants

[7] G. Carson, *Cornflake Crusade*; H. B. Powell, *The Original Has This Signature—W. K. Kellogg.*

producing paper products were built and operated by men trained in paper-making in the Kalamazoo Paper Company. Other paper plants were built about the same time in towns in the Kalamazoo River valley: Vicksburg, Plainwell, and Otsego. Among the enterprises that made the name "Kalamazoo" known was the Kalamazoo Stove Company; the legend "a Kalamazoo direct to you" became a nationally known trademark of this company's product. Other Kalamazoo industries manufacture mint oils, fishing tackle, and guitars. The manufacture of pills was started on a small scale in 1886 by Dr. William E. Upjohn, and this grew into one of the nation's leading pharmaceutical firms, The Upjohn Company.[8] The low muck lands around Kalamazoo were well adapted to celery culture and the Dutch settlers were successful in developing a popular type of celery. The vegetable was new to Americans, and at first was not too favorably received. But as sales increased, Kalamazoo celery became the standard of quality.

Kalamazoo affords a good example of shifting economic patterns. The stoves that once made "Kalamazoo" a byword no longer are made there. Little celery was grown around Kalamazoo after about 1950. The manufacture of buggies, cigars, coffins, corsets, and steel windmills, once thriving Kalamazoo industries, have became extinct. But Kalamazoo remains as a city of diversified manufacturing and stable employment. The city was relatively little affected by the auto industry. Its boom period came between 1900 and 1910, a decade before the great automobile boom in other Michigan cities. With two colleges and a university, in addition to an outstanding orchestra and art center, Kalamazoo is an important cultural center. Its downtown mall attracted nationwide attention in the 1960s.[9]

But of all Michigan cities Detroit had the most spectacular growth in the twentieth century, most of it between 1900 and 1930. The population increase in those three decades was almost eightfold. Villages like Highland Park and Hamtramck, incorporated in 1889 and 1901 respectively, grew into cities completely surrounded by the city of Detroit. Life in Detroit between 1900 and 1930 was reminiscent of the boom towns in the mining regions, only on a far bigger scale. The lovely shade trees, which did much to justify the claim that Detroit was America's most beautiful city, were cut down to widen the streets. The old mansions, abandoned by their owners when they moved to fashionable suburbs, were transformed into rooming houses. Tremendous numbers of foreign people, farm boys from Michigan, and people from

[8] L. Engel, *Medicine Makers of Kalamazoo.*
[9] W. F. Dunbar, *Kalamazoo and How It Grew.*

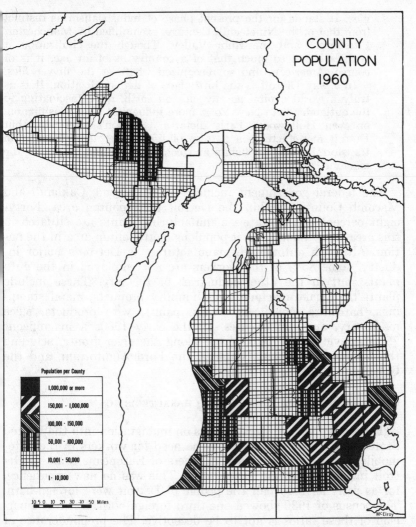

COUNTY
POPULATION
1960

Population per County

■	1,000,000 or more
	150,001 - 1,000,000
	100,001 - 150,000
	50,001 - 100,000
	10,001 - 50,000
	1 - 10,000

10 5 0 10 20 30 40 50 Miles

McElroy

the South flocked to the "motor city." It was an age of hurry,
bustle, confusion, construction, vast schemes, big financial deals,
and colorful personalities. One author summed up the Detroit
boom in these words:

In the same fashion as the embodied fossils give the age of
a stratum of rock, Detroit is dated and placed by its products.
It is the Twentieth Century. It belongs to a period of democra-
tized luxuries, with gas stations on every corner, chain stores,
moving-picture palaces, glittering automats, broadcast sympho-

nies. It stands for the present phase of industrialism as distinct
from that of the Nineteenth Century, exemplified by Manchester,
Pittsburgh, and the Ruhr Valley. Though the civilization it
typifies is not so much that of a country as of an age, it is of
course, American, and so recognized wherever the flivver flies.

In a way Detroit is the birthplace of that civilization. It is as
truly a world capital as any city on earth, more fascinating to
the outlander than New York, more influential than Washington,
or even Hollywood. Paris dictates a season's silhouette, but
Detroit manufactures a pattern of life, bolder than Moscow in
transforming human habits and communizing the output of the
machine.[10]

The federal government includes all of Wayne, Oakland, and
Macomb Counties within the Detroit metropolitan area. Forty-
eight percent of the state's manufacturing plants are situated in
this area. It is the fifth most populous metropolitan area in the nation. Although automotive manufacturing is Detroit's major industry, some 85% of the workers are not employed in the auto
plants, but in the other industries of the city. These include
plants that make machine tools, foundry products, metal stamp-
ings, hardware, chemicals, drugs, paints, wire products, office
machinery, and rubber tires. In the early 1960s a magnificent
75-acre civic center took shape along the river front, including
the Veterans Memorial Building, the Ford Auditorium, and the
Cobo Hall Convention Arena.[11]

CHANGES IN URBAN POPULATION CHARACTERISTICS

There were very few restrictions on immigration into the United
States until 1921. Attracted by the need for workers in the automobile plants, unprecedented numbers of Europeans came to Detroit in the years prior to that date. This was no new experience,
for as early as 1850 half the people of Detroit were foreign-born.
The census of 1930 showed one-third foreign-born. Yet a comparison of these ratios is apt to be deceptive. The preponderance of
the immigrants prior to 1900 came from Great Britain, Ireland,
Germany, and Canada. These folk were assimilated with relative
ease. But the immigrants who came in the twentieth century were
largely from southern and eastern Europe, and they were more

[10] Anne Hare McCormick, New York *Times,* Nov. 11, 1934, quoted in
A. Pound, *Detroit, Dynamic City,* pp. 367-368.

[11] For other histories of Detroit, see C. M. Burton, *The City of Detroit,
Michigan*; G. Catlin, *Story of Detroit*; M. Bingay, *Detroit Is My Own
Home Town*; Detroit City Planning Commission, *Detroit Master Plan*; G.
W. Stark, *City of Destiny, The Story of Detroit.*

inclined to settle together in certain parts of the city and to retain the customs, language, and habits of their kind. By 1930 Poles constituted the largest foreign-born group in Detroit, numbering 66,113. There were 28,581 Italians, 21,711 Russians, 11,162 Hungarians, 9,014 Yugoslavs, 7,576 Rumanians, and 6,385 Greeks. The Detroit settlements of Bulgarians and Macedonians were the largest in the nation. In some census tracts in Detroit in 1930 the proportion of foreign-born was as high as 60%.

Other Michigan cities received an influx of foreigners, though in smaller numbers. Half the population of Flint in 1920 was foreign-born. Lithuanians came to Grand Rapids in large numbers, while Dutch immigrants predominated in Muskegon, Kalamazoo, and other west Michigan cities. After the quotas were imposed on immigration in 1924, the influx was halted and assimilation gradually ran its course. But it required far more than a single generation for these nationality stocks to become adjusted to the new American urban environment.[12]

Another major source of Detroit's swelling population was the South. Both whites and Negroes were attracted in large numbers to Detroit and to other Michigan cities. Only 17,115 Negroes lived in Michigan in 1910, but by 1930 they numbered 169,453, or between 3% and 4% of the total population. The influx of Negroes was even more rapid after 1930. The census of 1960 enumerated 717,581, almost 10% of the total population of the state. The percentage of Negro population in the cities was much larger than in the state as a whole: almost 30% of the population of Detroit in 1960 was Negro. It goes without saying that this resulted in critical race-relations problems. The Negro was not denied political rights in Michigan, but he was forced to accept the most menial occupations. The poverty of Negro families meant that few could afford an education, and in Detroit and other major cities Negro housing was segregated and substandard. The tragic race riot in Detroit which took place in 1943 has been referred to earlier. Fundamentally, the cause for the riot was the increased economic prosperity of the Negroes who worked in war plants and the effort of certain white groups to keep them down. Housing was a particularly bitter bone of contention, since Negroes were charged higher rents than whites for the miserable hovels they lived in.[13]

Since World War II there has been a revolution in the status

[12] L. Rankin, "Detroit Nationality Groups," *Michigan History,* XXIII (1939), 129-207.

[13] J. C. Dancy, "The Negro People in Michigan," *ibid.,* XXIV (1940), 221-241.

of the Negro in Michigan. The legislature made history in 1955 by passing the Fair Employment Practices Act, placing legal sanction behind nondiscrimination in employment. Although the law did not result in any sudden elimination of discriminatory practices, it had the effect of battling such practices with legal tools. Slowly Negro workers in manufacturing plants, service occupations, and the professions increased in number. Higher incomes helped make education available to more Negro youth. Even so, unemployment among Negro workers, especially youth, remained at a far higher level than among whites. Furthermore, in every Michigan city segregation of Negro housing persisted in spite of many attempts to alleviate or eliminate it.

Southern whites also came to Michigan in large numbers. Many were migrant farm workers, but the majority found their way to cities. Generally, they lacked education. Coming mostly from rural districts, they were not adjusted to urban living. The families that moved to the cities from the farms and small towns of Michigan were on the whole better equipped to cope with the adjustment to urban living than were the foreign peoples or those who came from the South. Even so, they had to adopt new patterns of living, and the change brought many problems.

PHYSICAL ASPECTS OF THE CITIES

The physical appearance of Michigan cities changed drastically in the twentieth century, and particularly after World War I. The movement to the suburbs left vacant the ornate mansions built in the gilded age, which were either torn down, became apartment houses, or were adapted to other uses. Many were replaced by gasoline filling stations, certainly no aesthetic improvement. The number of servants employed declined as household appliances to make domestic toil lighter became available. With fewer servants smaller and more functional houses became the general rule.

As automobile traffic increased, city streets became hopelessly congested. Traffic lights came into use in the 1920s. The elimination of the streetcars, which ran down the middle of the streets, eased the situation temporarily, but not for long. Presently, huge parking lots and ramps were required for the storage of private cars coming downtown. Public buildings of ornate design, constructed in every city in the nineteenth century, gave way to simpler structures designed for utility. Expansion in downtown areas of cities was vertical. Skyscrapers fashioned of steel and concrete increased in number and size. The flight of retail stores to suburban shopping centers (especially food and drug stores) has been mentioned. The ubiquitous saloon of the pre-prohibition days gave way to "speakeasies" during prohibition and to the equally ubiquitous bars and taverns that sprang up after repeal. The dignified theaters of the nineteenth century and the opera houses of the small towns fell into decay as nickelodeons and then movie palaces were built. The latter, in turn, felt the pinch when television arrived and as outdoor movies became popular after World War II.

Even the sounds of the city changed. Early in the century there was a cacophony of factory whistles morning, noon, and night. On Sunday bells rang out from the church steeples and on weekdays from the schoolhouses. The vegetable peddler, the scissors grinder, and the junk collector each had his call and cry. The whistles of steam locomotives, some deep-throated and ominous, others shrill and shrieking, added to the urban din, as did their chugging and puffing. Along the streets was the ding-ding-ding of the bell on the trolley cars, while owners of new cars loved to sound their horns and klaxons. These sounds one by one were eliminated, and the cities became quieter. They also became cleaner as more and more homes, factories, and businesses changed from the use of coal for fuel to oil or gas.

RECREATION

Partly as a health measure, city-dwellers became devotees of sports in one form or another. Sports also served as a substitute for outdoor living and the hard muscular labor that so many men and women had known on the farm. Furthermore, athletic activities constituted a psychological compensation for the tedium and monotony of assembly-line production or office routine. Whatever the cause, sports of every kind became popular.

Baseball leaped into the spotlight in the early years of the twentieth century. Thousands of boys and young men played ball on "sandlots," where old and young were equally enthusiastic as spectators or fans. Detroit had a major-league baseball team after 1900, when Frank J. Navin obtained a franchise in the American League. Since that time the Detroit Tigers have been favorites throughout the state. Beginning in the 1930s, millions got their baseball third-handed, for they neither played the game nor attended it, but followed the radio description or watched the play on television. A Detroit schoolboy might not be able to identify Hazen Pingree or James Couzens, but he had no trouble with such Tiger "greats" as Ty Cobb, "Wild Bill" Donovan, Harry

Heilman, Mickie Cochrane, Charlie Gehringer, or Al Kaline. Minor-league baseball teams appeared in other Michigan cities, but television spelled their doom. However, the number of amateur baseball leagues continued to grow, and the "little leagues" sprang up for the younger set.

As a spectator sport football outrivals baseball for a short season. The immense stadium at Ann Arbor was built not to accommodate the University student body alone, but also thousands from Detroit and elsewhere in the state who come by train, bus, and automobile to see the games. In the early 1930s, professional football gained in popularity. Detroit's professional football team, at first called the Detroit Panthers and later the Lions, was organized in 1925 by James G. Conzelman. It became a member of the National Football League, which then included twenty teams. Among the famous players who wore the Lions uniform were Earl (Dutch) Clark, Roy (Father) Lumpkin, Byron (Whizzer) White, Frankie Sinkwich, Doak Walker, and Bobby Layne. The colleges and universities made football a major sport. Every high school had its team and in backyards, vacant lots, or any other handy place city youngsters worked off steam by kicking a football around.

Hockey, like baseball and football, became a popular professional sport. The Detroit Red Wings followed the Tigers and the Lions in the public eye as the seasons advanced. Basketball, played by high school and college youth, also had thousands of fans and its professional players. Boxing was another spectator sport; wrestling, which degenerated into something of a racket, still another.

But city-dwellers were not content to be simply spectators. Sports of all kinds seemed to become more popular as the cities grew. Roller skating flourished intermittently following the Civil War, rinks being built from time to time as the vogue waxed and waned. For a time croquet was a popular game, played on the lawns of thousands of homes. The game was suitable for the ladies to play, for it did not require undue exertion and the prim belle of the gay 'nineties could joyfully giggle as she tapped the ball with the daintily held mallet and caused her swain's heart to flutter. Lawn tennis was imported to America about 1875 and became popular around the turn of the century.

The increase in the number of YMCAs during and after World War I provided facilities for such sports as volleyball, squash, and handball. During the 1920s golf attained widespread popularity. Formerly a game played by rich men on private courses, it attracted many more players. By the mid-1920s there were 5,000 courses and 2,000,000 players in the country. Most participants were city-dwellers. In 1940 Detroit had ten public and many private and semi-private courses, Grand Rapids had seven courses, Kalamazoo had three public and several private ones. As one writer put it,

> There is a charm about this game that comes from kinship with a common purpose. There is the solid satisfaction of meeting with men who play the same shots, use the same clubs, and talk a common language. Golf has restored the powwow to the modern world, and the shower-bath is our counterpart of the old campfire in the hills. It is not bad fun . . . to gather at the nineteenth hole, swap jokes, plan the day's attack and debate the choice of weapons. It is not bad fun to wear clothes that are made for the open road in a world dressed up in office clothes and collars.[14]

Thousands of city-dwellers became ardent fishermen and huntsmen. They migrate each year for a time to the woods and streams of the northland in pursuit of the trout, panfish, deer and other game. So great is the exodus from the cities at the opening of the deer season that business operations are slowed down and factories work short-handed. Camping and life out of doors were encouraged by the increasing custom of providing workers with a vacation lasting two weeks or longer.

In the early years of the twentieth century pool and billiards were popular diversions for menfolk, though the "pool room" was generally regarded as somewhat wicked. It was a popular hangout for loafers, bums, and assorted unsavory characters. Perhaps this explains in part why, about the time of the depression of the 1930s, pool rooms tended to pass from the scene. But in the 1950s and 1960s there was a marked revival in pool and billiards, with many tables being installed in home recreation rooms. The sport that grew most lustily after World War II was bowling. All over the state, on the outskirts of cities and towns, large bowling alleys were constructed. This boom in bowling spelled prosperity for a Michigan firm, the Brunswick Company, which is one of the major suppliers of bowling equipment.

Through all these channels cityfolk escape periodically from the sedentary, indoor, and confined living conditions for which they are still poorly adapted both physically and emotionally. Even so, urban living created serious problems, particularly with regard to youth. Juvenile delinquency became a matter of increasing concern in the 1950s. Especially serious was the problem of unemployed youth who had dropped out of school. Many of these

[14] C. Merz, *The Great American Bandwagon*, p. 96.

young people, especially among minority groups, became law violators. A large number came from broken families or families where both parents worked outside the home.

URBAN PROBLEMS

Some of the problems that resulted from the rapid growth of Michigan cities in the twentieth century have already been noted. Others remain to be mentioned. For the central cities fire protection, water supply, police protection, and sewage disposal were carried out so efficiently that the public took such services for granted, although the need for them constituted critical problems in the fringe areas around the major cities. The pollution of streams into which sewage was dumped became such a nuisance that the legislature in 1929 established a Stream Control Commission and gave it extensive powers to halt this pollution.[15] Cities and industries dumping sewage into streams were ordered to build and operate sewage disposal plants.

The period following World War I saw marked increase in crime. The automobile provided the thief or murderer a quick getaway. There was wholesale violation of the Volstead Act, passed by Congress to implement the prohibition amendment. Rum-runners, as they were called, conducted a flourishing business, bringing liquor across the Detroit River from Canada and shipping it by truck to major midwest city bootleggers. Prostitution and gambling were other offenses with which city police forces had to deal. Periodically in the larger cities there were scandals, judicial inquiries, and prosecutions that aroused public indignation. Another major police problem was the enforcement of traffic safety laws. In the middle 1920s "stop streets" and automatic traffic signals became common. One-way streets and widened thoroughfares came later. After World War II the traffic problems became so acute that multilane expressways were built to carry traffic into and out of Detroit and Grand Rapids. Safety campaigns were promoted by civic organizations, schools, and the police, but the number of traffic fatalities continued to mount.

In order to bring about more efficient municipal administration many cities adopted some form of the commission-manager type of government. Under the Constitution of 1908 cities enjoyed the right of "home rule" and many took advantage of this to draw up charters providing for new kinds of city government. Between 1915 and 1925 the majority of Michigan cities adopted new char-

[15] The Stream Control Commission was supplanted by the Water Resources Commission in 1949.

ters. Some provided for the election of council members at large rather than by wards; more provided for a city manager. Michigan leads the nation in the number of cities having city managers.

Like many other large cities, Detroit had a corrupt and graft-ridden city government in the early twentieth century. The movement for a new city charter was promoted by the Detroit Citizens League, founded in 1912 with the automobile manufacturer Henry M. Leland as its president. A new charter was adopted in 1918. It provided for a nine-member city council elected at large to replace the old council made up of aldermen chosen by wards. The elected mayor was given extensive powers, including that of appointing department heads. James Couzens, first mayor elected under the new charter, brought into city government in Detroit a new regime of order, efficiency, and honesty. Couzens carried on the battle started by Pingree against the Detroit street railway company; this culminated in 1922 when the city took over the Detroit United Railway lines in the city.

Among the problems to which cities gave increasing attention was that of public health. The inspection of the milk supply, restaurants, meat, and food stores became important city functions. Dr. Caroline Bartlett Crane of Kalamazoo, a Unitarian minister, was a pioneer in bringing to public attention the need for such inspection. The control of contagious diseases was another facet of the public health movement. For the first time in the history of the state no deaths from diphtheria were reported in 1958; there was only one death from typhoid fever in Michigan between 1952 and 1958. Deaths from tuberculosis were down to 395 in 1958. Grand Rapids in 1945 started the fluoridation of its city water supply as a means of reducing tooth decay, and 70 other cities had followed suit by 1959.

One development of the twentieth century in Michigan cities was zoning. The zoning movement started in New York in 1916 and spread rapidly. In the 1920s most Michigan cities passed zoning ordinances setting aside certain areas for residential use, others for commercial, others for industrial purposes. In the 1930s and 1940s city planning became popular and most cities employed a city planner to study land use, traffic patterns, and related problems. Municipal ownership of public utilities was made possible by the Constitution of 1908, and several cities built or acquired electrical power plants. Kalamazoo built the first municipal airport in Michigan in 1926. Civic auditoriums, partly designed to attract conventions, were built at public expense in Grand Rapids and Saginaw before World War II, and in Detroit and Lansing in the 1950s.

Particularly related to urban growth was the development of organized labor. The scarcity of workers during the Civil War had the effect of encouraging the formation of trade unions, but in the postwar period they did not prosper. A new labor organization, the Knights of Labor, was organized in 1869, and a Detroit branch was founded in 1878. Its leading member was Charles Joseph (Jo) Labadie, a journalist, poet, idealist, and philosophical anarchist. For a time the organization flourished; it was reputed to have had 25,000 members in Michigan in 1886. Through its efforts the legislature in 1883 established a Bureau of Labor and two years later passed a law limiting the hours of labor for children. A sawmill strike in the Saginaw Valley in 1885 was led by the Knights of Labor. About the same time a strike hit the Muskegon sawmills. The strike leaders' slogan was "Ten Hours or No Sawdust." Governor Russell A. Alger sent the militia to Saginaw, and the operators hired 150 Pinkerton men to break up the strike. The strike ended when a new state law providing for a ten-hour day became effective.

The Knights of Labor suffered from promoting strikes the membership could not sustain, and it also was hurt by being unjustly blamed for the notorious Haymarket Riot in Chicago in 1886. Furthermore, skilled workers in the different trades had a different set of interests from that of the unskilled workers, who were also included within the Knights of Labor. Consequently, in the late 1880s the movement declined. Its leadership of organized labor was taken over by the American Federation of Labor, a combination of craft unions formed in 1881. The Michigan Federation of Labor, an organization made up of craft unions within the state, was organized in 1889. Jo Labadie was its first president. The craft unions refrained from any involvement in politics and concentrated on improving wages, hours, and working conditions.[16]

Although the Michigan Federation of Labor did not endorse candidates and engage in political campaigns, it did much to secure the passage of legislation favored by its members. Laws providing for factory inspection, the abolition of prison labor, municipal ownership of public utilities, and the suppression of child labor were backed. But the membership of labor unions until 1933 was relatively small, and the labor movement was weak. The bulk of the workers in the cities remained unorganized. Some unskilled laborers, excluded from the craft unions, were attracted about the

[16] V. H. Jensen, *Lumber and Labor,* pp. 45-70; S. Glazer, "The Michigan Labor Movement," *Michigan History,* XXIX (1945), 73-82.

time of World War I by an organization called the Industrial Workers of the World (I.W.W.), but it was considered too radical by the majority. A strike in the Detroit Studebaker plant in Detroit in 1913 was blamed on the I.W.W., and some lumber workers around Cadillac joined the organization. But the I.W.W. failed to make much of an impression, and it was not until Congress passed the National Recovery Act of 1933 during the Great Depression, with its clause recognizing the right of labor to organize and bargain collectively, that the labor movement began to gain ground rapidly.

The growth in numbers and power of labor unions during the 1930s has been related as part of the history of the automobile industry, with which it is so closely connected. The capitulation of Ford to the United Auto Workers in 1941 marks the end of large-scale resistance to organized labor. Since then there have been labor-management differences, strikes, and even violence, and management has developed a healthy respect for organized labor. Gangsters and racketeers on the loose after the repeal of prohibition found an outlet for their talents in labor unions. Slowly, however, most unions ridded themselves of these elements. In the 1950s organized labor, through its political action committees, became a potent force in Michigan politics. Closely allied with the Democratic party, the unions succeeded in delivering a huge vote in Detroit and, to a lesser extent in Flint, for Democratic candidates.

As the labor unions became more and more a potent political force, the power and influence of the typical city political boss declined. One of the important sources of power for the oldtime city politician was his influence over the vote of that mass of citizens living close to poverty, especially the immigrants. In each precinct the political boss had a man who doled out food and coal to the poor, helped them to get out of trouble with the police, found them jobs, and attended their weddings, wakes, funerals, and social affairs. For this he expected only one favor in return: their votes on election day. In Detroit elections were frequently held in saloons, and the ballot boxes were stuffed. The boss received his return from kickbacks on contracts awarded by his pals on the city council, bribes, and other types of gratuities. But changes in the 1920s and 1930s destroyed the foundations of the boss's power. Immigration was restricted by Congress. The New Deal resulted in the establishment of a multitude of public agencies to provide relief, unemployment payments, old-age assistance, aid to dependent children, social security, and employment information. The poor and needy no longer had to depend on the politician for help. Election laws were tightened up, registration of voters in advance was required, and voting machines were installed—all making it difficult or impossible to "fix" elections.

The worker found in his union an organization that sought to get for him better wages and working conditions. His union membership gave him a sense of belonging. No longer did the big boss hold over him the power of job or no job. Unfortunately, the New Deal had the tendency to shift political patterns so that they closely approximated the lines of economic and social classes. There was, without doubt, some loss of civic spirit as a consequence. But with the growing maturity of the labor movement and the general acceptance of the fact that organized labor is here to stay there was an increasing tendency for the managerial, professional, and wage-earning classes to work together on civic projects. The common effort required to achieve victory in World War II was, perhaps, a major turning point. Labor unions accepted the responsibility of doing their share in such civic efforts as Community Chest and United Fund drives. Labor came to be represented on important civic committees and commissions. Organized labor might differ from bankers, business-men, and physicians, for example, on election day, but on matters involving municipal affairs there was a cheering revival of city pride and common civic purpose.

* * * *

The movement of the population to the cities, which proceeded relatively slowly in Michigan up to about 1910 and proceeded with phenomenal speed after that time, was one of the most important aspects of the state's history in the past century. It changed the pattern of living and touched almost every political, social, and economic issue. Old problems were met, only to be succeeded by new ones. There is no sign that the growth of urban communities is at an end. In fact every indication points to the likelihood that urbanization will continue. The entire three-county area around Detroit is urban; and large urban complexes are developing elsewhere in southern Michigan. In fact the development of a solid urban bloc between Detroit and Chicago lies in the foreseeable future.

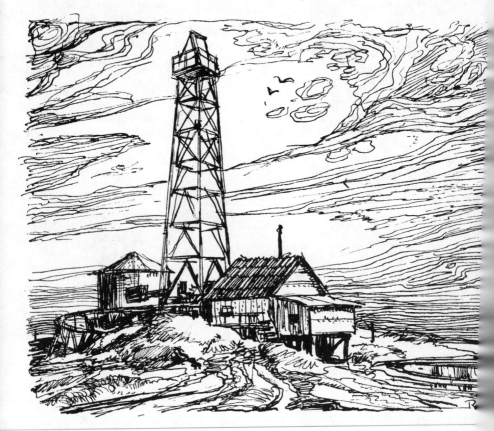

Oil well, central Michigan

21

THE TRANSFORMATION OF RURAL LIFE

In her delightful book *Home Grown*, Della T. Lutes recalls vividly the flavor of rural life in Michigan during the years following the Civil War. The frontier stage had passed in the southern-Michigan area where she lived. One had neighbors close by, schools and churches had been established, and there was no danger of want or privation. A few miles away there was a village in which supplies not produced on the farm could be procured, and Jackson, a city of considerable size, was not too far distant. It was relatively easy, however, to reach a wild, unsettled region by taking the train that ran north from Jackson through Saginaw and on to the Straits of Mackinac. The farmer was self-sustaining to a remarkable degree, as judged by standards of the twentieth century. Hardware, salt, sugar, wagons, shoes, and some clothing had to be obtained from outside, but for most foodstuffs the farmer depended on his own acres. For social recreation he relied on his own ingenuity. His house contained no bathroom or running water, no radio, few magazines, no refrigerator, no telephone, no vacuum sweeper. His sons and daughters learned to read and write in a one-room school; they were not likely to go to high school, and even less likely to go to college. They were more apt to "go west" or find a job in a city. The weather was the most important subject of conversation; family affairs were a close second, politics a poor third, and what happened outside the United States was

609

quite beyond the farmer's sphere of interest or concern. It seldom occurred to him to question the social and economic order. He spent little time pondering religious matters. Generally he would have vowed he believed in God and in the church, although he knew some church people who weren't above reproach and he would admit he was a little lax on church attendance. The prices his salable products brought were something he took for granted like death and taxes, though he was not above complaining if they got too low. However low they were, though, you could make a living.

The transformation from this type of life to rural conditions a century later constitutes a change that is probably greater than all those that took place in farm living during earlier American history. There is little in the history books about it. One may find segments of it described, but the whole story is a vital part of Michigan history. The changes may be classified under a few major headings: transportation, communication, mechanization, types of products, specialization, scientific farming, and farm organization.

TRANSPORTATION

Improved transportation has been a major factor in the transformation of rural life. The electric interurban made it easier for the farmer and his family to reach a village or city and to a small extent helped transport his products, especially milk. But it was the coming of the automobile, the truck, and the bus that effected a real revolution in transportation for the farmer. The automobile and truck made it possible for the farmer to get his products to market faster and in better condition. It brought him and his family closer to the cultural advantages of the cities. The automobile established a new pattern of courtship for young people. It made the consolidated school possible and brought the high school within easy reach of farm youth. It made possible an occasional trip so that the farmer and his family could see something of the country. Thus it was a major factor in breaking down provincialism and changing a traditionally restricted and narrow point of view.

Scores of little shifts in the way things were done on the farm may be attributed to the automobile. For example, one of the onerous tasks on the farm in Della Lutes' time was the churning of butter. In 1910 over 130,000 pounds of butter were churned on the farm for sale outside. By 1940, although milk production had doubled, less than one-quarter as much butter was churned

Covered bridge, Flat River, Michigan (near Smyrna)

on the farm as in 1910. The truck or the family car took the cream to the creameries, thus saving the farmer's family hours of monotonous toil. Prior to the coming of the automobile most of the fruit grown in western Michigan was shipped by boat across Lake Michigan to Chicago and Milwaukee. Since 1925 most of it has been shipped by truck. In 1920 only 2% of the livestock delivered to Detroit came by truck; by 1937 some 75% of it came that way. By 1920 about 40% of Michigan farms had an automobile; by 1940, 81.5% had one or more.

In no area did automotive transportation have a greater long-range effect in breaking down the isolation and provincialism of rural areas than in education. The one-room country school, attended exclusively by farm children, was the rule until around 1920. The greatest number of school districts Michigan ever had was 7,333 in 1910. After that, consolidation began slowly at first, then proceeded rapidly until by June 30, 1960 there were only 2,145. Fewer than 1,300 one- and two-room schools were left in Michigan by 1960. This meant that more and more farm children attended larger schools, where they had better educational opportunities and sat in classes with children from towns, villages, and cities. The school bus, which made consolidated or "reorganized" school districts possible, also enabled thousands of rural youth to attend high school and to prepare for college. In 1947 a total of 2,000 schoolbuses were transporting 105,733 students in 700 school districts in the state; by 1959 the number of schoolbuses had risen to 5,550, transporting 460,121 students in 843 districts.[1]

COMMUNICATION

Closely related to improved transportation was faster communication. The farmer of 1865 received mail only by calling at the closest post office, which might be many miles distant. Few farmers ever read a daily or even a weekly newspaper. Rural free delivery was started in Michigan in 1896. The village of Climax in Kalamazoo County was selected as the point of departure for the first carriers. One of them used a horse and buggy, the other a bicycle. The latter means of conveyance for the carrier proved impractical, and the horse and buggy were used almost exclusively up to the advent of the automobile. By 1899 some fifteen rural routes were in operation, and the service was thereafter extended to practically every part of the state. The innovation of parcel post in 1910 was of particular importance to the farmer. Now he could get the huge mail-order catalogs of Sears Roebuck, Montgomery Ward, and other firms, and he and the other members of his family were thereby introduced to a variety of merchandise undreamed of in the country store. They could order items, have them sent parcel post, and delivered by the carrier. Even the old catalogues served a useful function![2]

Then came the telephone. The Bell patent expired in 1893, making possible the organization of hundreds of local companies. It was some time before service was extended beyond the cities, but during the first decade of the twentieth century, private companies or local co-operative concerns built many lines into rural areas. The average farm home was on a "party line," which included several neighboring farmsteads, thus promoting neighborhood visiting and gossip. By 1920 there were telephones on nearly 50% of the farms.

Radio brought the words and other sounds of the outside world into the rural home. Wireless telegraphy had been in use for some years and had been utilized particularly by ships at sea in distress. One of the pioneers in this field was Thomas E. Clark of Detroit, who came to be known as "Wire-less Clark." Thousands of amateurs all over the land played with wireless telegraphy in the same way that their fathers had toyed with horseless carriages.

[1] *105th report of the Supt. of Public Instruction,* pp. 25, 26, 30.
[2] J. H. Brown, "How We Got the R.F.D.," *Michigan History, VI* (1922), 442-459.

As early as 1908 Clark carried on a conversation by "radiophone" from a station near Alpena with a ship eight miles out in Lake Huron. The honor of being the first broadcasting station in the world is usually given Station KDKA in Pittsburg, but Station WWJ in Detroit is a close cempetitor for primacy in this field. Operated by the Detroit *News*, WWJ broadcast its first scheduled program on August 20, 1920. Small stations soon sprang up in different parts of Michigan, and by the later 1920s receiving sets were becoming so inexpensive that almost any family could acquire one. They brought fine music, professional players, lectures, and news as well as popular music, "soap-operas," and Hollywood chitchat into the farm home. From a more practical viewpoint, radio quickly became a necessity to keep the farmer abreast of farm prices, weather forecasts, and scientific information in the field of agriculture. Station WKAR, operated by Michigan State University, specialized in this kind of information.[3]

And finally came television to bring the sight as well as the sound of the outside world into the rural living room. Until 1950 there were no television stations in Michigan outside Detroit, but by 1952 three outstate stations were on the air, and more quickly followed.

MECHANIZATION

A third transformation in rural life has come about through the increased use of machinery in the work of the field and the home. The combines used so extensively today are the lineal descendants of a machine devised near Climax, Michigan, in the late 1830s by John Hascall and Hiram Moore. The early combines were huge contrivances and were adaptable only to the vast stretches of the western prairies. More useful to the Michigan farmer was the binder, which came into being in 1879 to bind cut grain into sheaves, which were then placed in small "shocks" or in large stacks until the threshing machine was available. The latter, operated by a steam or gasoline engine, made its seasonal rounds of a community of farms and did away with the threshing of grain with flails on the barn floor. Threshing became a midsummer event on the farm. The men toiled like titans in the broiling sun, while women labored in the kitchen for hours on end to provide their best cookery for the famished workers at a noon dinner and again at supper time. Then during the 1940s the more compact combines began to appear in large numbers on Michigan

[3] R. L. Kelly, "History of Radio in Michigan," *Michigan History*, XXI (1937), 5-19.

farms. By 1950 the threshing rig, with its puffing engine, thresher, and bailer had become almost extinct. Little shocked or stacked grain may be seen today on Michigan farms, except in St. Joseph County where the Amish farmers still use the older method.

Other mechanical improvements included the Deere plow with its steel moldboard that appeared in the 1850s, and the Oliver plow, fabricated of chilled steel and put on the market about 1870. As has been noted earlier, the shortage of labor during the Civil War constituted a stimulus for the invention of farm machinery. The amount of machinery required by farmers increased steadily as hay loaders, cream separators, manure spreaders, spraying equipment, cornpickers and dozens of other contrivances became available.

The coming of the tractor effected one of the most significant revolutions in the history of American agriculture. Prior to the 1920s, when the tractor became common, the average farmer devoted a large proportion of his labor and his acres to planting, growing, and harvesting hay and grain for his work horses. As the tractor replaced the horse as a source of power on the farm, more acreage became available for the production of food and fiber. This marks the beginning of the nation's farm surplus problem. By 1930 there were 34,600 tractors on Michigan farms; the number increased to 66,500 in 1940, to 149,372 in 1949, and reached a total of 194,205 in 1959, an average of 1.7 per farm.[4] The number of horses and mules on Michigan farms declined from 396,000 in 1920 to 37,000 in 1959.

The farmer's wife shared with her spouse the conveniences the machine age contributed to the farmstead. The automobile, telephone, radio, and television set made the farm home a much less lonely place. To her the coming of electricity was a special blessing. This great servant not only lighted the house and the barns, but also operated the radio and television sets, cream separator, vacuum sweeper, poultry incubator, and innumerable other devices. At first, electrical current was generated by plants operated by gasoline engines in the basement or an outbuilding, but during the three decades from 1920 to 1950 lines from central power plants reached a large proportion of farmsteads. In 1920 only 8% of Michigan farms had electricity; by 1948 the proportion had risen to 96.6%, a percentage exceeded only by Ohio and Rhode Island. Privately owned public utilities got the jump on the federally-financed R.E.A. co-operatives in Michigan and kept ahead. The Consumers Power Company built the first rural electrical power line from Mason to Dansville in 1926. Consumers

[4] Michigan Dept. of Agriculture, *Michigan Agricultural Statistics*, p. 49.

served 58% of the Michigan farms with electricity by 1946; another 20% were customers of the Detroit Edison Company. The remaining 22% included customers of seven privately owned companies and 43 municipal plants, leaving only a very small fraction of the total as members of the R.E.A. co-operatives.[5]

TYPES OF PRODUCTS

These and other changes, as well as trial and error, brought about a transformation in the type of products that came from Michigan farms. Until almost 1900 wheat was the leading grain crop on the state. But Michigan could not compete with the prairie states and the prairie provinces of Canada; by 1950 Michigan had less than a third of the wheat acreage it had in 1880. However, Michigan remains one of the largest producers of winter wheat, used for making pastries and breakfast foods. In fact wheat is the most important cash crop in the state. Almost twice as much acreage is devoted to raising corn, but two-thirds of the corn is used for feeding livestock. Wool, shorn from the backs of sheep, was an important farm product in the nineteenth century, Michigan ranking third or fourth during most years. Sheep raising declined about 1900; Michigan in 1956 ranked 23rd among the wool-producing states. Swine have largely displaced sheep as the favorite of Michigan farmers. The number of pigs and hogs raised on Michigan farms increased from an estimated 301,000 in 1892 to 747,000 in 1962.

The disappearance of horses from Michigan farms, mentioned above, was reflected in crops raised. Timothy hay, used to feed horses, gave way to clover and alfalfa. The latter crop, called "lucerne" in the early days, was first sown by a farmer of French origin near Monroe in 1845 but for many years remained almost unknown. Alfalfa came into its own around 1920; production increased more than twelve times between 1920 and 1934. About 40% of the state's cropland was used for hay and pasture in 1962.

The growing of livestock and the sale of livestock products vastly increased during the century after the Civil War. In 1960 54% of the total farm income in Michigan came from livestock and livestock products. Dairy products alone accounted for 27%

---

[5] The Consumers Power Company and the Detroit Edison Company have furnished plaques to mark farms that have been owned by the same family for a century or more. The marking of centennial farms was inaugurated in 1948 by the Michigan Historical Commission. By the end of 1962 the total of centennial farms had reached 1,746.

of the farm income. Field crops brought the farmers 26% of their income, fruit and vegetables 15%, and other sources 5%.

SPECIALIZATION

Perhaps the most marked change of all in Michigan farm production during the past century has been increased specialization. The wide variety of soils and the sharp differences in climatic conditions have contributed to specialization. General farming, with emphasis on maximum production of products for home consumption, which was the general rule on Michigan farms in 1860, has almost disappeared. Sizable areas in the Upper Peninsula and in the northern portion of the Lower Peninsula have farms that specialize in growing potatoes. In the Saginaw Valley navy beans are the leading product of the farms; Michigan ranks first among the states in the production of field beans. After the passage of the Dingley tariff law in 1897, which provided protection of domestic sugar from foreign competition, the growing of sugar beets became a major specialty of the Thumb area. Michigan ranked sixth among the states in sugar beet production in 1961. In southwestern Michigan, notably in Berrien, Van Buren, and Allegan Counties, fruit is a major product. Michigan's fruit belt extends northward along the shore of Lake Michigan into Leelanau and Grand Traverse Counties. Michigan in 1961 ranked first among the states in the production of tart cherries, late cantaloupes, and late strawberries, second in plums, third in apples, fourth in peaches, pears, and sweet cherries, and fifth in grapes. The Benton Harbor fruit market is the largest outdoor fruit market in the world. Central and southwestern Michigan produce large quantities of peppermint and spearmint oil, with Michigan ranking fifth among the states in the amount of peppermint oil and third in spearmint oil. The muck lands of southern Michigan are devoted largely to the growing of vegetables; Michigan leads all other states in the production of late celery, cucumber pickles, and late tomatoes, and ranks fourth or better in beets, cabbage, carrots, cauliflower, onions, and sweet corn.

Increased specialization meant that the farmer became a producer more comparable to the manufacturer than to the farmer of a century ago. Instead of producing on the farm as much as possible of what his family needed for food and clothing, he concentrated more and more on one specialized crop or product, buying other food and supplies from the stores and markets like city people.

SCIENTIFIC FARMING

The farmer of the 1860s practiced an art that he had learned from his father and his neighbors. But as time went on he was forced by competition and perhaps by social pressure to rely increasingly on the scientist for gadgets and advice. More and more he depended on the specialists of Michigan State University (called Michigan Agricultural College until 1925 and Michigan State College from 1925 to 1955) to help him learn techniques and procedures that would increase the yield of his acres and raise his income. Michigan State was the first state agricultural college in the United States, and it was a leader in devising practical methods of serving the farmers. In 1875 extension work began. In towns all over the state "Farmers' Institutes" were held, where experts from East Lansing talked to the farmers about how scientific findings might help them better their lot. Regular bulletins describing agricultural experiments were distributed beginning in 1885. Federal aid for the establishment of experiment stations was provided in 1889. It was the agricultural college that developed new and better grains, such as American Banner wheat, Rosen rye, Markton oats, and Sparton barley. Better breeds of farm animals and new strains of fruits and vegetables have come in a steady stream from the experiment stations. Short-term courses were provided and an annual Farmers Week was set aside when farmers and their families came to East Lansing. The farmer was encouraged to keep systematic records and to use business methods. He learned how to fix his car, his truck, or his tractor if something went wrong. He continued to teach his sons what he knew about farming, but this no longer sufficed; many of these sons now spent four years at East Lansing acquiring scientific knowledge and skills to make them better farmers.

Among the faculty members at East Lansing who were leaders in the movement for scientific agriculture was Dr. Robert C. Kedzie. It was he who championed the idea of holding farmers' institutes in various parts of the state and who persuaded the legislature to reward farmers who planted roadside trees by reducing their taxes. Dr. Manly Miles demonstrated spectacular results from scientific fertilization, and William J. Beal established the first seed-testing laboratory in America, "first in a chain that led to the modern miracle of hybrid corn."[6] Most notable of all was Liberty Hyde Bailey, a native of South Haven, who after serving on the faculty of M.A.C. moved to Cornell and became one of

[6] M. Kuhn, *Michigan State, the First Hundred Years,* chaps. 2-3.

the leading authorities and writers in America on horticulture.[7]
Frank A. Spragg was noted for his work as a plant breeder. These
and many others not only developed a science of agriculture but
sold the Michigan farmer on it.

FARM ORGANIZATIONS

The farmer of a century ago was a rugged individualist, and
not infrequently an eccentric. As agriculture became less an art
and more a science, he lost some of his intense individualism,
his suspicion of new-fangled ideas, and his self-reliance. The
farmer of 1860 had plenty of capacity for teamwork, for he gave
and received help cheerfully and effectively at harvest time, during
sickness or trouble, at house raisings—in short, on many occasions
when help was needed. But when it came to tilling his acres, he
used his own ideas, and in buying or selling he wanted to make
the deal himself. Two factors were vital in breaking down this
attitude. The farmer found himself powerless to contend against
the railroads, upon which he had to rely to transport his products
to market, and the manufacturers of farm machinery who found
ways to keep up the prices they charged the farmer. Steadily declining prices for farm products in the latter part of the nineteenth
century caught the farmer in a pinch, and he could do little about
such problems by himself. As a consequence, he turned to farm
organizations having nationwide affiliations to fight in the state
legislature and in Congress against the big corporations. And he
found in such organizations a means by which co-operative organizations could be formed to build elevators, operate stores, and
market his products so as to reduce the middleman's costs. Furthermore, these organizations were closely related to political
parties that advocated an inflation of the currency through paper
money or silver, thus increasing prices of farm products. The
farmer turned to organization because he had to. And in doing so
he learned that such co-operation with his neighbors had its
pleasant aspects.

The Grange, or Patrons of Husbandry, was formed in 1867 and
its first Michigan branch was established in 1872. Organized at
first for educational and social purposes, it led the fight for lower
railroad rates. Local granges often operated co-operative stores
and elevators. By 1875 there were 600 local granges in Michigan.
Many built their own halls in rural areas. So successful was the
Grange that a somewhat similar organization called the Gleaners
was started in Tuscola County.

Farmers also formed an amazing variety of organizations based

[7] P. Dorf, *Liberty Hyde Bailey, an Informal Biography.*

on specialized aspects of farming: the Michigan State Horticultural Society (1870), the Michigan State Poultry Improvement Association (1925), the Michigan Berkshire Association (1906), and the Michigan Horse Breeders Association (1912), to mention a few. The most important farm organization in the twentieth century has been the Michigan State Farm Bureau, which came into being in 1919 as a central organization to look after such matters as transportation, taxation, and legislation for farmers. Hundreds of farm co-operatives became affiliated with the Farm Bureau. Farmers were urged to work together through the Farm Bureau on all matters of general concern. Fire and life insurance were made available after 1928 by this organization. In each county, through federal aid, a county agricultural agent and a home-demonstration agent were appointed to help the farmer and the farm wife with their problems.

The various farm organizations operated as pressure groups for favorable legislation and got a great deal of it passed. The compulsory licensing and inspection of canneries, provisions for grading grapes and potatoes, milk-marketing laws, and many others found their way to the statute books. Several state agencies were created for the benefit of the farmer, these being combined in 1921 into a State Department of Agriculture. An Apple Commission was created in 1939 to promote the consumption and sale of Michigan apples, and a Cherry Commission was created in 1947 to do the same for cherries.

Agricultural associations and societies had been formed prior to the Civil War to arrange for county fairs. Some counties, Allegan for example, have held county fairs each year for more than a century. An act passed by the legislature in 1915 provided state funds to help defray the cost of premiums paid farmers on their prize-winning products exhibited at county fairs. During 1959-60 a total of 92 county, district, and community fairs were held; in addition, 36 special agricultural shows were staged.

Farm organization attracted rural youth as well as adults. The 4-H club program was launched in 1917. State aid to 4-H clubs to the amount of $70,895 was given in 1959-60. The Future Farmers of America, an organization of boys studying agriculture in the schools, also received state aid amounting to almost $30,000 in the same fiscal year.[8]

FEWER FARMS . . . GREATER PRODUCTION

In the 1860's probably 85% of the people of Michigan depended upon agriculture for their subsistence. As noted earlier, the census

[8] Michigan Dept. of Agriculture, *19th biennial report,* pp. 21-22.

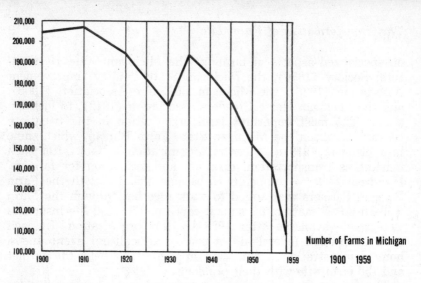

Number of Farms in Michigan 1900 1959

report for 1960 indicated that only 26.6% of the population of Michigan lived in rural areas or in towns under 2,500 population. But far less than this proportion of the people of Michigan depended mainly on agriculture for their living. In the first place, those living in small towns depended on trade, small manufactures, processing, or professional services for their income. Secondly, thousands who lived in rural areas had jobs in factories situated in nearby cities and cannot be regarded as farmers at all. And finally, many farmers depended on work off the farm for a considerable portion of their income. In 1929, only 15% of the people living on farms worked 100 days a year or more at some other employment; by 1959 the proportion had risen to 42%. Other income accounted for more than the value of agricultural products on 46% of Michigan farms in 1959. It has been estimated that in 1960, only about 5% of the families in Michigan were dependent upon farm income for their support.[9]

Michigan had only a little more than one-half the number of farms in 1959 that it had in 1910. The number of farms increased from 62,422 in 1860 to a high of 206,906 in 1910; thereafter there was a decline until the 1930s, when the depression caused a small movement back to the farm. But in the 1940s the number of farms began to decline once more, and in 1959 it stood at 111,817. As the number of farms has declined, the average size has increased somewhat. The average number of acres per farm declined from 113 in 1860 to 86 in 1890, then rose slowly to reach 132 in 1959. The total land in farms reached a high of 19,032,961 acres in 1920.

[9] Co-operative Extension Service, Michigan State University, *Michigan Agriculture: County Data and State Trends*, p. 15.

It declined slowly thereafter, increased slightly during the depression years, and was down to 15,100,000 acres in 1961. While the amount of land in farms declined by 21% between 1920 and 1961, the state's population increased by more than 100%. It has been estimated that one farm worker supported about four and a half people in 1857, and that a century later he supported twenty. Through scientific agriculture involving the use of fertilizers, insecticides, better seed, and improved methods, much more farm production can be achieved using less land. The average value of farm land and buildings per acre in Michigan in 1900 was $33. It rose to $75 in 1920, declining to a low point of $45 in 1935, then increasing rapidly to $190, where it stood in 1959.

An important and significant trend in the past century has been the decline of tenancy. The number of farms operated by tenants increased somewhat from 1880 to 1920, but after that date it began to decline, although there was some increase during the depression period. The percentage of Michigan farms wholly operated by tenants was 16% in 1900, 18% in 1920, 16% in 1930, 19% in 1935, and was down to 7% in 1959.

THE COUNTRY VILLAGE

The country village, closely allied as it was to the fortunes of the rural area around it, shared many of the changes that transformed country living during the century after the Civil War. It grew up, in most cases, as a trading center for a farming community. Its location was apt to be on a stream that provided water power for a sawmill or a gristmill; it was usually somewhere near the center of a township. In territorial times these villages sprang up along the main roads. After the Civil War, and especially in the North, they were built on railroad lines. Many a country village, established before the Civil War at a mill site or on an important road, withered or even disappeared entirely if it failed to be situated along one of the railroad lines that crisscrossed the state in the post-Civil War period. Some of these revived when the automobile and the truck replaced the railroad to a great extent as carriers of freight and passengers, and, conversely, some of the towns that sprang up along the railroads declined in importance or were abandoned. In northern Michigan numerous country towns that were founded during the great era of lumbering became ghost towns when the lumberman "cut and got out."

In appearance the Michigan country villages were similar to those in other midwestern states. There was invariably a "Main

Street" along which most of the stores and shops were situated. Branching out from this were cross streets, with business houses extending a short distance off the main stem and then giving way to homes. Where the New England influence was strong there was apt to be a town square around which the churches were clustered. Even the smallest village generally had two or three churches and invariably a schoolhouse. Somewhere in the village or near to it there was a sawmill as long as timber was available in the area. A mill to grind grain for the farmers was another standard feature of the country village. If there were any manufactures at all they were small and usually processed raw materials locally produced. There might be, for instance, a flour mill, a canning factory, or a stave factory. The store buildings along the main street usually were built two or three stories high, the upper floors sometimes housing the merchant and his family or providing rooms for one of the several local fraternal orders such as the Masons, Maccabees, or Odd Fellows. Social center of the town was the opera house, where traveling players, medicine shows, lecturers, farm institutes, teachers' institutes and the like held meetings.

In the years before the coming of the automobile, the railroad depot was the most exciting place in the village, especially at train time. Shortly after the morning, afternoon, or evening train had arrived and passed on, the post office became a gathering place for the entire town. Every village had one or two livery stables where one could hire horses, buggies, and carriages. There were the blacksmith shops, where the farmer could have tools and wagons repaired or made, and where he had his horses shod. The professional class included physicians, lawyers, and ministers; school teachers were not regarded as being professional people. There often were several lawyers, kept busy in the early days by the numerous land transfers and the decided propensity of the pioneers to take even picayune disputes to court. Ranking with the professional class as leaders of the community were the bankers. Most country villages had a weekly newspaper, largely devoted to local gossip and advertising, and paying little heed to national news, much less to foreign news. Most small towns had one or more hotels, whose patrons were mostly traveling salesmen.

The automobile brought revolutionary changes to the country village. Most of the lawyers moved to the county seat. Specialty stores such as jewelry and furniture shops tended to disappear. The livery stables were torn down; the creamery went out of business. The depot was deserted and in many cases closed up entirely. The blacksmith shops, which relied heavily on horseshoeing, disappeared. But there were other industries and businesses that replaced those that were lost. Garages took the place of the blacksmith shops, filling stations replaced the livery stables, and motels supplanted the oldtime commercial hotels.

There were other changes besides the coming of the automobile that tended to transform the country village. Merchandising, for example, was revolutionised by the coming of the chain store. The ubiquitous "A&P" began to establish its red-front stores in the smaller towns of Michigan about the time of World War I, and others followed. Often they sold for less than what the small town merchant paid. They helped drive many Grange and Gleaner stores out of business and forced the independent stores to form their own associations so they could buy goods in large quantity. The independent grocer hung on partly through offering credit and delivery service, but in time he was forced to adopt more efficient methods of doing business. The casual manner in which the oldtime country store was conducted became a thing of the past. The cracker barrel as a vantage point for the American who wants to tell the world what he thinks became an archaic expression. The country store became less a place for gossip and more a place of business.

The coming of the movies was one of the factors that doomed the village opera house. The traveling dramatic companies (sometimes designated as "stock companies") continued for some years to visit the country villages in the summer and play under canvas, but one by one they became extinct.[10] The building of high-school gymnasiums, which also served as auditoriums particularly during the 1920s, provided a center for community activity that was preferred to the opera house. The latter, being often situated on the second floor of buildings, could not be changed into a movie house because of fire regulations. So it fell into decay and oblivion. After a few years only the older people remembered the delights of the opera house. They recalled gazing in wonder at the performance of hypnotists and magicians, seeing their first flickering moving pictures, sharing horrors of the Count of Monte Cristo and the tragedy of Uncle Tom's Cabin, having the fun of being end-man in a minstrel show, and—on a hot June evening—receiving their high-school diplomas.

Patriotic celebrations, particularly the "grand and glorious" Fourth of July, were high spots in small town life. Farmers brought their families early in the morning. The local "Cornet Band" was at it all day, trying without too much success to keep together and make the welkin ring. Firecrackers punctuated the

[10] One of the last was the Slout Players, which had Vermontville as their headquarters.

Tourist industry: a horse-drawn "resort express," Grand Haven, 1940s

normally quiet atmosphere from early morn until late at night. There were oratory, athletic contests, baseball games, much lemonade (stronger stuff, too, if the town was not in a "local option" county, sometimes in the back alley if it was), and quantities of hearty food. Decoration Day (it was never called Memorial Day in the country village except by the hightoned folks) was a somewhat more solemn occasion. The venerable members of the Grand Army of the Republic were the center of attention. The veterans attended church in a body the Sunday prior to May 30, even some who never went any other time and were notorious for cussing and drinking. On Decoration Day the fife-and-drum corps or the village band led the parade to the local cemetery, and afterwards there was speaking and music. Then you went fishing, although it was not quite the thing to do. As the Civil War veterans passed on, veterans of later wars took their places. Gradually "Memorial Day" took precedence over "Decoration Day" in popular usage. The hit-or-miss village bands made up of adult men gave way to smartly uniformed high-school bands. As for the Fourth of July, country-town celebrations became a rarity, most residents preferring to take a trip, spend time at their cottages on a nearby lake, or simply spend the day quietly in the back yard.

Many country villages were enlivened each year in the late summer or fall by the county fair. Here one examined the exhibits of livestock, fruit, vegetables, and cookery, rather casually as a rule unless one had an entry. Most of the time at the fair was spent watching harness racing, visiting with friends and neighbors, and—if you were a youngster, eating red-hots, taffy, and ice cream or trying out the various "rides." The county fair developed frills as time went on: balloon ascensions were popular for many years; airplane flights were quite an attraction in the early years of aviation; auto races sometimes replaced harness racing for one of the fair days; and somewhat elaborate stage shows put on by professionals became more and more the vogue. A notable emphasis on 4-H club and Future Farmers of America exhibits characterized the county fairs after about 1930.

Along with the fairs came the development of community festivals and celebrations. Some of these were held in nearby cities. One of the earliest and most successful was the Blossom Festival at Benton Harbor-St. Joseph. The annual Tulip Time at Holland attracted enormous numbers to see the unique tulip lanes and enjoy the klompen dancers. The Hollanders managed to keep Tulip Time free of carnival attractions, which was not true of most community festivals. In the 1930s and 1940s an increasing number of these affairs were staged. Marcellus had its bluegill frolic, Lowell its Showboat, Cedar Springs its Red Flannel Days. And for almost every sort of celebration there was a queen. Michigan had a cherry queen, a dairy queen, a grape queen, and even a gas-engine queen, to mention a few among many. Centennials became a special occasion for community festivals.

Another influence of importance in the life of the country village during the first quarter of the twentieth century was the chautauqua. This institution originated at Chautauqua Lake in New York as a summer school for the study of the Bible and Sunday-school methods in 1874. The "Chautauqua Assembly" soon broadened out into the whole field of education, with popular entertainment included. It was so popular that it was copied in other places. In Michigan the Bay View Assembly developed, along the same lines as the Chautauqua Assembly, from an annual Methodist camp meeting, the first of which was held in 1875. The idea of taking the "chautauqua" to the people in their own towns originated about the turn of the century. The first company to form a chautauqua circuit was organized in 1904. Several others were soon formed. Each had its own "talent," consisting of lecturers, singers, bands, orchestras, ensembles, and entertainers. These were shuttled from one town to the next on a "circuit" and performed in tents supplied by the company. Usually the chautauqua lasted about a week. Farmers and their wives came to town to get an annual dose of "culture." Small-town merchants and professional people usually were guarantors of a minimum ticket sale. Before the days of radio and quality recordings, many people in rural Michigan got their first chance to listen to great music at the chautauqua. The chautauqua began to disappear in the 1920s with the advent of radio, and by 1930 it was virtually a thing of the past.[11]

Practically every small town dreamed of becoming a thickly populated city with busy factories and higher property values. Some of them went to great lengths to attract industries. The citizens of Hartford, Michigan once authorized a large bond issue for the express purpose of building a village jail, whereas the real object, as everyone knew, was to subsidize industry. The villages and smaller cities were not very successful in attracting industry until the decade of the 1940s. In some small towns industries already established continued through the depression years, but elsewhere once-busy factories closed down. One of the most tragic incidents of this sort was in Belding, which once boasted some of the biggest silk mills in the country. But during World War II, with the staggering demands on industry for war production and the drainage of manpower into the armed services, factory management began to look to the small towns. Here was a reservoir of labor, consisting of part-time farmers, married women wanting employment outside the home, and young women fresh out of high school. There were vacant buildings, and by this time most small towns had a good water supply and utilities required for manufacturing. A notable case of a small town that benefited from this wartime phenomenon was Bangor, which had no manufacturing prior to 1940 and subsequently had half a dozen busy plants employing several hundred people. The Wolverine Shoe Company, whose main plant was in the small town of Rockford, established branch plants in several nearby towns as its business grew.

Once established in the small towns, industrialists discovered there were marked advantages. For one thing, labor unions were not so strong. Living expenses were lower, overhead was less. The development of trucks capable of providing economical transit for

[11] G. MacLaren, *Morally We Roll Along;* K. Detzer, Karl, *Culture Under Canvas;* M. H. Miller, "The Chautauqua in Lansing," *Michigan History,* XL (1956), 257-274.

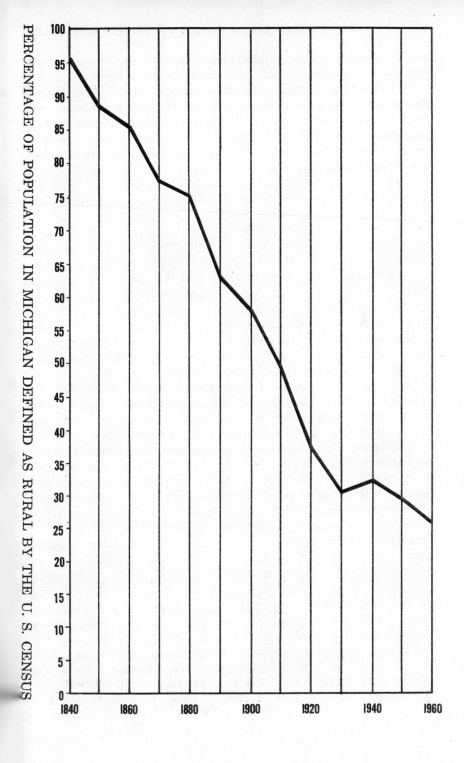

raw materials and finished goods made industry less dependent on rail service, another factor that aided the small town.

During the depression federal subsidies helped many small towns extend water systems, install sanitary sewage systems, and improve park and recreation facilities. The motorization of fire departments, which began in the second decade of the twentieth century, was a great boon to farmers. Better public utilities and better fire protection also aided in attracting industry.

There was a time in the early years of the twentieth century when ambitious youth, born on the farm or in a small town, almost universally migrated to the cities. Only a minority remained to spend their mature years in the same environment. The towns were run by the older folk, many of them retired farmers. The stimulus provided by the 4-H clubs, the Future Farmers of America, and better educational facilities had the effect of persuading more able youth to remain on the farm. And the availability of all the amenities of modern living on the farm or in the small town also tended to slow down the exodus of young people. Many young men who had had their fill of adventure during their years in the armed services gladly settled for a quiet life in a small community. As a result the number of younger people in business and the professions in small towns increased after World War II. These younger people voted additional millage for better schools, staged community festivals, organized service clubs, and gave more support to the churches and civic organizations.

The factors that once made the man or woman from the farming communities and country villages of Michigan quite different from their city cousins have been gradually eliminated. Up-to-date schools educate their children about the same as city schools; their automobiles make it possible for them to visit cities frequently on business or pleasure; their television sets and their newspapers keep them up-to-the-minute on national and world news. To be sure, not all the distinctive characteristics have disappeared; in politics, for example, the people of the rural areas and small towns tend to be more conservative than the majority of city people. Even here, however, the differences are disappearing. Conservatism depends more on the citizen's economic status and his social class than on where he happens to live, and the same may be said of liberalism. Much of what passes for rural-urban conflict is in actuality based on other factors, such as the rivalry between the Detroit metropolitan area and outstate Michigan (including cities as well as rural areas), partisan rivalry, and differences over the proper role of labor unions. For the most part, the changes of the century after the Civil War had the effect of making the farmer and small-town dweller less distinctive and more like Michiganians in the cities.

First state capitol building, Lansing

22

BIG GOVERNMENT
AND POLITICS, 1932-1963

The progressive movement of the first two decades of the twentieth century gave the people a more direct voice in their state government. In part because of this they began to demand more services. Voices were raised against big government, but they seldom were effective against the various pressure groups that, from time to time, demanded that the state government enter some new field of activity. The era of big state government began in the 1920s with the creation of many new boards, commissions, and other agencies and the expansion of the older departments. During the depression years of the 1930s, citizens turned for help to the state as well as to the federal government and demanded that positive action be taken to cure economic ills and provide assistance to the individual citizen. The war years, though causing a vast expansion of the federal government, constituted a brief breathing spell for state government. But in the postwar years expansion once more set in. Some state functions were shared with the federal government, and the latter sent back to the state capitals increasingly large sums for state aid in one form or another. But whatever loss there was of state powers to the federal government were more than matched by the responsibilities formerly exercised by local governmental units that were taken over by the state. And just as the federal government provided aid to the states, the state government distributed state aid to the local units.

In politics the three decades after 1932 were a period of close and often bitter party rivalry in Michigan, in contrast to the long period from 1854 to 1932 when the Republican party was dominant. The strength of the Michigan Democratic party increased steadily, for a variety of reasons, until, in the 1950s, Democratic candidates won state-wide elections almost as consistently as Republicans had won them prior to 1932. Due to apportionment that favored Republican strongholds, however, the Democrats were unable to control the legislature as they were the executive branch. Legislative reapportionment became a prime issue in the early years of the 1960s.

The constitutional framework of government was altered frequently during these three decades by the amendment process. Finally in 1961 the voters approved the calling of a convention to frame a new state constitution. Delegates completed their task in 1962, and the constitution they wrote was approved by the people by a narrow margin in April, 1963.

THE COMING OF BIG GOVERNMENT

At the turn of the century the government of Michigan was comparatively simple. Expenditures were confined to modest appropriations for the maintenance of the University of Michigan, the agricultural college, the normal schools and the College of Mines, for mental hospitals, prisons, a few other institutions, and the ordinary costs of the legislative, executive, and judicial branches. A few boards and commissions were the forerunners of the vast proliferation of such agencies that was to come later. As early as 1883 the state began to set qualifications for the practice of dentistry. There was a Railroad Commission, a Fish Commission, a State Game Warden, a Forest Commission, and a few others, none of which spent much money. The support of schools, poor relief, and the maintenance of roads were exclusively functions of local government.

Today's big state government is a far cry from the little state government of 1900. In the fiscal year 1959-60 the State Highway Department, an agency which did not even exist in 1900, spent more than $257,000,000. In 1910 the total taxes levied by the state amounted to $4,729,000. By 1932 they had risen to around $100,000,000. For the 1963-64 fiscal year state taxes were expected to yield $1,105,000,000; in addition to this, $311,414,490 was to be collected in other revenues, making the total state tax and other revenues reach almost a billion and a half dollars, or three hundred times the amount collected in 1910 and fifteen times the amount levied in 1932.

In part, this enormous increase in state-government expenditures was due to inflation; the purchasing power of the dollar in 1910 was about three times what it was in 1960, and the dollar was worth twice as much in 1932 as in 1963. The increase in the cost of state government was also due to the growth in the size of the population; the number of people served by the state government in Michigan has tripled since 1900 and doubled since 1920. Even taking into consideration these factors, however, the cost and scope of state government functions have increased to a point that would have seemed fantastic to earlier generations.

What are the reasons for this increase? Why has state government become so big? There are several basic explanations. For one thing, the state has become a collecting agency for a large portion of the taxes to support the schools and other local-government functions. In 1960 almost 60% of the total revenues collected by the state were returned to local government for schools, highways, and other purposes. Another major factor in big government arises from the greatly increased proportion of young people seeking higher education. Enrollments in colleges and universities in Michigan rose from about 20,000 in 1930-31 to 159,000 in 1960-61, and almost 80% of these students were in state-supported institutions. Higher education came to constitute the largest item in the state's general-fund budget. Another reason for the rising cost of state government has been the increase in the incidence of mental illness and the resultant rise in the cost of providing mental hospitals and other facilities for its treatment. The growth of big government also may be attributed in part to greater concern for the poor, the handicapped, the unemployed, and the aged. The state shares relief costs with the counties, provides old-age assistance, operates a state employment service, administers unemployment compensation, and performs other related functions quite beyond the scope of state government in 1900. The major role played by the Highway Department in big government has already been noted. When the reward system failed to provide highways adequate to the demands of car owners the state undertook to build major highways and collected revenues to be returned to counties and cities for local roads and streets. The regulatory functions of government have grown in size and number, too. The Water Resources Commission, which developed from the Stream Control Commission established in 1929, is an example of this. Furthermore, the people have demanded a variety of services such as the promotion of tourism and new facilities such as state parks and public fishing sites. State government has been called upon to promote economic development and to take such action as required to attract new industry to the state.

Starting about 1910 the regulatory activities of state government began to increase rapidly. The Railroad Commission was replaced by the Public Utilities Commission (now the Public Service Commission), and its functions were enlarged to include rate regulation of electric power, gas, and telephone companies. The workmen's compensation law, passed in 1912, required a new board to administer its provisions. A Department of Labor was formed in 1909. A Securities Commission was established by an act passed in 1915. Boards for the registration and licensing of accountants, optometrists, architects, and nurses were provided in acts passed in 1913 and 1915.

In 1921 a number of boards and commissions were consolidated into major departments, such as Conservation and Agriculture, reducing the number of state agencies from 98 to 65. But the legislature continued to create new boards and commissions, so that by 1960 there were twice as many as in 1921. Some $81,000,-000 in state and federal funds were spent on highway building between 1919 and 1924, and in the latter year the state began providing auto-ferry service at the Straits of Mackinac. The "Michigan Troops," organized during World War I as a substitute for the militia, which had been called into national service, had evolved into a permanent State Police by 1920, and law enforcement, which formerly had been a local government function, thus was shared by state government. In 1921 a corporation franchise tax was voted by the legislature as a means of providing new buildings at growing state institutions.

The depression years brought demands for economy in government, but also, and very much more insistently, demands for state government to aid the people suffering from unemployment. The sales tax, levied in 1933, brought in revenues that enabled the state to meet some of these demands. Old-age assistance, aid to dependent children, appropriations for relief, and a state employment service were among the new departures of this period that made government bigger. Furthermore, local school districts in some cases had so much tax delinquency that the legislature in 1933 began to provide massive state aid to schools. State aid to libraries was another innovation of the 1930s.

During World War II shortages of materials and manpower halted capital improvements at state institutions and curtailed for a time the growth of state government. In fact, the state treasury showed a gratifying surplus during the war years. Then in 1946 the sales tax diversion amendment was adopted, obligating the state to "kick back" five-sixths of the sales-tax collections to local units. But the legislature quickly tapped other sources of revenue, and state government continued to grow. By 1949 the Highway Department was spending $100,000,000 annually, and this staggering total increased two and a half times during the next decade. Appropriations for higher education tripled in the decade of the 1950s. A new department was created in 1947 to promote economic development. The records of big government accumulated at such a rate that a new records-storage center had to be built. Civil defense became a function of state government. An act passed in 1955 established a Fair Employment Practices Commission. A Mackinac Bridge Authority was set up. Starting in 1943 the state began to provide a retirement system for its employees. These are only a few of the indications of the manner in which big government got bigger in Michigan during the post-World War II period.

FINANCING BIG GOVERNMENT

How to pay the cost of big government became a problem of great concern and infinite complexity. From the earliest years the major source of revenue to operate state government was the tax on land, buildings, and personal property. This source of revenue was shared with counties, townships, and school districts. The elected officials of each of the local units and the state legislature determined how much revenue would be needed and the rate of taxation on assessable property needed to produce the amount. The sum of these determined how much tax the owner of real estate and personal property would be required to pay. Cities and villages were also permitted to levy taxes on real estate and personal property. The only other substantial source of revenue for the state was the tax on liquor, which was levied starting in 1879, and by 1910 was producing around $2,000,000 annually, almost half as much as the state's share of the real-estate and personal-property tax.[1] An inheritance tax, established in 1899, yielded a small amount.

The adoption of prohibition, of course, eliminated the liquor tax. As has been noted above, the legislature in 1921, upon the recommendation of Governor Alex Groesbeck, adopted a corporation franchise tax, apportioned according to the size of corporations. The first collection of this tax, due July 1, 1921, brought in $5,478,000, almost exactly one-half the amount the state then realized from the real estate and personal property tax. To meet

[1] *Michigan Manual*, 1915-1916, pp. 320-331.

rising costs of government, the legislature added certain other taxes: a tax on boxing and wrestling (1919), aircraft registration (1923), building and loan associations (1921), and an oil and gas severance tax (1929). The weight tax on automobiles, first levied in 1915, began to produce a sizable revenue in the 1920s, and in 1923 an additional tax was placed upon operators of trucks and buses. A gasoline tax was adopted in 1925.

The principal reliance of state government until 1933, however, continued to be on the state's share of the real-estate and personal-property tax. By 1932, as a consequence of the depression, tax delinquency all over Michigan, had increased to frightening proportions. In the November election that year, voters approved a constitutional amendment that limited the total tax on real estate and personal property to 1½% (15 mills) of assessed valuation.[2] The adoption of this amendment virtually forced the state legislature to seek a new source of income, since fifteen mills was inadequate to support state as well as county and township governments and the schools. This led to the passage of an act by the 1933 legislature (which had a Democratic majority) under which the state would forego in the future any share in the real-estate and personal-property tax, and instead would collect a 3% retail sales tax to finance state government.

The yield of the sales tax was gratifying, but the demands for state aid for welfare relief, schools, and other purposes were so great that other sources of revenue had to be tapped. Furthermore, an amendment adopted in 1939 forbade the use of revenues derived from the gasoline and weight taxes for anything else but highway purposes. With the end of prohibition, a tax was levied on the manufacture and sale of beer and wine. Largely as a result of pressure by retail merchants, a chain-store tax was adopted in 1933. The same year a tax was laid on horse-race wagering. In 1939 a tax was laid on intangible property (stocks and bonds), but half the expected return was allocated to local government units. A use tax on goods bought outside the state was authorized in 1937 and a tax on producing oil was laid in 1939. Employers were taxed from 1937 to build up an unemployment-compensation fund.

During World War II, as has been stated, revenues from established tax sources were more than adequate to meet state needs. But local government units were caught in a squeeze. Rising

[2] Home-rule cities could levy an additional tax under the provisions of this amendment. It also provided that voters of any assessing district might authorize the collection of additional millage. The original provisions were somewhat modified by subsequent amendments.

costs of materials as well as wages and salaries created a serious problem for them in view of the 15-mill tax limitation. At every legislative session mayors and school superintendents entreated the legislature for state aid. The response was meager. As a result of this situation, a constitutional amendment providing for the diversion of a part of the state sales tax to local units was placed on the ballot by petition and adopted by the people in 1946. Under the provisions of this amendment two-thirds of the total sales-tax revenue was to be returned to local school districts and one-sixth to cities, villages, and townships. The adoption of this "sales tax diversion amendment" marked the beginning of financial problems and difficulties for the state government that were still unsolved a decade and a half later. At the time it was approved, it diverted some 77% of the state's revenues to local governmental units.

The legislature in the years that followed sought to make up for the loss to state government of sales-tax revenues by levying new taxes and by striving for economy. At the same time, persistent pressures for more and better state services drove the lawmakers to adopt larger and larger budgets. Among the new taxes levied in an effort to balance income and expenditure in the state treasury were a cigarette tax (1947), a diesel-fuel tax (1947), liquor taxes (1957 and 1959), a watercraft tax (1947), and a business-activities tax (1953). But as government costs continued to rise these proved inadequate. An amendment adopted in 1954 limited the sales tax to 3%. Since the constitution limited the state debt to $250,000 it was impossible to borrow money in any substantial amount. By July 1, 1958 the state treasury showed a deficit of 21.1 million dollars. In order to meet payrolls amounts were borrowed from funds that had a balance to cover deficits in other funds. Payments of state aid to school districts were delayed, and contractors with the state had to wait beyond the usual time for the payment of their bills. The amount of the deficit increased to 95.4 millions by July 1, 1959.[3]

These recurring deficits and the possibility that the state might not be able to meet its payrolls got national attention. Michigan became known as the state that had gone broke. The reports were greatly exaggerated, but they gave the state a bad reputation. Michigan was by no means the only state that had financial problems in these years. But a variety of factors made the situation in Michigan more acute than elsewhere. Employment was sharply lower in the state's main industry, automotive manufacturing, as a result of automation, loss of defense contracts,

[3] 19th Annual Report, Michigan Department of Revenue, p. 10.

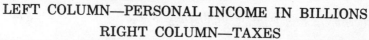

LEFT COLUMN—PERSONAL INCOME IN BILLIONS
RIGHT COLUMN—TAXES

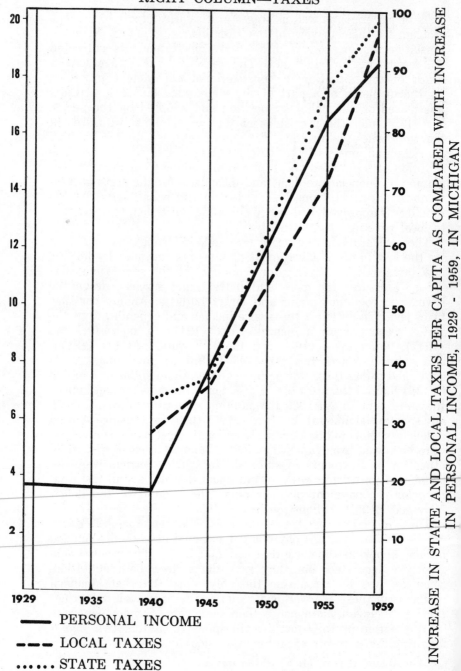

INCREASE IN STATE AND LOCAL TAXES PER CAPITA AS COMPARED WITH INCREASE IN PERSONAL INCOME, 1929 - 1959, IN MICHIGAN

——— PERSONAL INCOME

- - - LOCAL TAXES

...... STATE TAXES

decentralization, and the competition of foreign-built cars. As a consequence, the economic recession that started in 1958 had a more severe impact on Michigan than on other states. This resulted in a decrease in revenue from the sales tax and sharply increased demands on relief and welfare funds. The increase in the state's population from 1940 to 1950 had been 23% and the increase during the first part of the 1950s was equally large. This meant there were more children to educate, more people seeking jobs, more people requiring government services. Michigan also had certain built-in problems not shared by its neighbors. The northern half of the Lower Peninsula and the entire Upper Peninsula were thinly populated and lacked a sound economic base. As has been noted, lumbering and mining, which once had been the backbone of the region's economy, no longer could provide employment for its people. Thin and sandy soils and a cold climate made the region unsuitable for agriculture in a time of surpluses. Remoteness from major markets made it difficult to attract manufacturing industries. Hence, the southern part of the Lower Peninsula was in a position of providing the other two-thirds of the state with state aid for schools, relief, and highways. Michigan also had a unique situation with respect to its institutions of higher education, with between 70% and 80% of its college and university students in tax-supported institutions, while the national average was between 50% and 60%.

These were major factors in the tax and financial crisis that reached a climax in 1960. But the political aspect of the crisis received much more attention. Since 1949 Michigan had had a Democratic governor in the person of G. Mennen Williams, and a Republican legislature. As Williams won re-election time after time, relations between him and the legislature became more and more strained. The winning personality of Williams and his acute sensitivity to human needs, which had endeared him to a majority of Michiganians, had no effect on the Republican majority in the legislature. The governor's party was able to elect most of the top administrative officials, but the apportionment of legislative seats that favored the Republicans made it impossible for the Democrats to win control of the legislature. The Republicans repeatedly were thwarted in their attempts to oust Williams from the governor's office during the entire time when a Republican President, in the person of Dwight Eisenhower, occupied the White House in Washington. Party rivalry is normal and healthy, but in Michigan during the latter part of the 1950s it became bitter and vicious.

It was apparent by 1957 that expenditures of state government would have to be curtailed or else new tax revenues found. The Republicans blamed Governor Williams for reckless spending. The Democrats replied that every penny spent had to be appropriated by the Republican legislature. Actually, the increased need for funds for education, mental hospitals, relief, and other state programs made it quite impossible to reduce spending. Even the enemies of Williams came to recognize that the only answer was to increase tax revenues. But at this point a serious difference of opinion arose over tax philosophy. Governor Williams repeatedly urged that the state adopt a personal and

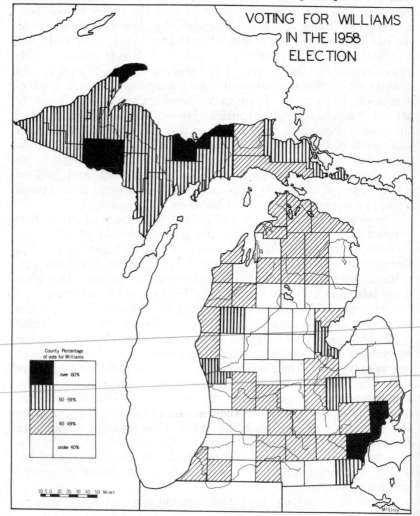

VOTING FOR WILLIAMS
IN THE 1958
ELECTION

County Percentage
of vote for Williams

over 60%

50 - 59%

40 - 49%

under 40%

10 5 0 10   20   30   40   50 Miles

McElroy

corporation income tax as the fairest and most equitable kind of taxation. He met with staunch opposition in the legislature and there was evidence that the majority of Michigan citizens, while demonstrating their support of Williams, were not favorable to an income tax. The voters had twice rejected proposals for a state income tax in the 1920s by overwhelming majorities. The federal income tax had become so high and the task of preparing annual federal income tax returns had become so onerous by the 1950s that the people shuddered to think of a state income tax. Newspaper polls showed popular opposition to such a tax, encouraging the Republicans in the legislature to maintain their intransigent opposition to Williams' proposals. They derided a study of the Michigan tax system which recommended an income tax as being the work of labor-union bosses.

The mounting deficit made it obvious that the legislature that convened January 14, 1959 would have to take some kind of action. Weeks went by, however, with no decision. At one stage it appeared that the treasurer would be unable to meet state payrolls, but various expedients were employed so that there was only a week's delay in one payday. There was some indication that the Republicans in the legislature deliberately put off a decision as long as possible in order to destroy Governor Williams as a possible presidential candidate in 1960 by giving him the image of a governor of a bankrupt state. Whether or not this was the motivation, the delay gave Michigan widespread unfavorable publicity. Finally, on August 29, the lawmakers passed a series of bills to increase tax revenues. The business-activities tax was increased and so was the intangibles tax. Main reliance was placed, however, upon a so-called "use tax" of 1%. In effect this was an addition to the 3% sales tax, although it covered certain items such as hotel bills that the sales tax did not. By calling the additional 1% tax a "use tax," the legislature sought to evade the constitutional limit of 3% on the sales tax. But the stratagem proved unsuccessful, for on October 22 the supreme court found the new tax unconstitutional. The legislature then reconvened and on December 18 enacted a "package" of "nuisance taxes" on telephone bills, liquor, cigarettes, and beer. The corporation franchise tax also was increased. Even with the income from these new taxes (which became effective January 1, 1960), expenditures for the fiscal year 1959-60 exceeded revenues by $9,211,630. In 1960 the legislature authorized the liquidation of the Veterans' Trust Fund, pledging the state to appropriate each year an amount equal to the annual interest the Fund had earned.

This brought 40.7 millions into the state treasury, reducing the accumulated deficit on July 1, 1960 to around 64 millions.

But this, of course, was no permanent solution to chronic deficits. Indeed, the nuisance taxes were intended only as a stopgap. The 1960 legislature decided to lay before the people a proposal to amend the constitution so as to permit a 4% sales tax. The question was submitted at the November 8, 1960 election, and was approved by a very narrow margin. The legislature then reconvened and enacted a measure increasing the sales tax to 4%. It was signed by the governor and became effective February 1, 1961. John B. Swainson, who had succeeded G. Mennen Williams as governor, recommended to the legislature a tax program that called for permitting the nuisance taxes to lapse, abandonment of the sales tax on food, and enactment of a personal and corporation income tax. The legislature, however, rejected his plan except for allowing the nuisance taxes to expire on schedule July 1, 1961. By that time the deficit was up again to almost 72 millions. Even with a full year's yield of the 4% sales tax, the following year produced another deficit, running the total to 85 millions on July 1, 1962. Some of the nuisance taxes were reimposed, and this, added to a sharp increase of business activity, resulted in a reduction of the deficit by July 1, 1963 to around 45 millions.

Governor George Romney, who succeeded Swainson on January 1, 1963, persuaded the legislature to "hold the line" on appropriations for 1963-64, and to postpone a decision on new taxes until a special session in the fall. The gratifying surplus of 1962-63, resulting in a reduction of the deficit by 40 millions, might appear to indicate that no change in the tax system was necessary. But two considerations pointed in the opposite direction. First, the state was faced with a "tidal wave" of students in its colleges and universities, requiring in the years ahead sharply increased appropriations for higher education. Mental health needs were becoming acute. There were demands for more funds from other state departments. The second consideration was the generally conceded fact that Michigan taxed business higher than neighboring states and others with which it had to compete for new industry.[4]

The tax problem was a serious one not only for state government but for local units as well. Cities and school districts sought new sources for funds as increasing populations and more demands for services continued to result in larger spending. Further-

[4] P. W. McCracken (ed.), *Taxes and Economic Growth in Michigan;* W. Haber *et. al., The Michigan Economy,* pp. 147-179.

Toll Gate E, toll house east of Grand Rapids, 1894

more, an important source of revenue to local units, the personal property tax, was under fire as being one of the taxes that were unduly heavy on business and industry. The elimination of this tax would require some other to take its place. More and more it came to be conceded that a state income tax was the best solution for Michigan's tax problem. Under the new constitution approved in 1963 such a tax could not be "graduated," but had to be laid at a "flat rate" on income of all sizes. Governor Romney submitted to the legislature in September, 1963 a comprehensive tax-revision plan. It called for the elimination of certain taxes, the reduction of others, and a personal and corporation income tax to take their place. By this time, however, existing taxes were not only erasing the deficit but also were building up a surplus. Romney argued that the purpose of his plan was not to produce more revenue but to make the tax system more equitable. He asserted that low-income families, senior citizens, and business were being taxed too heavily. In spite of his efforts to obtain backing throughout the state, Romney failed to persuade the legislature to adopt his reform program.

It was a far cry from the times of Governor Barry, who had bolstered the state treasury in the 1840s by having the grass on the capitol lawn cut and sold for hay, to those of 1964, when the people of Michigan would pay state and local taxes amounting to more than two billion dollars. Critics might bemoan big government and attribute it to bureaucrats incessantly striving for more money and more authority, but there could be no doubt that, for the most part, government grew big because citizens demanded that it serve them better and in a greater number of ways. Although taxes to pay for big government were as unpopular as ever, when it came to a test citizens preferred to pay higher taxes rather than to cut government services.

THE MANAGEMENT OF BIG GOVERNMENT

As state government became bigger and more complex, the problem of operating it efficiently became acute. In earlier times, when government did little and cost little, loose control and management was tolerable. It was a different matter after government became a big business.

When Alex J. Groesbeck was campaigning for the governorship in 1920 he promised to bring about a reorganization of state administration. Following his election he sought to introduce business methods into state administration. Upon his recommendation the legislature in 1921 consolidated a number of separate agencies into major departments. It also created the Administrative Board, to consist of seven elective state officials, with the responsibility for preparing a state budget, setting up a centralized purchasing system, and establishing uniform accounting for all state agencies.[5]

This arrangement worked well for a time, but soon the legislature began to create new boards and commissions. Over these the governor had little control. Periodic efforts were made during succeeding years to reorganize the executive branch of the state government. Commissions were appointed by Governor Murphy in 1938 and by Governor Sigler in 1947 to make recommendations in this field. The legislature also designated committees for the same purpose. In 1950 the so-called "Little Hoover Commission," appointed by the legislature, drew up a series of proposals dealing with reorganization of state government. Only a few of these were implemented.

From time immemorial those holding elective office in government have appointed their friends and supporters to lucrative government jobs. So long as government was simple and the

[5] In 1948, the Department of Administration was created to perform these functions under policies set by the Administrative Board.

duties of most public offices required no special training or skill, the so-called "spoils system" was seldom challenged. But as government became more complex, technical knowledge and skill were needed for many positions, and the practice of appointing favorites to such positions began to arouse opposition. In the federal government a beginning was made in 1883 in introducing a merit system of appointments through civil-service examinations. One objective was to give government workers more job security and to avoid a wholesale turnover whenever the presidency of the nation passed from one party to another. In Michigan, due to the domination of the Republican Party for many years prior to 1932, there was seldom such a turnover. But beginning that year, the two major parties alternated in winning the governorship each term for a decade. This intensified the need for a civil-service system in the state. The legislature in 1937 created a civil-service commission to handle appointments and dismissals of most state employees. Under the law office holders could be "blanketed in" by passing an examination. Since the state at the time had a Democratic governor, a majority of important officeholders were Democrats. In 1939 the Republican legislature, resenting the "blanketing in" of so many Democrats, exempted some 8,000 positions from the civil service. Public protest resulted in an initiatory petition that placed before the voters in 1940 a proposal to amend the constitution by writing into it a provision establishing a civil-service commission with power to appoint, dismiss, and set the salaries of all state employees except for elected officials, employees of the courts, employees of state educational institutions, and a few others. Each agency was allowed two "unclassified" positions—positions not under civil service. The amendment was adopted. Thus the governor and the legislature ceased to control the employment, dismissal, and salary rates of most state employees.[6]

Study commissions beginning in the 1920s repeatedly advocated for the governor a longer term and broader powers to administer state government. Little attention was paid to these recommendations for many years. Rivalry between Governor Williams and the legislature from 1949 to 1961 resulted in Republican opposition to increasing the governor's term or powers. Serving a two-year term, most governors spent a large part of their time campaigning for re-election. Furthermore, the structure of state government was such as to remove major administrative areas from the control of the governor. Such departments as

[6] J. K. Pollock, "Civil Service Developments in Michigan, *"Good Government, LVIII* (1941), 27-28.

Highway and Public Instruction were administered by elective officials, who might even be members of a different political party from the governor's. Over the various boards and commissions that he appointed the governor had little or no direct authority. His colleagues on the State Administrative Board were all elective. Governor Williams frequently had several Republicans on the Board. Governor Romney was the only Republican on the Board in 1963-64.

The constitutional convention that met in October, 1961 had a large Republican majority. Since Michigan had chosen a Democratic governor at the last seven elections there was some reluctance on the part of the majority of Republicans to increase the powers of the governor. But the arguments in favor of doing so in the interest of administrative efficiency were so strong that the delegates did provide in the new constitution for a considerably stronger governor. For one thing the state's chief executive, beginning in 1966, was to be elected for a four-year term. Another vital provision required the consolidation of all state agencies into not more than twenty departments, most of them headed by a single executive appointed by the governor with the consent of the senate. But the new constitution stopped short of providing the governor with full powers to manage state administration. Two of the largest departments were removed from his control by giving the elected State Board of Education power to appoint the superintendent of public instruction and by providing for the appointment of the highway commissioner by a bipartisan board. Furthermore, the secretary of state and the attorney general would continue to be elected officials. Ironically enough, even before the new constitution was approved by the voters, a Republican in the person of George Romney had been elected governor.

The administration of justice

Supreme-court justices, who were chosen by appointment of the governor under the state's first constitution, have been elective since 1850. The supreme-court justices under the constitution of 1850 also served as circuit judges, but were relieved of this duty after 1857. Under the law of 1857 there was to be a supreme court consisting of a chief justice and three associates. The size of the court was increased to five in 1887 and to eight in 1903, with two elected each biennium for eight-year terms.

During the 1930s there was considerable agitation for "taking the judges out of politics." Proposals to choose supreme-court justices by appointment rather than by popular election were rejected by the voters in 1934 and 1938. In 1939, however, a compromise proposal was adopted in the form of a constitutional amendment. Supreme-court justices were to be nominated at party conventions, but were to run on a nonpartisan ballot. Judges of all other courts were to be nominated and elected on a nonpartisan ballot.

There was much criticism of this plan as it pertained to the method of choosing supreme-court justices. It was something bordering on the ridiculous to presume that a candidate for supreme-court justice, nominated at a party convention, could run as a bona-fide, nonpartisan candidate. In the constitutional convention of 1962-63 there was a protracted discussion of the matter; alternative methods were finally rejected, and the 1939 method was retained with two modifications: a justice could run for re-election if he wished without being renominated; and a candidate might be nominated by initiatory petition as well as by party convention.

A court in each county was provided by the first state constitution, but the second constitution abolished county courts and substituted circuit courts. At first the state's counties were organized into eight circuits. By 1897 the number had increased to 35. The growth of population in the cities required more than one circuit judge in some counties. By 1960 there were 41 circuits and a total of 81 judges, including 18 in Wayne County, five in Oakland, and four each in Macomb and Genesee. With this large number of circuit courts and judges, the number of appeals to the supreme court became so large that there were long delays in obtaining decisions. The constitution framed in 1961-62 provided for the establishment of intermediate courts, standing between the circuit courts and the supreme court.

There have been comparatively few changes in the provisions for the probate court. Under the latest state constitution, however, the term of the probate judge is extended from four to six years. Since 1939, the probate judges as well as other judges have been chosen on a nonpartisan ballot. The Constitution of 1908 gives to probate courts original jurisdiction in all cases involving juveniles and dependents. This part of the court's responsibility became especially important as the problem of juvenile delinquency grew more critical in the 1950's.

From the earliest years the township justice of the peace was a part of Michigan's judicial system. Elected by the people of the township, the justice all too often lacked any legal training or more than the most elementary knowledge of the law. His remuneration came from fees levied upon litigants. Suited to a prodominantly rural state and a time when litigation usually fell into a few categories, the justice of the peace had become an anachronism in an age of big government. Consequently, the Constitution of 1961-62 provided for the abolition of the office of justice of the peace by the legislature within five years.

Much earlier the growth of cities had resulted in a volume of cases far beyond the competence of justices of the peace to handle. The police court of Detroit was authorized by legislative act in 1850 to hear, try, and determine all criminal cases arising in the city. The recorder's court in Detroit was established in 1857, with original jurisdiction in certain types of cases. The two were merged in 1920 as the Municipal Recorder's Court. With a jurisdiction equal to that of the circuit courts, it was presided over in 1960 by ten judges. The Superior Court in Grand Rapids, like the Municipal Recorder's Court in Detroit, has jurisdiction equal to that of the circuit court. Most of the other larger cities of Michigan have municipal courts with elective judges, but their jurisdiction is only that of the justice courts in the townships, although cases arising outside the city and within the county are sometimes tried before them.

THE LAWMAKERS

The making of state laws in an age of big government became a highly complex and technical as well as, in some instances, an intensely controversial procedure. The senate by 1852 had increased in size to 32, where it remained for the next 100 years. The size of the house became 100 in 1864 and remained at that figure until 1952. After 1850 one regular session was held each two years in the odd-numbered year, but occasionally there were special sessions. The second state constitution set the remuneration of legislators at $3 per day for the first forty days of the session, after which time they received nothing. By the turn of the century, however, the biennial sessions, beginning in January often lasted into May or June. In 1867 the legislative mill ground out no less than 520 laws, and from that time until 1907 no session produced less than 400. The legislature of 1907 broke all records by passing 754 laws.

The Constitution of 1908 made no basic change in the provisions for the legislature. Two-year terms for the legislators and biennial sessions were retained. Legislators' salaries, however, were increased to $800 for the regular session and $5 per day for the first twenty days of special sessions. Legislatures after 1909 enacted a smaller number of laws than in the preceding two decades, due to the decreased number of local acts. Under the terms of a constitutional amendment adopted in 1948 legislators were empowered to set their own salaries, which were increased thereafter until they amounted to $10,000 per year. A constitutional amendment adopted in 1952 provided for an increase of the number of house members from 100 to 110 and of senators from 32 to 34. As the demands for more legislation increased, and as legislative problems became more complex, the constitution was amended in 1951 to provide for annual sessions.[7]

As government grew bigger, proposed legislation often embraced matters so technical and complex that they were quite beyond the ability of legislators to comprehend. This problem was met in a variety of ways. In the first place, the governor, with the advice and counsel of department heads and experts, assumed the responsibility for proposing to the legislators a detailed budget and specific legislative proposals. Portions of the governor's program as well as bills introduced by legislators, were referred to committees, before which hearings were held. The average legislator might regard himself as being reasonably well informed in one or two areas, but usually relied on committee reports in others. Some legislative committees continued studies of long-range problems between sessions. Secondly, heavy reliance was put upon veteran legislators, who "knew the ropes" and could guide younger members through the jungle of government red tape. In 1941 a legislative service bureau was set up to provide technical assistance, to draft bills, and to otherwise serve the legislature. Finally, there were the lobbyists, who represented different pressure groups, and who provided the legislators with much valuable information (often slanted, however) on a wide variety of subjects.

Lobbyists representing many different "pressure groups" were maintained in Lansing to influence legislative action. Among the more influential interests represented by lobbies in Lansing were the automobile manufacturers, teachers, conservation clubs, retail merchants, and veterans' organizations. In 1943 rumors were afloat that votes of legislators were being purchased. A one-man grand jury was called upon by the attorney general to make an investigation. Ingham County Circuit Judge Leland W. Carr was given the assignment and Kim Sigler was appointed prosecutor. A lobbyist named Charles F. Hemans turned state's evidence

---

[7] The change from biennial to annual elections was necessitated by an amendment that made annual appropriations of funds for state aid dependent on tax receipts for the preceding year. For data on legislative sessions and laws, see *Michigan Manual, 1961-62* pp. 105-107.

and it was revealed that in a little black book he had made a record of payments to legislators from bankers, loan companies, racetrack operators, slot-machine owners, and others. Twenty of the defendants were convicted in 1944. In the continuing investigation Senator Warren G. Hooper of Albion, who was about to testify, was murdered. The killer was never found. Total convictions numbered 46 out of 125 indicted. Fines and jail sentences were imposed, the careers of several legislators were ruined, and the reputations of certain businessmen were smeared.

In order to identify lobbyists, or "legislative agents" as they sometimes were called, a law was passed requiring them to register. Periodically in the years that followed accusations were made of undue influence exercised by these persons in Lansing. While there may have been instances of bribery, the stock in trade of the legislative agent was in the main the influence of the group he represented and the power it might exert at the polls. They performed a useful purpose, as has been observed, in providing the lawmakers with data and arguments on controversial issues. In most instances, while they might wine and dine influential legislators, outright bribery was not attempted. Among the strongest of the lobbies were those of local government officials, such as the Township Officers Association, the Municipal League, the Sheriffs' Association, and others.

The apportionment of seats in the state senate and house of representatives became a highly controversial issue in the 1950s. In earlier years there had been little discussion of the matter. Under the state's first and second constitutions the legislature was given the responsibility for reapportioning the legislature after each federal census; there was also to be a state census between the federal censuses, after which there also was to be a reapportionment. The legislature generally carried out this duty of reapportioning each five years. The Constitution of 1908 provided for reapportionment only every ten years after each federal census. The house was to be apportioned according to population, but there was some question whether the language of the constitution also obligated the legislature to apportion the senate seats on the same basis.

The phenomenal growth of Detroit and the suburban area around it as well as other cities after 1900 was reflected in the 1910 census. Members of the legislature, the majority of whom represented rural areas, small towns, and cities, balked at carrying out the requirement that the legislature be reapportioned in 1913 and every tenth year thereafter. At that time Wayne County had four out of 32 senators and fourteen out of 100 representatives. A weak gesture toward reapportionment was made by the 1913 legislature by giving Wayne County one more senate seat; nothing was done about reapportioning house seats. When 1923 rolled around the legislature again failed to act at the regular session in spite of the recommendation of Governor Groesbeck. The governor called a special session and still there was no action. In the 1925 session, however, Groesbeck was able to push through reapportionment by agreeing to sign a bill levying a gasoline tax of 2¢ a gallon, which the legislature wanted. This reapportionment gave Wayne County seven more legislative seats.[8]

No action was taken in 1933 to reapportion legislative seats as required by the constitution. The senate failed to reapportion its seats in 1943, but the house passed a reapportionment act that gave Wayne County 27 seats. The population of that county entitled it to 38 seats. There appeared to be no reason to suppose that the legislature would carry out its responsibility to provide a fair reapportionment in 1953 any more adequately than it had in the preceding decades. As the gap between the population of senatorial and house districts became wider, public demand for reapportionment became more insistent. As a result a Michigan Committee for Representative Government was formed, and proposed a plan under which four counties in southeastern Michigan, which had 50% of the state's population, according to the 1950 census (Wayne, Oakland, Macomb, and Genesee), would have sixteen out of 33 senate seats and 49 out of 99 house seats. Another plan was proposed by the Michigan Committee for a Balanced Legislature, largely made up of outstate citizens. This plan increased the senate from 32 to 34 members, and the house from 100 to 110. The house was to be reapportioned by the legislature according to population every 10 years beginning in 1953, and if the latter failed to act within 180 days of the start of its first regular session, the duty was to devolve upon the state board of canvassers. The plan for the house, however, retained the moiety provision of the 1908 constitution, which meant that any county having a population equal to one-half of the population of the state divided by 100, was to have a representative. As this worked out, some larger counties had less representation in the house than the smaller counties. The plan provided fixed senatorial districts, the effect of which was to give the less populous areas of the state much more representation in the

[8] F. B. Woodford, *Alex J. Groesbeck*, pp. 229-234; C. W. Shull, *Legislative Reapportionment in Michigan*.

senate than they would have been entitled to on a population basis.

Both proposals were placed on the ballot in the November, 1952 election. The "balanced legislature" plan was adopted by a margin of about 300,000 votes out of over two million cast. The other proposal was defeated by almost 500,000 votes. In 1953 the house was reapportioned according to the provisions of the new constitutional amendment, and the first legislature of 34 senators and 110 representatives was elected in 1954. The largest representative district had a population of 67,110, according to the 1950 census, while the smallest had 32,913. Population of senatorial districts had a wider range: from 364,026 to 61,008.

Dissatisfaction with the 1952 amendment became stronger as urban populations in southeastern Michigan continued to grow faster than outstate areas during the 1950s. This was an important factor in the rise of sentiment in favor of complete constitutional revision. In the constitutional convention of 1961-62 the hottest issue was legislative reapportionment. Republicans, who held a majority of the seats in the convention, favored a continuance, with some modifications, of the balanced legislature, that is, with one house apportioned according to population and the apportionment of the other determined to some degree by geographic area. The Democrats, whose strength lay in populous southeastern Michigan, strongly favored a straight population basis for both houses.[9] The outcome was in the nature of a compromise. The provision written into the new constitution provided, as did the 1952 amendment, for the reapportionment of house seats every ten years on a population basis. Moiety, however, was raised from one-half to seven-tenths. This meant that a county had to have seven-tenths of the total population of the state divided by 100 in order to be entitled to a single representative. The new constitution also provided for the reapportionment of the senate each ten years. In apportioning senate seats a formula was to be applied that weighted population 80% and area 20%.

Democrats might have accepted this compromise had it not been for a United States Supreme Court decision, handed down while the convention was still in session. In the case of Baker vs. Carr the court ordered the Tennessee legislature to carry out the provisions of the Tennessee constitution, which called for reapportionment at periodic intervals according to population.

[9] Democrats, like Republicans, however, favored the retention of county lines, because party organization was by counties. Apportionment strictly according to population could not be achieved without laying out districts that cut across county lines.

This appeared to offer hope that the federal courts would order the Michigan legislature to be reapportioned on a straight population basis.

Meanwhile, a case brought by August Scholle, president of the Michigan A.F. of L.-C.I.O. was pending before the United States Supreme Court. In his suit, Scholle claimed that the 1952 amendment to the Michigan constitution violated the equal-rights provisions of the fourteenth amendment to the United States Constitution. The state supreme court had decided against him and he had appealed the case to the United States Supreme Court. After the decision in the case of Baker vs. Carr, the high federal court remanded the Scholle case to the Michigan supreme court for reconsideration. On July 18, 1962 the state supreme court, by a 4-3 vote, along party lines, found in favor of Scholle, canceled the primary election for the nomination of senators scheduled for August 7, and ordered the legislature to reapportion the senate according to population. However, a stay order was obtained from Justice Potter Stewart of the United States Supreme Court, and the primary election was held as scheduled. With the adoption of the new constitution, the question of the constitutionality of the 1952 amendment became academic. Scholle then started over, with a suit claiming the provisions of the new constitution also were in violation of the fourteenth amendment to the federal Constitution.

In 1964 the federal courts declared that the fourteenth amendment required that state legislatures be apportioned strictly according to population. The bi-partisan apportionment commission (provided for under the new state constitution) having failed to agree on a formula, the state supreme court specified house and senatorial districts of approximately equal population, and in November, 1964 legislators were elected from these new districts.

THE GREAT GAME OF POLITICS

The 78-year dominance of the Republican party in Michigan was ended by a major political upheaval in November, 1932. The Democrats elected William Comstock, their candidate for governor, all their candidates for other executive offices with the sole exception of secretary of state, and a majority of both houses of the legislature. Furthermore, for the first time since 1852 Michigan's entire electoral vote went to the Democratic candidate for president of the United States, Franklin D. Roosevelt. The reason for this political revolution was clearly the distress of the economic depression and the American habit of blaming the party in power for hard times. Many of the Democrats swept into office in 1932 were party faithfuls who had no expectation of being elected and, in some cases, little preparation for the responsibilities of the offices they had been chosen to fill. In the spring election of 1933 Democratic candidates won the offices of superintendent of public instruction and highway commissioner.

In 1934 the Republicans made a strong comeback. Secretary of State Frank D. Fitzgerald, who had been the sole Republican survivor in the 1932 debacle, was elected governor, and most of the other Republican candidates for state offices were successful. A Republican majority was returned to the legislature. Then in 1936 the tide turned again, with Democrat Frank Murphy being elected governor and Michigan's electoral vote again going to Roosevelt. It was apparent that Roosevelt's New Deal was popular with a majority of the voters. The magic of F.D.R.'s name on the ballot seemed sufficient to bring victory to state candidates. Once more in 1938, when there was no presidential election, the Republicans won the governorship in Michigan, re-electing Frank D. Fitzgerald.[9] In 1940 Roosevelt ran for an unprecedented third term and was elected. While Michigan's electoral vote in 1940 went to the Republican candidate, Wendell Wilkie, by a small margin, Democratic strength was sufficient to elect former Highway Commissioner Murray D. Van Wagoner governor.

In 1942, the familiar pattern was repeated: with no presidential election, Michigan returned to its old Republican habits and voters chose Republican Harry F. Kelly as governor. Two years later, for the first time since 1928, Michigan elected a Republican governor in a presidential election year. Kelly was re-elected, but the state's electoral vote in 1944 went to Roosevelt, even though the latter was running against a native of Michigan, Thomas E. Dewey, who was born in Owosso. Roosevelt nosed out Dewey by 22,476 votes in an election in which a total of 2,191,332 votes were cast. In 1946 Kim Sigler, who had won publicity as special prosecutor in the legislative bribery grand-jury investigation, was nominated by the Republican party for governor and won the election. But in 1948 Sigler was defeated in his bid for re-election by a Democratic political newcomer, G. Mennen Williams.

Williams was re-elected in 1950 by a margin of only 1,154 votes out of almost two million cast. Running for a third term in 1952, he won by only a slightly larger margin. No Michigan governor had ever been elected for more than three terms, but Williams shattered precedent by not only winning a fourth, but also a

[9] Fitzgerald died March 16, 1939, and was succeeded by Republican Lieutenant Governor Luren D. Dickinson.

fifth and a sixth term, all by substantial majorities. When Williams decided not to run in 1960 the Democrats nominated and elected John B. Swainson. The state's electoral vote in 1960 also went to the Democratic candidate for President (John F. Kennedy)—something that had not happened since 1936. During the period from 1948 to 1960 Democrats won an increasing number of state-executive offices besides that of governor. A majority of the supreme court came to consist of Democrats. Only the legislature remained a Republican stronghold in Lansing.

As has been observed, the Democratic attack on the Republican citadel in Michigan was successful in 1932, and probably to a certain extent during the rest of the 1930s, because the economic depression was blamed on the Republicans. The magic of Franklin D. Roosevelt's name was important in helping the Democrats win in 1936 and in 1940. The re-election of Harry F. Kelley in 1944, however, appeared to indicate that Roosevelt's influence on Michigan politics was waning, and it appeared that the state was returning to its old Republican habits.

The election of Williams as governor in 1948 and the subsequent Democratic successes must be attributed to other factors. There can be no question that Williams himself was one of the most potent political personalities ever to appear on the Michigan stage. He was a tireless campaigner. He appeared at countless community festivals, crowned queens, made speeches, called square dances, shook hands with millions, and developed a personal popularity rarely matched in political annals. His youthful smile and his green polka-dot tie became known everywhere in Michigan. He championed the cause of the little people, advocated more support for education, and in general was sensitive to human need. His appointments were excellent; there was hardly a breath of scandal during the dozen years he was governor. Though he was hated by his political opponents, who were fond of calling him "Soapy," he was idolized by many more. Democratic victories between 1948 and 1960 may be attributed in part to Williams' personal popularity.

But there were other factors. During most of the period, the chairman of the Democratic State Central Committee was Neil Staebler of Ann Arbor. Staebler was something of a genius as a party organizer, and in part the Democrats had him to thank for their winning ways. Another factor in the Democratic victories was the Negro vote. Prior to the 1930s Negroes were regarded as being supporters of the Republican Party, but they were won over to the Democrats in large numbers by the New Deal. In the period after 1945 in the northern states the Democratic party appeared more zealous than the Republicans in support of equal rights for minority groups. As has been noted earlier, Michigan had a huge influx of Negroes from the South after World War II, and there is strong evidence that they heavily favored the Democratic party. And finally, Democratic victories were won through the support of organized labor, and the success achieved by labor leaders, especially in Michigan, in recruiting union members to support and vote for the Democratic party. Republicans frequently accused both Williams and Swainson of being bossed by U.A.W. and other union leaders, though the extent to which this was true is a controversial question. In any event, organized labor was an important segment of the Democratic party in Michigan and played a vital role in the party's victories.

Republicans were cheered in 1961 when they were able to elect 99 out of the 144 delegates to the constitutional convention. In part this was due to the fact that the delegates were elected by legislative districts, which put the Democrats at a disadvantage. But even in some of the strong Democratic districts Republicans won. Out of the convention emerged a new political personality on the Republican side in the person of George Romney. Known as president of American Motors, Romney first attained political notice of organizing a nonpartisan movement called "Citizens for Michigan." He was elected as a member of the constitutional convention and was chosen as one of the vice-presidents of the convention. As leader of the Republican liberals, he quickly became a national figure. In 1962 he ran for governor as the Republican candidate. He conducted a hard-fought campaign, was supported by large campaign contributions, and won election in November. Democrats, however, were elected to all the other executive offices. In 1964 Romney was re-elected governor by a large majority in spite of a Democratic landslide.

Whatever the future might hold, there could be little question that Michigan had become a state where party rivalry was vigorous and where elections were hotly contested. The old Republican dominance was only a memory. In the thirty years after 1932 party lines more and more corresponded with economic and social lines. Businessmen, most professional people, and many of the "white collar" workers supported the Republican party, while wage-earners, especially union members, minority groups, social reformers, and intellectuals were generally Democratic in their preferences. Geographically, the Detroit area, Genesee County, and the western Upper Peninsula were Democratic strongholds, while the Republicans depended heavily on the rural areas and smaller cities of southern Michigan. Throughout the Lower Peninsula, except in the Detroit metropolitan area and Genesee County, township and county offices were filled by Republicans almost as universally as in the years before 1932. Until 1964, Republican congressmen were elected by large majorities in most outstate districts. Political rivalry, therefore, came to represent, to some degree, the cities versus the rural areas and small towns, but more clearly, the rivalry between the Detroit metropolitan area and the remainder of the state.

CONSTITUTIONAL CHANGE

The Constitution of 1908, third in Michigan's history, was amended 70 times during its 55-year history. Another 57 proposed amendments were rejected by the voters. This constitution was framed before the progressive movement of the first two decades of the twentieth century had reached its height. Several typical progressive reforms such as the direct primary were added by amendment. Subsequent amendments included such vital changes as the 15-mill tax limitation, sales-tax diversion, civil-service system, right of the legislature to fix salaries of elected officials, and reapportionment. Several amendments were adopted for the purpose of authorizing bond issues for soldiers' bonuses, highway construction, and mental hospitals. Others modified the framework of government, changed the name of a state agency or board, or dealt with some aspect of local government.

Three reasons may be cited for the large number of amendments that were added to the constitution. The Constitution of 1908, like that of 1850 but in sharp contrast with the Constitution of 1835, was long and detailed. As a result, a constitutional amendment was required for making even minor changes. The right of the people to initiate proposed constitutional amendments by petition made it possible for almost any sizable special-interest group, by concerted action, to get a proposal on the ballot to amend the constitution. Finally, the lack of trust on the part of citizens in their legislature and governor often moved them to write into the constitution provisions that were properly statutory rather than constitutional matters. The civil-service system and the sales-tax-diversion amendments may be cited as examples.

As a result of the frequent addition of amendments, the constitution became a patchwork, full of anachronisms and inconsistencies. This led to proposals for constitutional "revision," which really meant rewriting the document. The Constitution of 1908 provided that the question of general revision should be submitted to the people automatically every sixteen years, beginning in 1926. At other times the question might be placed on the ballot either by initiatory petition or legislative resolution. In 1926 the proposal for general revision was rejected by more than a two-to-one majority, but the vote in 1942 was much closer. The question was put on the ballot again in 1948. This time 855,451 votes were cast in favor of revision and 799,198 against. But the Constitution of 1908 had provided that in order to approve general revision, a majority of those voting in the election at which the question was submitted must vote in favor of it. Although a majority of those voting *on the issue* in 1948 approved revision, many voters had not voted on the issue at all. The number of votes in favor of revision was not a majority of those voting in the election; over two million votes had been cast for governor. Again, when the question came up automatically in 1958, a majority voting on the issue approved a general constitution revision, but not a majority of those voting in the election.

By this time sentiment in favor of revision was growing, however. The financial difficulties being experienced by the state government and growing problems of local government were important factors in convincing many citizens that in order to solve its problems the state needed a new constitution. The League of Women Voters and the Junior Chamber of Commerce took the lead in supporting the campaign for a new constitution. The difficulty of securing voter approval under the provisions of the Constitution of 1908 led the two organizations to initiate an amendment that would order constitutional revision by a majority approval of those voting on the issue. This amendment was placed on the ballot in the November, 1960 election and was approved by a majority of over 300,000. The amendment also specified that the question of revision should be submitted at the April election in 1961.

The two organizations that had led the campaign for the amendment adopted in November also worked in favor of the proposal for revision at the April, 1961 election. They were aided by many other civic groups, including Citizens for Michigan, which had been organized by George Romney. In opposition to revision were the Farm Bureau, local government officials and their organizations, and some other groups. In part, the opposition was due to the fear that a new constitution would make inroads on the existing system of local government, but in the main it arose from the belief that any new constitution would involve reapportionment of the legislature that would favor the Detroit area and the Democratic party. This latter consideration, however, created a favorable sentiment toward revision in the Detroit area. The proposal carried by a margin of 23,421 out of 1,169,445 votes cast. Wayne, Oakland, Macomb, and Washtenaw Counties voted heavily in favor of revision, but the vote was against it in most of the counties outside the Detroit area. What turned the tide was probably the work by civic organizations that produced enough favorable votes outstate added to those of the Detroit area to produce a majority.

The favorable vote also was made possible by another provision of the amendment adopted in November, 1960. Under the original provisions of the Constitution of 1908 a convention for general revision was to consist of three delegates from each senatorial district. Since the senatorial districts were so arranged as to favor the parts of the state outside the Detroit area, any revision by a convention made up of delegates chosen in this manner was staunchly opposed by Detroit leaders. They proposed that the constitution be amended so that the convention would be composed of delegates chosen from representative, rather than senatorial districts. The organizations working for revision came up with a compromise that called for one delegate from each senatorial district *and* one from each representative district. This was incorporated into the amendment that was approved in November, 1960.

There was considerable sentiment in favor of choosing the delegates on a nonpartisan basis, but this was overruled by the legislature, which enacted a measure providing for partisan nomination and election of delegates. The two major parties chose their nominees in a primary held July 25, and the election was held September 12, 1961. Of the 144 delegates elected, 99 were Republicans.

During the summer of 1961 a considerable amount of preparatory work was done by a commission appointed by the governor and financed by a grant from the Kellogg Foundation. The delegates assembled in a special hall fitted up in the Lansing Civic Center on October 3, 1961. First order of business was the selection of a convention president. Among the aspirants for the honor were George Romney, President John Hannah of Michigan State University, and Edward Hutchinson of Fennville. A Republican caucus, however, gave the honor to Stephen S. Nisbet of Fremont, former executive of Gerber Products Company and member of the State Board of Education. Democratic delegates made the selection of Nisbet unanimous.

The convention got down to work in short order. Committees were appointed to deal with education, legislative organization, the executive branch, the judiciary, local government, and other matters that would be involved in the new constitution. During the first three months time was largely devoted to committee hearings. From January through April, the convention hammered out the provisions of the new constitution. On May 11 the convention completed its work, but put off final approval of the document until August 1. On that day delegates reassembled, made some minor changes, and approved the final draft by a vote of 96 to 48.

The Constitutional Convention of 1961-62 was made up of ten women and 134 men. Several nonwhites were among the delegates. Although there were a number of delegates who had had extensive experience in government, some were political novices. On the whole, the calibre of delegates was high and they worked hard and conscientiously. They considered the practices of other states, the recommendations of political scientists, and the opinions of citizens as expressed at hearings. In not a few instances logical conclusions on what was best for Michigan were modified or rejected for the reason that delegates did not believe the voters would approve. In other cases the clash of opinion made compromise necessary. Special-interest groups demanded that safeguards and provisions in the old constitution be perpetuated in the new; the earmarking of funds for highways and for education are examples of such provisions. Matters that the delegates might have preferred to leave to the discretion of the legislature were dealt with in the new constitution in order to satisfy the demand of various interest groups.

Another factor that made the new constitution a bundle of compromises was partisan rivalry. At first there was a rather remarkable degree of party harmony in the convention, but before the end partisan bickering and rancor had been aroused to fever pitch. Among the Republicans there were two major factions, commonly called the liberals and the conservatives. The leader of the liberals was George Romney, while former State Treasurer D. Hale Brake was the acknowledged leader of the conservatives. The conservatives generally wanted the pattern of local government to be left largely as it was, favored the selection of state officials by election rather than appointment, and insisted on an apportionment of the legislature that would follow the existing pattern of favoring outstate Michigan over the Detroit metropolitan area. Many of the conservatives had opposed constitutional revision, and they were inclined as delegates to make as few changes as possible. The liberals, in contrast, wanted a new constitution that incorporated changes recommended by political scientists that would enable the state and local government to operate more efficiently and to meet the needs of the people more fully.

Democrats in the convention were inclined to co-operate with Republican liberals. But at a critical stage in the proceedings Romney negotiated a series of compromise agreements with D. Hale Brake, leader of the Republican conservatives. This infuriated the Democrats, who claimed that Romney already was eyeing the governorship and that he made his peace with the conservative Republicans as a means of uniting his party for the coming election campaign. From this point forward party acrimony was bitter and all chance of unanimity in the final outcome was dissolved. In the end all but a few Democrats voted against approval of the document, while Republicans were almost unanimous in favoring it.

Several of the salient provisions of the constitution framed by the Constitutional Convention of 1961-62 have been discussed above: reapportionment, changes in the judiciary, the executive branch, taxation, and finance. Another deserving mention is county home rule. There was a strong movement by the Republican liberals to give the people of each county the right to draw up and adopt such forms of county government as they believed was best fitted to their need. Conservatives opposed such a provision on the ground that it would enable cities to dominate county government. A compromise was reached which provided that the legislature would be given the power to provide for county home rule. The article on education in the new constitution received high praise from both sides of the political fence. It provided for a new elective State Board of Education with broad responsibility for planning and co-ordinating public education in the state. But its powers over the governing boards of state colleges and universities was sharply limited. Each of these institutions was to have its own governing board, largely independent of control by the legislature or the governor. The governing boards of the three largest state universities were to continue to be chosen by election; the others were to be appointed by the governor with the consent of the senate. The superintendent of public instruction, instead of being elected, was to be appointed by the State Board of Education.

The new constitution guaranteed civil rights to every citizen and provided for a civil-rights commission to safeguard these rights. A bipartisan legislative council with a full-time staff was provided for. The new constitution eliminated the spring elections in odd-numbered years. The term of senators was extended to

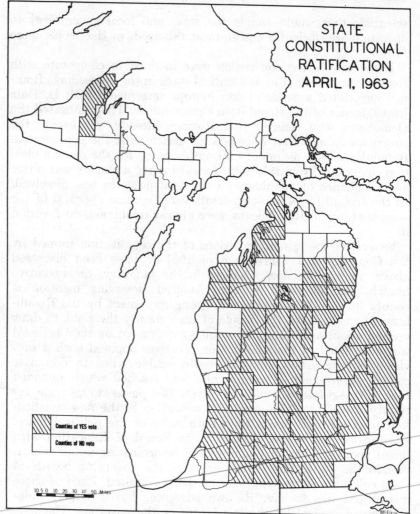

STATE
CONSTITUTIONAL
RATIFICATION
APRIL 1, 1963

Counties of YES vote

Counties of NO vote

10 5 0 10 20 30 40 50 Miles

MCElroy

four years, as was that of the governor. The governor and senators were to be elected in November of the even-numbered years when there was not a national presidential election, starting in 1966, so as to concentrate attention of voters on state issues and state candidates.

Following adjournment of the convention, a lively campaign was waged for and against the proposed constitution. The Democratic state convention came out against approval, largely because Democrats hoped that the federal courts would order reapportionment of the legislature under the 1908 constitution strictly on population lines. Democratic Highway Commissioner John Mackie also opposed the new constitution because it would take the election of the highway commissioner out of the control of voters, and also because certain provisions regarding the right of eminent domain in the new constitution would make it more difficult to obtain land for highways. Considerable opposition to the new constitution was also voiced by the Republican conservatives, though the action of the Democratic Party in opposing the constitution had the effect of driving many Republicans who might otherwise have opposed it to come out for it. Some Democratic leaders, notably former United States Senator Prentiss Brown, announced their support. Once more civic organizations conducted a vigorous drive in favor of approval.

The voters passed judgment on the proposed new constitution on April 1, 1963, and approved it by a margin of only about 7,000 votes. A partial recount was demanded, but the result was not changed. Detroit produced a negative majority, though not large enough to defeat the new constitution. Suburban areas around Detroit in several cases voted in favor of approval. Outstate Republican conservative strongholds in many cases produced an adverse vote, but the work of civic organizations plus the factor of Democratic opposition had the effect of turning the tide in favor of approval in populous counties such as Kalamazoo and Kent.

The constitution adopted in 1963 was somewhat more brief than that of 1908. It was more logically organized and co-ordinated. It incorporated a number of changes that were generally conceded to be desirable, notably the four-year term of governor and the educational provisions. But it did not go as far in giving Michigan a framework of government based on sound principles as many had hoped. There were provisions in it that would call for amendment in the not-too-distant future. But on the whole it was an improvement over the Constitution of 1908, more geared to the needs of a twentieth-century industrial state.

23

THE GROWTH
OF SOCIAL CONSCIOUSNESS

In Michigan, as elsewhere in the nation and in the world, the twentieth century brought a greater consciousness of human suffering, of the plight of the poor and the handicapped, and of the needs of the less fortunate members of society, than had existed in any previous age. In part this was due to a greater volume of information on social conditions and higher levels of education. Perhaps also it was due to a more widespread acceptance of Christian principles. As individuals, through private organizations, and through governmental agencies, Americans sought to take action to alleviate distress, to help the needy, the sick, and the handicapped, and to adopt social reforms designed to make life better for all the people.

During the latter part of the nineteenth century social Darwinism had been popular, and by some this was interpreted as meaning that progress came through a social organization that did not interfere with the natural law of the survival of the fittest. But such a concept was never generally accepted, and the progressive movement, which affected so many aspects of American life in the early twentieth century, had a distinctly humanitarian aspect. The growth of social consciousness and the changes that came about in response to it are reflected in the history of Michigan during the century after 1865 in a wide variety of ways. In dealing with violators of the law the emphasis came to be on correction and reform rather than on punishment. The state government provided institutions and clinics for the treatment of mental illness and other diseases, while local communities built general hospitals. Provisions were made for the rehabilitation of the handicapped. Women won legal, educational, and political rights. The experiment of prohibition was tried. Citizens formed dozens of health, welfare, and recreation agencies and raised funds to support them. And finally, Michigan played its part in three major wars that were justified to a large extent on the ground that they were crusades for human rights and decency.

FROM PUNISHMENT TO CORRECTION

The century and a quarter after Michigan was admitted into the Union was a period when the treatment of criminals was humanized. The idea of punishing criminals gave way to that of correcting them or reforming them, and the emphasis shifted from confinement to prevention.

At the time Michigan became a state one of the first problems to which the legislature directed its attention was that of providing a state prison. The first legislature to convene after the admission of the state into the Union authorized the construction of a prison at Jackson. The concept of a prison at that time had become one of providing a place where a person could be restrained from doing further harm to society. Although the whipping post had been used in Detroit in the early 1830s, the idea of inflicting physical suffering upon criminal offenders as a punishment for their wrongdoing was giving way to a more humane attitude. The prison at Jackson was modeled after that at Auburn, New York, which provided individual cells for prisoners but allowed them to work together in groups during the day. The first prison built at Jackson was a wooden building surrounded by a palisade, but a new structure with stone walls was started in 1841.

Michigan was the first state in the Union to abolish capital punishment. One of the reasons for this was an incident that took place in 1838 at Sandwich, across the river from Detroit on the Canadian side. A man named Fitzpatrick was convicted of a crime on circumstantial evidence and was hanged for the offense. A few months later a man named Sellers confessed on his deathbed that he had been guilty of the crime for which Fitzpatrick had been convicted and executed. This caused a revulsion of feeling on both sides of the border. The abolition of capital punishment came about when a revised code of laws that set the maximum penalty for murder as imprisonment at hard labor for life was adopted on May 18, 1846. There was some resistance to the change, one of those opposing it being the Rev. George Duffield, pastor of the First Presbyterian Church of Detroit. But there was no widespread demand for the restoration of capital punishment, and so no change was made. Several times in the years that followed, however, a wave of crime or some particularly horrendous offense brought demands for the restoration of the death penalty. Though the question was submitted to the people after the adoption of the initiative, capital punishment was never reinstated.[1]

Even before the Civil War it was recognized as being inhumane and unwise to throw youthful offenders into prison with hardened criminals. In 1855 the legislature established at Lansing a "house of correction for juvenile offenders," later called the "Michigan Reform School," and subsequently the "Boys' Industrial School." The purpose of this institution has always been to provide remedial and corrective measures to help the boy to eventually become a useful and self-supporting citizen.[2] The Michigan Reform School for Girls, later named the "Girls' Training School," was established at Adrian in 1879 to perform a similar service for youthful female offenders. The trials of criminal cases involving children were carried on in the same way as those where adults were charged, until the twentieth century. The Constitution of 1908 provided for a special division of the probate court in each county to act as a juvenile court and to deal with cases where youthful offenders were being tried. This action was in line with a nationwide movement for juvenile courts that grew out of the writings of Judge Ben Lindsay.

Over the years more humane treatment of criminals replaced earlier practices. The whipping post was abolished. The legislature in 1875 prohibited the "water cure" and lashes inflicted on the bare body at the state prison. The rule of solitary confinement for serious offenders, a treatment that few could survive for more than ten years, was modified. In 1877 a reformatory was established at Ionia for "first offenders." Since about 1887 women convicted of felonies were sent to the Detroit House of Correction. The Northern State Prison was built at Marquette in 1889. For criminals who were proved to be insane the Ionia State Hospital was opened in 1885. Michigan was one of the first states to

---

[1] G. Catlin, *The Story of Detroit,* pp. 420-422; D. B. Davis, "The Movement to Abolish Capital Punishment in America, 1787-1861," *American Historical Review,* LXIII (1957), 23-47.

[2] M. Barnes, *The Prison System of Michigan.*

develop the parole system. Since 1896 good behavior in prisons has been rewarded by paroles under supervision, as a means of gradually reorienting the prisoner to the duties of citizenship. The principle of probation was recognized as early as 1903. Gradually it came to be recognized that in most cases crime arises out of broken families, poverty, and emotional imbalance rather than from the innate malevolence of the individual.[3] Camp Pugsley near Traverse City, established in 1958, was the nation's first state-operated probation camp for youths up to 22 years of age. Vocational training and outdoor work under conservation-department supervision were provided for young offenders who, in the opinion of the sentencing judge, lacked suitable probation opportunities in their home communities. Beginning in 1948 conservation work camps were established for adult prisoners to improve state parks and recreational areas.

The old state prison was abandoned in 1930 and a new one was constructed north of Jackson called the Southern Michigan State Prison. It has the dubious distinction of being the largest walled penal institution in the world and houses some 5,500 prisoners.

HOSPITALS

The care of the sick long remained one of the exclusive functions of the home. Society was concerned only when a disease was communicable or contagious. The first general hospital in the state was opened in Detroit in 1845 by the Sisters of Charity. It was called St. Vincent's. As has been noted earlier, Harper Hospital in Detroit was established during the Civil War for sick and injured soldiers. Hospitals were long regarded as pesthouses. Due to a lack of knowledge concerning asepsis and its importance, disease was often spread rather than cured in hospitals. Not until the latter part of the nineteenth century, when the use of antiseptics and anesthesia became common, were many hospitals built. During the 1880s and 1890s private benefactions made possible the founding of general hospitals in many of the larger cities. Grace Hospital in Detroit was incorporated in 1888. By the turn of the century Battle Creek, Bay City, Grand Rapids, Hancock, Ishpeming, Kalamazoo, Lansing, Manistee, Marquette, Menominee, Mt. Clemens, and Saginaw had general hospitals.

The University Hospital at Ann Arbor had its beginnings as an adjunct of the Medical School soon after 1850. A program of construction to provide better facilities in this institution was

[3] W. F. Hopp, *The Michigan State Prison, Jackson, 1837-1928.*

started by the state in 1899. Aided by private benefactors as well as state appropriations, this hospital had some 1,300 beds by 1948. A large out-patient clinic was opened in 1952. Many of the patients at the University Hospital were without resources and were treated at public expense.

Many general hospitals were built by religious and other private groups. The memory of large donors is perpetuated in the names of some of these institutions, such as Henry Ford Hospital in Detroit. The Federal Hospital Survey and Construction Act, passed by Congress after World War II, enabled many Michigan communities to build new hospitals and to enlarge old ones. A 1946 survey by the American Medical Association showed that Michigan had 183 general hospitals. In 1947 state aid was provided for hospital buildings. By 1959 Michigan had 245 general hospitals, 466 nursing homes, and 106 privately operated homes for the aged.

The care of the mentally ill was recognized as a state function as early as 1848. In that year the Kalamazoo Asylum for the Insane was established by legislative act, but it was not until 1859 that the institution received its first patients. Up to this time mentally ill persons were cared for in homes. Often in violent cases they were confined in an attic, a shed, or even an iron cage kept in the yard. Many were mistreated and neglected. Dorothea Dix, famous for her work in calling attention to the plight of mentally deranged people, spoke before the Michigan legislature to call attention to the problem. For some years, however, few families would permit their loved ones to be committed to an asylum; to do so was considered almost a social disgrace. But in the first decade of the twentieth century the public began to think of mental illness in the same category as physical affliction. Meanwhile other asylums had been established by the state: at Pontiac in 1873, at Traverse City in 1881, and at Newberry in 1893. In 1911 and 1912 the names of these institutions were changed to State Hospitals. A fifth one was established at Ypsilanti in 1929. Tremendous advances were made in the treatment of mental cases, leading to a steady increase in demand for institutional treatment. Private mental hospitals were established to supplement the state hospitals. The Wayne County Hospital at Eloise was originally built to receive mental patients from Wayne County, but most of its patients came to be cared for by the state. A seventh state hospital was built at Northville. By 1960 these seven hospitals had a resident population of 20,600.

The growing incidence of mental illness became a matter of increasing concern. The large state hospitals were not adequate to house all the patients needing treatment. Outpatient clinics were operated at several of them. By 1960 some 1,200 patients were cared for in private families under supervision of the State Department of Mental Health. Much attention was given to preventive measures. During the 1940s and 1950s a total of 17 child-guidance clinics were opened in different parts of the state for the early treatment of emotionally disturbed children. Two all-purpose clinics and six adult clinics were also set up. These clinics were jointly supported by the state and the counties. The Hawthorn Center, a children's psychiatric residential center, the Lafayette Clinic in Detroit, mainly for research and professional training, and the Children's Psychiatric Hospital in Ann Arbor also became part of the state-supported mental-health program. In addition to mentally ill and emotionally disturbed children, the mentally retarded also receive state aid. Seven state facilities at Coldwater, Lapeer, Mt. Pleasant, Fort Custer, and Plymouth were devoted to the care, treatment, and training of some 10,000 mentally retarded children by 1960.[4]

The state has assumed the responsibility for maintaining institutions for other kinds of illness and disability. Michigan had the first state law providing for tax-paid hospitalization for tuberculosis patients. The first tuberculosis sanitarium provided by Michigan was built at Howell in 1905. By 1960 there were other sanitariums at Gaylord, Kalamazoo, and Hancock, a tuberculosis unit at the University Hospital in Ann Arbor, and fourteen approved county, city, and private tuberculosis hospitals. Free chest X rays were provided for the early detection of tuberculosis. Several Michigan doctors, including Dr. John Alexander and Dr. Cameron Haight of the University of Michigan, and Dr. E. J. O'Brien of Detroit, were pioneers in the field of chest surgery for the treatment of the disease. The use of antibiotics was another factor in reducing the death rate from tuberculosis in Michigan from 103 per 100,000 in 1900 to 5 per 100,000 in 1958. So rapid was the decline of tuberculosis as a major killer that in 1959 a large number of beds in the state sanitariums were turned over for the use of patients from the state mental hospitals who needed care but not treatment, mainly senility cases.

Another disease, the treatment of which has been assumed as a state responsibility, is epilepsy. In 1895 an institution was opened at Lapeer by the state for the care and treatment of epileptics. After 1914 this became an institution for mentally retarded children, with the severe epileptic cases being treated at a new

[4] Department of Mental Health, *Program and Activities.*

institution established at Wahjamega. By 1960 there were 1,900 patients, with a long waiting list.

During the 1920s the legislature sought to encourage counties to build and operate hospitals for indigent patients by providing state aid, and many counties took advantage of this. Municipal hospitals to take care of poverty-stricken persons who fell ill were maintained in several cities, while others provided funds for the treatment of such patients in general hospitals. The expansion of poor relief in the 1930s included funds for paying the hospital bills of indigent patients.

"THE HALT, THE LAME, AND THE BLIND"

The assumption of state responsibility for the handicapped was recognized in 1848 by the passage of an act by the legislature that appropriated the proceeds to be derived from the sale of 24 sections of salt-spring lands for the establishment of an "asylum for the deaf, dumb, blind, and insane." In addition to the institution for the insane at Kalamazoo the state provided a school for deaf and blind children at Flint in 1854. A separate school for the blind was opened in Lansing in 1879.

As the number of deaf children increased, the state, instead of building additional schools for them, provided state aid to school districts providing special classes for the hard-of-hearing. The first law giving such aid was passed in 1899. Under an act passed in 1923 similar aid was provided to districts that maintained special classes for blind and crippled children. Since 1921 federal aid has been used for the vocational rehabilitation of the handicapped.

As early as 1871 a state school for dependent children was opened at Coldwater. Since 1929 such children have been cared for in licensed homes and have attended regular schools. The service clubs, including Rotary, Kiwanis, and Lions, have made important contributions to the care of crippled children. Rotary was instrumental in the formation of the Michigan Society for Crippled Children in 1921. Private charity has been devoted to the welfare of children since the earliest years. An orphan asylum existed in Detroit as early as 1836. Among the associations devoted to child welfare are the Michigan Children's Aid Society, started in 1891, the Children's Aid Society of Detroit, and the Children's Fund of Michigan to which the late Senator James Couzens gave $10,000,000. In the 1950s Goodwill Industries established branches throughout Michigan to provide employment for the handicapped as a self-supporting venture.

The relief of poverty

The problem of providing relief for the poor is by no means a new one. Even when Michigan was on the frontier there were men who were too lazy to work or were incapacitated for work through some disability. That poverty existed is demonstrated by the passage of a law by the Territorial Council in 1827 making the township the unit for dispensing poor relief. This continued to be the pattern for more than a century. However, a law passed in 1830 authorized counties to erect poorhouses, the first of which was built by Wayne County in 1832. Eventually all but one of the state's 83 counties built a poorhouse. Township supervisors, cities, or neighborly help provided relief for temporary poverty cases, but those who were unable to support themselves over any extended period of time were sent to a poorhouse. Conditions in these institutions were sordid. The disgrace attached to being sent to a poorhouse was immortalized by the lachrymose verses of Hillsdale's poet, Will Carleton, in his "Over the hills to the poorhouse."

Until the 1930s it was usually regarded as a disgrace for a person to accept support from a public agency. Pride in self-reliance prevented most people from asking for such assistance except in cases of the direst need. The Puritan notion that poverty is due to sloth, lack of industry, indulgence, drunkenness, laziness, or some other shortcoming prevailed in an age when America provided almost unlimited opportunity for those who were willing to work. But a marked change in attitude came about during the depression years after 1930. The unprecedented amount of unemployment compelled acknowledgment of the fact that poverty might be the consequence of the maladjustment of the economic system, that the individual might be without the means of providing for himself and his family through no fault of his own. This altered point of view led to revolutionary changes in relief and welfare administration after 1930.

In cases where want was clearly the result of circumstances beyond the control of the individual, some provision had been made even prior to 1930 for assistance short of poor relief. Before 1912 an employer was not held responsible for the care and support of an employee injured while at work if it could be proved that the employee, or even a fellow employee, had been negligent. Since it usually was possible to establish such negligence, persons unable to work on account of injuries sustained on the job became objects of charity. In that year, however, the legislature passed a Workmen's Compensation law, which held the employer fully responsible. In 1913 a mother's pension act was passed. It provided an allowance ranging from $2 to $10 a week to mothers lacking other means of support, depending on the number of children. But until after 1930 there was no provision for the aged or the unemployed save such scanty aid as the township or city might provide, or, as a last recourse, the county poorhouse.

Following 1929, unemployment in Michigan reached new highs. In rural communities most families managed somehow to get along, although even there conditions were critical in some parts of the state. The problem was greatest in the cities. The Great Depression was, of course, nationwide, but it hit Michigan harder than most other states. The automobile industry, which dominated manufacturing in the state, quickly reflects adverse economic conditions. If times are hard people can make do with the old car. Another factor that caused Michigan to be hard hit by the depression was the marginal nature of farming in the northern part of the Lower Peninsula and in the Upper Peninsula. Thousands of farmers on the thin, sandy soils of these areas were barely able to make a living in normal times, and when prices fell and demand slackened for farm products they found themselves in desperate straits. Finally, in the copper-mining counties production had been decreasing in the 1920s as Michigan mines were unable to compete successfully with Rocky Mountain copper mines; the depression, which drove prices down and down, caused almost all the mines to close. In Keweenaw County two-thirds of the families were on relief; in Houghton County one-third were without means of support. About 20% of the nonagricultural workers of the state were unemployed by 1930; the figure was up to 29% in 1931, and in 1932 it reached 43%.

In 1932, public relief cost more than $30,000,000. Of this amount about $24,000,000 was paid from taxes by cities, townships, and counties. The remainder was provided by the state government. A large share of the automobile-license fees was returned to the counties for relief. The legislature also raised the bonding limit of cities to enable them to borrow money for relief. In Washington President Herbert Hoover turned a deaf ear to pleas for a federal relief program. However, the Reconstruction Finance Corporation loaned money to the states for relief. Michigan received a total of $21,000,000 from this source by 1933. The situation caused not a few to advocate radical remedies. In the election of 1932 a communist candidate for governor received 7,906 votes. Mayor Frank Murphy of Detroit allowed critics of the social and economic system to "blow off steam" in Grand Circus Park, though many criticized him for doing so. An abandoned warehouse was used to house homeless men, and Murphy declared that no one should starve. Many of the idle in Detroit and elsewhere in Michigan listened to the radio talks of Father Charles E. Coughlin, the radio priest of Royal Oak. He violently attacked President Hoover and the businessmen of the nation, and in the presidential campaign of 1932 he told his listeners that the alternatives were Roosevelt or ruin. The tirades of Father Coughlin were not needed to swing the election to Roosevelt. Not only did Michigan give him a large majority of its popular vote, but also sent a Democratic governor and legislature to Lansing.

At that time the President was inaugurated on March 4, rather than on January 20, following his election. The interim between the November, 1932 election and the inauguration of President Roosevelt four months later was a trying and uncertain time throughout the nation, and especially in Michigan. It is not surprising that citizens with plenty of woes of their own, paid little attention to the news that Adolf Hitler, in early 1933, became the dictator of Germany. Not only were unprecedented numbers out of work, but the meager savings that some had managed to hold on to were jeopardized by a wave of bank failures, and finally the closing of all the banks. The withdrawal of funds by depositors to meet current needs or because of doubts regarding the soundness of financial institutions caused many banks to be hard-pressed. Many had their funds invested in mortgages on buildings, investments that may have seemed perfectly safe a few years before. But during the depression the value of real estate plunged to such a low point that the mortgages in many instances far exceeded the amount for which the property could be sold. To tide them over, banks secured loans from the Reconstruction Finance Corporation. Unfortunately, Congress had provided that all such loans be made public; the result was that when a bank borrowed from the R.F.C., depositors became wary and withdrew their funds faster than ever.

A banking crisis was precipitated in Michigan early in February, 1933. The Union Guardian Trust Company, a unit of a large banking chain in Detroit, had borrowed $15,000,000 from the R.F.C. in 1932; in January, 1933 it asked for $50,000,000 more. But R.F.C. examiners reported that the institution's collateral did not warrant such a loan. An offer was made to provide part of the amount if large local depositors would loan the rest. General Motors and Chrysler agreed to the plan, but Henry Ford, in spite of a personal appeal by President Hoover, refused. In Washington, Senator James Couzens advised the President not to try to save the Michigan banks if their holdings did not warrant it, and threatened to "scream from the housetops" if a loan were given without adequate security. A crisis was reached on February 13, a banking holiday following Lincoln's birthday, which fell on a Sunday. It was decided that Union Guardian could not open for business Tuesday morning. Since this would certainly cause a run on other banks, Governor William Comstock was called into conference. He soon recognized that the closing of Union Guardian would create panic conditions in the state unless something were done. Therefore he issued a proclamation continuing the bank holiday until February 23, and word of his decision greeted citizens all over Michigan when they turned on their radios that Tuesday morning.

Michigan was not the first state to close its banks. Banks already had been temporarily closed in Nevada, Iowa, and Louisiana. But the news came, nevertheless, as a shock. Many people found themselves with little or no cash on hand. But somehow they got along. Merchants extended credit. Friends and neighbors helped each other. On February 21 Governor Comstock extended the holiday, but allowed banks to pay out limited sums. Other states also were forced to close their banks, and the day after he was inaugurated President Roosevelt declared a national bank holiday. Congress on March 9 passed an act that gave federal examiners power to decide which national banks were sound enough to reopen, and which should be liquidated. The Michigan legislature passed an act March 21 providing for a similar procedure for state banks.

Not until 1949 was the liquidation of the state banks and trust companies that had been closed during the depression completed. A total of 436 state banks and trust companies had been closed. Of this number 207 were allowed to reopen and their depositors suffered no loss. Of the remainder, 170 were authorized to reorganize and 59 were placed in receivership. Reorganized banks made payments to depositors aggregating 93.8% of the amount of deposit at the time they were reorganized; the closed banks paid off 85.4% of their deposits. Of the total on deposit in all state banking institutions at the time of the crash 96.11% was eventually returned to depositors.[5] Although no great permanent loss was suffered there were fears at the time of the crisis that little would be salvaged. A repetition of the 1933 experience was made impossible by the passage of the Federal Deposit Insurance law.

The closing of the banks, added to increasing unemployment, created a situation in 1933 that made it impossible for local com-

[5] Annual *Report* of State Banking Commissioner (1949), p. 10.

munities even with state aid to continue to meet the needs for relief. President Roosevelt, unlike President Hoover, did not hesitate to involve the federal government in providing relief to people in need. The Federal Emergency Relief Administration was set up under an act passed by Congress March 22, 1933. A federal relief administrator was appointed for each county, and the costs were borne by the federal and state governments, townships and cities being relieved of the burden. After 1935 the federal government withdrew from direct relief, and in 1939 the Michigan legislature passed an act that gave each county the responsibility for establishing a department of social welfare. Costs were shared by the state and the counties, but the policies governing direct relief were determined by each county.

Meanwhile, through a wide variety of means, efforts were made to reduce the number of persons on direct relief. The federal government sought to provide work for those needing help. The Civil Works Administration in 1933 and 1934 and, after 1935, the Works Progress Administration made funds available so that workers could be employed on public projects such as building parks, installing sewers, and a variety of other activities. The W.P.A. had projects for white-collar workers, including artists and writers as well as unskilled laborers. The Public Works Administration made federal aid available for major projects such as public buildings. The Civilian Conservation Corps gave unemployed youth an opportunity to do useful work such as reforestation in return for food, lodging, and a small stipend. The National Youth Administration enabled many students to remain in college through payments by the federal government to the colleges for the employment of students. These programs reduced the number of persons on direct relief.

On July 7, 1933 a state law providing old age assistance was approved by Governor Comstock. Later, Congress made federal assistance available for this program, and in 1937 the state law was amended to bring it into conformity with the federal system. In each county a Bureau of Social Aid was established to dispense regular payments to needy citizens over the age of 65 who had been residents of the state at least five years. In addition to old-age assistance, the Bureau of Social Aid in each county grants aid to dependent children and to the blind. This program is financed by state and federal funds.

In 1936 the legislature of Michigan set up an Employment Security Commission, which was given the duty of operating a state employment service and superintending the payment of unemployment-insurance benefits. A fund was to be built up through contributions from employers so that unemployed workers, for a limited time, could secure unemployment compensation. This made Michigan eligible for federal benefits under the Social Security Act passed by Congress in 1935. This act also provided for payments from employers and employees to provide payments to retired workers.

By 1939, therefore, an entire new concept of social welfare had taken form. The temporarily unemployed person could draw unemployment-compensation benefits. He could use the state employment service to find other work. If injured on the job, he was covered by Workmen's compensation, an obligation of his employer. After retirement, if he came under the social-security law, he could draw regular payments for the rest of his life. If he were not under social security and were in need, he could receive old-age assistance. The federal and state governments provided aid for dependent children and the blind. And finally, there was direct relief, financed by state and county funds. Under the Social Welfare Act of 1939, the State Department of Social Welfare co-ordinated and administered a large part of this program. In 1960 medical assistance for the aged was provided. Some comprehension of the extent of these programs may be gained by noting these facts: (1) An average of 54,667 Michigan citizens received old-age assistance between 1960 and 1962; (2) in the same period there was an average of 31,763 recipients of aid to dependent children and 1,719 who received aid to the blind; (3) aid to the disabled, authorized by a 1951 law, was received by an average of 5,701 persons during the 1960-62 period; (4) a total of 13,585 different persons received medical assistance for the aged from July 1, 1961 to June 30, 1962; (5) direct relief during the year 1961-62 was provided for an average of 147,998 persons; (6) in 1960-61 the total amount of federal and state funds paid through the Michigan Social Welfare Commission was $136,000,-000, while counties dispensed an additional $46,000,000.[6]

RECREATION, HEALTH, AND SOCIAL AGENCIES

Charity is one of the cardinal Christian virtues, sometimes viewed as a means to salvation, but in more recent years regarded as a social responsibility. The word "charity" tended to disappear as the idea gained acceptance that the support of agencies dedicated to social betterment was a civic obligation. The number of such agencies proliferated during the first half of the twentieth

[6] Twelfth biennial *Report* of the Michigan Social Welfare Commission.

century until they became so numerous that few citizens could comprehend the scope of their activities.

The Boy Scout movement, originating in England in 1908, reached Michigan about 1910. The first Boy Scout Councils, formed in 1911 and 1912, were centered at Grand Rapids, Flint, and Lansing. Troops were organized rapidly; business and professional men volunteered as troop leaders, while churches and schools co-operated fully. The movement helped to bring about a rebirth of interest in out-of-doors activities, but its cardinal purpose was to build good citizens. The Girl Scouts formed their first Michigan troop at Detroit in 1916; by 1938 there were 617 troops in the state. About 1920 the first group of Camp Fire Girls was formed at Grand Rapids, and this organization also grew rapidly. The Young Men's Christian Association is somewhat older. A "young men's society" organized in Detroit prior to the Civil War was the predecessor of the Detroit Y.M.C.A. When the first state convention was held in 1868, some fifteen associations sent delegates. But the greatest growth came after 1900. Activities expanded along several lines. Athletic activities were important from the first; the Y.M.C.A. pioneered in the introduction of basketball. As early as 1903 the Jackson and Grand Rapids associations were operating boys' camps. Camp Hayowent-ha, built on Torch Lake north of Traverse City, and opened in 1904, is reputed to be the first permanent boys' camp in the western states. The camp movement grew by leaps and bounds after World War I, with many different organizations sponsoring summer camps for boys and girls. The first Y.W.C.A. was organized in 1885 at Kalamazoo. Through a program of physical training, education, and social activities the Y.W.C.A. sought to provide a wholesome center for the use of young women employed away from home. By 1934 a total of 17 cities had Y.W.C.A. associations in Michigan.

These were but a few of many social agencies that grew up in cities and even in smaller communities during the first two decades of the twentieth century. Others came later. Many of them sought to obtain funds for buildings and for operation expenses by annual "drives." By the time of World War I the number of drives for funds to support social agencies had become so great that some sort of co-operative effort to raise money was clearly called for. Combined drives were held in Grand Rapids and Detroit in 1917 to support war relief agencies as well as local agencies. The "community chest" plan was adopted by most major Michigan cities between 1917 and 1922. It soon became the accepted way to raise funds to carry on the work of such organizations as the Boy Scouts, Girl Scouts, Y.M.C.A., Y.W.C.A., Salvation Army, orphanages, homes for the aged, child-welfare clinics, and a variety of other agencies.

A number of these, like the Y.M.C.A., belonged to national associations but all of them had their local programs. During the period from 1920 to 1950, however, many state and national agencies which did not have local branches were formed for research and educational purposes. National and state organizations concerned with research into the causes, treatment, and public information concerning almost every major type of human illness were organized. In addition a host of recreation and welfare agencies came into being. All sought public support. Some were worthy while others were proved to be promotion schemes that profited mainly their sponsors. In 1948 Henry Ford II, bombarded as were other prominent and wealthy citizens by hundreds of appeals from these groups, proposed a state organization to investigate the worthiness of each agency, to decide what share of its budget Michigan should pay, and what portion of that figure should be raised in each community. As a result of this, the Michigan United Fund came into being. By 1962 it embraced some 36 agencies. In most Michigan communities the annual fall drive for funds included both the local community chest and Michigan United Fund. The Red Cross, after being included in the early community-chest drives, withdrew for a number of years, and later, in most communities, rejoined the federated drive. But some organizations such as the American Cancer Society, the "March of Dimes," and the Michigan Tuberculosis Society continued to conduct their own campaigns for funds.

With the vast expansion of public agencies for welfare and relief in the 1930s, private agencies turned more and more to programs not directly related to the relief of poverty. The organizations they sponsored became in reality service agencies rather than agencies for helping the needy. As cities grew and as more work became routine or sedentary, greater need was felt for recreation facilities. A group of women in Detroit put into operation the first supervised playground in Michigan in 1901. The movement became so popular that in 1919 a $10,000,000 bond issue was authorized by Detroit voters for parks and playgrounds. Grand Rapids began playground programs in 1902, and other cities soon followed. Started by private initiative and financed by private donors in its early days, the playground and recreation movement soon was accepted by cities as a municipal responsibility. By 1922 there were supervised playground projects in nineteen Michigan cities. A decade later the number had increased to forty. Parks were equipped with picnic tables, bathing beaches were opened, baseball diamonds, golf courses, and tennis courts for public use were laid out, while high schools and colleges built stadiums and gymnasiums to accommodate thousands of spectators.

Recreational facilities were designed not only for the use of Michigan citizens, but also for the tourists and vacationists who contributed increasingly to the state's economy, particularly in the northland. The State Conservation Department, formed in 1921 by combining a number of different agencies, took a leading

STATE
INSTITUTIONS

☀	State Capital
✚	State Hospitals
⊤	Tuberculosis Sanitaria
■	Institution for Epileptics
▲	State Schools
C	Correctional Institutions
E	State Supported Colleges & University

10 5 0 10 20 30 40 50 Miles

role in providing parks, public fishing sites, and other recreational facilities. Research, education, and legislation were sponsored by the Department and by the many conservation clubs in Michigan to make for better fishing and hunting. A State Park Commission formed in 1919 had acquired about a dozen small areas when it was integrated into the Conservation Department in 1921. By 1962 there were 65 state parks and fifteen state recreation areas. A total of more than 19,000,000 people used the state parks in 1960. In addition many counties and townships as well as cities provided parks, public beaches, and recreation areas.

The great increase in the number of private and public associations and agencies involved in health, welfare, and recreation programs is one of the most striking and significant developments of the twentieth century. No longer was the individual family dependent on its own resources when disease struck, when misfortune befell its members, or when it sought recreation. It could turn to any one of hundreds of public and private sources for help, services, and facilities. To a considerable extent all this was the consequence of a greater social consciousness, and the growing acceptance of the principle that a prosperous society, with an economy of abundance, should see to it that the good things of life are made available to the poor as well as the rich. The continuation of private association as a means of meeting health, welfare, and recreation needs is significant. It was an indication that the genius for voluntary association to accomplish that which is beyond the power of the individual to do for himself was still in a healthy state.

THE STATUS OF WOMEN

No social change in the period from 1860 to 1960 was more profound or perhaps less recognized in historical accounts of the period than the change in the status of women. It was the battle for the ballot waged by the suffragettes that attracted the greatest amount of attention. Yet the winning of political rights was perhaps the least important of all the gains made by women in the century. It only symbolized a changing status that had many other ramifications.

First came the battle for legal rights. At the time of the Civil War the legal position of women in Michigan, as in most other states, was essentially in conformity with the English common law. A woman lived under the tutelage of her father until she married; thereafter, under her husband's. Spinsters could not even control their own property. The legislature of New York took the lead in removing many of these disabilities by an act passed in 1860. Other states, including Michigan, followed suit during the next few years. By 1893 the joint signature of a husband and wife were required in the sale of a homestead; a widow was given a claim to a share of her husband's property, which formerly had gone entirely to his children. But the husband could still seize any of his wife's earnings outside the home. A few years later the legislature also abolished this restriction.

Along with the struggle for legal rights came the quest for equal educational opportunity. Boys and girls attended elementary schools together, but prior to the Civil War few girls went beyond the primary grades. Those who did usually attended "female seminaries" where courses such as sewing, literature, French, and etiquette were offered. The first college in America to grant an academic degree to a woman was Oberlin, which admitted women to its college courses in 1837. Michigan Central College (predecessor of Hillsdale College) granted in 1850 the first academic degree conferred upon a woman in Michigan. Until after the Civil War several colleges maintained separate "female departments" or "female colleges." In 1855 there was agitation for Michigan to establish a public college for women. One of the leaders in this movement was Miss Abigail Rogers, who started Michigan Female College in Lansing, hoping it would be taken over by the state. Another woman prominent in the movement to make higher education available to women was Mrs. Lucinda Hinsdale Stone, wife of the president of Kalamazoo College and head of the "Female College" conducted in connection with Kalamazoo College. It was at her urging that the Rev. George Willard, Episcopal rector in Kalamazoo and regent of the University of Michigan, took the lead in persuading the regents to allow women to be admitted to the University. Miss Madelon Stockwell of Kalamazoo in 1870 became the first woman to be admitted. The colleges in the state quickly followed the University in admitting women to full collegiate status.[7]

Along with legal rights and educational opportunity, women won opportunity for economic independence. School teaching and domestic labor were the chief occupations by which women could earn a living in 1860. So long as women were dependent upon men for a livelihood real emancipation was impossible. The invention of the typewriter opened a new field for the employment of women. Typewriters came into general use about 1890. The telephone exchanges that were being established offered further opportunities. In factories and even on farms toil was lightened

[7] W. F. Dunbar, *The Michigan Record in Higher Education*, pp. 97-103.

by new machines that could be operated by women. As American doughboys marched off to war in 1917 their places in offices, factories, and farms were taken by women. By 1920 it was possible for any woman with reasonable ambition and industry to earn her living. In 1960 almost 27% of the labor force in Wayne County consisted of women.[8]

On the political front the first wedge was an act of 1867 that permitted women taxpayers to vote in school elections. In 1881 women who were parents or guardians of school children were granted the same right. In 1870 the Michigan Suffrage Association was formed, but a proposal in 1874 to amend the constitution to give a woman the ballot was overwhelmingly defeated by the voting males. Nevertheless, two women managed to vote in 1871: Miss Mary Wilson in Battle Creek and Mrs. Nannette B. Gardner in Detroit. Mrs. Gardner, a wealthy widow, persuaded the officials to permit her to register because she had no husband to protect her interests, and thereafter she was allowed to vote.[9] The Michigan Equal Suffrage Association, organized in 1884, continued the battle for the ballot until final victory was achieved. But it was a long pull. A law enacted in 1893 enabling women to vote in municipal elections was declared unconstitutional by the supreme court. In the constitutional convention of 1907-1908 hearings were held and there were hot debates over the question of women's suffrage, but in the end the delegates defeated by a margin of 57 to 38 a proposal to incorporate in the new constitution a provision allowing women to vote. A compromise was adopted, allowing women taxpayers to vote on issues involving the expenditure of public money.

During the next decade one of the chief subjects of discussion throughout the state was women's suffrage. The Progressive Party in 1912 endorsed it, as did Governor Chase Osborn. A proposed amendment permitting women to vote was turned down by a slender margin in the April, 1913 election. Though endorsed by many civic organizations, the proposal was fought by the Michigan Association Opposed to Equal Suffrage, composed of both men and women. Active in the forces fighting against women's suffrage were the liquor interests, which feared that if women secured the right to vote, prohibition would be adopted. But many citizens opposed to the change were impelled by loftier motives. The venerable Cardinal Gibbons stated that woman suffrage "will tend to increase the searing social evil, divorce," and he opined further that it would "bring about moral looseness, dis-

[8] *Michigan Statistical Abstract* (1960), p. 59.
[9] F. C. Bald, *Michigan in Four Centuries*, p. 316.

cord, and dishonor in the sacred family circle."[10] But the mood of the time was favorable to reform. Furthermore, the work of women in helping to achieve victory in World War I gave the movement impetus. An amendment to the state constitution providing for women's suffrage with certain limitations was passed in 1918. Following the adoption of the nineteenth amendment to the Constitution of the United States in 1920, the state constitution was further amended to sweep away all political disabilities of women.

During the 1920s ancient taboos, restrictions, and prejudices that hampered women and denied them equal rights with men were vigorously attacked. The older generation was shocked by the "revolt of youth." Women bobbed their hair, shortened their skirts, and smoked cigarettes. Frankness in the discussion of sex dealt Victorian prudery a death blow. There can be little doubt that moral standards reached a low point in the 1920s, yet the situation was never so bad as the elders imagined. The era of "whoopie" came to an abrupt end with the Great Depression, and the excesses of the 1920s were but a memory. What endured was the emancipation of women from many foolish and outmoded restraints that custom and tradition had thrust upon them.

Another phase of the emancipation of women has been the modification of the divorce laws to make separation easier in the case of unhappy marriages. The divorce rate nationally rose from 1.6 per 1,000 population in 1920 to 2.0 in 1940. Since then it has been fairly stable, except for an increase in the years immediately after World War II. In 1959 the rate in Michigan was 2.0, as compared with a national average of 2.2.

PROHIBITION

Prohibition, like women's suffrage, came in part out of the idealism of World War I. The temperance cause in 1917 was almost a century old. As a result of the temperance crusade of the 1840s and 1850s a state prohibition law was passed in 1855. It was never completely effective, especially in the cities. The legislature backtracked as early as 1861 by permitting the manufacture and sale of wines and beer not to be drunk on the premises. In Detroit liquor of all sorts was openly sold, and in 1875 the prohibition act was altogether repealed.

There followed a long battle by the temperance forces against John Barleycorn. It took different forms. The Prohibition Party,

[10] Quoted in K. Fox, "The Movement for Equal Suffrage in Michigan," *Michigan History,* II (1918), 90-109.

formed in 1869, was made up of crusaders rather than practical politicians. It helped to spread propaganda, but accomplished little else. John Russell, one of the party's founders, was a Michigan temperance leader. More effective than the Prohibition Party was the Women's Christian Temperance Union, the members of which, distinguished by white ribbons, labored in season and out against the evils of the liquor traffic. The most powerful temperance organization, however, was the Anti-Saloon League, the Michigan branch of which was organized in 1896. Working largely through the churches, this group carried on a vigorous campaign against liquor through lectures, printed materials, and temperance meetings. It supported candidates for public office who favored prohibition, regardless of party. The League swung a large bloc of votes and politicians came to respect its power.

As has been noted earlier, license fees levied on manufacturers and vendors of liquor came to constitute a major source of state revenue. But they did little to discourage the business. An 1877 law required saloons to close on election days and prohibited sales to Indians and minors. Any county was empowered to prohibit the sale of liquor within its boundaries, upon approval of the voters, under a "local option" law passed by the legislature in 1887. Van Buren was the first county to "go dry"; others followed suit, then repented, and only Van Buren remained in the "dry column" by 1907. It had become apparent that there was too much seepage across county lines for local option to be effective. The Anti-Saloon League now concentrated on state-wide prohibition as its objective. In 1916 state voters endorsed a state prohibition amendment by a substantial majority. Although Detroit and some other major cities voted "wet," there were enough "dry" votes, combined with the overwhelming majorities for prohibition in the rural counties, to spell victory. Michigan became dry on May 1, 1918, over a year before the eighteenth amendment providing for national prohibition became effective.

The temperance forces joyfully proclaimed that John Barleycorn was dead and buried, but this proved to be a mistaken notion. Under the illusion that the battle had been won, the ill effects of alcohol were no longer taught in church and school, and a new generation of youngsters grew up unacquainted with the evils of alcoholism that had been so widely taught in earlier years. In thousands of homes, beer, wine, and assorted forms of home brew were concocted. "Blind pigs" and "speakeasies" dispensed liquor in the cities and even in the smaller towns. Detroit became a center for the smuggling of liquor from Canada into the United States across the Detroit River. Hoodlums and gangsters thrived on the business. Trucks transported cargoes of liquor from secluded boathouses along the Detroit River to various points in the Middle West. Sometimes rival gangs "hijacked" such cargoes. And this, of course, contributed to the crime wave of the 1920s.[11] All this brought about criticism of prohibition and demands for repeal. When the depression struck after 1929 and tax delinquencies grew, there was growing sentiment for legalizing liquor so that the state could collect taxes on it. In 1932 the voters overwhelmingly approved the repeal of the state prohibition amendment, and on April 10, 1933 a state convention chosen to pass upon the twenty-first amendment to the United States Constitution, which repealed the eighteenth amendment, voted 99-1 for approval. The era of prohibition was over.

Regulation of the liquor traffic and the power to license vendors in Michigan was entrusted to a Liquor Control Commission created in 1933. The oldtime saloon never returned in precisely the same form, and cities retained the right to prohibit the sale of liquor by the glass. More and more, addiction to liquor came to be regarded as a disease. In 1951 the legislature created the State Board of Alcoholism to promote programs and conduct studies in this field. Perhaps the most effective agency for combatting alcoholism as a disease was Alcoholics Anonymous, which established branches throughout the state to assist persons trying to break the habit of overindulgence. The Prohibition Party continued to put candidates for public office on the ballot with the forlorn hope of restoring prohibition, but they received little support. One of the major concerns was the part played by drinking in automobile accidents, and many civic organizations joined to urge citizens not to drink if they had to drive a car afterward. Several Michigan cities still prohibited the sale of liquor by the glass in 1960, but the number was diminishing. For the most part, education on the evils of overindulgence was relied on to prevent addiction.

SOCIAL CONSCIOUSNESS AND WAR

Except for the fighting on the western plains to subdue the Indians, the wars in which the United States has participated since 1865 have been conceived as humanitarian crusades. The Spanish War of 1898 was caused in large measure by the resentment of Americans against atrocities committed in Cuba by the Spanish authorities. American entrance into World War I grew out of the revulsion of the people against German atrocities in Bel-

[11] F. C. Bald, *op. cit.,* pp. 383-85.

gium, the loss of lives through unrestricted use of submarines by the Germans, and the growing conviction that German militarism constituted a menace to the whole world. The Second World War engulfed the United States when the Japanese attacked Pearl Harbor in 1941, but the brutality and threat to freedom posed by the Axis powers already had conditioned Americans for war. Both in 1917 and in 1941 Americans believed their own security and independence were threatened, and hence it was not idealism alone that brought about American participation. Yet it is signficant that the United States entered none of these wars with any aspirations for territorial gains. Essentially they were, at least in the minds of most Americans, crusades for a humanitarian cause.

In 1898 war was glamorous, especially to the young men who, as small boys, had listened enviously to the stories of gallantry and adventure recounted by their fathers and grandfathers who had fought in the Civil War. But the men who made up the four regiments that Michigan contributed to the Spanish War found the experience anything but glamorous. One regiment did not reach Cuba at all. The others participated in the brief campaign, but there was little glory in it. Not enemy bullets, but typhoid fever and yellow fever caused most of the casualties. Poorly equipped and inadequately provided for, the soldiers found army life quite different from what they had imagined. A few hundred Michigan guardsmen were enlisted in the navy, and the state was represented in the forces that were sent after the war to suppress the Filipino insurrection.

The war was over quickly and its effects on civilian life were almost nil. Cuba, freed from Spanish rule, became nominally independent, although it was virtually a protectorate of the United States until 1934. Michigan men, along with other soldiers, helped to suppress the Filipinos under Aguinaldo, who wanted immediate independence for their country. The American rule that was established over them and the military interventions in Latin America that followed in the early twentieth century were jusified as being America's share in bearing the white man's burden. The very fact that Americans needed some moral justification for extending national boundaries is evidence of social consciousness.

When Woodrow Wilson became President he introduced moral principles as a guideline in foreign policy. He refused to recognize Victoriano Huerta as President of Mexico because the latter attained his position through assassination and without popular consent. When war broke out in Europe Wilson at first called for strict neutrality but as the fighting continued and increased in fury, and as American lives were lost through submarine attacks on merchant ships, the President once more began to think of American foreign policy in terms of right and wrong. The stories of German atrocities in Belgium as well as the sinking of the *Lusitania* and other ships carrying American passengers aroused a feeling of moral indignation in the popular mind. No one can say how much this had to do with the final involvement of the United States in World War I, but that it was a potent factor cannot be denied. And it is notable that when President Wilson called on Congress on April 6, 1917 to declare war against Germany he disavowed any desire on the part of this nation for conquest or aggrandizement. He called it a war to end war, a war to save the world for democracy, and his appeal thrilled the American people and helped make the war a crusade for right and justice.

During the nineteen months that elapsed between April 7, 1917, when Congress declared war, and November 11, 1918, when the armistice was signed, there was hardly a man, woman, or child in the nation not affected in some way by the war. In Michigan a total of 873,383 men were registered for military service under the selective service acts, and 135,485 were inducted into the armed services. Some 5,000 Michigan men were killed in battle or died of disease while in the service, and 15,000 were wounded. But the war touched civilians as well as soldiers. America was called on to provide food for the allied armies and everyone was urged to produce and conserve foodstuffs. There were four "Liberty Loan" drives during the war and a "Victory Loan" drive after the armistice; it was estimated that one out of every four persons in the state bought "Liberty Bonds" or "Liberty Stamps." The Red Cross, the Y.M.C.A., the Knights of Columbus, the Salvation Army, and many other American and foreign war-relief agencies sought and received financial contributions. Even before war was declared, a War Preparedness Board had been created by the legislature, and it had a major role in food production and conservation. Food was not rationed, as it was later in World War II, the government relying on voluntary observance of "meatless days" and "wheatless days" to save food. "Four-minute men" gave talks in churches and theaters to sell Liberty Bonds and volunteer workers collected funds for a wide variety of war work.

There was dedication to the achievement of victory in what was regarded as almost a holy cause. By common consent political parties united behind the war effort. Mixed with wartime idealism, however, was hatred of the enemy and the evil he was purported to represent, and this gave rise to many absurdities that in retrospect seem tragic. Weird stories were circulated about the activities of German sympathizers, causing thousands of loyal German-Americans to become suspect. The automotive industry had attracted many foreign peoples to Michigan; at the time of the war there were some 80,000 Germans and 20,000 Austrians in the state. Though most of them were thoroughly loyal to their adopted country, fantastic stories went the rounds about their doings. Housewives heard the rumor that enemy aliens were putting ground glass in the sugar supplies. One old German who had built a high tower overlooking Lake Michigan was reputed to have a wireless set used to relay messages back and forth between the Fatherland and Mexico. It became unpopular to play German music and the teaching of German in high schools and colleges was abandoned, French and Spanish taking its place. Hamburger became "liberty sausage" or "salisbury steak," while frankfurters became "hot dogs" because Hamburg and Frankfurt were names of German cities. The little town of Berlin near Grand Rapids changed its name to Marne, although the annual fair held in the town continued to be called the "Berlin Fair." Those who failed to buy Liberty Bonds or support war drives of other kinds frequently had their houses smeared with yellow paint. Such activities set the pattern for the revival of the Ku Klux Klan after the war.

Fort Custer, near Battle Creek, had its origin in World War I, when it was called Camp Custer. It was one of 32 cantonments established in 1917 to receive enlisted and drafted men for training. Through the work of the Battle Creek Chamber of Commerce about 8,000 acres of land were acquired and leased to the government. Construction of buildings, mostly wooden, began on July 15, 1917, and the first selectee entered the camp on September 5. An extension of the Camp started in the summer of 1918 was not completed until after the armistice. Three thousand buildings were hastily erected; most of them were dismantled after the war. The first military air base in Michigan was established near Mount Clemens in 1917 and named in honor of Lieutenant Thomas E. Selfridge. In addition to being the reason for the origin of these two important military installations, World War I had other lasting effects on Michigan. The fact that two-fifths of the men examined for military service during the war were adjudged physically unfit was a major reason for the adoption of required physical-education courses in schools and colleges. The necessity for conserving fuel gave rise to the adoption of "daylight-saving time" during the war. Michigan, which up to then had set its clocks by Central Standard Time, eventually made Eastern Standard Time official. The Michigan State Police had its origin in World War I.

Soldier and civilian alike fell victim to the terrible epidemic of Spanish influenza that swept the country in the fall and winter of 1917-18. At Camp Custer some 10,000 patients were admitted to the camp hospital, most of them suffering from influenza; some 2,000 of these developed pneumonia and 674 died. In cities and rural areas the civilian population was stricken. Schools, theaters, and churches were closed. At the University of Michigan 57 men enrolled in the Student Army Training Corps died of influenza.[12]

The National Guard units of Michigan and Wisconsin were combined to make up the Thirty-Second or "Red Arrow" Division. These men had a taste of military campaigning in 1916 as members of the American expeditionary force that invaded Mexico in pursuit of the bandit Pancho Villa. The division was trained for service in World War I at Waco, Texas, and was sent to France in the first three months of 1918. From May 18 to the armistice it was almost constantly under fire, participating in the Battle of the Aisne, the Oise-Aisne offensive, and the Meuse-Argonne action. Casualties were heavy, and many of the officers and men were decorated for heroism by the American and foreign governments. The Eighty-fifth Division, made up largely of Michigan and Wisconsin men, arrived in France early in August, 1918. Part of this division was sent to Archangel, Russia, in the allied campaign against the Communist government that had made a separate peace with Germany. The purpose of the expedition was to bring Russia back into the war. Known as the "polar bears," these men were not brought home until the autumn of 1919. Many Michigan men also served in the famous Forty-second, or "Rainbow" Division.[13]

The aftermath of World War I is a tragic story. The idealism of Woodrow Wilson had caught the imagination of the American people; they believed they were fighting for a lofty and noble cause, that this was a war to end war, a war to make the world safe for democracy. This high idealism was shattered by the events of the postwar period. After protracted bickering at the Paris Peace Conference, Wilson was forced to compromise his

[12] A. A. Hoehling, *The Great Epidemic.*
[13] C. Lumdrum (comp.), *Michigan in the World War: Military and Naval Honors of Michigan Men and Women;* G. Fuller (ed.), *Historic Michigan,* II, 949-962. Vols. II, III, and IV of *Michigan History* contain numerous articles on Michigan during World War I.

principles and ideals in order to get the allied statesmen to approve the covenant of the League of Nations, a world organization on which Wilson pinned all his hopes for justice and a lasting peace. By the time Wilson finally brought home the Treaty of Versailles containing the League covenant the idealism of wartime had largely disappeared, and partisan rivalry, which had been suspended during the war, was back with a vengeance. The Treaty and the League met strong opposition in the Senate, to which Wilson submitted them for approval. Some senators were honestly convinced that the United States should return to its traditional isolationist policy; others opposed the League because of personal antagonism toward Wilson or because they saw in it an opportunity for partisan advantage. Opponents of the President insisted on extended hearings, and while these were in progress the country was flooded by propaganda against the Treaty and the League, some of which was false and misleading. In the end, however, the defeat of the Treaty and the League was due to Wilson's stubborn refusal to accept any reservations. Congress brought the great crusade to an inglorious close by passing a simple resolution declaring the war against Germany and her allies at an end.

To the American people it was clear that the war had not saved the world for democracy, for in Russia a communist dictatorship ruled, and it was obvious that many democratic governments were unstable. National rivalries seemed to have been intensified rather than diminished by the war, and there were several minor conflicts, such as that between Russia and Poland, that demonstrated that the "war to end war" had not, in fact, ended war at all. The veterans of World War I seemed unconcerned about the loss of the fruits of their victory; the new veterans' organizations stressed nationalism rather than internationalism.[14] And their view seemed to be that of the nation. The intolerance generated by the hatred of the Germans during the war was now manifest in the arrest and deportation of people suspected of being sympathetic toward communism. The Ku Klux Klan was revived with the avowed purpose of promoting

[14] The Michigan Department of the American Legion received its charter August 1, 1920. Much of the effort of the Legion was directed to the relief of the disabled; the first tuberculosis hospital to be operated by the American Legion for treatment of servicemen was built by the Michigan Department at Fort Custer and was dedicated November 7, 1921, by Marshal Ferdinand Foch. See E. L. Carlson, "The American Legion in Michigan," *Michigan History,* XXIII (1939), 15-21. By 1938 the Legion had 347 posts with a membership of 30,275 in Michigan.

"100% Americanism," and it helped spread rumor and suspicion against Jews, Catholics, Negroes, and foreigners. In Michigan as well as in other northern states the Klan became so strong in the 1920s that it threatened to become a potent political force. Meanwhile, the progressive movement, which had brought so many reforms in the decade before World War I, came to an abrupt end, and one of these reforms, prohibition, was so far from being successful that it contributed to the disillusionment of the time.

Even during the 1920s, however, there were signs that social consciousness had not entirely disappeared. Some measure of naval disarmament was achieved at the Washington Disarmament Conference in 1921, and at the end of the decade a treaty designed to "outlaw war" was approved. Americans responded generously to the needs of the Japanese following the great earthquake of 1926. It was a great period of school construction, and social agencies continued to grow.

The domestic problems brought to the fore by the Great Depression tended to obscure the international scene for most Americans. They had come to accept the theory that American participation in World War I had been a great mistake, and that the nation had been dragged into the war by British propaganda, by the munition makers, and by bankers who wanted to secure the loans they had made to the allies. War was pictured as both horrible and futile. College youth took oaths never to fight in another war. But along with this pacifism was a general revulsion against the atrocities the Japanese army committed in China, Hitler's persecution of the Jews, and the "purges" in Soviet Russia. Congress passed a series of acts, however, designed to keep this nation out of any future war. After World War II began in 1939 Americans continued to hope their country could stay out of it, though many were convinced that eventual involvement of the United States was inevitable. This proved true when the Japanese attacked Pearl Harbor on December 7, 1941, leaving the United States no alternative but to take up arms against the Axis powers.

World War II was a different sort of war than that of 1914-1918 in many respects. The lofty idealism that had so inspired the American people in 1917-18 was almost totally absent. In its place was a kind of hard-headed realism that accepted the war as necessary to save the United States from the Axis aggressors. But while the conflict was still in progress, churches and other organizations urged that plans be laid for a just peace and a world organization to maintain it. Senator Arthur Vandenberg of Michigan, who had been a leading champion of isolationism for many years, became convinced that the United States must continue to play a role in world affairs after the war was over. Through his efforts and those of Secretary of State Cordell Hull, the idea of a bipartisan foreign policy became a reality.[15]

The signal contribution Michigan made to the winning of World War II through the production of war materials has been described earlier. A total of 613,542 Michiganians served in the armed forces during World War II. The Thirty-second Division, which had won the name "Red Arrow" for its drives through the German lines in World War I, fought in the South Pacific during World War II with great valor, and received the special commendation of General Douglas MacArthur. Most of the men who served in the armed forces in World War II passed through the draft boards that were set up in every community.

There was a great influx of people into Michigan to work in the war plants, beginning the population bulge that continued during the 1940s and 1950s. Even more than World War I, World War II was a total war, and sacrifices were required of every citizen. Food, gasoline, and tires were rationed; new cars were unavailable. Those who stayed at home cultivated victory gardens, bought war bonds, and subscribed to war-relief agencies. Army, navy, and air-corps units were assigned to the different colleges and universities in the state for training. Boys and girls collected scrap metal and milkweed pods, the floss from which was used to fill life jackets. And families gathered around the radio each evening to hear the latest war news and its interpretation by commentators and analysts.

Spontaneous celebrations throughout the state marked the end of the war on August 14, 1945. Men, women, and children flocked to the downtown sections of the cities to cheer and shout. Half a million people jammed downtown Detroit and a hundred thousand converged on Campau Square in Grand Rapids. But mixed with the festive spirit was no such feeling as had existed in 1918 that victory would assure a lasting peace or that the war had been a triumph for democracy. The United States and other free countries had been in dire danger in 1941, and the war had been fought against what at first were heavy odds. Victory had been hard-won, and though it was obvious that troubles lay ahead the nation was, for the time being, secure.

[15] A. H. Vandenberg, Jr., *The Private Papers of Senator Vandenberg.*

SOCIAL CONSCIOUSNESS AND EQUAL RIGHTS

In the period since World War II there have been many manifestations of social consciousness in Michigan. There was a vast expansion in the number of social agencies, both public and private. Chapters of the American Association for United Nations were established in the principal cities. Numerous organizations were formed to promote the travel of Americans abroad and the reception of foreign visitors. But in no field was social consciousness more marked than in race relations. The many Negro servicemen in World War II and the excellent record they made gave rise to the feeling after the war that if they were called upon to fight for their country they should enjoy equal rights in peacetime. The outstanding performance of Negro athletes in amateur and professional sports was another factor in promoting the cause of minority rights. The racism preached by Hitler created a revulsion against racial prejudice here in the United States. And finally the cold war, which involved a contest for the neutralist nations and their peoples between East and West, and the fact that many of these neutralist nations had non-white populations, was an influence that propelled the United States to the necessity of squaring practice with theory in the matter of minority rights.

The large influx of Negroes from the South to work in war-production plants continued after the war as civilian production was resumed. And still more jobs became available when the nation began its rearmament program in 1950, with large orders for defense materials coming to Michigan. By 1960 the Negro population of Detroit constituted almost 30% of the total, and in other cities in the state there was a large increase. The Negro vote became important in politics, a fact that played no small part in advancing the cause of equal rights. The terrible race riot in Detroit in 1943 had been indicative of what might happen if steps were not taken to ease the tensions that arose as the Negro population grew. Many communities established "Human Relations Councils" and several appointed official Human Rights Commissions.

School segregation, which played such a large role in racial conflict in the South during the years after the United States Supreme Court in 1954 ordered the schools to be desegregated, was not a serious problem in Michigan. But there were other problems of a critical nature. One was housing. In almost every large city the Negro population was housed in "Negro districts" where slum conditions prevailed, and Negroes were prevented from buying or renting homes in other parts of the cities. Another type of discrimination was in public accommodations; Negroes frequently found it difficult or impossible to find hotel rooms or restaurants that would serve them. They were often denied service in barber shops. And finally, there was job discrimination. Regardless of their education and training, few Negroes could find employment except at menial or servile tasks.

Many whites joined Negroes in the fight against these conditions and in the crusade for equal rights. Negroes were employed in greater numbers in shops, in stores, and as teachers, social workers, physicians, nurses, and government workers. After a protracted struggle, the legislature in 1955 passed a law forbidding discrimination in employment and creating the Fair Employment Practices Commission to administer the law.[16] Progress was made, too, in making public accommodations available to Negroes. The most difficult problem was housing. Real-estate brokers and property owners' organizations resisted any effort to eliminate the right to discriminate in the sale of houses. An administrative ruling was made that barred real-estate dealers from practicing discrimination, but this rule was successfully challenged in the courts. Although Governor Romney proposed an "open occupancy" law for the state in 1963, the legislature failed to act. As a result several cities moved towards the adoption of ordinances making it unlawful to discriminate in the sale of real estate.

The new state constitution framed in 1961-62 and adopted by the voters in April, 1963 contained a strong section on civil rights. In fact, proponents of the new constitution claimed that its equal-protection and anti-discrimination provision was the strongest in any state constitution. An eight-member, bipartisan civil-rights commission was provided for and given the duty "to investigate alleged discrimination against any person because of religion, race, color, or national origin in the enjoyment of the civil rights guaranteed by law and by this constitution and to secure the equal protection of such civil rights without any discrimination."[17]

Efforts were made, also, to recast educational materials and procedures to promote the cause of equal rights. In 1963 the Detroit Board of Education provided eighth-grade students with a 52-page booklet entitled *The Struggle for Freedom and Rights* to supplement their history textbooks, which, it was claimed, presented the Negro as a "dependent, servile creature."[18]

[16] Act 25, Public Acts of 1955.
[17] Article V, Section 29.
[18] *Michigan in Books,* Volume V, No. 3 (Winter, 1963), published by the State Library, contains an excellent bibliography on Negro life in Michigan.

Although there was still a long way to go before minority groups in Michigan could enjoy equal rights, great progress was made during the eighteen years following World War II. An aroused social consciousness among the citizens of the state once more was achieving progress toward greater social justice and a more complete realization of the ideals and goals of a democratic America.

Interlochen

24

THE ENRICHMENT OF CULTURAL LIFE

Along with population growth and increasing material wealth,
the century after the Civil War brought an enrichment of cultural life: the life of the mind and the spirit of man. Education
became universal and was extended over a longer span of years.
The proportion of the people belonging to the churches increased
markedly. More people read newspapers, magazines, and books,
while new media of mass communication emerged. The arts, developing slowly at first, flourished to a greater degree as the
twentieth century advanced. Michigan shared in this refinement
of civilized living, and in several ways made unique contributions
to it.

While cultural progress is clear and unmistakable, it would be
unrealistic not to observe that the century also had its seamier
side. The improvement of the standards of taste did not keep
pace with the increase in material wealth, the leisure to create
and enjoy beauty, and the opportunity to cultivate the mind and
the spirit. The *nouveau riche*, in the houses they built, in the art
objects they acquired, and in their mode of living, frequently
demonstrated execrable taste. And in the twentieth century,
when so many more families were enabled to live beyond the
margin of subsistence, there was a flood of cheap and tawdry
gadgets marketed and eagerly purchased. Films were made and
radio and television programs were presented to attract the

699

largest possible mass audience, and the result was vulgar and
mediocre. The "commercial artist" catered to the popular taste.
Newspapers sought larger circulation by featuring sensational
stories and helping make professional spectator sports almost a
mania. But there were evidences in the later years of the century
since the Civil War that the standards of popular taste were
improving. Manufacturers of automobiles and household appliances
were paying more attention to good design, there was a veritable
renaissance in the visual arts, and even the moving pictures were
beginning to reflect a growing popular demand for something
beyond the grandiose, the spectacular, and the eternal triangle.

EDUCATION

From the earliest days Michigan held a position of leadership
in public education in the nation. It utilized the land grants received from the federal government for education more wisely
than did its neighboring states. Michigan's was the first state
constitution to provide for a state superintendent of public instruction. Michigan could boast of the first state agricultural college in the nation and the first teacher-education institution west
of the Alleghenies. The University of Michigan was the first really
successful state university, and it became a model for other state
universities. Alongside the system of public education, private
elementary and secondary schools appeared, many supported by
churches. Independent colleges, also in most cases church-sup-
ported, were established, but they developed more slowly than
in many other states, due to some degree at least to the extraordinary success of the public colleges and the University of
Michigan. In the century that followed the Civil War Michigan
continued to enjoy in some respects a position of leadership in
public education, although this leadership was less marked than
in the earlier period.

By the time of the Civil War a primary school was available to
children in most of the settled parts of the state, although they
often had to go considerable distances to attend it. The Constitution of 1850 had accepted the principle of free schools. By
the time of the Civil War "rate bills" (tuition charges upon
parents) were rapidly disappearing. But it was not until 1869
that the legislature enacted a law requiring all public schools to
be free and open without charge to the pupils of the district in
which they were located. Michigan lagged somewhat behind
Ohio, Illinois, and Indiana in making all of its schools free.

The next advance was the acceptance of compulsory education. Michigan was one of the first states to pass a compulsory-education law. An act of 1871 required all children between the ages of eight and fourteen to attend school at least twelve weeks each year. In 1883, partly due to the work of the Knights of Labor, the term was extended to four months and it became illegal to employ a child until he had attended school the required time. But there was no adequate provision for enforcing these early compulsory-education laws, and they were evaded by many parents. It was not until 1905 that a law required all children between the ages of seven and sixteen to attend for the entire school year and provided for truant officers to enforce the law.

A system of public education beyond the common school and reaching to the college level was clearly envisioned in the act of 1817 establishing the Catholepistemiad or University of Michigania. The first state constitution also implied that Michigan should sustain an entire system of education from the lowest grades to the highest. But there was, nevertheless, a sturdy resistance to the expenditure of tax revenues for the operation of schools beyond the primary grades. While conceding that a common school education for all at public expense was justifiable in a democracy, there were many who asked with regard to schools beyond the elementary level, "Why should I be taxed to educate another man's child?" It should be borne in mind that the University of Michigan, the State Agricultural College, and the State Normal School had all been founded on the basis of federal land grants, and that it was expected that they would be supported and maintained largely from the income derived from these grants.

Secondary education had been provided in territorial times by private academies. In the early days of statehood the branches of the University were designed to serve as secondary schools, but the federal land grant proved inadequate to support both them and the University proper. As a consequence state support was withdrawn and the branches reverted, in most instances, to the status of private academies. Detroit established the first public high school in the state in 1844. Several other cities followed suit in the 1850s. In the cities and larger towns there was a single primary school at first. As the place grew, additional districts and additional one-room schools were established. In the 1850s the legislature permitted the consolidation of the several school districts within a city to form a "Union School District." The one-room schools were abandoned and a single school was built called a "Union School." It now became possible to divide the students into grades, and those of the highest grades constituted the "high school." An act passed by the legislature in 1859 specifically empowered a school district containing more than 200 children to "grade the scholars" and to establish a high school. But in 1873 three citizens of Kalamazoo brought suit to prevent the local school board from levying taxes to support a high school. When the circuit court rejected their plea they appealed to the state supreme court. In 1874 Justice Thomas M. Cooley rendered the unanimous opinion of that court that the Kalamazoo School Board was within its rights in levying a tax to support a high school, pointing out that, beginning with 1817, there was a clear intent on the part of the people of the state to foster a complete system of education. The "Kalamazoo Case" laid the legal foundation for the growth of high schools not only in Michigan but also in other states. Justice Cooley was a jurist with a national reputation, and this gave the opinion weight. The case is cited in every major history of education in America.[1]

Even before the supreme-court decision in the Kalamazoo Case had been rendered the legislature had begun to spend tax revenue for the institutions of higher learning. Modest appropriations had been made to support the Normal School from the beginning, but it was not until 1867 that a definite commitment was made for tax support to the University of Michigan. In that year the legislature passed a law levying a tax of one-twentieth of a mill on all property in the state for the support of the University. As time went on the appropriations for both the University of Michigan and the other public colleges and universities increased. By 1960 higher education took a larger share of the general fund of the state than any other branch of the state government.

In 1860 there were only three state-supported institutions of higher learning, enrolling a few hundred students. By 1960 there were nine state-supported colleges and universities enrolling over 95,000 students; in addition there were sixteen community colleges, enrolling over 27,000 students and supported by both state and local tax funds. The Michigan School of Mines (now Michigan Technological University was established at Houghton in 1885. Three additional normal schools (now regional universities) were established between 1895 and 1903 at Mount Pleasant, Marquette, and Kalamazoo. Wayne University, founded in 1933 by the Detroit Board of Education as a consolidation of several

---

[1] A. P. Nevins, "The Kalamazoo case," *Michigan History,* XLIV (1960), 91-100; W. F. Dunbar, "The High School on Trial: The Kalamazoo Case," *Papers* of the Michigan Academy of Science, Arts, and Letters, XLV (1960), Part II, 187-201.

separate colleges that had developed in Detroit (beginning with a medical school in 1868), was taken over by the state and renamed Wayne State University in 1957. Ferris Institute (now Ferris State College), founded as a private school, became a state-supported institution in 1950. And in 1963 a tenth state-supported, degree-granting college, Grand Valley State College, was opened near Grand Rapids.

The community college movement in Michigan began with the opening of Grand Rapids Junior College in 1914. At first this and other similar colleges offered only the usual college courses of the freshman and sophomore level, but beginning in the 1930s they began to provide "terminal courses" of a vocational and technical nature. At about the same time the legislature authorized broader support for these colleges. Originally they were financed by local school boards and tuition fees. Then, in a series of acts, the legislature permitted several school boards or even an entire county to support a community college, and finally approved multi-county support. State aid to community colleges began in 1947.

One of the other major developments of the century after the Civil War in Michigan education was the introduction of a wide range of vocational and technical courses. Michigan State University was founded in 1855 as a college where students could study agriculture and the mechanical arts. Michigan Technological University, originally the Michigan School of Mines, was created to provide technicians for the state's extensive iron- and copper-mining industries. The Detroit Institute of Technology was founded in 1909, and subsequently the Lawrence Institute of Technology came into being. The needs of the automobile industry for trained technologists were met by the General Motors Institute, which grew out of an automotive trade school started at Flint in 1916, and by Chrysler Institute in Detroit, founded in 1931. The pioneer in the field of business schools and colleges was the one opened by Uriah Gregory in Detroit in 1848. After the Civil War the number of such schools increased rapidly in Detroit and other cities to teach students the skills required in clerical and other business employment. One of the most successful was started in Ypsilanti by Patrick R. Cleary in 1883. Several of the denominational colleges opened "commercial departments" to teach such skills as telegraphy, penmanship, and bookkeeping. Woodbridge N. Ferris, in founding what was first called Ferris Industrial School at Big Rapids, aimed to provide practical courses not taught in the public schools.

Until almost the turn of the century the high schools devoted their entire attention to college-preparatory subjects. One of the pioneers in vocational education in the public schools was Bay City, which taught business, sewing, cooking, carpentry, and wood turning by 1891. Muskegon and Ishpeming provided courses in shopwork, foundry, cooking, sewing, and mechanical drawing by 1896. And by 1900 Ann Arbor, Calumet, Detroit, Flint, Grand Rapids, Menominee, and Saginaw were offering vocational courses in their high schools. Thereafter, more and more schools provided classes in typing, shorthand, manual training, and domestic science. In 1908 North Adams High School in Hillsdale County introduced a full course in agriculture. The Smith-Hughes Act, passed by Congress in 1917, gave a great impetus to vocational education by offering federal aid to schools giving vocational courses. The Michigan legislature at once passed the Tufts Act to meet the federal requirements, and Michigan became one of the first states to qualify. A State Board for Vocational Education was set up to administer the program. By 1950 more than 50,000 students in 334 high schools were taking vocational courses. Since 1921 the state, with federal aid, has also provided an extensive program of vocational rehabilitation for the handicapped.

Another major trend in Michigan education since the Civil War has been a greater equalization of educational opportunity. Until about 1900 the public schools were financed almost wholly by funds raised through local taxes. The school districts of the state varied widely in the value of taxable property per schoolchild, and thus there was a wide gap in the quality of education provided in the richer districts from that available in the poorer ones. The only equalizing factor was the small amount distributed annually from the interest on the primary-school fund, originally derived from the sale of section sixteen in each township reserved for education. After 1901 this fund was substantially increased by becoming the recipient of a tax on railroads imposed as a result of the arduous efforts of Governor Hazen S. Pingree. Subsequently, taxes levied by the state on insurance, express companies, and telephone and telegraph companies were added to the fund. Then, starting in 1907, the legislature made annual appropriations of state aid to the poorer districts. Total state aid in 1928, including the payments from the primary-school-interest fund, amounted to about $28,500,000.

State aid in far larger amounts became necessary as the depression of the early 1930s hit the state. Many citizens could not pay their property taxes, and in 1932 a constitutional amendment was adopted that limited the total tax on real estate and personal property to 15 mills on the assessed valuation. In 1933 the legislature levied a 3% sales tax, and the anticipated revenue from this tax enabled the legislature to step up state appropriations to the schools. Without such aid many schools in the poorer districts would have had to be closed. During the 1940s the costs of operating schools steadily climbed. At the same time the state was accumulating a surplus from sales taxes. This led to the proposal of the sales-tax-diversion amendment in 1946. As adopted by popular vote, it provided that two-thirds of the revenue from the sales tax be returned to local school districts. This provided the schools with ample funds for a few years, but rising costs, including higher teachers' salaries, coupled with a vast influx of students as a consequence of the increased birthrate, again created financial problems for the schools. They sought and obtained appropriations from the legislature beyond the amount earmarked by the sales-tax-diversion amendment. By 1960 state aid amounted to $205 per pupil. Even so, school budgets increased so rapidly that specially voted millage was sought in many districts.

The objective of equalized educational opportunity was the goal not only of state aid to local districts but also of district reorganization. Prior to 1903 farm youth living outside a district supporting a high school were forced to pay tuition in order to get an education beyond the eighth grade. In that year a law was passed that allowed school districts that did not have a high school to levy a tax to pay tuition and transportation of pupils to an approved high school, and in 1909 it became mandatory for a district to do so. Although there were not a few one-room schools where able and devoted teachers gave boys and girls a good primary education, there were many in which teachers were poorly trained and ill-equipped to teach. The advantages of the graded school were obvious. This led to a movement for the consolidation of school districts. As related in an earlier chapter, the number of school districts in the state was reduced by consolidation (or "reorganization" as it came to be called) from 7,333 in 1910 to 2,145 in 1960. A considerable number of districts by 1960, furthermore, maintained no school. Fewer than 1,300 one- or two-room schools were left. And the goal of the department of public instruction was to eliminate all those that did not maintain schools graded from kindergarten through the high school.

Still another trend during the hundred-year period since the Civil War has been better-trained teachers. In 1865 a teacher was considered qualified if he could convince the local school board that he was competent to teach. The State Normal School at Ypsilanti provided training for only a small fraction of the teachers required by the schools of the state. The University of Michigan in 1879 established a professorship in the Science and Art of Teaching, the first American university to do so, and the second in the world. But this innovation helped only to provide a few more well-trained high-school teachers. It did nothing for the elementary teachers. As the demand grew for more trained teachers, the denominational schools and even the business colleges offered "normal courses." In Detroit a normal school to train teachers for the city's schools was opened. And as has been noted, the state founded three schools between 1895 and 1903 to provide a larger number of trained teachers, especially for the elementary schools. Teachers' Institutes were held in Michigan as early as 1846, but were conducted on a voluntary basis for many years. In the 1880s, however, counties, with the help of a small allocation of state funds, provided compensation and expenses for teachers attending the institutes, which afforded a short training course lasting from one to four weeks. In spite of these efforts it was reported in 1903 that only 6% of the teachers in the rural schools had a minimum of one year's training. The new state normal schools and the county normals helped increase this percentage to 36 by 1921. The county normals admitted students who had graduated from the eighth grade and provided them with one year's training, graduating 10,000 between 1903 and 1921. In 1921 the legislature decreed that beginning in 1925 all teachers must have at least one year of professional training. The State Board of Education required two years of training before the life certificate would be granted, and this was raised to three years in 1928. Four years of training were specified for the life certificate in 1932, and eventually the life certificate could be earned only by completing a full college course, teaching successfully for three years, and completing at least ten semester hours of graduate courses.

Educational theory has been in a constant state of flux during the century under review. The theory developed by Friedrich Froebel in Germany that education is the guidance of the development of the child from stage to stage and that the chief agency in that development is spontaneous play activity led to the establishment of kindergartens. The demonstration kindergarten at the Philadelphia Exposition in 1876 attracted widespread attention, and kindergartens were introduced into Michigan schools about this time. By 1900 they had become common. The old injunction that to spare the rod would spoil the child was gradually abandoned, and corporal punishment slowly disappeared from the schools. About the turn of the century the study of

Greek and Latin in schools and colleges suffered a sharp decline as more stress was placed on science, literature, and history. About the same time the need for vocational education attracted widespread attention. In the early years of the twentieth century the ideas of John Dewey began to affect education. Dewey held that the school is an embryonic community and that the mission of the school is to give the child a guided experience in democratic living.[2] "Progressive education," which stemmed in part from Dewey's ideas, enjoyed a great vogue in the 1920s and 1930s. In 1936 the superintendent of public instruction initiated a long-range study of the schools' curriculums. The Michigan Study of the Secondary School Curriculum was begun in 1937, financed in part by foundation funds. These studies resulted in greater emphasis on meeting the needs of individual students, in making the school a center of community life, and in stress upon democratic procedures in the classroom. After World War II educational "progressives" made much of social adjustment as the aim of the schools, and advocated the training of the whole child, rather than purely intellectual development. But the launching of the first Sputnik by the Russians in 1957 had the effect of re-emphasizing rigorous intellectual effort, improving scientific studies, and paying more attention to the gifted child.

The improvement of the status of teachers and the advancement of teaching to the rank of a profession have been another notable development of the century. The Michigan Education Association has been a major factor in this change. Preliminary steps were taken to organize the Association during a teachers' institute held in connection with the dedication of the first normal-school building at Ypsilanti in 1852. Semiannual meetings were held for a number of years. At the meeting held in April, 1854 two notable figures in the history of American education, Horace Mann and Henry Barnard, were present. Some of the reforms advocated in the early days of the M.E.A. were abolition of rate bills, compulsory education, free textbooks, and teachers' institutes. Improvement of salary levels for teachers has been a continuous goal of the organization. In its early years the M.E.A. was largely dominated by the faculty members of the colleges and the normal schools. Feeling that the organization was doing little to advance their interests, teachers lost interest in it. Only 136 out of the 13,000 teachers in the state belonged to it in 1874. A number of reforms were made in that year, but even as late as 1905 the M.E.A. had only 901 members in the entire state. In that year the general meetings of the Association were given

[2] Dewey served on the University of Michigan faculty from 1884 to 1894.

official status as teachers' institutes so that members did not lose pay while attending them. This seems to have been a needed "shot in the arm," and membership soared to an unprecedented 4,488 in 1906. For many years Henry M. Pattengill published his *Moderator Topics*, giving news of Michigan teachers. This was replaced by a quarterly publication in 1919 and by the monthly *Michigan Education Journal* in 1923. By 1921 the Association had grown so large that districts and regions were set up, and in 1922 the first executive secretary, Ernest T. Cameron, was appointed. Growth in membership after 1922 was rapid, and the M.E.A. became a potent pressure group during legislative sessions. By 1951 the Association had a headquarters staff of 22. On February 15, 1963 M.E.A. membership stood at 64,102. The annual budget was in excess of $800,000.[3]

Although Michigan has relied heavily on public schools and institutions of higher learning for the education of its youth, independent and church-related schools and colleges have developed alongside the tax-supported system. The Roman Catholic Church by 1960 had 256 elementary schools and 102 high schools in Michigan, with a total enrollment of 188,959. The Lutheran and Seventh Day Adventists also supported parochial schools, while the members of the Christian Reformed Church established "Christian" elementary and high schools in communities where there were sizable numbers of people of Dutch origin. In 1959, there were 211,277 students enrolled in non-public schools, as compared with 1,548,704 in public schools.[4]

In 1865 there were only five church-related institutions of higher education in Michigan: Kalamazoo, Albion, Olivet, Adrian, and Hillsdale Colleges. By 1963 there were 28 independent colleges and universities, most of them church-related, and six church-related seminaries. The Roman Catholic Church alone had established eight colleges, one university, and four seminaries. The University of Detroit developed from Detroit College, established by the Jesuit order in 1877. The Catholic colleges, except for Aquinas, founded at Grand Rapids in 1931 are colleges for women. They include Madonna (1946), Marygrove (1910), Mercy (1934), Nazareth (1924), and Siena Heights (1919).

[3] J. C. Springman, *The Growth of Public Education in Michigan;* G. L. Jackson, *The Development of State Control of Public Instruction in Michigan.*

[4] Sister M. A. Dalton, "The History and Development of the Catholic Secondary School System in the Archdiocese of Detroit" (unpublished doctoral dissertation); J. F. Stach, "A History of the Lutheran Schools of the Missouri Synod in Michigan, 1845-1940" (unpublished doctoral dissertation); *105th Report of the Superintendent of Public Instruction.*

Founded in the 1960s were De Lima Junior College at Oxford and Maryglade College at Memphis.

The Protestant denominations were also active in founding colleges. Hope College was chartered in 1866, developing out of a school founded in Holland by the Dutch immigrants in the 1850s and supported by the Reformed Church. A few miles away in Grand Rapids the Christian Reformed Church founded a school in 1876 that ultimately became Calvin College. The Seventh Day Adventists opened a college in Battle Creek in the 1870s. It was moved to Berrien Springs in 1901 and renamed Emmanuel Missionary College. In 1960 the denomination moved Potomac University from Washington, D.C. to Berrien Springs and merged it with Emmanuel Missionary College under the name Andrews University. Suomi College developed out of a school started by Finnish immigrants at Hancock in 1896. Alma College was founded by Michigan Presbyterians in 1886. Spring Arbor College developed from a school opened by the Free Methodists in 1873, becoming a junior college in 1923 and a four-year college in 1963. Michigan Lutheran College in Detroit was established in 1936. Members of the Church of Christ founded Michigan Christian Junior College at Rochester in 1961.

Several independent schools and secular colleges also form part of Michigan's educational system. Several schools were established at Bloomfield Hills by the Cranbrook Foundation, formed to administer the estate of George and Ellen Scripps Booth of Detroit. The most notable of these are the Cranbrook Academy of Art, founded in 1928 and internationally known for the training of architects, painters, and sculptors, and the Cranbrook Institute of Science, established in 1931. The Merrill-Palmer Institute in Detroit, founded in 1920, offers a number of specialized courses. Chrysler Institute of Engineering, Detroit, General Motors Institute, Flint, and Detroit Institute of Technology are among the state's leading technical schools. The report of the superintendent of public instruction in 1963 listed no less than 74 colleges, universities, seminaries, and advanced schools.

Although there was a continuing concern for the quality of education, the paramount problem faced by the state's schools after 1945 was rapidly mounting enrollments. The proportion of boys and girls continuing their education through high school increased sharply during the depression decade of the 1930s. In that decade, while the state's population increased 8%, high-school enrollments went up 56%. The birth rate began a sustained rise during World War II. During the two decades from 1940 to 1960 the population growth of Michigan was one of the

largest in the nation. In the 1950s the proportion of high-school
graduates going to college began to rise almost as spectacularly as
the proportion of primary school students attending high school
had done in the 1930s. All these factors combined to bring into
the schools and colleges a tidal wave of students. Colleges and
universities in 1960 enrolled 159,182 students, as compared with
122,808 a decade earlier, and the "war babies" had not yet
reached college age. Public-school enrollment stood at 1,043,566
in 1950—about what it had been in 1930. But by 1963 it had
zoomed to 1,800,000. To house the students, school districts,
colleges, and universities built feverishly. It became difficult to
find a sufficient number of qualified teachers for the schools and
faculties for the colleges and universities. Financing the costs had
become a major problem for both local communities and the
state.

Schools in earlier times were regarded exclusively in terms of
the upbringing and training of children. But by 1963 Michigan
schools were serving adults as well. Soon after the beginning of
the twentieth century public evening schools were organized in
Detroit and Kalamazoo. The idea spread slowly to other cities.
Programs for the foreign-born, many of whom were illiterate, and
for others who wished to complete the requirements for an
eighth-grade diploma were the chief features of these schools in
earlier years. Adult education was greatly stimulated by federal
aid during the depression. In 1943 the legislature granted authority to all school districts, except those not maintaining a high
school, to operate adult-education programs. State aid for adult
education began in 1944. The G.I. Bill of Rights made it possible
for World War II veterans to receive vocational training, and
Veterans' Institutes were established between 1947 and 1951 in
213 school systems. Interest in adult education continued to
increase during the 1950s; a total of 222,906 students were enrolled in 10,857 classes in 1959-60. All of the state-supported
colleges and universities developed field service or "extension
classes" to meet the demand for adult education at a higher
level. By 1960 over 15,000 people were attending extension
classes and taking correspondence courses.

From time to time during the century after 1865 there were
criticisms of educational practices, but the record leaves no doubt
that the people of Michigan retained and strengthened their faith
in education. In fact this faith was so great that the schools
were sometimes expected to take over responsibilities with regard
to young people that properly belonged to the family, the church,
and other agencies. The school, along with the church, was

regarded even more strongly than in earlier days as the bulwark of a free people.[5]

THE CHURCHES

Judged by the number of their members, the growth of churches in Michigan since the Civil War has been almost as marked as that of the schools. The five major Protestant denominations had a total membership of only 60,560 out of a total population in the state of 749,113 in 1860, or around 8%. In 1870 the Roman Catholic Church claimed 170,000 members in Michigan out of a total population of 1,184,509, or about 14%. By 1960 it was estimated that about 62% of the people of the nation were church members, and it is reasonable to suppose that this was approximately true in Michigan. A century ago church members were held to strict adherence to the doctrine and practices of the churches to which they belonged, and any deviation might result in expulsion or excommunication. There can be little doubt that many people in 1960 were church members in name only. The church, furthermore, has lost its status as the center of community social life. The coming of the automobile, movies, radio, and television, and the growing vogue of sports, together with the emergence of the school as the center of community life have provided other means of mingling with one's fellow man. The primacy of the church in education has been taken away by the publicly supported schools and colleges. Charity, once dispensed in large measure through the church, is now entrusted to a variety of public and private agencies. The theory of evolution and the critical study of the Bible had some effect in weakening the hold of the church on its members. In the 1920s there were bitter conflicts between modernists and fundamentalists. People became much less interested in the fine points of theology and more concerned with material values.

At the same time there was a growing feeling of need for security by the individual in a rapidly changing world, and this has played no small part in the growth of church membership. If the church is less effective in public affairs than it once was, its emphasis on spiritual values continues to be recognized as vital. The conflict between communism and the American system also served to encourage adherence to the church and spiritual values as contrasted with the atheistic tenets of the communists.

[5] *The Michigan Record in Higher Education* by this author is the first in a projected series of four volumes on the history of education in Michigan to be published by the Michigan Historical Commission through the John M. Munson Fund.

The Roman Catholic Church enjoyed a phenomenal growth in Michigan in the century following the Civil War. The 170,000 Catholics in the state in 1870 had increased to 844,106 in 1926, and in 1962 the Church claimed 1,396,346 members in the Archdiocese of Detroit. The influx of Poles, Hungarians, Irish, and Italians to work in the automobile plants was one factor in the rapid growth of Catholic membership, since most of these people were Catholics. Between 1916 and 1926 Detroit had the second largest increase in church membership of any American city, and most of that increase was Catholic.

The extent of the Catholic educational system in Michigan has been noted in the preceding section of this chapter. Catholic hospitals have been established in most of the state's major cities, starting with St. Vincent's in Detroit in 1845. By 1958 the Catholic Church had 31 general and four special hospitals in Michigan. Several religious orders played an important part in the establishment of schools, colleges, and hospitals. The Sisters, Servants of the Immaculate Heart of Mary, who belong to an order founded at Monroe in 1845, started the school that later became Marygrove College. The Felician Sisters, the first of whom arrived in Michigan in 1874, were staffing 33 schools and two orphanages by 1937. The Sisters of St. Joseph came to Kalamazoo from New York State in 1889 and around their growing community Borgess Hospital and Nazareth Academy and College developed. The Sisters of St. Dominic, members of an order founded in the thirteenth century in France, came to Adrian in 1878, and through their efforts Siena Heights College was established. Another group of Dominican Sisters settled in Grand Rapids, and their educational work resulted in the founding of Aquinas College there.

The establishment of separate dioceses in different parts of the state reflect the growth of the Catholic Church. The diocese of Upper Michigan was created in 1853. The Diocese of Grand Rapids dates from 1882, of Lansing from 1937, and of Saginaw from 1938. On August 3, 1937 the Archdiocese of Detroit was created. Its archbishop, Edward Mooney, was made a cardinal of the Church in 1945, one of five in the United States. Cardinal Mooney died in 1958.

Caspar Borgess, who was bishop of the Diocese of Michigan from 1870 to 1887, was notable for his interest in education and his work in forming parishes for immigrants speaking foreign tongues. A parish for Bohemians was formed in 1870 and one for Belgians in 1884. The second-oldest Polish congregation in the United States had been formed in Huron County in 1854; Detroit

Polish parishes were formed in 1871 and 1873. Fourteen years later Father Joseph Dabrowski started a Polish high school and seminary in Detroit; this school was later moved to Orchard Lake and men of Polish origin preparing for the priesthood came from all over the nation to attend its seminary. Bishop Samuel Foley presided over the Detroit diocese from 1888-1918; he was succeeded by Bishop James Gallagher (1918-1937). It was during the reign of these two bishops that the Church enjoyed its most rapid growth, especially in the Detroit area. The first bishop of the Diocese of Grand Rapids was Henry Joseph Richter, whose unusually long reign lasted from 1882 to 1916. One of the most beloved of Catholic bishops was Frederic Baraga, first bishop of the Diocese of Upper Michigan. He came from an aristocratic family in Slovakia, labored for many years among the Indians of the Grand River Valley, Cross Village, and the Upper Peninsula, and served as bishop until his death in 1868. A county in the Upper Peninsula is named in his honor.[6]

The membership of the Methodist Church in Michigan was larger than that of any other Protestant denomination by 1865 and remained in that position throughout the century following. The Methodist circuit rider of pioneer days was an effective instrument in promoting the spread of Methodism, and the well-developed central organization of this church, with its bishops, supervisors, and assigned pulpits, appears to have been an important factor in its subsequent growth. The Methodist Episcopal Church, as the largest body of this denomination was called until 1939, grew in membership from 41,490 in 1870 to 114,326 in 1906, and to 142,141 in 1936.[7] The Methodist Episcopal churches in the South were reunited in 1939 with those in the North; at that time, also, the Methodist Protestant Church joined this united body, which henceforth was known as the Methodist Church. The Methodist Protestants had three "circuits" in Michigan as early as 1842, and had founded Adrian College. Remaining separate were the Wesleyan Methodists, founded originally by strong antislavery elements within the denomination, and the Free

[6] G. W. Paré, *The Catholic Church in Detroit, 1701-1888;* J. W. McGee, *The Catholic Church in the Grand River Valley;* J. K. Jamison, *By Cross and Anchor. The Story of Frederic Baraga of Lake Superior.*

[7] Although the National Council of Churches of the U.S.A. compiles statistics on church membership in the United States and publishes them annually in a volume entitled *Yearbook of American Churches,* the figures are not broken down by states. A United States census of churches and religious bodies issued in 1906, 1916, 1926, and 1936 was discontinued and reliable data on church membership by states after 1936 are difficult to obtain.

Methodist Church. The Wesleyans had adherents in Michigan as early as the 1850s. The first Free Methodist Society was organized in 1863 and the Michigan Conference of this denomination was formed in 1866. During the following decade the Free Methodists opened the school that subsequently became Spring Arbor College.

Among the features of Methodism that had great popular appeal were the democratic character of the service, simplicity, emotional fervor, and the doctrine of "free grace." The Methodists, more than any other denomination, developed the camp meeting, which grew out of the great revivals in the early nineteenth century. One of the oldest camp-meeting sites in Michigan is Crystal Springs, near Dowagiac. Bay View Assembly, founded in 1875 in imitation of the original "chautauqua" at Lake Chautauqua in New York, was sponsored by the Methodists and was a kind of sophisticated version of the summer camp meeting. Following the formation of the Epworth League for Methodist young people, this organization grew rapidly in Michigan. It sponsored a recreational and educational program at Epworth Heights near Ludington. Methodists also supported a number of hospitals and social agencies, Albion and Adrian Colleges in Michigan, and the Garrett Biblical Institute in Illinois (now Garrett Theological Seminary).[8]

The Baptist Church grew in membership and also greatly expanded the sphere of its activities during the century after 1865. Membership increased from 20,051 in 1870 to 49,275 in 1936. Baptist young people's societies in Michigan date back to 1859; later they became affiliated with the Baptist Young People's Union of America. Baptist women, like those in other Protestant churches, formed missionary societies; a foreign-missionary society was organized in 1879 and a home-missionary society a dozen years later. After the union of the regular Baptists and the Free Will Baptists in 1916 the denomination gave support to both Kalamazoo College and Hillsdale College. During the 1940s there was a serious cleavage among Baptists on the question of fundamentalism versus modernism. The liberal wing of the denomination adhered to the American Baptist Convention while conservative churches formed separate associations.

Other Protestant churches were also active in support of mis-

[8] E. H. Pilcher, *History of Protestantism in Michigan;* R. C. Crawford, "Reminiscences of Pioneer Ministers in Michigan," *Mich. Pioneer and Historical Colls.*, XVII (1890), 226-238; W. R. Prescott, *The Fathers Still Speak; a History of Michigan Methodism;* J. D. Brush, "Father Was a Preacher," *Michigan History,* XLVII (1963) 226-242.

sionaries. The Congregationalists, with the aid of the American Home Missionary Society, established many churches in the north country during the boom days of lumbering. Presbyterians gave support to female seminaries in Monroe and Kalamazoo, and the denomination established Alma College in 1887. The Congregational Church, which had merged with the Christian Church by 1936, had a membership of 41,942 in that year, while the Presbyterians had 67,286 members in its largest group, and 1,685 in smaller Presbyterian sects.

The first Lutheran congregation in Michigan was organized at Ann Arbor in 1833 by Frederick Shmid. With the large German immigration the number of Lutherans increased rapidly. Their churches adhered to different synods; in fact, if the members of the various Lutheran bodies are considered as one group, they outnumbered the Methodists by 1936. The largest Lutheran body in the state at that date numbered 130,248 members; the second largest had 56,528. In the period after 1945 Lutherans were distinguished by the large number of churches of contemporary design that they built. Michigan Lutheran College was founded at Detroit in 1936.

Several other churches drawing their membership largely from a single nationality developed into large denominations. The Reformed Church, with a membership largely made up of people of Dutch ancestry, tripled in membership between 1906 and 1936. The Christian Reformed Church, which developed out of a split in the Reformed Church just prior to the Civil War, quadrupled its membership in the same period. Members of Jewish congregations in Michigan had reached 99,366 by 1936. Separate Methodist and Baptist denominations consisting of Negro members grew up. A society of Negro Methodists was formed in Detroit as early as 1841. Negro Methodist churches in 1936 claimed about 18,000 members, while Negro Baptists numbered about twice that figure.

Several of the smaller denominations that had their beginnings in Michigan prior to 1860 grew rapidly in the postwar period. The United Brethren In Christ sent missionaries to the St. Joseph Valley as early as 1830; a General Conference of the denomination was organized in 1853. The earliest workers in the Evangelical Church appeared in Michigan about 1839, and a church was established at Ann Arbor in 1845. Its members were largely Germans. The Unitarian and Universalist Churches, recognized for their liberalism in doctrinal matters, were both quite vigorous in the period before the Civil War, but their membership failed to keep pace with population growth in the century that followed.

Much more vigorous was the development of churches founded

in Michigan after 1865. The first Christian Science practitioners came to Detroit in 1885, and the first church services were held in 1889. In the years that followed, Christian Science societies were formed in the state's principal cities. Battle Creek became the center of the Seventh Day Adventist Church in the period after 1865. A group of Adventists from Maine had arrived in Battle Creek in 1855 and continued there the publication of a religious paper they had started earlier. But it was the coming of Elder James White and his wife Ellen that gave Battle Creek its pre-eminence in the denomination. Mrs. White, who had frequent dreams and went into trances in which she believed she received divine revelations, was accepted by members of the church as its leader. The Seventh Day Adventist Church claimed 10,000 members in Michigan by 1936.

The Mormon faith, like the Adventist and Christian Science denominations, originated in the United States, developing from the teachings of Joseph Smith in western New York. Two Mormon missionaries are known to have visited Pontiac in 1834, and Joseph Smith himself is reported to have preached there later the same year. Following the assassination of Smith, the largest group of Mormons followed Brigham Young to Utah and established the Church of the Latter Day Saints.[9] One splinter group accepted the leadership of James Strang; the story of Strang and his Mormon colony on Beaver Island has been related earlier. A larger number adhered to a son of Joseph Smith and founded the Reorganized Church of the Latter Day Saints. A church was founded by members of this group at Galien in 1861. Many other congregations were organized in the years that followed and the Reorganized church became the largest Mormon group in Michigan.

In cities, and even in many rural communities, the growth of small sects conservative in doctrine, preaching the "old time religion," and relying heavily on emotional appeal, was a noteworthy sequel to the modernist-fundamentalist split of the 1920s. The older Protestant denominations tended to introduce formal ritual and to appeal to the head rather than to the heart. Imposing church edifices were built and leadership in church organizations went to socially prominent members. All this repelled many worshipers, who sought a warmer and more personal religious faith and fellowship. Assemblies of God, the Nazarene churches, and a large number of smaller denominations rose to meet this need. Services frequently were held in vacant store buildings,

[9] George Romney, elected governor of Michigan in 1962, was a member of this church.

garages, or tents, but in many instances more permanent church structures and regularly organized denominations evolved in due course. The first Nazarene church in Michigan was founded at Grand Rapids in 1909 by persons with various former church affiliations who organized themselves into a "Holiness Band." By 1936 the denomination had 5,560 members in Michigan.

At the opposite extreme from the new evangelical churches was the Episcopal Church, which had its time-honored ritual. The first Episcopal parish in Michigan was St. Paul's in Detroit, organized in 1824. The diocese of Michigan, formed in 1832, was presided over for 42 years (1836-78) by Bishop Samuel A. McCrosky, a legendary figure in Michigan Episcopalian history. Growth of membership led to the creation of the Diocese of West Michigan in 1874.

During the century many unusual religious organizations were formed, some of them ephemeral, others more permanent. At Benton Harbor a Kentuckian named Benjamin Purnell, claiming he was the Seventh Angel, established the House of David in 1903. Members lived and worked together as a colony. They practiced vegetarianism and the men never shaved. Charges of immorality ultimately led to the arrest of Purnell and the colony split into two groups following his death.[10] After World War II Mackinac Island became the headquarters of the Moral Rearmament movement, founded by Frank Buchman, and an imposing collection of buildings were erected to house adherents of the movement who came from all over the world.

It would be impossible to estimate the scope of the contribution of the churches to the people of Michigan over the century since 1865. Certainly they brought inspiration and hope to those bereaved, helped give life meaning, and contributed greatly to the maintenance of moral standards. Church workers provided education, nursing care, and social aid to untold thousands. The notable increase in the proportion of the population belonging to churches, however it may be explained, can hardly be set down as anything but a gain.[11]

[10] M. M. Quaife, *Lake Michigan,* pp. 262-281.

[11] *The Congregational Churches of Michigan For the First Fifty Years;* C. Hayne, *Baptist Trail-makers in Michigan;* M. E. D. Trowbridge, *History of the Baptists in Michigan;* G. H. Waid, *Centennial History of the Michigan State Baptist Convention;* C. C. Trowbridge, "History of the Episcopal Church in Michigan," *Mich. Pioneer and Historical Colls.,* III (1881), 219ff.; F. C. Smith, *The Diocese of Western Michigan;* J. Comin and H. F. Fredsell, *History of the Presbyterian Church in Michigan;* L. M. Franklin, "Jews in Michigan," *Michigan History,* XXIII (1939), 77-92.

LIBRARIES

The importance of libraries as repositories of the cultural heritage of the race and as sources of information has been recognized since the earliest days in Michigan. The first three state constitutions all stipulated that monies collected from fines for penal offenses should be set aside for the support of libraries. The present State Library dates from 1828. The legislature has passed many acts to encourage the establishment and maintenance of libraries.

Prior to the Civil War, however, there was relatively little done to establish public libraries. In 1861, only 12% of the townships were appropriating any funds for libraries. The desire of the people for libraries had to be met by private library organizations, often called "subscription libraries." A City Library was organized at Detroit in 1817 and shares of stock were sold to obtain funds. It was merged with the Detroit Young Men's Society in 1832. The Detroit Mechanics' Society, formed in 1818, also maintained a library. The Historical Society of Michigan, which came into being in 1828 with Governor Lewis Cass as its president, collected manuscripts and articles on the history of Michigan. In Kalamazoo, a Ladies' Library Association was organized in 1852 and incorporated in 1859. In 1879, this association erected a large building, reputed to be the first in the nation built exclusively for the use of a woman's club.[12] A women's library association was formed in Flint in 1853. Subsequently similar associations were formed in other cities and even in small villages and towns.

Funds realized from the collection of fines constituted the financial basis of the Detroit Public Library, opened in 1865. The Grand Rapids Public Library originated in 1871 with the consolidation of the school district libraries. The Kalamazoo Public Library was founded about the same time, also originally as a school library. Private gifts made public library buildings possible in such cities as Battle Creek, Hillsdale, Kalamazoo, and Grand Rapids. Many cities benefited from the donations received from Andrew Carnegie for library construction. Typical of these were Niles and St. Joseph. Gradually, as the public libraries developed, private library associations disappeared or directed their attention to other objectives.

While cities of the state developed public libraries, rural areas

[12] The Association was still active and the building was still in use in 1963. See G. E. Foote, *History of the Ladies' Library Association.*

and small towns remained for many years with no library service or only subscription libraries. The legislature passed a county library act in 1917, but little action was taken under its provisions until 1933, when federal funds were made available. The depression years of the 1930s brought a heavy demand on libraries. Unemployed workers found in libraries a means by which their idle time could be occupied profitably. Thirty county and village libraries were established through federal aid between 1934 and 1936. But there were still large areas in the state without libraries. Governor Frank Murphy in 1938 declared that nearly a quarter of the people of Michigan did not have access to a library, and that another 30% had only nominal service. State aid was provided on a broad scale starting in 1937. The W. K. Kellogg Foundation of Battle Creek performed a great service to rural communities of southwestern Michigan by providing thousands of new books for local libraries. Another important contributor to making books available to areas lacking libraries was the State Library in Lansing, through its "bookmobiles" and its lending services. In 1963-64 more than $1,000,000 was appropriated by the state legislature for libraries, and federal aid provided an additional $300,000. This supplemented funds raised by cities and school districts for library operation.

The colleges and the universities gradually built up large collections of books, periodicals, and documents. Much more emphasis was placed on the importance of libraries after the abandonment of the classical course of study around 1900. The University of Michigan alone in 1958 had 2,717,029 volumes in its libraries. The donations of an alumnus and former regent of the University of Michigan, William L. Clements of Bay City, made possible the William L. Clements Library, one of the nation's greatest depositories of original materials on the colonial and revolutionary periods in American history. A Detroiter, Clarence M. Burton, collected original source materials on the history of Michigan and the Northwest, which became the nucleus of the Burton Historical Collection of the Detroit Public Library. The Michigan Historical Collections at the University of Michigan, the Clarke Memorial Library at Central Michigan University, and smaller archival collections at other institutions provide the historian with the raw materials he needs for recreating the past of the state. The State Archives at Lansing is the repository for all state records of historical value. Under state law no local governmental unit may destroy its records without approval of the State Administrative Board, after certification by the Michigan Historical Commission that the papers proposed for destruction have no historical value. The J. M. Longyear Research Library in Marquette is a rich depository of records related to Upper Peninsula history.

The appearance of low-priced paperbacks in the 1950s and the advent of television had the effect of changing the character of the demand on libraries. Relatively greater emphasis was placed on reference and informational services. Special books and story-hours for children became popular. Most libraries established audio-visual services, including record and film lending. Although libraries in 1963 were changing in character, the use of their services was steadily increasing.

NEWSPAPERS

In 1850 only three daily newspapers were being published in Michigan, but most cities and villages had weeklies. As the population grew many of the weeklies became dailies and new daily newspapers were established. During and after the Civil War newspapers were fiercely partisan in their editorials and did not hesitate to slant the news to fit their particular political preference. Not a few were published at a loss by party leaders and their supporters as a means of influencing public opinion. In some cases such newspapers expired after a few weeks or months or, as more often happened, were consolidated with another newspaper. Changes in ownership were frequent. Up to the year 1885 an amazing total of 253 newspapers had been started in Detroit. Every sizable city had at least two newspapers, one supporting the Republican cause, the other championing the Democratic party.

By the turn of the century a change was in evidence, as publishers began to regard their newspapers more as business ventures and less as partisan outlets. In this transition James E. Scripps of Detroit became a figure of national importance. He came to Detroit in 1859 to become business manager of the *Advertiser and Tribune.* This newspaper supported the Republican party while the *Free Press* was the Democratic organ. In 1873 Scripps founded the Detroit *Evening News,* an historic event in the history of journalism in the United States. Scripps believed a newspaper should be self-supporting, not dependent on political handouts. In order to accomplish this his first job was to increase circulation so as to attract advertisers. The paper was smaller than those being published at the time, and the news was condensed. It sold at 2¢ a copy, in contrast to the 5¢ price of other newspapers. Scripps enlisted other members of his family to secure funds to buy fast cylinder presses and to take over various responsibilities in the office. His brother, George H. Scripps, sold his Illinois farm and became business manager of the paper; his sister, Ellen B. Scripps, joined the editorial staff, and his half brother, E. W. Scripps, came to help increase circulation. New features were introduced and sensational news was featured. Circulation increased rapidly, and the venture was so profitable that E. W. Scripps established the Cleveland *Press* along similar lines. This was the beginning of the Scripps-Howard newspaper chain. James E. Scripps remained in Detroit to manage the *News*. The success of this newspaper naturally led other publishers to imitate it. Partisanship became less prominent, with more emphasis on features and the kind of news designed to attract readers and thus to win advertising contracts.[13]

Since about 1914 many daily newspapers in Michigan have been consolidated. When the Detroit *Times* suspended publication in 1960 the state's largest city was left with only two major newspapers, the *Free Press* and the *News*. A few years before, the consolidation of the Grand Rapids *Herald* with the Grand Rapids *Press* had made Detroit the only city in the state with more than one daily newspaper. About fifty dailies were still being published in Michigan in 1963. There were several reasons for these consolidations. Advertisers found it less expensive to buy space in one newspaper with general circulation, even at higher rates, than in two or more with overlapping circulation. Increasing costs of labor and the demand for more features, widespread news coverage, and attractive format were other factors.[14] The single daily newspaper that evolved from consolidations in all Michigan cities except Detroit was no longer strongly partisan, usually reflecting in its editorials prevailing public opinion in the community, although on occasion there were evidences of crusading fervor.

Another evidence of the trend toward newspapers becoming a segment of big business in America was the development of companies owning newspapers in several cities. The largest such company in Michigan was the Booth Publishing Company. George G. Booth of Detroit, who had married a daughter of James E. Scripps, acquired the Grand Rapids *Press* in the 1890s and in due course it came to have the largest circulation of any outstate paper. Early in the twentieth century Booth's brother, Ralph, obtained control of newspapers in four other Michigan cities, and these were brought together with the *Press* under the management of the Booth Publishing Company. Three others news-

13 E. W. Scripps, *Damned Old Crank; a Self-portrait of E. W. Scripps.*
14 F. L. Mott, *American Journalism*, pp. 635-37.

papers were acquired by 1922. The Booth chain, since that date, has included the Grand Rapids *Press*, the Flint *Journal*, the Muskegon *Chronicle*, the Jackson *Citizen-Patriot*, the Kalamazoo *Gazette*, the Ann Arbor *News*, the Bay City *Times*, the Saginaw *News*, and the Ypsilanti *Press*. Two other outstate dailies, the Lansing *State Journal* and the Battle Creek *Enquirer-News* were acquired by Federated Publications, Inc.

In towns and villages not large enough to support a daily newspaper a weekly publication invariably sprang up. In 1963 there were some 350 weekly or semiweekly newspapers. The country editor spent long hours to make both ends meet. Far more profitable than the newspaper was the job printing done in the newspaper office. The weekly newspapers, like the dailies, tended to become less partisan, but editors did not hesitate to express their views on local, state, and national affairs. Subscriptions were hard to collect in the early days; one publisher tried this bit of doggerel to bring in payments:

> Breathes there a man with soul so dead,
> Who never to himself hath said,
> Tonight before I go to bed,
> I'll go and pay the printer?
>
> Yes, there are some we know full well,
> Who never such a tale could tell.
> But they, we fear, will go to—well,
> The place that has no winter.

Another publisher, in soliciting firewood in payment for subscriptions, admonished his readers not to bring wood "that the devil can't split." His rival announced to his readers that they should bring any kind of wood they had, and if the devil couldn't split it, he'd split it himself. During the early years the editor-publisher of a country newspaper did not occupy a very high social position and often was the butt of a good deal of ridicule, but in later years he assumed the status of a community leader.[15]

Numerous foreign-language newspapers have been published in Michigan. As early as 1850 Holland had a Dutch-language newspaper. Between 1876 and 1930 no less than 33 Finnish newspapers and periodicals were published in Michigan.[16] German, Italian, and Polish newspapers appeared in Detroit, which also

[15] E. H. Mudge, "The Old-time Country Newspapermen," *Michigan History*, XXX (1946), 754-58.

[16] J. L. Kolehmainen, "Finnish Newspapers and Periodicals in Michigan," *Michigan History*, XXIV (1940), 119.

had a newspaper especially for Jewish readers and others especially for Negro readers.

The oldest periodical published in Michigan is the *Michigan Farmer*, founded in 1843. There are numerous religious periodicals; among the oldest of these are the *Banner*, founded at Grand Rapids in 1868 for members of the Christian Reformed Church, the *Christian Advocate*, established at Adrian in 1874 for Methodist readers, and the *Christian Herald*, founded prior to the Civil War to serve the Baptist Church. The number of trade, professional, and business publications increased rapidly after World War I. Probably the oldest of these is the *Michigan Tradesman*, published at Grand Rapids. Many veterans' organizations and civic associations publish periodicals in the state.

By 1963 the mass of printed and duplicated material that poured from presses and other machines was so great that the chief problem of the reader was to pick and choose. In 1865 only a few books were available, and still fewer periodicals. Since people could have but a few they chose the best. The quantity of printed material now produced is so staggering that the average Michiganian finds it difficult to select what he wants to read. In spite of the lure of television and many other diversions, reading of some sort, however, appears to be holding its own or actually increasing.

THE ARTS

The arts require taste, leisure, and intelligence in order to flourish. Unquestionably the primary necessity of providing food, clothing, and shelter in a new land left little time for the pioneer to devote to the arts. Yet it is possible to overstress this cause for lack of interest. The German people who settled in Michigan exhibited a lively interest in music from the earliest years because they had a taste for it. One of the retarding influences in the development of the fine arts in Michigan was the Puritan tradition, which regarded beauty as a snare of the devil and those who devoted themselves to music, drama, or painting as lost souls. As has been observed, the New England Puritan influence was stronger in Michigan than elsewhere in the Middle West. But little by little in the period after the Civil War, courageous people dared to manifest interest in the arts.

The sudden acquisition of wealth from lumber, railroads, or some other profitable business venture often did the cause of art more harm than good. Men who had spent their lives making money suddenly assumed the role of connoisseurs of the arts, and the results were dreadful. They built huge mansions in imitation of a medieval castle or a Gothic cathedral and furnished them with outlandish bric-a-brac. They hired dancing masters and musicians to "finish" their daughters and sent their sons to college to learn the classics in a frenzied effort to buy culture. They spent fabulous sums to obtain second-rate paintings from Europe but did little to encourage struggling young native artists.

The depression decade of the 1930s may be regarded as a kind of turning point in matters of popular taste. In the years that followed more and more attention was paid to good design in the manufacture of such everyday things as household appliances and automobiles. More and more people found in the arts a needed outlet for their urge to do creative work. Popular magazines did much to promote a more widespread understanding of the visual arts. Meanwhile radio and recordings, by making music an everyday experience, had the effect of stimulating interest in good music. The coming of television ultimately had a salutary effect on the making of films; viewers wanted something out of the ordinary when they went to a theater, and the result was a marked improvement in artistic standards in the production of motion pictures.

Music was the first of the arts to gain converts. In pioneer times ballads, folk songs, and fiddlers' dance tunes comprised the musical fare. As has been noted, the Germans brought to Michigan a devotion to music that spread beyond the limits of that nationality. In the years after the Civil War every community had its brass band, usually called by some such grandiloquent name as "Silver Cornet Band," which played on patriotic occasions and for dancing. As early as 1881 the Ann Arbor High School offered a music course. In 1927 a member of the School of Music in Ann Arbor, Joseph E. Maddy, founded the national high-school music camp at Interlochen, which in the years that followed was to become nationally known. In 1962 it was expanded into a year-round school for youth of high-school age gifted in the arts. The chautauqua programs of the first two decades of the twentieth century introduced thousands of Michiganians to serious music. Radio programs broadcast after 1920, when the first station (WWJ) went on the air, were devoted mostly to popular music, but there was also some symphonic and operatic music broadcast, and the very surfeit of popular music turned many people to an interest in music of a more lasting character.

The growing interest in music was reflected in the organization of music clubs. A Michigan Federation of Music Clubs was formed and in 1916 it became affiliated with the National Federation. The

University of Michigan has been a vital force in the musical life of the state. Concerts were sponsored by the University Choral Society, formed in 1879. The spring festival, which brought to Ann Arbor each year the leading orchestras and musical artists of the world, was started in 1894. The Detroit Symphony Orchestra, founded in 1914, became one of the nation's leading orchestras under the direction of Ossip Gabrilowitsch. Symphony orchestras were established in Grand Rapids and Kalamazoo in 1921.

Meanwhile music was introduced into practically all the schools of the state. Among the many interesting activities of Henry R. Pattengill, superintendent of public instruction from 1893 to 1896, was the compilation of a "knapsack" of songs for school children, which remained in use for many years. By the 1920s many high schools had developed excellent bands and orchestras.

Michigan shared with the rest of the nation the craze for popular music, starting about the time of World War I. Many singable tunes were composed and sung during the months of American participation in that conflict. After the war, dance orchestras and dance "bands" increased in number with great rapidity. Around Detroit and at the more populous summer-resort lakes huge "pavilions" and "casinos" were built to accommodate the throngs who paid to listen to and to dance to the rhythms of "name bands."

Interest in painting and sculpture developed more slowly than enthusiasm for music. Painters who devoted themselves largely to portraiture were not uncommon in Michigan cities prior to the Civil War, but only the wealthy few demonstrated much awareness of the visual arts for many years after 1865. Although the Detroit Art Association was formed in 1875 to provide art exhibitions, there was no public art gallery in Michigan until 1888. In that year the Detroit Museum of Art was made possible through private donations. The organization was known in later years as the Detroit Institute of Arts; its holdings, including some world-famous paintings, were housed after 1927 in a magnificent building designed by Paul Cret.

During the century after 1865 Michigan produced some notable artists. Robert Hopkin, who came to Detroit from Scotland in 1832 at the age of fourteen, became a popular landscape and marine painter, surviving until 1909. The Scarab Club, an association of Detroit artists, was originally called the Hopkin Club in honor of this painter. William B. Conely was well known as a portrait painter in Kalamazoo and Detroit from 1873 to 1911. Most famous of all was Gari Melchers, son of a German wood carver who came to Detroit in 1855. His paintings won international recognition; no other Michigan artist had so many honors bestowed on him both in Europe and America. His murals for the Detroit Public Library show the landing of Cadillac's wife at Detroit, an incident in the "Conspiracy of Pontiac," and "The Spirit of the Northwest." By 1875 Detroit could boast of a sizable group of artists, some of them with a national reputation. Lewis T. Ives and his son Percy were among the most notable Detroit artists in the latter part of the nineteenth century. Many distinguished Americans and Michiganians sat for Percy Ives, among them being President Grover Cleveland, Hazen S. Pingree, Thomas W. Palmer, and Russell A. Alger. Joseph W. Gies, a native of Detroit, did figure subjects and landscapes as well as portraits. Another Detroit native, Francis Petrus Paulus, was, like Gies, closely associated with the Detroit Museum of Art. He worked abroad from 1902 to the time of World War I, when he returned to his native city and remained there the remainder of his life.

Although Detroit was the center of art life in Michigan, other cities made their contributions. Frederick Stuart Church, born in Grand Rapids in 1842, attained popularity in New York as a magazine illustrator. His "Pandora's Box," "Beauty and the Beast," and "Sorceress" won him great renown. Among the artists who were active in Grand Rapids in the 1930s was Alexander Flynn, a portrait painter, Anton Lang, the famous wood carver from Oberammergau, and Stanislav V'soske, a designer. A Saginaw native, Eanger Irving Gousem, born there in 1860, won distinction as a painter of Indian pictures. Frederick Carl Frieske, born at Owosso in 1875, won international honors for his paintings. Ezra Winters, whose murals and friezes may be seen in public buildings in Washington, D.C., New York, and Detroit, spent his early life in Manistee and Traverse City. De Jonge Smith, a muralist of distinction, and Algred Hutty, a noted etcher, came from Grand Haven.

The widespread interest in art in Michigan is evidenced by the growth of art education in the twentieth century. In Detroit the Arts and Crafts Society, formed in 1907, became established as an art school of major importance. Arts instruction at the University of Michigan began as early as 1852, when a professorship of fine arts was established. Art departments and art schools were established later in almost all the state's colleges and universities. The founding of the Cranbrook Academy of Art in 1928 was an event of major significance in the history of art in Michigan. The Cranbrook Academy soon became known throughout the nation and the world. In 1910 a summer school of art was established at the summer-resort town of Saugutuck in western Michigan. Offering courses in crafts, graphic arts, and painting, this school is accredited by all the chief art schools. Another summer art school was established at Leland, on the Leelanau Peninsula, by Michigan State University.

Associations for the purpose of providing galleries for art exhibitions as well as encouraging art instruction were formed in various parts of the state in the first three decades of the twentieth century. The Ann Arbor Art Association dates from 1909 and was active in providing a number of items for the permanent collection in Alumni Memorial Hall of the University of Michigan. The Grand Rapids Art Gallery, which dates from 1910, sponsored an annual showing of work by western Michigan artists. The Hackley Art Gallery in Muskegon was established in 1911 through a bequest from C. H. Hackley, a wealthy lumberman. It has a widely representative collection of paintings, including works by Corot and Whistler. The Kalamazoo Institute of Arts was organized in 1924. It established an "art center," which was housed after 1961 in a magnificent new building, the gift of Mr. and Mrs. Donald Gilmore. Starting in 1952 this association sponsored an annual outdoor "clothesline" art show. The Saginaw Art Museum, founded in 1947, sponsors an annual showing of work by northern Michigan artists.

Detroit is one of the few cities in America that supports art with public funds. Under a new city charter an Arts Commission was established as a municipal department in 1919. The Art Museum, which had been managed by a private association from 1885 to that time, turned over to the city its properties, valued at $3,000,000, although it continued to administer the funds and endowments of the corporation. The city adopted the name "Detroit Institute of Arts."[17]

THE THEATER

In spite of the antagonistic attitude towards the theater on the part of most of the Protestant churches, traveling theatrical troupes visited Detroit and other Michigan cities even in pre-Civil War times. As early as 1830 a barn near the Steamboat Hotel in Detroit was used as a theater, and a building was constructed especially to accommodate touring players in 1848. The Athenaeum Theater was erected during the Civil War, but it burned down in 1869. A few weeks later, however, the Detroit Opera House was

[17] C. H. Burroughs, "Painting and Sculpture in Michigan," *Michigan History,* XX (1936), 395-410; XXI (1937), 39-55 and 141-158.

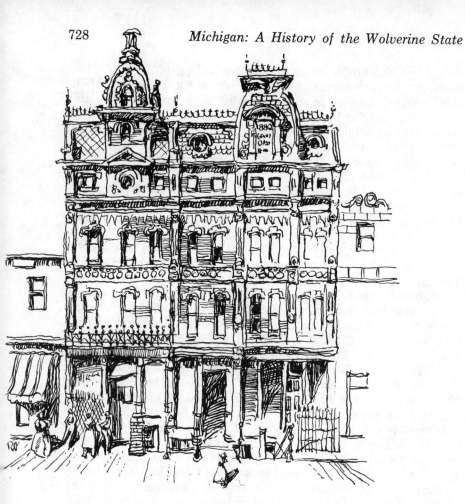

Typical Michigan opera house, ca. 1890

opened, and for forty years it remained the center of Detroit musical and theatrical life. Many other theaters were constructed in later years. The Lafayette was opened in 1925 and the Cass in 1926.

In outstate cities the evolution of the theater followed a pattern similar to that in Detroit. At first theatrical productions were given in halls used for general civic purposes. About the time of the Civil War buildings especially designed for concerts and plays and usually called "opera houses" were erected in the larger cities. Grand Rapids had its first opera house in 1859, and Powers' Grand Opera House, opened there in 1873, seating

1,600 people, was the largest and best equipped for many years in western Michigan. In Kalamazoo an "Academy of Music" (actually a theater) had its grand opening in 1882. Buck's Opera House in Lansing was constructed in 1872. Between 1870 and 1900 opera houses were built in the smaller cities and even in villages. The Midland Opera House was opened about 1880. It was situated on the second floor of a store building, like most of those in the smaller cities and towns. South Haven had an opera house as early as 1879. The Beckwith Theater in Dowagiac was built as a memorial to Philo D. Beckwith, inventor of the Round Oak Furnace and founder of Round Oak Company, for years Dowagiac's leading and distinctive industry. Buchanan had an opera house as early as 1880. Bellevue, with a population of only a few hundred, boasted an opera house in 1876. Another example of the small-town opera house was that in Cedar Springs, built in 1880. It had a large stage and several dressing rooms. A rural scene was painted on the front curtain by a local artist; around it, as was the custom, appeared advertisements by local merchants. The hall was lighted by acetyline lamps. Seats were removable so that the hall could be used for dances, chicken suppers, school fairs, graduation exercises, mouth organ and fiddlers' contests, political rallies, and home talent plays. The owner, a Republican, refused to rent the hall, however, to the Democrats when they wanted to hold a rally.

The theater enjoyed great popularity in the Copper Country around the turn of the century. In the 1890s Houghton had two theaters, as did Hancock, while Lake Linden, Calumet, and Laurium each had its own opera house or theater. In 1898 Laurium built an opera house to seat 1,300 people. Not to be outdone, the people of Calumet spent $70,000 for an elaborately decorated theater, which opened March 20, 1900, with a production of *The Highwayman* by a professional troupe before an audience of 1,200. The Kerredge Theater, which opened in Hancock in 1902, had a seating capacity of 1,565, a stage 40 feet deep and 70 feet wide, ten dressing rooms, and a thousand incandescent electric lamps. For the opening performance box seats sold for $40. Excellent train service to the Copper Country enabled traveling theatrical companies to appear there between engagements at Chicago and Minneapolis-St. Paul.[18]

Typical of the dozens of stock companies that toured Michigan

[18] W. F. Dunbar, "The Opera House as a Social Institution in Michigan," *Michigan History,* XXVI (1943), 661-673; E. E. McDavitt, "The Beginnings of Theatrical Activities in Detroit," *Michigan History,* XXXI (1947), 35-47; G. N. Fuller (ed.), *Michigan, a Centennial History,* II.

between 1890 and 1914 was the one owned and managed by M. A. (Al) Hunt called Hunt's Stock Company. Hunt, a native of Bangor, started his career as a showman and musician in a traveling show band. Later he joined the "rube band" of Tucker's Show. Tucker, who resided in Decatur, was one of the most popular of the small-town showmen. Always genial, he received a hearty welcome when he returned to the same towns year after year. He was handsome, stockily built, and wore a conspicuous black moustache turned up at the ends. During all performances he wore overalls tucked into high boots. After several years of apprenticeship with Tucker, Hunt started his own troupe, consisting of twelve men and women. As the movies came in, the opera houses where Hunt's troupe played closed their doors, but Hunt continued, putting his show under canvas. Business was good until the depression. The venture was discontinued in 1931 and most stock companies folded up about the same time. The Slout Players, with headquarters at Vermontville, however, continued to play the small towns until the 1950s.

A combination of factors spelled the doom of the small-town and small-city opera houses and theaters during the decade between 1910 and 1920. The prime factor was, perhaps, the coming of the movies. But the building of high-school auditoriums was important, too, because they replaced the opera house as the center of community activities. The chautauqua played its role in dooming these once pretentious and prosperous theaters.

In the larger cities the decline of the legitimate theater was slower. Touring companies playing both serious drama and musical comedy did good business up to the close of the 1920s, although the number of attractions was smaller than in the days before the movies. Vaudeville had a tremendous vogue from about 1910 to 1929. All the principal cities had their vaudeville houses, playing daily matinees and evening performances with weekly or semiweekly changes in programs. Sound pictures, radio, and the depression killed vaudeville shortly after 1929.

Motion pictures were first demonstrated in 1894. Bertram C. Whitney brought the first moving-picture machine to Michigan in 1896 and installed it in the Detroit Grand Opera House as an oddity. It projected about a thousand feet of celluloid film. The first Detroit movie house was the Casino Theater, opened in 1905. Very quickly in Detroit and outstate cities dozens of "nickelodeons" appeared in the decade after 1905. Usually occupying vacant store buildings and charging five cents for admission, they showed short films. By the time of World War I longer films were being shown, and most Michigan towns had at least one moving picture theater. A pianist provided "mood music," and in the larger cities orchestras were used to provide musical settings for the films. Before many years the production, distribution, and exhibition of films had developed into a big business. Enterprisers secured control of theaters in several cities and established "circuits" for the showing of movies as well as vaudeville acts. In Michigan the largest such organization was the Butterfield Circuit, formed by Walter S. Butterfield, a native of Indiana. In 1906 he acquired the Hamblin Opera House in Battle Creek and remodeled it as a popular-price vaudeville house. A few months later he opened the Bijou Theater in Kalamazoo. By 1929 he had a chain of 55 theaters. As vaudeville became less popular Butterfield supplemented and finally replaced the vaudeville acts with motion pictures. Expansion continued during the depression and afterward; by 1948 the Butterfield circuit included a total of 115 theaters in 33 Michigan cities. Another successful operator was Claude Cady of Lansing. The Cady theaters eventually became part of the Butterfield circuit.

The coming of television in the 1950s and the construction of outdoor moving-picture theaters dealt a severe blow to the ornate movie palaces built by Butterfield and others. Many of the smaller and older moving-picture theaters were closed, and most small towns saw their once-popular movie houses discontinued. But the larger cities continued to support the moving picture theater. The development of colored and wide-screen movies, which gave the viewer a greater sense of realism, helped save the movie theater. The coming of television also forced the motion-picture producers to pay more attention to artistic values in the films made for projection in moving-picture theaters.

In spite of the competition of films, radio, and television, interest in the legitimate theater did not die out. Traveling theatrical troupes still visited Detroit and other Michigan cities, though much less frequently than earlier, and Detroit still had several legitimate theaters. Of more importance, however was the development of the community theater. In Detroit Miss Jessie Bonstelle established a resident professional theater company in 1925. Three years later the company was reorganized as a nonprofit group called the Civic Players, and its theater became the Detroit Civic Theater. Miss Bonstelle was known as the maker of stars. Among the great figures of the theater whose talents were recognized by her were Katherine Cornell, Ann Harding, Frank Morgan, Melvyn Douglas, and William Powell.

Jessie Bonstelle was chiefly interested in the professional theater. But amateurs played a major part in rescuing the legitimate theater from oblivion. During her career in Detroit many amateurs were forming organizations of what was at first known as the "Little Theater" movement. Fundamentally this was a response of communities to the decline of the road show. That decline was becoming apparent by 1910 as a consequence of higher rents, higher transportation costs, and dissatisfaction of theatergoers with the dramatic fare supplied by New York booking agencies. In the early stages of the "Little Theater" movement it was sometimes identified with the "Art Theater," an organization formed to provide an outlet for the creative work of play writers, actors, directors, designers, musicians, and dancers. The art theater never attained a very large popularity outside New York. Two other phases of the Little Theater movement, however, had significance throughout the nation.

One of these was the organization of community theaters. The Ypsilanti Players are regarded as being the first Little Theater group in Michigan, but the Flint Community Players have been in longest continuous operation. The Ypsilanti project started in an old carriage house, with a tiny stage and seats for 200 people. No salaries were paid; deficits were absorbed by Daniel Quirk, a local businessman. Some excellent plays were presented. In Detroit a number of amateur theatrical groups developed, the most important being the Players' Club and the Contemporary Theater. Sheldon Cheney, who joined the latter group, became editor of a magazine called *Theatre Arts*, a publication that exerted a national influence in the Little Theater movement. Outstate other amateur theatrical groups were being formed. The earliest was founded in Allegan in the 1920s; for its use Griswold Auditorium was provided. Grand Rapids was the next to develop a community theater. In Kalamazoo the Civic Players originated in 1929, and through the generosity of Dr. W. E. Upjohn a beautiful and fully equipped theater was constructed for its productions. Community theaters were established in other Michigan cities in the 1930s and subsequently. In some cases full-time directors, managers, and technicians were employed, but in the main these theaters were for the amateur. The Community Theater Association of Michigan was formed in 1949. By 1963 there were 35 outstate community theaters belonging to this organization, with another twenty in Detroit.

Most Michigan high schools stage dramatic productions, and in some there is serious study of dramatic art. In the colleges, too, there has been increasing attention to the theater. As early as 1928 the institution now known as Wayne State University opened a training course in drama and the experimental theater.

The University of Michigan's play-production group was formed the same year. During the summer, as the Michigan Repertory Playhouse, this group has presented for many years a play each week for a period of five weeks in the Lydia Mendelssohn Theater, a splendidly equipped playhouse.

Another development in more recent years has been the summer theater located near vacation centers. Shortly after World War II Jack Ragotzy started an amateur group called the Village Players at Richland, near Gull Lake and within a few miles of both Kalamazoo and Battle Creek. Later he acquired an old barn near Augusta and refurbished it as a theater. Professional actors replaced amateur players, and a summer-long series of plays was presented each year. Summer theaters were opened in the 1950s in such summer-resort towns as Saugutuck, South Haven, Paw Paw Lake, Grand Haven, Manistee, and Petoskey. In the Copper Country the old Calumet opera house was reopened as a summer theater, playing musical comedy.

Thus the legitimate theater continued to flourish in Michigan in spite of all its competitors. The patterns of theatrical activity had undergone many changes since 1865, but the enduring value of the theater and its perennial attraction were still apparent. The popularity of the theater, the films, and television may have reflected in part a need for escape from a world that was becoming more and more complex and bewildering. The media through which dramatic performances were presented all tended to seek patronage through the sensational and not infrequently the vulgar. Still, for the audience and for the players, the presentation of a dramatic performance was on many occasions an ennobling experience.

LITERATURE

Michigan has produced a number of writers who have achieved national recognition and a host of others whose works have varying degrees of merit. Many of these have used Michigan materials; others show little trace of Michigan nativity or background in their literary works. Typical of the latter are Ring Lardner, the noted humorist, who was a native of Niles; the distinguished novelist Edna Ferber, born in Kalamazoo; Clarence Buddington Kelland, popular story writer who was a native of Portland, Michigan; and Bruce Catton, a prolific writer on the Civil War who was born at Petoskey. Ernest Hemingway, one of the most distinguished novelists of the twentieth century, lived in Michigan for many years, as did the well-known satirist Peter DeVries.

There have also been, of course, numerous authors not born in Michigan who have used Michigan settings for their works.

The period of the Civil War and Reconstruction was not conducive to literary production. But beginning about 1870, publications from the pens of Michigan authors began to appear in greater number. As the pioneer days waned older people sought to recapture the memories and spirit of earlier times. The Michigan Pioneer Society was organized in 1874 and began the publication of an annual volume of *Collections*. State histories by Charles R. Tuttle and James V. Campbell were published in the 1870s and Silas Farmer produced his voluminous history of Detroit in 1889. Most of the earliest county histories were published in the 1870s and 1880s.

Perhaps the best known Michigan writer of fiction in the latter part of the nineteenth century was Constance Fenimore Woolman, whose mother was a niece of James Fenimore Cooper. Her novels won the praise of Henry James, and Alexander Cowie, in his monumental work on the American novel, published in 1948, devotes eleven pages to her work. Probably her best-known work is *Anne, a Tale of Mackinac*, the material for which she gathered during a summer on Mackinac Island. The setting is Mackinac Island during the Civil War.

The verse best liked by Michigan readers of the late nineteenth century dripped with sentimentality. Will Carleton's "Over the hills to the poorhouse" had exactly the quality to endear it to thousands. A bronze tablet was erected in 1925 just a little east of Hillsdale on the grounds of the old poorhouse that made Carleton famous. In the same category was Ben King, "the sweet singer of old St. Joe," who wrote many humorous and sentimental verses. Rose Hartwick's "Curfew shall not ring tonight" was long a favorite for schoolroom recital. Another of this ilk was Julia Moore, known as the "sweet singer of Michigan," whose verse was immensely popular in the 1880s.

In the early years of the twentieth century several Michigan authors attained a national reputation for their fiction. Rex Beach, a native of Michigan, wrote more than a score of novels and many short stories. Born at Atwood, he was best known for his stories of the Klondike, although in some of his writings he makes use of the Michigan scene. James Oliver Curwood, who attained an immense popularity in the first quarter of the twentieth century, occupied a palatial house that was a showplace in Owosso. Among his best sellers were *The Honor of the Big Snows* (1911), *The Flower of the North* (1912), and *The Valley of Silent Men* (1920). Perhaps the ablest of all the writers of the "he-man" type of fiction was Stewart Edward White, born in Grand Rapids. His novels deal with life in the lumber camps. *The Blazed Trail* (1902), *The Forest* (1903), and *The Riverman* (1908) were his best-known novels. Harold Titus, an enthusiast for conservation, also wrote works on the out-of-doors, describing the beauties of the forests and lakes of the Grand Traverse region, which was his home. Another writer of robust fiction was Karl W. Detzer, whose stories of the Michigan State Police and the Great Lakes are particularly well known.

The day of the lumberman was romanticized by a number of writers besides Stewart Edward White. Eugene Thwing, in his novels *The Red-Keggers* and *The Man from Red Keg*, used the Saginaw country as his setting. The legend of Paul Bunyan, whose epic feats were the subject of tales told in the lumber camps from Maine to Washington, is well known largely through the collections of Bunyan stories published in 1925 by James Stevens and by Esther Shephard. E. C. Beck of Mount Pleasant published a notable collection of lumberman's ballads in the 1940s, and recited and sang them with great gusto to delighted audiences.

Farm life in Michigan was depicted with a liberal dash of nostalgia in the books written by Della T. Lutes in the 1930s and 1940s. Typical of these are *The Country Kitchen* (1936), *Millbrook* (1938), and *Cousin William* (1942). In contrast, Godfrey Dell Eaton, in *Backfurrow* (1925), describes life in a poor farm region of Michigan as one of stupidity, beastliness, and bitterness. Helen Rose Hull, who was born in Albion, explored the woman's place in the scheme of things in her novels, one of which, *The Islanders* (1927), depicts Michigan as it was passing out of the pioneer stage into a more complex society. Arthur Pound, in his *Once a Wilderness* (1938) and *Second Growth* (1935), interprets Michigan's transition from an agricultural to an industrial state.

The automobile industry has provided Michigan authors and other writers with material for dozens of biographies, histories, and novels. The fame, significance, and enigmatic character of Henry Ford have attracted a host of biographers. Outstanding are the three volumes on Ford and his company written by Allan Nevins (1954-1962). Arthur Pound tells the early history of General Motors in his *The Turning Wheel* (1934), while Walter Chrysler, founder of the other "Big Three" automobile manufacturing company, tells his own story in *The Life of an American Workman* (1950). Writers of fiction also have used the automobile industry as a setting for their stories. Lawrence H. Conrad, who lived near Detroit and was the son of a father devoted to the ideals of handicraft and bitterly opposed to mass production, authored a novel entitled *Temper* (1924), giving a realistic account of the tempering of the soul of a steelworker in an automobile factory. Other novels of the auto industry include Wessel Smitter's *F.O.B. Detroit* (1938) and Gordon Webber's *What End But Love* (1959).

The nationalities that make up the people of Michigan have been the subject of many works of fiction and nonfiction. Arnold Mulder describes the ways of the Dutch in his novels *The Domine of Harlem* (1913), *The Outbound Road* (1919), and *The Sand Doctor* (1921), and in his book on *Americans from Holland* (1947). David C. DeJong, in his *With a Dutch Accent* (1944), also deals delightfully with the immigrants to Michigan from the Netherlands. Meindert DeJong, brother of David C. DeJong, has received international recognition (Hans Christian Anderson Award) for his children's books. Leonard Cline has written a novel in the typical realistic fashion about a Finnish settlement in the Upper Peninsula entitled *God Head* (1925). Newton G. Thomas' *The Long Winter Ends* (1941) tells the story of adjustment to the ways of a new land by a Cornish miner group near Hancock. Florence E. McClinchey, in her *Joe Pete* (1929), tells how the pressure of white supremacy made a hard life even more difficult for an Ojibway Indian of northern Michigan.

The Upper Peninsula has had its own historians, interpreters, and novelists. An Upper Peninsula lawyer, who served for a time as a justice of the Michigan supreme court, John F. Voelker, has written several novels and stories with Upper Michigan as a setting. One of these, *The Anatomy of a Murder* (1958), was a bestseller and was used as the title and subject of a successful motion picture. John B. Martin's *Call It North Country* (1944) contains a wealth of stories and tall tales of the surveyors, settlers, lumberjacks, fur traders, and miners of the Upper Peninsula. *Northwoods Sketches* (1949) contains observations on the Upper Peninsula by a former governor, Chase S. Osborn, one of the many who loved the region. Mildred Walker's *Fireweed* tells how the second generation in an Upper Peninsula lumber town flourished briefly, like fireweed, after the giants of the forest were cut. The folkways of a Swedish family in the Upper Peninsula are recalled in a book entitled *Latchstring Out*, by Skulda Baner. Louis Reinman, a native of the Upper Peninsula, wrote many stories of the region that were published in the 1950s, the best known being *Between the Iron and the Pine*. Richard Dorson, in his *Bloodstoppers and Bearwalkers* (1952) deals with the folklore of Upper Michigan.

The history of the Great Lakes is told in a series published by the Bobbs-Merrill Company: Harlan H. Hatcher's *Lake Erie* (1945), Fred Landon's *Lake Huron* (1944), Milo Quaife's *Lake Michigan* (1944), and Grace Lee Nute's *Lake Superior* (1944). George Cuthbertson in his *Freshwater* (1931) and Walter Havighurst in his *Long Ships Passing* (1942) relate the history of navigation on the Great Lakes. Storms and shipwrecks on the Great Lakes have attracted a great deal of interest. Among the books dealing with this subject are Dana T. Bowen's *Shipwrecks of the Lakes* (1952) and Frank Barcus' *Freshwater Fury* (1960).

The early history of Michigan continues to hold fascination for twentieth-century writers. *Wolves Against the Moon* (1940) by Julia Altrocchi is a dramatic story of white men and Indians with Mackinac Island as its locale. A story of pioneering in the 1870s on Little Traverse Bay is delightfully told by U. P. Hedrick in his *Land of the Crooked Tree* (1948). The life of the circuit rider in pioneer days is depicted by Cecile Matschat in *Preacher on Horseback* (1940). Iola Fuller was awarded the Hopwood Prize at the University of Michigan for her *Loon Feather*, published in 1940. The story is told by Oneta, daughter of the Indian chieftain Tecumseh, and it deals with the difficulties of adjustment faced by the Indians when the lumbermen moved into their hunting grounds.

Books and articles about Michigan continue to pour from the presses in ever-increasing numbers. In spite of the fact that the United States was plunged into the maelstrom of world affairs after World War II to an extent it had never been before, there was in the 1950s an extraordinary growth of interest in state and local history. Publishers found a ready market for biographies, histories, and fiction about Michigan. It seemed as if, in their quest for meaning in contemporary life, thoughtful people were seeking to understand more clearly how their society evolved and the nature of their origins and growth. This had the effect of greatly stimulating the demand for printed materials. What was published varied widely in literary merit; certainly a great deal of it was ephemeral, but it is probable that a considerable amount of it will prove to have lasting significance.[19]

MUSEUMS

Another agency of cultural enrichment is the museum. There are many kinds of museums, most of which are represented in

[19] An excellent summary of Michigan literature may be found in K. I. Gillard, *Our Michigan Heritage*. See also A. Mulder, "Authors and Wolverines" *Saturday Review* (*March 4, 1939*) and *Michigan, a Guide to the Wolverine State*, pp. 145-151.

Michigan: science museums, industrial museums, historic houses, fort museums, and general historic museums. In the first building erected for the University of Michigan when it opened in 1841 a room was set aside for what was then called a "cabinet" and which would now be called a museum. By 1963 the University of Michigan had more than a dozen separate museums, containing collections in such varied fields as archaeology, musical instruments, plants, and animal life. Museums in Michigan are maintained by state agencies, cities, school districts, private associations, and individuals. A directory of Michigan museums issued by the Michigan Historical Commission lists more than 80 historical museums and exhibits, located in 45 of the state's 83 counties.[20]

Art museums and art galleries have been described in an earlier section of this chapter. Among the museums with notable collections of natural history are the Grand Rapids Public Museum and the Kingman Museum in Battle Creek. The Grand Rapids Public Museum developed out of a collection started by the Grand Rapids Lyceum of Natural History, dating back to 1854. The Kingman Museum occupies a beautiful building in Leila Arboretum, situated in the western part of Battle Creek. One of the state's distinctive exhibits is found in the Netherlands museum at Holland, which depicts the life and customs of the Dutch people as they adapted to the Michigan environment while preserving many of their folkways and handicrafts. The Cranbrook Natural History collection at Bloomfield Hills is a notable one. Another unique venture is the Detroit Children's Museum.

The State Pioneer Museum at Lansing grew from a collection started by Mrs. Marie B. Ferry about 1900. In 1903 it was placed under the supervision of the Michigan Pioneer and Historical Society but later became the responsibility of the Michigan Historical Commission. Among the best known of its kind in the nation is the Detroit Historical Museum, started in 1928 from a collection of historical materials gathered by Clarence M. Burton. For several years it was housed in the Barlum Tower. Impetus was provided for the establishment of a major museum in Detroit by the approach of the city's 250th anniversary. The Detroit Historical Society by 1952 had over 3,000 members and was the largest historical society in the nation. Over $400,000 was raised by popular subscription in 1943, and the City Council voted an additional $500,000 to provide a spacious and beautiful new museum building at the corner of Woodward and Kirby. It was dedicated

[20] *Michigan Museums and Historic Exhibits,* issued by Michigan Historical Commission.

in 1951. The Detroit Historical Commission was appointed in 1946 by the mayor to supervise the maintenance and staffing of the museum. The Detroit Historical Museum pioneered a new concept of historical museums. Most such institutions accumulated tremendous numbers of objects quite unrelated to each other and displayed them in such profusion as to baffle the viewer. At the Detroit Museum it was decided that since museums are primarily educational in their purpose, the exhibits, to be effective, ought to be displayed in such a fashion as to create living history and to illustrate a single idea, concept, or period. The new technique involved the extensive use of dioramas, and of taste and ingenuity in the construction of exhibits. In the dozen years after the museum building was dedicated three additional museums were added. The Fort Wayne Military Museum was established in 1949 when the United States government transferred to the City of Detroit the historic portion of the old Fort Wayne. The Dossin Museum of Great Lakes history, originally located on board the *J. T. Wing,* an old sailing schooner, is now housed in a new building on Belle Isle. At the Michigan State Fair Grounds the historic house where Ulysses S. Grant lived while serving as company officer and quartermaster at the Detroit Barracks in 1849 is open two weeks each year during the Michigan State Fair.

There are a number of museums maintained and operated by professional staffs in other Michigan cities. The Kalamazoo Public Museum pioneered a plan of loaning exhibits for use in the home or schoolroom. At Dearborn the local historical society in the 1940s secured a building that once was part of the United States arsenal for use as a museum. Other historical museums operated by local historical societies are found in Muskegon, Niles, and Marquette. In the 1950s and early 1960s a host of small museums sprang up, usually under the direction of a local historical society and staffed by volunteer workers. Among these were museums at Marshall, Manistique, and Escanaba. Michigan State University, Wayne State University, and other public and private colleges and universities have museums open to the public.

Several manufacturing companies maintain museums. The Wisconsin Land and Lumber Company promoted the Paul Bunyan Museum at Blaney Park. The Ford Motor Company rebuilt at Dearborn the Ford Rotunda exhibited at the Century of Progress Exposition in Chicago in 1933, containing murals, models, and displays showing the scope of Ford manufacturing operations. The Baker Furniture Company established a museum for furniture research at Grand Rapids in 1941.

The most extensive exhibit of Americana in Michigan is found in Greenfield Village and the Ford Museum at Dearborn. Greenfield Village was built on a 200-acre tract of land by Henry Ford. It is said to be America's first outdoor museum. Ford, who had once said "History is bunk," purchased about a hundred historic buildings that were moved to Greenfield Village to show how Americans lived and worked during the first three centuries of their history. The Henry Ford Museum was built to exhibit the vast collection of Americana that Ford began to assemble as early as 1906. In the same area Ford established schools to carry out his "learning-by-doing" ideas in education. Greenfield Village, the Museum, and the schools constitute the three divisions of The Edison Institute, dedicated on October 21, 1929 by President Herbert Hoover as a memorial to Thomas A. Edison on the fiftieth anniversary of the incandescent light. Greenfield Village and the Ford Museum became one of Michigan's major tourist attractions. In 1960 more than a million visitors were received.

In the Straits of Mackinac area there was another successful museum development. A museum at Fort Mackinac on Mackinac Island had been in existence for a number of years, but not much attention was paid to it and there were few visitors. Largely through the efforts of Stewart Woodfill, chairman of the Mackinac Island State Park Commission, the legislature of the state was persuaded to enact a law authorizing the Commission to issue $150,000 in revenue bonds with which to refurbish the museum. Interest was to be paid and the principal retired by admission fees. The work of preparing and arranging artifacts, dioramas, and paintings illustrative of the fort's history was carried out under the direction of Dr. Eugene Petersen. In 1958 Fort Mackinac, with its "new look," was opened, and the number of visitors exceeded all expectations. The venture was so successful that another and larger bond issue was authorized to restore Fort Michilimackinac on the Lower Peninsula side of the Straits. The original fort here had entirely disappeared. In the 1930s it was partially restored as a W.P.A. project. The new program of restoration, based on careful historical research, was begun in 1959. A new palisade and a few buildings were started the first year. At Fort Michilimackinac, one of the most successful features was the archaeological "dig," carried on in full view of visitors, which yielded what was probably the richest store of eighteenth-century artifacts in the nation. The number of visitors increased each year, reaching about 350,000 in 1963.[21]

[21] E. Petersen, *Michilimackinac: Its History and Restoration;* M. S. Maxwell and L. H. Binford, *Excavation of Fort Michilimackinac, Mackinaw City, Michigan, 1959 Season.*

Meanwhile on Mackinac Island other restorations took place in a program designed to make this one of the nation's greatest historic spots. Even before the old fort was refurbished a project was launched to rebuild the retail store where the French fur trader Alexis St. Martin had been accidentally shot in 1822, and where Dr. William Beaumont was summoned from the fort to treat his wounds. As has been related earlier in this narrative, the experiments and observations carried on following this accident led to the writing of a book on the processes of digestion that made medical history. Funds were raised by the Michigan State Medical Society to build an exact replica of the old Astor store as a memorial to Dr. Beaumont. Construction took place in 1953, and the memorial was dedicated July 17, 1954.[22] Along Market Street, on which the Beaumont Memorial is situated, are buildings erected by the American Fur Company shortly after the War of 1812. Further along is the Biddle House, parts of which may date from 1780. It is the oldest structure on the Island and one of the oldest in the Old Northwest. This house was completely restored by the Michigan Society of Architects in 1959.

Historic buildings have been preserved elsewhere in the state. On Beaver Island one may visit the old Mormon Print Shop where James Strang printed his newspaper. At Sault Ste. Marie the Indian Agency house and the Bishop Baraga House are open to visitors. The house where former Governor Frank Murphy was born is preserved at Harbor Beach; other governors are commemorated by the Moses Wisner home in Pontiac and the John S. Barry House at Constantine. The historic Walker Tavern still stands at Brooklyn. There are many privately owned museums open to the public, such as the Poll Museum near Holland and Luckhard's Museum in Sebewaing. The Conservation Department maintains historic exhibits at Fort Wilkins, at Copper Harbor, and at Fayette. This is not an exhaustive list of Michigan museums and exhibitions, and many historic sites remain unmarked and undeveloped. More and more the tourist and vacation industry is recognizing the importance of history in attracting visitors to Michigan. Even more important is the role that living history plays in impressing upon citizens of Michigan, and especially on youth, the rich heritage that is theirs and the responsibility they have to preserve and enhance that heritage.

JOINERS

The typical American has gained a wide reputation as a "joiner." Dating from the time of the Mayflower Compact, the

[22] H. B. Selleck, *Beaumont and the "Mackinac Island Miracle."*

American has demonstrated a marked proclivity for voluntary organization to meet some need beyond the power of the individual. In Michigan the number of clubs, societies, and associations that sprang up over the years is beyond counting. Those related to various interests, such as education, religious worship, artistic expression, and agriculture, have been mentioned above.

In the years following the Civil War fraternal orders attained a high degree of popularity. They became so numerous and absorbed such a large part of the interest of the people that many churches opposed them. There was a Masonic lodge in Michigan as early as 1764 and there were many Masons among the pioneers. But the growth of the order was interrupted by a wave of anti-Masonry that swept the nation in the 1830s. The revival of Masonry in Michigan began in 1840 when a convention was held in Mount Clemens to reorganize the lodge. Three of the old lodges were revived and a Grand Lodge of Michigan was instituted in 1844. Progress from this point was rapid, and by the close of the century there was a Masonic lodge in virtually every city and town in the state. The first Odd Fellow lodge in the state was organized in 1843 at Detroit; by 1865 more than a hundred lodges of this order had been founded in Michigan. The Eastern Star lodge, associated with the Masons, and the Rebekahs, for wives of the Odd Fellows, both had their start in the state before the Civil War. The Maccabee order originated in this state under permission granted by the legislature in 1881. The original ritual of the Knights of Pythias was written by an Upper Peninsula schoolteacher in 1859; the order's first lodge in the state was organized in Detroit in 1871. These and many other lodges were designed as fraternal and social organizations, and all of them aided those of their members who were sick as well as the widows and children of those who died. Several developed life-insurance programs of considerable size and importance, among them the Maccabees and the Gleaners.

In the first two decades of the twentieth century the noonday luncheon clubs had their origin. The first of these was Rotary International, the first club of which in Michigan was formed in Detroit in 1910. Two of the major luncheon or service clubs had their origin in Michigan: the Exchange Club in 1911 and Kiwanis International in 1915. In 1963 there was no village or town of any size that did not have at least one service club.

Important among the organizations in every Michigan community since the Civil War have been the veterans' associations. Until after 1900 the Grand Army of the Republic, an organization of Civil War veterans, wielded enormous influence on the political affairs of the state, as well as providing a social outlet for its members and giving them a pressure group to press for pensions and other benefits. The United Spanish War Veterans grew out of a number of organizations formed by the men who served in the armed forces in 1898. Although this organization never attained the proportions of the G.A.R., it had about 65 local "camps" in Michigan as late as 1935. The Veterans of Foreign Wars originated from one of the organizations of Spanish War veterans which was formed in 1899. Its present name dates from 1913. A large accretion of World War I veterans to its membership led to the establishment of the Department of Michigan in 1920. A national home for widows and orphans of members was built at Eaton Rapids. Another great increase in membership came after World War II. The Disabled American Veterans (D.A.V.) and the Amvets, the latter composed exclusively of World War II veterans, were two other large veterans organizations represented in Michigan. Largest of all was the American Legion. Michigan was represented by 46 delegates at the meeting in New York in 1919 at which this organization was formed. The Michigan Department received its charter the next year. In addition to its work on behalf of the veterans the American Legion promoted a program of "Americanization," sponsored such projects as the Wolverine Boys State and patriotic speaking and essay contests.

Women have proved no less zealous than men in forming clubs and associations. Women's clubs were formed in Kalamazoo in 1852, Battle Creek in 1864, Grand Rapids in 1869, and Detroit in 1872. A state-wide organization to fight the battle against John Barleycorn was formed when the Women's Christian Temperance Union came into being at Grand Rapids in 1875. A State Federation of Women's Clubs originated at a meeting held in Bay View in 1894. The earliest chapters of the Daughters of the American Revolution were organized in Michigan in 1893. Women's auxiliaries were attached to all the veterans' groups and there were similar groups associated with the various lodges. Women in business and the professions have formed the Business and Professional Women's clubs, the Altrusa Club, and Zonta International.

During the last two decades of the nineteenth century and the first two decades of the twentieth, scores of state associations were formed by trade, manufacturing, labor, and professional groups. Typical of these are the following: Michigan Retail Hardware Association (1895), Retail Lumber Dealers' Association (1889), Michigan Bankers' Association (1875), Michigan State

Horticultural Society (1870), Michigan Academy of Science, Arts, and Letters (1894), and Michigan Federation of Labor (1889).

These are but a few of the organizations and associations that have been formed to meet some specific need felt by their members. Most of them serve a social purpose and satisfy, to a greater or lesser degree, the yen most Americans feel to "belong." But they go beyond that. In many instances they maintain legislative agents or lobbyists in Lansing to promote legislation desired by their members. They perform countless civic services for the less fortunate members of society. Some have rituals and pageantry that may be regarded as constituting the democratic counterpart of the role played by royalty and aristocracy in other countries. There is hardly a single organization that does not have a full compliment of committees and subcomittees to consume the spare time of members. The Michiganian of 1963 is driven by necessity to conclude that he cannot possibly read all the books and magazines, see all the movies and plays, enjoy all the recreation facilities, nor join all the organizations. Either by chance or by choice he must select some and reject others. A culture of abundance has replaced a culture of scarcity.

Peacetime Nuclear Plant, Big Rock Point, Charlevoix, Michigan

25

INTO THE SPACE AGE

Not far from Sault Ste. Marie, where Father Jacques Marquette started the first permanent settlement in Michigan in 1668, a great air base has been constructed by the United States government. It is named in honor of Iven C. Kincheloe, Jr. of Cassopolis, an Air Force pilot who, before his death in 1958, set an altitude record of 126,000 feet in the X-Z research plane.[1] Just as Father Marquette was a pioneer in the exploration of primitive Michigan, so Iven Kincheloe was a pioneer in the exploration of space. The three centuries that have elapsed since Father Marquette founded the little mission on the St. Mary's River have been filled with drama and achievement, as recounted in the earlier pages of this narrative. It seems probable that the next three centuries will witness events of equal excitement and significance.

Developments of the middle years of the twentieth century have resulted in a new kind of world. The capacity for the production of food and fiber as well as manufactured goods has increased so rapidly that an economy of abundance has replaced an economy of scarcity. International relations have undergone a revolution as a consequence of the development, through science and technology, of weapons capable of destroying all life on earth. The United States, which during most of its history enjoyed the opportunity to grow and prosper independently of the rest of the

[1]Secretary of Defense Robert McNamara, late in 1965, announced that this base would be closed in 1970.

747

world, can no longer do so, but must share the world's problems and responsibilities. Conditions of life have made nations as well as individuals interdependent, thus creating new problems for government. The population explosion has been unprecedented, and the number of people needing food, clothing, medical care, and education in the world has almost outrun the fantastic gains in productive capacity. What role will the American states play in this new kind of world? What part will Michigan play?

It is not the function of the historian to be a crystal gazer. He can only assess the future in terms of the past and the present. The tendency during the past half-century has been for local government units to lose some of their functions to state government, for the states to shift some of their responsibilities to the national government, and for the national government to depend heavily for the performance of some of its work on a world organization. There is every reason to presume this trend will continue. The trend has been resisted stoutly by conservatives, and there is no doubt it will continue to be resisted. But rapid communication, the ease of travel, interdependence, and the growth of trade all point outward from the local community to the larger world. Neither local government nor the states, however, are likely to wither away in the process. History and tradition exert a strong pull on Americans. Furthermore, there are many common needs that can be met most efficiently and agreeably by local and state action.

The growth of population and the increasing proportion of the people living in urban communities have created critical problems for local government. These have been compounded by the move away from the central cities to the suburbs. Many thousands of Michiganians residing in urban communities lack municipal governments and have to rely on township governments that were designed for governing rural, not urban communities. Superimposed on the township, village, and city governments are the school districts, some large and some small. Within a single large Michigan urban community one finds a great number and variety of local governmental units, often overlapping and conflicting. County governments, which might serve the needs of a larger metropolitan area, have been kept by the constitution and laws in a standard pattern, with administrative machinery and legislative powers totally inadequate to carry increased responsibilities. If the provisions in the new state constitution for county home rule are implemented by appropriate legislative action it may well be that county government, in urban areas, can be refashioned to perform needed functions for a large metropolitan district. It is abundantly clear that the chaotic condition and inadequacy of local governmental units in Michigan invites the loss of the powers of local government to the state. If government at the local level is to be kept alive and vital, changes are mandatory.

In at least three vital areas state government has already taken over functions that once belonged exclusively to local units. To facilitate the construction and maintenance of arterial highways the state has been given this responsibility, and even the building and maintenance of county roads and city streets are financed largely through tax revenues collected by the state and returned to local units. Then there is the field of education. From its earliest years Michigan has had a department of public instruction, but until the third decade of the twentieth century its functions were mainly informational. It was because school districts differed so widely in their financial capacity for supporting schools that state aid on a large scale began during the depression years of the 1930s. Finally, there is the relief of poverty, which was also an exclusively local-government function until the twentieth century. The desirability here, as in the field of education, of equalizing the cost of welfare relief between counties was a major cause for state intervention. County welfare boards still control to some extent policy on relief, but funds for relief of the poor, the handicapped, the unemployed, and the aged come largely from state and federal sources, and this carries with it the implication of a large amount of control.

Just as the state has been used as a means of equalizing the financial burdens and facilities for highway building, schools, and poor relief, so the national government has been called on to equalize the burdens and facilities among the states. Federal aid has been provided for education so that children in a state with fewer resources to pay for schools will not be denied educational opportunities. Federal aid for highways has been a means of constructing interstate roads spanning the nation. Federal aid for the poor, the unemployed, and the handicapped has been given on the ground that poverty, unemployment, and handicapped persons constitute a national problem. By the same sort of justification federal aid has been provided in other areas: library aid, airport construction, sewage disposal, urban renewal, soil conservation, and recreational facilities—to mention a few. Although there has been a continuing protest against the loss of the powers of local and state governments to the national government, the trend seems irreversible. But this has not meant any atrophy of state government. As citizens demand new services, the states have taken on new responsibilities far exceeding those that have been lost.

The effort to halt the loss of the powers of state government to the federal government has been thwarted to a great degree by the same forces that have applied to the loss of local-government functions to the states. In Michigan, as in many other states, urban communities have been denied their fair share of representation in the state legislature by the apportionment of seats favoring nonurban areas. The decision of the Supreme Court of the United States in the case of Carr vs. Tennessee in 1961 meant that states would be compelled to reapportion their legislatures in such a manner as to give the urban resident equal representation. The situation as it existed in Michigan for many years was that the legislature, dominated by outstate members and interests, paid little heed to the needs of the state's largest city, Detroit, and also ignored to a lesser degree the needs of the state's other cities. Laws governing the annexation of adjacent areas to cities, for example, were largely dictated by the powerful township lobby. Cities were denied the power to lay many types of taxes. The consequence was that cities looked increasingly to Washington rather than to Lansing for help. Reapportionment on a one-man one-vote basis appears to hold promise for some improvement in terms of legislative attention to urban problems. The losses of state powers to the national government in the years ahead are likely to be reduced only in proportion to the capacity of state governments to meet needs that local communities by themselves cannot meet.

What are the prospects for the Michigan economy in the space age? The peculiar problems Michigan has faced have been sketched in the preceding pages. The high degree of dependence on a single industry, automotive manufacturing, has resulted in an economy that has been subject to violent fluctuations. Higher taxes have been required by the necessity of providing for the needs of about two-thirds of the area of the state that is sparsely populated and lacking the basis for a sound economy, by the necessity of providing tax-supported higher education for a much larger percentage of college youth than attend public institutions in other states, and by certain other unique characteristics of Michigan. The tax burden on business has probably served to deter some industries from coming to Michigan and has contributed to the loss of some already in the state. The Upper Peninsula, with its dwindling lumber and mineral industries, its thin, sandy soils and cold climate, which discourage agriculture, and its remoteness from markets that has made it unattractive for manufacturing, is an economic problem in itself. The northern half of the Lower Peninsula has similar economic problems. Michigan labor has been highly skilled and highly organized, factors that have affected economic growth. The loss of defense contracts and the extent of automation were other factors contributing to widespread unemployment and economic distress in the last half of the 1950s.

There are, however, hopeful signs for the future. With the spread of labor organization it appears less likely that Michigan industries in the future will find in the southern states a haven where labor costs and taxes are lower. It must be pointed out, however, that in the South costs for heat and light and other factors attributable to the climate, such as snow removal, will continue to give that region some advantage over Michigan for industry. The decentralization of the automobile industry, largely due to the advantages that accrue from not having to transport finished vehicles over long distances to get them to market, is likely to continue, and to the extent it does, Michigan will become less a single-industry state. The state agency working for economic growth, together with local chambers of commerce, are seeking more diversified industries for Michigan. One great advantage the state has is an abundant supply of water, a factor of major importance in many industries such as those producing chemicals. The pool of skilled labor in Michigan is another advantage. The great boom following World War II in the automotive industry, to which defense contracts were added, probably served to lessen the attention paid to research and development of new products by the industry. Since the economic recession of the late 1950s, much more attention is being paid to the importance of research, and large research centers have been developed, notably around Ann Arbor. All this holds promise for the years ahead.

Although an expansion of the vacation and recreation industry seems to hold the greatest promise for northern Michigan in the immediate future, there are long-range factors that stand to benefit the region in a variety of ways. The enormous increase in the nation's population seems likely to bring to an end within the foreseeable future the problem of agricultural surpluses. The soils of northern Michigan can be made productive when the time comes that increased production of food and fiber is needed, and because of the population growth this seems less remote than it did in the 1930s and 1940s. Much the same situation applies to the mining of iron and copper. There are vast amounts of cop-

New International Bridge to Canada, Sault Ste. Marie, Michigan

per and iron ore in Upper Michigan, but the expense of bringing them to the surface and refining or smelting them has made production uneconomical in competition with other sources. But the nation is using up its mineral resources at a rapid rate, and the day may not be far away when it will be profitable to spend whatever needs to be spent to mine this Upper Peninsula ore.

The Upper Peninsula stands to profit, too, by the growth of world commerce. The foreign-trade-expansion law of 1962 seems destined to greatly increase trade between the United States and foreign countries in the years ahead. There will be vastly larger exports and imports. And it is altogether probable that much of this increased commerce will move through the St. Lawrence Seaway. Michigan, with its many ports, stands to benefit more than most states by such a possible increase in world trade. Cities in the Upper Peninsula such as Marquette, Sault Ste. Marie, Escanaba, Houghton, and Munising—which may be regarded as remote from the great domestic markets—are actually less remote, in some cases, than certain Lower Peninsula cities from world markets such as London, Hamburg, and Rotterdam. There is every reason to presume that as the nation's economy becomes less dependent on the domestic market and more dependent on foreign markets, Michigan, and especially northern Michigan, will be especially benefited.

The need for recreational facilities is certain to increase during the years ahead. Michigan has great stretches of unspoiled wilderness for those who love the out-of-doors. Isle Royale is a prime example. Efforts are being made through the National Parks Service and the state Conservation Department to pre-empt large areas from private use and dedicate them to the use of the public. In 1963 a seashore area around the Sleeping Bear Dunes in northern Lower Michigan and an area east of Munising in the Upper Peninsula were in process of being acquired by the national government for recreational use. If, as is possible, the Upper Peninsula in the years ahead witnesses a revival of mining, farming, and manufacturing, it will become even more urgent to reserve large areas from such uses for recreation.

The variety of national and racial stocks that form the basis of Michigan's population in 1963 hold promise for a rich and varied cultural development in the space age. It seems safe to predict that as the state grows older there will be greater care for the preservation of historic sites and historic buildings. The striking development of musical activities, the theater, and the visual arts during the middle years of the twentieth century seems likely to be further accentuated.

Some of the needs Michigan must meet already have been indicated: a reform of local government that will make it more adequate to the needs of an urban, industrial state; an improvement in the efficiency of state government; a great diversification of industry; preparation for an expanding world commerce; and the conservation of recreational and historical resources. In earlier portions of this history of Michigan attention was focused on the problem of financing state and local government. In 1963 the problem of deficits in the state treasury was temporarily, at least, solved, and the state was actually accumulating a surplus. But Governor George Romney pointed out that while the amount being collected was adequate, taxation was inequitable. Too much of the tax burden, he insisted, was being borne by business, by senior citizens, and by those with low incomes. A tax-reform program that he presented to the legislature and that was designed to eliminate these inequalities was rejected. But the need for tax reform was admitted even by many legislators who voted against the governor's program. Although the state treasury in 1963 not only completely eliminated the deficit that had accumulated but began to show a surplus, there were many unmet needs. Vastly larger sums would be needed for higher education if the "war babies" were to have a chance for college training. More funds would be needed for mental health. There was a movement afoot to build mental-health facilities in each area rather than to build more huge state hospitals, and federal aid was entering the picture. But it seemed certain that large sums would be needed by the state, whatever methods and techniques were employed to meet this growing problem. Higher education and mental health were only two of many state functions that would require much larger sums in the years ahead.

The problem of race relations had assumed national proportions by 1963. In Michigan the Negro population increased from 442,296 in 1950 to 717,581 in 1960. Only four northern states had as large a Negro population as Michigan had. Almost one-third of the population of Detroit was Negro. There was no serious problem in Michigan with regard to school segregation, as was the case in the South. Substantial progress was made after World War II in eliminating discrimination in employment, although this aspect of the problem was by no means completely solved. Gains had been made, too, in the matter of equal rights in public accommodations. Probably the most serious aspect of race relations in Michigan focused on housing. In most cities Negro citizens lived in segregated areas and these areas were, through necessity, expanding. The inevitable result was tension. In the larger cities movements were underway to secure ordinances that would forbid discrimination in the sale or rental of housing facilities.

These were some of the problems faced by Michigan at the dawn of the space age. There are likely to be others, unforeseeable in 1963, that future generations of Michiganians will be called upon to meet. They will be as difficult and perplexing as any that have been faced in earlier times. But insight and inspiration will come from the heritage of the past. The history of Michigan should warn those who shape the state's destiny in the future not to waste natural resources, to seek to build a more diversified and stable economy, and to seek out wise, enlightened, and dedicated leaders. It should demonstrate that liberty under law is the best guarantee of social justice, prosperity, and happiness. It should point the way to voluntary association as the first resort when a need cannot be met through individual effort, and the wisdom of restricting government to those services that cannot be provided either through individual enterprise or through voluntary co-operation.

The College and Cultural Center which has been built in Flint looks to the future. It is a 38-acre complex of buildings housing the Flint Community College, the Flint College presently connected with the University of Michigan, the Mott Library, the Bower Theatre, the De Waters Art Institute, the Longway Planetarium, and the Flint Public Library. An auditorium and a museum are being added. Private contributions to the Center have totaled more than $25 million. The Mott Foundation, established by Charles S. Mott, has been a major supporter of Flint's cultural development as well as of a community health program. The Foundation's programs have attracted national and international attention.

Citizens of the future will find inspiration in the men and women who built Michigan. In the lives of the seventeenth-century Jesuit missionaries, such as Father Jacques Marquette and Father Claude Allouez, dedicated service was combined with a spirit of adventure. Douglas Houghton and Dr. William Beaumont will be emulated by young men and women entering the field of science. Anna Howard Shaw, Laura Haviland, Caroline Bartlett Crane, and Lucinda Hinsdale Stone will inspire women who dedicate themselves to a worthy cause. George Armstrong Custer will be a symbol of courage to Michigan youth. Lewis Cass, Chase Osborn, Mennen Williams, and George Romney will be symbols of devoted public service. Henry P. Tappan will inspire the scholars of the future, John Dewey the philosophers, Father Richard the ministers. John D. Pierce will be remembered and revered by those who devote their lives to education. There are many others whose lives and achievements belong to Michigan history and who will have meaning and significance for tomorrow's Michigan. Many of them were pioneers who forsook security and comfort, set high goals for themselves, and accomplished much. The hope of the future is that there will be more like them, willing to forego personal gratification and ease to brave the dangers of the unknown.

BIBLIOGRAPHY

Adams, Henry. *History of the United States During the Administrations of Jefferson and Madison*, 9 vols. New York, 1889-91.

Aiken, Martha. "The Underground Railroad," *Michigan History*, VI (1922).

Alford, C. M. "The Conquest of St. Joseph," *Missouri Historical Review*, II (1908).

Alilunas, Lee. "Michigan's Cut-Over Canaan," *Michigan History*, XXVI (1942).

Allen, Clifford (ed.). *Michigan Log Marks*. East Lansing, 1941.

Allie, Roob. *Everyman's Almanac*. Detroit, 1952.

American State Papers, Finance, Vol. V.

Anderson, Fannie. *Doctors Under Three Flags*. Detroit, 1951.

Applegate, Tom S. "A History of the Press in Michigan," *Michigan Pioneer and Historical Collections*, VI (1883).

Arnold, Delevan, A. *A Kalamazoo Volunteer in the Civil War*. Kalamazoo, 1962.

Automobile Manufacturers Assoc., Inc. (compilers). *Automobiles of America: Milestones, Pioneer Roll-Call, Highlights*. Detroit, 1962.

—————. *Automobile Facts and Figures*. Detroit, n. d.

Babst, Earl D. and Vander Velde, Lewis G. (eds.). *Michigan and the Cleveland Era*. Ann Arbor, 1948.

Bailey, Thomas A. *A Diplomatic History of the American People*. 6th ed., New York, 1958.

Bain, James (ed.). *Travels and Adventures of Alexander Henry*. Boston, 1901.

Bakeless, John. *Background to Glory*. Philadelphia, 1957.

Bald, F. Clever. *Detroit's First American Decade, 1769 to 1805*. Ann Arbor, 1948.

————. *Michigan in Four Centuries*. Rev. ed., New York, 1961.

————. *The Sault Canal Through 100 Years*. Ann Arbor, 1954.

Barnard, Harry. *Independent Man: The Life of Senator James Couzens*. New York, 1958.

Barnes, Charles. "Battle Creek as a Station on the Underground Railroad," *Michigan Pioneer and Historical Collections*, XXXVIII (1912).

Barnes, Gilbert H. *The Anti-Slavery Impulse, 1830-1844*. New York, 1933.

Barnes, M. *The Prison System of Michigan*. Lansing, 1899.

Barnhart, John D. *Henry Hamilton and George Rogers Clark in the American Revolution, With the Unpublished Journal of Henry Hamilton*. Crawfordsville, Indiana, 1951.

Bates, George C. "Reminiscences of the Brady Guards," *Michigan Pioneer and Historical Collections*, XIII (1888).

Bauman, Robert F. "Kansas, Canada, or Starvation," *Michigan History*, XXXVI (1932).

Bay, John E. "The Moravians in Michigan," *Michigan Pioneer and Historical Collections*, XXX (1906).

Bayliss, Joseph and Estelle. *River of Destiny*. Detroit, 1955.

Beck, E. M. *Lore of the Lumber Camps*. Ann Arbor, 1948.

————. *Songs of the Michigan Lumberjacks*. Ann Arbor, 1941.

Beers, J. H. *History of the Great Lakes*. 2 Vols. Chicago, 1899.

Bellaire, John I. "Michigan's Lumberjacks," *Michigan History*, XXVI (1942).

Bemis, Samuel F. *The Diplomacy of the American Revolution*. New York, 1935.

Berry, Chester D. *Loss of the "Sultana" and Reminiscences of Survivors*. Lansing, 1892.

Bestor, Arthur E., Jr. *Backwoods Utopias*. Philadelphia, 1950.

————. "Patent-Office Models of the Good Society: Some Relationships Between Social Reform and Western Expansion," *American Historical Review*, LVIII (1953).

Billington, M. O. "The Haldimand Papers," *Michigan Pioneer and Historical Collections*, XIX (1891).

Billington, Ray Allen. *Westward Expansion*. New York, 1949.

Bingay, Malcolm. *Detroit Is My Own Home Town*. Indianapolis, 1946.

Blair, E. H. *Indian Tribes of the Upper Mississippi and the Great Lakes Region*. Cleveland, 1911.

Blois, John T. *Gazeteer of the State of Michigan*. New York, 1839.

Bodley, Temple. *George Rogers Clark*. New York, 1926.

Bond, Beverly, Jr. *The Civilization of the Old Northwest*. New York, 1934.

Bonk, Wallace J. "The Botanic Luminary, A Michigan Incunabulum," *Michigan Alumnus Quarterly Review*, LXVII (1961).

Boyd, Thomas A. *Mad Anthony Wayne*. New York, 1929.

Brinks, Herbert. "The Effect of the Civil War in 1861 on Michigan Lumbering and Mining Industries," *Michigan History*, XLIV (1960).

Brock, Thomas D. "Paw Paw Versus the Railroads," *Michigan History*, XXXIX (1955).

Brotherton, R. A. "The Discovery of Iron Ore: Negaunee Centennial, 1844-1944," *Michigan History*, XXVIII (1944).

Brown, Alan S. (ed.). *A Soldier's Life*. Kalamazoo, 1962.

————. "Southwestern Michigan in the Campaign of 1860," *Michigan Heritage*, II (1960).

————. "William Austin Burt: Michigan's Master Surveyor," *Papers of the Michigan Academy of Science, Arts, and Letters*, XLVII (1962).

Brown, Ida C. *Michigan Men in the Civil War* (Bulletin No. 9 and supplement, Michigan Historical Collections). University of Michigan, Ann Arbor, 1959-1960.

Brown, J. H. "How We Got the R.F.D.," *Michigan History*, VI (1922).

Brown, Prentiss. *The Mackinac Bridge Story*. Detroit, 1956.

Brush, Jane D. "Father Was a Preacher," *Michigan History*, XLVII (1963).

Buley, R. Carlyle. *The Old Northwest*. 2 Vols. Bloomington, 1951.

————. "Pioneer Health and Medical Practices in the Old Northwest Prior to 1840," *Mississippi Valley Historical Review*, XX (1934).

Burlingame, Roger. *Henry Ford, A Great Life in Brief*. New York, 1955.

Burr, C. B. (ed. & comp.). *Medical History of Michigan*. 2 Vols. Minneapolis, 1930.

Burroughs, Clyde H. "Painting and Sculpture in Michigan," *Michigan History*, XX (1936), XXI (1937).

Burt, Horace E. "William Austin Burt, Inventor," *Michigan History*, VI (1922).

Burt, William A. "Autobiography," *Michigan Pioneer and Historical Collections*, XXVIII (1898).

Burton, Clarence M. *The City of Detroit, Michigan*. 5 Vols. Detroit, 1922.

————. "Detroit in the Year 1832," *Michigan Pioneer and Historical Collections*, XXVIII (1898).

Butler, Albert F. "Rediscovering Michigan's Prairies," *Michigan History*, XXXI (1947), XXXII (1948), XXXIV (1949).

Byers, David C. "Utopia in Upper Michigan," *Michigan Alumnus Quarterly Review*, LXIII (1957).

Calkins, Edmund A. "The Railroads of Michigan Since 1850," *Michigan History*, XIII (1929).

Calkins, Elisha. "Report of St. Mary's Falls Ship Canal, 1857," *Michigan History*, XXXIX (1955).

Campbell, Murray and Hatton, Harrison. *Herbert H. Dow, Pioneer in Creative Chemistry*. New York, 1951.

Cannon, George H. "The Life and Times of William A. Burt," *Michigan Pioneer and Historical Collections*, V (1882).

Carlson, Emil L. "The American Legion in Michigan," *Michigan History*, XXIII (1939).

Carman, Harry J. and Syrett, Harold C. *A History of the American People*. 2 Vols. New York, 1952.

Carson, Gerald. *Cornflake Crusade*. New York, 1957.

Carstensen, Vernon (ed.). *The Public Lands*. Madison, 1963.

Carter, Clarence E. (ed.). *Territorial Papers of the United States*. 17 Vols. Washington, 1934-1950.

Caruso, John A. *The Great Lakes Frontier*. Indianapolis, 1961.

Catlin, George. *The Story of Detroit*. Detroit, 1921.

Central Electric Railfans' Association. *Electric Railways of Michigan*. Chicago, 1959.

Chambers, John S. *The Conquest of Cholera, America's Greatest Scourge*. New York, 1918.

Chase, Lew Allen. "Early Days of Michigan Mining: Pioneering Land Sales and Surveys," *Michigan History*, XXIX (1945).

————. "Michigan's Share in the Establishment of Improved Transportation Between the East and the West," *Michigan Pioneer and Historical Collections*, XXXVIII (1912).

————. "Michigan's Upper Peninsula," *Michigan History*, XX (1936).

————. "Silver and Gold in Michigan," *Michigan History*, XXX (1946).

Classis Holland Minutes, 1848-1858. Grand Rapids, 1943.

Cleaves, Freeman. *Old Tippecanoe: William Henry Harrison and His Times*. New York, 1939.

Cleveland, Reginald and Williamson, Samuel T. *The Road is Yours: The Story of the Automobile and the Men Behind It*. New York, 1951.

Clymer, Floyd. *Henry Ford's Wonderful Model T, 1908-1927*. New York, 1955.

Cobb, Charles L. "Ho! Gogebic County," *Michigan History*, VI (1922).

Cohen, Joseph J. *In Quest of Heaven*. New York, 1957.

Cole, Maurice (ed.). *Voices From the Wilderness*. Ann Arbor, 1961.

Collier, T. Maxwell. "William H. Seward in the Campaign of 1860," *Michigan History*, XIX (1935).

Comin, John and Fredsell, Harold F. *History of the Presbyterian Church in Michigan*. Ann Arbor, 1950.

Compendium of the Tenth Census. Washington, 1883.

Comstock, O. C. "Internal Improvements," *Michigan Pioneer and Historical Collections*, I (1875).

Congregational Churches of Michigan for the First Fifty Years. n.p., ca. 1892.

Coon, D. S. "The Quincy Mine," *Michigan History*, XXIV (1940).

Co-operative Extension Service, Michigan State University. *Michigan Agriculture: County Data and State Trends.* East Lansing, 1962.

Copley, A. B. "The Pottawattomies," *Michigan Pioneer and Historical Collections,* XIV (1889).

Crawford, R. C. "Reminiscences of Pioneer Ministers in Michigan," *Michigan Pioneer and Historical Collections,* XVII (1890).

Crow, Carl. *The City of Flint Grows Up.* New York, 1945.

Cubberley, Ellwood P. *The History of Education.* Boston, 1920.

Culbertson, George A. *Freshwater: A History of the Great Lakes.* New York, 1932.

Cunningham, Wilbur M. *Land of Four Flags.* Grand Rapids, 1961.

Curtis, Francis. *The Republican Party.* 2 Vols. New York, 1904.

Cutcheon, Byron M. *The Story of the Twentieth Michigan Infantry.* Lansing, 1904.

Dain, Floyd R. *Every House a Frontier.* Detroit, 1956.

Dalton, Sister M. Arthemise. "The History and Development of the Catholic Secondary School System in the Archdiocese of Detroit." Unpublished doctoral dissertation, n.d.

Dancy, J. C. "The Negro People in Michigan," *Michigan History,* XXIV (1940).

Danforth, Mildred M. *A Quaker Pioneer: Laura Haviland, Superintendent of the Underground.* New York, 1961.

Darling, Birt. *City in the Forest: The Story of Lansing.* New York, 1950.

Davis, Calvin O. *Michigan's High Schools* (Bulletin No. 39, Michigan Education Association). Lansing, 1941.

Davis, David Brion. "The Movement to Abolish Capital Punishment in America, 1787-1861," *American Historical Review,* LXIII (1957).

Delanglez, Jean. *Life and Voyages of Louis Jolliet, 1645-1700.* Chicago, 1948.

Denison, Merrill. *The Power to Go: The Story of the Automobile Industry.* Garden City, 1956.

Department of Mental Health. *Program and Activities.* Lansing, 1960.

Detroit City Planning Commission. *Detroit Master Plan.* Detroit, 1951.

Detroit Post and Tribune. *Zachariah Chandler: An Outline Sketch of His Life and Public Services.* Detroit, 1880.

Dilla, H. M. *The Politics of Michigan, 1865-1878.* New York, 1912.

Donaldson, Thomas. *The Public Domain: Its History.* Washington, 1884.

D'Ooge, Martin L. "The Dutch Pioneers of Michigan," *Michigan Pioneer and Historical Collections,* XXXVIII (1912).

Dorf, Philip. *Liberty Hyde Bailey, An Informal Biography.* Ithaca, New York, 1956.

Downes, Randolph C. *Council Fires on the Upper Ohio.* Pittsburgh, 1940.

Drake, Daniel. *Discourses on Northern Lakes and Southern Invalids.* n.d.

Dunathan, Clint. "Fayette," *Michigan History,* XLI (1957).

Dunbar, Willis F. "The High School on Trial: The Kalamazoo Case," *Papers,* Michigan Academy of Science, Arts, and Letters, XLV (1960).

————. *Kalamazoo and How It Grew.* Kalamazoo, 1959.

————. *The Michigan Record in Higher Education.* Detroit, 1963.

————. "The Opera House as a Social Institution in Michigan," *Michigan History,* XXVII (1943).

————. "The University and Its Branches," *Michigan Alumnus Quarterly Review,* LVI (July 20, 1940).

Dunham, Harold H. "Some Crucial Years of the General Land Office, 1875-1890," *Agricultural History,* XI (1937).

Durant, Samuel W. *History of Kalamazoo County.* Philadelphia, 1880.

Dutton, C. J. *Oliver Hazard Perry.* New York, 1935.

Eccles, W. J. *Frontenac, The Courtier Governor.* Toronto, 1959.

Emery, B. Frank. "Fort Saginaw," *Michigan History,* XXX (1946).

Engberg, George B. "Who Were the Lumberjacks?" *Michigan History,* XXXII (1948).

Engel, Leonard. *Medicine Makers of Kalamazoo.* New York, 1961.

Etten, W. J. (comp. and ed.). *A Citizen's History of Grand Rapids, Michigan.* Grand Rapids, 1926.

Everett, Philo M. "Recollections of the Early Explorations and Discovery of Iron Ore on Lake Superior," *Michigan Pioneer and Historical Collections,* XI (1888).

Farmer, Silas. *History of Detroit and Michigan.* Detroit, 1884.

Felch, Alpheus. "Early Banks and Banking in Michigan," *Michigan Pioneer and Historical Collections,* II (1880).

————. "The Indians of Michigan and the Cession of Their Lands to the United States By Treaties," *Michigan Pioneer and Historical Collections,* XXXVI (1894-95).

Fisher, James. "Michigan's Cornish People," *Michigan History,* XXIX (1945).

Fitzgibbon, J. "King Alcohol, His Rise, Reign, and Fall in Michigan," *Michigan History,* II (1917).

Fladeland, Betty. "Alias Franklin Thompson," *Michigan History,* XLII (1958).

————. "New Light on Sarah Emma Edmonds, Alias Frank Thompson," *Michigan History,* XLVII (1963).

Flexner, James T. *Mohawk Baronet: Sir William Johnson of New York.* New York, 1959.

Foote, Mrs. George E. *History of the Ladies' Library Association.* Kalamazoo, 1941.

Ford, R. Clyde. "The Life Work of John D. Pierce," *Michigan Pioneer and Historical Collections,* XXXV (1907).

Forty-Fourth Annual Report of the Superintendent of Public Instruction. Lansing, 1881.

Fox, Karolena. "The Movement for Equal Suffrage in Michigan," *Michigan History,* II (1918).

Franklin, Leo M. "Jews in Michigan," *Michigan History*, XXIII (1939).

Fredeen, H. E. "The Story of Isle Royale," *Michigan History*, XXV (1941).

Fuller, George N. *Economic and Social Beginnings of Michigan.* Lansing, 1916.

————— (ed.). *Historic Michigan.* New York, n.d.

—————. *Laws of the Territory of Michigan.* 4 Vols. Lansing, 1871-1884.

————— (ed.). *Messages of the Governors of Michigan.* 4 Vols. Lansing, 1925-27.

————— (ed.). *Michigan, A Centennial History.* New York, 1939.

Gardner, Emelyn and Chickering, Geraldine J. (comps.). *Ballads and Songs of Southern Michigan.* Ann Arbor, 1939.

Gardner, Washington. "Civil War Letters," *Michigan History*, I (1917).

Gates, William B., Jr. *Michigan Copper and Boston Dollars.* Cambridge, 1951.

Gillard, Kathleen I. *Our Michigan Heritage.* New York, 1955.

Gilpin, Alec R. *The War of 1812 in the Old Northwest.* East Lansing, 1958.

"The Gladwin Manuscripts," *Michigan Pioneer and Historical Collections,* XXVII (1896).

Glasscock, Carl B. *Motor History of America, or, The Gasoline Age: The Story of the Men Who Made It.* Los Angeles, 1945.

Glazer, Sidney. "The Beginnings of the Economic Revolution in Michigan," *Michigan History*, XXXIV (1950).

—————. "The Michigan Labor Movement," *Michigan History*, XXIX (1945).

Godbout, Archange. "Louis Jolliet et son dernier historien," *Culture* (Quebec), XIV (1953).

Goebel, Dorothy B. *William Henry Harrison.* Indianapolis, 1926.

Goodman, Warren H. "The Causes of the War of 1812: A Synthesis of Changing Interpretations," *Mississippi Valley Historical Review,* XXVIII (1941).

Goodykonntz, Colin B. *Home Missions on the American Frontier.* Caldwell, Idaho, 1939.

Gordon, John M. "Michigan Journal, 1836," *Michigan History*, XLIII (1959).

Green, James A. *William Henry Harrison: His Life and Times.* Richmond, 1941.

Greenleaf, William. *Monopoly on Wheels: Henry Ford and the Selden Patent.* Detroit, 1961.

Greenman, Emerson F. "The Indians of Michigan," *Michigan History,* XLV (1961).

Haber, William, McKean, Eugene C., and Taylor, Harold C. *The Michigan Economy: Its Potentials and Its Problems.* Kalamazoo, 1959.

Hacker, Louis M. "Western Land Hunger and the War of 1812," *Mississippi Valley Historical Review*, X (1924).

Hamil, Fred C. *Michigan in the War of 1812.* Lansing, 1960.

Hamilton, Claude T. "Western Michigan History," *Michigan History,* XIII (1929).

Hanna, Frances C. *Sand, Sawdust, and Saw Logs: Lumber Days in Ludington.* Ludington, 1955.

Harlow, Alvin F. *Old Post Bags.* New York, 1928.

———. *The Road of the Century.* New York, 1947.

Hatcher, Harlan. *A Century of Iron and Men.* Indianapolis, 1950.

———. *Lake Erie.* Indianapolis, 1945.

Havighurst, Walter. *George Rogers Clark, Soldier of the West.* New York, 1952.

———. *The Long Ships Passing.* New York, 1942.

———. *Vein of Iron: The Pickands-Mather Story.* New York, 1958.

Hayne, Coe. *Baptist Trail Makers in Michigan.* Philadelphia, 1936.

Heimann, Robert K. *Tobacco and Americans.* New York, 1960.

Henry, Robert S. "The Railroad Land Grant Legend in American History Texts" (*The Public Lands.* Edited by Vernon Carstensen. Madison, 1963).

Hibbard, Benjamin H. *A History of Public Land Policies.* New York, 1924.

Hill, Arthur S. "The Romance of a Railway," *Michigan History,* XXIII (1939).

Hilton, George W. and Due, Joseph F. *The Electric Interurban Railways in America.* Stanford, 1960.

———. *The Great Lakes Car Ferries.* Berkeley, 1962.

Hirschfield, Charles. *The Great Railroad Conspiracy.* East Lansing, 1953.

———. "The Great Railroad Conspiracy," *Michigan History,* XXXVI (1952).

Hobart, William. "The Crosswhite Case," *Michigan Pioneer and Historical Collections,* XXXVIII (1912).

Hoehling, A. A. *The Great Epidemic.* New York, 1961.

Holbrook, Stewart. *Burning an Empire: The Story of American Forest Fires.* New York, 1943.

———. *Holy Old Mackinaw, A Natural History of the American Lumberjack.* New York, 1938.

———. *Ironbrew.* New York, 1939.

———. *The Yankee Exodus, An Account of Migration From New England.* New York, 1950.

Hopp, W. F. *The Michigan State Prison, Jackson, 1837-1928.* Jackson, 1928.

Horsman, Reginald. *The Causes of the War of 1812.* Philadelphia, 1962.

Hoyt, Charles O. and Ford, R. Clyde. *John D. Pierce.* Ypsilanti, 1905.

Hubbard, Bela. *Memorials of a Half Century.* New York, 1887.

———. "A Michigan Geological Expedition in 1837," *Michigan Pioneer and Historical Collections,* III (1881).

Hulbert, William D. *White Pine Days on the Tahquamenon.* Lansing, 1950.

Huntington, Ellsworth. *Mainsprings of Civilization.* New York, 1945.

Hybels, Robert J. "Lake Superior Copper Fever, 1841-47," *Michigan History,* XXXIV (1950).

Hyma, Albert. *Albertus Van Raalte and His Dutch Settlements in the United States.* Grand Rapids, 1947.

Ingersoll, John N. "The Clinton and Kalamazoo Canal Celebration," *Michigan Pioneer and Historical Collections,* V (1882).

Innis, Harold A. *The Fur Trade of Canada.* New Haven, 1930.

Isbell, Egbert B. "The Catholepistemiad of Michigania," *Michigan Alumnus Quarterly Review,* XLIII (1937).

Jackson, George L. *The Development of State Control of Public Instruction in Michigan.* Lansing, 1926.

James, James A. (ed.). *George Rogers Clark Papers.* Springfield, 1912.

————. *The Life of George Rogers Clark.* Chicago, 1928.

————. "To What Extent Was George Rogers Clark In Military Control of the Old Northwest at the Close of the Revolution?" (*Annual Report* of the American Historical Association for 1917). Washington, 1920.

Jamison, James K. *By Cross and Anchor. The Story of Frederic Baraga of Lake Superior.* Paterson, New Jersey, 1946.

Jamison, Knox. "The Survey of the Public Lands in Michigan," *Michigan History,* XLII (1958).

Jenks, William L. "Augustus Elias Brevoort Woodward," *Michigan History,* IX (1925).

————. "The History and Meaning of County Names in Michigan," *Michigan Pioneer and Historical Collections,* XXXVIII (1912).

————. "Michigan's Five Million Dollar Loan," *Michigan History,* XV (1931).

————. "Michigan Immigration," *Michigan History,* XXVIII (1944).

Jenney, William. "Governors of Michigan Territory," *Michigan Pioneer and Historical Collections,* III (1881).

Jensen, Vernon H. *Lumber and Labor.* New York, 1945.

Johnson, Ida A. *The Michigan Fur Trade.* Lansing, 1919.

Johnston, J. E. "The Griffon, Ship of Tragedy," *Telescope,* VII (1958).

Jopling, James E. "Cornish Miners of the Upper Peninsula," *Michigan History,* XII (1928).

Karman, Thomas A. "The Flint Sit-Down Strike," *Michigan History* XLVI (1962).

Karpinski, Louis C. *Bibliography of the Printed Maps of Michigan, 1804-1880* Lansing, 1931.

————. "Early Michigan Maps: Three Outstanding Peculiarities," *Michigan History,* XXIX (1945).

Katz, Irving I. "Ezekiel Solomon: The First Jew in Michigan," *Michigan History,* XXXII (1948).

————. *The Jewish Soldier From Michigan in the Civil War.* Detroit, 1962.

Kellogg, Louise P. *The British Regime in Wisconsin and the Old Northwest.* Madison, 1935.

————. (ed.). *Early Narratives of the Northwest, 1634-1699.* New York, 1917.

————. *French Regime in Wisconsin,* n.d.

Kelly, Robert L. "History of Radio in Michigan," *Michigan History,* XXI (1937).

Kennedy, J. H. *Jesuit and Savage in New France.* New Haven, 1950.

Kercher, L. C. Kebker, V. W., and Leland, W. C., Jr. *Consumers' Co-operatives in the North Central States.* Minneapolis, 1941.

Kidd, J. H. *Personal Recollections of a Cavalryman.* Ionia, 1908.

Kimball, Solon T. *The New Social Frontier: The Fringe* (Michigan Agricultural Experiment Station Special Bulletin No. 360). Lansing, 1949.

Kinnaird, Lawrence. "The Spanish Expedition Against Fort St. Joseph in 1781: A New Interpretation," *Mississippi Valley Historical Review,* XIX (1932).

Kirk, Russell. "A Michigan Soldier's Diary, 1863," *Michigan History,* XXVIII (1944).

Kirkland, Caroline M. *A New Home or Life in the Clearings.* New York, 1953.

Kistler, Mark O. "The German Theater in Detroit," *Michigan History,* XLVII (1963).

Knight, George W. *History and Management of Land Grants for Education in the Northwest Territory.* Papers of the American Historical Association, I, No. 3. Washington, 1891.

Kolehmainen, J. L. "Finnish Newspapers and Periodicals in Michigan," *Michigan History,* XXIV (1940).

Kuhn, Madison. *Michigan State, The First Hundred Years.* East Lansing, 1955.

Lanman, James H. *History of Michigan.* New York, 1837.

Larzelere, Claude S. "The Boundaries of Michigan," *Michigan Pioneer and Historical Collections,* XXX (1906).

————. "The Red Men in Michigan," *Michigan History,* XVII (1933).

Lederle, John W. and Aid, Rita Feiler. "Michigan State Party Chairmen: 1882-1956," *Michigan History,* XLI (1957).

Leech, Carl A. "Deward: A Lumberman's Ghost Town," *Michigan History,* XXVIII (1944).

Lenderink, Rodney. "The Electric Interurban Railway in Kalamazoo County," *Michigan History,* XLIII (1959).

Lewis, Ferris E. "Frederic: A Typical Logging Village in the Twilight of the Lumbering Era," *Michigan History,* XXXII (1948).

Lewis, Martin D. *Lumberman from Flint, The Michigan Career of Henry H. Crapo, 1855-1869.* Detroit, 1958.

Lindley, Alfred B. "The Copper Tariff of 1869," *Michigan History,* XXXV (1951).

Lucas, Henry S. *Netherlanders in America: Dutch Immigration to the United States and Canada, 1789-1950.* Ann Arbor, 1955.

Lundrum, Charles (comp.). *Michigan in the World War: Military and Naval Honors of Michigan Men and Women.* Lansing, 1924.

Lyon, Lucius. "Letters of Lucius Lyon," *Michigan Pioneer and Historical Collections,* XXVII (1896).

MacLaren, Gay. *Morally We Roll Along.* Boston, 1938.

MacLennan, Hugh. "By Canoe To Empire," *American Heritage,* XII (1961).

Margry, Pierre. *Découvertes et établissements des Français dans l'Amérique.* 6 Vols. Paris, 1876-86.

Marquette Centennial. Marquette, 1949.

Martineau, Harriet. *Society in America.* 3 Vols. London, 1837.

Mary Rosalita, Sister. *Education in Detroit Prior to 1850.* Lansing, 1928.

Mason, Philip P. *Iron Ore Mining in Michigan Past and Present.* Detroit, 1958.

————. (ed.). *Schoolcraft's Expedition to Lake Itasca.* East Lansing, 1958.

Mathews, Lois K. *Expansion of New England.* Boston, 1909.

Maxwell, Moreau S. and Binford, Lewis H. *Excavation of Fort Michilimackinac, Mackinaw City, Michigan, 1959 Season.* East Lansing, 1961.

Maxwell, William Q. *Lincoln's Fifth Wheel.* New York, 1961.

May, George S. *A Bibliography of Printed Sources on Michigan and the Civil War.* Detroit, 1962.

————. *War 1812.* Lansing, 1962.

May, Philip P. and Pentecost, Paul J. *From Bull Run to Appomattox.* Detroit, 1961.

Maybee, Rolland, H. *Michigan's White Pine Era, 1840-1900.* Lansing, 1960.

McCain, Anne. "Charles Edward Stuart of Kalamazoo," *Michigan History,* XLIV.

McCoy, Raymond. *The Massacre of Old Fort Mackinac.* 2nd ed., Bay City, 1939.

McCracken, Paul W. (ed.). *Taxes and Economic Growth in Michigan.* Kalamazoo, 1960.

McDavitt, Elaine E. "The Beginnings of Theatrical Activities in Detroit," *Michigan History,* XXXI (1947).

McGee, John W. *The Catholic Church in the Grand River Valley.* Grand Rapids, 1950.

McLaughlin, Andrew C. *Lewis Cass.* Boston, 1891.

McMurtrie, Douglas C. *Early Printing in Michigan.* Chicago, 1931.

Mencken, H. L. *The American Language.* New York, 1937.

Merz, Charles. *The Great American Bandwagon.* New York, 1928.

Michigan Adjutant General's Office. *Record of Service of Michigan Volunteers in the Civil War, 1861-1865.* 46 Vols. Kalamazoo, 1903-1915.

Michigan Civil War Centennial Observance Commission. *Michigan Women in the Civil War.* New York, 1963.

Michigan Dept. of Agriculture. *Michigan Agricultural Statistics.* Lansing, 1961.

————. *19th Biennial Report.* Lansing, 1960.

Michigan Dept. of Revenue. *19th Annual Report.* Lansing, 1960.

Michigan Historical Commission. *Michigan Museums and Historic Exhibits.* Lansing, 1961.

Michigan Manual, 1915-1916. Lansing, 1916.

Michigan Manual, 1961-62. Lansing, 1962.

Michigan Social Welfare Commission. *Twelfth Biennial Report.* Lansing, 1962.

Michigan Statistical Abstract. East Lansing, 1960.

Michigan Writers' Project. *Michigan, A Guide to the Wolverine State.* New York, 1941.

Miller, Melvin H. "The Chautauqua in Lansing," *Michigan History,* XL (1956).

Millis, Wade. "When Michigan Was Born," *Michigan History,* XVIII (1934).

Mitchell, Sylvia C. "La Mothe Cadillac . . . A Stormy Figure of New France," *Bulletin of the Detroit Historical Society,* XI (July, 1955).

Moore, Charles (ed.). "The Beginnings of Territorial Government in Michigan; Manuscripts in the Department of State, Washington, D. C.," *Michigan Pioneer and Historical Collections,* XXXI (1901).

———— (ed.). *The Saint Mary's Falls Canal . . . Semicentennial.* Detroit, 1907.

Moore, Vivian Lyon. "A Pocahontas of Michigan," *Michigan History,* XV (1931).

Mott, Frank L. *American Journalism.* New York, 1950.

Mudge, Edson H. "The Old-Time Country Newspapermen," *Michigan History,* XXX (1946).

Mulder, Arnold. *Americans From Holland.* New York, 1947.

————. "Authors and Wolverines," *Saturday Review* (March 4, 1939).

Murdock, Angus. *Boom Copper: The Story of the First U. S. Mining Boom.* New York, 1943.

Myers, Gustavus. *History of the Great American Fortunes.* 3 Vols. New York, 1907-1910.

Nevins, Allen. *Ford, Expansion and Challenge.* New York, 1957.

————. *Ford: The Times, the Man and the Company,* New York, 1954.

Nevins, Archie P. "The Kalamazoo Case," *Michigan History,* XLIV (1960).

Niemeyer, Glenn. *The Automotive Career of Ransom E. Olds.* East Lansing, 1964.

Norton, Clark F. "Early Movement for the St. Mary's Falls Ship Canal," *Michigan History,* XXXIX (1955).

————. "Michigan Statehood, 1835, 1836, or 1837," *Michigan History,* XXXVI (1952).

Nowlin, William. "The Bark-Covered House, or Pioneer Life in Michigan," *Michigan Pioneer and Historical Collections,* IV (1881).

Nute, Grace L. *The Voyageur.* New York, 1931.

Owen, C. W. *The First Michigan Infantry.* Coldwater, n.d.

Paine, R. D. *The Fight For a Free Sea.* New Haven, 1920.

Paré, G. W. *The Catholic Church in Detroit, 1701-1888.* Detroit, 1951.

Pargellis, Stanley. "Braddock's Defeat," *American Historical Review,* XLI (Jan. 1936).

Parkman, Francis. *LaSalle and the Discovery of the Great West.* Boston, 1906.

Patterson, John C. "Marshall Men and Marshall Measures in State and National History," *Michigan Pioneer and Historical Collections,* XXXVIII (1912).

Paxson, Frederick L. *History of the American Frontier, 1763-1893.* Boston, 1924.

Peake, Ora R. *A History of the United States Indian Factory System, 1795-1822.* Denver, 1954.

Peckham, Howard. *Pontiac and the Indian Uprising.* Rev. ed., Chicago, 1961.

Percival, John T. "Railroads in Ottawa County," *Michigan Pioneer and Historical Collections,* IX (1886).

Perkins, Bradford. *Prologue To War. England and the United States, 1805-1812.* Berkeley, 1962.

Perry, Charles T. *Henry Philip Tappan.* Ann Arbor, 1933.

Peterson, Eugene. *Michilimackinac: Its History and Restoration.* Mackinac Island, 1962.

Pickard, Madge E. and Buley, R. C. *The Midwest Pioneer: His Ills, Cures, and Doctors.* New York, 1946.

Pierce, John D. "Origin and Progress of the Michigan School System," *Michigan Pioneer and Historical Collections,* I (1876).

Pieters, Aleida J. *A Dutch Settlement in Michigan.* Grand Rapids, 1923.

Pilcher, E. H. *History of Protestantism in Michigan.* Detroit, 1878.

Pollock, James K. "Civil Service Developments in Michigan," *Good Government,* LVIII (1941).

Porter, K. W. *John Jacob Astor, Businessman.* 2 Vols. Cambridge, 1931.

Potter, Theodore E. "A Boy's Story of Pioneer Life in Michigan," *Michigan Pioneer and Historical Collections,* XXXV (1907).

Pound, Arthur. *Salt of the Earth, The Story of Captain J. B. Ford and the Michigan Alkali Company.* Boston, 1940.

————. *The Turning Wheel: The Story of General Motors Through Twenty-Five Years.* Garden City, 1934.

Powell, Horace B. *The Original Has This Signature—W. K. Kellogg.* New York, 1956.

Pratt, Julius. *The Expansionists of 1812.* New York, 1949.

————. "Fur Trade Strategy and the American Left Flank in the War of 1812," *American Historical Review,* XL (1935).

Praus, Alexis (ed.). *The Cholera in Kalamazoo.* Kalamazoo, 1961.

Pray, Carl E. "An Historic Michigan Road," *Michigan History*, XI (1926).

Prescott, William R. *The Fathers Still Speak: A History of Michigan Methodism.* Lansing, 1941.

Prucha, Francis P. *Broadax and Bayonet: The Role of the Army in the Development of the Northwest, 1815-1860.* Madison, 1953.

Putnam, Daniel. *A History of Michigan State Normal School at Ypsilanti.* Ypsilanti, 1899.

Pyne, William H. "Quincy Mine: The Old Reliable," *Michigan History*, XLI (1957).

Quaife, Milo M. *The Capture of Old Vincennes.* Indianapolis, 1927.

———— (ed.). *The John Askin Papers.* 2 Vols. Detroit, 1928-1931.

————. *The Kingdom of St. James.* New Haven, 1930.

————. *Lake Michigan.* Indianapolis, 1944.

————. "The Romance of the Macinack Country," *Michigan History*, XIII (1929).

Rankin, Ernest H., "Lake Superior—1854," *Inland Seas*, XIX (Winter 1963).

Rankin, Lois. "Detroit Nationality Groups," *Michigan History*, XXIII (1939).

Reber, J. Benjamin. *History of St. Joseph.* St. Joseph, 1924.

Rector, William G. *Log Transportation in the Lake States Lumber Industry.* Glendale, California, 1953.

Rhodes, Charles D. "William Rufus Shafter," *Michigan History*, XVI (1932).

Richards, Allan R. "The Traditions of Government in the States," *The Forty-Eight States.* New York, 1955.

Richards, William C. *The Last Billionaire.* New York, 1948.

Riddell, William R. *Michigan Under British Rule: Law and Law Courts, 1760-1796.* Lansing, 1926.

————. *William Dummer Powell.* Lansing, 1924.

Riegel, O. W. *Crown of Glory.* New Haven, 1935.

Rintala, Edsel K. *Douglass Houghton, Michigan's Pioneer Geologist.* Detroit, 1954.

Robbins, Roy M. *Our Landed Heritage.* Princeton, 1942.

Robertson, John. *Michigan in War.* Lansing, 1882.

Rogan, Harry N. (comp.). *Tallyho.* Automobile Club of Michigan, n.d.

Rosenberg, Charles E. *The Cholera Years.* Chicago, 1962.

Russell, J. A. *The Germanic Influence in the Making of Michigan.* Detroit, 1927.

Russell, Nelson V. *The British Regime in Michigan and the Old Northwest, 1760-1796.* Northfield, Minnesota, 1939.

Sagendorph, Kent. *Stevens Thomson Mason, Misunderstood Patriot.* New York, 1947.

Salmon, Lucy. *Education in Michigan During the Territorial Period.* Lansing, 1885.

Schlesinger, Arthur M., Jr. *The Age of Jackson.* Boston, 1945.

Schoolcraft, Henry R. *Historical and Statistical Information Respecting*

the History, Condition, and Prospects of the Indian Tribes of the
United States. 6 Vols. Philadelphia, 1851-57.

Scripps, E. W. *Damned Old Crank: A Self-Portrait of E. W. Scripps.*
New York, 1951.

Selleck, H. B. *Beaumont and the "Mackinac Island Miracle."* East Lansing, n.d.

Sewell, Richard. "Michigan Farmers and the Civil War," *Michigan History,* XLIV (1960).

Shannon, Fred A. "A Post-Mortem on the Labor-Safety-Valve Theory,"
Agricultural History, XIX (January, 1943).

Shaw, Wildred B. (ed.). *The University of Michigan, an Encyclopedic Survey,* Part I. Ann Arbor, 1941.

Shearman, Francis W. *System of Public Instruction and Primary School Law of Michigan.* Lansing, 1852.

Shull, C. W. *Legislative Reapportionment in Michigan.* Detroit, 1961.

Simonds, William A. *Henry Ford: His Life, His Work, His Genius.* Los
Angeles, 1946.

Skinner, Constance L. *Beaver, Kings, and Cabins.* New York, 1933.

Smith, Arthur D. H. *John Jacob Astor.* Philadelphia, 1929.

Smith, Donald L. *The Twenty-Fourth Michigan of the Iron Brigade.*
Harrisburg, 1962.

Smith, Franklin C. *The Diocese of Western Michigan.* Grand Rapids,
1948.

Smith, Stanley B. "Notes on the Village of Schoolcraft in 1850," *Michigan History,* XL (1956).

Smith, W. V. "The Puritan Blood of Michigan," *Michigan Pioneer and Historical Collections,* XXXVIII (1912).

Sorenson, Charles E. *My Forty Years With Ford.* New York, 1962.

Soule, Annah May. "The International Boundary Line of Michigan,"
Michigan Pioneer and Historical Collections, XXVI (1896).

————. "The Southern and Western Boundaries of Michigan," *Michigan Pioneer and Historical Collections,* XXVII (1897).

Springman, John C. *The Growth of Public Education in Michigan.*
Ypsilanti, 1952.

Stach, John F. "A History of the Lutheran Schools of the Missouri
Synod in Michigan, 1845-1940." Unpublished doctoral dissertation.

Standard Guide. Mackinac Island and Northern Lake Resorts. n.p.,
1904.

Starbuck, James C. "Ben Franklin and Isle Royale," *Michigan History,* XLVI (1962).

Stark, George W. *City of Destiny, The Story of Detroit.* Detroit, 1943.

Starring, Charles R. "Hazen S. Pingree, Another Forgotten Eagle,"
Michigan History, XXXII (1948).

————. "Lucinda Hinsdale Stone: A Pioneer in the Education of
Women in Michigan," *Michigan History,* XLII (1958).

Stassman, W. Paul. *Economic Growth in Michigan.* East Lansing, 1959.

State Banking Commissioner. *Annual Report.* Lansing, 1949.

State Library. *Michigan In Books.* Vol. V. No. 3 (winter, 1963).

Steck, Francis B. *Marquette Legends.* New York, 1960.

Steinman, David B. *Miracle Bridge at Mackinac.* Grand Rapids, 1957.

Stephenson, O. W. *Ann Arbor: The First Hundred Years.* Ann Arbor, 1927.

Stern, Philip V. *Tin Lizzie, The Story of the Fabulous Model T Ford.* New York, 1955.

Stevens, J. Harold. "The Influence of New England in Michigan," *Michigan History,* XIX (1935).

Stevens, James. *The Saginaw Paul Bunyan.* New York, 1932.

Stevens, Wayne E. "The Michigan Fur Trade," *Michigan History,* XXIX (1945).

Stocking, William. "Prominent Newspaper Men in Michigan," *Michigan Pioneer and Historical Collections,* XXXIX (1915).

Streeter, Floyd B. "History of Prohibition Legislation in Michigan," *Michigan History,* II (1917).

——. *Political Parties in Michigan, 1837-1860.* Lansing, 1918.

Sullivan, Mark. *Our Times.* New York, 1926.

Sullivan, William A. "The 1913 Revolt of the Michigan Copper Miners," *Michigan History,* XLIII (1949).

Superintendent of Public Instruction, 105th Report of the. Lansing, 1961.

Sward, Keith T. *The Legend of Henry Ford.* New York, 1948.

Taggart, F. "The Capture of St. Joseph, Michigan by the Spaniards in 1781," *Missouri Historical Review,* V (1911).

Taylor, Howell. "Michigan's Pioneer Architecture," *Michigan History,* XXXVII (1953).

Thompson, Robert L. *Wiring a Continent: The History of the Telegraph Industry in the United States, 1832-1866.* Princeton, 1947.

Thwaites, Reuben G. "The Fur Trade in Wisconsin, 1812-1825," *Wisconsin Historical Collections,* XX (1911).

——. *How George Rogers Clark Won the Northwest.* New York, 1903.

—— (ed.). *The Jesuit Relations and Allied Documents.* Cleveland, 1896-1901.

Tingley, Ralph R. "Postal Service in Michigan Territory," *Michigan History,* XXXV (1951).

Tocqueville, Alexis de. *Oeuvres et correspondence inédite.* 2 Vols. Paris, 1861.

Tourist and Investor. An Illustrated Guide to the Lake Superior District. Hancock, 1895.

Trepagnier, William J. "The Tin Lizzie," *Motor News* (May, 1959).

Trowbridge, C. C. "History of the Episcopal Church in Michigan," *Michigan Pioneer and Historical Collections,* III (1881).

Trowbridge, M. E. D. *History of the Baptists in Michigan.* Detroit, 1909.

Tucker, Glenn. *Tecumseh.* Indianapolis, 1956.

University of Michigan. *Records of the University, 1817-1837.* Ann Arbor, 1935.

Utley, Henry M. and Cutcheon, Byron M. *Michigan as a Province, Territory, and State.* 4 Vols. New York, 1906.

_____. "The Wildcat Banking System in Michigan," *Michigan Pioneer and Historical Collections,* V (1884).

Vale, Joseph G. *Minty and the Cavalry.* Harrisburg, 1886.

Van Buren, A. D. P. "The Fever and Ague—'Michigan Rash'—Mosquitoes—The Old Pioneers' Foes," *Michigan Pioneer and Historical Collections,* V (1882).

_____. "The Log Schoolhouse Era in Michigan," *Michigan Pioneer and Historical Collections,* XIV (1889).

_____. "The Old Academy and Seminary, the Classic Schools of our Pioneer Days," *Michigan Pioneer and Historical Collections,* XVIII (1896).

_____. "A Quarter Century of Teaching," *Michigan Pioneer and Historical Collections,* X (1888).

_____. "Our Temperance Conflict," *Michigan Pioneer and Historical Collections,* XIII (1888).

_____. "Temperance in Pioneer Days," *Michigan Pioneer and Historical Collections,* V (1882).

Vandenberg, Arthur H., Jr. *The Private Papers of Senator Vandenberg.* Boston, 1952.

VanDeusen, John G. "The Detroit Campaign of Gen. William Hull," *Michigan History,* XII (1928).

VanFleet, J. A. *Old and New Mackinac.* Ann Arbor, 1870.

VanOosten, John. "Michigan's Commercial Fisheries of the Great Lakes," *Michigan History,* XXII (1938).

Wahlgren, E. *The Kensington Stone, A Mystery Solved.* Madison, 1958.

Waid, George H. *Centennial History of the Michigan State Baptist Convention.* Lansing, 1936.

Walsh, Justin E. "Radically and Thoroughly Democratic: Wilbur F. Storey and the Detroit Free Press, 1853-1861," *Michigan History,* XLVII (1963).

Wargelin, John. "The Finns in Michigan," *Michigan History,* XXIV (1940).

Warner, Robert M. *Chase Salmon Osborn, 1860-1949.* Ann Arbor, 1960.

_____. "Chase S. Osborn's 1910 Primary Election Campaign," *Michigan History,* XLIII (1959).

Wax, A. S. "The Calumet and Hecla Copper Mine," *Michigan History,* XXIV (1940).

Weatherwax, Paul. *Indian Corn In Old America.* New York, 1954.

Webber, William L. "Discovery and Development of the Salt Interest in the Saginaw Valley," *Michigan Pioneer and Historical Collections,* III (1881).

White, George H. "Sketch of the Life of Hon. Rix Robinson," *Michigan Pioneer and Historical Collections,* XI (1888).

White, Peter. "The Iron Region of Lake Superior," *Michigan Pioneer and Historical Collections,* VIII (1885).

Wildes, Harry E. *Anthony Wayne, A Name In Arms.* Pittsburgh, 1960.

Williams, Alpheus. *From the Cannon's Mouth.* Detroit, 1959.

Williams, Ephraim S. "The Treaty of Saginaw in the Year 1819," *Michigan Pioneer and Historical Collections,* VII (1886).

Williams, Frederick D. *Michigan Soldiers in the Civil War.* Lansing, 1960.

————. "Robert McClelland and the Secession Crisis," *Michigan History,* XLIII (1959).

Williams, Ralph D. *The Honorable Peter White.* Cleveland, 1905.

Wittke, Carl. *History of Canada.* New York, 1928.

————. "The Ohio-Michigan Boundary Dispute Re-examined," *Ohio Archaeological and Historical Society Quarterly,* XLV (1936).

————. "Ora Labora, A German Methodist Utopia," *Ohio Historical Quarterly,* LXVII (1958).

Wood, Edwin O. *Historic Mackinac.* 2 Vols. New York, 1918.

Woodford, Frank B. *Alex J. Groesbeck, Portrait of a Public Man.* Detroit, 1962.

————. *Father Abraham's Children.* Detroit, 1961.

———— and Hyma, Albert. *Gabriel Richard, Frontier Ambassador.* Detroit, 1958.

————. *Mr. Jefferson's Disciple: A Life of Justice Woodward.* East Lansing, 1953.

————. *Lewis Cass, The Last Jeffersonian.* New Brunswick, 1950.

Wrong, George M. *The First and Fall of New France, II.* New York, 1928.

Yarnell, Duane. *Auto Pioneering, The Remarkable Story of Ransom E. Olds, Father of Oldsmobile and Reo.* Lansing, 1949.

INDEX OF NAMES AND PLACES

(This index includes numerous town, city, and county names not followed by the name of a state. All such entries are names of places located in Michigan.)

775

INDEX OF SUBJECTS